PROCEEDINGS

THE

WORLD
FOOD

CONFERENCE
OF 1976

PROCEEDINGS

THE
WORLD
FOOD
CONFERENCE
OF 1976

JUNE 27-JULY 1
IOWA STATE UNIVERSITY
AMES, IOWA, U.S.A.

THE IOWA STATE UNIVERSITY PRESS
A M E S

© 1977 The Iowa State University Press
Ames, Iowa 50010. All rights reserved

First edition, 1977

International Standard Book Number: 0-8138-1825-7
Library of Congress Catalog Card Number:

CONTENTS

v

FOREWORD

The World Food Conference of 1976 began in 1972 when the idea for such a meeting was circulated in an interoffice memorandum at Iowa State University.

What developed was a unique approach to the problem of hunger in the world. For the first time, the best and the brightest minds in the multidisciplinary universe of world food teaching, research, and service were given an opportunity to communicate directly and intensely across the boundaries of specialization.

Not only was its multidisciplinary and worldwide nature unique. The World Food Conference of 1976 was a carefully constructed nonpolitical gathering designed to promote rational and objective discourse influenced as little as possible by nationalistic and political forces.

By virtually every measure, this meeting of international scientists exceeded the expectations of its planners and participants. Although a firm effort was made to limit the number of participants to 600, nearly 660 were registered. Approximately 1,600 persons attended each of the several plenary sessions. Although it had been anticipated that 50 nations would be represented, specialists from 70 nations were in attendance. During and following the Conference, participants saluted The World Food Conference of 1976, its theme, its unusual organization, and its execution.

The published Proceedings constitute one major product of the Conference. They are the official record of the 42 major addresses and of the efforts of participants in a dozen specialized workshops, who concentrated for many hours over a four-day period on specific and diversified world food concerns.

The Proceedings identify areas that will require continued and intensified emphasis if the problems of hunger and malnutrition are to be effectively met and, in any substantial degree, alleviated on our planet.

The Proceedings also help to insure that the humanitarian and intellectual efforts expended, by so many in making The World Food Conference of 1976 a fruitful experiment in the cross-fertilization of thought, will enjoy extended life and influence.

Of course, many other efforts on several fronts must be made if the benefits of The World Food Conference of 1976 are to be extended, interpreted, and used where they are most needed. Audio tape recordings of The World Food Conference presentations, for example, have "highly inspired" an African prime minister who is also an agricultural scientist. International mass communications media have helped to extend the influence of the Conference. A recently-completed documentary film of the Conference is also available as one means of informing general audiences of the aims and activities of The World Food Conference of 1976.

The World Food Institute of Iowa State University, the sponsor of the Conference, was created by Iowa's State Board of Regents in 1972. It continues to encourage the involvement and commitment of scientists and educators, within their own institutional and organizational environments, in following up on the recommendations and assessments resulting from the Conference. The World Food Institute has been encouraged, in this regard, by the recent passage of "The International Development and Food Assistance Act of 1975" by the Congress of the United States.

Solutions to food problems, however, will be achieved by nothing less than zealous efforts by many persons, organizations, institutions, and governments and their commitment to invest substantial resources in a wide range of human inquiry and action.

Just as The World Food Conference of 1976 began with a memorandum, it is our hope that a significant and lasting contribution to the alleviation of human suffering will begin with the publication of these Proceedings.

Marvin A. Anderson
Executive Director
The World Food Conference of 1976

Walter F. Wedin
Director
World Food Institute

PREFACE

We are talking about poor, hungry, hopeful people.
Hundreds of millions of men, women, and children
whose futures, whose prespectives on life, whose
values and whose capacities to appreciate being alive
depend largely on our willingness and ability now to
take up the challenge of providing them with and
helping them to provide themselves with an adequate
supply of food. If we do not take up this challenge
now with deeds and actions that actually bring about
change, we will not have adequately provided for our
own children's future.

> John A. Hannah, Executive Director
> The World Food Council, Rome, Italy
> at The World Food Conference of 1976

The general objective of The World Food Conference of 1976
was to broaden and intensify the involvement of scientists and
educators in solving world food needs through concerted efforts
among universities, research organizations, extension service
and their many disciplines.

The World Food Conference attempted to meet that objective
by bringing face to face hundreds of specialists to explore
"The Role of the Professional in Feeding Mankind." These specialists included internationally renowned nutritionists, economists, sociologists, animal scientists, food technologists,
plant scientists, soil scientists, agricultural engineers, vet-
erinarians and others. Together they examined in depth various aspects of food related problems.

Publication of these Proceedings provides a record of the
conference activity. These pages reflect the thoughts--often

x i

conclusive, sometimes divergent--of some of the world's best
thinkers in food related disciplines. Important options are
spelled out for the consideration by all who have the responsibility, resources and inclination necessary for action.

Success of the conference in terms of its objectives and
participation was unmistakable. Whether that success will be
translated into better yields, improved diets, less hunger,
better health and less global tension, however, depends on the
degree to which these suggestions are implemented within the
world's decision making and political processes. The next step
is yours.

Frank Schaller
J. Artie Browning
Harry E. Snyder
H. Vandewetering
Mary Halstead

ACKNOWLEDGMENTS

SUPPORT FOR THE WORLD FOOD CONFERENCE OF 1976
     The World Food Conference of 1976, a project of the World
     Food Institute of Iowa State University, has received sub-
     stantial assistance and valuable counsel from units within
the University, other Land-Grant institutions, agencies of the
federal government, foundations and individuals. The major
financial support required to make the Conference possible has
been provided by the following:

Sponsors
John Deere, Moline, Illinois
American Revolution Bicentennial Administration
Cook Industries, Inc.
Farmland Industries, Inc.
Iowa American Revolution Bicentennial Commission
Allis-Chalmers Corporation
DEKALB AgResearch, Inc.
Land O'Lakes, Inc.
Pioneer Hi-Bred International, Inc.
The Rockefeller Foundation

Contributors
Cargill, Inc.
General Mills Foundation
Massey-Ferguson, Inc.
FS Services, Inc.
Grocery Manufacturers of America, Inc.
Ralston Purina Company
Agricultural Equipment Division, International Harvester Com-
pany
Central Soya Company, Inc.
Funk Seeds International

COMMITTEES FOR THE WORLD FOOD CONFERENCE OF 1976

EXECUTIVE DIRECTOR--Marvin A. Anderson

Steering Committee
William W. Marion, Chairman--Marvin A. Anderson, Joe M. Bohlen,
Wesley F. Buchele, Brian D'Silva, George H. Ebert, Kenneth J.
Frey, Norman E. Hutton, David L. Lendt, Phillip A. O'Berry,
Peter J. Reilly, Charlotte E. Roderuck, Harry E. Snyder,
William H. Thompson, John F. Timmons, George R. Town, Walter F.
Wedin

SUBCOMMITTEES

Program
Charlotte E. Roderuck, Chairman--Joe M. Bohlen, Phillip A.
O'Berry, Kenneth J. Frey, Harry E. Snyder, Vaughn C. Speer,
John F. Timmons

Participants
Kenneth J. Frey, Chairman--Joe M. Bohlen, Brian D'Silva, Peter
J. Reilly, J. T. Scott

Interpretation and Translation
Norman E. Hutton, Chairman

Public Information
David L. Lendt, Chairman--George H. Ebert, Marjorie P. Groves,
James W. Schwartz, William H. Thompson

Proceedings
Frank W. Schaller, Chairman--J. Artie Browning, Harry E.
Snyder, H. Vandewetering, Mary Halstead

Registration
Debbi Nelson, Bonnie Overturf and Mary Klassen

Local Arrangements
George H. Ebert, Chairman--H. K. Baker, Clarence W. and
Virginia Bockhop, Wesley F. and Mary Buchele, Harold R.
Crawford, Robert L. Crom, Selma Duncan, Leonard Z. and Helen
Eggleton, John N. Hathcock, Mary Jane Hazen, H. B. Howell,
Norman E. Hutton, David L. Lendt, Larry E. Loenser, Beverly S.
Madden, Bert Mahlstede, Glenn Murphy, Grace E. Olsen, Charlotte
E. Roderuck, Robert E. and Dorothy Rust, Frank W. Schaller,
Gladys Scholtes, Naomi Shank, William H. Thompson, Roger
Volker, Thomas E. Walsh, Margaret C. Warning, John H. and Helen
Wessman, Thomas W. and Jane Wickersham, William G. and Jean
Zmolek

1

Plenary Papers

CLIFTON R. WHARTON, JR.

The Role of the Professional in Feeding Mankind: The Political Dimension

The invitation to participate in this conference was most welcome--partly because participation provides relief from some of the concerns and problems that consume much of the time and energy of university administrators these days. Partly because the invitation was a welcome reaffirmation that I am viewed by some as still a practitioner of the Third World developer's art. But most importantly, the invitation was welcome because of the opportunity it affords to meet with many friends of long standing with whom I have held dialogue on many of the issues to which this conference is addressed.

It is in the spirit of continuation of the dialogue with these old and respected colleagues, and new ones as well, that I have prepared my remarks and look forward to your reactions and views. Thus, I am returning to my old professional love and to my old friends.

In one sense, it seems as though I have not been away. If your papers, journal articles, books, and the general news stories are valid measures, the food/population problems are just as severe as ever or more so.

The world is not only threatened with temporary food shortages, but with chronically acute shortages, as far as we can see ahead. Food reserves are dangerously low, and production to feed the underfed millions is not at all assured. For example, only 21 out of 62 countries reached the 3.4 percent annual growth target set forth in the United Nations Food and Agriculture Organization (FAO) World Indicative Plan

Clifton R. Wharton, Jr., is President, Michigan State University, East Lansing, Michigan.

for the period 1961-63 to 1975.

The population side of the equation continues its inexor-
able press. Between 1961 and 1971 population grew faster than
food production in 42 out of 92 developing nations. The stark
fact is that many thousands, if not millions, of people in the
food deficit nations are very likely to die of starvation in
the next decade before excessive population can be brought
under control.

And the issues of international distributive justice are
still with us. The USA, Canada, Western Europe, Japan, and
other industrial nations continue to consume a disproportionate share of food and energy in terms of global resources.

My assigned task was to deal with the universality and
diversity of the world's food problems and their solutions from
the perspective of people and food in one world. But these
problems are not new and much of what might be said would be
old and repetitive. Moreover, the technical, economic, and
human factors that are involved in diagnosing and resolving
problems of food production and distribution will be handled
most competently by other speakers in this conference--such as
Drs. Hannah, Burton, Castillo, Oluwasanmi, Aziz and Chandler.
Having benefited from their previous works in these areas, I
have decided to strike out in a different direction.

THE "CONSENSUS" AND THE "GAP"

In preparing for today, my thoughts turned back almost 30
years to when my interest in foreign aid and technical
assistance was stimulated by General George Marshall's
announcement of his European plan and the subsequent announcement by President Harry Truman of a plan for the developing
world. Any historical review of the years since then reveals
impressive strides and progress.

But the review also leads me to two interesting conclusions:

First, there is a very sizable consensus within the various
professions and disciplines as to what is required technically
to achieve significant, sustained agricultural development.

I have been impressed in recent years by the frequency with
which one can read a journal article, speech, or book in which
the statistics that are used, the arguments or analyses that are
advanced, and the conclusions that are reached have a high degree of conformity. Conformity in the sense that, while there
may be minor variations on appropriate strategies, there is
among us a far greater consensus today than there was 15 or 20
years ago.

If one goes back to the earliest days when agricultural
development in the developing world was set as a deliberate

policy goal, there existed a similar degree of conformity in
what were then perceived to be the solutions. But the conformity was largely without any evidence based upon experience or
research focused upon the needs, resources, and conditions of
developing nations. Much of the consensus, when tested, turned
out to be invalid. Few of us today would argue for those early
panaceas of undifferentiated and unadapted technological transfer or of simplistic and imitative building of a land-grant university as ideal strategies to achieve agricultural development
abroad.

Our situation today is that we have had almost 30 years of
experience testing and implementing a variety of projects, programs, and strategies. We have conducted extensive research
under a variety of socio-economic and agronomic conditions in
most regions and nations of the developing world. Much has
been learned; much remains to be learned. For example, only
recently have some come to realize the importance that must be
given to the productivity and welfare of the subsistence farmer, the small farmer, the peasant agriculturist. Similarly,
some of my colleagues in the biological sciences still only
grudgingly recognize the importance of the social sciences and
interdisciplinary approaches to impact successfully the complex
intricacies of agricultural development. On the whole this
cumulative experience has brought us to the stage where, while
we may disagree on minor details, by and large we have significantly large areas of consensus among the various disciplines
and professions about the key factors and strategies to impact
the complex process called agricultural development.

Second, despite this consensus and despite the admitted
progress that has been made over the years, few nations or
regions have achieved the levels of agricultural development
that match our state of knowledge on the "art" of agricultural
development. Despite the predictable constraints, I believe
that any objective assessment of our progress to date would
conclude that we have not come even reasonably close to what we
know to be possible. There is a significant gap between the
potential and the actual--and the gap appears to be growing.

These two conclusions juxtaposed have recently become a
growing concern, and I have been trying to wrestle with the
question "Why?" Why does the global food crisis persist at
such an acute level--a level that is higher than is warranted
with our tested and proven knowledge? Is it merely the normal
lag in the process of implementation between all research and
its application? Or have other variables been ignored that may
be significant?

There is one possible explanation in which I have become
increasingly interested and which, paradoxically was sharpened
by the theme of this conference.

The theme of this conference is "The Role of the

Professional in Feeding Mankind." Professionals may be classified into several groups, each of which is an important actor
in the world food "drama." But have we been defining "professional" too narrowly?

There is perhaps a neglected cluster of professionals who
are rarely mentioned in discussions of the global crisis. I
refer to the role of "professional politicians."

The politicians are the persons who must adopt, finance,
advocate, and defend the policies, programs, and projects recommended by the scientific and technical professionals. Have
we neglected the politicians' critical role? Have we, who consider ourselves as agricultural development professionals, paid
sufficient attention to the political professionals?

Often the professional politicians see the policies formulated, choices to be delineated, and issues to be resolved from
quite different perspectives than do the agricultural development professionals. How many times has a perfectly valid scientific solution--or even a set of equally viable alternatives--
been frustrated by the decisions of the political professional?
Is there a dimension to this that has been responsible for the
frustration one feels as one looks at the attainable versus the
reality in the continuing global food crisis?

(Parenthetically I must add that, in light of the low es-
teem in which a few politicians are currently held, I am using
the term "politician" as T. V. Smith once defined the much
maligned word: "A politician is a person who can compromise
the issues without compromising himself.")

Without downgrading the role or contribution of persons we
normally consider as "professionals," I believe we must expand
our definition of professionals by including politicians. Most
important, this redefinition must be applied equally in the
developing world, the industrial world, and the post-industrial
world--if we are to achieve the levels of agricultural develop-

PROFESSIONAL POLITICIANS IN THE DEVELOPING WORLD

There are two political requirements for achieving significant, sustained agricultural development: the political leadership must have a genuine commitment to the goal
of agricultural development; and they must have an understanding of the process. (Admittedly, a number of other political
requirements such as political stability are also key variables.)

On the issue of commitment, one is forced to ask the question, "Why have so many governments failed to adopt policies or
to carry out programs and projects even in those problem areas
where there is virtually universal agreement on the technical

strategies required?" In some nations, even where there is expressed commitment to the agricultural process, the gap between reality and commitment is wide. Why has this happened? Is it because we have not concentrated our attention in this critical arena?

I realize that the policy area in its full political trappings is probably the most sensitive arena into which foreign aid and technical assistance could venture. One of the traditional "commandments" of foreign aid by outsiders has been: "Thou shall not intrude into the national political policy-making of host nations." Candidly, I admit that I have taken that same position for many, many years. And I believe the prohibition was correct--at least for former times. But as I look at how our problems internationally are becoming more and more strongly interrelated in a resource-limited world, I am beginning to wonder to what extent we may not find ourselves increasingly forced to adopt a stronger position on the issues that impinge on food policy and policy implementation in all nations.

I fully realize that this is a very, very sensitive subject. But one cannot ignore the extent to which either the failure to adopt the right food policies or the adoption of wrong policies in many cases has had a reverberating multiplier impact in other nations around the world. This has been true both for the developing nations and for the industrial ones. The international impact of domestic policies works both ways. Indeed, the disputes and conflicts experienced at the first and even most recent meeting of the World Food Council are dramatic examples of these political issues coming to the fore. The growing acerbity in the debates of the United Nations and its agencies are symptomatic of the burgeoning politicization of world development issues. We in the USA have never really faced up to the political dimension of the agricultural development process in the developing world and are now being forced to consider that set of variables in international arenas.

From another perspective, it could be argued that the situation today is far more appropriate than ever before for a candid dialogue on the political issues of agricultural development among the concerned parties.

One of the most significant changes in recent years has been the growing recognition by political leadership in the developing world that their "tenure in office" depends to a great extent on their capacity to lead and to achieve agricultural development. This change has been especially notable in the food-deficit nations where policies to improve agricultural production in their own countries and to secure help from food surplus countries to meet the basic food needs of their people have assumed increasing primacy. This growing sensitivity has been evident regardless of the political ideological form of government or how the political leadership was attained.

The basic ingredient in this newly emerging political sentiment among political leaders has been the adoption of pronouncements and policies that will favor agriculture, the rural areas, and the farming poor. More specifically, some of the various expressions of this new political sentiment include: 1), getting people back on the land and acknowledging that the future of the Third World lies with peasant or small farmers; 2), allocating more resources and social services to rural areas to increase agricultural production and the quality of rural life; and 3), adopting policies that address centuries old institutional rigidities related to the ownership and operation of land.

More than at any previous time, there is an awareness of the need to adopt strong policies that favor agriculture or that reflect a higher priority for this sector. Thus, the time may now be far more propitious to face the constellation of political issues that we have traditionally avoided.

The second neglected dimension is fostering a greater understanding of the agricultural development process among the professional politicians. In all candor, I believe that we have been less than successful in achieving the desired, minimal levels of understanding among political leaders.

Lest you believe that my view is wholly negative, I readily concede that we have had some impact upon the next tier-- those agricultural and developmental professional experts who advise the professional politician. Such persons do play a significant role in establishing the framework for policies and resolving the very complex issues and choices that confront heads of state and other political officials. Our influence among these advisory professionals has included such activities as workshops, training materials, advanced degree training, and the services of advisory teams. Efforts also have been made, such as those by Art Mosher, to reach the middle echelon worker or bureaucrat and provide such officials with a better understanding of the agricultural development process.

Yet, while it is manifestly true that we have had "advisory teams and experts"--both national and foreign--who have sat at the elbow of ministers and even prime ministers or presidents in Third World nations, the fact remains that on the whole our impact has been minimal. How many times can we point to individuals or instances where we or our works have facilitated the professional politicians to acquire a sound understanding of the agricultural development process and of a proper strategy to bring it to pass?

But our greatest area of neglect has been our low level of concern for this political dimension, broadly defined. If we are to become more serious about the political variables in the agricultural development formulae, we should be seeking answers to such questions as the following:

What are the political consequences of alternative agricultural policies, reallocation of resources, land reform measures, and related questions? In a given country, which citizens or groups stand to lose as a result of the policy change
we are considering as part of new rural development strategy?
In other words, who is likely to oppose the change? How are
they connected to the political decision-makers? How can the
strength of their opposition be blunted?

Are there ways of introducing change or is there a pace of
change that will either neutralize opposition or stengthen the
hand of supporters? Will the political professionals, that is
the high level governmental decision-makers, see their political futures as tied closely to one or another segment of those
likely to gain or lose as a result of the agricultural development strategy under consideration?

How can we maximize consensus behind the policy that makes
good use of scientific knowledge?

What are the international consequences of alternative
policies? How can food surplus nations be persuaded that the
deficit nations are taking all reasonable measures to help themselves?

We should understand that when confronting development
policy, a political leader is often faced with the dilemma of
maintaining the popularity or support he or she needs to stay
in power, on the one hand, and, on the other, making tough decisions that may work hardship and be unpopular over the short
run. The tough decision may be dictated by the relevant technology, and over the long run, may be critically important to
increased food production and to the broader population. But
it may also lose supporters. For example, enforcing minimum
price supports on grain to benefit producers is likely to raise
prices temporarily to urban consumers. Or investing in rural
infrastructure often comes at the cost of restricting urban services. Or expanding lower level education for rural youth may
temporarily hold down the expansion of urban universities. Land
reform decisions are among the most difficult and call for careful analysis and bold decision-making that balance equity and
production variables. In these situations, the political decision-makers may be faced with choices that directly affect
their own future in office. Only the professional politician
can judge the correct balance, but as developmental professionals we must seek understanding of the trade-offs involved
and be prepared with research delineating the relevant variables. This role is essential if we are to continue as useful
advisers and to have the ear of the political professionals.

PROFESSIONAL POLITICIANS IN THE INDUSTRIAL
AND POST-INDUSTRIAL NATIONS
The issue of our neglect of the professional politician

is not limited to those in the developing world. Those in
the industrial and postindustrial nations of the world
must be included in this calculus as well. Indeed, there is
reason to believe that their role in the agricultural development process is of equal importance.

This is true whether such persons occupy positions in
national bilateral programs or in international organizations.
For example, Robert MacNamara's adoption of low income, peasant
agriculture as a high priority developmental goal for the World
Bank has had an incalculable impact upon efforts in the Third
World. Similarly, Dr. John A. Hannah's longstanding commitment
to the centrality of agricultural development was reflected
during his recent tenure as leader of the US Agency for International Development. In both instances, I view their roles as
that of professional politicians impacting and carrying out
policies related to agricultural development.

Even in the advanced industrial and postindustrial nations
there is a need to include the professional politician more
deliberately in our calculus. Let me choose the USA as a case
in point.

Recent actions by the US Congress, such as the addition of
Title XII to the Foreign Aid Act, reflect the resurgence of
awareness and commitment to the centrality of agricultural development abroad if the chronic world food crisis is to be
satisfactorily treated. Yet, despite these developments, the
policy debate has been limited. Once the impact of the first
USSR wheat agreement eased and the Arab oil embargo declined,
attention shifted away from the food/energy crises. But the
march toward an ever tighter global economy marches inexorably
forward.

The world economy is global and is gradually forcing a
realization that neither the rich nations nor the poor can
achieve their goals in independent isolation. We in the USA
must recognize this reality if we are to play our proper role
in meeting the challenge of people and food in one world.

There are several vital policy issues that must be faced
and debated by our elected officials, our political leaders.
For example, how do we deal with our "food power?" The USA and
the few other food surplus nations have the awesome power to
decide the fate of the human masses of the world. The USA, for
example, has a larger proportion of the world grain market than
the Arab countries have of the energy market. Furthermore, the
USA gained more from the rise in food prices than we lost in
oil prices. Some wag has said that "the Arabs have the crude
but America has the food." And food is power which we must
find ways of using--both wisely in our own long-term self-interest and in the interest of humanity.

World leaders and our own thoughtful critics know that
many policies have not always been oriented to the needs of the

maximum number of human beings or the poorest of the poor.

The USA and other food surplus countries need to debate the policy alternatives to determine what should be our contribution to global food problems. While recognizing that most of the world's food must be produced in the food deficit countries, should we produce food at our full capacity without due regard for the long-term protection of our basic fertility and natural resources?

When dealing with a universally needed commodity, can the USA and the other food surplus nations show the way toward a developmental humane policy? Can we use our food power more even-handedly and gain wide respect in the world community for such policies?

What are the optimal policies and procedures for resolving the understandable conflict between prices paid to producers, whether controlled or freely negotiated in world markets, and the effect of such prices on the cost of living of urban dwellers? How do we balance the prices paid to producers for contributions to world food reserves with the effect of such prices on the cost of living in both the giving and receiving countries?

Should the allocations of food on concessionary terms or to world food reserves be made under policies and procedures designed to strengthen the political commitment of leaders of food deficit nations and the policies that they espouse to maximize their own production and minimize their continued dependence upon us? Can this be done without charges of economic imperialism?

How do we develop a sound national food policy that includes international considerations and more than purely economic factors?

How do we use our "food power" with restraint for the high purpose of advancing human welfare for the largest number?

In seeking to resolve the complex and often conflicting policy issues involved above, elected politicians in the industrial and postindustrial nations will need the best scientific and technical advice possible, the insights of the experienced old development hands. Our elected officials will also need to direct and utilize the services of a veritable army of competent public servants who can devise the short and long-term policies and procedures to give effect to our national aims and purposes. Most important, the professional politician will need the encouragement and support of an informed and enlightened public who are committed to make the maximum contribution possible to the alleviation of world suffering.

Thus, farsighted and sensitive political leadership aided by knowledgeable scientists and researchers and by competent public servants who can assist in devising creative operational policies and procedures, and supported by an informed and

sympathetic public opinion, can help resolve inevitable conflicts of interest. They can forge wise and humane political
decisions and put the USA and other food surplus nations in a
position to make a maximum contribution toward alleviating
world hunger.

CONCLUSION
      My purpose has been not so much to provide answers as to
      raise questions. All of us will continue to work to de-
      velop and improve our respective disciplinary and inter-
disciplinary contributions to world agricultural development--
new developments in fertilizer uptake, better processes for
hybridization, improved economic incentives, more efficient
marketing/storage arrangements. These and many other developments will continue from our creative and fertile genius.
These will come. But taking advantage of and adopting that new
technology, that new scientific development, that consensus
developmental strategy also rests with the political process.
Thus, a pivotal role will be played by those who are involved
in making the decisions on agricultural development policy and
its implementation--the professional politician. Further, we
must include those politicians in the industrial nations as
well as the developing nations.
      In conclusion, I hope that I have made clear that I see
"The Role of the Professional in Feeding Mankind" in a context
that widens the ordinary usage of the term to include professional politicians and their advisers who are confronted with
differing aspects of the world food crisis. Politicians, who
despite their differing requirements and constraints, are committed to agricultural development and understand the process.
      The emphasis I have given to these other actors, not usu-
ally thought of as "professionals," is in no way meant to diminish the importance of the biological scientists, technical
agriculturists, economists, social scientists, and others from
all countries whose contributions to helping resolve global
food problems is basic and undisputed. I genuinely believe
that we need to widen the spectrum in order to embrace all aspects and dimensions of the problem. There is not only room
for adding these "others" to our deliberations, but without
their inclusion we are not facing the realities of the situations. Indeed, their exclusion may well account for our limited success to date. There have always been significant
political variables at work that related to the agricultural
development process, but to a large extent we have failed to
include the political dimension in our developmental assistance
strategy.
      There is little doubt that the greatest source of unity
among the nations of the Third World is their universal desire

for economic development and human progress. The new international economic order for which they are striving will in the final analysis be resolved by the political process both domestically and internationally. Agriculture and the people dependent upon agriculture continue to constitute the largest single segment of this basic world problem. Those of us whose insights, knowledge, and energies have concentrated upon this highest priority sector have a significant role to play. And our role as professionals will be enhanced by broadening our definition to include the politician.

When I look at the key world developmental issues over the next 25 years--food policy, population policy, distributive justice, resource "wars"--I have concluded that most solutions will be rooted in the ability of the political processes, both national and international, to deal with them effectively. And remember that, if the political process fails to deal with these basic human issues of hunger and survival, the inevitable alternatives will be growing interpersonal violence, domestic upheaval, and wars.

REFERENCES

Mosher, A. T. 1966. Getting Agriculture Moving. Praeger, New York.
Mosher, A. T. 1969. Creating a progressive rural structure, to serve a modern agriculture. Agricultural Development Council, New York.
Mosher, A. T. 1971. To create a modern agriculture, organization and planning. Agricultural Development Council, New York.
Mosher, A. T. 1975. Serving agriculture as an administrator. Agricultural Development Council, New York.

SARTAJ AZIZ

The World Food Situation— Today and in the Year 2000

Food is one of the most complex economic, political and moral problems of our times. Despite a great deal of discussion and debate, particularly in the past four years, the underlying issues are still very confused and different groups of people in different parts of the world continue to look at the food problem from their own particular angle. The food situation itself and forecasts about its future are clouded by so many imponderables that predictions swing from deep pessimism to cautious optimism. International discussions about environment, population, food, habitat and water are all part of a sudden realization that without a major restructuring of relationships and concepts, the world simply cannot continue the patterns of production and distribution of the past 25 years for the rest of this century.

Similarly, the search for solutions to the food problem quickly run into deep moral and political dilemmas which go far beyond the problem of food. Will the rich nations of the world continue to treat the world as a vast market or is there any hope of its evolution into a genuine international community? Is there any common ground between self-interest and the moral imperatives of feeding the whole of mankind? Is it possible for developing countries to achieve, within a system based on freedom of ownership, mobility and consumption, a minimum of equality to secure everyone's basic needs of food, clothing, shelter, medicine and education? But before we get into these complex questions, let us look at the present world food

Sartaj Aziz is Deputy Executive Director, World Food Council, United Nations, Rome, Italy.

situation and the outlook for the future.

THE PRESENT FOOD SITUATION

In 1972 the world faced an unexpected food crisis partly because total grain production in that year fell, for the first time since the War, by 33 million tons, instead of increasing by 25 million tons to meet the annual increase in demand. This depleted the North American grain stocks on which the world had depended for two decades. In the next three years, world production of cereals[1] increased from 1,280 million tons to only 1,360 million tons, or an average of 2.0 percent per year, hardly keeping pace with the average increase in demand. As a consequence, grain prices throughout these four years were two or three times higher than the pre-1972 levels. Many countries suffered shortages and distress, while higher food prices kept commercial demand for cereals relatively low. About half of a million persons died of starvation in many parts of Africa and Asia. Food suddenly became a global issue.

In 1975, the developing countries harvested bumper crops, and crops in the USA and Canada, encouraged by high prices, also reached record levels. Although European crops were badly affected by adverse weather, the world food situation began to improve in the short run. Prices of wheat in June 1976 are considerably lower than the record level reached in October 1974. If crops in 1976 turn out to be as good as expected, we may even begin to rebuild stocks from their precarious levels of the past four years. In other words the short-term food situation has "improved". It should, however, be emphasized that current prices of wheat and rice are more than twice as large as the pre-1972 level of $60 and $140 a ton respectively. Even after allowing for inflation the real cost of food has increased, and an average Indian with a per capita income of $130 and an average consumption of 200 kgs has to spend about 20 percent of his income on cereals alone at current world prices, while he needed to spend about 10 percent at world prices before 1972.

The improvement in the food situation is in effect more superficial than real. When we go beyond the statistical assessment of the current food situation to look at factors which really brought about the food crisis of 1972-75, we find them largely unchanged.

The food reserves which for two decades provided stability of food supplies and prices were based on incidental surpluses mainly in the USA and Canada, rather than a consciously designed international system. Despite discussions in many

---

1. Throughout this paper cereals include rice expressed in paddy equivalent.

different fora the world is nowhere near a dependable system of
food security. The need to rebuild grain reserves to protect
the world against undue fluctuations in supplies and prices is
widely accepted, but opinions and interests differ about the
size and management of such reserves. The USA has proposed at
the International Wheat Council, a food security reserve of 30
million tons but in a loosely managed system that will not
interfere with the commercial markets or prices. The European
Economic Community (EEC) and some other exporting countries
are prepared to share a part of the burden, providing stocks
are built up as a part of a formal grains agreement and are
triggered by price movements within agreed limits. In other
words, the USA wants to have food security at market prices and
most developed importing countries are looking for market stability. Meanwhile the risks of continued insecurity are growing and are particularly ominous for the developing countries.
Most developed importing countries have already secured their
future import requirements by signing long-term purchase agreements.

     The gradual slow-down in food production in developing
countries from an average of 3.1 percent in 1952-62 to 2.9 percent in 1962-70, which increased their net cereal imports from
3 million tons in 1950-51 to 33 million tons in 1969-71, has
also continued. Despite an increase of 5 percent in 1975, the
average annual increase in food production for 1971-75, is 2
percent. The total cereal imports of developing countries have
consequently increased from 33 million in 1969-71 to about 50
million tons in 1975-76. The cumulative excess costs of these
imports in the past three years, because of higher food prices
has been estimated at $12 billion.

     The chronic problem of hunger and malnutrition, which in
many ways is the real food problem, has perhaps become more
serious, notwithstanding the temporary relief provided by the
large 1975 crops. In 1972 the number of people suffering from
serious under-nutrition was estimated at 460 million (about 20
percent of total population in Africa and Asia and 13 percent
in Latin America). Even if the proportion of such people has
not increased, the absolute number has gone up and the world is
probably moving away from its declared goal of abolishing hunger and malnutrition in a decade, 20 months after this was
agreed at the World Food Conference in Rome in November, 1974.

     Finally, and perhaps most seriously, the policies in de-
veloped and developing countries which in effect brought about
the recent food crisis in the first place, have remained largely unchanged. In the developed countries the problems of
evolving a new set of agricultural, food and trade policies for
a period of food scarcity have hardly been tackled. Even in
the developing countries, which are becoming increasingly aware
of the importance of agricultural development, very few

countries have been able to devise strategies and policies that
can attack the food problem in a fundamental sense. In addition to these four major factors, any assessment of the present
food situation must take note of many other striking factors:
the continued maldistribution of food in the world, with over-
consumption in the developed countries and widespread undernourishment in the developing countries; a dramatic change in
the patterns of world grains trade, with 80 percent of world
exports coming from only one region (USA and Canada) and the
developing countries as a group now importing almost half the
world grain exports, and centrally planned economies of East
Europe emerging as substantial importers; a marked improvement
in fertilizer availability, but with no longer-term international policy to prevent cyclical swings in supplies and prices
that has characterized the world fertilizer situation for the
past 15 years.

THE FUTURE OUTLOOK
     The food prospects for 1990 and perhaps the year 2000 will
     depend very much on what we do, or choose not to do, in
     the next five years. Any assessment of the future food
outlook is only partly a statistical exercise, primarily to
determine the likely demand for food. But whether that demand
can be met adequately or whether the world faces recurring
famines and food shortages, will depend very much on the
efforts of the developing countries to increase their production, on the willingness of developed countries to assist these
efforts, on the agricultural and trade policies of main food
exporting and importing countries, and finally on the feasibility and efficacy of international arrangements to manage the
world food economy.
     Thus any meaningful assessment of the food outlook for the
next ten or twenty years must go beyond statistical projections
into the policy implications of all three inter-related aspects
of the food question: (1) the projected demand for food; (2)
the likely production or supply of food; and (3) the likely
distribution of available food supply. Each of these three
elements involves difficult political issues and conflicts of
interests between different groups of countries.

Demand for Food
     The demand for food can be predicted much more easily and
     with a greater degree of accuracy than its supply. It
must be emphasized, however, that statistical projections can
be made on reasonably sound assumptions for a decade or so.
Those projections made for longer periods become progressively
less reliable and vary with policy changes or inherent

adjustments in the preceding period.

The two main determinants of changes in demand over the long run are population and income growth. The projected demand for cereals, wheat, rice and coarse grains for the years 1980, 1990 and the year 2000 are presented in Tables 1, 2, 3 and 4 at the end of this paper. The implications of these projections for per capita demand for food are given in Table 5. The main conclusions that can be drawn from these projections are summarized below:

1) In the developed countries total demand for cereals is likely to increase over the 30-year period by 72 percent or 1.8 percent per annum, from 387 million tons to 665 million tons, but the demand for coarse grains is expected to increase by about 90 percent, from 275 million tons to 520 million tons. In fact about 80 percent of the total projected increase in the demand for cereals in the developed countries is attributable to feed uses of grains.

2) In the developing countries the total demand for cereals could, however increase from 387 million tons to 1,015 million tons, or by 162 percent, if the underlying assumptions turn out to be realistic. This will imply an annual average increase of 3.3 percent for the 30-year period for cereals. (The average increase will be somewhat higher if non-cereal foods were to be included.)

3) In the centrally planned economies consisting mainly of East Europe, USSR and China, the demand for cereals is likely to increase at the slowest rate--about 70 percent over 30 years (or 1.8 percent per annum)--despite an increase of 128 percent in the demand for feeds. This is because the average population growth rate in China and some other centrally planned Asian countries in this group is much slower than that in other developing countries and the proportion of grain fed to livestock in USSR and East Europe will be a somewhat smaller proportion of total consumption than in the developed countries, increasing from 50 percent in 1970 to 59 percent in the year 2000 against 73 percent in the developed countries.

4) If the current consumption trends were to continue, per capita consumption in developed countries would increase from about 3,000 calories to 3,242 calories and protein consumption from 95 to 100 grams. Such increments could certainly be categorized as further 'over-consumption'. In the developing countries the average increase in consumption from 2,211 calories to 2,615 calories will be unevenly distributed between different regions, but would provide a welcome improvement if it can be achieved. It is also clear that except for the middle income developing countries, the demand for cereals for direct consumption will not decline appreciably.

If the projections for the period 1990-2000 were based on
low population assumptions of the UN for the developing countries, the demand growth for that period would be only marginally lower. These demand projections do therefore provide a
fairly realistic order of magnitude for the future.

Food Availability
        Factors which are likely to affect the supply of food in
    the future are much more uncertain and unpredictable, and
include the physical resource base, availability of financial
resources, technological progress, access to internal and international markets, and social and institutional factors. It is
clear, however, that the projected increase of less than two
percent per annum in the demand for cereals in the developed
countries and the centrally planned economies is less than the
average increase these two groups of countries have achieved in
the preceding two decades (see Table 6). It is therefore reasonable to assume that despite some years of bad harvests, these
groups of countries will be able to increase their production
of cereals to meet their own long-term demand. The developed
exporting countries could also produce a sizeable surplus to
meet the commercial demand for cereals from other countries and
a marginal quantity for concessional sales to developing countries.
        The projected increase of 3.3 percent in the demand for
cereals in the developing countries is, however, considerably
faster than the average increase of 2.8 percent in production
attained by these countries in the past two decades, and of 2.5
percent in the past five years (1970-75). The average increase
of the past two decades is quite remarkable and is faster than
that achieved by the developed countries. But the bulk of it
was eaten up by unprecedented population growth. The key question in the food debate is therefore whether the developing
countries as a group can produce over the next 25 years an additional 600 million tons of cereals (or 550 million tons if the
lower demand projections are used) over and above their current
production of about 400 million tons.
        It is in the context of this key question that two dis-
tinct lines of argument have been presented in the current debate on the food problem. The pessimists emphasize many unfavourable factors and predict mass starvation within this generation. The pressure of the growing demand for food, they
point out, ecologically undermines some of the major food producing systems in the world. There is over-fishing, over-graz-
ing, deforestation and soil erosion in many parts of the world.
Many experts predict worsening weather patterns and an unusual
frequency of droughts and floods. Some draw attention to the
changing economics of agricultural production with cultivation

moving into marginal land and modern technology requiring ever
larger inputs of energy and capital. Future increments in production, they argue, are possible only at prices that cannot be
sustained by consumers, particularly those in developing countries. There is also a great deal of skepticism in the current
strained atmosphere of international cooperation about increasing the flow of external resources for food production to the
required levels. On top of these are the social and political
constraints which prevent the small farmer and landless workers
from participating in the process of economic and social development.

Another group of economists and scientists, however, argue
that mass starvation can be avoided if the food problem is
tackled resolutely both at the national and international
levels. There is no shortage of physical resources of land and
water for several decades to grow more food. With the backlog
of existing technology, production in most developing countries
can be doubled in 10 to 15 years. In fact only through larger
food production and the resultant favourable economic and social climate, it is emphasized, can the demographic transition
to a lower population growth be reached in the future.

The main distinction between these two lines of argument
is not one of fact but of judgement about what might happen in
the future. The pessimistic line is obviously more sensitive
to the outer limits set by finite physical resources of land,
water and fossil fuels and the inner limits imposed by constraints on man's ability to manage complex technological and
political systems. The optimistic view is based on the assumption that pushed for survival, man will have no option but to
expand the frontiers of these limits to make the best use of
available physical and human resources. It also assumes that
much larger financial resources will be forthcoming to undertake the major effort involved and political and economic institutions which are a part of the agricultural system will be
restructured for the purpose.

In the light of this very wide range of possibilities
there is no point in concentrating on supply projections in
purely statistical terms. Different countries or regions have
different resource endowments and different capacities to use
them. The agricultural system of each country is affected not
only by its own internal political and economic institutions,
but also by external trade and economic relationships. Between
the purely subsistence agriculture and highly capital and energy intensive modernized agriculture there is a wide variety of
systems that are constantly evolving in different parts of the
world. What each country or region will produce in the next
25 years will depend on positive and negative influences of
all these factors taken together.

The commitment of the international community at the World

Food Conference held in November 1974, to abolish hunger and
malnutrition within a decade, is based on the optimistic prospect of increasing food production in the developing countries
at an annual rate of about 4 percent per annum. The World Food
Council has already begun work on the concrete implications of
this goal in terms of requirements for investment and inputs
and by identifying a group of food priority countries whose
food problem is more serious or whose production potential is
significant, to allow adequate concentration of efforts on
these countries. But there is no assurance so far that adequate financial and policy support will be forthcoming for the
attainment of this goal.

If these efforts succeed only in maintaining the average
annual growth of 2.8 percent attained in the past 20 years, the
food gap of developing countries will increase to 85 million
tons by 1985. The gap will, of course, be larger if the slow-
down that has occurred in the first half of the 1970s cannot
be reversed.

Distribution of Food

The distribution aspects of the food problem, the third
element in the future outlook for food, is almost as important as the production aspect, but has received very little
attention in the food debate so far.

At the international level, a solution of the food problem
is closely connected with the problem of international distribution of food and that in turn is intimately linked to the
agricultural and trade policies of the US which accounts for
more than 60 percent of world grain exports. But the US policies, unlike the past two decades, are no longer fully determined by the US Government. Since 1970, as a matter of deliberate policy, the role of the Government in agriculture has
been curtailed through the liquidation of Government held
stocks, reductions in food aid and elimination of price support
operations. Thus paradoxically, while the dependence of the
world on the US grain exports has been increasing, the US Government has been shifting this responsibility to the uncertain
and erratic forces of the market. Even the modest international framework agreed at the World Food Conference to regulate
the world food economy within certain agreed parameters of objectives and guidelines has not yet been created. These comments on the present precarious state of affairs do not imply
any reflection on the efficacy of the market system in an ideological sense. The market has a very useful role to play in
providing incentives to producers and determining prices, but
agriculture is such a volatile sector that no country can
afford to leave the entire management of such a critical commodity as food to vagaries of the market. Even the US has not

done so in the preceding 20 years. If we depend only on the market, the rich will eat and the poor will starve, the rich farmer will benefit and the small farmer will go bankrupt.

Another aspect of international distribution of food is the problem of over-consumption in the rich countries. The relationship between affluence in some countries and hunger in others has not been fully investigated but it is clear that as long as the available food supply is distributed according to commercial demand rather than nutritional needs, the over-consumption in the rich countries will be an important cause of hunger and malnutrition in years of food shortages. Today about 30 percent of the world population in the rich countries uses about two-thirds of the world grains supply, about 60 percent indirectly as livestock feed. In other words, per capita consumption of grain in the rich countries is three times that in the developing countries. The total quantity of grain fed to livestock (about 400 million tons) is more than the quantity consumed by human beings in India and China taken together. This relative over-consumption is of course harmful in itself. In the last 20 years the average longevity of the US citizen has not increased at all, despite a 30 percent increase in food consumption, because of diseases associated with over-consumption. But how would a reduction in grain consumption in the rich countries help to improve nutrition in the poor countries? The only long-term solution is a corresponding transfer of incomes to the poor to create an effective demand for food, but that will take time. In the meanwhile, it is necessary to determine a kind of food consumption ceiling or maximum and a food consumption floor or minimum along with selected policy instruments that can be used to curtail consumption at least in years of bad crops when prices go up beyond agreed limits. Even if marginal shifts are achieved in consumption, the supply in the world markets will improve and developing countries with food shortages will be able to buy food at reasonable prices.

At the national level the problem of food distribution is not merely a question of distributing free or subsidized food in schools or factories, but is linked to the whole pattern of onwership of land and other assets, income distribution and employment opportunities. Even if all the required financial resources, inputs and technology were available, the poorest quarter of the population, which has very little land or no land and no employment prospects, will not be able to benefit from them and will remain hungry. The crux of the food problem lies in evolving a pattern of development that will involve the small farmer and the landless labourer in employment and production. China, with about one-fifth of the world population, has already demonstrated the success of a development strategy based on basic human needs and a more egalitarian approach to the distribution of the fruits of progress.

CONCLUSIONS AND MAIN ISSUES
> This brief analysis of the current food situation and its
> future outlook leads to some significant conclusions.
> These and the issues they raise are summarized below:

The short-term food situation has 'improved' in a superficial sense, but the main long-term factors which brought
about the recent food crisis are still very much there.

The future demand for cereals is likely to grow at about
3.3 percent per annum in the developing countries and at less
than 2.0 percent per year in the developed countries and the
centrally planned economies over the next 25 years. Changes in
assumptions about population growth and incomes will not drastically alter these projections at least for the period up to
1990.

The developed countries and the centrally planned countries could conceivably increase their food production at a
rate that covers their projected demand for food, but the required increase needed in the developing countries is considerably faster than the growth achieved in the preceding 15 years.
The key question is whether developing countries can accelerate their food production on a sustained basis over the next
20-25 years.

There is considerable potential for increasing production
in developing countries by expanding the area under cultivation
and by improving yields from existing areas in the majority of
developing countries. This will require much larger investment from domestic and external sources, assured supply of all
inputs at reasonable prices, intensified research and training
efforts. Even more important, a sustained increase in production will require a major restructuring of political and economic institutions and other measures to provide larger incomes
and employment opportunities to the poorest segment of the population in developing countries.

The distribution aspects of the food problem, both at the
national and the international level are almost as important as
the production aspect. Without an orderly system of food distribution, either in an agreed international framework or a
combination of active national policies, the world food economy
will remain at the mercy of uncertain market forces.

The over-consumption of food in the rich countries, besides being undesirable in itself is at least one factor in the
relative scarcity of supply for the poor. It is important to
devise policy mechanisms that will discourage over-consumption
at least in years of bad crops.

At the national level the problem of food distribution is
intimately linked to patterns of ownership, income distribution
and employment opportunities. Technical solutions to the food
production problems can go only some distance and may even be

counter-productive unless they can tackle the distribution aspects of the food problem.

To sum up, the food problem of the next 25 years is essentially manageable, but it will require a tremendous national and international effort. In seeking solutions, it is important not to look for simple alternatives such as larger production versus better distribution, or population control versus larger production. All three elements--increased production, improved distribution and lower population growth--are interrelated and must be pursued simultaneously.

While these longer-term tasks are being undertaken, the world must evolve a dependable system of food security and food distribution that will effectively replace the system that disappeared in the early 1970s and prevent future disasters. The principal responsibility for this rests, I feel, with the United States. As Barbara Ward said recently:[2]

There is perhaps a profound significance in the fact that all these problems of world community have come to a head just as America approaches its Second Centennial. Certainly no nation is called upon today for a comparable effort of leadership. To hold in one's hand the living or dying of half a million children, to be the only power capable of beginning the building of grain reserves, to be the chief state with power and wealth enough to rise above the narrow temptations of naked market power--here is a challenge unequal in history. And if it is not met, it is with foreboding that America's friends will recall the words of Thomas Jefferson, founding father and tutelary genius of the new republic: 'Indeed, I tremble for my country when I reflect that God is just'.

---

2.   Barbara Ward in her foreword to "Hunger, Politics and Markets"--New York University Press, 1975.

TABLE 1. Developed market economies: demand for cereals 1970 actual, 1980, 1990 and 2000 projected

	1970			1980			1990			2000		
	Food	Feed	Total[a]	Food	Feed	Total[a]	Food	Feed	Total[a]	Food	Feed	Total[a]
	.... million tons											
Wheat												
North America	15.7	8.1	26.1	16.1	9.6	28.0	16.9	11.3	30.8	16.5	13.4	32.8
Western Europe	37.4	14.2	55.9	36.2	18.3	59.2	34.6	22.1	61.6	41.0	26.7	73.7
Oceania	1.5	.9	2.9	1.8	1.1	3.4	2.0	1.4	4.0	2.2	1.7	4.5
Others	5.5	.7	6.7	6.6	1.1	8.5	7.8	1.3	10.1	8.9	1.6	11.6
Total[b]	60.1	23.9	91.7	60.7	30.1	99.2	61.4	36.2	106.5	68.6	43.5	122.7
Coarse Grains												
North America	3.7	140.3	157.4	4.0	169.9	192.6	4.3	206.5	233.6	4.2	251.0	282.9
Western Europe	4.9	79.4	99.0	4.7	105.0	129.0	4.4	127.1	154.9	4.5	154.0	186.8
Oceania	.1	1.7	2.6	.1	2.5	3.7	.1	3.2	4.7	.1	4.2	6.0
Others	3.3	10.9	16.4	3.9	17.3	24.7	4.6	23.3	33.1	5.2	31.5	44.3
Total[b]	12.0	232.2	275.4	12.7	294.7	350.0	13.5	360.2	426.3	14.0	440.6	519.9
Rice												
North America	1.0	.4	1.5	1.2	.4	1.7	1.4	.4	1.9	1.5	.5	2.1
Western Europe	1.4	.0	1.6	1.6	.1	1.8	1.8	.1	2.0	1.9	.1	2.2
Oceania	.1	--	.1	.1	--	.1	.1	--	.1	.1	--	.1
Others	14.3	.8	16.4	14.9	1.0	17.2	14.7	1.1	17.2	15.2	1.4	18.0
Total[b]	16.8	1.2	19.6	17.7	1.4	20.8	17.9	1.7	21.2	18.7	1.9	22.4

[a] Includes other uses.
[b] The totals do not necessarily add up due to rounding.

TABLE 2. Developing market economies: demand for cereals 1970 actual, 1980, 1990 and 2000 projected

	1970			1980			1990			2000		
	Food	Feed	Total[a]	Food	Feed	Total[a]	Food	Feed	Total[a]	Food	Feed	Total[a]
	.... million tons											
Wheat												
Africa	6.5	--	7.2	9.3	--	10.5	13.1	--	14.6	22.2	--	24.2
Latin America	14.0	.5	16.1	19.3	.8	22.2	26.5	1.2	30.6	34.3	1.8	40.0
Near East	20.1	2.0	27.9	25.2	3.5	35.8	30.0	6.4	44.9	38.1	11.7	59.9
Far East	31.9	.4	36.2	45.0	.4	50.3	64.2	.8	72.1	84.6	1.5	96.3
Total[b]	72.7	2.9	87.6	98.9	4.7	119.0	134.1	8.4	162.4	179.6	14.9	220.9
Coarse Grains												
Africa	26.8	1.3	33.0	35.8	4.0	45.9	48.9	7.2	65.0	65.9	13.0	91.7
Latin America	12.3	20.3	38.5	15.6	31.6	55.9	19.7	48.9	80.6	24.4	75.6	116.8
Near East	7.3	7.6	17.4	9.1	13.2	26.2	11.3	23.8	41.1	14.4	42.7	66.6
Far East	32.2	2.4	38.9	40.9	5.2	51.4	51.2	9.5	67.7	59.9	17.4	86.5
Total[b]	78.7	31.5	128.1	101.6	53.9	179.6	131.4	89.3	254.6	165.0	148.8	361.9
Rice												
Africa	5.0	.1	5.7	7.2	.1	8.2	11.2	.3	12.9	17.1	.5	19.8
Latin America	9.8	.0	11.3	13.2	.1	15.1	17.0	.1	19.6	22.3	.1	25.6
Near East	4.1	--	4.4	6.2	--	6.7	9.3	--	10.0	12.2	--	13.2
Far East	132.9	1.0	150.2	181.5	2.1	206.0	243.3	3.9	277.3	312.3	7.3	360.1
Total[b]	152.2	1.2	172.0	208.6	2.3	236.5	281.5	4.2	320.4	378.2	7.9	433.1

[a] Includes other uses.
[b] The totals do not necessarily add up due to rounding.

27

TABLE 3. Centrally planned economies: demand for cereals 1970 actual, 1980, 1990 and 2000 projected

	1970			1980			1990			2000		
	Food	Feed	Total[a]	Food	Feed	Total[a]	Food	Feed	Total[a]	Food	Feed	Total[a]
						.... million tons						
Wheat												
Asian Centrally Planned Economies	30.3	5.5	40.2	40.1	11.1	58.0	52.3	17.6	78.5	65.9	27.9	104.8
USSR and Eastern Europe	52.6	37.7	113.1	53.5	47.7	127.6	55.3	56.3	142.4	54.7	66.3	153.0
Total[b]	83.0	42.6	153.2	93.6	58.8	185.6	107.5	73.8	220.9	120.6	94.2	257.8
Coarse Grains												
Asian Centrally Planned Economies	34.8	7.6	47.2	42.8	23.2	72.1	51.2	36.9	97.1	58.3	58.6	130.0
USSR and Eastern Europe	17.3	77.1	115.3	15.6	94.0	132.1	12.9	111.4	149.1	15.4	132.0	174.8
Total[b]	52.2	84.7	162.5	58.4	117.2	204.2	64.1	148.3	246.2	73.7	190.6	304.8
Rice												
Asian Centrally Planned Economies	99.0	2.2	116.5	117.6	4.4	139.6	121.8	6.9	147.6	142.2	10.8	173.2
USSR and Eastern Europe	2.1	.0	2.3	2.8	.0	3.2	3.7	.0	4.1	4.4	.0	5.0
Total[b]	101.1	2.2	118.9	120.4	4.5	142.8	125.5	6.9	151.7	146.6	10.8	178.1

[a]Includes other uses.

[b]The totals do not necessarily add up due to rounding.

TABLE 4. World: demand for cereals 1970 actual, 1980, 1990 and 2000 projected

	1970			1980			1990			2000		
	Food	Feed	Total[a]	Food	Feed	Total[a]	Food	Feed	Total[a]	Food	Feed	Total[a]
							million tons					
Wheat	215.7	69.4	332.5	253.2	93.7	403.7	303.0	118.4	489.8	368.8	152.6	601.3
Coarse grains	142.8	384.4	566.0	172.3	465.8	733.7	209.0	597.8	927.1	252.8	780.1	1186.6
Rice	270.0	4.6	310.5	346.7	8.2	400.1	424.8	12.8	493.4	543.5	20.6	633.6

[a]Includes other uses.

Sources Tables 1, 2, 3 and 4.

The demand projections are derived from the application of regional income elasticities to the growth of private consumption expenditures per caput which was projected to grow at the rates corresponding to the trend assumption for gross domestic product shown in Table 26 of the "Assessment of the World Food Situation present and future" United Nations World Food Conference (E/CONF.65/3) i.e. for developed market economies the growth assumed is 3.6 percent per annum; for Eastern Europe and USSR 5.3 percent; for developing market economies 3.6 percent; and for Asian centrally planned economies 2.5 percent. Total demand was calculated by multiplying the projected per caput demand by total regional population assuming the United Nations medium variant, which is based on "World Population Prospects, 1970-2000, As Assessed in 1973", Working Paper ESA/P/W.P.53, March 1975 Population Division, United Nations. For the more developed countries the rate of population growth 1975 to 2000 is assumed to be 0.7 percent per annum and for the less developed countries the growth is 2.2 percent per year. The projected demand under the low population growth variant for the more developed countries would be 3.9 percent less than under the medium variant: it would be 5.4 percent higher under the high population variant. For the less developed countries the figures would be 7.4 percent less and 6.3 percent more respectively.

TABLE 5. Per capita demand for cereals 1970 actual, 1980, 1990 and 2000 projected

		1970			1980				1990				2000			
	P[a]	C[b]	Pr[c]	FV[d]	P	C	Pr	FV	P	C	Pr	FV	P	C	Pr	FV
Developed market economies	724.4	3091	95.0	100.0	792.4	3146	97.3	104.81	861.0	3232	101.1	111.45	923.3	3241	100.7	114.30
North America	226.3	3318	105.5	100.0	248.7	3354	106.7	102.78	275.0	3409	109.3	106.29	296.0	3342	108.2	107.77
Western Europe	353.9	3133	93.7	100.0	375.2	3206	96.9	106.85	395.6	3311	101.5	115.77	414.5	3377	106.6	120.08
Oceania	15.4	3261	108.1	100.0	18.4	3287	109.4	102.85	21.5	3335	111.7	107.51	24.3	3368	112.8	109.12
Other developed	128.8	2554	79.1	100.0	150.0	2636	81.6	107.56	168.9	2745	85.4	118.05	188.4	2772	88.8	123.21
Developing market economies	1754.7	2211	56.1	100.0	2291.2	2333	59.4	108.33	2996.7	2481	63.7	119.90	3692.6	2615	67.4	127.67
Africa	279.2	2188	58.4	100.0	368.0	2273	61.7	108.11	497.7	2413	67.0	122.57	654.9	2476	68.9	128.09
Latin America	284.2	2528	65.0	100.0	373.8	2660	69.0	107.94	488.9	2795	73.4	117.37	619.9	2875	75.6	122.06
Near East	170.7	2495	69.3	100.0	226.7	2611	72.8	111.46	303.2	2682	75.8	123.46	380.4	2765	78.1	129.17
Far East	1016.5	2082	50.7	100.0	1317.4	2208	53.8	107.51	1699.9	2375	57.8	119.04	2029.1	2553	62.4	129.06
Centrally planned economies	1142.0	2506	72.2	100.0	1317.4	2608	75.7	109.81	1488.2	2708	79.9	123.98	1637.4	2764	82.0	128.39
Asia c.p.e.	794.1	2174	60.4	100.0	936.3	2339	65.6	115.00	1071.8	2473	70.8	135.25	1196.6	2574	73.8	142.24
USSR + Eastern Europe	347.9	3265	99.3	100.0	381.1	3268	100.5	107.80	416.3	3312	103.3	118.12	440.8	3279	104.3	122.34
World	3621.0	2480	69.0	100.0	4401.0	2562	71.1	103.76	5345.9	2665	74.2	109.96	6253.3	2746	76.1	111.75

[a] Population (millions).
[b] Calories (per day).
[c] Proteins (grams per day).
[d] Farm Value (index, 1970=100).

30

TABLE 6. Rates of growth of food production 1952 to 1975 (percent per year)

	1952-62		1962-70		1971-75	
	Total	Per Capita	Total	Per Capita	Total	Per Capita
Developed market economies	2.5	1.3	2.3	1.3	1.9	1.0
Western Europe	2.9	2.1	2.2	1.4	2.0	1.4
North America	1.9	0.1	2.2	1.0	1.7	0.8
Oceania	3.1	0.9	2.9	1.2	2.9	1.3
Eastern Europe and USSR	4.5	3.0	4.3	3.3	2.3	1.5
Total developed countries	3.1	1.8	2.9	1.9	2.0	1.1
Developing market economies	3.1	0.7	2.8	0.2	2.5	-0.2
Africa	2.2	--	2.5	--	0.7	-2.0
Far East	3.1	0.8	2.8	0.3	2.8	0.3
Latin America	3.2	0.4	3.1	0.2	2.5	-0.3
Near East	3.4	0.8	3.2	0.4	3.8	0.8
Asian Centrally Planned Economies	3.2	1.4	2.7	0.9	2.4	0.7
Total developing countries	3.1	0.7	2.9	0.5	2.5	0.1
World	3.1	1.1	2.9	0.9	2.2	0.3

Source: Food and Agriculture Organization; Production Yearbook, Rome, Italy.

GELIA T. CASTILLO

The Farmer Revisited: Toward a Return to the Food Problem

When God created the world, He allocated His blessings in many ways incomprehensible to us so that it is impossible to detect what decision-making model He applied in determining who gets what, where, how much and why. To some He assigned the desert; to others He gave mountains, lowlands, and swamps; some received snow and others the monsoons; some too much water and others, no water at all. He also made us of different shades from white to brown 'to black with no indication as to why some would have fair skin, tall nose, and blonde hair while there are those of us who are tanned, pugged-nosed, and short. However, we can have a pretty good guess as to why some were made women and others, men. In the allocation process, one occasionally suspects that He might have played favorites for a few more generously anointed with oil while some managed to inherit all the natural calamities--drought, flood, earthquake, cyclone, etc. To my country He bestowed mixed blessings--a lot of smiles, several International Beauty Queens, and an average of 19.6 typhoons a year (in 1964 a maximum of 30 tropical cyclones occurred and the mimimum was 13 in 1950-51). On the other hand, our Southeast Asian neighbors were conferred the right to oil and the freedom from the fury of the winds. It is just as well that we do not comprehend God's motives, otherwise there would be no end to the negotiations and to the bargaining for more concessions. Given this Master Creation called Earth and its inexplicable inequalities, we in the 1970s are super-

---

Gelia T. Castillo is Professor of Rural Sociology, University of the Philippines at Los Baños, College, Laguna, Philippines.

ciliously trying to fashion an equal world, hopefully with
enough food for all.

For a long time now we have been waging a War on Hunger
with varying outcomes and short-lived successes. When the new
rice variety was born in 1966, hopes ran wild. The press
dubbed it "miracle rice" and endowed it with unimaginable vir-
tues. The only thing it could not do was fly. After the initial euphoria, Dr. Clifton R. Wharton, Jr. (1969) opened Pandora's Box and from then on, every conceivable social and
biological evil in the world has been attributed to the Green
Revolution. While all these misgivings on the new agricultural
technology were raging, the issue turned away from growth and
productivity to equity, employment, population, pollution, habitat and women. If we scan the international development literature presently bulging in our library shelves, we would
encounter such titles and phrases as: "Limits to Growth";
"Models of Doom"; "Prophets of Gloom"; "Spoils of Progress";
"Seeds of Disaster"; "Demons of Discontent"; "Harvests of the
Hungry"; "The Politics of Pollution"; "Economics of the Environment"; "Economic Gains and Political Costs"; "the worst pollution of mankind: mass rural poverty"; "Changing tolerance for
income inequality"; "Contradictions of the Green Revolution";
"the Green Revolution--a plot by the imperialist-capitalist
Ford and Rockefeller Foundations"; "Plunderers of the Third
World"; "Women-Equality, Peace and Development"; "Assault on
World Poverty"; "Development from Below"; "Integrated agricultural and rural development"; "Smallholder Agriculture"; "Integrated Development of Small Farmers in Areas of Change"; "Marginal men"; "The Poor of the Earth"; "Who Benefits from Economic Development?" and finally the most popular of all--"the
rich are getting richer and the poor are getting poorer".

A cursory examination of what is being said about developments around the world gives one the impression that most of
what we have done or are currently doing is "wrong" or at
least, "not right". Illustrative of this type of disillusionment is most picturesquely expressed by a ranking FAO official
who says:

> there is a growing belief in our House and elsewhere, that
> much of the development approaches assiduously implemented
> over the last three decades have pushed most of our basically
> agrarian societies--and this takes in the Third as well as
> the Fourth and Fifth Worlds of recent categorization--into a
> dead end. The recurrent food problem, with its threat of
> becoming a chronic feature of our landscape, is only one man-
> ifestation of earlier strategies gone bankrupt.

In summary he suggests that

> sustained agricultural growth will come only when our poli-

cies undo the heavy burden of outdated policies, break the
yoke that vested interests strap on the small farmers, locking them . . . into invisible but oppressive economic prison
camps (Umali, 1976).

Along with this disillusionment comes a message loud and
clear that while everything else might be "wrong", the Chinese
seem to be the only ones who are "right". The Chinese experience appears to be so "liberating" that even the elites who sit
on capitalist chairs join in singing praises to non-elitism and
egalitarianism. As they say: "If you have not been to China,
you have not lived." Part of the aftermath of many pilgrimages
to Peking is the rise of the barefoot doctor, the barefoot
technician, and the barefoot manager and, of course,--the poor
peasant look among the children of the rich interpreted in
dingy-looking, but expensive, fashionably recycled faded denims.
In search of solutions to the problems of mankind, we have
a series of World Conferences on Food, Population, Environment,
Human Settlements, Employment and Women with each concluding
with some kind of a World Plan of Action. There are such proposals as a Global Food Strategy; A New Growth Pattern; and
Fuller Integration of Women in Development. Each of these
attempts to embody the equity dimension. Although all self-
respecting professionals pay lip service to the need for a more
equitable income distribution, I am not so Utopian as to
believe that a new international economic order is forthcoming
in the next decade or whether it is forthcoming at all.
Although I am also a born optimist, I have no illusions that
the rich of the earth whether in the developed or the developing countries would substantially and deliberately alter their
lifestyle so that the lower 40 percent might have a better lot
in life. If they do change, it is probably because they are
convinced that it is to their best self-interest. Moving
closer to home those of us who hue and cry about the social
injustices and inequalities in this world are happily at the
upper end of the income distribution of whatever country; and
are arguing for equality on a full stomach; with the vocabulary
of at least 16 years of schooling; and not about to write off a
day's development consultancy, a small project's research hon-
oraria; or even more boldly, take a cut in our "princely salaries" (Anonymous, 1976)--even in the service of the poor, the
small farmer and the marginal men we so eloquently champion.
Our credentials, therefore, as serious advocates of an equal
world are far from impeccable.
I am not so self-righteous as to accuse the developed
world of "eating little children" nor am I going to ask the
rich to eat less so the poor can eat more. We should not ask
anybody to give up something which we ourselves are not prepared to forego. Nobody should be asked to be a "martyr" even
in the name of development.

OBJECTIVES OF THE PAPER
    The most remarkable aspect of all the grim hindsights on
    the Green Revolution is the speed with which we turned to
    the issues of equity, employment, and ecology forgetting
almost completely what brought about the new agricultural
strategy in the first place. This paper is, therefore, only a
very modest attempt to revisit the farmer and his world to help
remind us once again what food production is. There are no
magic solutions hidden or bare in this presentation.
    The objectives of the paper are two-fold:

    1. To present in capsule, a portrait of the farmer:
        a. As an occupational category
        b. As a family man
        c. As a farmer
        d. As a consumer
        e. As a target of development programs
    2. To briefly identify the roles of the professional as
        he relates to the farmer and the food problem.

    For the very obvious reasons, the farmer who will be
described here is Filipino but he is presented not as a universal farmer but as an illustrative case. The rationalization
for inflicting this on an international audience arises from
the fact that my limited exposure to other parts of the world
has taught me that farmers all over the developing world are
similar, but they are fascinatingly different in their many
similarities. Accidents of geography, history, culture,
ethnicity, religion, political ideology, and most of all, physical environment make for all the differences. Not all the
descriptions portrayed here will fit farmers in other countries
but I hope that at least some of the issues will be relevant.
The decision to focus on the farmer rather than on some other
actor in the food drama was dictated by the fact that unless
proven otherwise, food most everywhere is produced by farmers.
Furthermore, practically all international development agencies
have chosen the farmer, particularly the small farmer as the
central figure in their programs.

PORTRAIT OF THE FARMER

The Farmer As An Occupational Category
    The Philippines, despite our dance troupes, fashion mod-
    els, and Fifth Avenue buildings is really a nation of vil-
lages with about 70 percent of our population living in rural
areas. In the comforts of our white-collar existence, we sometimes forget that the most important figure in food production
is not at all aware that there is a World Food Conference. If

they did, they would be wondering why we were invited and they were not. As of 1974, more than one-half (55 percent) of our labor force earn their livelihood from farming. This picture has changed only very slightly from the 58.8 percent 20 years ago. Furthermore, 70 percent of the self-employed and 88 percent of the unpaid family workers in the country are in agriculture. For a more accurate picture of the situation, it is necessary to examine specifically the rural sector because the national statistics tend to mask the existing realities. Over a ten-year period since 1965, the proportion of the rural male labor force engaged in farming has remained close to 80 percent. Even for the 10-14 year olds who drop out from school, there is an increasing agriculturization of the employment picture for both males and females. The total labor force in farming is almost 7.5 million with 22 percent of them female. The increase in the size of the agricultural labor force is 65 percent from 1956 to 1974. Males increased by 74 percent and females, only 40 percent. These figures have been cited in order to emphasize that rural industry and manufacturing have failed to increase their capacity to absorb rural labor. Perhaps it is a pretty good guess that agriculture will be the major source of employment for a long time to come. In the case of rural females in agriculture, their lower rate of increase is due to the "escape" from farming provided by jobs in urban areas mainly as domestic helpers. Next to commerce which is an euphemism for peddling, hawking, and vending, domestic service is the most significant source of employment for village girls who migrate to the city. It is not unusual for them to send remittances home through savings or cash advances from their employers to buy fertilizers and other farm inputs or to pay off mortgages on a small piece of land (Castillo, 1976, pp. 131-188).

The rhetoric of the Green Revolution has centered considerably on the resulting inequalities between the large and the small farmer because the latter has been "left behind" by a strategy that purportedly favored the better-off. In the Philippines, this is not the issue. There is a serious inequality in the distribution of incomes but one aspect of this is "the large discrepancy between the average incomes of farm families and those of non-farm families" (Mangahas and Rimando, 1976, p. 107). Based on a minimum cost food basket which meets the recommended nutrient requirement given the price of marketed goods in selected localities, Tan (1976) estimates that 70 percent of Filipino families are poor, but farmers, farm laborers, fishermen, hunters, loggers and related workers registered the highest incidence of poverty among all the occupational groups. Eighty-four percent of them are poor. They received the lowest income of all. On the other hand, administrative, executive, and managerial workers have the highest income and the lowest incidence of poverty (18 percent); followed by professional,

technical and related workers (22 percent); clerical workers
(28 percent); miners, quarrymen (33 percent); sales workers
(52 percent); service workers (57 percent); transport and communication workers (62 percent); craftsmen and production process workers (67 percent); and manual laborers (80 percent).
The significant inequality, therefore, that deserves prior
attention is that between farmers and non-farmers particularly
white-collar workers such as professionals and executives
rather than the inequality among farmers, who as a category,
are the poorest in the country. As a means of narrowing this
gap, Mangahas and Rimando (1976) suggest such measures as "a
research-induced biological improvement in the plants being
cultivated which will also help ease the food adequacy" and
land reform or the shifting of farmers from one form of tenure
to another higher income form although this approach is not
necessarily helping in solving food shortages.

The analysis by Tan (1976) showed that schooling is the
most important factor which determines the incidence of poverty. The

incidence declines almost monotonically from 82 percent for
those with Grades one through three of schooling, to 40 percent for those with 4 years of high school, to 20 percent
with 4 years of college. The incidence further drops to 14
percent as the heads of families achieve more than 4 years of
college.

In this connection, agricultural education is a big enterprise
in my country but farming is mostly in the hands of people with
low educational attainment. The mean years of schooling for
the rural labor force is four years but 15 percent of them have
not had any formal schooling and those in farming have the lowest educational attainment among the different occupational
groups. The more agricultural the region is the higher the
proportion of males employed with no schooling (Castillo,
1974). As a matter of fact, it is low education which puts
them in farming. These bits of information have implications
both for income distribution and for productivity. Considering the composition of the poor and the position of farmers and
farm laborers at the lower end of the income distribution, to
focus mainly on the inequalities among farmers is to ignore the
more serious poverty problem and the larger inequality within
the society.

The Farmer As a Family Man
Because the rice farmers are most numerous and cultivate
the most area and because of the primacy of rice as a food
item, most of the presentation here will be about them. The
typical rice farmer is in his early or mid-40s. He has about

4 or 5 years of schooling but about 10 percent or more did not
go to school at all. He has been farming for 20 years and
started to do so at about the age of 18. His wife would have
borne about 6.5 children by the end of her reproductive life.
His household size which includes him and his wife is smaller,
only 6.08 because an average of 1.94 persons have already left
the household permanently. The labor potential which includes
members aged 15 and above is 3.14. This represents farmer,
wife and 1.14 children. In practice, however, farm work starts
as early as 6 or 7 years so part of another 1.92 younger children are available. This means children miss school during the
peak of planting or harvesting or drop out early because of the
family's need for labor. About three-fourths of rural households are nuclear. Married children set up their own households since it is relatively easy to build houses even if they
are of very light materials. This practice makes for more than
80 percent home ownership, but only half of these homes are
built on owned residential lots. Because farmers work on the
land, we do not usually think of them as squatters, but many of
them are. For some reason, families in nuclear households
breed about 1.3 children more than those with extended arrangements, hence farm families are more prone to child-bearing
under this system.

The number of children affect both food and labor force.
Practically no Filipino wife would deliberately choose child-
lessness, and the preferred number is still more than 4
although the actual size is about two more than that (Castillo,
1976). When asked how many children they could support if they
had three hectares of irrigated and five hectares of non-
irrigated land, 37 percent of farmers studied in land reform
areas in Central Luzon think they could support 7 to 9 children
or more (Flores and Clemente, 1975). In another study, more
than 75 percent of farmer-parents said "yes" when asked if life
chances of their children would be better if there were fewer
of them. Their reasons for the affirmative response are:
first, there would be fewer mouths to feed, fewer to clothe,
and fewer to send to school, hence less expenses; second, there
would be more resources available to fewer children. These two
sets of responses are qualitatively different. When one thinks
of "fewer children means fewer mouths to feed", the motivation
to increase productivity may also be diminished. As we often
hear, "What is the use of working so hard when you have only
two children?" The second category of response implies a non-
diminished need for resources to achieve a better quality of
life. But more revealing than these two observations, are the
reasons parents gave for saying that even with fewer children,
life chances for them would not be any better. They have very
eloquently pointed out that there is no necessary relationship
between number of children and state of livelihood because
there are parents who have only one or two children and are

still poor. Furthermore, they argued that fewer children means
fewer breadwinners and, therefore, lower family income
(Castillo et al., 1975). All the evidence indicates that
whether in delivery of services, knowledge, attitudes or practice of family planning, rural wives lag behind those from the
urban areas especially Metropolitan Manila. A more frustrating
lag is the slow translation of knowledge and attitudes into
actual family planning behavior, without which a decline in
population growth rate will not materialize. Farmers make a
complicated trilogy of contributions to the food problem. They
produce the food, the producers of the food as well as the consumers of the food they produce. It is difficult to unravel
when one factor represents a constraint or a potential for
increasing productivity. At the macro level, it is easy to see
why we need to have fewer children, but at the individual farm
level, we can ask the question: "When one is poor, has little
or no land of one's own, has little or no education and meager
material wealth and there is not much future in sight, why
shouldn't he have at least six children as his only capital for
survival and hope for the future?" Unlike other occupational
groups, farmers affect both the numerator and the denominator
in the food-population equation, and from what we see, they
seem to be more efficient in producing the denominator. Fortunately or unfortunately most farmers do not want their children
to become farmers, if they can help it. They want them to have
college education as a way out of farming and into white-collar
and skilled occupations. On the part of their children, farming is not really a preferred occupation. It is something to
fall back on when their first choice of professional or skilled
jobs with regular income fails to materialize. There is an
ambivalence in their attitude toward farming. To them, farming
as an occupation offers a good potential "if" conditions happen
to be "right" and favorable. Farming is a risky enterprise and
is not a definitely positive and dependable source of income.
Hard, physical work involved and the risk of crop failure are
the specific negative features of farming which make it unat-
tractive to many (Castillo, 1973a; Castillo et al., 1973 and
1975; Flores and Clemente, 1975; Rivera, 1976). The chances
that future farmers will have more schooling depend very much
on whether alternatives outside farming exist for rural youth.
The higher their educational attainment, the greater is the
likelihood that they will move out of the village and out of
farming leaving only those who dropped out of school earlier.
Agricultural manpower, therefore, is likely to remain a reluctant manpower for some time to come. Furthermore, contrary to
popular belief, farming is not always an alternative available
to farm youth, anyway, because there is not enough land to
accommodate all six children in farming. The most they could
hope for is to work as hired farm labor or unpaid family worker.
Either way, it is nothing exciting to look forward to.

On the female side of the farmer's family, his wife is the family treasurer and a joint participant in decision-making even in matters pertaining to the farm such as applying for production loans, purchasing inputs and farm implements, adoption of new practices, disposal of farm products and even on how much to save (Castillo, 1976). Although we are very proud of this fact, we do not know what impact her participation has on the quality of the farm-related decisions. What information, knowledge, and skills, for example, does she bring to bear in this process which would make for better decision outcomes? Perhaps it will pay to invest in the enhancement of her ability to contribute positively to the farmer's role in food production.

The Farmer As a Farmer

In discussing the farmer as a farmer, we return to the notion that despite our social and ideological concerns, farming is basically a physico-biological process. The problems most frequently mentioned by farmers relate to immediate production problems such as irrigation, insects, disease, rats, floods, droughts, high cost of inputs, and low yields. Being better-off or worse-off depends upon the success or failure in production, and whether you ask them before or after a typhoon. Land reform, credit or price support can only enhance the production process, but none of them can replace it. The large farmer-small farmer categorization which is currently in vogue is too simple a dichotomy to reflect the complexities of reality in crop production. Even if we concentrate only on the rice farmer, there is an infinite number of dichotomies and trichotomies which make up the basics and the surrounding circumstances in farming. Let us explore a few of them.

Suitability of land for rice production. Rice, like any other plant, seems to grow well in some places, but not in others. There is Class I land ideally suited for rice production; Class II suitable for rice production but with increasing limitations; Class II-A can be profitably planted to rice by adding purchased inputs such as fertilizers, chemicals, power and labor; Class II-B land cannot be profitably farmed because production is too low to yield a profitable return on purchased inputs; Class II-B and Class III are only farmed when resources have zero opportunity cost and Class IV is unsuited for production (Herdt and Barker, 1976).

In real life, we are trying to grow rice under all these conditions. A farmer who grows rice on a hectare of Class I land is probably better-off than someone who is trying to grow it on 7 hectares of Class III land. How did Farmer A happen to have Class I land and Farmer B, Class III? Who knows?

Source and amount of water available. There are farms
which are fully-irrigated, partially irrigated, rainfed, lowland, upland and even "floating". Among the irrigated farms
some have gravity systems, others, deep wells and pumps. The
costs involved are widely different.

Intensity and diversity of cropping. These include
single-crop, double-crop, multi-crop, mono-culture and multi-
ple-cropping, not to mention the dry season and the wet season.

Vulnerability to the whims of nature. There are floods,
droughts and typhoons. We also have the typhoon-free areas and
the typhoon belts.

Accessibility of farm and home to development services.
Needless to say, farms along the roads have a decided advantage
over those where you have to walk half a day to reach it.

Tenure status. Farms are operated under different systems
such as owner-operator, part-owner, share tenant, leaseholder
or lessee, amortizing owner, combination farmer (who as the
name implies is owner-operator, lessee, share tenant and landlord all at the same time but different small pieces of land),
squatter farmer, sub-tenant, and farmer administrator with
hired labor. Even under share tenancy, we have 70-30, 65-35,
50-50 with landlords and tenants sharing the inputs and outputs
in different proportions. Seventy-thirty is not necessarily
better than 50-50, because the tenant shoulders more of the
costs, although he also gets more of the harvest. The lessees
have fixed rentals, but the level at which they are fixed varies not only in different areas but even in the same village.
They can range from 5 to 30 sacks of rice per hectare depending
upon productivity of the land, relationships between landlord
and tenant, and the year when the farmer shifted from crop-
sharing to leasehold.

Type of landlord. We have all kinds of landlords: big or
small; resident or absentee; traditional or modern; paternalistic or non-paternalistic; managing or non-managing; and fully
or partially dependent on rice. The nature of the relationships and the sharing arrangements are conditioned by the above
factors.

Access to other income sources. Some farmers are better-
off than others not because of their farm but because they have
off-farm and non-farm jobs.

Number of land parcels farmers cultivate. In one study in
Central Luzon, 47 percent of the rice farmers have more than
one parcel of land which are not always in the same vicinity.

Furthermore about 35 percent have more than one landlord. One parcel may be more productive than the other, and one landlord more generous than the other.

The complexities brought about by the combinations of coexisting factors make it difficult to predict the "winning combination" as far as participation in the benefits of agricultural development is concerned. As one farmer so aptly put it: "When the harvest is good, I want to be a leaseholder. When the harvest is bad, I want to be a share tenant." Although there are "bundles of positives" and "bundles of negatives" in response and institutional endowments, there are also compensatory factors in between such as the usual larger size of rainfed as against irrigated farms, etc. Incidentally, small farms have also registered higher yields per hectare than larger ones (Castillo, 1975b).

In addition to all the above-mentioned complexities, there is tremendous variation in farm size and yield per hectare even in a village with only 106 hectares of riceland and only 55 farm families. The farm sizes ranged from below one hectare to five hectares and more. The yields per hectare varied from 20 to more than 100 sacks per hectare. The yield variability was observed for both the 2 hectares and above (large) and the below 2 hectares (small) (Hayami et al., 1975).

Finally, the Filipino rice farmer is a small farmer. We have some big landholdings, but farm operating units average less than 3 hectares. Any agricultural development strategy, therefore, has to be a small-farmer strategy. Besides being small, our rice farmers are "trapped" in a sense, because they have few or no alternatives. When asked about their reasons for farming, they said: "This is the only way I know how to earn living"; "I was born a farmer, I will die a farmer"; "There's no place where I can build my house except on the farm"; "farming is for the poor and the little-educated"; "I feel secure with my land"; "farming is not so difficult after all". The most positive response came from 25 percent who said "I like farming very much" (Rivera, 1976).

The "rich farmer" is few and far between and when we find him, he almost always has nonfarm sources of income or maybe he is farming as a tax write-off. If there were more rich farmers, farming might be a more coveted rather than a "residual" occupation. When productivity levels are low, levels of living are low, and farmers as a category are at the bottom of the economic ladder. Anything we do in agricultural development will lead to further inequalities among farmers. On the other hand, investments in the countryside are steps toward loosening the farm-nonfarm gap. Let it not be said that we would rather opt out of opportunities to increase food production in favor of keeping farmers more equal but poor. This is what is implied when yield-increasing technology is condemned because it has created increasing disparities among farmers.

The Farmer As a Consumer

Most of the time we think of the farmer as a producer. What he sells beyond his family's needs is regarded as marketable surplus. Again, this is an oversimplification which needs to be elaborated upon. The majority of farmers sell their rice crop immediately after threshing to meet immediate cash needs. In general, "storing for purposes of getting a better price was not practiced. What was stored was only the rice for home consumption, but this was also sold when the need for cash became critical" (Rivera, 1976; Lasap and Sulabo, undated). A recent study of farmers in a predominantly rice-growing area showed that almost half of them bought the greater portion of their rice needs, and 18 percent bought half of their needs after disposing of their crops immediately after harvest. Only one-fourth of them do not buy rice at all. During the months of September and October, 74 and 46 percent, respectively, of the farmers indicated that there was scarcity of food in their households. In November, 16 percent and in April and May about 12 percent of the farmer-households admitted to food scarcity. More than 7 percent said they miss their meals and 63 percent are unable to meet their food requirements adequately. One of the most important items they dream of enjoying if there ever should be a good harvest is good food which includes among other things, fried chicken, barbecue, roasted pig and dog meat (Rivera, 1976). Most of the farmers spend two-thirds to three-fourths of their income on food (Villaviza, 1974).

In the final analysis, the rice farmer is a net purchaser of rice and therefore, he is both a beneficiary and a victim of high rice prices. Part of the marketable surplus is only an "interim surplus". Furthermore, a study of energy intake and expenditure of some workers found that farmers' calorie intake is lower than that of drivers and shoemakers but their calorie expenditure is highest of the three groups. Farmers also have the lowest protein and fat intake. Although housewives were reported to have the lowest intake, they also have the lowest calorie expenditure. Farmers registered the greatest deficit in work calories (de Guzman et al., 1974).

The stereotype of the farmer splurging much of his money and produce on fiestas and other recreational activities finds little support from empirical evidences. Two studies report 2 to 4 percent of their income goes for annual and occasional celebrations (Villaviza, 1974; Flores and Clemente, 1975). About half of the farmers reported no formal recreation. They spend their free time in lively "bull sessions" in front of small village stores. Going to the movies is enjoyed by 22 percent and 8 percent indulge in cockfighting, card games and mahjong (Flores and Clemente, 1975). The average farmer, therefore, is not throwing away his money on "fun and games".

The Farmer As a Target of Development Programs

Despite the poverty of our farmers, their level of schooling, their small farms and their share tenancy status,
they have responded positively to the new rice technology. In
less than 10 years, 62 percent of the total rice area in the
Philippines is planted to the modern semi-dwarf varieties.
Furthermore, annual output growth in rice production is
explained almost completely by increased yield rather than by
expansion in hectarage. Our farmers, therefore, cannot be
faulted for being traditional, resistant and unwilling to take
risks (Castillo, 1975; Hardt and Barker, 1976; Mangahas and
Rimando, 1976).

But all these innovations and improvements in productivity
have yet to solve our rice problem. Actual yields still lag
considerably behind the experiment station potentials. When
the former Director of the International Rice Research Institute (IRRI) reflected on this matter, he said:

The only real disappointment I felt was that somehow we
did not understand sufficiently why the Asian farmer who had
adopted the new varieties was not doing better. Somehow I
felt that the rice scientists who had obtained yields of up
to 5 to 10 metric tons per hectare on the IRRI farm still
could not explain why so many Filipino farmers (for example)
obtained on the average less than one metric ton per hectare
increase in yield after shifting from the traditional to the
high-yielding varieties (Chandler, 1975, p. 15).

Economists and agronomists have identified

two distinct gaps between farmer's yield and experiment station yield. Gap one, the 'environmental effects', shows the
difference between the maximum possible yield of the technology under experiment station conditions and the maximum
yield in farmers' environments. The second gap shows the
difference between farmers' actual yields and the maximum
potential under their conditions. . . . In some circumstances, the gap between the best yields in experiment stations and the maximum potential under most farmers' conditions may be just as wide as the second gap (Herdt and
Barker, 1976).

In farm level observations from this "constraints" study,
mean yields were 2 tons per hectare during the wet season and
2.8 during the dry season. Heavy rains, floods, and typhoons
caused low yields. In the dry season, farmers attributed yield
loss to rat damage, shortage of water, lack of fertilizer,
insect infestation and weeds. The failure of the wet season
crop has reduced the use of fertilizer, herbicides, and insec-

ticides in the dry season. Lack of awareness is not a significant constraint since 95 percent of the farmers have heard of
the 16 practices studied. Inputs were also apparently available.

The widespread adoption of the new seeds and their accompanying components has given us the impression that our farmers
are sophisticated. Their ability to use each input correctly
is, however, another matter. For example, while most of the
farmers had used chemical fertilizers for over a decade only
one-third correctly identified the time at which it should be
applied. Knowledge of correct weed control practice is also
very low. While they use insecticides and can recognize the
damages caused by insects, the identification of the insects
responsible for damage is not good. Although practically all
of them use the new varieties, the seeds they use are seldom
pure, for they obtain them from other farmers and they plant
their seedlings much older than the ideal age.

We, therefore, have a situation characterized by high
awareness of yield increasing technology and by high adoption
but by low level of technical knowledge. Consequently, there
is a high incidence of incorrect use of the technology. Bern-
sten (1976) suggests that "part of the yield gap could be
reduced and that costs could be lowered by teaching farmers how
to use presently employed inputs properly." This latter task
depends on the intensity of extension exposure. Unfortunately
even in the study sites which are priority areas for rice production and land reform programs, farmers received only an
average of less than 3 visits during the season. In most
cases, "the purpose of the visit was to process papers which
were required for obtaining an input loan. The education component of extension was largely neglected. At the same time
over 75 percent of the farmers wanted the technician to visit
him more frequently--indicating their receptivity to new knowledge and a positive attitude towards the extension technician."
The relevant issue, therefore, is no longer adoption-non adoption but sufficient knowledge to adopt and use the technology
properly. This is a definite role for the extension worker.

As part of our development thrust, we have agricultural
credit programs and efforts to organize farmers for capital
build-up and more effective delivery of agricultural services.
Evidences show that many farmers have shifted credit sources
from landlords to banks. It is also evident that farmers are
learning to use institutional credit for production purposes
(Castillo, 1975; Lasap and Sulabo, 1975; Rivera, 1976). However, credit repayment remains a serious problem. In the past,
farmers were said to be caught in a perpetual state of indebtedness blamed on "exploitation" by their landlords. Today they
are still in a state of indebtedness but to the bank, not to
the landlord. The high costs of production and successive crop
failures due to major forces have contributed to low repayment

rates (Collado, 1976). On the other hand, there are indications that closer technical supervision of both the production
process and the use of credit contributes to better production
and improved loan collections. Even among those who have been
able to repay loans, there is some ambivalence toward credit.
Although they acknowledge the need for it, they would prefer to
have no debts so they will be free from worries. They are
likewise uncertain that borrowing capital can help improve
agricultural production and augment the household budget (Lasap
and Sulabo, 1975; Anwarul Karim, 1976). Credit, therefore, is
not perceived as an "unqualified good thing" because of the
accompanying risks and obligations.

With respect to organizations intended for their welfare,
farmers are "slow joiners". The advantages to them as individual members have to be substantial and clearly demonstrated
before they would consider membership. If benefits in life
could be obtained in some other way, without joining any organization, farmers seem to prefer to act on their own as individuals or as family. Altruism for the good of the community and
of other members, even the less fortunate ones, is not the most
salient selling point of farmers' associations (Castillo, 1975;
Flores and Clemente, 1975; Valiente et al., 1976). The experiences of some small-scale intensively supervised farmers'
associations have shown that it takes at least five years
before some degree of organizational viability emerges (Lasap
and Sulabo, 1975; Anievas, 1975). We seldom have this patience
and persistence to pursue farmers' organizations beyond the
initial organizational phase. Enthusiasm wanes rapidly after
that and newer programs come into view.

Our land reform program which was expected to contribute
the twin objectives of equity and productivity has fallen short
of expectations on both counts. Several studies conducted by
different researchers done independently of each other have
shown that contrary to the assumption that owner-operators
would have the incentive to produce more because any increases
in production would accrue to them, share tenants were found to
be as innovative and as productive as owner-operators. The
reason why the latter are better off is because they do not
have to pay land rentals. Land reform or change in tenure status per se, therefore, has not contributed to increased productivity (Castillo, 1975; Mangahas, 1974; Flores and Clemente,
1975).

On the equity objective, it was discovered in the process
of implementation that contrary to the prevailing image of the
landlord as a big landlord, 80 percent of them have small holdings of less than 7 hectares, and less than one percent own
more than 100 hectares. Although the latter own 30 percent of
the tenanted areas, the greatest resistance to land transfer
comes from the small, not the big landlords who were the first
to enter into fixed rentals and amortizing arrangements with

their tenants. Since the majority of our landlords are small,
there is not that much land to redistribute. Furthermore,
there are share tenants who refused to be "liberated" from
their bondage to the landlord. Good relations with the landlord and the sharing of risks with them are their rationale for
preferring the old system (Castillo, 1975; Mangahas, 1974;
Flores and Clemente, 1975). Under a fixed rental or amortizing
system, farmers shoulder all the risks involved and have to pay
rentals regardless of success or failure in production. Those
who shifted from share tenancy to leasehold and to amortizing
ownership considered being their own boss and getting an
increased share of the produce as their reasons for shifting
tenure status. Those who said their life situations have
improved do not attribute this to land reform but rather to
increased production (Castillo, 1975; Rivera, 1976).

THE ROLE OF PROFESSIONALS
    In trying to meet world food needs, we the professionals
    play a number of roles, some of which are more directly
    relevant than others. We have in our midst: policy-
makers; professionals turned politicians; problem conceptu-
alizers and model builders; articulators and interpreters of
policy; translators of plans into programs and programs into
projects; designers of field strategy; and finally at the bottom of the totem pole, the doers. As far as actualization of
food production goals is concerned, the most crucial but the
most maligned, least rewarded and seldom appreciated among the
professionals are the doers represented by the extension workers. They are the conduit for agricultural technology, technical knowledge and skills, agricultural credit, organizational
services, land reform and general development information.
There are those who argue that if the technology is sound and
profitable, it will diffuse without the aid of extension workers. But where farmers are poor and have minimum education as
has been pointed out earlier, diffusion and adoption can take
place rapidly without the necessary knowledge to use technology
correctly. Just as important is the extension worker's role in
the more equitable delivery of development services, because he
is the farmer's link with the outside world. Quite often it is
he who determines which farmers will receive the new seeds, the
credit, the fertilizer, etc. Where the farmer-extension worker
ratio is very unfavorable, one cannot expect the extension
worker to give priority to the more "difficult" sector of the
farming community, because the "better-off" farmers are really
not well-off and not sophisticated. With the advent of irrigation, new technology, credit, and land reform, farmers recognize the value of competent and more frequent contact with

extension workers. They have no desire to be left behind
(Castillo, 1973b, 1975; Lall, 1975; Rivera, 1976; Anwarul
Karim, 1976; Bureau of Agricultural Economics, 1975; Chua,
1975; Valiente et al., 1976). On the positive role of extension, a recent study has shown that extension substitutes for
the effects of schooling in less developed villages. In the
more developed ones, extension and formal schooling complement
each other to increase rice production. The need for a sustained, viable, and dependable extension system is also suggested by the finding that "the effect of extension contact in
a year does not depreciate in the same year but the effects
diminish at a rate of 50 percent in the following years. The
more rapidly the recommended inputs change, the more rapidly
the effect of extension participation will diminish" (Halim,
1976; Tapay, 1976).

Extension work is not a glamorous job. Work overload, low
pay, meager transportation allowance, difficulty in convincing
farmers on the merits of innovations, presence of factional
groups among farmers, lack of confidence in the worker, unrec-
ognized performance, etc. are frequent complaints (Llano, 1973).
Anyone who has seen the extension agent at work in our villages
knows what these mean. All of us ought to try it sometimes if
only to teach us some humility and a little bit of sincerity
in what we profess.

The group of professionals who are simultaneously "heroes"
and "villains" in food production are the creators of technology. They are "damned if they do and damned if they don't",
but so far, they are the only ones who have a direct input into
the production process. The rest of us are peripheral.

In assessing the magnitude of our food problem and the
progress made toward its solution, we have data gatherers, data
processors, and data sanctifiers. It is amazing how very crude
data from our respective countries take on an authoritative
character the moment they have been computerized and released
by international agencies in the different capitals of the
world. Although we have highly trained manpower in these agencies, the basic data-gathering process leaves much to be
desired. We need to make more investments at the field level
not only in terms of expertise but also in terms of more
attractive incentives.

With respect to evaluation of agricultural programs, we
have apologists, critics, but mostly hindsighters. The latter
are professionals who know all the answers after the fact has
been accomplished, and never before. Side by side with the
hindsighters are the professional preachers of egalitarianism
who live with all the trappings of elitism and the comforts of
"dirty" capitalism.

One criterion which we should apply in judging our worth
as professionals concerned with the food problem is the extent

to which we live by what we say and whether what we say or do
makes a little bit of a difference in the lives of the poor and
the hungry. Some agencies are very vulnerable to criticism
because the work they do is directly relevant to the problem.
They contribute toward making the farmer a participant in the
development process. Much of what we say or do, farmers never
know about, let alone profit from, but they appreciate roads,
irrigation, electrification, credit, new seeds, fertilizers,
hand tractors, etc. They are impatient with words which produce no tangible impact on their production and their lives.

In a lament about earlier strategies gone bankrupt and
agriculture that has slowed to a crawl, FAO's Assistant
Director-General cites the staggering human costs in terms of
further impoverishment of the poor and the marginal men, mostly
sharecroppers, tillers of small farms, subsistence fishermen
and slash and burn farmers. As he puts it:

> Modern technology, the new seeds, pesticides, small
> machines etc. has by-passed them. Services gravitate we now
> know into areas where there is water management and control.
> A lopsided structure has therefore emerged. It is one that
> favors the better-off and in a real chilling sense, it is a
> prison camp. It locks our small farms into debilitating
> poverty. In FAO and other places, there is the crystallizing
> conviction that the beginning of a rural breakthrough may be
> found in the very victim of the lack of that rural growth--
> the farmer. It may seem a strange paradox but the victim
> could well be the liberator (Umali, 1976).

There is no rural breakthrough and certainly nothing new
in the conviction that to promote rural growth, we have to
reach the farmer. What has been missing all along is the cour-
age to implement the conviction with most, if not all of our
resources, in as many places, for as long as it takes. It is
very doubtful whether any of the past strategies designed to
reach the farmer were really ever "assiduously implemented."
The bane of our development programs is that we look for new
strategies, new slogans every year because the old one last
year no longer justifies our existence. For once, let us be
innovative by implementing an old conviction. The rural breakthrough lies in being able to match fiery rhetoric with persistent action. The world has probably all the literature it can
stand. We are rich in promise and short in performance. As
Charles Haddon Spurgeon once said: "They promise mountains but
perform molehills" and then we make mountains out of molehills.

The challenge of today is to translate our misgivings into
implementable alternatives; our technical knowledge into operational field projects so that food may actually be produced
rather than simply discussed.

REFERENCES

Anievas, T. C. 1975. Some socio-economic changes among farmers in the UPLB/SEARCA social laboratory, Pila, Laguna, Philippines. Unpublished Ph.D. thesis, University of the Philippines, Los Baños, Philippines.

Anonymous. 1976. Princely salaries in UN agencies. Bulletin Today May 22.

Anwarul Karim, A. M. 1976. Profile and loan repayment behavior of small vice-farmer members of Samahang, Nayons in Laguna Province. Unpublished Ph.D. thesis, University of the Philippines, Los Baños, Laguna, Philippines.

Bernstein, R. H. 1976. Rice farming in Central Luzon: Input usage, cultural practices, and yield constraints. Paper presented at International Rice Research Institute Seminar, March 20, Los Baños, Laguna, Philippines.

Bureau of Agricultural Economics. 1975. An agro-economic study of Iloilo: Farm management and socio-economic aspects. Research Report No. 5, Quezon City, Philippines.

Castillo, G. T. 1973a. Perspectives on rural out-of-school youth: The undiscovered majority. In Proceedings of the workshop on manpower and human resources. Institute of Economic Development and Research, University of the Philippines, Los Baños, Laguna, Philippines.

Castillo, G. T. 1973b. Between promise and performance: The role of agricultural extension in the diffusion and adoption of agricultural innovations. University of the Philippines, Los Baños, Laguna, Philippines.

Castillo, G. T. 1974. Some characteristics of the Philippine educational system and the case for non-formal education. Southeast Asian Spectrum 3:66-75.

Castillo, G. T. 1975. All in a grain of rice: A review of Philippine studies on the social and economic implications of the new rice technology. Southeast Asia Center for Graduate Study and Research in Agriculture. Los Baños, Laguna, Philippines.

Castillo, G. T. 1976. The Filipino women as manpower: The image and the emperical reality. University of the Philippines, Los Baños, Laguna, Philippines.

Castillo, G. T., A. M. de Guzman, S. L. Pahud and L. Paje. 1973. The Green Revolution at the village level: A Philippine case study. In R. T. Shan (Ed.) Technical Change in Asian Agriculture. Australian National University, Canberra.

Castillo, G. T., D. M. Arboleda, L. P. Domingo and V. M. Lasap. 1975. Alternatives for rural youth: Three village level case studies. University of the Philippines, Los Baños, Laguna, Philippines.

Chandler, R. F., Jr. 1975. Case history of IRRI's research

management during the period 1960-1972. Asian Vegetable
Research and Development Center, Shanhua, Taiwan.

Chua, L. 1975. Benchmark survey on the farming activities and
off-farm jobs of farmers in Maramag, Musuan, Bukidnon.
Central Mindanao University, Philippines.

Collado, G. M. 1976. Credit as a catalyst in agricultural
development: The Philippine experience. International
workshop on accelerating agricultural development. SEARCA,
Los Baños, Laguna, Philippines.

de Guzman, P. E., et al. 1974. A study of the energy expenditure dietary intake and pattern of daily activity among
various occupational groups. Philippine Journal Science
103:6-8.

Flores, T. G. and F. A. Clementa. 1975. Socio-economic profile of tenants and landlords/landowners in the Philippines. Report of the Philippine Council for Agricultural
Research, Agrarian Reform Institute, University of the
Philippines, Los Baños, Laguna, Philippines.

Halim, A. 1976. The economic contribution of schooling and
extension to vice production in the province of Laguna,
Philippines. Unpublished Ph.D. thesis, University of the
Philippines, Los Baños, Laguna, Philippines.

Hayami, Y., L. Maligalig and N. Fortuna. 1975. Socio-economic
characteristics of a rice village in Southern Luzon: A
report of benchmark survey for anatomy of peasant economy.
International Rice Research Institute, Los Baños, Laguna,
Philippines.

Herdt, R. W. and R. Barker. 1976. Networks, environments, and
new rice technology for farmers. International Rice
Research Institute, Los Baños, Laguna, Philippines.

Lall, V. S. 1975. Diffusion of IR 26 rice variety in compact
and non-compact farms in Camarines Sur, Philippines.
Unpublished Ph.D. thesis, University of the Philippines,
Los Baños, Laguna, Philippines.

Lasap, S. L., Jr. and E. C. Sulabo. Undated. Mobilizing human
resources through institutional approach: Case studies on
farmers' associations, Social Laboratory Action Research
No. 2, University of the Philippines, Los Baños, Laguna,
Philippines.

Lasap, S. L., Jr., E. C. Sulabo, L. L. Lumactod, C. A. del
Rosario, T. N. Sierra and I. S. Cuñada. 1975. The UPLBCA/
SEARCA social laboratory after 5 years: An assessment of
performance. Department Agricultural Education, University
of the Philippines, Los Baños, Laguna, Philippines.

Llano, D. S. 1973. Problems relative to teaching adult farmers as identified by extension workers. Unpublished M.S.
thesis, University of the Philippines, Los Baños, Laguna,
Philippines.

Mangahas, M. 1974. Economic aspects of agrarian reform under
the New Society. Discussion paper No. 74-20. School of

Economics, University of the Philippines, Los Baños, Laguna, Philippines.

Mangahas, M. and R. Rimando. 1976. The Philippine food problem. In: Philippine Economic Problems in Perspective. Institute of Economic Development and Research. University of the Philippines, Los Baños, Laguna, Philippines.

Rivera, F. T. 1976. The production-consumption behavior of farmer-cultivator households in six Nueva Ecija barrios. Unpublished Ph.D. thesis. University of the Philippines, Los Baños, Laguna, Philippines.

Tan, E. A. 1976. Income distribution in the Philippines. In: Philippine Economic Problems in Perspective. Institute of Economic Development and Research. University of the Philippines, Los Baños, Laguna, Philippines.

Tapay, N. E. 1976. The effects of farmer's education on production and income. Unpublished M.S. thesis, University of the Philippines, Los Baños, Laguna, Philippines.

Umali, D. L. 1976. FAO strategies and experiences in agricultural development. Paper presented at the International Workshop on Accelerating Agricultural Development, Los Baños, Philippines. April 26-30.

Valiente, A. M., Jr., L. S. Sayaboc, C. F. Mendoza, M. V. Manuel, and E. H. Federizon. 1976. A socio-economic study of farmers in selected towns of Cagayan. Special Studies Division Planning Service, Office of the Secretary, Dept. of Agriculture, Diliman, Quezon City, Philippines.

Villaviza, Q. N. 1974. Socio-economic factors associated with the spending behavior of lowland rice farmers. Unpublished Ph.D. thesis. University of the Philippines, Los Baños, Laguna, Philippines.

Wharton, C. R., Jr. 1969. The Green Revolution: Cornucopia or Pandora's box. Foreign Affairs 47:464-476.

ROBERT F. CHANDLER, JR.

The Physical and Biological Potentials and Constraints in Meeting World Food Needs

The assigned topic is a broad one. As this audience well knows, there is no simple answer to the world food problem, charged as it is with complexity and often with bafflement. All that I can hope to do here, in such knowledgeable company, is to provide certain background information and to express certain opinions in the hope that my remarks may prove useful in our conference discussions on the factors affecting food production capacity.

Because Dr. Gelia Castillo is presenting, at this same session, a paper on the socio-economic and cultural potentials and constraints in meeting world food needs, I shall restrict my comments to the physical and biological factors (which, furthermore, are within the scope of my professional background). I wish to emphasize at the outset, however, that I fully appreciate the important role that social, economic and cultural factors play in meeting world food needs. In fact, in many situations they are the key elements determining food supply.

Since my experience in international agriculture has been largely with rice and since rice and wheat combined feed such a huge segment of the world population, I shall draw my specific examples from those two crops. The general theme of the conference having been defined as, "The role of the professional in feeding mankind," I shall stress principally the contribution that plant science is making toward increasing the yield potentials of those vital cereal grains and shall list some of the

---

Robert F. Chandler, Jr. is former director, International Rice Research and Asian Vegetable Research and Development Center, now retired. Templeton, Massachusetts.

major constraints that appear to limit yield. I shall then
recommend actions that I think would accelerate progress in
food production. Finally, I shall predict world rice production in 1990, simply to give some indication of the increases
we may expect.

THE SCIENTIFIC BACKGROUND OF THE GREEN REVOLUTION

Greater progress in meeting the food grain needs of the
less-developed countries of the world has been made during
the past 10 years than in any period of even several decades in the past. Of the many factors responsible for this advance, by far the most decisive was the development, by agricultural scientists, of the short, stiff-strawed, fertilizer-
responsive varieties of rice and wheat which have essentially
doubled the yield potential of mankind's two most important
food crops.

The rapid increase in grain production that occurred in
the countries that widely planted the new varieties is frequently referred to as the "Green Revolution." Incidentally,
to my best knowledge, the term was first used by the then Administrator of the US Agency, for International Development,
William S. Gaud. On March 8, 1968 in Washington, D.C., he addressed the Society for International Development on the subject, "The Green Revolution: Accomplishments and Apprehen-
sions."

Because of the vital role that plant breeding played in
this giant forward step, I shall sketch the more important
events that took place within that discipline.

For centuries and until a decade or so ago, the typical
rice plant of the tropics was tall, with long drooping leaves.
Developed to survive under prevailing conditions of inadequate
insect, weed and water control and the non-use of chemical fertilizers, its yields were dependable but low. When, in an
effort to increase yields, fertilizer was applied to those traditional varieties they became even taller and leafier and
lodged (fell over) before harvest. The larger the amount of
fertilizer applied, the earlier and more severe the lodging.
Scientists had established the fact that the earlier in its
life a rice plant lodged, the less grain it produced. Thus the
tropical rice farmer was faced with a dilemma: if he did not
apply fertilizer, yields would be low because of poor nutrition;
yet if he tried to boost his yields by applying fertilizer, he
obtained little or no increase in grain. Indeed, he might get
a lower yield than when no fertilizer at all was used.

The response of the traditional wheat plant to fertilizer
and modern management methods was essentially the same as that
of the rice plant; the same improvements in wheat varieties
were needed, if yields were to be brought out of the relatively

static levels that existed before 1965.

The Green Revolution was triggered off by the intense up-
surge in rice research that resulted from the establishment of
the International Rice Research Institute (IRRI) in the Philippines, and in wheat research from the programs conducted by the
International Maize and Wheat Research Center (CIMMYT), and by
the subsequent international activities of both organizations.
However, such spectacular progress in the improvement of rice
and wheat would not have been possible had it not been for the
work previously done in Taiwan (on rice) and in Japan (on
wheat). I shall now briefly present those developments.

Rice Development

Immediately after World War II, rice breeders on Taiwan
had crossed a short, stiff-strawed Indica rice variety,
Dee-geo-woo-gen, with a medium-tall variety, Tsai-yuan-chon,
noted for its drought resistance. Several years later a selection from among the progeny of this cross proved to be exceptionally high-yielding; it was named Taichung (native) 1. This
was the first Indica variety to satisfy most of the requirements of a modern, tropical rice plant; namely, short stiff
straw, short upright leaves, heavy tillering ability, early
maturity and insensitivity to day length. However, it lacked
disease resistance and superior grain quality. Nevertheless,
Taiwan plant breeders made a significant contribution to the
development of many high-yielding rice varieties which were
bred not only by IRRI but by national rice research programs
throughout the tropics and subtropics. I would guess that over
90 percent of the current modern varieties used in Asia (excluding mainland China), Latin America and Africa contain the
dwarfing gene of either Dee-geo-woo-gen or I-geo-tse, from
Taiwan. Thus, from Asia, the home of the rice plant, came the
germ plasm that opened up new horizons for the ancient crop of
rice.

Wheat Development

Asia also provided the source of dwarfness that was so
essential for making rapid progress in increasing the
yield potential of wheat. During the US occupation of Japan
following World War II, Dr. S. C. Salmon of the US Department
of Agriculture was attracted by a short, stiff-strawed, heavy-
tillering Japanese wheat varisty, called Norin 10. He sent it
to Dr. Orville A. Vogel, a wheat breeder of the USDA working at
Washington State University. After several years of crossing
Norin 10 with US varieties, Dr. Vogel was able to surmount
the problem of sterility and of other genetic difficulties resulting from the introduction of the foreign germ plasm. He

produced two genetic lines--one known as Norin 10 x Brevor and
the other as Norin 10 x Baart--which served as superior sources
of dwarfness for breeding programs around the world. From this
material Dr. Vogel developed the Gaines variety which established new wheat yield records in the Pacific Northwest. Furthermore, it was these same lines that Nobel laureate Dr. Norman
E. Borlaug of CIMMYT (at that time the Rockefeller Foundation's
Mexican Agricultural Program) used in developing the series of
Mexican varieties that formed the basis for the Green Revolution
for wheat in Asia, especially in India and Pakistan.

Influence of IRRI and CIMMYT
     I do not need to repeat here the well-chronicled activi-
     ties of IRRI and CIMMYT that stimulated a worldwide inter-
est in breeding and testing modern rice and wheat varieties.
They influenced many a national government not only to support
additional rice and wheat improvement research, but also to
multiply and distribute seed to farmers. These programs were
well under way by 1966; since then millions of hectares of improved varieties of rice and wheat have been planted in the developing countries. IRRI's impact has been not in Asia alone,
but in Latin America and Africa as well. CIMMYT's influence is
worldwide, wherever wheat is grown. However, its greatest impact has been in the subtropics and the lower latitudes of the
temperate zone.
     Although IRRI and CIMMYT were started and originally sup-
ported by the Rockefeller and Ford Foundations, they are now
receiving funds from a "consortium" of over 30 foreign aid agencies, both private and governmental. It is called "The Consultative Group on International Agricultural Research" (CGIAR).
This organization not only supports IRRI and CIMMYT but 7 other
international centers around the world. This is the greatest
effort made in history to apply scientific research toward the
solution on a global basis of mankind's food problem. Now let
us see whether this effort is paying off, as far as rice and
wheat are concerned.

THE IMPACT OF MODERN RICE AND WHEAT
VARIETIES ON GRAIN PRODUCTION
     A realistic way to analyze the impact of modern varieties
     and improved technology on rice and wheat production is to
     examine FAO statistics for the period 1961-65, before the
Green Revolution got under way, and then to compare those data
with the figures for 1973.
     In Table 1, I have summarized that information, showing
the area cultivated, the total production and the yield per hectare. An examination of this table reveals that the world area

TABLE 1. Area, production and crop yield for rice and wheat

Region	Area planted (000's ha)				Production (000's mt)				Yield (kg/ha)			
	1961-1965		1973		1961-1965		1973		1961-1965		1973	
	Rice	Wheat	Rice	Wheat	Rice	Wheat	Rice	Wheat	Rice	Wheat	Rice	Wheat
World	123,389	210,892	134,163	222,268	251,925	254,390	320,714	377,017	2,042	1,206	2,390	1,696
Asia	113,752	62,452	121,953	75,004	232,202	55,950	293,793	89,191	2,041	896	2,409	1,258
Central and South America	5,236	8,206	6,503	7,533	9,030	11,629	11,748	11,865	1,723	1,417	1,808	1,338
Africa	3,177	7,658	3,903	9,010	5,541	6,381	6,945	8,929	1,744	833	1,780	1,045
Europe	326	28,583	404	26,545	1,517	59,349	1,920	82,123	4,661	2,077	4,758	3,072
Oceania	35	6,806	60	9,199	161	8,470	336	12,348	4,620	1,245	5,562	1,342
USSR	158	66,620	462	63,155	390	64,207	1,761	109,680	2,461	964	3,812	1,737
USA and Canada[a]	705	30,577	878	31,822	3,084	48,404	4,201	63,689	4,374	1,583	4,794	2,001

[a]Canada, of course, produces no rice.

planted to rice increased from 123 million hectares in the 1961-
65 period to 134 million hectares in 1973. This is a rise of
only 8.7 percent. During the same period the yield per hectare
climbed from 2.0 to nearly 2.4 tons, an increase of 17 percent.
Although this increase in yield is disappointingly low, it does
reveal that yield per hectare increased about twice as much as
did the land area planted to rice. The combined effect of area
and yield paints a somewhat more optimistic picture; total rice
production was 27 percent higher in 1973 than during the static
period of 1961-65.

The improvement in the production of wheat was considerably greater than in that of rice. Although the total world
area planted to wheat, in the period under discussion, increased by only 5.3 percent, average yield per hectare increased by 40 percent. Total wheat production went up by 48
percent.

In considering the rice production problem we must realize
that 90 percent of the world's rice is produced in Asia. In
Table 1, it can be seen that there is no substantial difference
between the average rice yield (kg per ha) for the world and
for Asia. Furthermore, over half of Asia's rice is produced in
two countries--India and China.

Many of us who were directly involved in improving the
productivity of the rice plant and its management expected that
by 1976, a decade after IRRI developed its first-named, widely
distributed variety, IR8, rice production in Asia would have
increased by at least 50 percent. Obviously, we were wrong.
The best that we can do now is to examine more carefully the
constraints to production on farmers' fields in an attempt to
find out why average yields are so far below those consistently
being obtained on experimental fields or in carefully supervised on-farm trials.

That subject will be discussed in the next section of this
paper. Because of my past experience, I shall draw my examples
from rice. In many instances, however, yield constraints
affecting the rice crop are equally applicable to wheat.

THE PRINCIPAL CONSTRAINTS TO RICE YIELD

Water Control

I believe that most authorities would agree that inadequate water control is the most important yield-limiting
factor in those countries that grow large quantities of rainfed
rice. On examining rice production figures for Asia, we find
that almost without exception the lowest production occurs in
years of deficient rainfall. Conversely, high production years

(1975, for example) are marked by adequate monsoon rains.

The rice plant is semi-aquatic. It suffers from soil mois-ture tensions that do not seriously reduce yields of many of the common upland crops. Although rice breeders are attempting to develop drought-resistant varieties, it seems unlikely that any cultivars will be created that possess the resistance of maize, sorghum or millet, for instance. I contend that growing rice under rainfed conditions, particularly when the paddies are not bunded, will continue to be hazardous. Future trends, I believe, will be to grow crops other than rice on unbunded up-land soils.

Excessive rainfall can cause serious damage by flooding. However, the frequency of deep-water injury is much less than that of drought injury.

There is, nevertheless, a deep-water problem which may not involve inundation but which is harmful to the rice crop. When monsoon rains are heavy, or even only adequate, for upland rice, low-lying areas may be covered with flood waters at depths of 30 to 70 centimeters for prolonged periods. Such water depths can seriously reduce yields of many of the short-statured, mod-ern rice varieties. Plant breeders are attacking this problem vigorously, and it is expected that high-yielding varieties will soon be developed that can tolerate reasonably deep flooding for sustained periods.

In a later section of this paper I shall discuss the impor-tance of irrigation and of the solar radiation that is associ-ated with deficient rainfall.

Fertilizer Use

While the use of fertilizer in the less-developed coun-tries has increased by 10 percent annually over the past decade or so, the lack of proper nutrition still remains, next to water, as one of the most important yield-limiting factors when the short, stiff-strawed modern varieties are grown. When adequate water control exists, the use of fertilizer on rice and wheat pays handsomely, often with cost-benefit ratios of 2 to 4, even at the current high price of fertilizer.

The less-developed countries of Asia, Latin America and Africa contain about 75 percent of the world's population and account for about 86 percent of the global population growth rate, yet they utilize only about one-fifth of the chemical fertilizer produced in the world. Many farmers apply no fer-tilizer to rice and wheat, and those who do often use amounts less than half the quantity recommended. Without doubt the lack of adequate mineral nutrition, particularly of nitrogen, is a serious constraint to rice production in the poorer coun-tries of Asia.

Control of Insects, Diseases and Weeds

Modern varietal improvement programs place great emphasis on breeding for resistance to insects and diseases. The reason for this, of course, is that insects and disease are important yield constraints and because chemical control of them is expensive. Furthermore, in many of the less-developed countries the chemicals are not available. In a number of studies conducted by IRRI agronomists and agricultural economists to identify yield-limiting factors on farmers' fields, it was found that next to inadequate water control, insect damage (and, in certain years and places, disease attack) was the most serious constraint to high yield. It should be added, however, that even insect attack is a highly variable factor. In some areas in certain years, insect control is not important simply because heavy insect populations do not happen to build up during the rice-growing season.

Plant breeders are making excellent progress in developing rice varieties that are resistant to insect attack. The problem is complicated by the development of new insect biotypes that are able to feed on varieties that were resistant to the original insect populations. However, as in the control of wheat rust and of the rice blast disease, both of which continually produce new biological races, active plant breeding programs undoubtedly can keep pace with the appearance of new insect biotypes.

It seems clear to us, now at least, that insecticides and fungicides will not be required for either rice or wheat, except when there are serious outbreaks of such leaf-eating insects as army worms and grasshoppers, against which varietal resistance has not yet been found.

Weed control is often inadequate on rice farms, adding another yield restriction. IRRI scientists found that many Philippine farmers weeded their rice so late in the growing season that little benefit resulted from their efforts.

It seems clear that although weeds in flooded rice paddies often reduce yields, they need not be a serious problem among Asian rice farmers who cultivate only a hectare or two of rice, as most do. A diligent farmer, who prepares his land well and hand-weeds twice during the early part of the growing season (before the maximum tillering stage), should not need to use expensive herbicides. However, I predict that as herbicides become cheaper and more effective they will be commonly used on direct-seeded rice under rainfed conditions.

Other Constraints to Rice Yield

Although, undoubtedly, inadequate water and pest control and insufficient fertilizer are the most important constraints to the yield of modern varieties of rice and wheat,

obviously there are many institutional, economic and cultural
factors that play a highly important role. Government policies
regarding the pricing of crop harvests as well as the inputs to
produce them, credit systems, the land tenure situation and a
host of other factors are involved. These elements are being
covered, of course, by other speakers, who are authorities in
the social sciences. I wish to mention, however, one additional factor that I consider to be extremely important in determining the rate of adoption of the new technology. I refer to
the development of a well-trained, adequately supported extension staff, deployed to the countryside and working hand in hand
with the farmer.

As an example of the need for such a service, I cite a recent experience in the state of Orissa in India, where, less
than a year ago, I participated in a food production study. I
was astounded to find that there were almost no on-farm trials
of any kind among farmers growing rainfed rice in the uplands.
In general, those farmers were growing the same rice varieties
that they were using when I first visited Orissa 20 years ago.
There were few extension workers, and most farmers had no one
to encourage them to change their rice production methods. As
an instance, photoperiod sensitive varieties are still being
grown and thus the crop does not mature before late November or
early December. However, the monsoon rains are over by early
October. Great reductions in yield are occurring simply because the rice crop flowers and matures in the absence of rain.
If modern high-yielding varieties that are non-photoperiod sensitive were grown, the crop could be harvested in early October,
or even late September, and so escape the drought. I would
guess that that change alone would increase yields, on the average, by at least 50 percent.

The Central Rice Research Institute (CRRI), located at
Cuttack, Orissa, is the principal rice research station of
India. This institution has developed modern disease- and in-
sect-resistant varieties that are photo-insensitive. Nevertheless, I saw almost no impact of CRRI's program at a greater distance than 15 miles from Cuttack.

In talking to farmers, I found none who were unwilling to
test new varieties and methods, provided they could see for
themselves evidence that they would gain by changing their practices. What I am saying is that the farmer himself is generally
not the limiting factor. More often it is the local government
official who is holding back progress. I could give scores of
examples of this from my own experience. Naturally (as with
most of us) these agricultural officers are often unaware of the
inadequacy of their efforts. Generally, they are well-educated,
intelligent, articulate and hard-working. Too frequently, however, they are urban-raised and have had almost no experience
in the practice of farming. Furthermore, they are bogged down

in excessive report writing and in duties that really have
little to do with increasing crop production in their districts.
I believe that there is much that governments can do to release
agricultural science from the confines of bureaucracy and put
it to the service of farming.

THE POTENTIAL FOR FOOD GRAIN PRODUCTION
In this paper I have attempted to outline the role that
agricultural science has played in developing modern rice
and wheat varieties that, under good management, will produce twice as much grain as was possible with traditional varieties. I have shown also that the impact on rice production
in the less-developed countries has been less than originally
expected and have mentioned some of the major restraints to
high yield. Now let us take a look at the future and discuss
some of the actions needed if we are to continue to provide
minimum food and nutrition for mankind.

Water Resources
First and foremost, I feel strongly that the world must
make much better use of its water resources than has been
true in the past. In Asia and Africa alike, vast amounts of
river water flow to the oceans without being utilized. In the
case of rice at least, we should take our lessons from such
ancient and experienced cultures as the Chinese and the Japanese. They have learned through the ages that growing rice
under rainfed conditions is extremely risky. They know that
even during the rainy season supplemental irrigation is crucial
for high yield. Today 80 percent of the rice of China (including Taiwan) is irrigated. In Japan, the corresponding figure
is 98 percent. Japan produced a national average of 6 metric
tons per hectare of paddy rice in 1973--the highest yield in
all Asia. China, with some 35 million hectares of land devoted
to rice production had an average yield of 3.2 metric tons.
This is a remarkable achievement for a nation cultivating rice
over such a vast area, with its inescapable environmental diversity.
I believe that the world should pay more attention to the
development of irrigation systems whereever possible in semi-
arid regions. This is primarily because low-rainfall areas receive much more solar radiation and because the crops grown in
dry regions (or in dry seasons) suffer much less from disease
attack.
There is, for example, abundant scientific evidence of an
extremely high correlation between solar radiation and rice
yield during the last 45 days before harvest, provided that
other factors are not limiting. The yields of rice in the

Philippines, for instance, are often twice as high in the dry
season as in the wet.

Egypt, Spain, Portugal and Australia (to illustrate the
point further) grow only irrigated rice under rainfall-defici-
ent conditions. Their national average yields are over 5 metric tons per hectare, considerably more than twice the world
average.

A decided advantage of irrigation in the tropics, of
course, is that it allows several crops to be grown in a single
year. The Chinese doubtlessly have practiced multiple cropping
for hundreds of years, although their methods did not receive
worldwide attention until the beginning of the 20th Century.

Farming Systems

The development of suitable year-round farming systems for
the tropics is one of the truly important contributions
that agricultural scientists can make toward increased food
production. Theoretically, the tropics should be the bread
basket of the world. Nevertheless, primarily because of the
underuse of natural resources, food production is well below
the potential as determined by climate and soil.

If the financial resources of the more affluent nations
are to be directed toward the world food problem, I can think
of no better use than to devote them to harnessing the waters
of the planet's great rivers, such as the Ganges, the Indus,
the Bhramaputra and the Mekong in Asia; the Niger, the Volta
and the Senegal in Africa; and the Amazon and other important
rivers in Latin America.

I realize that in many rice-growing countries, 60 to 80
percent of the rice is grown under rainfed conditions and that
this situation is likely to remain for some years to come. Accordingly, research and development programs must continue to be
directed toward solutions to the problems that farmers face under such conditions. Rice scientists, therefore, must continue
to develop varieties that have greater resistance to drought,
that are early maturing for harvest by the time the monsoon
rains cease, and that have strong resistance to the insects and
diseases that are so prevalent during the rainy season.

In India, Bangladesh and Vietnam, and in several West African countries, there are large areas subject to deep flooding
during the rainy season. Those lands will produce no economic
crop except floating rice. Consequently, it is important that
rice breeders develop better varieties for deep-water conditions. Recently, the rice breeders of Asia have intensified
their efforts in this direction.

I am convinced that the world cannot feed itself without
using chemical fertilizer on rice and wheat. It is important,
of course, to apply no more than the optimum economic dose.

Furthermore, research must be continued to find ways of increasing fertilizer efficiency, particularly with respect to nitrogen. Under current management methods, nitrogen losses in the
soil are too great. In addition, scientists must study the
possibilities of improving soil fertility through the conservation and use of crop residues. Today, in Asia at least, rice
straw is often wasted by burning or other means, when it should
be returned to the soil after harvest.

Admittedly, the cost of fertilizer is too high in the less-
developed countries. This is partially due to the low level
of efficiency at which their fertilizer factories are operated.
It has been stated that India's fertilizer plants function, on
the average, at no more than 50 percent of their capacity.
Ways must be found to improve this condition, if fertilizer
prices are to be brought down.

Applied Research

As mentioned earlier, there is a great dearth of capable,
well-trained and dedicated extension workers deployed
throughout the countryside. Among their duties, one of the
first and most essential is to conduct adaptive (or applied)
research trials to identify the simplest and most profitable
set of varieties and cultural practices that will produce consistently higher yields in a particular environment. Obviously,
these initial trials must be carried out in close cooperation
with the scientists at experiment stations in the region.

Recent studies by CIMMYT among maize farmers in Africa,
for example, showed that when suitable varieties were made
available to farmers, adoption rates and fertilizer use were
high. Conversely, the scientists contended, the principal reason for the low adoption rates that occurred in certain regions
covered by the study was that appropriate varieties for the environment had not been made available to the farmers.

It is my conviction that rapid progress in getting farmers
to innovate will not occur unless adaptive research trials and
on-farm demonstrations are carried out widely, and unless dedicated and well-trained extension workers are available in sufficient numbers to work closely with small farmers, leading
them toward greater productivity and higher income.

Potential for New Lands

Obviously, in a paper of this sort one should discuss the
potential that exists for cultivating new areas of land.
The amount of still unused land varies greatly among the regions of the world. It is estimated that Asia and Europe are
already using over 86 percent of their arable land and that
what is not being cultivated is much less productive than the

area now being used. On the other hand, Africa and South America are currently utilizing only 15 to 30 percent of the potentially arable land.

From these facts, we must conclude that Asia's future crop production potential lies in increasing crop yields on land now being cultivated, while Africa and Latin America can depend upon area expansion as well as upon yield increases. Unfortunately, there are some serious problems in quickly expanding crop area in those latter regions. The Amazon Basin, for instance, has serious problems of poor accessibility and low manpower resources. In Africa, much of the land preparation today is by the hand hoe. If African agriculture is to be brought out of the doldrums, it appears that mechanization of an appropriate type must be developed and used.

I agree with those who consider that the farmer himself, in general, is able and willing to adopt the new technology, provided he becomes convinced that it is to his advantage to do so. Also, of course, the socio-economic and cultural factors must, where necessary, be changed to the advantage of the farmer.

In spite of the complexity of agricultural development in the less affluent nations, I believe that if the countries themselves, with the assistance of development agencies, make an all-out effort to remove as many constraints as possible, steady progress will be made. I am confident that governments and farmers alike will become increasingly aware of the advantage of adopting modern rice and wheat varieties and the cultural practices that should accompany them. Government programs, usually with foreign aid, will continue to expand irrigation systems and flood control operations. Without doubt, rice yields and total production will continue to rise during the years ahead.

Predicting Future Production

Not long ago, I was asked to prepare a paper (unpublished) predicting world rice production in 1990, some 15 years in the future. Simply to provide another calculated guess of what will happen in the next decade and a half, I am reproducing those estimates in this paper. They are summarized in Table 2.

In preparing this table, I used certain FAO projections for 1974 and, in making the predictions for 1990, drew mostly upon my experience in visiting most of the rice-producing countries of the world.

The estimates are conservative but perhaps are more realistic than are some more optimistic predictions made by others. The rice-producing world, I am sure, could do much better than this, but I truly doubt that it will.

.Asia, of course, will continue to dominate the rice scene.

TABLE 2. Estimated rice production data for 1974 and predictions for 1990

Country or Continent	1974 Estimates			Predictions for 1990		
	Area 000's ha	Production 000's mt	Yield mt/ha	Area 000's ha	Production 000's mt	Yield mt/ha
Asia	121,050	288,180	2.4	137,145	405,000	2.9
Central and South America	6,482	12,142	1.9	10,800	27,200	2.5
USA	1,006	5,148	5.1	1,300	6,630	5.1
Africa	4,050	7,510	1.8	6,600	15,500	2.4
Europe	410	1,940	4.7	470	2,276	4.8
USSR	495	1,761	3.8	600	2,400	4.0
Oceania	64	358	5.6	100	580	5.8
World totals	133,557	317,039	2.4	157,015	459,586	2.9

I have guessed that average yields will increase by a half-ton per hectare and that the area planted to rice in Asia will increase by only 16 million hectares, or 13 percent. However, I anticipate that over the 15-year span production will increase from 288 million metric tons to 405 million, or by 40 percent. Because of the great opportunities that exist for rice-area expansion in Latin America and Africa, I have indicated a probable increase of considerable magnitude for those regions and have estimated, also, that yields will rise considerably along with the increases in area devoted to rice.

I do not expect any increases in yield in the USA or in Europe, for yields there are already high and probably have leveled off. Any expansion in area will depend, of course, upon the market situation, which is never easy to predict.

If, based upon my estimates, we calculate the average annual increase in world rice production over the next 15 years, we see that it comes to 2.4 percent. This, by pure coincidence, equals the present rate of population increase for Asia, where the bulk of the rice will be produced and consumed. What can we conclude from all this? Mainly, if my conservative figures should be attained or exceeded, we can safely assume that no long-term disastrous famines will occur in the rice-dependent nations of Asia for the next decade and a half.

As far as food production per se is concerned, there is real scope for improving yields, for the simple reason that present yields are so low. Certainly, in the long run yields can be doubled. We can say, therefore, that the population of the Indian subcontinent, for example, theoretically could double and the average individual still could eat much as he does there today, inadequate though his diet may be.

Population Growth and the Food Supply

However, to turn Malthusian for a moment, the total land area of the world is a constant. There likewise will be no increase in the amount of solar radiation that hits the surface of our planet. Accordingly, there are limits to the natural resources available for food production. As a consequence, there must be a limit to the rate of population growth. Unfortunately, the reductions in population increase rate that have occurred so far have been largely in the more developed countries where crop yields are high and the degree of affluence in the economy is far above that of most of Asia. Somehow, mankind must find means of population control that can reach all families, whether rich or poor, literate or illiterate, urban or rural. This, obviously is an enormous task but one which must be accomplished if the world is to save itself from ultimate disaster.

As has been said by many authorities, it is a race against

time. How much time we have depends upon the progress that
will be made in producing more food and in implementing successful birth control programs. At the present rate of advancement, I can see mankind holding its own, in the food-population
balance through the year 2,000. Beyond that, however, the outlook becomes too clouded for forecast and too uncertain for any
sort of comfort. There is every need to take seriously the
warnings of Malthus. If they are to remain a hypothesis and
not become a dreadful reality, population control must become
not merely a goal but an accomplished fact. The achievements
of modern agricultural science have bought for mankind a limited extension of time in which to work out his destiny.

GLENN W. BURTON

Overcoming Constraints and Realizing Potentials in the Physical and Biological Aspects of Feeding People

The conference was over. For four days the world's experts had met together. The blackboards that lined the walls of the conference room were full. Problems, potentials, constraints, and strategies had been listed. Slowly the janitor, sent to clean the boards, read the headings and a few of the many words listed under them and said "I can say it with three words." Walking to the blackboard he erased a few words, picked up a piece of chalk and wrote "YOU GOTTA WANNA."

Our concern is feeding more people. In the next few moments I shall list a few of the physical and biological constraints that must be overcome if we are to do this. I shall suggest important potentials that may serve as goals and I shall describe a few strategies that should help to realize them. But I know the janitor was right. To feed the people, governments, farmers, you and I, everyone involved has GOTTA WANNA--as if our next meal depended on it.

Driving from the airport to the Research Laboratory at Oak Ridge, Tennessee several years ago, we passed a Volkswagen with a huge sign on its back. On its black background, huge green letters spelled these words, "HAVE YOU THANKED A GREEN PLANT TODAY?" Have _you_ thanked a green plant today? If not, let me

---

Glenn W. Burton is Research Geneticist, Agricultural Research Service, U.S. Department of Agriculture, and the University of Georgia, College of Agriculture, Experiment Stations, Coastal Plain Station, Tifton, Ga. 31794.

The paper is based on cooperative investigations of the USDA Agricultural Research Service, U.S. Department of Agriculture, and the Agronomy Department, University of Georgia.

71

tell you why you should. The bread, the cake, and the vegetables you will eat today were once green plants. The ham and
eggs you enjoyed for breakfast were once green plants. The
gasoline that brought you here was once a green plant. Most of
the energy that makes possible our sophisticated way of life
was once green plants.

Green plants feed the world. They are the first link in
the food chain. If we are to feed more people, we must learn
how to grow more good green plants. Not all green plants are
good; Weed Science (Ennis et al., 1975) listed some 2,000 species of weeds--green plants that cause economic losses in crops
--in the USA and Canada.

Only a few of the 250,000 named green plant species are
important as food plants. Mangelsdorf (1966) states:

During his history, man has used at least 3,000 species of
plants for food and has cultivated at least 150 of these to
the extent that they have entered into the world's commerce.
The tendency through the centuries has been to use fewer and
fewer species and to concentrate on the more efficient ones,
those that give man the greatest return for his land and
labor. Today the world's people are actually fed by about
15 species of plants: rice, wheat, corn, sorghum, barley,
sugarcane, sugar beet, potato, sweet potato, cassava, common
bean, soybean, peanut, coconut, and banana.

In 1956, Simon and Schuster, Inc., New York City, published a fascinating novel by John Christopher entitled No
Blade of Grass. The book described a new virus disease so devastating that it destroyed all grasses it attacked. Starting
first with rice in the Orient, the virus rapidly spread around
the world, leaving in its wake no blade of grass and only a few
people who had survived starvation. The story, dealing mainly
with the response of man to starvation, dramatized most effectively man's dependence on grass for food.

Today the cereal grasses are man's most important source of
food. One species alone, rice, furnishes 60 percent of the energy for at least half of the people in the world. Thus, 30
percent of the human energy of the globe comes from one grass,
rice. Wheat ranks second and maize third as human foods. To
these, add barley, rye, oats, sorghum, and millet and you have
listed the plant species that directly or indirectly supply over
three-fourths of our energy and more than half of our protein.

The cereal grasses will probably always be man's most important food source. Here are some of the reasons behind this
statement: One or more of the cereal grasses are adapted to
our major climates. Barley and rye originally grew in cold
climates; wheat and oats, in the temperate zone; and rice,
corn, sorghum, and millet in the tropics. But thanks to their

flexibility and the efforts of plant breeders, both primitive and modern, they now grow successfully outside their zones of origin.

The cereal grasses are adapted to a great diversity of soil and water conditions. They range from rice, growing on rich, fertile soil flooded with water, to pearl millet, producing grain on 16 cm of infertile soil with only 10 cm of rainfall.

Most of the world's food is now produced on 3 percent of its surface. Another 2 to 3 percent of the earth's crust could produce cultivated crops, but only after draining, clearing, leveling, irrigating, etc.--all expensive, time-consuming operations. With hectarage limited, only high-yielding crops can feed tomorrow's hungry billions. The cereal grasses admirably meet this requirement.

Cereal culture is well suited to mechanization. A few can feed many when the food is produced by cereal grasses. This cuts food costs and frees man to develop his other interests.

The seeds of the cereal grasses are high in nutrients. The dried seeds are easy to handle, store, and transport with a minimum of processing. Urbanization, the agglomeration of people for industrialization of the economy, is rapidly spreading throughout the world. These people, far from food sources, can be most easily fed with crops that are easy to handle, store, and transport.

What are the potentials of some of our major food crops--the grass cereals? In 1966, Mangelsdorf (1966) reported world record yields for corn, wheat, and rice of 190, 140, and 134 q/ha, respectively. These yields at that time satisfied Webster's definition of "potential"--that which is possible. World average yields reported at that time for corn, wheat and rice were 18, 11, and 12 q/ha, respectively. A number of constraints made the difference.

CONSTRAINTS

In 1975, Herman Warsaw of Saybrook, Illinois harvested 338 bushels of corn from a measured, witnessed acre (212 q/ha) (Pfeifer, 1976). With this yield, Warsaw raised the potential yield of corn 11 percent. What constraints did he overcome? Pfeifer stated that Warsaw's soil was very good. He had spent years building the fertility above what most farmers would consider adequate. Other obvious constraints--genotype, water, pests, and temperature could hardly have been limiting factors. But why had his previous yields been much less? Until such potential yields can be repeated at will, one must conclude that their are hidden constraints. Discovering these hidden constraints is one of the challenges facing research. Until they can be described and understood, such hidden constraints cannot be overcome.

To feed people, constraints must be overcome on the farm.
Learning how to overcome constraints in the research laboratory
is essential. But it will not feed people until it becomes
farm practice and increases yields on a state-wide basis. How
can the world overcome constraints that keep farm production
low? Many of the answers can be found in the story of peanut
production in Georgia.

From 1920 to 1949, "Neglect" (little support from research,
extension, or industry) was the principal constraint that kept
Georgia's peanut yields around 800 kg/ha. Government price
supports ranging from 75 to 90 percent of parity had supplied
price incentives since 1941 but with low yields, the incentive
was small.

In the early 1950s, research pathologist, L. W. Boyle
(1956) discovered that the constraint imposed on peanut yields
by southern blight caused by Sclerotium rolfsii could be removed
by complete deep burial of crop residue and controlling weeds
without throwing soil on the peanut plant. Chemical weed control methods developed by weed research specialist Ellis Hauser,
supplied weed control without throwing soil on the plant and
increased flowers per plant and yield. In 1954, J. Frank Mc
Gill, an outstanding county agent, became full-time extension
peanut specialist, included these research findings in a production package, and set about to overcome the human constraint
that resisted change. Result and method demonstrations, demonstration clinics, annual peanut production schools in each pea-
nut-growing county, and "ton-per-acre clubs" were a few of the
strategies that helped sell the program. McGill's expertise and
untiring efforts earned the growers' confidence that resulted
in rapid adoption of constraint-removing practices coming from
research. Georgia's peanut yield in 1960 was 1,340 kg/ha.

Greater research effort directed to removing constraints
(often identified by McGill and growers) developed better cultivars and improved insect and disease control. Industry added
new pesticides and equipment to the ever-changing peanut production package and by 1970, Georgia produced 2,486 kg/ha of
peanuts on 213,000 ha of land.

Florunner, a new cultivar with greater yield potential,
was introduced in 1970 and occupied 93 percent of the hectarage
by 1975. The constraint imposed by limited water on 20 percent
of the sandiest peanut soils was removed with irrigation during
this 5-year period. These two breakthroughs, added to the peanut production package and applied by growers highly receptive
to new technology, set a 5-year world record for yield (increasing from 2,790 kg/ha in 1971 to 3,700 kg/ha in 1975). In just
25 years Georgia's peanut yields have been increased 4.6 times.

The strategy is simple. It depends on people--dedicated
people who care. There must be a leader who is energetic,

knowledgable, enthusiastic, and capable of gaining the cooperation and respect from all who are involved. He must be anxious
to devote his all to feeding people.

There must be a team of capable research workers--special-
ists who make discovering ways of overcoming biological constraints the top priority in their lives. There must be a reward for such effort; otherwise, they may be tempted to devote
their time and talents to research that may contribute little
or nothing to eliminating food production constraints. Too
many scientists in some of the world's hungriest nations spend
their time on such research.

There must be continued interchange between the farmer who
applies the new technology to grow more food and the scientist
who creates it. Laboratory solutions will probably need modification on the farm. The scientist must be made aware of new
constraints as soon as they appear. Working closely with the
farmer may be the best way for the scientist to discover the
nature and scope of each new constraint.

The inputs required to overcome the constraint must be
supplied. Discovery of a chemical that will protect a crop
from the ravages of a disease or some other pest will not save
the crop. The chemical must be available, growers must be induced to use it, and someone must show them how. In countries
like the USA, industry assumes this responsibility. In the
hungry nations, governments must accept this role.

Overcoming food production constraints costs money. Financial resources must be supplied. If the private sector cannot provide financing at a reasonable rate of interest, governments must.

For everyone involved in overcoming constraints, there
must be incentives--there must be rewards. For the farmer,
particularly, there must be financial rewards. He cannot be
expected to assume the extra financial risk without being assured of a reasonable profit. The magnitude and certainty of
this profit will determine the rate at which the new practice
will be adopted. In most of the world, governments must supply
the fiscal incentive. There are other incentives. For many,
the satisfaction of helping to feed the hungry will be a great
reward. Recognition by government or peers of the best workers
in a particular discipline can be a great motivating force.
Production contests, citation of winners, and an analysis of
how they did it can be a great incentive and an educational
tool in any nation or society.

In Mexico a few years ago, Norman Borlaug, Rockefeller
Foundation scientist, furnished the leadership for increased
wheat production. Borlaug bred better cultivars and cooperated
with other scientists and farmers to discover and overcome constraints. The government supplied the needed inputs, incentives, and credit. Within 10 years, Mexico's wheat yields were

doubled. Continued cooperative efforts among scientists, educators, government, and farmers doubled production again in the
next 10 years.

Taking his high-yielding wheats to Pakistan and India and
enlisting the help of local scientists, educators, governments,
and farmers, Borlaug helped these hungry nations to rapidly increase food production. For Borlaug, it was more hard work and
self-sacrifice, with the satisfaction of feeding the hungry being his main reward. The world heartily agreed when in 1970
Borlaug received the coveted Nobel Peace Prize in recognition
of his outstanding contribution to peace and humanity.

In India, the rapid increase in the yields of wheat and
rice was dubbed the Green Revolution. It was based on the development of new short-stiff-stalked, photoperiod-insensitive,
nitrogen-responsive cultivars. Without them, there could have
been no revolution. Nor could these high-yielding cultivars
alone have made much difference. The Green Revolution involved
recognizing and overcoming a number of major yield constraints
at one time. Although cultivars were the first of these constraints, fertilizer, water control (usually irrigation), pest
control, and improved management were also essential inputs that
increased yields. The Green Revolution demonstrated in a most
forceful way how removing yield constraints could dramatically
increase food production. It saved the lives of millions who
might have died from starvation. Unfortunately, the Green Revolution has not reached its full potential. By 1969, only 12
percent of the Indian farmers growing the high-yielding cultivars were following all recommendations. Inadequate fertilization, irrigation, pest control, management, incentives, and/or
credit were responsible for the partial failure of the Green
Revolution.

In 1965, Indian pearl millet breeders released HB1 hybrid
millet, a cross between our Tift 23A and D.S. Athwal's Bil 3B.
In tests throughout the 11 million-hectare pearl millet belt
from 11 to 31 degrees north latitude, HB1 had yielded 88 percent
more grain than the best open-pollinated cultivar. Under the
enthusiastic leadership of Dr. K. O. Rachie, a Rockefeller
Foundation scientist, Indian pearl millet breeders, starting in
1961 in a great cooperative effort, had developed a male parent
for our cytoplasmic male sterile Tift 23A (Burton, 1965) to make
an outstanding hybrid. Hybrid millet hectarage increased rapidly, limited only by lack of good seed. With fertilizer, irrigation, pest control, and better management, yields were reported that exceeded by 10 times those once realized from the
old cultivars without additional inputs. In 1969, B. R. Murty,
Indian millet coordinator, reported that 20 percent of the increased food production associated with the Green Revolution
could be credited to hybrid millet. Then two new constraints
appeared: a new race of downy mildew, caused by <u>Sclerospora</u>

<u>graminicola</u>, and ergot, caused by <u>Claviceps</u> <u>microcephala</u>. Until methods for removing these constraints are found, the land planted to this important grain crop will probably continue to decline. The need for continued vigilance in identifying and overcoming yield constraints is apparent.

REMOVING CONSTRAINTS

<u>Teaching</u>
        The remainder of this paper will consider action or research that may help to remove constraints limiting yields of several of the world's major sources of food. Because research is expected to solve such problems and because of some of its spectacular breakthroughs, there is a growing tendency in universities around the world to support research at the expense of teaching. We dare not forget that without good teaching, there will soon be no one to do research. Without good teaching that informs and inspires students to make this a better world, there will be no one to carry the findings of research to those who need them.

<u>Land</u>
        Land is one of the major physical constraints for increased food production in the world. It is generally agreed that the land suitable for food production in the world is about twice the 1.4 billion hectares presently used. Much of this land is in sparsely populated areas of Africa and South America. To develop these lands, provide transportation, and set up a food production industry and distribution system will take time and much money. For the next few years, increasing the land area in crops through drainage, irrigation, clearing, etc. offers the most promise. The developing nations are doing this. In the past 20 years, they have increased their land area suitable for crops 32 percent, whereas the developed countries have continued to farm the same hectarage (Willett, 1974).
        For the next few years, increasing yields on the hectares growing crops offers the main hope for feeding the world's rapidly increasing population. To do this, we must identify and overcome such physical constraints as soil fertility, weather and production management.

<u>Fertilizer</u>
        Applying fertilizer to most of the world's croplands will increase yields. The constraints imposed by inadequate supplies of fertilizer must be overcome by building more

fertilizer plants and providing the energy and raw materials
required for fertilizer production. I personally believe that
oil for the production of nitrogen fertilizer must receive a
higher priority than oil for military machines.

Research to pin-point the fertilizer needs of each crop
could greatly increase the efficiency of fertilizer use. Research that proved that a 4-1-2 ratio of $N-P_2O_5-K_2O$ was as
effective as the 4-12-4 farmers had used to produce Coastal
bermudagrass hay saved hay producers thousands of dollars and
saved the world many tons of two of its most important fertilizer elements, phosphorus and potassium (Jackson et al.,
1959).

Most crops recover less than half of the fertilizer elements used to make them grow. Some crops and cultivars can recover more fertilizer than others, suggesting that the efficiency of fertilizer use could be improved by breeding for this
character.

Inoculated legumes are able to satisfy their nitrogen requirements from the elemental N in the atmosphere. There is
increasing evidence to indicate that several microorganisms
within or in close contact with the roots of certain grass genotypes can fix elemental nitrogen for the associated grass (Day
et al., 1975). The great potential for this research warrants
the increased attention it is receiving.

Water

Extreme sandiness, shallowness, rockyness, and poor soil
structure are constraints limiting yields. Irrigation,
carefully applied, can help to remove these constraints. Subsoiling a Marlboro sand soil under rows of soybeans increased
rooting depth and nonirrigated yields up to 60 percent (Parker
et al., 1975). Over a 4-year period, planting cotton after
Pensacola bahiagrass on a soil with a dense subsoil increased
seed cotton yields from 1,353 kg/ha for continuous cotton to
2,895 kg/ha for cotton following sod. With continuous cotton,
99 percent of the roots were confined to the 33-cm thick plow
layer above the dense subsoil. Roots of cotton following sod
extended to depths of 180 cm and over 20 percent were below the
plow layer. The bahiagrass roots were able to penetrate the
dense subsoil and left channels through which the cotton roots
were able to grow. The increased water storage associated with
the deeper rooting of the cotton plants increased water and
soil nutrient availability that in turn increased yields
(Elkins et al., 1973).

pH

Extremes in pH limit the yields of many crops by releasing
excessive quantities of aluminum and other elements that

may be toxic or by tieing up iron at high pH levels to cause chlorosis. Lime on acid soils and acid residue fertilizer such as ammonium sulfate on alkaline soils will help to solve these problems but on very acid clay soils, the amount of lime required may be uneconomic. Choosing species and breeding cultivars with greater tolerance of pH extremes and associated problems offer another solution to this problem.

Salts

Some of the world's once productive soils have been abandoned because of accumulated salts. Faulty irrigation with improper drainage is usually the main cause of salt accumulation and draining and flushing the salt out of such soils can reclaim them. Sometimes a change of crops to a more salt-tolerant cultivar or species will permit continued use of the land. Growing a highly salt-tolerant crop such as Coastal or Coastcross-1 bermudagrasses and removing the forage as green chop or hay to feed livestock will lower the salt content in the soil and supply excellent livestock feed at the same time. Cultivars of all crops can be bred to have greater salt tolerance.

Weather

How can man overcome the constraints set by weather? Devices to create smoke or circulate air can save a citrus crop from frost but they cost too much to protect most other food crops. Fortunately, cultivars and species vary in their cold tolerance. Rye can be grown north of the wheat belt. Spring varieties of wheat, barley, and oats can be grown in colder climates than their higher-yielding winter forms. Selecting cultivars of summer annuals such as corn that germinate at lower temperatures will extend their use into colder climates. Greater heat tolerance can be bred into important food plants.

Inadequate water, the other major constraint in weather, can be overcome by irrigating where water for irrigation is available. Irrigated cropland, constituting 15 percent of the world's cultivated land, supplies 30 percent of man's food (Willett, 1974). But losses of irrigation water by runoff and deep percolation are substantial. Drip-irrigation, a significant development in water management, makes water go farther and requires less energy than most other irrigation systems. It is still restricted to high-value crops in arid regions but represents the kind of. improvement in water use that must be developed.

Much irrigation water is lost because of inadequate fertilization, pest control, and cultural methods. Using cultivars,

fertilizer, pest control and management practices which will
make water the limiting factor will insure the most efficient
use of this valuable and limited resource.

Most of the world's cultivated hectares cannot be irrigated. Here research must discover ways to capture and conserve rainfall. Plants must be bred that have deeper and more
efficient root systems, fewer stomata, and thicker cuticles to
enable them to use the limited rainfall more efficiently. Two
examples from our own research illustrate the potential in such
a plant breeding effort.

Coastal bermudagrass is an F_1 hybrid that yields about
twice as much forage as common bermudagrass when soil moisture
is adequate. On a very sandy soil in an extremely dry year,
Coastal bermuda produced six times as much forage as common
bermuda because its deep, efficient root system and leaf characteristics enables it to stay green and make growth following
every shower of rain. Under this severe drought, common bermudagrass turned brown and was not able to respond to the light
rains during the summer (Burton et al., 1954 and Burton et al.,
1957). Kilograms of water used per kg of dry matter produced
for common and Coastal bermudagrass, respectively, were 1,546
and 803 in a wet year and 4,336 and 641 in a very dry year.

A single recessive gene, tr, that removes all trichomes
from pearl millet (Powell and Burton, 1971) alters the cuticle
such that it reduces transpiration. Leaves of the tr mutant
transpired 26 percent less water than leaves of its normal isogenic counterpart (Hanna et al., 1974). These isogenic lines
yield the same in Georgia where rainfall is abundant. If we
find that the tr mutant uses water more efficiently and yields
more in an arid climate, the tr gene could be easily transferred to other lines to increase their water use efficiency.

On the edge of the desert, it may be necessary to grow a
crop after a single good rain that may be accumulated in a
catchment basin. Shortening the time from planting to maturity
by breeding could improve food production in such environments.

Pests

Pests cause an estimated 30 percent loss in the world's
food supply (Ennis et al., 1975). Among the pests are
more than 160 bacteria, 250 viruses, 8,000 fungi, 10,000 insects, 2,000 weeds, nematodes, birds, and rodents. In 1963 and
1964, insects and rodents that attacked grain in the field and
in storage in India destroyed 13 million tons of grain. In the
Sudan area alone, the tiny grain-eating quelea birds consume an
estimated 3,000 tons of grain daily. We must reduce these
losses.

In many cases, pest-related losses can be prevented
through better storage, quarantine (where possible), and

planting clean or treated seed. Special cultural methods can
sometimes control serious pests. Burying all plant debris and
controlling weeds without throwing soil on the peanut plant has
virtually eliminated southern blight losses in peanuts.

In the USA, chemicals play an important role in protecting
crops. Upchurch and Heisig (1964) estimate that without pesticides, crop and animal production would be reduced 25 percent,
the price of farm products would rise 50 percent, and consumers
would be forced to spend 25 percent more of their income for
food. The beautiful blemish-free fruits and vegetables we have
come to expect in the market place would cease to exist.

Biological methods have helped to control some pests.
The introduction of pathogens, predators, and parasites capable
of reducing pest populations has been successful in about 20
cases and partially successful in more than 100 (DeBach, 1964).
This method has also helped to control several weeds such as
the pear cactus in Australia and St. Johnswort in the western
USA.

Plant breeding offers one of the most effective methods of
removing or reducing the constraints that pests impose on our
major food crops. Literally hundreds of diseases and insects
that could destroy the world's major food crops are controlled
by resistant cultivars. Controlling pests by plant breeding is
not easy. It involves discovering genes for resistance in land
races or wild relatives and transferring them into the susceptible cultivars. Desirable characteristics must be retained
and the undesirable traits that resistant sources often carry
must be eliminated. New races of the pests make breeding for
resistance a never-ending battle. Only pest-resistant sources
compatable with the susceptible cultivars of major food crops
can be used because the transfer must still be made by hybridization. Breaking this barrier is one of the major objectives
of plant cell culture research. I believe that one day it will
be possible to isolate purified DNA for pest immunity from totally unrelated species and introduce it into susceptible crop
plants. When this can be done, the short life of a resistant
cultivar (5 to 15 years because of genetic change in the pest)
should be greatly extended and food losses due to insects, diseases, and nematodes should be minimized. I believe the potential of such research warrants more support than it now receives.

Until we can transfer pest resistance from unrelated, in-
compatable sources, we must depend on compatable sources of
genes for pest resistance and we must use conventional plant
breeding methods to make the transfer. The need for collecting
and preserving the world's rapidly disappearing land races and
wild relatives of our major food crops is apparent.

For the immediate future, integrated systems that combine
genetic resistance with all other methods of pest control offer

the best hope for overcoming pest losses. The potential of increasing food supplies 30 percent by removing constraints
caused by pests calls for more research, directed toward the
development of such integrated systems.

Nutrition
     One of the major constraints that must be removed to feed
     people well are the deficiencies of protein and essential
amino acids in our major food crops. All food constituents
(protein, amino acids, oil, starch, sugar, etc.) are under genetic control and can be modified by plant breeding. The
opaque-2 (O_2) recessive gene doubles the lysine and tryptophan
content in corn. The recessive flouri-2 (fl_2) gene in corn
doubles lysine and increases methionine content of the grain by
more than 50 percent. In 'Hyproly' barley, a single gene con-
fers both high protein and high lysine content. Breeding programs are underway to improve protein content and amino acid
balance in all major cereals. 'Lancota' hard red winter wheat
recently released in Nebraska illustrates the potential of such
research (USDA, 1975). Culminating 20 years of cooperative
USDA-state research, Lancota combines 10 to 20 percent more
protein with the yield, disease resistance, milling, and baking
qualities of leading cultivars in Nebraska. Replacing other
cultivars grown in Nebraska with Lancota would produce 45 million kg more protein per year at no extra cost.
     Raising the quantity and quality of protein in the major
cereals high enough to provide a balanced diet without a supplement should be a primary objective in their genetic improvement. I can think of no cheaper or better way to solve the
world's protein problem. Other foods, vegetables, fruits, and
animal products could then be added to this basic cereal diet
to supply variety and zest. But those unable to afford more
than the basic cereal diet could still enjoy the good health
associated with adequate nutrition.

Breeding Methods
     Raising the yield potential of our major food crops by
     applying better breeding methods can help to feed the
world's people. One such method has been developed by Frey
(1975) and his associates here in Iowa. From wild oats (Avena
sterilis) they have transferred genes to cultivated oats that
have given resistance to five diseases, improved protein content in the grain and straw, raised grain oil content 12 percent, and increased grain yields 25 to 30 percent, twice the
yield increase from 55 years of conventional oat breeding.
     To maximize yield and efficiency of production, plant
breeders should try to produce commercial F_1 hybrids of all

major food crops. The superiority of the F_1 hybrid in yield (particularly under stress) and in many other characteristics has been well established. Corn hybrids yield some 50 percent more grain than the old open-pollinated cultivars, and pearl millet hybrids may produce 100 percent more grain and 50 percent more forage than the open-pollinated cultivars they replaced (Burton and Powell, 1968). Fruits, vegetables, and grasses that can be propagated vegetatively or by apomixis on a commercial basis have carried the benefits of hybrid vigor to the grower. Lack of a suitable mechanism for the commercial production of F_1 hybrid seed has denied the world the benefits from hybrid vigor in many seed-propagated food crops such as rice, oats, barley, and soybeans.

Cytoplasmic male sterility (cms) is the mechanism used in the commercial production of most F_1 hybrid seed. Unfortunately, cms has not been discovered in many major food crops. A technique that would create cms mutants in such crops would allow the exploitation of hybrid vigor and a consequent major advance in food production. Results of research begun at Tifton, Georgia, in 1975 suggest that such a technique may now be available. By soaking seeds of the homozygous Tift 23DB pearl millet maintainer for the cytoplasmic male sterile Tift 23DA in 1,000 ppm of ethidium bromide in water at 5°C for 40 hours, we produced in the M_1 generation one male sterile mutant (whole head, mixed, or sectored head) per 274 heads in a head population of 19,200. One male sterile sector was found in 30,100 heads from untreated seeds (Burton and Hanna, 1976). Advancing male sterile mutants in the greenhouse two generations suggests that the male sterile mutants are cytoplasmic. Preliminary studies carried out cooperatively with Darrell Morey, small grain breeder at Tifton, Georgia, indicate that ethidium bromide can create male sterile mutants in the M_1 generation in rye. In a small greenhouse population of soybeans treated with ethidium bromide, Joe W. Burton, ARS, USDA, North Carolina State University, Raleigh, N.C., found one M_1 generation male sterile plant. The stability of these cytoplasmic male sterile mutants and the discovery of fertility restorer genes for them are facets of current research required to establish the usefulness of this technique.

Animals

Any discussion concerned with feeding the world's people cannot ignore animals. Pets (cats, dogs, and horses) in the USA compete with humans for food as they consume $2.5 billion of food annually, six times that spent on baby food (Wittwer, 1975). Pet health care costs close to $5 billion per year and competes with farm animals for veterinary services.

Converting plant foods (grains) to animal foods before

they are fed to people reduces materially the number of people
that can be fed. But much of the earth's land is too cold, too
dry, or too rough to grow food crops. These lands can feed
people only as they consume the animals that feed on the plants
that grow there. Straw and other crop wastes can feed animals
that, in turn, can help feed people as they furnish draft power
and fertilizer (dung) to grow crops and produce meat, milk, and
fuel (dung) to cook their food. Ruminants could produce substantial amounts of food for people if they were fed only crop
wastes and high-quality forages bred to grow on land too rough
for crop production. These forages, largely grasses and legumes, as they produce food for people through animals, could
also control soil erosion, conserve water, greatly reduce the
sedimentation of rivers, lakes, and irrigation reservoirs and
help to beautify the environment. I believe that research designed to develop better forages and more efficient ruminants
to convert them into food for people warrants much greater support than it presently receives.

CONCLUDING REMARKS
     Time has allowed me to consider only some of the poten-
     tials and constraints that I consider most important in
     feeding people. Your choice would have been different
from mine. I believe, however, that most of us would agree
with Roy I. Jackson, Deputy-Director General, Food and Agriculture Organization of the United Nations when he says, "In a
world organized for the full use of technology and proper sharing of effort there would be no danger of running out of food
either this year or this century. In the real world in which
we live, running out of food is a recurrent danger" (Jackson,
1974). I believe the world can feed itself for the remainder
of this century if it will remove the constraints it knows how
or can learn how to remove. It cannot feed itself unless it
changes its ways. The janitor was right--"WE GOTTA WANNA" and
the "WE" is every person (farmer, research worker, teacher,
government official, and representative of industry) who has a
responsibility for feeding people.

REFERENCES

Boyle, L. W. 1956. Fundamental concepts in the development of
     control measures for southern blight and root rot on pea-
     nuts. Plant Disease Reporter 40:661-665.
Burton, G. W., E. H. DeVane, and R. L. Carter. 1954. Root pen-
     etration, distribution, and activity in southern grasses
     measured by yields, drought symptoms and P^{32} uptake. Agron-
     omy Journal 46:229-233.

Burton, G. W., G. W. Prine, and J. E. Jackson. 1957. Studies of drought tolerance and water use of several southern grasses. Agronomy Journal 49:498-503.

Burton, G. W. 1965. Pearl millet Tift 23A released. Crops and Soils 17:19.

Burton, G. W. and J. B. Powell. 1968. Pearl millet breeding and cytogenetics. Advances in Agronomy 20:49-89. Academic Press, New York.

Burton, G. W. and W. W. Hanna. 1976. Ethidium bromide induced cytoplasmic male sterility in pearl millet. Crop Science (In Press).

Day, J. M., M. C. P. Neves, and J. Dobereriner. 1975. Nitrogenase activity on the roots of tropical forages grasses (Pennisetum purpureum, Digitaria decumbens). Journal Soil Biological Biochemistry 7:107-112.

DeBach, P. 1964. Biological Control of Insect Pests and Weeds. Reinhold, New York.

Elkins, C. B., F. Lowry, and Jordan Langford. 1973. Alleviation of mechanical impedance to cotton rooting in a dense subsoil by use of sod. Agronomy Abstracts. pp. 122. American Society of Agronomy, Madison, Wisconsin.

Ennis, W. B., Jr., W. M. Dowler, and W. Klassen. 1975. Crop protection to increase food supplies. Science 188:593-598.

Frey, K. J. 1975. Plant breeding in the seventies: useful genes from wild plant species. Journal paper number J-8136. Iowa Agriculture and Home Economics Experiment Station, Ames, Iowa.

Hanna, W. W., W. G. Monson, and G. W. Burton. 1974. Leaf surface effects on in vitro digestion and transpiration in isogenic lines of sorghum and pearl millet. Crop Science 14: 837-838.

Jackson, J. E., M. E. Walker, and R. L. Carter. 1959. Nitrogen, phosphorus, and potassium requirements of Coastal bermudagrass on a Tifton loamy sand. Agronomy Journal 51: 129-131.

Jackson, R. I. 1974. Situation serious. John Deere Journal. Vol. 3, No. 4. Moline, Illinois.

Mangelsdorf, P. C. 1966. Genetic potentials for increasing yields of food crops and animals. Prospects of the World Food Supply - a symposium. National Academy of Science, Washington, D.C., pp. 48-55.

Parker, M. B., N. A. Minton, O. L. Brooks, and C. E. Perry. 1975. Soybean yields and lance nematode populations as affected by subsoiling, fertility, and nematicide treatments. Agronomy Journal 67:663-669.

Pfeifer, R. P. 1976. Record yields and your operation. Crops and Soils 28:5-7.

Powell, J. B. and G. W. Burton. 1971. Genetic suppression of shoot-trichomes in pearl millet, Pennisetum typhoides. Crop Science 11:763-765.

Upchurch, L. M. and C. P. Heisig. 1964. The economic impor-
    tance of pesticides to the US consumer. Economic Re-
    search Service, US Department of Agriculture, Washington,
    D.C.
USDA. 1975. Protein-packed wheat. Vol. 34, No. 25.
Willet, J. W. 1974. The world food situation and prospects
    to 1985. Foreign Agriculture Economic Report Number 98.
Wittwer, S. H. 1975. Food production technology and the re-
    source base. Science 188:579-584.

H. A. OLUWASANMI

Socio-Economic Aspects of Feeding People

One of the major issues facing the world today is how to feed a rapidly increasing population which creates an ever-growing pressure on available world resources. Although the poor everywhere are exposed to hunger and suffer from malnutrition, the major hunger zones of the world are to be found in the developing or poor regions of the world. In these regions per capita farm output is only a fraction of achieved yields in the developed countries, income per person less than a third of such incomes in the advanced countries, and the rate of population growth almost twice as high as in the developed countries.

The food problem is in part a problem of income levels, in part a question of improved agricultural production, and in part an issue of the rate at which population is growing. Where output of farm products is increasing at the same or at a higher rate than population and there are increasing opportunities for the rural population to earn additional incomes both within and outside agriculture, the problem of hunger becomes one of adjustment in agricultural production and a more efficient distribution of the resulting farm products. It is because these parallel developments of agriculture and of non-agricultural industries are not occurring fast enough in most developing countries that the world is faced with the food situation. Expressed in these broad terms, hunger is essentially a problem of overall development.

H. A. Oluwasanmi is former Vice-Chancellor, University of IFe, Ile-IFe, Nigeria and currently visiting Professor, Land Tenure Center, University of Wisconsin, Madison, Wisconsin, USA.

About two decades ago, when most of the present-day developing countries attained independence, there was great optimism that backwardness could be overcome by the application of the findings of science and technology to the organization of agricultural and industrial production. The enthusiasm about the limitless possibilities of science in bringing about change in the conditions of the poor was not confined to the new nations. The advanced countries as well as the UN expressed their optimism about the possibility of progress in the newly independent countries by allocating billions of dollars in technical assistance to the development of agriculture, to the creation of research facilities and to the building of basic infrastructure. To be sure, these international efforts at agricultural development have yielded significant results, so significant in fact in some respects that the term "Green Revolution" has been appropriately applied to them.

Despite the massive infusion in the last two decades of both foreign assistance and domestic capital into agriculture, resulting in the increased use of such nontraditional inputs as fertilizers, improved seeds and insecticides, agriculture in many developing countries, particularly in Africa, has remained esconced in its traditional moulds. In the Africa region the farmer has continued to farm his two-acre plot with the hand hoe and matchet and to maintain the fertility of his land by the age-old device of rotating bush fallow with crops. Any increase in total farm output has been due more to additional inputs of land and labour than to significant improvements in productivity. Adoption of new agricultural technology has not been sufficiently widespread to make significant impact on traditional modes of agricultural organization and production to a degree that will lead to food surpluses for an increasing population.

In considering this largely static state of affairs it is customary to list inadequacies of credit, marketing, storage and transportation, and the assumed conservatism of the peasant farmer as the main factors limiting the adoption of new agricultural techniques and improvement in farm production. While these factors are certainly important in explaining the relative backwardness of agriculture in the poorer regions of the world, they are only a part of the total institutional setting within which agricultural innovation must take place and whose operation is crucial to the process of agricultural development.

The less developed countries enjoy a unique advantage in their efforts to raise agricultural production. They do not have to discover afresh the basic technological and biological improvements that have resulted in the more efficient use of labour and raised output per unit of land in the advanced industrial countries. The failure of agriculture in the

developing countries to exploit this unique advantage in raising enough food to feed their population is less a failure to
mechanize farming operations or to introduce modern inputs than
a failure to come to serious reckoning with those institutional
forces that facilitate or impede rapid improvement in agricultural production.

I propose to consider some of the nontechnical factors
impeding improvement in agricultural production under three
major headings: forms of farm organization and landholding;
population; and agricultural supporting services and infrastructure.

FARM ORGANIZATION AND LANDHOLDING

The form of economic organization and structure of land
ownership appropriate to rapid agricultural development
are yet unsettled issues in many developing countries,
particularly in Africa. The debate centres around the suitability of either the large, managed farm or the family farm
for improved agricultural production. The argument in favour
of either form of organization is well known and will bear no
repetition here. The plantation was the major form of managed
farm in Africa. During the colonial period a large number of
large-scale plantations were established in West and Central
Africa by foreign concerns from the metropolitan countries.
These plantations were limited to such export crops as cocoa,
coffee, oil palm and rubber and were operated entirely by paid
labour. They organized their own marketing, credit and supplies. The development of plantations was continued by some of
the governments that succeeded the colonial powers as an effort
to increase foreign earnings. Except in the Kenyan highlands,
where European settlers produced food as well as cash crops,
commercial plantations played no role in food production.

Some independent African governments have adopted the land
settlement scheme as a device for restructuring the organization of agricultural production and for boosting farm output.
Young, literate farmers are settled on tracts of land acquired
for the purpose. Each settler is provided with a house and is
expected to work his land with assistance from his family and
such hired help as may be needed during peak periods. The initial capital costs of opening the land and providing housing
and other amenities as well as the maintenance cost before the
first crops are harvested are treated as credit to the settler
which must be repaid over an agreed period of time. Although
operations on the settlements are supervised in the formative
stages by government functionaries from the ministries of agriculture, the idea is that responsibility for managing the farms
and for providing services to the settlements will ultimately
devolve on the settler through his own multi-purpose

cooperative organization. In addition to producing cash crops
the farmer grows food crops and raises poultry on a two-acre
farm near the farm house.

Managed farms in the form of plantations and settlement
schemes account for only a small fraction of agricultural output in the continent of Africa and apply mainly to the export
sector. Food production remains in the hands of small peasant
operators. The predominance of peasant family farms arises in
the main from the nature of traditional African tenure.

Rules of African Land Tenure

In most African countries land is <u>owned</u> by a group and not
       by individuals. The land-owning group may be a village,
a clan or a family. It is by virtue of membership of this
group that an individual has access to the <u>use</u> of land. The
farmer enjoys unlimited security in the use of the land and the
disposition of his crops. He cannot be dispossessed of his
land by the head or any member of the group, nor can he be refused the use of a part of the family land. Under the rules of
traditional tenure the farmer is permitted to grow such economic crops as cocoa and rubber on his portion of the family
land and can transfer such improvements to his immediate heirs.
He can also pledge these crops, though not the land itself,
against loans or debts. However, no member of the landowning
group can transfer any portion of the family land to an outsid-
er by sale or mortgage. After all, you can only sell what you
own.

The operation of these basic rules of African traditional
tenure vary in detail from community to community. Its most
enduring feature, which requires further study and preservation
as the old rules are modified, is the delicate manner in which
group and individual rights coexist within the same context.
This, together with the rule which gives every individual who
can make beneficial use of it a piece of the family land, has
enabled most African countries to avoid the social tension,
unhappiness, and even revolutions that often characterize land-
lord-tenant relationships elsewhere in the developing world.

The ban imposed by traditional tenure on the transfer of
land by sale or mortgage is seen as a major barrier to the development of African agriculture. This rule is said to impede
the flow of credit to the farms because lending institutions
will not accept as security property over which the cultivator
has no absolute right of disposition and since the farmer himself will be reluctant to borrow to make improvements on property which he cannot transfer to his immediate heirs. For this
reason development of individual tenure is urged as an alternative system of land ownership that will accelerate the process
of agricultural development. According to Lugard (1965, p.

295) individual ownership is the final stage in the process of
tenurial evolution:

> The labourer who works on land which is not his own, whether
> as the serf, or even as the paid servant of an estate owner,
> or as unit in a communal estate, has little interest in its
> improvement during, and none beyond his own life-time. . . .
> Individual proprietorship is no doubt inimical to the supply
> of wage labour for large estates, but it makes for individual
> progress, thrift, and character. It is the strongest induce-
> ment to good farming, and politically an asset to the Govern-
> ment, to which the peasant owes the security of his holding.

The perception of African tenure as the primitive begin-
nings in the evolution of economic and social institutions led
policy-makers in the colonial era to enact laws and issue administrative directives designed to ensure the desired outcome
of individual ownership in land. Except in the areas of the
continent where European settlers expropriated native lands and
imposed alien concepts of landholding, traditional African tenure systems have retained their essential features. The modifications that have occurred in the system have been more in response to changing economic conditions than to the force of
legal enactments and administrative directives. Thus, the cultivation of such perennial crops as coffee, cocoa, oil palm and
rubber has meant the identification of the farmer with a particular piece of the family land for a much longer period than
is usual where only annual crops are cultivated. As we have
seen, permanent crops can be transferred to immediate heirs and
can be pledged against debt although the land itself remains
theoretically the property of the landholding group which has
ultimate right of disposition. This is a reserved right which
is rarely used. The ban on the sale of family land by individual members has not stopped farmers from making permanent improvements on the land where it is perceived that this will
lead to improvement in their economic condition. In the western parts of Nigeria, for example, over one million acres of
land are in cocoa--owned, operated and controlled by individual
peasant operators having secure user rights.

Solution of the Tenure Question

The solution of the tenure question is of crucial importance to any programme designed to improve food production.
The development of individual ownership of land does not offer
the solution which its proponents claim for it. Indeed, in the
current African situation where, as a result of development,
land has acquired enhanced economic value, individual ownership
of rural land may hinder rather than accelerate agricultural

production. Wherever land has been left to the free forces of
the market the more affluent members of society have used their
superior economic power and political influence to acquire this
most basic asset of the community. The result has been the
creation of a landless, impoverished and unhappy peasantry subject to the sway of demogogues and political adventurers.

African tenure has so far managed to avoid this dire situation by ensuring that the small peasant holder retains a high
degree of self-respect and human dignity. What is required is
a tenure system which, while preserving the traditional user
rights of the farmer, enables him to gain access to the use of
modern techniques of farming. The farm settlement schemes,
state farms, and cooperative farming projects established in
different parts of Africa were designed to achieve this objective. Although none of these schemes can be said to be yet an
economic success, the principle of joint ownership and individual proprietorship embodied in them represents the first realistic attempt to deal with the land tenure issue. These experiments at a comprehensive reformation of African agrarian structures need further study and modification.

POPULATION
    The growth of population is a major factor in the changing
    agrarian structures in the developing countries. The
    seemingly inevitable rapidity with which population is in-
creasing in these countries and the effect of such growth on
agriculture may be illustrated by what has happened to the population of one of them during the last fifty years.

The Nigerian population rose from 19.9 million in 1931 to
30.4 million in 1953. In 1963 the population stood at 54.2
million and it is estimated that it will grow to 86.2 million
in 1980 (Federal Office of Statistics, 1972). The annual rate
of growth of about 2.5 percent is typical of the growth pattern
in the less developed countries. The proportion of the Nigerian population actively engaged in agriculture averaged 70 percent during the 45-year period for which partial census data
exist. This figure is expected to decline to about 68 percent
by 1980 (Food and Agriculture Organization, 1966, p. 400).
Quite apart from the inefficient use of resources involved in a
situation in which over two-thirds of the population is tied
down to the production of food crops and other raw materials,
the growing pressure of population on agricultural land has resulted in the breaking up of holdings into smaller units and a
sharp reduction in the period of fallow.

As we have seen, every individual has a right to the use
of a piece of the land for his family to grow his food and
other crops. His cropping cycle includes periods in which part
of his land is left to bush fallow to allow the soil to regain

lost fertility. The longer the period of fallow the more fully
fertility is restored.

As long as there is enough land to go round the admirable
rule of tenure which secures to each individual unlimited access
to the use of land not only ensures adequate supply of food, it
contributes significantly to the preservation of social stability. In addition, abundant supply of land permits the full
operation of the traditional system of bush fallow. However,
with increasing pressures of population and the extensive cultivation of permanent crops the land available to each farmer
for the production of food crops has progressively declined.
The division of the land among surviving heirs has resulted in
fragmentation of holdings into smaller units with a farmer having to spread his operation over three or four plots separated
by fairly wide distances.

The consequences of the shortening of the fallow period
and the fragmentation of holdings for food supply may be illustrated by the increasing imports of food by many developing but
supposedly agricultural countries. The food situation in
Nigeria will serve as our example of the failure of agricultural policy in the developing countries.

In 1960 the value of food imports was 23.9 million naira;
imports of food rose in value to 57.7 million naira in 1970 and
stood at 232 million naira in 1973. Yet despite the phenomenal
increase in food imports since 1970:

> Nigeria has found herself short of basic foodstuffs many of
> which could have been grown at home . . . the price of such
> things as beef, eggs, poultry and pigs had gone up to such a
> level that it has become almost impossible for the low income
> groups to afford them. Taking November 1974 as the base in-
> dex of 100 (and this does not allow for the fact that food
> prices have been increasing since the civil war) then the in-
> dex in Lagos almost a year later stood at 154. The rise in
> staple foodstuffs was huge. Gari went up to an index of 185,
> maize 152, and plantains 240. Fresh beef rose to 176 and
> fresh chicken to 226. Even salt went up to 218. Firewood and
> other fuel and light sources also rose by over 50 percent.
> (Rake, 1976)

Although increased income from oil is a major factor in
the rising demand for food imports, the fact that population
has grown at a faster rate than food production is as important
as the oil boom in explaining the current food shortages in
Nigeria.

SUPPORTING SERVICES AND INFRASTRUCTURE

Measures designed to improve both the technical competence
of farmers and the quality of the resources available to

them, to restructure the tenure system, and to control the growth of population will no doubt lead to some improvements in agricultural output. But sustained agricultural development depends as much on these measures as on the existence of a net- work of supporting services organized into a system of assis- tance to the farmer. Without an efficient system of marketing, supply, credit, transportation, storage, education, health and roads "all other efforts will be in vain--the farmer will be like a man battering on barred doors" (Weitz, 1971, p. 111).

In both the literature of agricultural development and in practical planning and operation of development or assistance schemes, greatest attention is paid to measures which will im- prove the technical competence of farmers and the quality of their physical inputs. The relative neglect of the nontechni- cal measures of agricultural development stems from what agri- cultural planners in developing countries perceive as the cru- cial factors in the development of agriculture in the advanced countries.

The scant attention paid by planners to agricultural sup- porting services may also be due to the more complex character of these services and the difficulty of finding adequate finan- cial and manpower resources with which to create and operate such a system of services simultaneously with the planning and operation of the more technical elements of the development programme.

To be sure, advanced technology and scientific innovations resulted in vast increases in labour productivity and enabled the farming family to operate larger farms in the USA.

This development would not have occurred, however, without the simultaneous expansion of supporting services. The trans- fer of activities such as seed and feed production and the marketing of products to nonfarm business enterprises has facilitated greater specialization within the farm itself. (Weitz, 1971, p. 32).

The supporting system plays as crucial a role as scientific innovations in the effort to increase farm output. To be able to purchase new and improved inputs the farmer needs access to cheap sources of credit; he will also want assurance that these inputs are conveniently located and are available at reasonable prices. He will not use fertilizers if it involves him in trav- elling long distances to supply depots and paying prices which are beyond his means. If he has no facility for storing the bumper harvests or a ready market for the products of the new technology, the farmer will prefer to stick to his traditional subsistence crops instead of taking what appears to him to be avoidable risks.

The organization of an efficient system of agricultural

services involves considerable financial outlays and a corps of
highly skilled managers to operate them. The absence of these
factors in sufficient quantities has hampered the development
of comprehensive systems of services in many developing countries.

Location of the Supporting Systems

To be of maximum use to farmers, the various elements of
the supporting system must be widely dispersed. Since the
demand for service comes from a large number of small farmers
the "branches of the supporting system must be brought as close
as possible to the rural community for them to be really useful
and compete successfully with the traditional service suppliers
. . . who are usually found in or near the village itself. . ."
(Weitz, 1971, p. 113).

In many developing countries the tendency is for these
services to be concentrated in large centres of population.
For instance, banks and other lending agencies are found usually
in capitals and provincial headquarters where they are out of
reach of the mass of farmers; major highways bypass villages
and farms without provision for effective rural link roads
which will make for easy and quick transportation of farm produce to the market; the warehouses and central stores of major
dealers in agricultural supplies (seeds, equipment, fertilizers
and insecticides) are often located in cities with the result
that farmers are forced to deal with retailers who charge
prices that put the services beyond their control; the most
knowledgeable and skillful members of the extension services
are based in headquarters, leaving the instruction of the farmers to the most poorly educated elements of the extension
system.

The reasons for concentrating agricultural supporting services in a few focal points are obvious and cannot be ignored
even when governments organize and operate them. In many poor
countries capital to create these services and the skilled personnel to operate them are limited; communications facilities
are poor; and roads, such as they are, are in a poor state of
maintenance. The result is that most marketing services are
left to middlemen, and credit to village moneylenders who
charge exhorbitant, almost extortionate prices for their services.

Perhaps the most important reason for the concentration of
these services in a few centres is the advantage of scale. In
order to make a decent return on his capital the supplier of
services will need to operate above a certain minimum level.
This level will be dictated by the particular service. Whatever the service, the number of economic units which can be
created will depend on the amount of capital which the supplier

can mobilize and the willingness of managers and other technical staff to move to rural areas. There is therefore a conflict between what Raanan Weitz (1971, p. 116) calls the principle of maximum territorial dispersal and the need to concentrate all the "services that function on a similar scale . . .
in a single location." For example, to bring education close
to the farmer will require that every village, no matter its
size, should have a school. And yet village schools are notoriously inferior to similar institutions in urban centres.

> To main reasons account for this situation: the limited scale
> of operation and the shortage of qualified teachers. A vil-
> lage population is often too small to be able to afford a
> full-fledged, high quality school. Furthermore, trained
> teachers and other professionals tend to prefer a job in the
> city and are usually unwilling to work in a remote village.
> There are many reasons for this preference, but one of the
> most important is the desire to work in a place that has a
> network of services of a high enough quality to satisfy both
> professional ambitions and social needs. (Weitz, 1971,
> p. 115)

The social and economic reasons why teachers prefer to remain in large population centres are similar to those which
make other carriers of agricultural change (extension workers,
bank managers and cashiers, merchants dealing in agricultural
supplies and equipment, technicians and mechanics--want to concentrate their services in a few urban centres. It is for
these same reasons that young, educated people are migrating
from the countryside into the cities, leaving farming to the
older folk.

The conflict between the principle of maximum dispersal of
agricultural supporting services and the need for a measure of
concentration of these services in a few focal points can be resolved by a restructuring of the spatial organization of rural
communities. This will involve the deliberate creation in strategic centres in the countryside of communities that are intermediate between cities and the small, widely scattered villages
that are typical of most developing countries. The population
of this intermediate community or "rural town" may be as low as
2,000 or as high as 20,000. Each "rural town" will serve farmers within a radius of between 5 and 10 miles. Where rural
roads are poorly developed, and foot and bicycle the main means
of reaching the farms, a "rural town" should ideally serve
farmers within a 5-mile radius. Where, on the other hand, rural roads are fairly well developed and farmers have access to
motor bicycles and even trucks for moving supplies and farm
produce, a "rural town" will be able to serve farmers within a
10-mile radius and even slightly more. The population of

farmers served by each "rural town" must be such as to make it possible for the supporting system to operate on a scale that will "guarantee efficient utilization of resources and the provision of services at a reasonable cost." In the prevailing conditions in the developing countries a minimum population of 5,000 farmers will be needed to guarantee the scale of operation that will enable the system to achieve these objectives. The maximum population served by a "rural town" should not be more than 50,000. As experience is gained and more managers and technicians trained, a "rural town" should be designed to serve between 2,000 and 25,000 farmers.

The figures used in the above paragraph are purely notional; they merely help to delimit the boundaries and magnitudes of the problem of creating agricultural supporting systems capable of providing maximum assistance to farmers in the developing countries in their efforts to improve food production and feed their increasing populations at a higher level of nutrition.

The various elements of the supporting system--banks, markets for farm products and for farm supplies and equipment, tractor maintenance and repair services, facilities for research or verification trials, schools, health centres, and major recreational facilities such as theatres, stadia and cinema houses --will be located in the "rural town". Rural roads will link the villages to the "rural towns" and the latter to main highway arteries of the nation. This arrangement satisfies the requirements of maximum dispersal of service units in that farmers located in various villages can reach the required services within hours rather than days as at present. Their children can be taken by bus to better staffed and equipped schools in the "rural towns". Moreover, the concentration of service units in a "rural town" will make it possible to "bring together a large enough group of professionals to create a self-supporting social unit" (Weitz, 1971, p. 118). The farmers within a given radius of a "rural town" as well as the professionals drawn to the area to service the supporting system will have access to good medical services which individual villages, acting on their own, cannot provide.

Who Owns or Operates the Supporting System

The land settlement schemes in Africa and elsewhere were designed to perform some of the functions envisaged here for "rural towns". In Kenya, Ghana and Nigeria the settlement schemes were planned as model farming communities with each farmer operating his holding along cultural lines laid down by the settlement authorities. In the former Eastern Nigeria, for example, each settlement was to comprise 10,000 to 12,000 acres of land in a single block subdivided into 12- to 14-acre

holdings per settler. The operation of his holding is the individual responsibility of the settler. The settler lives in
one of the 6 villages which make up a settlement. Each village
has 120 families. "The villages consist of a grid street plan
around which are located the settlers' homes, a community centre, a junior primary school, the village square and playground,
a communal yam barn, and a fuel (firewood) plantation." (Floyd,
1967). The high cost of establishing these settlments severely
limits the number of farmers that can benefit from the scheme.
After more than 15 years of operation less than 1,500 farmers
are involved in the farm settlement scheme of the former Western
Nigeria. In the Nigerian case, where there are already established intermediate-scale towns, an alternative programme of
agricultural improvement based on existing communities would
have been more appropriate for the maximum dispersal of the
various elements of the supporting services for agriculture.

It is the aim of most governments of developing countries
to bring to the rural areas modern urban amenities, pipe-borne
water, electricity, roads, schools, hospitals, etc. It is real-
ised that the absence of these facilities limits the ability of
the farmer to improve production. In many instances the provision of these facilities makes little or no impact on agriculture. Because of their location new and expensive highways
have been known to render farms even more remote from their
markets; depots for farm supplies are often located in centres
which farmers must spend a considerable time to reach; lending
institutions are to be found in the big centres of population
where the better schools and health facilities are also located;
and extension agents and research facilities are almost invariably found in ·headquarter towns. The result is that the farmer
is left, for the most part, at the mercy of middlemen and moneylenders. The creation of the rural communities envisaged in
this paper will bring closer to the farmer the services he needs
to improve the output of his land.

The question of who operates or owns the supporting system
is a matter of detail which will need to be settled in accordance with the social philosophy of each developing country. An
ideal situation would be one in which the government and private
entrepreneurs act as partners in developing the various elements
of the supporting system. Obviously, it is the responsibility
of government to provide education and health services of the
same quality to people in the countryside as to those residing
in urban centres. Failure to do this may limit the incentives
of farmers to improve production and cause their children to
migrate in large numbers to cities, with adverse consequences
for agriculture. Government also has responsibility for providing research facilities and organizing an efficient extension
service. With the demand made upon government financial resources by other sectors of the economy, it may be more

appropriate to encourage existing private financial institutions to put their considerable resources at the disposal of the farmer with the government only providing guarantees where necessary. Farmers' cooperatives charged with responsibility for the marketing of farm produce of their members will minimize the problem of the middlemen and remove the disincentive effects of the operation of the giant marketing boards.

In many developing countries the farmer has no voice in making the decisions that affect his profession. Decisions as to planting materials, method of operation, type of lending institution, and the system of tenure considered suitable for improved agricultural production are made at national or state capitals and handed down to subordinate bureaucrats at provincial or divisional headquarters for implementation. The result of inadequate consultation at the local level with the prospective users of agricultural services or with their representatives is misunderstanding of government motives and the mislabelling, by frustrated bureaucrats, of sensible but cautious farmers as conservatives who prefer their traditional ways to modern, scientific innovations designed to improve their output of farm products. A strong local government of the proposed "rural towns" with adequate representation of farmers will remove this misunderstanding and create the favourable political climate for the operation of an effective agricultural supporting system.

SUMMARY OF SOCIO-ECONOMIC MEASURES

The socio-economic measures for improving food production in the developing countries, particularly of Africa, can be summarized under three broad heads:

1) A reform of the traditional tenure system which continues the arrangement whereby the individual operator enjoys unlimited use of the land for the production of his food crops and ultimate ownership of land is vested in the community. While the individual has the freedom to dispose of his produce as he deems fit and his heirs can inherit any improvement made on the land, he will not be permitted to transfer the land by sale or mortgage without the consent of the community. The assurance that the usufruct of the land is for life and that improvements are heritable will provide farmers with enough incentives to invest in farm improvement. Cooperative or government guaranteed credit will ensure that farmers have access to the capital they require to acquire new inputs. The gradual evolution of the tenure system will avoid the situation which has developed in the urban areas where land speculation has resulted in massive corruption. The grafting of new forms of tenure on the old will lead to a systematic and orderly

development of a tenure system adaptable to each stage in the
process of agricultural development and will avoid the emergence of a landless peasantry. The experience of planners in
Israel, as eloquently summarised by Raanan Weitz (1971), is of
interest to those seeking the reform of African tenure into
structures that are alien to existing social practices:

> Agricultural production in the newly settled areas lagged be-
> hind the expected and required rate. Knowing that these dis-
> tressing conditions had to be corrected, we began to seek a
> remedy. And, as often happens in life, in our search for a
> new approach we stumbled upon some basic home truths. We
> learned, above all, the necessity of preserving the existing
> social framework of different ethnic groups, of refraining
> from subjecting them to pressure in an attempt to introduce
> immediately a new way of life. We had to be careful not to
> push the people beyond themselves, not to attempt to destroy
> their customs, beliefs, and traditions, but instead to graft
> new economic, social, and organizational concepts on to the
> old. In this way we encouraged their feelings of hope and
> pride and began to stimulate a desire for development.

2) The creation of an effective system of agricultural
services that meets both the aims of maximum dispersal of the
elements of the system and the need to concentrate similar
units of the system in a number of focal points that will bring
their costs within the reach of the farmer. If these services
are located too far from the villages, farmers will not use
them. If, because of extensive dispersal, it is not possible
to operate at a size where dealers can reap the rewards of the
economies of scale, the price of the services may be beyond
what the farmer can afford. The concentration of these services at focal points near the farmers enables a more efficient
operation and brings together in one place a number of professions (teachers, doctors, nurses, bank managers, clerks, technicians, etc.) who can form a viable social unit.

3) The creation of intermediate communities between the
large centres of population where modern social amenities tend
to be concentrated and the villages virtually devoid of such
amenities. These intermediate communities or "rural towns" will
act as points of concentration for the social and economic services so essential to the development of agriculture and to the
welfare of rural peoples. The creation of schools, health centres, banks, extension administration, facilities for research
and local verification trials, markets, and recreational facilities in centres where they are within easy reach of the farmers will make it possible to attract into rural areas professionals and technicians needed to operate and maintain these
agricultural supporting services.

REFERENCES

FAO. 1966. Agricultural Development in Nigeria, 1965-1980.
    Rome, Italy.
Federal Office of Statistics. 1972. Digest of Statistics 21:1.
    Lagos, Nigeria.
Floyd, B. and M. Adinde. 1967. Farm settlement in Eastern
    Nigeria: a geographical appraisal. Economic Geography 43:
    192.
Lugard, F. D. 1965. The Dual Mandate in British Tropical
    Africa. Anchor Books, Connecticut, USA.
Rake, A. 1976. The collapse of agriculture. African Develop-
    ment 10:236.
Weitz, R. 1971. From Peasant to Farmer. Columbia University
    Press, New York, USA.

JOHN A. HANNAH

The Challenge of Providing Food for Hungry People

I am happy to be here this evening invited to speak on the topic of the "Challenge of Providing Food for Hungry People." It is a challenge.

To my mind, it is the greatest challenge of the last quarter of the 20th century.

It is a challenge for you, who are professionals in the production, or processing or delivering food for the people of America. It is a challenge to the farmers and consumers of food all over the world.

It is not simply the challenge of producing more food, but also the challenge of understanding what the food problem of the world is and where and how it must be solved.

The world food problem has been a source of international concern repeatedly in the past quarter century and long before that, but the challenge was not taken as a problem of very serious concern to the whole world until the World Food Conference in Rome in November 1974, 19 months ago. Your discussions during this past week are one of the consequences of the World Food Conference. I would like to speak this evening of some other important consequences and how they relate to this challenge we all must face.

WHAT IS THE CHALLENGE?

First, let me re-state it. The challenge is how is the

John A. Hannah is Executive Director of the World Food Conference, United Nations, via delle Terme di Caracalla, 00100 - Rome, Italy.

world to feed its <u>hungry</u> people in the years immediately
ahead. It is embodied in the Declaration on the Eradication of Hunger and Malnutrition in these words:

> Every man, woman and child has the inalienable right to
> be free from hunger and malnutrition in order to develop fully
> and maintain their physical and mental faculties. Society
> today already possesses sufficient resources, organizational
> ability, and technology and hence the competence to achieve
> this objective.

This Declaration was adopted by the World Food Conference and
endorsed by the General Assembly of the United Nations in December 1974 following the World Food Conference.
This challenge, even its formulation, was critically influenced by the statement of the Secretary of State of the United
States at the World Food Conference when he said:

> The profound promise of our era is that for the first
> time we may have the technical capacity to free mankind from
> the scourge of hunger. Therefore, today we must proclaim a
> bold objective--that within a decade no child will go to bed
> hungry, that no family will fear for its next day's bread, and
> that no human being's future and capacities will be stunted by
> malnutrition.

I emphasize this formulation because it is important to
recognize that the issue is not simply one of producing more
food <u>for</u> people <u>in</u> <u>general</u>. The world has done this consistently in the past--populations have increased rapidly and life
spans have been extended--and will undoubtedly continue to do so
in the future. The four billion people alive today have more
food available than the 2.5 billion people alive in 1950 had--
about one fifth more per person. But this is <u>on</u> <u>the</u> <u>average</u>!
Underneath this <u>average</u> is the real food problem and the real
challenge we face today.

THE MAGNITUDE OF THE PROBLEM
Over the past quarter century a growing imbalance in food
production and consumption has emerged in the world. The
developed countries--of which the United States is one of
the most developed and by far the most significant producer and
exporter of food in the world--have mastered the techniques and
the policies appropriate to producing not only <u>enough</u> food but
more than enough. They have been able to do this in part
because they are developed, which means their people have the
education and incomes appropriate to a high level of food consumption and production. This capacity to produce more than

enough food gave rise to two important phenomena that characterized the food world from the end of World War II until 1972
with:

    1. The accumulation of large stocks of grain which pro-
tected the world against unexpected calamities; and
    2. The provision of food aid for emergencies and for poor
countries whose food supplies were inadequate and who were
unable to import large amounts of food commercially.

    But in the developing countries, less desirable phenomena
were emerging. During the 1950's food production in the developing countries was growing about as rapidly as in the developed
countries and more rapidly than population. In the 1960's however, the developing countries experienced both more rapid population growth and a slowing down in their rate of increase in
their food production. By the middle of the 1960's food production in the developing countries was no longer keeping up with
population growth. During the first five years of the 70's, it
slipped even more seriously. As a result, the developing coun-
tries--into which are born about 85 percent of all the children
of this earth--were no longer able to feed themselves let alone
improve their level of nutrition.
    These developments have had two important and sobering con-
sequences. The developing countries, which were virtually self-
sufficient in their food supplies in 1950 were importing between
15 and 20 million tons of grain in 1970, half of which was in
the form of food aid. By 1975 the gross imports of these countries had reached about 45 million tons. Every projection of
the food situation for 1985, nine years from now, points to a
doubling or tripling of these cereal imports--from 85 to 100
million tons per year or more--unless there is a fundamental
improvement in the capacity to product food in the food deficit
developing countries.
    Thus, the first challenge is to increase food production in
the developing countries. In recent years, each year additional
developing countries cease being self-sufficient in food production and the food import requirements of those already in food
deficit increases.
    The second and more complex, but even more important, chal-
lenge is to see to it that increased food supplies are actually
consumed by those people who need additional food most. At the
time of the World Food Conference, November 1974, 460 million
people were estimated to suffer from serious malnutrition--460
million people--that is almost twice the population of the
United States. It is possible to quibble about whether the figure should be 400 million or 500 million, but the phenomenon--
the experience of hunger and malnutrition--is not in question.
Most of these malnourished people live in Asia, another large

proportion live in Africa, and there are large groups of malnourished people in Latin America as well. These people live
mostly in rural areas, although malnutrition is evident to any
observant visitor to a large city in a developing country. The
least well nourished are the women and children--the future citizens of this world and those who will be most instrumental in
teaching them about the world.

If the challenge to erradicate serious hunger and malnutrition in a decade is to be seriously faced--and you and I know in
our hearts that it should be--we must attack the problem where
it is and this is not simply a matter of increasing food production.

The third challenge is the development of a new, realistic
and adequate system of food security, which inevitably means a
system of food stocks. The food stocks, essentially grain
stocks in the developed grain exporting countries, which we
relied on for more than two decades, came to an end in 1972-1974
as a result of food shortages that plagued a number of countries
at that time and as a result of the efforts of many grain
exporting countries over previous years to reduce their surpluses.

After two decades of trying to cope with the burden of surplus grain stocks in North America which tax payers had to pay
for and farmers disliked because they depressed grain prices, it
is understandable that there is a degree of relief that these
surpluses are gone. But for the world as a whole this is a very
dangerous situation. Food, especially the basic cereals, rice,
wheat, other food grains that are the principal diet for poor
people, and the pulses which are a source of protein, is the
most necessary of all human needs. When there is a little bit
too much food, prices are low and farmers have little incentive
to expand production. When there is not quite enough food,
prices can reach incredibly high levels and hungry, poor people
get hungrier and poorer. That is particularly true in the least
developed countries lacking foreign exchange to pay for food.

I think that it is generally recognized that the pattern of
world food production, food aid and food surpluses that prevailed during the past two decades was unsatisfactory. It produced the progressively deteriorating conditions that came to
light with such force during the world food crisis of 1972-74.
These patterns of production and consumption and the policies
which underlay them cannot be continued without disastrous
results and they should not be returned to. But we must be
realistic. The slowing down of food production in the developing countries cannot be reversed immediately and it cannot be
reversed by those countries alone without outside assistance.

This means, first, that additional external resources, both
capital and technical assistance, must be provided by those
countries in a position to do so. Second, there is a useful
role for food aid. Not careless food aid. Not food aid as a

by-product of surplus disposal programmes. Food aid must have
a real intent and purpose: designed to feed hungry people; to
support efforts in developing countries to advance their own
food production or to advance other development efforts that
will provide increases in income necessary to buy more food; and
to assist in the transition from negative to positive food production policies. Third, it means a responsible attitude toward
world food security which must include some kind of coherent and
adequate system of food reserves, especially cereal grain
stocks.

All of this is part of the challenge as I see it. It is a
challenge with three major facets:

First, to increase the food production capacity of the
poor, food deficit countries where gross malnutrition is most
serious;

Second, to raise the level of nutrition of the world's poor
and hungry people; and

Third, to make the world secure against those calamities of
nature and man which cannot be predicted but which we all know
will occur from time to time.

WHY IS IT IMPORTANT TO SOLVE THESE PROBLEMS?

Here in Iowa, this year when we are celebrating the results
of two hundred years of a glorious experiment which has
served Americans so well, it is difficult for you to see,
or to feel intensely, just how these food problems relate to
you. But I assure you they do. They are profoundly relevant to
you and they will be important and immediate elements of the
daily lives of your children and grandchildren, and of mine.

The 4 billion people on this earth now will have increased
to 6 billion and more at the end of this century, 24 years from
now. Even with the best of population control efforts, little
can be done to change this situation and nothing can be done to
substantially change the population impact on food in the next
decade. The food deficits of the developing countries projected
by 1985, are too high to be considered manageable. They are
only a fraction of those that can be projected for the years
beyond 1985 unless immediate and adequate steps are taken to
change the pattern of the last two decades.

But it is most important that we realize that, more important than percentages of population increases or quantities of
food available to feed them, is the fact that we are talking
about poor, hungry, hopeful people: hundreds of millions of
men, women and children whose futures, whose perspectives on
life, whose values and whose capacities to appreciate being
alive depend largely on our willingness and ability now to take
up the challenge of providing them with and helping them to provide themselves with an adequate supply of food. If we do not
take up this challenge now with deeds and actions that actually

bring about change, we will not have adequately provided for
our own children's future.

THE WORLD FOOD CONFERENCE

The World Food Conference of 1974 not only raised the challenge of feeding hungry people; it also called for the
establishment of institutions to ensure that this would be
done: the World Food Council, the International Fund for Agricultural Development; the Committee on Food Aid Policies and
Programmes; the Committee on World Food Security; and The Con-
sultive Group on Food Production and Investment in Developing
Countries.

Each of these institutions has an important role to play
along with the larger international and regional institutions
dealing with food.

I hope you will pardon me if now I speak of the first two
which I have been especially close to and for which I have great
personal hope.

The International Fund for Agricultural Development

The World Food Conference, in its Resolution XIII, called
for the establishment of an International Fund for Agricultural Development if sufficient additional resources could be
generated to support such a Fund.

The Secretary-General of the United Nations assigned me the
responsibility of determining whether such funds could be generated and to organize the inter-governmental discussions necessary to bring such a Fund into being. It is a matter of great
personal satisfaction for me to be able to tell you that in less
than two years this Fund, which started as only an idea, has
become a reality. In Rome, just three weeks ago, 80 countries
agreed to establish such a Fund. At that meeting, more than 936
million dollars was firmly pledged by governments of the world
toward the target of one billion dollars which will set the Fund
in motion.

The Fund is a unique institution. The major contributors
are the Organization for Economic Cooperation and Development
(developed countries of western Europe, the US, Canada, Japan,
Australia, and New Zealand) and the OPEC countries. Its underlying financial support is new. Its voting structure is also
new, divided equally between the developed countries, the OPEC
countries and the developing potential recipient countries. The
developing countries will have a substantial role in determining
the policies and activities of the Fund. It has already been
determined that the first priority in the Fund's activities will
be the stimulation of food production in the poorest developing
countries with first emphasis on the food deficit countries. I
see in this Fund both a clear indication that the countries of

the world are ready to provide the resources necessary to begin
to solve the world food problem and at the same time are willing to do so with a new type of institution which will help to
bridge the gap that has so often separated the rich and the
poor.

The World Food Council

The World Food Council is another product of the World
Food Conference. It was created to give guidance and
direction to international efforts to solve the world food
problem. To do so it will monitor the policies and programmes
of the international agencies dealing with food and those of
governments to ensure that the major food problems are tackled
and that the necessary resources and political support are generated to solve them.

The World Food Council consists of 36 member governments
and a secretariat of about a dozen professional people, with
supporting staff, of which I am proud to be the Executive Director. Representation in the Council is also unique. Almost two-
thirds of its members are developing or OPEC countires. The
rest are developed and socialist countries. The United States
is a member of the Council and so is the Soviet Union. This is
an important fact since participation by the USSR in international organizations dealing with food has been minimal. The
present membership consists of nine African countries, eight
from Asia, seven from Latin America, four from the Socialist
countries of eastern Europe and eight members from western
Europe and other developed countries. They are: Argentina,
Australia, Bangladesh, Canada, Chad, Colombia, Cuba, Egypt,
France, Federal Republic of Germany, Guatemala, Guinea, Hungary,
India, Indonesia, Iran, Italy, Japan, Kenya, Libyan Arab Repub-
lic, Mali, Mauritania, Mexico, Pakistan, Romania, Rwanda,
Somalia, Sri Lanka, Sweden, Thailand, Trinidad and Tobago, USSR,
United Kingdom, US, Venezuela, Yugoslavia.

The World Food Council has a long way to go to live up to
the responsibilities assigned to it. As a new international
body it has had to face the problem of how to work together to
solve specific problems when these problems are often the result
of very real political differences between countries. It is the
first body in the United Nations system made up of Ministers of
Governments.

The Council is making progress. It has just concluded its
second annual session in Rome, June 14 through 16, where it
began to consider some of the serious issues which must be faced
if the world food problems are to be solved, increased food production in the food deficit developing countries, food aid and
the complicated problems of food security.

It took up the issue of how to ensure that food production
increases take place in those developing countries where they

are most needed or where they can most efficiently be produced. It endorsed recommendations which centred on:

1. The identification of developing countries in greatest need of increased food production and least likely to be able to do so without specific additional assistance;

2. The need to identify quickly and precisely how food production can be increased in these "food priority countries" and the internal and external resources necessary to achieve these specific production increases;

3. Recommended mechanisms to deal with policy and other constraints that "food priority countries" must overcome if they are to effectively utilize larger resources in their food production efforts; and

4. Recommendations to help direct external resource flows for food and agriculture so that they are better adapted to overcome specific food problems.

To bring about needed improvements in food aid, the Council endorsed recommendations to establish a dependable, annual flow of food aid at the level of 10 million tons of cereal grain so that it would be possible to begin to transform food aid into a device which:

1. Improves the nutritional level of poor, hungry people in the developing countries;

2. Supports food production efforts or other efforts in poor countries to generate income so that more food can be purchases; and

3. Does not result in disincentives for food producers.

The Council also recognized that despite the need for a system of world food security, there had been little progress since the World Food Conference. It endorsed recommendations calling for an emergency relief programme of at least five hundred thousand tons of grain and recommended that the International Wheat Council and the General Agreement on Tariffs and Trade (GATT) consider a modified form of grain reserves, in the range of 15-20 million tons, as an intermediate step in the eventual development of a truly satisfactory world grain stock policy.

CONCLUSION

Ladies and Gentlemen, these are only beginning steps but they are in the right direction. Repeatedly in the past the world food problem has been dramatically presented and then quietly allowed to drift from the minds of those who were concerned. The World Food Council was established to ensure that this did not happen again, that the world's attention will be constantly focused on the need to make fundamental improvements and that ways to accomplish this will be brought to the attention of international agencies and national governments. The dimensions of the world food problem are known--where it is, who suffers the most and, within limits, why it is. We have a reasonably good idea of how to solve the problem.

I purposely noted at the outset that both the Declaration on the Eradication of Hunger and Malnutrition and Secretary of State Kissinger's statement made it clear that the world has the resources and the technical capabilities for solving the world food problem and for making certain that "no child go to bed hungry and no family fear for its next day's bread."

The problem is not simple--for a week you have considered many of its complexities at this Conference--but the problem is solvable.

It is my profound hope that the World Food Council can serve as the vital link between those who possess the resources and the techniques and those who are only poor, hungry and hopeful.

The World Food Council has begun to take up that challenge; you here at this Conference have been dealing with that challenge.

I am confident that this time the world will recognize that what it knows it should do it can do.

That is the Challenge of Providing Food for Hungry People.

2

Impacts of the World Food Situation on People, Environment, Development

FERNANDO MONCKEBERG B.

Impacts of Food Availability on Health

To eat adequately is one of the fundamental needs of every living being. The history of man has been the history of the fight for food, and the greater part of his activity has been aimed to this objective (Prentice, 1946). The fight was a difficult one and hunger, undernutrition and misery were always his usual companions. It is only during the last epochs and due to the enormous amount of knowledge accumulated by man, that the availability of food has increased, and man has been able to develop other activities. At present, nobody can deny that man has acquired knowledge enough so as to permit an adequate food availability for the whole of humanity. Nevertheless, we must recognize that this has not been made a reality. Today in spite of all the knowledge acquired, millions and millions of human beings continue suffering undernutrition and hunger. It is a fact that these conquests of knowledge have not benefited men equally (Monckeberg, 1974). While some have food in more than enough amounts, others remain in very primitive conditions. Moreover, during the last years, a separation that seems to be getting worse had appeared between these two groups. Evidently, knowledge has not spread homogeneously, nor has it been applied uniformly.

The availability of sufficient food to be consumed by man is not an easy task and depends on numerous factors. Where there exists hunger and undernutrition, there also coexists inefficiency of all the infrastructures of society. Hunger and undernutrition always coexist with misery (Monckeberg,

Fernando Monckeberg B. is Head, Department of Nutrition and Food Technology, University of Chile, Santiago, Chile.

Valiente, 1976). Undernutrition damages the individual as well
as society, and the same damages are also increased and produced by misery. In misery there is a vicious circle conditioning damage: hunger, undernutrition, disease, ignorance,
insalubrity, crowding, leading to more hunger. The undernourished individual is always in an inadequate environment, and
the damage produced by undernutrition is aggravated by this
environment (Monckeberg et al., 1972). This is why we cannot
ignore the environmental factors inherent to misery, when evaluating and analyzing this damage.

Undernutrition and misery provoke the most severe damages
during those stage of life when growth is quicker, that is to
say, during the first years of life (Monckeberg, 1967). Evidently, the intensity of the damage depends on the severity of
undernutrition and misery. Undernutrition has been compared to
an iceberg. The projecting part represents the severe cases,
which are the minority, while the submerged part represents the
majority of cases, that are less severe.

In children with severe undernutrition, the damage produced is evident, compromising practically every organ and
function. The immunological mechanisms are altered (especially
the mechanisms of cellular immunity) (Schlesinger et al.,
1973). The processes of digestion, absorption, metabolization
and excretion are also modified, as described by many investi-
gators (Monckeberg, 1967). Recently, special attention has
been called to the disturbances produced in the development of
the central nervous system, expressed as a lowering of intellectual capacity and behavioral abnormalities (PAHO, 1972;
Kallen, 1973; Richardson, 1973; Scrimshaw et al., 1967;
Monckeberg, 1972). The percentage of children suffering from
severe undernutrition varies between 1 and 4 percent in the
different underdeveloped countries (OMS, 1973).

The less severe cases of undernutrition are much more frequent, affecting almost 70 percent of the children under 6
years of age. The damage produced is not so marked, being pro-
portional to the degree of undernutrition. They show a
decreased adaptation capacity and defense before their environment. In this way, risks increase, expressed as a higher morbidity, a greater severity of diseases and finally a higher
mortality rate. In Latin America, 50 percent of the deaths
occur before 15 years of age, while in USA, only 4 percent of
the deaths occur before the age of fifteen (OMS, 1973). No
doubt this is due to subalimentation as well as to adverse
environmental factors: crowding, insalubrity, ignorance.

The most evident manifestation of chronic subalimentation
during the first years of life is physical growth retardation.
Figure 1 shows the growth pattern of different groups of Chilean children, with similar genetic conditions, but belonging
to three different socio-economic groups. It can be observed
that those showing a greater growth retardation, are precisely

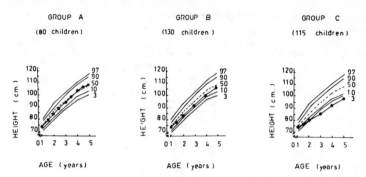

FIG. 1. Average growth curve in three groups of Chilean children belonging to three different socio-economic
groups: A--Medium socio-economic level; B--Low medium
socio-economic level and C--Low socio-economic level.

those belonging to the lowest socio-economic level. This also
coincides with a high incidence of retardation of psychomotor
development.

   With the present experimental data, we can assume that
retardation of growth and maturational development is the
direct consequence of chronic subalimentation. Nevertheless,
we cannot infer the same conclusion as regards the retardation
of psychomotor development. It is true that there is a very
positive correlation between the degree of physical growth
retardation and intelligence quotient (Figure 2). However, we
cannot assume the existence of a cause-effect relationship,
because there are many other factors acting negatively upon the
development of intellectual capacities. In man, subalimentation is never an isolated phenomenon, because the groups suffering from undernutrition, also suffer from many other adverse
factors, inherent to misery (Monckeberg, 1972).

   For some years, it has been a well known fact that health,
intelligence, adequate social behavior and intellectual efficiency are in very close relation to the socio-economic conditions in which the child develops: the better the socio-
economic condition, the higher the levels reached for these
parameters. Experiences carried out in animals show that the
development of the central nervous system is modified according
to social experiences (Lesser et al., 1965). Rats submitted to
isolation and to lack of stimulation suffer biochemical alterations of the central nervous system similar to those produced
by severe undernutrition. These animals also show abnormal
behavior and retarded psychomotor development (Frankova, 1973).

   Observations made in man do not permit definite conclusions, because from a practical viewpoint, it is impossible to

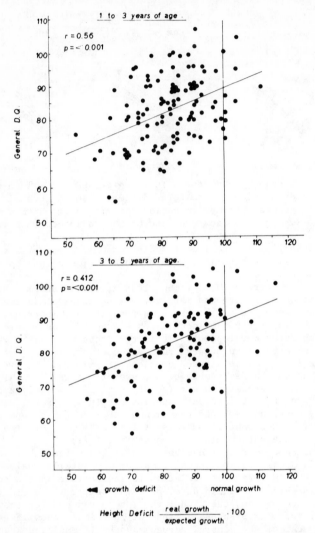

FIG. 2.   Height and mental development quotient in pre-school
children from 1 to 3 years old and 3 to 5 years old.

A significant correlation can be observed between the
percentage of deficit of growth and the general development quotient. The percentage of growth deficit was
calculated by dividing the real growth by the
expected growth for age in accordance with the 50 Iowa
percentile and multiplying by 100.

make a well defined separation between the two contributing variables. Undernutrition and low socio-economic level are always very close together. However, it has been observed that even those children with an acceptable nutritional state but with an inadequate socio-economic environment show low efficiency in psychomotor development tests (Table 1). Birren and Hess (1968) conclude that poverty affects intellectual development due to social as well as biological agents. In children submitted to these conditions, these can be observed: a) lower efficiency of intellectual functions, b) lower efficiency in specific tests analyzing cognitive conditions, and c) lower efficiency in learning performance.

TABLE 1. Development quotient in well-nourished (weight over the 10th Iowa percentile) and malnourished (weight under the 3rd Iowa percentile) children of a close population (slum area)

Area	Malnourished (96 cases)	Wellnourished (24 cases)	p
Motor	72 ± 12	93 ± 12	< 0.001
Language	68 ± 15	79 ± 14	< 0.001
Adaptative	74 ± 11	86 ± 11	< 0.001
Personal social	70 ± 11	87 ± 11	< 0.001
General	71 ± 9	87 ± 9	< 0.001

It does not seem logical to think that the intellectual retardation observed in the weaker socio-economic groups is due to genetic factors, because there are demonstrations that an early and simultaneous improvement of nutritional conditions and psychosensorial stimulation prevent this retardation (McKay, 1973).

The relationship between nutritional and environmental factors and intellectual development of the child can be seen more clearly when its influence upon the recovery of a severely undernourished child is studied. The pediatric experience shows that severe undernutrition, marasmic type, produced during the first year of life is very difficult to treat. The risk of dying is very high (30 percent), even with the best of medical care (Monckeberg, 1967). The resuming of growth is very slow and takes months to reinitiate, even in the absence of concommitant infections. Recent experiences demonstrate that this very difficult recovery is due to not taking into account factors apart from the medical and nutritional treatment. A group of 70 infants with severe undernutrition were submitted to a special treatment at a Recovery Center. A house near a pediatric hospital was made available, and the infants were cared for by volunteers of an adequate socio-economic and

cultural level. The treatment consisted basically of feeding
based on cow's milk, motor and cognitive stimulation during one
hour daily and affection, trying to imitate what a mother could
normally give. The results were surprising, because physical
and psychical recovery started immediately at an accelerated
rhythm. Figure 3 shows the percentage of weight gain, compared
to that observed with a conventional treatment at a pediatric
hospital, in which children only received medical treatment and
adequate feeding. Table 2 shows the same results, observing
that psychical recovery was almost complete, reaching practically normal psychomotor levels after 150 days. Mortality
rate was also very different. There were no deaths in the special treatment group; the mortality rate was 29.5 percent under
conventional treatment. These results force a restatement of
the previous assertion about the irreversibility of the damage
produced by severe undernutrition acquired during the first
months of life (Monckeberg, 1973). They also demonstrate that
the nutritional factor is only part of an environment that must
be considered as a whole.

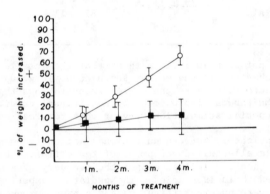

FIG. 3. Weight increased in 70 severe malnourished infants
         after four months of treatment.

Very positive results have also been obtained for pre-
school age children. The experiments carried out in the city
of Cali (Colombia) by McKay and Sinisterra (1973) were precisely done in preschool children of different ages (between 3
and 5 years old). Children were chosen who belong to very low
socio-economical levels and who live in slum areas of the city
of Cali, where undernutrition has a high prevalence. Four
groups of children were studied analyzing the following vari-

TABLE 2.   Evolution of 320 infants (under one year of age),
           with severe undernutrition. Group A: 250 infants
           treated conventionally in pediatric hospitals. Group
           B: 70 infants submitted to a treatment of psycho-
           motor stimulation and affection

Days of treatment	0	50	100	150
% weight deficit	A: 56 ± 8 B: 53 ± 5	A: 54 ± 13 B: 36 ± 8 $p < 0.001$	A: 48 ± 12 B: 21 ± 8 $p < 0.001$	A: 40 ± 8 B: 2 ± 4 $p < 0.001$
% height deficit	A: 76 ± 10 B: 82 ± 13	A: 70 ± 17 B: 50 ± 14 $p < 0.001$	A: 65 ± 16 B: 32 ± 8 $p < 0.001$	A: 60 ± 14 B: 20 ± 6 $p < 0.001$
Developmental quotient	A: 53 ± 12 B: 58 ± 15	A: 60 ± 11 B: 71 ± 10 $p < 0.01$	A: 64 ± 14 B: 86 ± 8 $p < 0.001$	A: 65 ± 12 B: 91 ± 8 $p < 0.001$

ables: a) adequate feeding covering all the requirements,
b) health care, c) cognitive stimulation. This last point
included five areas of intervention: 1) verbal production,
elemental comprehension in quantity and quality; 2) temporal
and spatial relations; 3) manipulation of normal work; 4) maintenance of attention and concentration in the work and
5) attainment of the capacity of independent decision.
    The conclusions of this experiment that has lasted for
four years may be summarized in the following terms: a) when
only adequate feeding is given, without any other action, physical growth reinitiates and weight and height increase are normal, but the intelligence developmental quotient is not significantly modified; b) instead, when in addition to feeding, a
program of psychological and social stimulation is developed,
very important changes can be obtained in cognitive and social
development, with almost complete recovery from the delayed
psychomotor development.
    Both experiences confirm what was previously stated: the
physical, psychical and behavioral damage observed in individuals living in misery is produced by many factors and undernutrition is only one of them.

ADVERSE ENVIRONMENTAL FACTORS
    Evidently in poverty there are factors having a negative
    influence upon the psychomotor as well as physical devel-
    opment of the child. These environmental factors sum up
to those produced by undernutrition.

Factors Retarding Psychomotor Development
     The environment of misery is grey and flat, it does not
     stimulate the imagination nor the curiosity. Everything
lacks luminosity. The color variation is limited, and there is
no play stimulus so necessary to initiate the development of
the child's abilities.
     Parents show a marked limitation of language, and give a
very scarce verbal stimulation. It is a constant finding, that
amongst the specific cognitive deficiencies observed in these
children, there is a constant speech retardation (Seeshore,
1951; Cazden, 1966). Parents also show a significant correlation between verbal score and socio-economic level. Low income
families present a very restricted verbal score, which means an
inhibition of symbolic forms with very scarce abstract and cat-
egoric speech (Bernstein, 1961; Cazden, 1968). Under these
conditions, motivation is only conditioned to everyday facts
with no real projection towards the future. All these facts
restrict the information and motivation of the child limiting
the alternative possibilities of knowledge.
     On the other hand, in extreme poverty the relations
between children and adults are diminished with very scarce
common activities between the members of the family. This is
evidenced as indifference towards the child. Affection and
understanding are minimal. Under these circumstances, there is
not only a negative influence upon the development of cognitive
functions, but it affects personality as well. For example, it
has been observed that children belonging to low socio-economic
levels have very poor "self-esteem". This restricts personal
motivation with an incapacity to integrate efficiently into
society (Minuchin et al., 1967).
     In misery, the family is distorted and disorganized. The
father's image is distorted or simply does not exist (Pollit,
1969; Graham et al., 1963; Cravioto et al., 1967). It is
usually the mother that has the greater responsibility in the
family group (Monckeberg, 1967). Nevertheless, the responsibility is limited because of her low educational level and her
numerous offspring, and because she must use the greater part
of her time doing her house work or working outdoors. The
intelligence quotient of mothers living in slum areas is consistently low. Using the Wechsler Scale, almost 80 percent of
the mothers show a score under 79 (Table 3). All these factors
lead to an environment where there is lack of stimulation and
very few opportunities to learn. It seems logical to think
that the deficit in psychomotor development is the consequence
of the summing up of different factors: lack of stimulation,
scarce affection, insecurity and undernutrition. They potentiate each other producing damage to the individual that properly
should be called "sociogenic-biological damage".
     The damage produced by undernutrition is more severe the
earlier it develops. The lack of stimulus also starts its

TABLE 3. Intelligence quotient of mothers of slum area and
          middle class

	Slum area (%)	Middle class (%)
Normal (over 91)	6	96
Subnormal (between 80-89)	17	4
Deficit (less than 79)	77	0

retarding action early in life. Thus, for example, different
investigations have shown that the intelligence quotient of
children belonging to low socio-economic groups is even lower
when they have been subjected to early social deprivation
(Willerman et al., 1970; Werner et al., 1967; Kublok, 1967).
This fact is particularly important, because the damage
observed is probably due to the different adverse factors early
in life plus those that continue their negative influence during preschool age.

Environmental Factors Aggravating Undernutrition
     Undernutrition is not only conditioned by lack of food,
     because even when this exists, the environment of misery
is so adverse that food utilization is greatly impaired. In
Chile for example, (Monckeberg, 1967) there are big programs of
food distribution for children under 6 years of age. Theoretically undernutrition should have disappeared at that age, but
nevertheless it persists. For example, there is a free distribution of: powdered milk (3 kilograms per month) to every
child between 0 and 2 years of age totaling 13 thousand tons
per year; infantile foods with a 20 percent protein to every
child between 2 and 6 years of age (2 kilograms per month)
totaling 16 thousand tons per year; and powdered milk (2 kilograms per month) for pregnant women and lactating mothers,
totaling 9 thousand tons per year. It may be true that undernutrition has decreased, nevertheless it still persists (Table
4).
     There is a very important part of the population with
inadequate sanitary conditions, with high crowding indexes,
with very low quality houses and with a low educational and
cultural level. As a consequence of this there is a high morbidity aggravating undernutrition. On the other hand, feeding
bottles are easily contaminated. Thus for example, in a recent
investigation done in a slum area population, it could be
demonstrated that approximately 80 percent of the feeding bottles contained Shigella, Salmonella or E. Coli, when the mother
was giving it to the child. This means diarrhea and gastroin-
testinal disturbances. In the summer months, 30 percent of the

TABLE 4. Percentage of malnourished children (0-6 years of age) in Chile

Year	1968	1975
Normal	36	83
1° degree	46	13
2° degree	14	3
3° degree	4	1
	100	100

calories of children living in such a population were lost due to diarrheas (Monckeberg, 1967).

The incomes for families do not allow sufficient food, and very frequently, the milk and foods given for children under 6 years of old are consumed by the whole family (Monckeberg, 1974). In this socio-economical level, alcoholism is very frequent: 30 percent of the fathers are excessive drinkers (Monckeberg, 1974). There is no knowledge as regards nutrition, and there are many beliefs and taboos that do not allow a good utilization of the budget.

All these facts explain why the damage produced by undernutrition cannot be separated from the damage produced by misery. Misery and undernutrition potentiate each other by closing a vicious circle, the effects of which are transmitted from generation to generation. Thus for example, a significant correlation could be found between the intelligence quotient of mothers and the degree of their children's undernourishment (measured as growth retardation) (Figure 4). In other words, a mother with an important psychical deficit has a very high possibility of her own child growing up undernourished, while those with normal intelligence quotients have better possibilities of feeding their children adequately, even when socio-economic conditions are not good.

In general, those individuals living in misery are the product of many generations that have lived in similar circumstances. It is as yet not clear whether this misery repeated through generations does or does not have more profound changes. This question has been studied in experimental animals having shown a very slow recovery. Steward (1973) described an experiment with rats in which he provokes subalimentation and marginality by submitting the rats to a restricted diet and lack of stimulus during nine successive generations. Progressively he could observe biochemical and psychical changes. Later, in the tenth generation he refed the rats with a complete diet observing that many of the alterations take more than two generations in reaching normality.

The damage produced by misery doesn't allow the individual to integrate usefully into society. The negative effect

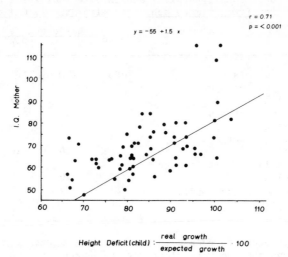

FIG. 4.   Intellectual quotient of the mothers and growth
          (height) of children.

becomes evident during school age. In a recent study, a very
significant decrease in school performance has been observed in
those children submitted to subalimentation and cultural deprivation. In Latin America, of every 100 children that start
primary school only 20 are able to finish it. It is evident
that the sociobiological damage is the main cause of this poor
performance and of high school desertion (Table 5) Monckeberg, 1973). It can be asserted that children that are able to
finish primary school are those whose environmental conditions
were sufficiently generous with them, so as to permit the
expression of the greater part of their genetic potentialities
during their growth period. It is today's reality that the
individual that is unable to complete his primary education is
definitely left out from society. This means that he will have
to be resigned to subemployment, very low salaries or unemployment, thus closing the vicious circle of misery and marginality. Furthermore, this situation is transmitted from one generation to another with very few possibilities of escaping from
it.

        To prevent the damage is urgent, but because the damage
that hurts the individual, not only affects him but the whole
of society, the prevention is especially important in those
poor countries where the greater part of the population is
under these conditions.

        To fight misery requires completely new planning, making
great efforts towards programs of direct and integrated

TABLE 5. Nutritional, physical and intellectual state of chil-
          dren from primary school in Alto Jahuel, Chile

	Basic course			
	1°-2°	3°-4°	5°-6°	7°-8°
Number of students	403	260	160	80
Height deficit for age (average) %	10	7	7	3
Weight deficit for age (average) %	15	8	9	3
Caloric deficit for age (average) %	16	10	10	+ 2
Animal protein deficit for age (average) %	32	20	17	6
I.Q. (Wisconsin) (average)	81	87	92	101
School performance	50	57	60	66

actions, in order to change this sub-world generating misery.
This concept must be very clear for the economists, sociologists, teachers and physicians. It is not easy to fight misery, not even wealth can defeat it, when it has become part of
the individual. The complexity of modern society requires more
and more effort everyday from the individuals if they really
want to become part of it and enjoy the benefits of human
knowledge. Misery has escorted and damaged man during the
whole history of humanity, but today the separation between
those that are capable of integrating into society and enjoying
its benefits and those that are definitely left out has
widened. Nutritional goals alone are not enough. "Man must
live not on bread alone". Today this phrase from the Gospel
acquires its full dimension.

REFERENCES

Bernstein, B. 1961. Social class and linguistic development:
     a theory of social learning. Education, Economy and Soci-
     ety. Glencoe Free Press.
Birren, J. E. and R. D. Hess. 1968. Influences of biological,
     psychological and social deprivation upon learning and per-
     formance. In Perspectives on Human Deprivation. Biologi-
     cal, Psychological and Sociological. US Department of
     Health, Education and Welfare, pp. 89-183.
Cazden, C. B. 1966. Subcultural differences in child lan-
     guage: an inter-disciplinary review. Merrill-Palmer Quar-
     terly 12:185.
Cazden, C. B. 1968. Development Medicine and Child. 10:600.
Cravioto, G., H. G. Birch, E. DeLicardie and L. Rosales. 1967.

The ecology of infant weight gain in a pre-industrial society. Acta Paediatrica Scandinavica 56:71.

Frankova, S. 1973. International Symposium, Stokolm.

Graham, G. and E. Morales. 1963. Studies in infantile malnutrition. I. Nature of the problem in Peru. Journal of Nutrition 79:479.

Kallen, D. J. 1973. Nutrition, Development and Behavior. US Department of Health, Education and Welfare, MIT Publication (National Institute of Health) 73-242.

Kublok, H. 1967. Prediction from assessment of neuromotor and intellectual status in infancy. Psychopathology of Mental Development. New York, Grune Stratton, pp. 387-400.

Lesser, S., J. Fifer and D. H. Clark. 1965. Society for Research in Child Development 4:30.

McKay, H., A. McKay and L. Sinisterra. 1973. Behavioral intervention studies, with malnourished children. Nutrition, Development and Behavior, MIT Publication 242.

Minuchin, S., B. Montalva, B. Guerney, B. Rodman, and F. Schumer. 1967. Families of the Slums. Little Brown and Co., Boston.

Monckeberg, F. 1968. Adaptation to caloric and protein restriction in infants, calorie deficiencies and protein deficiencies. McCance, R. A. and Widdowson, E. J., Churchill Ltd., London.

Monckeberg, F. 1968. Nutrition and Behavior. Nutrition, Development and Social Behavior. National Institute of Health Publication No. 73-242.

Monckeberg, F., S. Tisler, V. Gattas, L. Vega and B. Elsemberg. 1972. Malnutrition and mental development. American Journal of Clinical Nutrition 25:766.

Monckeberg, F. 1973. Revista Centro Estudios Educativos (Mexico) 3:67.

Monckeberg, F. 1974. Jaque al Subdesarrollo. Editorial Gabriela Mistral, Santiago, Chile.

Monckeberg, F. and S. Valiente. 1976. Antecedentes y acciones para una política nacional de alimentación y nutrición de Chile. Editorial Gabriela Mistral, Santiago, Chile.

Organización Mundial de la Salud. 1973. Inf. Tecn. No. 522, Ginebra.

Pan American Health Organization. 1972. Nutrition. The Nervous System and Behavior. Scientific Publication No. 25.

Pollit, E. 1969. Ecology, malnutrition, and mental development. Psychosomatic Medicine 31:193.

Prentice, E. 1946. El hambre en la historia. Espasa-Calpe, Argentina, SA, Buenos Aires.

Richardson, F. 1973. Brain and Intelligence. National Educational Press, Hyattsville, Maryland 20781, USA.

Seeshore, H. G. 1951. Differences between verbal and performance IQs on the Wechsler intelligence scale for children. Journal Consult Psychology 15:62.

Scrimshaw, N. and E. Gordon. 1967. Malnutrition, Learning and
    Behavior. The MIT Press, Cambridge, Mass., USA.
Schlesinger, L. and A. Stekel. 1973. Rev. Chil. Ped. 44:455.
Steward, R. 1973. A marginally malnourished rat colony. The
    effect of maternal malnutrition on the development of the
    offspring. Nutrition Reports International, White Plane,
    New York 10605.
Werner, E., K. Simonian, J. M. Bierman and F. E. French. 1967.
    Cumulative effect of perinatal complications and deprived
    environment on physical, intellectual, and social develop-
    ment of preschool children. Pediatrics 39:490.
Willerman, L. and S. H. Broman. 1970. Infant development,
    preschool IQ, and social class. Child Development 41:69.

JEAN A. S. RITCHIE

Impact of Changing Food Production, Processing and Marketing Systems on the Role of Women

This short paper is limited in scope to inter-relationships between changing agricultural patterns and food use and the roles of age and sex groups in some societies in Africa. Even then, to talk of Africa is obviously overambitious, as the societies and cultures of the Continent offer an infinite variety of patterns and problems.

Eighty to ninety percent of African families earn their living from farms, fisheries, livestock breeding or rural businesses or industries connected with these. It is hoped that some of the dilemmas of Africa recorded here will serve as bases for discussion for those of other regions, since subsistence farmers the world over share many problems of food supply and development.

Although the topic of the paper is concerned with the impact of changing food and agricultural systems on people, it is impossible to divorce this from the impact of changes in people, on technologies and systems, and on the resultant availability of food. This year is near the mid-point of the Second Development Decade of the United Nations, with the goal "to bring about sustained improvement in the well-being of the individual and to bestow benefits on all". It is also the beginning of the United Nations declared Decade for Women "Equality, Development

---

Jean A. S. Ritchie is FAO Planning for Better Family Living Advisor, U.N. Economic Commission for Africa, P. O. Box 3001, Addis Ababa, Ethiopia.

The views expressed in this paper are those of the author and do not necessarily represent the views of the Food and Agriculture Organization of the United Nations.

129

and Peace" during which it is hoped to eliminate some of the inequalities to which women are subjected in most countries of
the world. The achievement of the aims of this decade in
Africa will depend to a great extent on the introduction of economic and technological changes in the production, processing
and marketing of food and other agricultural produce since the
economies of Africa are based on the efficiency of the farmer.
Increased productivity will depend not only on agricultural inputs but on efficient use of all human resources, women as well
as men. The present roles and relationships assigned to women
form a barrier to such progress. These roles have arisen from
numerous influences in the past and are strongly affected by
20th century changes.

The neglect of the subsistence economy, largely in the
hands of African women, has retarded the potential growth of
food production. As a result, family cash income continues to
be low. This has imposed severe constraints on the demand for
consumer goods which in turn has affected the availability of
jobs for both men and women in the industrial sector. Failure
to look at society as a whole and to establish an equitable
balance between food production and cash crops has been a major
obstacle to development in many countries.

Some of these complex inter-relationships are discussed in
the following pages and some of the situations are emphasized
for which remedies are urgently needed if United Nations' development goals are to be reached and the disaster of famine
averted.

TRADITIONAL SEX ROLES

In the early history of Sub-Sahara Africa, men and women
had recognized complementary roles in caring for the family
and society. Men were hunters, and women were food gatherers. This pattern can still be seen among the peoples of the
Kalahari in Botswana (FAO/ECA,[1] 1976). This was followed by
systems of shifting cultivation in which efficiency was maintained through a division of labour between the sexes (Reynolds,
1975). Brown (1970) has suggested that a major factor determining the sex roles was women's responsibility for the care of
children. To allow them to do this satisfactorily, their other
tasks had to be near home, easily interrupted and resumed, not
of a kind requiring rapt attention, and not dangerous.

In many traditional African societies, for example among
the Ga and Akan peoples of Ghana, women played significant social and political roles and enjoyed prestige in their own right
and great independence (Smock, 1975). Their economic contribution to the welfare of the family was recognized and appreciated,

---

1. ECA is the UN Economic Commission for Africa.

even though they rarely controlled land or the basic rituals to
maintain the good will of ancestors or the most powerful of the
secret-societies (Van Allen, 1974). Men helped them with the
strenuous jobs of cutting trees and clearing bush, but women
bore the responsibility for feeding the family and still do.
Africa south of the Sahara has always been a female farming
area, and in many countries, women have over the last century
augmented their cash resources by selling surplus food or articles they have made.

THE IMPACT OF COLONIAL RULE
        The early missionaries and administrators who came to
        Africa during colonial times brought with them 19th cen-
        tury European concepts. They believed that the women's
place was in the home, and they had little respect for women's
intelligence, business acumen or capability for independent
thought and action. They assumed that men were the owners of
land, the breadwinners and wage-earners and that they fulfilled
all the economic roles in society. They distorted the local social patterns and roles to comply with their pre-conceived
ideas. Thus men were hired for work in plantations and as servants, a change which upset the agricultural cycle (Ritchie,
1967, p. 21). Men were given technical training for a variety
of jobs including agriculture. Women were taught domestic
skills and "ladies" work with emphasis on embroidery and western
cooking even though they still had to grow the food their families needed. With the advent of "companies", such as those
established in Ghana to grow cocoa for export, it was unusual
for women to be employed, even in societies like the Akan, where
a considerable proportion of traditional cocoa farmers were
women (Hill, 1970), or like the Acholi of Uganda where cotton
was started as a woman's crop (Boserup, 1970, p. 54).
        As a result of these changes in agricultural and in social
patterns, women's significant political and social roles were
frequently undermined, and the degree of equality and authority
many had achieved was weakened or destroyed. The more servile
traditional relationships were retained as the basis of the status of women in many African societies (Van Allen, 1974).

THE IMPACT OF THE INTRODUCTION OF CASH CROPS
AND OF CHANGES IN AGRICULTURAL TECHNOLOGY
        Changes in agricultural technology followed the introduc-
        tion of cash crops and were largely limited to this aspect
        of farming. Raw materials such as oil, cocoa, coffee
beans, tea, rubber and sisal were needed for the expanding economies of the industrializing countries. Because of the mistaken
assumptions concerning sex roles, a dual economy was created;

men now became farmers for cash while women continued to produce food within a subsistence economy and were also expected
to weed and tend their husbands' crops. Thus women's labours
increased although their control over the family income diminished.

In most societies men considered cash crop earnings as
their own property and rarely gave much to their wives. In the
Bouske region of the Ivory Coast, for example where cash crops
bring in good returns, the percentage of the family income allocated to women is only 10-15 percent compared to 50 percent in
traditional villages (FAO, 1973).

Men have been able to invest some of the profits of their
cash crops in extra land and farm inputs while the productivity
of women farmers has remained low or even declined (Reynolds,
1975). Moreover, women's freedom and opportunities to trade
with surplus food or home-made articles has diminished as the
demand for labour on their husbands' cash crops has increased.
This has led to their greater economic dependence on their husbands. Quarrels over money have resulted in some societies, to
increased instability of marriage (Rigby, 1972).

The introduction of only one modern technique may divert
labour from food production and consequently reduce domestic
food supplies. A study of agricultural change in Teso district
of Uganda (Uchendu and Anthony, 1975, p. 100) has shown that
while ox-drawn ploughs were introduced for the cultivation of
cotton as a cash crop in the first decade of this century best
estimates indicate that, even now, there is only one seeder or
weeder in Teso to 100 ox-ploughs. Labour bottlenecks have thus
been built up because of the failure to introduce an efficient
series of technical innovations, and the burden of hand weeding
and picking on an extensive scale falls largely on the women.

Mechanization can also reduce the land available to women
for food crops. In most parts of Africa South of the Sahara,
each wife has traditionally been allotted a piece of land on
which to grow food for her family. Her rights have been assured by her society, and in most cases, she could sell surplus
foods to buy necessities. The introduction of tractors has in
some places led to land consolidation and to a greater demand
by men for land for cash crops cultivation. Men still control
most of the allocation of land, and consolidation and title
registration have sometimes made women's rights more precarious.
Few women have been in a position to buy farms of their own
(Boserup, 1970; de Wilde, 1967). Fencing of consolidated land
can lead to women losing grazing facilities for their cattle.
This leaves some with the choice of either selling their cattle,
and foregoing the proceeds of the sale of butter and cheese, or
the alternative of keeping the cattle at home which leads to
the task of cultivating or gathering fodder and possibly fetch-
ing water for the animals (ECA, 1974).

Thus, with the introduction of modern agricultural techniques, a woman's role may become more burdensome and her economic importance may decrease if her husband's cash crops become very profitable.

It should not be assumed, however, that women in all societies conform to exogenous decisions regarding agricultural change. Pala (1975) reports from a study in South Nyanza, Kenya, that women make the basic decisions concerning planting, cultivating, labour use and the sale of small food surpluses to meet their cash needs. Where cash crops compete with food crops for labour, they may neglect the former until work on the food crops is finished. Some women refuse to work on crops such as tobacco when they know that they will receive no share of the profit.

Modernization, while benefiting some families, may sometimes have unfortunate results for others. It has been estimated that in the area of the Chilalo Agricultural Development Unit in Ethiopia 6,500 tenant farm families lost the land they cultivated between 1966 and 1972 probably as a result of mechanization (Cohen, 1975, p. 369 and p. 373).

THE DIVISION OF LABOUR IN EARLY MODERNIZING ECONOMIES OF AFRICA

It is difficult to get sufficient empirical evidence to generalize about the division of labour between sexes.

However, the limited available information indicates that the changes in roles which have persisted since early colonial times have led to an unbalanced distribution of work. In addition to their role as farmers, described above, women have many other roles in African societies. They fetch wood and water, cook, clean and maintain the home, look after the children and provide their early education, care for the extended family, take much of the responsibility for social duties in the community, process and store the food, and market the produce. They have important roles as wives, and especially as mothers, and as consumers who influence demand for various goods.

It has been found that women frequently contribute the majority of working hours on self-help schemes. The Government of Kenya has estimated that women provide about 80 percent of the self-help labour. Ninety percent of the roads in Lesotho have been built by women under a food-for-work programme (ECA, 1974). The largest modern hotel in Mogadiscio, Somalia was built by women's self-help work contribution.

Many examples are available which indicate that women work longer hours than men (Lele, 1975, p. 26). A review of some data available in the ECA, from research findings, missions, country reports and meetings, suggests that the percentage of total hours put in by women on different jobs might roughly take the pattern shown in Table 1 with, of course, many variations

TABLE 1.   Percentage of total labour (hours) per task contrib-
           uted by African women

Production and supply activities	% by women	Household activities	% by women
Food production	70	Bearing, rearing and early education of children	100
Domestic food storage	50	Cooking for the extended family	100
Food processing	100	Cleaning, washing, etc.	100
Animal husbandry	50	House building	30
Brewing	90	House repair	50
Marketing	60		
Supply of water	90	Community work	
Supply of fuel	80	Self-help projects	70

and exceptions (ECA, 1974). With men, increases in agricultural activity tend to be at the expense of off-farm activities.
With women the tendency is to sacrifice leisure (Lele, 1975).

THE INFLUENCE OF AGRICULTURAL COOPERATIVE
SOCIETIES AND CREDIT FACILITIES
       Traditional cooperative societies have long existed in
       Africa for the purpose of saving, mutual aid or work-shar-
       ing.   Many market women and farm women formed their own
groups, because they had no access to other types of loans.   In
modern Africa, the cooperative movement has spread widely and
agricultural banks have been established, but cooperative membership is usually restricted to male heads of households and
loans are mostly available to men.   Experience in Lesotho, where
the majority of cooperative members and officers are women, has
proved them to be capable and honest managers.   It is a move
forward that the establishment of family membership, with either
the husband or the wife representing the family's interests, is
now being discussed in East African countries.

THE INFLUENCE OF CHANGES IN TRADE AND MARKETING PATTERNS
       It has been pointed out in much of the literature that by
       tradition the women of Africa, especially those of West
       Africa, are traders.   For example two-thirds of Yoruba
women in Nigeria are engaged in trade (Boserup, 1970).
       In modernizing economies several factors are endangering
this role of women: the influx of cheap manufactured household
goods which substitute for the home-made articles women used to
sell; the squeezing out of petty traders by large commercial

undertakings (ECA, 1971); and the type of education given to
children which now may be appropriate but which results in modern girls being less successful as traders than their illiterate mothers. Already slight declines in the percentages of
traders who are women have been recorded in Nigeria and Benin
(ECA, 1974).

THE INFLUENCE OF SOME POPULATION FACTORS
        Population growth rates in some African countries exceed
        3 percent per year, and the greater numbers of people have
        put pressure on the land in some areas as well as increas-
ing the need for jobs and services. Lack of land resources has
been one of the obvious causes of rural to urban migration. A
vicious circle may be created since urbanization raises the demand for food, but the changes in agricultural patterns described earlier and the increases in rural family size have resulted in food production which lags behind population growth.
Although the African agricultural production has kept pace with
that of the developed countries, this increase has been nullified by a high population growth rate (FAO, 1974).
        Frequent child bearing tends to reduce the working effici-
ency and health of women. Added to this problem is the inadequate quantity of food many women consume. Surveys carried out
by the Food Science and Nutrition Institute at the University
of Ibadan have indicated that women, in the parts of Nigeria and
Ghana studied, consume a lower proportion of their requirements
than do men. Those findings confirm a general impression that
in comparison to what is given to children and other family members, women tend to give a disproportionate share of available
food to their husbands. Women thus are apt to have less food
and as there is abundant evidence that a low calorie intake results in low work output, their productivity is apt to be affected (FAO, 1962).
        Short birth intervals and too many mouths to feed from
existing inadequate food supplies often result in children with
low birth weight. These children are in a high risk category
(ECA, 1974). Furthermore, the rapid increase in demand for food
is already leading to steep rises in prices which are likely to
result in decreases in quality of diet among the poor (FAO,
1974).
        The current population growth rates, unprecedented in human
history, give cause for concern that progress in developing
countries is being to a large extent offset by increased population size (Bhattacharjee, 1975).

THE IMPACT OF ATTITUDES TOWARDS WOMEN'S ROLE
IN ECONOMIC DEVELOPMENT
        The colonial regimes in Africa gave no credit to women's
        contribution to economic progress although the whole

approach was dependent on women staying on the farms and growing food for the workers (Reynolds, 1975, p. 10). The high
profits made by companies operating in Africa would have been
impossible without the unpaid work of the wives of low-paid
labourers. These wives fed, clothed and cared for themselves
and their children at no expense to the company. Far from the
traditional agricultural sector being a drag on the modern sector as is sometimes claimed, the modern sector has been dependent for its profits on the efforts of women subsistence farmers
(Van Allen, 1974). Even today, labour statistics from many
countries class male farmers as actively employed but not their
wives (ECA, 1974). There is still a tendency among planners
and administrators to see the roles of women in western terms
although many farm households are headed by women, de facto if
not de jure. In Kenya, one-third of rural households are
headed by women (ILO, 1973), and similarly high or higher figures are found in Niger, in Malawi, and in other countries with
a high proportion of migrant labour.

In most parts of Africa, attitudes toward women and children prevailing from earlier tradition or stemming from colonial days still persist. Girls often are expected not to attend
or to leave school in order to help their mothers and husbands.
New goals toward ownership of consumer goods and land and
toward education of children (especially boys) have partially
supplanted such traditional goals as that of having large families which had power and respect within the society. Nevertheless in many areas of Africa a woman is still valued and judged
by her capacity to bear children, especially sons. Every new
child is still welcomed as an extra pair of hands (Sinha and
Kötter, 1975).

In some areas, women as human beings are still viewed as
something less than men. Pala (1975) has pointed out that employment laws in some countries group women and children together, giving them a juvenile status. Women may be de facto
heads of households but still unable to buy or sell cattle or
to make decisions on planting permanent crops. The decision-
making roles on agricultural matters are usually well-defined:
decisions with long-term implications such as sale of land or
the planting of trees being a male prerogative.

As elsewhere in the world, male attitudes are frequently
patriarchal; what is good for the man is automatically assumed
to be good for his family. Most men are quite pleased with
this ideology, to the point of sometimes opposing the few
attempts which have been made to include women in their own
right in the modernizing process (PAG, 1975). It is not uncommon for men to take the attitude that relieving women of some
of their work burden would make them idle and possibly give
them leisure time to be unfaithful. Their wives' first task is
to minister to their personal wants and comforts (ECA, 1974).

When rural women migrate to towns with their husbands or on their own, they lose the security of their extended family and frequently are unemployable because of lack of employable skills or little or no education. Their chances for incomes are likely to be only in the brewing of beer, in petty trade, or in prostitution. The role of child-bearing may be their only source of personal satisfaction and respect. Some, on the other hand, return from time to time to the village to farm, thus continuing to contribute to the family economy and preventing the reallocation of the land (Van Allen, 1974, p. 64).

In general, the relative unimportance attributed to the role of women in current African society by the men who have most of the decision-making power is reflected in the make-up of the budgets of both national and international development programmes. Women's projects receive low priority and, if funds are insufficient, it is these programmes which suffer first from budget cuts (PAG, 1975). It is noted that the roles of women have been defined in many African societies, limiting their options, but that one seldom hears of the "roles of men" (Reynolds 1975).

OTHER BLOCKS TO NATIONAL DEVELOPMENT

In spite of progress made in modern agricultural science and technology, rural families in Africa are not yet making the full contribution required of them when development depends on agricultural earnings. Among the inhibitors of progress can be government paternalism and reluctance to delegate responsibility to rural people; inability of governments to produce innovations which are attractive enough and low enough in risk to motivate farmers; mistrust of research centres whose work, they consider, is unrelated to their own local problems (Lele, 1975, p. 184); too few extension agents, many of whom are not always adequately equipped to meet farmers on their own level; and the concentration of extension services on men and cash crops with consequent neglect of the needs of women in the subsistence agricultural sector.

It is clear that although development has not yet reached most people in rural Africa, in the areas where it has had an impact, men have received more benefits than women. Where women have been reached by extension programmes, these have largely dealt with the improvement of home and family tasks and rarely with improved crop production or other economic functions.

FAO recognizes the importance of the familial role and that training for farm and home tasks cannot always be divided among the sexes arbitrarily. There is a trend toward multi-purpose family-focussed extension programmes which strive to train men, women and youth in the act of improved farm and home management. Just as women need training in agriculture skills, so men also

need training in nutrition, population education and improved
use of family and community resources (FAO, 1975b).

The emphasis on agricultural extension for men has led to
some spectacular failures. For example, Chinese experts in
Senegal taught men to improve rice-growing techniques with no
success in increased production. The Chinese had not realized
that women, not men, are the rice producers in that country
(Delalande, 1966). The poor transfer of new agricultural skills
learned by men to their wives was demonstrated at the Makerere
University farm, Uganda, where the women's crops were frequently
in poor condition. Women, given the opportunity and training,
can master improved agricultural techniques. A good example is
the participation of more than 4,000 women in their own commercial onion production schemes in the Gambia. It is certain that
if food production is to outstrip population, much more attention must be given to helping women in their roles as farmers.

As the situation is now, the gap between men and women's
participation in development is widening. The Uganda poet Okot
p'Bitek has illustrated this dramatically in his Song of Lawino
and Song of Ocol (p'Bitek, 1966 and 1970).

> "Husband, now you despise me ....
> You no longer want me
> Because I am like the things left behind
> In the deserted homestead
> You insult me
> You laugh at me
> You say I do not know the letter A
> Because I have not been to school ....

> "Woman
> Shut up
> Pack your things
> GO!

> Take all the clothes
> I bought you
> the beads, necklaces
> And the remains
> Of the utensils
> I need no second-hand thing"

A NEW AWARENESS IN THE SEVENTIES

The Second Development Decade, the seventies, has seen the
gradual but sure growth of new awareness of the necessity
of involving women fully in development activities. As
one Africa President expressed it: "People say that women must
be included in efforts for development because they constitute
50% or more of the community. The truth is greater than that.
Women are the community." An ECA document on the new

international economic order (in draft 1976) raises the question by understatement: "There is not much evidence at present that the role of women and children in agriculture, particularly food production, processing and marketing, is seriously taken into account by policy-makers and planners, who continue, mistakenly, to treat this subject and associated nutrition problems . . . as peripheral".

Resolutions arising from recent major World Conferences have focussed on the inter-relationships between the provision of food and shelter, the status of women and the well-being of the rural family within the total context of rural development. This theme is re-iterated in the objectives of Habitat (the UN Conference on Human Settlements, 1976). It is becoming increasingly recognized that adequate food, appropriate management of resources, betterment of the near environment, an improvement in the quality of life and participation of the whole family in the process are imperative for the success of any plan for integrated rural development.

The United Nations World Food Conference, held in Rome in 1974 called on governments to intensify their efforts in both the formal and non-formal education of rural people with emphasis on what is relevant to their needs, taking into account the special role of women in agriculture and rural life in many societies (World Food Conference Resolution II).

The World Plan of Action of the International Women's Year (1975) and the resulting resolutions adopted by the UN General Assembly and most of the UN specialised agencies including FAO have provided new directions for the world to intensify efforts to accelerate the integration of women into the rural development process. The rural women of many countries are recognised as major contributors to the agricultural labour force, with important roles in food production, harvesting, marketing and processing. The Plan calls for measures to help these women become modern agricultural producers, for the development of self-help and self-employment activities and for the provision of training to extend the range of rural women's economic roles.

FAO, the lead UN agency in food and agricultural development, has adopted two resolutions which seek to improve the role of women in agriculture, rural development and food and nutrition policy. The resolutions encourage a rural development approach which prepares women to fulfill a balanced role in the farm and home enterprise and in the improvement of the rural habitat. FAO further supports public policy which strengthens national institutions that can provide women and their families the opportunities for full participation in development. The World Bank in distinguishing between relative and absolute poverty has also begun to give consideration to women's economic contributions in the rural areas and the agricultural sector.

As indicated above, the entire UN System is emphasizing

the integration of women into the development process and giving consideration to women as human resources for economic as
well as social development.

It is sometimes said that this integration would disrupt
the cultural patterns of African societies. It must be realized, however, that the role assigned to women during colonial
days and the introduction of innovations in rural Africa during
the 20th century have already resulted in radical disruptions
in Africa as in other continents.

Many of the Governments in the Africa region share in this
new awareness of the need to involve women. For example, there
are a number of women cabinet Ministers and Permanent or Principal Secretaries, some appointed in unlikely fields such as
commerce, law, urban development and national planning. However, more recognition is still needed so that rural women can
be prepared to advance and participate more fully in the development process of their countries.

SOME FURTHER MEASURES WHICH MAY AID IN STRENGTHENING THE ROLES OF RURAL MEN AND WOMEN IN DEVELOPMENT

As noted above, favourable actions have already been proposed such as the World Plan of Action of International
Women's Year plus the regional plans (UN, 1975) and the
resolution on the establishment of a new economic order (UN,
1976). An FAO resolution (FAO, 1975) invited member states to
support measures insuring that women share in the benefits of
development in the rural sector and participate, on an equitable basis with men, in the policy-making, planning and implementation process in all agricultural and rural development
programmes. The ECA Conference of Ministers passed a similar
resolution in Nairobi in 1975.

The need to discover and promote low-risk techniques to
increase the production of food crops and release labour for
high-value export crops has been emphasized (Lele, 1975, p. 30).
Numerous organizations are now funding projects on simple but
appropriate technologies for saving labour and increasing productivity in all farm, home and community efforts. The importance of the participation of the family as a basic social unit
in integrated rural development is being stressed by FAO
(DeLaney and Barghouti, 1972).

Many proposals have been made concerning the improvement
of rural development extension services. Frequently, no consideration has been given to stating explicitly the aims of
adult education. Education for women is advocated but for
what? (Kennedy, 1975). Is it, for example so that they will
fetch a higher bride price (Mitchnik, 1972) or to enable them
to play a greater role in the development of their country? To
be effective, learning must be linked to the needs and problems

of the learner, which in Africa are likely to be related to agriculture.

Since extension agents do not often have time or resources to contact large numbers of individual families, the importance of learning through group discussion methods is being emphasized. Groups in which farmers can discuss their own particular needs and problems and which aim at developing self-reliance and a more equitable relationship between extension workers and farmers are advocated.

The individual performance of extension staff is considered more important than numbers (Lele, 1975, p. 71). There is need for more women rural development extension workers as the present systems favour male heads of households (Bond, 1974).

Both FAO, through its technical assistance programmes, and ECA, through its Training and Research Centre for Women, have responsibilities for helping their member countries integrate women more closely into development. Among its activities, ECA encourages member governments to establish national Commissions and technical bureaux, or other governmental machineries, to assure that women are considered together with men in all actions for development.

RESEARCH NEEDS

The above discussion is based on the very limited data available on the subject, at present. Much research on the comparative roles and participation of men and women, boys and girls, is still needed. Present data do not explain the great diversity of women's economic roles across cultures, nor do they allow detailed estimation of the social and economic costs of under-utilizing fully 50 percent of a country's human resources (Weisblat, 1975). The World Plan of Action of the International Women's Year as well as the ECA Regional Plan for Africa (UN, 1975) list suggestions for research. A recent meeting in Kenya gave others. Both FAO and ECA are developing proposals to assist national institutes to conduct research related to women in development. The effect of changing agricultural and marketing patterns on the roles of different social groups has been placed high on the list. Current FAO studies are being completed on the "Role of Women in Credit" and the "Role of Women in Marketing".

Misconceptions of the actual roles of women explain why the allocation of social and economic investment by African governments has not been fully effective, and further study is needed to clarify women's roles in different countries. Other vital areas needing study are the contribution of women to economic development as well as to family and national well-being; the division of work and time spent by women on unproductive labour; changes in land tenure systems and their effect

on women; the relationships between development and population
factors; the attitudes of men and women to exercising the right
to control fertility; and the availability of food supplies in
relation to women's role in production, distribution and storage of food and to nutritional status.

Both ECA and FAO favour the promotion of action-oriented
research of the applied type: research intended for specific
audiences including high-level policymakers. Country studies
which apply similar methodologies make it possible to replicate
studies and to transfer findings to those countries which share
common problems and resources. Proposed studies on the allocation of local resources in the context of the family and rural
development, it is anticipated, will lead to greater under-
standings of women's roles.

CONCLUDING REMARKS

In this paper, I have tried to illustrate the fact that
changes have resulted in the polarization of interests of
African men and women; the question that now needs to be
answered is: Can the complimentarity which traditionally
existed between the roles of African men and women in rural
society and which has been distorted over the years, be re-
established by development? Somehow it is hoped that some solutions can be reached in this decade (1975-1985) which has been
declared by the United Nations as the Decade of Women--Equal-
ity, Development and Peace.

REFERENCES

Bhattacharjee, J. P. 1975. Food and agricultural development:
    a medium-term view. Paper presented at the Seminar on Pop-
    ulation and Food and Agricultural Development, Rome, Decem-
    ber 1-5. FAO, Rome.
Bond, C. A. 1974. Women's involvement in agriculture in
    Botswana. Overseas Development Ministry (U.K.) Advisory
    Team, Botswana.
Boserup, E. 1970. Women's Role in Economic Development. St.
    Martius Press, New York, N.Y.
Brown, J. 1970. A note on the division of labor by sex.
    American Anthropologist 72:1073-1078.
Cohen, J. M. 1973. Ethiopia After Haile Selassie. African
    Affairs 72:369-373.
Delalande, P. 1966. L'aide étrangerè à la vulgarisation
    agricole au Sénégal, Université de Dakar. In Boserup,
    Women's role in Economic Development. St. Martius Press,
    New York, N.Y.

Delaney, J. and S. Barghouti. 1972. Multi-disciplinary approach to solving population problems of rural families. Paper presented at FAO/UNFPA seminar on Population Problems as Related to Food and Rural Development in the Near East, Cairo, December 11-20. FAO, Rome.

de Wilde, J. C. 1967. Experiences with Agricultural Development in Tropical Africa, Vol. I, the Synthesis. The John Hopkins Press, Baltimore, Maryland.

ECA, 1971. Report of the Regional Conference on Education. Vocational Training and Work Opportunities for Girls and Women in African Countries. Rabat, Morocco.

ECA, Women's Programme Unit. 1974. Africa's food producers: The impact of change on rural women. Paper prepared for American Geographical Society.

ECA, 1974. The data base for discussion on the interrelationships between the integration of women in development, their situation and population factors in Africa. Paper presented at the Regional Seminar on the Integration of Women in Development with Special Reference to Population Factors, June 3-7, ECA, Addis Ababa, Ethiopia.

ECA/FAO, Women's Programme Unit. 1976. The role of women in population dynamics related to food and agriculture and rural development in Africa. FAO, Rome.

FAO. 1962. Nutrition and Working Efficiency. Freedom from Hunger Campaign. Basic Study No. 5. Rome.

FAO. 1973. Report to the 25th Session of the Commission on the Status of Women. FAO, Rome.

FAO. 1974. FAO Preliminary Assessment of the World Food Situation, Present and Future. E/Conf. 65/Pre.6, Rome, April.

FAO. 1975a. Draft Report of Commission i-Part 6 from the Eighteenth Session of the Conference of the FAO of the United Nations, Rome, Italy, November 8-27. FAO, Rome.

FAO. 1975b. Home Economics in Rural Development - Expert Consultation, Rome 4/1975. FAO/ESH/75/3.

FAO. 1976. The Family in Integrated Rural Development. May 1976. FAO, Rome.

Hill, P. 1963. Migrant Cocoa Farmers of Southern Ghana. Cambridge University Press, Cambridge.

ILO. 1973. Report to the 25th Session of the Commission on the Status of Women, ILO, Geneva.

Kennedy, E. 1975. The role of women in food production and the planning of the family. Paper presented at the Seminar on Population and Food and Agricultural Development, Rome, December 1-5. FAO, Rome.

Lele, U. 1975. The Design of Rural Development: Lessons from Africa (1st ed.) John Hopkins University Press, Baltimore, Maryland.

Mitchnik, D. A. 1972. The Role of Women in Rural Development in the Zaire. OXFAM, Oxford.

Pala, A. O. 1975. A preliminary survey of avenues for and constraints on women's involvement in the development process in Kenya. Paper presented at WFUNA/ECA/SIDA Seminar on the Changing and Contemporary Role of Women in Society, Addis Ababa, December 1-10.

p'Bitek, O. 1966. Song of Lawino. (5th ed.) Kenya Litho Ltd., Nairobi.

p'Bitek, O. 1970. Song of Ocol. (1st ed.) Afropress, Nairobi.

Protein Calorie Advisory Group. 1975. The role of women in food production and nutrition-implications for research. Draft paper for PAG project. United Nations, New York, N.Y.

Reynolds, D. R. 1975. An Appraisal of Rural Women in Tanzania. Regional Economic Development Services Office, Agency for International Development, Washington, D.C.

Rigby, P. 1972. Social patterns and family life: Family economics and management of family resource. Paper presented at Seminar/Workshop for the Development of an Integrated Programme for Better Family Living in Uganda, July 17-20. Inter-Ministerial/Inter-Organizational Coordinating Advisory Committee on Programmes for Better Family Living (PBFL) Uganda. FAO, Rome.

Ritchie, J. 1967. Learning Better Nutrition: A Second Study of Approaches and Techniques. (3rd. ed.) FAO, Rome.

Sinha, R., and H. R. Kötter. 1975. Population Aspects of Integrated Rural Development. Paper presented at Seminar on Population and Food and Agricultural Development, Rome, December 1-5. FAO, Rome.

Smock, A. C. 1975. The Changing Roles and Status of Women in Ghana. Ford Foundation, New York, N.Y.

Uchendu, V. C., and K. R. M. Anthony. 1975. Agricultural Change in Teso District, Uganda (A Study of Economic, Cultural and Technical Determinants of Rural Development). East Africa, Literature Bureau, Nairobi.

United Nations. 1975. General Assembly Resolution 3505. Integration of women in development. U.N., New York, N.Y.

United Nations. 1975. Meeting in Mexico: The Story of the World Conference of the International Women's Year (Mexico City, 19 June-2 July). United Nations, New York, N.Y.

Van Allen, J. 1974. Women in Africa: modernization means more dependency. Center Magazine: May/June.

Weisblat, A. M. 1975. A seminar report: Role of rural women in development. Based on a Conference of Rural Women in Development, Princeton, New Jersey, December 2-4, 1974. Agricultural Development Council, Inc. Research and Training Network, New York, N.Y.

R. J. OLEMBO

Environmental Issues in Current Food Production, Marketing and Processing Practices

At the Seventeenth Session of the Food and Agriculture Organization (FAO) Conference, a view was expressed that

the major environmental problems facing agriculture, forestry and fisheries were not only the avoidance of environmental pollution, but the ensuring, in the development process, of the maintenance of the productive capacity of the basic natural resources for food and agriculture through rational management and conservation measures.

One year later, Dr. M. K. Tolba (1974) then Deputy Executive Director of the newly established United Nations Environment Programme (UNEP) told the World Food Conference meeting in Rome that

development without destruction--maximization of the production of food without destroying the ecological basis to sustain production--is in essence, the theme . . . any strategy to increase food production on a sustained basis should explicitly take account of the complementarity of environment and development.

Food remains, undoubtedly, the world's most pressing and urgent problem. The world's population now well in excess of four billion is continuing to grow at the rate of 2.2 percent

R. J. Olembo is Acting Deputy Director, Division of Ecosystems and Natural Resources, United Nations Environment Programme, Nairobi, Kenya.

per year, and there is no hard evidence of a levelling-off.
(See, for example, the Environment Fund, 1975). Moreover, this
growth is greatest in countries least able to match the demands
for food with the increases in population, the countries of the
Third World of Africa, Asia and Latin America. Many reports
indicate famine in various developing nations, and a recent
study states that death rates are rising in at least 12 and perhaps 20 nations, largely in Central Africa and Southern Asia
(National Academy of Sciences, 1974). As can be seen from
Table 1, this situation seems chronic. While in global terms
we may grant that it is theoretically possible to produce
enough food for the much larger numbers of people expected to
be alive in the year 2000, starvation prevails and spreads
among developing countries (Brown and Finsterbusch, 1971), even
though there are some who interpret differently the facts upon
which this conclusion is based (Eberstadt, 1976). This is the
paradox which makes it obvious that the food problem must continue to occupy the centre stage in all forums where development
is planned and discussed. According to FAO estimates, the minimum requirement is to raise the average annual increase in the
rate of food production in developing countries from 2.6 percent over the last twelve years to at least 3.6 percent during
the next twelve years. If this is not done, the developing
countries as a whole might well face annual deficits of grain
of 85 million tons in normal years and over 100 million tons in
bad years.

The food problem and the energy crisis are two typical examples of the urgent and proliferating problems to which no nation, however powerful, can find solutions on a unilateral
basis. These problems go beyond the capacity of even small
groups of more favoured nations to solve. They demand a global
'one earth' framework within which the exercise of national
sovereignty and the acceptance of national and regional responsibility can provide a basis for action. The organizers of this
Conference are to be commended for providing yet another excellent opportunity during which we can examine our response to
this major concern of our times in order to sharpen our perception and knowledge in tackling it.

In recognizing that we must urgently and dramatically increase food production, it is equally important to ensure that
the strategies adopted to increase food production on a short-
term basis can be sustained and be effectively integrated with
the long-term policies. If we do not do so, we run the risk of
finding ourselves in a far more precarious situation in the
1980s because we will have relied upon short-term ad hoc and
self-defeating strategies. Such long-term strategies must explicitly involve environmental dimensions, that is the careful
husbanding of natural resources, respect for biological laws
and ecological balances as well as adjustments of production,

TABLE 1. Post-World War II reported famines in the Third World
(not exhaustive[a])

Region	Year and Country
Latin America	1949 Ecuador
	1951 El Salvador
	1954 Haiti
	1960 Chile
	1967 Colombia
	1970 Peru
	1972 Nicaragua
Africa	1958 Tunisia
	1960 Morocco; Mauritania
	1960-61 Republic of Congo
	1962 Algeria
	1967-70 Nigeria
	1972 Burundi
	1973 Sudan
	1971-74 Angola; Chad; Mali; Niger; Mozambique; Mauritania; Upper Volta; Senegal; Dahomey; Togo
	1973-75 Ethiopia
Middle East	1945-49 Syria-Palestine
	1954 Iraq
	1962 Iran
	1969 Syria
Asia	1945-49 China
	1950-56 Pakistan; India; Korea
	1959 Taiwan
	1961, 1964, 1968, 1975 Vietnam
	1970 Cambodia
	1970-71 Afghanistan
	1972 Philippines
	1970-75 Bangladesh

[a]After J. Mayer, 1975.

supply, and reserves to demands. The aims of such strategies should not be growth at the cost of deterioration of the environment and destruction of natural resources, but rather development with concern for environment and resources.

In this paper I wish to examine, some of the important elements, factors and issues which when integrated constitute a statement of an environmental policy in food production. I

limit myself to land-based production systems, although, of
course, the special problems associated with the harvesting of
freshwaters and oceans are of great importance as well.
Whether we take the pessimistic view which sees the world rapidly approaching the point where it will have lost the capacity
to feed itself (The Environment Fund, 1974), or the leisurely
attitude which traces all shortages in food production to transient factors and which sees that the necessary expansion in
agricultural production can be achieved for many years to come
without a dramatic increase in real costs of production (Sanderson, 1975; USDA, 1974), there are long-term factors, which if
not taken into account, will make for greater instability in
world food production. Environmental considerations are among
these long-term factors. Though many of these relate to the
local environment, a number have serious global implications.

EXPANDING THE CULTIVATED AREA: PRESSURES ON NATURAL ECOSYSTEMS
     In the face of the compelling urgency to increase food pro-
     duction, the first step is to bring more land into cultiva-
     tion. The earth's land surface is estimated to be 1.13
billion ha (US President's Science Advisory Committee, 1967) and
at the moment about 10 percent of the total is under cultivation
for agricultural purposes (Brown and Finsterbusch, 1971). Expressed in these terms there would seem to be plenty of reserve
land to be used for food production. However, viewed in the
context of ecosystems and based upon the analysis of soils and
climate in particular, the area capable of supporting crops is
small, the most generous estimate of potential arable land being
3.2 billion ha (US President's Science Advisory Committee,
1974). Furthermore, not all countries are lavishly endowed with
arable land. Little, if any, potential for new farmlands exists
in Asia and Europe and relatively little in the USSR. Canada
with its immense north, Brazil's unexplored Amazon jungle, Australia's great but "dead heart" and the barren African Sahara
cannot be considered great reserves of potentially arable land.
Apart from the US with perhaps 20 million ha of potentially
arable land still untapped, the tropics are thought to possess
the greater portion of potentially arable land.
     The point must be made that man might be extending agricul-
tural practices into areas most unsuitable for this form of
land use. Since this extension is of recent origin, environmental and ecological consequences are only now beginning to be
documented. Mahler (1972) made a brief survey of these, and
more recently, Erik Eckholm (1976) through the support of UNEP
has completed a study of proven cases of the negative ecological
consequences of irrationally manipulating ecosystems, especially marginal and vulnerable ones, in a manner not conducive to
their stability.

In addition to serving as sources of fuel, most forests
and woodlands of the humid and sub-humid tropics are now being
converted into arable land with the expectation that they will
become breadbaskets for millions. The shift from forests to
farms, is a necessity for people who badly need the land's produce. As these ecosystems are fragile, if clearance occurs on
ecologically strategic slopes or on soils unsuited to agriculture or in careless ways, it becomes self-defeating. In the
wake of clearing and deforestation come soil erosion, siltation, and ultimate desolation which, in the longer term, severely damage the land's productivity. Moreover, forests influence
the wind, temperature, humidity, soil and water in ways often
discovered only after the trees are cut and these functions already sabotaged. Unfortunately, as a study by FAO in 1967
noted "much of land colonization is indiscriminate . . . an
ill-advised use of the land. It is merely a process of trial
and error. Very often the chosen forest land cannot support
agriculture." If we have to ensure the long-term stability and
productivity in these ecosystems, we must be discriminating in
our forced management of their resources.

Highlands and mountain ecosystems are other areas now coming under intense pressures of agriculture. Highlands occupy
one-fourth of the earth's surface and in the face of shrinking
arable cropland it is not surprising that they are looked to
for increased food production. Unfortunately, and despite
their rugged appearance, highlands and mountains are most delicate ecosystems; they react sensitively and sharply to any destructive changes and at the same time are very slow to recover from imposed ecological changes. Experts are in general
agreement on this point. For example, examine the following
summaries. ". . . High mountain ecosystems . . . are unusually
prone to sudden, rapid and reversible loss of soil if slope
stability and vegetation cover are disturbed (United Nations
Education, Scientific and Cultural Organization, 1973). Based
on an analysis of case histories from India to Nepal, from East
Afrtican Highlands to South American Andes, Eckholm (1976) concludes that

> on the basis of already available knowledge, it is no exagger-
> ation to suggest that many mountain regions could pass a
> point of no return within the next two or three decades.
> They could become locked in a downward spiral from which
> there is no escape, a chain of ecological reactions that will
> permanently reduce their capacity to support human life.

When steep slopes are foolishly assaulted, fertile soils slip
away, the productive capacity of the hills declines and the
cause of increasing food production is left even more difficult
to serve. In the wake of this hillside devastation, the fertile

valleys below them are choked to the point where their own
capacity for sustained agricultural productivity is seriously
threatened through increased flooding, water-logging and silt
accumulation.

Perhaps the areas most sought-after as possibilities for
increasing arable croplands are the arid and semi-arid zones.
However, as Brown and Finsterbusch (1971) note, further opportunities to expand farm area in these zones are not likely to
arise until the cost of desalinization is reduced to a point
where it is profitable to use seawater in large scale irrigation or until it is technically possible and economically feasible to alter rainfall patterns to shift some of the rainfall
to arid land masses capable of being farmed. Even where man
can succeed in extending arable crops into semi-arid zones,
care must be taken not to extend the process of desertification
and aridization. The lessons of the American Dust Bowl and the
Soviet Virgin Lands are grim reminders that agricultural activities which are to be carried out upon a tract of land should
depend upon its natural qualities. Marginal lands can only be
properly utilized if the appropriate technology available is
correctly employed. Otherwise, whatever short-term benefits
are derived will result in long-term environmental costs which
will eventually completely negate the gains in increased food
production.

The painful conclusion must be made that hopes for expanding the cultivated areas to match increasing populations are
for the most part unattainable or have high environmental
costs.

INCREASING PRODUCTIVITY THROUGH MANAGEMENT
In the knowledge that dramatic increases in agricultural
production are tempered by the fact that the surface of
arable land cannot continuously be extended and that the
existing arable land may not always be available to agriculture for economic or political reasons, the rational management
of land under cultivation becomes an increasingly critical factor in the fight against world hunger. According to Baumer
(1975), developing countries cultivate 30 percent more land
than developed countries, but their production is inferior by
that 30 percent. India has almost the same acreage (150 million ha) under cultivation as the United States. With a comparable soil and water potential, its crop is only two-fifths
as much (Wittwer, 1975). Improved yields on the cultivated
land in these countries would therefore, be a logical first
step. Recognition of this situation seems widespread, but the
methods proposed for effecting these desirable increases in the
developing countries do not always seem to achieve the necessary results.

Technology
        For example, there is an indiscriminate transfer of highly
    developed technologies suited to the large scale agri-bus-
iness of the developed countries without attempting to adapt to
the social, cultural and economic conditions of the developing
countries. In most of these countries, the need is for solutions applicable to small farmers and homesteaders, the rural
population. These must be the technologies which would function most effectively at the lowest level of society, being
modified, changed and substituted as sophistication grows.
They should also be based on ecological considerations and be
fully in harmony with and enhance the quality of the environment. They should, in the final analysis, promote self-reliance and require little capital for their adoption, and allowances should always be made for time-lags in the adoption of
new technolgies. Wittwer (1975) has published results of a
study of the time taken to adopt new agricultural technologies.
He states, for example, that complete adoption of hybrid corn
in the United States took 36 years, a 50 percent adoption of
high yield in wheat in India has taken 6 years and a 50 percent
adoption of high yield rice in the Philippines also has taken
6 years.
        Apart from adopting imported appropriate technologies,
greater effort should be made to use technology that is already
available. A case in point is the use of wind as a source of
energy and terraced or contour-lined cultivation. These are
excellent, cheap and non-polluting techniques tested for thousands of years, yet very far from being used as completely as
they could. UNEP is currently spearheading pilot schemes in
Senegal and Sri Lanka under the name of "Rural Energy Centres"
through which renewed attention is to be focussed on the rural
use of non-traditional sources of energy such as wind, biogas
and solar energy. Of particular interest is the re-examination
of "Firewood and Substitutes" as energy sources. Other renewable non-polluting sources of energy can be found, and research
should be carried out on tidal energy, wave energy, geothermal
energy and perhaps even energy resulting from rainfall.
        While we must leave the detailed discussion of the rela-
tionship between agricultural production and energy to another
contributor to this Conference (Dr. Pierre Crosson), we should
repeat that the crucial role energy plays in the overall food
production system behooves us to strive for those sources of
energy which will not exert further environmental stresses on
the agricultural ecosystems. Similarly, while scientifically
planned inputs of a specific type of energy to land yield
extraordinarily favourable results, a saturation point can be
reached wherein extra inputs are wasted and cause serious environmental degradation. Some agricultural technology approaches to non-polluting and environmentally-sound energy

systems include the enhancement of photosynthetic efficiency, conversion of agricultural and industrial by-products into energy sources or into fertilizers, and the enhancement of biological nitrogen fixation. I will return to some of these topics as they are key elements in improving food production in the developing countries.

Soil Loss

In a situation where shortage of arable land is already imposing severe limitations to increased food production, man cannot condone agricultural practices which lead directly to loss of productive soil. It has been estimated that the total area of biologically productive soil which has been destroyed and degraded due to past agricultural practices is 2 billion ha. If this present trend continues, 650 to 720 million ha of good farmland will be lost by the year 2000 (United Nations Environment Program, 1974). If we continue to lose 6 to 7 million ha of soil annually, we have to bring a significantly new amount of land under cultivation each year just to retain the status quo. With the attendant investment costs, this is a severe price to pay.

Whilst a greater portion of this loss is attributable to farming marginal lands without the adequate and ecologically appropriate precautions, a large amount of soil loss is from good agricultural land. The United States Soil Conservation Service estimates that 3.4 billion tons of soil are lost through erosion from approximately two-thirds of the privately-owned land in the United States. Grant (1975) reported that in the United States, 4 million ha formerly pastures, woodlands and idle fields were converted to crops during 1974-75. Out of these, 2 million were not adequately managed from a conservation point of view. The average loss of topsoil due to erosion on these lands was 27 tons per ha. It has been estimated that about 80 percent of the land surface of Madagascar has been eroded (Biswas, 1976). In tests carried out in the Sudan from 1957 to 1962, Baumer (1968) demonstrated that the soil loss near El Odaya (Kordofan Province) was 450 to 600 t/km^2/year. Globally, FAO estimates that about one-sixth of the world's agricultural land suffers from wind and water erosion.

Soils of the tropics have come under increasing attention in the past few years (Centro International de Agricultura Tropical, 1974; International Institute of Tropical Agriculture, 1974; Sanchez and Buol, 1975; Soil Science Department North Carolina, 1973). Because vast areas of tropical savannah can be easily cleared of vegetation and are easy to till, they are considered to have a great and underused agronomic potential. Similarly, densely forested parts of the tropics are frequently viewed as potentially viable agricultural areas because of

their adequate rainfall and temperature conditions. Generalizations about the properties of these soils can be misleading
and inaccurate. However, many reviews conclude that a large
group of the soils in the tropics are of low base status and
are highly leached. Such soils require enormous inputs to
correct their low fertility. Also, whether we like it or not,
large scale clearances of zones of such soil status are attended by severe management problems. On the other hand, the
productivity of the high base status soils has been proved, and
the injection of appropriate technological packages has provided examples of dramatic and sustained increases in production. The cautious conclusion, therefore, is that if careless-
ness is avoided and technically and environmentally-sound practices are adopted, there is some optimism that the soils of
the tropics can make a major and sustained contribution toward
world food production.

Deterioration of soil fertility and loss of agricultural
land due to increase in salinity or alkalinity are other common
environmental problems in many parts of the world. At one
time, Pakistan alone was losing 24 thousand ha of fertile cropland every year, and currently 10 percent of the total Peruvian
agriculture is affected by land degradation due to salinization.
Among other major areas affected by salinization are the Helmud
Valley in Afghanistan, the Punjab and Indus Valley on the
Indian Sub-continent, Mexicali Valley in Northern Mexico, and
the Euphrates and Tigris basins of Syria and Iraq. A study of
the major irrigation schemes in the Punjab shows that seepage
from unlined canals has in the past 10 years raised the water
table seven to nine metres above the previous high in records
kept since 1835. Globally, at least 200 thousand ha of land is
lost every year due to salinization and water-logging.

Water Management

Water is the second important resource in agricultural
production, and in most instances, is the decisive and
chief limiting factor. Consideration of its management is in-
separable from that of the land with which it is associated.
Man has practised irrigation to increase crop production for
several thousand years, but the real momentum of irrigation on
a large scale started in the 19th Century with several major
undertakings in India, Egypt and other countries. During the
19th Century, the irrigated acreages of the world increased
nearly 5.5 times--from 8 to 45 million ha. Currently, 230-240
million ha are under irrigation; China has the largest irrigated acreage of any country. Whilst globally irrigated cropland constitutes about 15 percent of the total cultivated land,
it yields up to 30 percent of the food for mankind. In

particular, the high yielding varieties and the increasing use of yield enhancement technologies require more moisture.

Irrigation increases crop yields by improved water availability for intensive agriculture, but it also creates severe ecological and environmental problems. One of the main problems of irrigated agriculture, that is secondary desalination and alkalinization, already has been discussed above. Groundwater resources of many areas have been steadily depleted, because water was constantly extracted for irrigation without considering the natural replenishment rates, and this directly affects the hydrological cycle. Examples can be drawn from such diverse countries and regions as Saudi Arabia, Israel, South Africa, the US, India and many others. After a short period of increased food production following irrigation, the yields were drastically reduced and in some cases, actual farming of the irrigated areas ceased completely because pumping had become uneconomic or the wells had dried up. A study by FAO (1969) has suggested some guidelines in the safe development of water resources.

The most serious effect of irrigation, however, is the spread of water-borne diseases and the consequent effects upon millions of human beings and their animals. In the tropical and semi-tropical regions of the world, irrigation schemes have enhanced and often created favourable ecological and environmental conditions for such parasitic and water-borne diseases as schistosomiasis, filariasis and malaria. While these diseases are not new, the unprecedented expansion of perennial irrigation systems has extended them into previously unaffected areas. In the current programme of UNEP, a great deal of attention is being paid to the integration of ecological and other methods of control of such water-borne diseases. FAO and the World Health Organization (WHO) are being brought together to consider what ecological measures should be taken to ensure that the gains in agricultural production resulting from irrigation schemes are not lost as a result of increased prevalence of water-borne diseases.

Other ecological and environmental problems occur concomitantly with the construction of dams for irrigation and other purposes. Corrective measures have had to be taken to remove the severe environmental problems created by dam construction in a number of places. One can cite the well-documented problems associated with the Aswan Dam in Egypt, and there are many similar cases in Africa, Asia and South America where man has had to pay heavy prices for irrigation schemes in terms of overall health of the region as well as in ecological deterioration. More research is required to find ways to minimise these adverse effects and thus to maximise the benefits irrigation has on a long-term basis.

Crop Protection

If man could completely control the loss of food due to
pests, much more food would be available for human consumption. On a global basis, pests cause an estimated 30 percent annual loss of worldwide production of crops, livestock
and forests. Borgstrom (1973), puts the annual losses from
weeds, pests and plant diseases to some 40 percent of the total
crop in Latin America. A 1969 estimate indicated that if the
insects of tropical Africa could be effectively controlled,
Africa would be able to feed eight times the people currently
living on that continent. Here again, is reason for optimism.
Even if no further increases in cultivated areas occurred,
effective control of pests in the cultivated fields would raise
the amount of available food several fold.

Devising methods of avoiding crop losses is thus a challenge. Among the tools available for crop protection, the one
which relies heavily on chemical control has, in the recent
past, been the one most widely practised. Chemical pesticides
have been most successful in achieving short-term gains. In
fact, the chemical pesticides developed after World War II were
so successful that there was some hope they would provide the
answer to all pest insect problems (Ennis et al., 1975). However, many undesirable effects, particularly of an ecological
or environmental nature, began to appear. These have been adequately described in many scientific articles, papers and books
and do not warrant detailed repetition here (Bergman, undated
and FAO, 1969). Most populations of pests are dynamic with
great capacities to reproduce and to survive and rapidly adapt
to new changes in the environment. Heavy and wholesale applications of chemical pesticides cause changes in the environment. In such circumstances, some change occurs in the pest
as it adapts to a new situation. This process of evolution
through natural selection leads to the appearance and prolifer-
ation of new strains, more vicious in the damage they cause to
the food crops and usually more resistant to the available
pesticides. Moreover, certain new agricultural practices in
fact increase incidences of pests and encourage the development
of new insect and disease problems that require a new management system, thus creating a vicious cycle. Obviously there
are expensive trade-offs.

In recent years, strong and informed scientific opinion
has turned to the advocacy of an integrated approach to pest
management. Such an approach calls for an effective integration of all available pest control techniques. Those purely
preventive methods which emanate from the ecological and cultural manipulation of seeds and seedlings, the genetic methods
based on the availability of disease-resistant varieties, biological control methods, cultural and physical methods, and the

selective use of chemical pesticides can all be effectively
integrated into efficient production systems. In cooperation
with FAO, UNEP is placing a high priority on development of integrated pest control systems. Taking cotton as an example, a
project to that end is now in its initial stages of development. To implement it successfully will require the cooperation of many multidisciplinary groups as well as public agencies, donors, and the farmers themselves.

Fertilizers
      Fertilizers are indispensable as a management tool of in-
      creased food production, and this is not only confined to
the high-yielding varieties. The complete dependence of world
agriculture on fertilizer is such that during the critical
months of the energy crisis extreme pessimists saw a new fatal
blow to agricultural productivity. Recently, Nelson (1974)
attributed 30 to 40 percent of increased agricultural productivity in the United States to fertilizer usage. Another study
has credited more than 50 percent of increased yields in developing countries to the increased fertilizer use there (Anonymous, undated). And yet at the same time, documentary evidence
points to the fact that fertilizer use also has detrimental
side-effects (Phillips, 1972; UNESCO, 1974).
      Among the many effects of washed-away fertilizers are
eutrophication, pollution of drinking water sources, and increase in certain diseases due to more vigorous and healthier
vectors because their water environment is enriched. There are
also many problems associated with the application of chemical
fertilizers to tropical soils (Mukerjee, 1963). One of the
more serious of these is the locking up of phosphorus in un-
available form in ferralsols. The policy should again be the
maximisation of profits from fertilizer use and a minimisation
of undesirable effects. This objective can be achieved if
fertilizers are used with the maximum efficiency on the farm.
If the right fertilizer is chosen for the crop, correctly formulated and applied in the right quantities at the appropriate
times, it would minimise the amount of nutrients liable to be
leached into the drainage system. Greater research efforts are
needed in the formulation of fertilizer requirements and in
better understanding the nutrient levels of our crops, especially in developing countries. Also required is an understanding of the appropriate methods of fertilizer application, so as
to minimise blind and costly applications. For instance, the
"mudball" technique which facilitates the slow release of nutrients near the plant roots promises many advantages.
      Apart from encouraging efforts in more efficient use of
fertilizers, UNEP is encouraging renewed interest in other
forms of non-polluting fertilizers. New research on

recuperation and better use of any form of organic and mineral wastes is being encouraged. The modern way of life generates a lot of by-products which, unfortunately, have not found widespread re-use. Agriculture, industry and millions of homes produce tons of so-called wastes which, after proper treatment, can be used to improve soil fertility and allow a sustained agricultural production. UNEP considers that residues should be completely used, wherever they can give some nutrients to plants, improve soil quality or provide other forms of useful products. The much neglected area of biological sources of fertilisation should be reawakened, and new concerted research efforts undertaken, with the first focus being on biological nitrogen fixation where some promising breakthroughs are being reported (Döbereiner and Day, 1974, 1975). The role of microorganisms also in the fixation of phosphorus should be kept in close attention. We require a fuller understanding of the interactions between fertilizers and the adjacent ecosystems. In particular, data are required on the effects upon the environment of a given application of a specific nitrogen-based fertilizer, because nitrogen is highly mobile, has diverse sources and is linked inexorably with the role of microorganisms. We need detailed and continuing surveys of the nitrate and nitrite content of surface water and their relation to contributions from fertilizer and organic wastes.

Monocultural Practices and the Erosion of Genetic Variability

Monocultural practices where in the agricultural ecosystems are characterised by a uniform vegetation are a growing trend in modern agriculture. The kingpin in this practice is the high-yielding variety, a product of many years of highly sophisticated plant genetic engineering. The improvement of major crops by deliberate breeding programmes rather than by selection of variants arising from fortuitous crosses in the field has become widespread. The resulting high yielding varieties have spread to most parts of the globe especially as a result of the massive agricultural development financed largely by development aid after World War II. Accompanied by large applications of fertilizers and buttressed by generous levels of pesticide treatment, such high yielding varieties have performed well, extending the fruits of the 'green revolution' to a number of countries and providing a welcome fillip to the quest for more food. Figure 1 depicts the increase in the production of major cereal crops during the period after World War II.

It can be seen from the figure that the biggest gains were recorded in Asia, where in fact, the most dramatic replacements of indigenous wheats and rices have been taking place, spurred in part by the research breakthroughs recorded at the

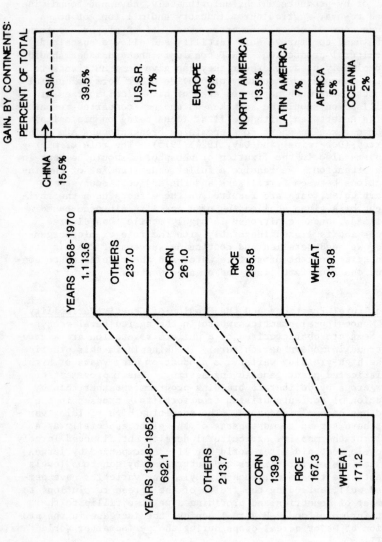

GAIN, BY CONTINENTS:
PERCENT OF TOTAL

CHINA 15.5%

ASIA 39.5%

U.S.S.R. 17%

EUROPE 16%

NORTH AMERICA 13.5%

LATIN AMERICA 7%

AFRICA 5%

OCEANIA 2%

YEARS 1968-1970
1,113.6

OTHERS 237.0

CORN 261.0

RICE 295.8

WHEAT 319.8

YEARS 1948-1952
692.1

OTHERS 213.7

CORN 139.9

RICE 167.3

WHEAT 171.2

FIG. 1. Increase in the production of major cereal crops during the period after World War II in millions of metric tons: (Source: FAO Production Yearbooks 1966-70).

International Rice Research Institute (IRRI).

The widely-grown modern varieties of many crops have been specifically bred to respond to improved cultivation and management practices. But as the original landraces are replaced, their inherited adaptations to their environment and resistances against many important pests and diseases may be lost to the plant breeder whose task is to stay ahead of the race by producing the higher yielding varieties of food and other crops which will be required to meet increasing needs. The potential value of these traditional varieties lies in the genes they contain, not only for presently sought-after characters, but for traits which though unrecognised at present, may become invaluable in the future.

The need for an international programme to promote deliberate efforts at genetic resource conservation has now been recognised. The resolutions of the Stockholm Conference on the Human Environment in 1972, the subsequent creation of the International Board of Plant Genetic Resources of the Consultative Group of International Agricultural Research (CGIAR) and the joint programmes of the FAO and UNEP are actions designed to strengthen and coordinate these efforts.

IMPACTS OF MARKETING AND PROCESSING

The greater part of this paper has dealt with the impacts on environmental quality of the food production processes. There are also, environmental aspects of the utilization of the produced food, particularly food storage, processing and marketing. However, the documentary evidence for this third dimension of the food issue (Borgstrom, 1973), is poor, and the area is neglected. Food spoilage resulting from decomposition through biochemical changes, decay or undesirable fermentations through microorganisms and destruction through pests must be kept under control. The current practices in storage and food processing must also conform to the requirements of environmental quality.

Similarly, environmental problems associated with food distribution and marketing require concerted surveillance. For example, there is the problem of transferring crops to the cities to be processed and consumed with the resulting litter dumped in waste piles. Rather than recycling back the organic matter to croplands, this 'waste' is for the most part dumped into surface water. The food consumed also ends up as human waste, and is transported by water as sewage to plants for treatment. There the polluting matter is reduced to a varying degree but a significant portion is released into adjacent waters as raw sewage. Consequently, the waters take care of mounting loads of sewage and other waste, thereby choking the natural water cycle.

CONCLUSION

These are but a few examples to indicate the complex intricasies of food and ecology. They reinforce the view that if mankind is going to survive and to secure food for this and future generations, much greater attention should be paid to this intimate interaction.

Scientific analysis provides alternative strategies for decision-making. Decision-making itself is an act of political judgment. Those who decide on strategies to solve the world food problem must do so in the full knowledge of the web of interdependence that exists between this and other major problems of population, energy, the availability of other raw materials and development. It is not in any one of them, but in the interaction amongst them, that meaningful solutions can be fashioned.

REFERENCES

Anonymous. US Policy and World Food Needs. Government Printing Office, Washington, D.C.

Baumer, M. C. 1968. Ecologie et amenagement des pâturages au Kordofan, République du Sudan, Montpellier.

Baumer, M. C. 1975. Statement to the 21st General Conference of International Federation of Agricultural Producers, Washington, October 29-November 6, 1975. (In press: World Agriculture).

Bergmann, E. D. Undated. The Future of Insecticides--a problem of human environments. A publication of the Department of Chemistry, Hebrew University, Jerusalem.

Biswas, A. K. 1976. Personal Communication.

Borgstrom, G. 1973. World Food Resources. Intext Educational Publishers, New York.

Brown, L. R. and G. Finsterbusch. 1971. Man, food and environment. In W. W. Murdoch (Ed.) Environment: Resources, Pollution and Society.

Centro Internacional de Agricultura Tropical (CIAT). 1974. Seminar on Soil Management and the Development Process in Tropical America, Cali, February 10-14.

Döbereiner, J. and J. D. Day. In Papers read at the International Symposium in Pullman in 1974 and at Ibadan in 1975.

Eberstadt, N. 1976. Myths of the food crisis. In the New York Review of Books, February 19.

Eckholm, E. P. 1976. Losing Ground. W. W. Norton and Co. Inc., New York.

Ennis, W. B., Jr., W. M. Dowler and W. Klassen. 1975. Crop protection to increase food supplies. Science 188:593.

The Environment Fund. 1974. Declaration on Population and Food. Washington, D.C.

The Environment Fund. 1975. 1975 World Population Estimates.
    Washington, D.C.
Food and Agriculture Organization of the United Nations. 1967.
    Wood and World Trends and Prospects. Basic Study No. 16,
    Rome.
Food and Agriculture Organization of the United Nations. 1969.
    Influence of Man on the Hydrological Cycle (guide to poli-
    cies for the safe development of land and water resources),
    Rome.
Food and Agriculture Organization of the United Nations. 1969.
    Report of FAO-WHO expert meeting on pesticide residues.
    Study No. 84. FAO, Rome.
Food and Agriculture Organization of the United Nations. 1972.
    Proceedings of the Expert Panel on Effects of Intensive
    Fertilizer Use on the Human Environment, Rome.
Food and Agriculture Organization of the United Nations. 1973.
    Report of the 17th Conference, Rome.
International Institute of Tropical Agriculture (IITA). 1974.
    Conference on Soil Conservation and Management in the Humid
    Tropics, Ibadan.
Grant, K. E. 1975. Erosion in 1973-74: The record and the
    challenge. Soil and Water Conservation 30:1.
Mahler, P. J. 1972. Agricultural Development and the Environ-
    ment. Geoforum 10/72.
Mayer, J. 1975. Management of Famine Relief. Science 188:571.
Mukerjee, H. N. 1963. Determination of nutrient needs of
    tropical soils. Soil Science 95:276.
National Academy of Sciences. 1974. Population and Food: Cru-
    cial Issues, Washington, D.C.
Nelson, L. B. 1974. In a paper read at the Annual Meeting of
    the American Society of Agronomy, November.
Phillips, J. 1972. Problems in the use of chemical fertil-
    izers. In T. Farrar and J. P. Milton (Eds.). The Careless
    Technology, New York.
Sanchez, P. A. and S. W. Buol. 1975. Soils of the tropics and
    the world food crises. Science 188:598.
Sanderson, F. H. 1975. The great food fumble. Science 188:
    503.
Soil Science Department, North Carolina Experiment Station.
    1973. Research on Tropical Soils, Raleigh.
Tolba, M. K. 1974. Statement to the World Food Conference,
    Rome. UNEP, Nairobi (Unpublished).
United Nations Environment Programme. 1974. Overview on land,
    water and soils. Papers prepared for third session of the
    Governing Council, Nairobi (Unpublished).
United Nations Education, Scientific and Cultural Organiza-
    tion. 1973. Impact of human activities on mountain eco-
    systems. Expert Panel on Project 6, Man and Biosphere
    Series, Paris.

United Nations Education, Scientific and Cultural Organization.
    1974. Ecological assessment of pest management and fertil-
    izer use, Paris.
US Department of Agriculture, Economic Research Service. 1974
    The World Food Situation and Prospects to 1985. Foreign
    Agricultural Economic Report No. 98.
US Presidents Science Advisory Committee. 1967. The World
    Food Problem, Report of the Panel on the World Food Supply,
    Vol. 2, Washington, D.C.
Wittwer, S. H. 1975. Food Production. Technology and Re-
    sources Base. Science 188:579.

PIERRE R. CROSSON

Relations between Food Production, Processing and Distribution Alternatives and Energy

To adequately feed the world's expanding population and meet other social and economic goals of development the amount of energy effectively used per person and per hectare in agricultural production, processing and distribution will have to be greatly increased from present levels, especially in the developing countries. Extension of low energy techniques still widely used--the man or woman with only a hoe, or bullock and plow, oxcart transport to the nearest village--will not produce the surpluses needed to feed rapidly growing urban populations, often located far from places of agricultural production. Only more energy, vastly more than can be provided by man and animals alone, will do the job. The question then is not whether more energy will be needed but what forms it might take. There are many alternative forms, and combinations of forms. None of them is free. Each carries with it a set of economic, environmental and social costs. For any given level of food production, processing and distribution the objective of public policy should be to induce farmers, food processors and distributors to adopt that alternative which, in combination with other resources, gives the lowest total economic, environmental and social costs. Obviously the lowest cost energy alternative will vary with time and place. This paper discusses some of the energy alternatives that might be employed in food production, processing and distribution, attempting to clarify the principal issues involved in choosing among these alternatives. The objective is not criteria for choice in specific circumstances

Pierre R. Crosson is Fellow, Resources for the Future, 1755 Massachusetts Avenue, N.W., Washington, D.C. 20016.

but rather general guidelines for establishing criteria.

SOME DEFINITIONS
      Reference was made to the economic, environmental and
      social costs of energy alternatives. Economic costs need
      little explanation. The concept of environmental costs
also now is familiar. It incorporates all those uncompensated
costs inflicted by one individual or group on another individual or group, for example, air pollution from combustion of
coal, oil spills in the ocean, or damages from nuclear wastes.
      Social costs need more explanation. They include all
costs associated with the development, production, distribution
and use of alternative forms of energy not counted as economic
or environmental costs. A particular form of energy generates
social costs when its deployment in the society causes tension
among persons or groups which impede achievement of non-energy
social objectives. For example increased use of petroleum to
fuel farm machinery may encourage movement of people from farm
to cities where their demands for housing and other public services cause a diversion of effort and resources otherwise available for investment in rural development. Increased exploitation of a forest for fuel may cause conflict among villages,
each of which by tradition has a claim to the forest resource,
thus impeding village cooperation in building a better road or
more efficient irrigation system.
      The concept of social costs admittedly is vague. Yet that
such costs exist and may be important is undeniable. Discussion of alternative forms of energy use in agriculture must
allow for them in principle, however hard it may be in practice,
to clearly identify or measure them.

FORMS OF ENERGY IN AGRICULTURE
      Except for nuclear and geo-thermal energy, all forms of
      energy on earth stem directly or indirectly from the sun.
      In agriculture the principal forms of energy used, apart
from human and animal, are direct solar radiation converted to
chemical energy by the photosynthetic activity of plants, and
fossil fuels. Energy absorbed through photosynthesis has contributed to increased food production wherever food crops have
replaced forms of vegetation. However, the rapid increases in
food production, processing and distribution achieved in some
areas in recent decades have resulted from increased use of fossil fuels embodied in fertilizers, pesticides, and energy to
drive farm machinery and food processing and distribution systems. Achievement of even faster growth in food availability to
meet rising world demand will require an even more rapid
increase in consumption of fossil fuels, or development and
application of substitute forms of energy. The economic, envi-

ronmental and social costs of fossil fuels relative to these costs for alternative sources of energy, therefore, is the proper focus for discussion of energy use in food production, processing and distribution.

Costs of Fossil Fuels

Economic costs. The several fold increase in the economic costs of fossil fuels since 1973 has raised serious questions about the economic viability of the agricultural technologies based on these fuels, and has spurred interest in development of alternative technologies. A major concern has been the effects of higher fuel costs on the cost of nitrogen fertilizer, the production of which is dependent on fossil fuels both for feedstock and for energy to drive the production process. It now is clear that this concern was excessive. The principal reason for the run up in nitrogen fertilizer prices in 1973 and 1974 was a shortage of capacity, not the increase in the price of fossil fuels. This was argued even in mid-1974 when nitrogen fertilizer prices were already high and still rising (US Department of Agriculture, 1974). The argument was considerably strengthened by the subsequent sharp fall in fertilizer prices at a time when prices of fossil fuels continued to rise.
    While it was a mistake to attribute so much of the 1973-74 increase in prices of nitrogen fertilizers to higher prices of fossil fuels, there is no doubt that higher fuel prices increased the cost of production of these fertilizers. Unless fuel prices decline, which is uncertain if not unlikely, production costs will remain high. Nonetheless, the US Department of Agriculture (Reidinger, 1976, p. 15) projects growth in world consumption of nitrogen fertilizer at more than 6 percent annually from 1973-74 to 1980-81, compared with 8 percent annual growth in the previous five years. Growth of consumption in the developing countries is projected at more than 10 percent annually in this period, slightly below the rate from 1968-69 to 1973-74. It is not clear how much if any of the slowdown is attributable to higher prices of fertilizer, but in any case, the higher prices, at least in the view of the US Department of Agriculture, do not appear to be a serious deterrent to continued growth in consumption of nitrogen fertilizers.
    Fossil fuels are used directly in food production to drive irrigation pumps and farm machinery as well as an energy source for food processing and distribution activities. The higher prices, and in some instances limitations on the availability of these fuels since 1973, had serious negative impacts on pump irrigation (i.e., irrigation with groundwater) in some places. The press in 1974 carried stories of Indian farmers standing in line to receive rations of diesel fuel which often were inadequate for pumping requirements and other farm uses. More

recently, several studies of situations in the United States
have shown that the attractiveness of pump irrigation relative
to dryland farming is very sensitive to the price and especially the availability of fossil fuels (Casey et al., 1975;
Condra and Lacewell, 1975; Dvoskin and Heady, 1976).

The effects of the price and availability of energy on the
economic attractiveness of pump irrigation are especially serious because the continued spread of the technology associated
with the Green Revolution likely will require substantial further increases in the world's irrigated area. Pump irrigation
is particularly important in this process because it permits a
more flexible and hence more efficient, system of water management than the typical surface irrigation scheme. Pump irrigation capacity can be expanded in smaller increments than most
surface irrigation systems and generally is shorter lived.
Hence pump irrigation systems tie up less capital for shorter
periods of time, permitting quicker responses to changing economic and technological conditions. Pump irrigation systems,
unlike surface systems, typically have been privately financed,
thus giving farmers strong incentives to plan and operate them
efficiently. Finally, pump irrigation permits farmers greater
flexibility than surface systems in deciding when and in what
amounts to apply water to their fields. It is significant that
the spread of the Green Revolution technology in Asia was especially rapid in the Punjab region of the Indian sub-continent
where pump irrigation was the rule. Reidinger (1974) points
out that the advantages of increased flexibility of pump irrigation systems were great enough to induce many Indian farmers to
invest in them, even in areas under the command of surface systems.

Environmental costs. The environmental costs of the fossil
fuel technologies employed in agricultural production, processing and distribution are mostly indirect and mostly centered in
production activities. Effluents from food processing activities may contribute to serious water pollution, but this is
independent of the form of energy used. Trucks and autos used
in food distribution activities may contribute to air pollution
in urban areas, but the amounts must be trivial compared to
other sources of such pollution.

The environmental costs of fossil fuels in agricultural
production are indirect. They result from pollution by nitrogen fertilizers and pesticides, both largely fossil fuel products. Run-off of nitrogen fertilizers may contribute to accelerated eutrophication of surface waters and to concentrations of
nitrates in both ground and surface waters high enough to constitute a health hazard if the water is used for drinking. Pesticide residues may damage birds, fish and other wildlife, disrupt ecological systems and cause illness, death, and perhaps
genetic and birth defects in humans.

That nitrogen fertilizers and pesticides exact environmental costs is beyond question. The importance of these costs, however, is uncertain. Too little is known about how these materials move through the environment and of the damages they do there. Even if we had perfect knowledge of the physical characteristics of these damages we still would have no clear measure of their importance since we frequently lack a mechanism (e.g., a market) for calculating their social value. What, for example, is the loss in social value caused by pesticide damage to an ecological system?

A review of the evidence on environmental costs of nitrogen fertilizers in the United States leads me to conclude that at present levels of use these costs are not so high as to require measures to restrict their use. Projected levels of use to 1985 suggest the same conclusion for that date.[1] Firm conclusions about the environmental costs of present and projected levels of pesticide use in the United States are harder to justify because of greater uncertainty about the behavior and consequences of pesticides in the environment. However, there are two aspects to prospective patterns of pesticide use in the United States which suggest that the environmental costs of these materials may decline, or at least that they will not rise in proportion to pesticide consumption. The first is the increasing substitution of organophosphorous insecticides for organochlorine compounds, a process reflecting, apparently, both economic advantages of the organophosphorous compounds and the action of the Environmental Protection Agency in banning use of DDT and other organochlorine compounds. For reasons developed at some length elsewhere (Crosson and Frederick, 1976, Chapter 5), the environmental costs of the organophosphorous compounds may be less than those of the organochlorines. The second aspect of emerging patterns of pesticide use suggesting that environmental pressures of pesticides may rise less than in proportion to the rise in pesticide consumption is the increasing share of herbicides relative to insecticides. A study by the Department of Health, Education and Welfare (1969) concluded that herbicides do not constitute a serious threat to the environment. A more recent study by the National Academy of Sciences (1975b) accepted that conclusion.

In developing countries consumption of fertilizers and pesticides per hectare of land in crops is much less than in the United States. Growth in consumption of these materials in those countries at a rate of 8 to 10 percent annually over the next 10 to 15 years--in line with current projections by the US Department of Agriculture and the Food and Agriculture Organization--would raise per hectare consumption roughly to present levels in the United States. If I am right in thinking that

---

1. The review of the evidence leading to this conclusion is in Crosson and Frederick (1976, chapter 5).

present levels of consumption of these materials in the United
States do not constitute a major environmental threat (nitrogen
fertilizers) or an uncertain but possibly diminishing threat
(pesticides), then I may be justified in the same conclusion
regarding present and prospective levels of consumption in the
developing countries. I feel comfortable with that conclusion
with respect to present levels of consumption of these materials but uneasy with respect to projected levels. The reason
for the unease is that it may be an error to extrapolate the
experience of the United States, a country of the temperate
zone, to the developing countries, many of which lie wholly or
in large part in the tropics. There is reason to believe that
in the tropics soils and ecological systems may react differently than in the temperate zone to given concentrations of fertilizers and pesticides (Crosson and Frederick, Chapter 7).
Moreover, use of the organochlorines is not subject to the same
social constraints in the developing countries as in the United
States, and illiterate farm workers in those countries would
have more difficulty in following label prescriptions for safe
use of the organophosphorous compounds. Accordingly, the experience of the United States may be a poor guide to future environmental costs of fertilizer and pesticide consumption in the
developing countries.

Social costs. The discussion above of the concept of the
social costs of energy use stressed the vagueness of the concept. Nevertheless it is possible to discern at least two
important sets of social costs that may be attributable in part
to the use of fossil fuels in agriculture: the costs arising
from farm-to-city migration induced by farm mechanization, and
the costs arising from conflict over the distribution of the
increased income produced by energy intensive technologies.
While these costs have been incurred in both developed and
developing countries, it is in the latter that they now seem
most important. Accordingly, the discussion of social costs is
focused on the developing countries.

Urban populations in the developing countries have been
growing at 4 to 6 percent annually for the last several decades,
rates which double population every 12 to 18 years. In some of
the larger cities, for example Mexico City, Sao Paulo, Calcutta,
population already has reached 8 to 10 million and is still
growing. The social benefits of this process are high, but so
are the costs in diversion of resources to provision of public
services and, less certainly, in growing feelings of alienation
among recent arrivals having difficulty adjusting to the urban
environment, psychic damages resulting from crowding, and so on.

Roughly one-half the urban population growth in the developing countries is attributable to migration from farms. How
much of this results from the displacement of farm workers by
mechanization is uncertain. No doubt the amount varies from

place to place, and in some circumstances, e.g., where Green
Revolution technology permits multiple cropping, mechanization
is associated with _increased_ demand for farm labor. Moreover,
while the availability of economically priced fuel is a necessary condition for mechanization, it clearly is not sufficient.
Indeed, in many parts of the developing world subsidized credit
and favorable exchange rates likely are more important in
encouraging farm mechanization than is the price and availability of fuel. Nonetheless, the availability of relatively cheap
fossil fuels must have provided some inducement to mechanization and, therefore, must have contributed in some uncertain
measure to the rising social costs of urbanization in the developing countries.

The principal components of the Green Revolution technology, apart from improved seed varieties and management, are
fertilizers, pesticides and irrigation water. The technology,
therefore, is based in large measure on fossil fuels. There is
a considerable literature on the effects of the spread of the
Green Revolution on the distribution of income between large
and small farmers in the developing countries. The most common
hypothesis is that large farmers benefit more than small farmers
because the technology requires use of fertilizer, pesticides
and, in some instances, machinery on a scale beyond the reach of
the small farmer. Moreover, runs the argument, large farmers
are more likely to have favorable access to surface irrigation
or the resources needed to invest in a well.

The evidence relevant to the hypothesis is mixed. My read-
ing of it suggests to me that many small farmers were able to
adopt the Green Revolution technology and to reap increased
income from it, but that large farmers did relatively better.
Hence, in general, relative income position of the small farmer
deteriorated, but his absolute income increased.[2] The social
cost of this would depend upon whether the small farmer's perception of changes in his welfare was influenced most by changes
in his relative income or in his absolute income. Frankel's
study (1973) of the income distribution effects of the Green
Revolution in India and Pakistan suggests that relative income
may be more important, but the evidence is quite inconclusive.
Perhaps more to the point, Frankel concluded that conflict over
the distribution of income gains from the spread of the Green
Revolution in India and Pakistan sharpened adversary relations
between large and small farmers in the affected areas, creating
the potential for explosive, and to some extent destructive,
social protest.

This discussion of the social costs of fossil fuel technologies in agriculture can be no more than suggestive, given the

---

2. For a sampling of the literature relevant to income distribution effects of the Green Revolution see Griffin (1972),
Frankel (1973), and Herdt and Barker (1975).

difficulty of clearly defining and identifying these costs. The suggestion is that these costs are real and that they may be important. They are relevant, therefore, to the evaluation of fossil fuel technologies relative to technologies based on alternative forms of energy. It is important to note in concluding this section, however, that the discussion has dealt only with social costs, not benefits of the spread of fossil fuel technologies in agriculture. These benefits obviously have been enormous and would of course have to be taken into account in a complete evaluation.

ALTERNATIVES TO FOSSIL FUEL

Discussion in the literature of energy alternatives to fossil fuels in agriculture has focussed primarily on food production rather than on processing and distribution. The principal alternatives considered have been non-fossil fuel substitutes for nitrogen fertilizer and pesticides, use of biomass to generate petroleum or methane gas, and increased use of direct solar energy by improving the efficiency of photosynthesis. Another "alternative" discussed is simply more efficient use of existing fossil fuel technologies.

At present most of these alternatives cannot compete economically with fossil fuels in food production except in special circumstances. For example, analysis of the large scale substitution of animal manure for nitrogen fertilizer in the United States suggests that this would not be economical except on farms within a radius of about one mile of an animal feedlot (Heichel, 1976, p. 68). The reason is that the value of the manure is too low to justify transporting it a greater distance. Increasing the capacity of legumes (e.g., soybeans) to fix nitrogen and developing this capacity in cereal crops show promise in reducing the need for manufactured nitrogen, but discussion of these techniques indicates that they will not soon be economically feasible for farmers, either in the United States or in developing countries (National Academy of Sciences, 1975a, p. 154; Wittwer, 1974, p. 217). Considerable work is underway to develop pest resistant varieties, biological controls, and integrated pest management techniques as substitutes for chemical pesticides. After a review of this work, however, the National Academy of Sciences (1975a, p. 97) saw no convincing evidence that the alternative techniques would displace chemical pesticides in the foreseeable future.

Photosynthesis presently converts a very small percentage of the sun's energy to production of food. For example corn, a relatively efficient converter, uses only about 0.4 percent of the sunlight calories available to it to produce food useful to an animal (National Academy of Sciences, 1975a, p. 113). Research to increase the efficiency of photosynthesis is following several lines, such as altering plant leaf structure to capture a larger amount of sunlight, reducing the rate of pho-

torespiration (which wastes energy) in carbon 3 plants such as
soybeans and wheat, and carbon dioxide enrichment of the atmosphere in which plants grow. While this research shows promise,
the process of photosynthesis still is quite imperfectly understood, and none of the efforts to improve it has yet contributed to increased energy efficiency at the farm level (National
Academy of Sciences, 1975a, p. 113).

The technology exists to convert the biomass represented
by crop residues and animal wastes to petroleum or methane gas.
Heichel (1976) asserts that only 15 percent of the biomass of
these materials in the United States would be sufficient to
produce 150 million barrels of oil annually, enough to meet
current on-farm requirements for petroleum. However, the process for doing this is not economically competitive with fossil
fuels. Makhijani (1975, p. 101) argues that biogasification of
plant and animal wastes to produce methane gas is economically
promising for widespread use in the near future. The process
has been recommended by an agency of the Indian Government as
an energy source for villages. Much of the experience with the
process, in fact, has been in India where thousands of small
biogasification plants have been built on small farms (Makhijani, 1975, p. 102). So far the fuel produced in these plants
has been used primarily for domestic purposes. The gas can be
stored, however, and used to power tractors, pumps and other
farm machinery.

While the economics of biogasification to produce methane
may be promising, the environmental implications of the process
are not clear. Stripping the land of crop residues would
greatly increase its exposure to erosion, already a major problem in the developing countries and threatening to become one in
the United States. On the other hand, greater availability of
methane for household use would reduce the demand for wood for
that purpose, thus slowing the deforestation of mountain slopes
and the resulting erosion of those areas.[3] The balance of
these environmental consequences of biogasification is unknown,
but the issue would have to be carefully weighed in judging the
viability of biogasification as an alternative to fossil fuels.

One of the most attractive "alternatives" may be adoption
of a variety of known techniques for economizing on the use of
fossil fuels. Among these are more efficient water management
to offset the increased cost of pumping; foliar application of
fertilizers, application through irrigation systems, and more
timely application to maximize crop uptake; more sparing use of
insecticides, aiming to keep insect pest damage below the economic threshold rather than at total elimination of the pest;
and minimum tilling. Of these various economizing practices
minimum tillage looks especially promising on both economic and
environmental grounds.

---

3. Wood is not suitable for biogasification.

With minimum tillage the breaking of the soil by disking
and plowing is avoided. Instead a chisel plow, or its equivalent, is used to punch holes in the earth to receive the seed.
Plant stubble from the previous harvest is not removed.
Because the technique requires fewer machine operations it
saves fuel relative to conventional tillage techniques.
However, preservation of crop stubble encourages insect populations, and weed control is less than with conventional techniques; consequently minimum tillage requires heavier applications of insecticides and herbicides than conventional techniques, offsetting some of the energy savings represented by
lower fuel requirements. There is, however, a net saving of
energy (Heichel, 1976, p. 68; Wittwer, 1974, p. 220). Minimum
tillage apparently sacrifices little if anything in yields compared to conventional tillage and has proved to be economically
viable under a wide variety of conditions in both the United
States and developing countries (Heichel, 1976; Wittwer, 1974;
Jacobs and Timmons, 1974; Elias, 1969; Greenland, 1975). Studies in such widely disparate farming areas as Iowa (Jacobs and
Timmons, 1974) and Nigeria (Greenland, 1975) indicate that in
comparison with conventional tillage minimum tillage reduces
erosion by a factor of 10 or more. This saving in environmental costs is offset to some extent by the greater use of pesticides required by minimum tillage. However, in my judgment
erosion under present and prospective conditions in both the
United States and the developing countries poses a greater
environmental threat than pesticides, indicating to me that the
net environmental costs of minimum tillage probably are less
than those of conventional tillage.

There is little basis for judging the social costs of the
various energy alternatives to fossil fuels since some of the
alternatives have never been employed at all at the farm level
(e.g., increased biological nitrogen fixation, more efficient
photosynthesis) and others only on a relatively small scale
(biogasification, minimum tillage). I see no reason to believe
that the social costs of the alternatives would be higher than
those of fossil fuel technologies, and in some cases they may
be lower. One of the economizing responses to higher fossil
fuel prices, for example, might be to adopt more labor intensive practices, such as more labor and less herbicides for weed
control. This shift, increasing the demand for labor on the
farm, might slow migration to the cities, thus lessening the
social costs of urbanization.

RELATIVE IMPACT OF ENERGY ALTERNATIVES ON FOOD
PRODUCTION, PROCESSING AND DISTRIBUTION
In the United States food processing and distribution use
a greater proportion of the energy consumed in the food
sector than food production does. However, neither food

processing nor distribution is as energy intensive as food production, defining energy intensity in terms of the percentage
of energy costs in total costs of the activity (Committee on
Agriculture and Forestry, 1974). In the developing countries I
would expect the energy intensity of food production to be even
higher relative to processing and distribution since the latter
activities probably are less well developed compared to production than in the United States.

The greater energy intensity of food production makes that
activity more sensitive to changes in the price of energy than
food processing and distribution. Moreover, the range of technological alternatives consistent with productive agriculture
is greater in production than in processing and distribution.
The Green Revolution has demonstrated that high farm level productivity can be achieved with widely varying ratios of capital
to labor, depending on circumstances. The range of capital-
labor substitution for the high levels of output needed in the
future is much smaller in food processing and distribution.
For those levels of output the man with a pack on his back or
an oxcart is no substitute for a truck.

The greater energy intensity of the production activity
and the wider range of technological alternatives available to
it suggest that the greater part of the adjustment to higher
energy prices will be in food production rather than in processing and distribution. The greater the adjustment in production, i.e., the greater the fossil fuel savings in that activity, the smaller would be the required adjustment in processing
and distribution.

CONCLUSION

For the foreseeable future most of the large increase in
energy needed to meet the world's rising demand for food
will have to come from fossil fuels. The energy alternatives that would involve large scale substitution for fossil
fuels cannot compete economically with these fuels except in
certain limited circumstances. Among these alternatives the
use of biomass to generate methane gas may hold most economic
promise, and this technique would seem to deserve increased
attention, especially in the developing countries. In considering biogasification, however, it would be important to examine
the possibility that the technique might entail high environmental costs in the form of erosion.

Probably the most promising "alternatives," at least over
the next 5 to 10 years, are various techniques which economize
on the use of fossil fuels. Continuation of high prices of fossil fuels automatically increases the economic attractiveness of
these practices, providing incentives to farmers everywhere to
adopt them. These practices probably would also yield savings
in environmental costs since they involve smaller inputs of fer-

tilizers and pesticides per unit of production, and minimum
tillage greatly reduces erosion compared to conventional tillage. The savings with respect to erosion may be very large;
however, they will not be fully reflected in farmers' calculations of the advantages of minimum tillage relative to conventional tillage because farmers do not bear the costs of erosion.
They are borne instead by people downstream who must deal with
silt laden waters. Consequently public policies to reinforce
the effect of high fossil fuel prices on farmers' incentives to
adopt minimum tillage may be justified.

The fact that the world must continue to rely mainly on
fossil fuels to meet rising demands for energy in food production, processing and distribution does not mean that those
demands cannot be met. It does mean, however, that the costs
of adequately feeding the world's growing population may rise.
This possibility, and how to deal with it, should be in the
forefront of our thinking about how to respond to the world
food problem.

REFERENCES

Casey, J. E., R. D. Lacewell and L. G. Jones. 1975. Impact of
    limited fuel supplies on agricultural output and net
    returns: southern high plains of Texas. The Texas Agricul-
    tural Experiment Stations MP-1175, College Station, Texas.
Committee on Agriculture and Forestry. 1974. The US food and
    fiber sector: energy use and outlook. US Senate, 93rd
    Congress, 2nd session. Government Printing Office, Washing-
    ton, D.C.
Condra, G. D. and R. D. Lacewell. 1975. Effect of alternative
    product and input prices on demand for irrigation water:
    Texas high plains. The Texas Agricultural Experiment Sta-
    tion, College Station, Texas.
Crosson, P. R. and K. Frederick. 1976. The world food situa-
    tion: resource and environmental issues for the United
    States and the developing countries. Under review for pub-
    lication by Resources for the Future, Washington, D.C.
Dvoskin, Dan and E. O. Heady. 1976. US agricultural produc-
    tion under limited energy supplies, high energy prices, and
    expanding agricultural exports. Center for Agricultural
    and Rural Development. Iowa State University, Ames, Iowa.
Elias, R. S. 1969. Rice production and minimum tillage. Out-
    look on Agriculture. 6:67.
Frankel, F. R. 1973. The politics of the green revolution:
    shifting patterns of peasant participation in India and
    Pakistan. In T. Poleman and D. K. Freebairn (eds.). Food,
    Population and Employment: The Impact of the Green Revolu-
    tion. Praeger, New York.

Greenland, D. J. 1975. International Institute of Tropical
    Agriculture. In Proceedings: soil and water management
    workshop. US Agency for International Development. Wash-
    ington, D.C.
Griffin, K. 1972. The Green Revolution: an economic analysis.
    United Nations Research Institute for Social Development.
    Geneva.
Heichel, G. H. 1976. Agricultural production and energy
    resources. American Scientist. 64:64.
Herdt, R. W. and R. Barker. 1975. Small farmers and changing
    rice technology. The International Rice Research Institute,
    Los Banos, Philippines.
Jacobs, J. J. and J. F. Timmons. 1974. An economic analysis
    of agricultural land use practices to control water quality.
    American Journal of Agricultural Economics. 56:791.
Makhijani, A. 1975. Energy and Agriculture in the Third World.
    Ballinger Publishing Company, Cambridge, Massachusetts.
National Academy of Sciences. 1975a. Agricultural production
    efficiency. Washington, D.C.
National Academy of Sciences. 1975b. Pest Control: an assess-
    ment of present and alternative technologies. Vol. 1.
    Report of the Executive Committee. Washington, D.C.
Reidinger, R. B. 1974. Institutional rationing of canal water
    in northern India: conflict between traditional patterns
    and modern needs. Economic Development and Cultural Change.
    23:79.
Reidinger, R. B. 1976. World fertilizer review and prospects
    to 1980/81. Economic Research Service, USDA. Foreign Agri-
    cultural Economic Report No. 115. Washington, D.C.
United States Department of Agriculture. 1974. The world food
    situation and prospects to 1985. Economic Research Service,
    USDA Foreign Agricultural Report No. 98. Washington, D.C.
United States Department of Health, Education and Welfare.
    1969. Report of the Secretary's Commission on pesticides
    and their relationship to environmental health. Washington,
    D.C.
Wittwer, S. H. 1974. Maximum production capacity of food
    crops. Bioscience 24:216.

BRIAN D'SILVA

Land and Water Constraints in Indian Agriculture— An Overview

In a discussion of the world food situation, it is only
natural that India should come in mind. The reasons for this
are many. Not only has India received large amounts of food
aid and technical assistance in the past, but also its approach
in solving food and population problems is often compared and
contrasted with that of the People's Republic of China.

From all indications, China today is capable of adequately
feeding its population and great strides have been made in reducing the population growth rate.[1] The situation in India is
different. There has not been a single year since the early
1950s when India has not been a net importer of food. Food imports compared to food production averaged 6 percent for the
period 1951-1975, with a low .8 percent in 1955 and a high 16
percent in 1966. This raises a question that many people have
asked--why does this situation persist in India?

The purpose of this paper is not to judge, but to present
an overview of the problem and the constraints under which the
Indian nation has to work. India just harvested a bumper crop

---

1. A representative of China at the UN World Population Conference held in Bucharest, Romania, from August 19-30, 1974,
made the following statement, "Although, today our population
has increased by nearly 60 percent over that of a twenty-odd
years ago, our (food) production has increased by a larger
margin. On the basis of developing production, we have eliminated starvation and unemployment, . . ."

Brian D'Silva is a Graduate Research Assistant, Department
of Economics, Iowa State University, Ames, Iowa, USA.

of 114 million tons, compared to 106 million tons in 1974-75
and 90 million tons in 1973-74. One could cite numerous reasons for the shortfall in 1973-74, among them adverse weather
and the sharp increase in the price of crude oil. In 1975-76,
weather conditions were favorable and there were no significant
increases in the price of crude oil, but one cannot depend on
good weather and stable crude oil prices forever. There remains the task of providing for adequate nutrition of the
Indian population. To get a clearer idea of the steps which
need to be taken, one may begin with an appraisal of the present state of human, land and water resources in India.

The present population of India is estimated at over 614
million. Even if present efforts to reduce the birth rate
prove successful, population will probably reach 900 million by
the year 2000. This, of course, is a conservative estimate
based on the validity of the assumption that the birth rate
will be reduced as per government expectations.

Annual food imports are currently about 6 million tons,
acquired at a cost of more than a billion dollars. Crucially
needed foreign exchange must be used for this. Together with
the crude oil bill, this will impose a ceiling on the government's budget for developmental expenditures. India's trade
balance showed a deficit of $1,490 million in 1974-75. A simi-
lar deficit is forecast for 1975-76 (The Economist, 1976).

All this means that if India desires to achieve self-sufficiency in food production and at the same time provide for adequate nutrition of an increasing population, there will be considerable pressure on the nation's land and water resources.
This calls for proper management and utilization of these resources.

DEPLETION AND RECOVERY OF LAND AND WATER RESOURCES
India[2] has a geographical area of 320 million ha. Out of
this, 140 million ha are seriously affected by wind or
water erosion. An additional 7 million ha suffer from
waterlogging and salinity in the coastal areas. Flooding
affects 20 million ha. All told 167 million ha need immediate
treatment so that further degradation of India's soil resources
may be prevented (Vohra, 1975, p. 13). Vohra describes the
situation in the following manner:

Visual evidence of our neglect of the soil is available wherever one might go in this country of ours. Denuded hillsides,

_____
2. B. B. Vohra, Additional Secretary, Ministry of Agriculture,
Government of India, was originally scheduled to deliver this
subplenary lecture. This paper draws heavily on Mr. Vohra's
speeches over the past five years, published as a book entitled, "Land and Water Management Problems in India."

ravines, waterlogged and saline areas, drought-stricken villages, silted-up tanks and drying wells are to be encountered
almost everywhere. Floods ravage large areas year after year
even as the Rajasthan desert maintains its leeward creep. In
certain coastal areas, particularly Kerala, erosion by the
sea is a major problem. In the north eastern parts of the
country shifting cultivation cintinues to strip once heavily
forested slopes of all vegetation.

One only has to read certain chapters of Erik Eckholm's
book, "Losing Ground: Environmental Stress and World Food
Prospects," to get a graphic description of the effects that
deforestation, soil erosion and description are having from the
Himalaya foothills and the Indogangetic plain to the Thar desert of the Indian subcontinent.
    This soil erosion in India causes the displacement of
nearly 600 million tons of fertile top soil each year, an inch
of which Vohra states has taken "Mother Nature" between 500 and
1,000 years to build and is estimated to contain 5.37 million
tons of nutrients valued at approximately $730 million. This
loss of top soil affects both the present and future generations. Improved soil conservation and management practices
must be implemented immediately.
    Approximately 20 million ha in India are irrigated by
canals. These canals are part of the major irrigation projects
completed during the past quarter century at a cost of nearly
$5 billion. But there have been problems with these irrigation
systems. These projects were considered to be completed when
distributaries for supplying water to blocks of about 200 ha
were completed. The average size of land holdings is about 3-5
ha, and so there remained a gap in the delivery system. Adequate consideration has not been given to the construction
of channels to bring the water to the farm. Without such channels or delivery systems, it is not possible to make proper
use of available water supplies. Waterlogging became a serious
problem on newly irrigated lands unless proper drainage was
provided. With proper management and improved planning the
productivity of a large percentage of irrigated lands would be
increased.
    Water is an essential input for the new varieties intro-
duced by the so-called "Green Revolution." These varieties
require that precise quantities of water be provided at the
proper time. In a country like India where uncertain weather
has been the rule rather than the exception, the fullest possible use of irrigation water is crucial.
    Nearly 35 million ha in India can be irrigated this way
through the use of underground water. So far only 15 million ha
have been developed, which leaves another 20 million ha to be
developed. There are obvious benefits as well as problems associated with this decision. Let us first enumerate the benefits.

Underground water is easy for the farmer to use. He does not have to worry about the construction of secondary channels or the availability of water. The farmer has direct control over the use of water, since it will come from under his land. It facilitates the utilization of water at the proper time as required with the new varieties. It ensures that the decision of optimum usage of water will be the farmer's alone.

The construction of big surface irrigation works requires many years. They are capital intensive with no immediate financial returns. With the tapping of onfarm underground water the gestation lag is very short. The benefits can be seen within a growing season.

With surface water irrigation works sediment builds up and this is an important problem. The rate of siltation is often greater than anticipated at the time of construction of these works. With underground water there is no such problem. Storage costs for underground water are nil. There is also less possibility of loss of water because there is no need to worry about evaporation.

The use of underground water does of course have problems. There is a substantial cost involved in installing tube wells. This cost will vary with the size of the well. Small farmers in most cases will not be able to finance the required outlay unless credit can be provided through the government. Fortunately, this is being done. Land tenure arrangements need to be designed so as to encourage investment in tube wells. One possibility is the consolidation of holdings in some states so that investment in tube wells becomes profitable both from the private and social viewpoints.

The pumps used to operate the tube wells require a source of power. During the 1972 oil crisis, it became apparent that India could not depend on cheap crude oil. Production dropped in the northwestern states because crude oil became too expensive. This calls for an alternative source of power. Fortunately, India has embarked on a massive rural electrification program, utilizing the large dams which have been constructed for that purpose.

In order that underground water be utilized properly, further research needs to be done as to its availability, location and rate of recharge. We need to know the nature and distribution of the sub-soil acquifers throughout the nation and plan accordingly. This requires considerable skills and fieldwork.

There is yet a larger problem which needs to be tackled. Farmers must be persuaded to utilize underground water as a source of irrigation water rather than leaving everything to nature or to the government. There are few unintelligent farmers around the world. But a farmer lives within his environment and a change in this environment will affect him. So, convincing him to utilize this change to his benefit as well as

that of the community and the nation is another task which
needs to be attacked.

PUBLIC ADMINISTRATION OF LAND AND WATER RESOURCES

Each state in India has prepared a perspective plan for
the optimum management of its land and soil resources.

The State Land Use Planning Board is responsible for this
task. The board is chaired by the Chief Minister of the States.
The State Land Use Boards are coordinated by a Central Land
Use Commission whose responsibility will be all matters "re-
lated to the optimum management of the country's land resources"
(Vohra, 1975, p. 8).

Drought-prone areas have received special emphasis in the
Fifth Five Year Plan. A program was designed to improve the
management of soil and water resources, at a cost of nearly
$500 million. The Plan provides $1 billion for the further improvement of large scale irrigation projects. Underground
water irrigation programs, too, are being emphasized. Time
will tell the effectiveness of these various programs.

The design of programs and plans for organizational structures are but a small part of the total development effort.
What is required, is a change in attitudes and approaches among
all concerned.

For even though scientists and researchers may develop new
techniques or come up with new discoveries, there remains the
task of convincing the decision makers to accept these recommendations and implement them. This is no small task. Even if
we assume that this can be achieved, we have the necessity of
working through existing institutions or developing new ones.
Organizational change to implement political decisions is another area of concern and this change does not come easy. Finally, there is the greater task of convincing the farmer at
the local level to make use of new practices and this is a
challenge. For this we need teams of professionals, not in the
capital but out in the field. It is here that the final decisions will be made that spell the success or failure of national policies.

Swedish scientists Malin Falkenmark and Gimnar Lindh
(1974) comment, "The transfer of knowledge is a task of formidable proportions, as the knowledge must reach to the level of
the peasant who irrigates his crops. He is the key factor:
without him it will not be possible to realize the necessary
crop production." This then is the crucial test.

Finally, as this conference addresses the problem of food,
a problem that has a definite human aspect to it, I hope that
we do come up with solutions which keep in mind the human
nature of the problem, so that we may have "Human Solutions for
Human Problems."

REFERENCES

Eckholm, E. 1976. Losing Ground: Environmental Stress and
    World Food Prospects. W. W. Norton, New York. USA
Falkenmark, M., and G. Lindh. 1974. How can we cope with the
    water resources situations by the year 2015? Ambio, III:
    114. Sweden.
Vohra, B. B. 1975. Land and Water Management Problems in
    India. Cabinet Secretariat, Government of India. New
    Delhi, India.

WILLARD W. COCHRANE

The Impact of Different Forms of Foreign Assistance on Agricultural Development

THE SETTING

Agricultural production increased relatively rapidly in the less developed world during the 1950s and 1960s. During the long period 1957-1967, for example, agricultural output for all developing countries (excluding mainland China) grew at a rate of 2.7 percent per year. This is a very good record, by any standards. In the Green Revolution period of 1967 to 1971, the rate of growth in agricultural output in these countries spurted upward to something approaching 4 percent per year. Since 1971 the growth in agricultural output has sputtered and slowed down in the less developed world, in part, at least, as the result of several poor to bad crop years.

But the very good production record through 1971 was nullified by rapid population growth. Per capita agricultural production held just about constant on a trend basis for the less developed world as a whole over the long period 1957-1975. The average consumer in the less developed world in terms of food availability was no better off in 1975 than he was in 1957, except in those areas where food supplies were supplemented by imports from the developed regions (FAO, 1970, pp. 1-2; ERS, USDA, WAS-9, 1975).

What is likely to happen to agricultural production growth rates in the long-run future is a much debated subject. Some experts hold that once the recent cycle of adverse weather is behind us, the production growth rates of the 1950s and 1960s

Willard W. Cochrane is Professor of Agricultural Economics, University of Minnesota, St. Paul, Minnesota 55108.

in the less developed world will be restored, and the food situation in those regions will become tolerable, if not satisfactory (Johnson, 1975; USDA, 1974). Other experts hold that food
production in the less developed world will lag behind population growth in the long run and Malthusian controls over population growth will take over, unless extraordinary measures are
taken internationally to deal with the deteriorating food situation (Mesarovic and Pestel, 1974; International Food Policy
Research Institute, 1976). I am inclined toward the latter
position. Agricultural production will be maintained at rates
of growth approaching 3 percent per year over the long run with
great difficulty. If such rates are achieved, it will be
because very great efforts are made to increase agricultural
production increasing both the real cost of producing food and
the real price of food to the average consumer.

Why is this so? There are a number of reasons which I
will only briefly mention here. First, the potentially arable
land in the world is scarce, and new and additional land can be
brought into cultivation only at higher and higher development
costs. Second, the water available for irrigation in the world
is extremely scarce and serves as a serious restraint to further modernization of the agricultural production plant.
Third, the energy crunch is already with us, and although no
one can predict the ultimate outcome, high energy prices for an
extended period seem certain to serve as a deterrent to
increased productivity in agriculture. Fourth, turning to the
demand, rates of population growth in the less developed world
do not seem to be declining importantly and many predict a
doubling of the world population by 2010, if Malthusian controls do not take over before that time and force a decline in
the rate of population growth. Fifth, if economic development
in the developed world continues at the rapid pace of the last
15 years, the per capita consumption of animal products will
continue to increase, along with a strong export demand for
grains from North America to produce those animal products.
Sixth, how do we know that the cycle of adverse weather is
behind us? Some climatologists are telling us to expect
greater weather variability in the monsoon and semi-arid
regions of the northern hemisphere in the years to come than we
experienced in the 1960s and 1970s.[1]

With some luck with the weather, then, long-run future
growth rates in agricultural production in the less developed
world could revert to those rates achieved in the 1950s and
1960s, but it seems more likely that production growth rates in
the decades ahead will tend to lag behind the rates achieved in

---

1. For an expansion of these arguments see the paper entitled
"The Price of Farm Products in the Future" by Willard W.
Cochrane in the Fall 1976 issue of The Annals entitled Rural
America.

the 1950s and 1960s. This means that, given present rates of
population growth in the developing countries and the increased
exports of grain from North America to the Soviet Union,
Eastern Europe, and Japan, average per capita supplies in the
developing countries will decline on a trend basis unless
extraordinary measures are taken in the international community
to cope with this development.

This trend problem is further complicated by an important
variability in grain production in the world resulting from
weather variability. And this production variability, given
the extreme inelasticity of demand for the grains, causes grain
prices to fluctuate widely and unpredictably. This weather-
induced variability in production, and the wildly fluctuating
grain prices which accompany it, are annoying and frustrating
to the developed countries, but they can be disastrous to the
very poor countries living on the edge of subsistence. If outside food aid is not forthcoming immediately, a short grain
crop in a very poor country means starvation and death to many.

The less developed countries (LDCs) are confronted with
two interrelated problems: a long-run trend problem in which
the real price of food is likely to rise and a short-run instability problem in which grain production varies unpredictably
from year to year, and grain prices fluctuate wildly. To cope
with these two problems it is obvious that the less developed
countries must devote more resources to agricultural production
first, to increase rates of growth in agricultural production
and second, to stabilize those growth rates. In the tropical
LDC this increased investment in agricultural production and
distribution will involve many things: higher quality labor
through education, new and improved plant varieties through
research and development, improved and expanded water management and irrigation, increased production and usage of fertilizer, increased and improved grain storage, government price
stabilization programs for farmers and on and on. All these
investment activities have one thing in common; they involve
the increased employment of scarce resources, hence they are
costly to the society involved. But if the rate of investment
in agricultural production and distribution is not stepped up
considerably in the typical LDC, the future of the typical LDC
is bleak indeed. In fact, rates of investment in agricultural
production in the less developed world must be increased significantly over the next two decades, if widespread hunger and
famine are to be avoided in those regions.

AUGMENTING INVESTMENTS IN THE FOOD AND AGRICULTURAL
SECTOR THROUGH FOREIGN ASSISTANCE

How is this increased investment in the food and agricultural sector of the typical LDC to be made? In the main
it must be made by the LDCs themselves; it must be

squeezed out of the meager production surpluses of the countries involved. But many of these countries are so desperately
poor--with per capita incomes of $200 or less per year--that
they cannot increase their net national investment importantly
and quickly. These countries require foreign assistance. And
they are receiving assistance. The total flow of resources to
the less developed countries from all sources--bilateral, multilateral, official, private, centrally planned, and Development
Assistance Committee countries (DAC)[2]--amounted to $35 billion
in 1973 and $40.8 billion in 1974 (OECD, 1975). This is a lot
of money in absolute terms; but relatively, it does not represent a prodigious effort. For the DAC countries as a whole, it
represents less than 1 percent of the GNP of those countries.

Foreign assistance to the food and agricultural sector of
the LDCs may come in three principal forms: food aid, economic, or capital, assistance, and technical assistance. Official disbursements from DAC countries (bilateral and multilateral) for food aid amounted to approximately $1.1 billion in
1973. Economic, or capital, assistance for the food and agricultural sector from DAC countries amounted to approximately
$2.0 billion in 1973. And bilateral technical assistance for
agriculture from the DAC countries amounted to approximately
$280 million in 1973. We may then conclude that, of the total
flow of resources from the DAC countries to the developing
countries in 1973 (some $24.7 billion), between 13 and 15 per-
cent went into the food and agricultural sectors of those countries (OECD, 1975, Chapter IV). In percentage terms the flow
of resources from the DAC countries to the food and agricultural sectors of the developing countries has been small in
recent years. Of the total flow into the food and agricultural
sectors, the largest amount was in the form of economic, or
capital, assistance, the next largest amount was in the form of
food aid, and that going into technical assistance was really
very small.

Having established the magnitudes of foreign assistance
resource flows into the food and agricultural sectors of the
developing countries, let us now explore the conceptual role of
these different forms of assistance. Food aid involves the
direct transfer of food products, most often in the form of
grains but sometimes in other product forms, from the donor
country, or multilateral agency, to the recipient country.
Since this form of assistance avoids the lengthy investment
process, as well as the production process, it is a relatively
speedy form of assistance. It is the only form of assistance

---

2. Participating in the work of the Development Assistance
Committee are: Australia, Austria, Belgium, Canada, Denmark,
France, Germany, Italy, Japan, the Netherlands, Norway, Portu-
gal, Sweden, Switzerland, the United Kingdom, the USA and the
Commission of the European Economic Communities.

that is useful in coping with crop failures and famine. Food
aid also has a role to play in building stocks to be used in
either a national, or international, reserve stock program that
has the objective of evening out supplies between crop years,
and hence contributing to increased price and income stability.

One problem with food aid is that it often fails to contribute to the development process. In starving times, the
food received as food aid is simply eaten up, and once it is
gone, it is gone. The productive plant is not expanded or made
more productive. But food aid need not always have this zero
effect. Food received as food aid can be used as a wage good
to pay underemployed and unemployed workers to build roads, to
construct irrigation works, and to plant forests. In this way
the productive plant is improved and expanded and the productive capacity of the country is increased.

Thus, food aid can be used in many ways. In the past its
greatest use has been in combating hunger and starvation
resulting from a crop failure. In the future its greatest use
could be in connection with the building of an international
food reserve and security system, again, to protect people living on the edge of subsistence from crop failure.

Economic, or capital, assistance involves the granting or
loaning (under concessional terms) of funds to an LDC by a
donor country or by a unilateral agency to be used to acquire
resources to support a productive enterprise (e.g., build an
irrigation works, build storage facilities, support the development of agricultural banks). Such funds almost always are
linked to a physical or capital project. Sometimes the funds
are tied to the acquisition of certain specified resources, and
not unusually, in bilateral economic assistance arrangements,
those funds must be expended in the donor country.

The purpose of economic, or capital, assistance is to
build capital structures, institutions and organizations needed
in LDCs to increase their productive capacity. But if the LDC
in question is interested in increasing the real per capita
incomes of its citizens as rapidly as possible, it will not use
scarce foreign economic assistance to support just any project.
It will use those scarce resources to support those projects
with the greatest social profitability. This social profitability will be determined in turn by honest, competent bene-
fit-cost studies.

In point of fact, the largest category of foreign economic
assistance for agricultural development provided by DAC countires in 1973 and 1974 was the category water management and
development. As a priority this makes sense, because agricultural modernization in most LDCs is absolutely dependent upon
improved and expanded water management. The great advantage to
economic, or capital, assistance is the opportunity it provides
LDCs to build needed production structures and institutions
that require foreign produced inputs where the LDC involved is

short on foreign exchange. If used wisely, foreign economic, or capital, assistance can serve to break critical production bottlenecks in the national production and distribution systems.

Technical assistance involves the transfer of productive knowledge and technical skills and practices, as well as the capacity to generate productive knowledge and technical skills and practices, from the developed donor countries, or international agencies, to the LDCs. Technical assistance takes many forms: the training of nationals from the LDCs in developed countries, the loan of scientists and technicians to LDCs, assistance in building research and development institutions in the LDCs, support for libraries and laboratories, and the building of effective extension and adult education programs in the LDCs. The purpose of all this is to upgrade the technical skills of farmers and improve the technical practices employed by farmers in the developing countries, and thus increase agricultural productivity in those countries.

But one thing that we have learned over the past 25 years is that agricultural technology tends to be location-specific. This means that the specific production technologies of such economically advanced countries as Japan, or the USA, or the Netherlands cannot be picked up and transferred directly to all developing countries. It means that the capacity must be generated for each agroclimatic region in the less developed world to adapt production technologies to the specific requirements of the region. And we have further learned that the building of this capacity in the typical LDC is a long, slow process.

Even though the building of the capacity to generate location-specific production technologies in LDCs is a long, slow process, this does not mean the process should be delayed further or avoided. To the contrary, it must be undertaken if the LDC in question is to modernize its agricultural plant and sustain a desired rate of increase in agricultural productivity over the long run. In a finite world there is no other way. And technical assistance from the developed world is absolutely essential to the development of this capacity by providing: (1) training and education for students from the LDCs, (2) technical experience and advice, and (3) financial support of research and development. But all concerned must remember continually that the purpose of the technical assistance is to build capacity within the LDC, not to bypass that critical development.

THE IMPACT OF VARIOUS FORMS OF FOREIGN ASSISTANCE ON THE LDCS
Let us consider first, food aid. We will focus on the record of the USA, since it was by far the leading provider of this form of aid in the 1950s and 1960s. The USA distributed food in the form of aid to the LDCs in the 1950s and 1960s like it was a free good, which indeed it was to the

US government, since it had title to vast stocks of food which
it could not sell in the commercial markets. Thus the USA literally pushed food aid on the developing countries in this
period. On the other hand, the USA has been most niggardly in
its provision of food aid since 1972. This resulted from the
fact that the USA depleted its surplus stocks in 1972-73 and
was reluctant to cut down on the supplies moving to commercial
buyers abroad or its own consumers. To an important degree,
then, the principal supplier of food aid in the world, the USA,
has dispensed that form of aid, not in terms of the needs of
the LDCs, but rather in terms of its own food surplus situation.

In making the above generalization it should be recognized
that in the long period 1952-72, when the USA held surplus
stocks, it in fact held the reserve stocks for the world and
protected many an LDC from famine conditions in bad crop years.
Certainly the massive shipments of grain to India in 1965-66
following the failure of the monsoon saved that country from
widespread famine. When the surplus stocks were available in
the USA, they were used to avert hunger and starvation abroad.

It is often argued that food aid shipments depressed farm
prices in the LDCs involved and thus acted as a deterrent to
agricultural development. The validity of this argument must
be ascertained for each LDC receiving food aid. Food aid to
LDCs experiencing a short crop obviously acted to keep food
prices from skyrocketing, and some LDCs did use food aid shipments to depress domestic food prices in noncrisis periods.
But all did not, and food aid did not need to be used in ways
that acted to depress domestic food and farm prices. In sum,
and in the judgment of this writer, the price-depressing
aspects of food aid is a much overworked argument.

What the huge surplus stocks in the USA and the generous
provisions of food aid by that country in the 1950s and 1960s
may have done is the following: they interacted to lull government decision makers in LDCs to sleep with regard to the
development needs of their agricultures, and as a result governments in the LDCs have systematically underinvested in agricultural development. This was the great and adverse consequence of the food aid policy of the USA as it was practiced in
the 1950s and 1960s on the LDCs.

The impact of economic, or capital, assistance on development in the LDCs has been very different from that of food aid.
The impact has been limited because the flow of this form of
assistance has always been limited. And in the 1970s it has
become extremely limited. The failure of Western developed
nations in general, and the USA in particular, to provide capital investment funds to the less developed countries with any
degree of generosity has been one of the principal deterrents
to economic growth and development in the less developed world
in the 1960s and 1970s. The capital investment funds desper-

ately needed by one LDC after another to build power grids,
transport systems, irrigation works, and fertilizer factories
have not been forthcoming from the developed world in the
amounts needed, hence the building of these elements has lagged,
and with it, economic development.

But limited or not, economic assistance often has not been
used in ways designed to support and promote economic development. Governments from both the recipient and donor countries
have in too many cases selected capital projects for assistance
funding for personal, political, or national monument reasons
rather than on the basis of social profitability. Thus, much
economic assistance has gone into personal enrichment and
national aggrandizement rather than into the support of economic growth. The shift toward the provision of economic aid
through international agencies and more experience with the
process of development in the LDCs are, however, helping to
correct this particular problem in the foreign assistance field.

In the technical assistance area the recipient and donor
countries have learned slowly through trial, failure, and much
anguish that most modern agricultural technologies from the
developed West cannot be transferred, with good results,
directly to LDCs. In most cases the technologies involved must
be modified and adapted to the socio-economic-agroclimatic conditions of the LDCs. The recipient and donor countries have
also learned together that the building of research and development capacity in the LDCs is a long, slow, painful process.
Personnel must be trained, value systems of researchers and
administrators must be changed--changed to emphasize performance rather than status--and a research and development organization must be brought into being, must gain experience by
doing and problem solving, and finally, must generate the technologies specifically adapted to local areas. All this takes
time, much time--more time than the recipient and donor countries have been willing to recognize in the past.

A DESIRABLE MIX OF FOREIGN ASSISTANCE

What should be emerging from the foregoing discussion is
that there is no one best form of foreign assistance.

Each has its place, and each its need. A very poor country living on the edge of subsistence will, if it suffers a bad
harvest, or a series of short crops, require food aid to avoid
widespread hunger and famine among its people. A very poor
country that is desirous of building such infrastructural elements as transport systems and irrigation works and such agro-
service units as fertilizer plants and grain storage facilities
to support and promote economic growth will almost certainly
require economic assistance to render this possible in a reasonable period of time. And a very poor country that seeks to
modernize its national agricultural plant will require techni-

cal assistance to build and operate a research and development
complex with the capacity to provide the location-specific
technologies required in the modernization process.

The proper mix of these various forms of foreign assistance will vary by less developed country. Thailand, for example, is not likely to require any food aid in the foreseeable
future, but it needs foreign economic, or capital, assistance
to manage the flood waters on its Central Plain, and it is
receiving effective technical assistance in the agricultural
sector. Food aid, on the other hand, will be an important component of total foreign assistance to Bangladesh for a long
time to come. In the case of India, technical assistance
should play a lesser role in the future, but it desperately
needs foreign capital to build physical infrastructure and
agro-service industries.

The mix of foreign assistance can and should vary in
accordance with the resource endowments of the LDC involved,
the stage of development that it is in, and the development
goals of the country. In the judgment of this writer this
desirable mix of foreign assistance can best be determined by
the LDC working with an international agency like the World
Bank or a consortium of international agencies. In this context the political aspirations of the donor countries can be
minimized, and the criterion of social profitability can be
emphasized in the provision of assistance.

INVESTMENT IN AGRICULTURE
The mix of foreign assistance is important to agricultural
development in the less developed world. But it is not
the number one problem of the less developed world. The
number one problem is the failure of less developed countries
themselves, and the aid-giving countries working with them, to
invest sufficiently in the agricultural sector. It is not
uncommon for less developed countries to have 70 to 80 percent
of their population living in rural areas, for their agricultural sector to generate from 40 to 50 percent of their gross
domestic product, and for their development expenditures
devoted to agriculture and irrigation to amount to only 15 to
25 percent of their total development expenditures. We have
already seen that of the total flow of resources from the DAC
countries to the developing countries in recent years, some 15
percent or less went into the food and agricultural sectors of
those countries. In short, both the LDCs themselves and the
aid-giving countries have been starving the agricultural sectors of the LDCs with respect to investment for two decades.
In the typical case the major sector, agriculture, receives a
minor share of the country's development funds. And the aid-
giving developed countries have acquiesced in this situation or
even contributed to it.

What the typical LDC must do, if it wants to get both its dominant sector, agriculture, and its overall general economy moving rapidly, is to up its development expenditures in the agricultural sector (including irrigation and water management) to 40 or 50 percent of total developmental expenditures for the next five to ten years. With such an investment expenditure in agriculture for say, ten years, the productivity of agriculture should increase sufficiently in most LDCs (but not all) to (1) enable those countries to increase significantly the per capita food consumption of its people, (2) increase significantly the per capita real incomes of rural people, and (3) permit those countries then to reduce gradually the percentage of total development expenditures devoted to agricultural development.

In the long run the percentage of development expenditures devoted to agricultural development should decline as the agricultural sector declines relative to other sectors in the national economy. But in the immediate run the productivity of the agricultural sector of almost every LDC needs to be increased greatly to provide the additional food required (1) by their rapidly growing populations and (2) to increase the per capita food consumption of those populations. Logic dictates that this will not happen where the agricultural sector receives only 15 to 20 percent of the total development expenditures, but the sector must provide a livelihood for 70 to 80 percent of the population. In the immediate run the aid-giving nations should seek to encourage the less developed nations to change, and to change radically, the mix of development investment expenditures within their countries. The Organization for Economic Cooperation and Development (OECD, 1974, pp. 31-32) was doing just this in 1974 when it wrote

> We believe the first need is to reorder development priorities in favour of an all-out effort to raise agricultural production, through broad rural development, in Third World countries. . . .
> It is for the developing countries to take the lead in adopting more balanced strategies of investment which give greater priority to agricultural and rural development. To be effective they will need to mobilize popular support and understanding that the relative backwardness and neglect of the rural sector is restraining the wider development of their national economies, and that the way forward is through a major transformation of the social and economic structure affecting food and agricultural production. Developing the rural sector will broaden the market for industrial and service industries, and will remove the constraint of food as a wage good thereby stimulating higher growth throughout the national economies of the developing countries.

SUMMARY AND CONCLUSIONS

There is no one superior form of foreign assistance. Each
has a necessary and proper role to play, depending upon
the situation and conditions in the LDCs involved. A
desirable mix of the various forms of assistance will depend
upon the resource endowments, and upon the stage of development
and development goals of the LDCs involved. But almost every
LDC needs to give a higher priority to investment in agriculture during the next ten years. The aid-giving countries can
and should assist the LDCs in reestablishing their priorities
in the direction of agricultural development and in effectuat-
ing those priorities.

REFERENCES

Cochrane, W. W. Fall 1976. The price of farm products in the
    future. The Annals, forthcoming.
International Food Policy Research Institute. February 1976.
    Meeting food needs in the developing world: the location
    and the magnitude of the task in the next decade. Report
    No. 1. Washington, D.C., USA.
Johnson, D. G. 1975. World food problems and prospects.
    American Enterprise Institute for Public Policy
    Washington, D.C., USA.
Mesarovic, M. D. and E. Pestel. 1974. Mankind at the Turning
    Point. Readers Digest Press, New York, USA.
Organization for Economic Cooperation and Development, Develop-
    ment Assistance Committee. November 1974. Development
    Assistance Efforts and Policies Review. Paris, France.
Organization for Economic Cooperation and Development, Develop-
    ment Assistance Committee. November 1975. Development
    Assistance Efforts and Policies Review. Paris, France.
United Nations, Food and Agricultural Organization. 1970. The
    State of Food and Agriculture. Rome, Italy.
US Department of Agriculture, Economic Research Service.
    December 1975. The World Agricultural Situation. Washing-
    ton, D.C., USA.
US Department of Agriculture, Economic Research Service.
    December 1974. The world food situation and prospects for
    1985. Foreign Agricultural Economic Report No. 98. Wash-
    ington, D.C., USA.

MARTIN J. FORMAN

New Alternative Strategies for Combating Malnutrition

Despite the widespread existence of malnutrition in developing countries, there was little <u>awareness</u>, and hence little attention, being paid to the problem until a few years ago. In the early 1940s, the world was pre-occupied with war. In the late 1940s and 1950s, attention was focused on rehabilitation of economies which had been disrupted by the war, on the struggle for independence by former colonies, and on the political and economic development of lesser developed countries (LDCs). It was not until the late 1950s and early 1960s that more than a few people became aware of yet another problem which seemed to be part of a poor nation syndrome--malnutrition.

Field workers began to describe the symptoms which are associated with various nutrient deficiencies and country surveys began to reveal that these deficiencies were relatively widespread in many of the LDCs. More and more people knew of the existence of the problem but a miniscule number of programs were being designed to address the problem.

It was not until the mid-1960s that this widening awareness began to change to genuine <u>concern</u>. This was due mainly to research findings which pointed out a relationship between protein deficiency in early childhood and a retardation of physical and mental growth. In the US a landmark publication of the US National Academy of Sciences and a report of the President's Science Advisory Committee helped to stir up widespread concern by documenting and implicitly endorsing research findings that

---

Martin J. Forman is Director, Office of Nutrition, US Agency for International Development, Washington, D.C. 20523.

linked malnutrition to retarded physical and mental development.
The UN Economic and Social Council called for the developed and
lesser developed countries to take action to avoid an "impend-
ing protein crisis" and forecast grave consequences if such action were not taken. An Indian Minister of Agriculture voiced
alarm that neglect of the country's chronic malnutrition problem among pre-school age children could lead to a generation of
people with dwarfed mentality.

In the late 1960s and early 1970s this concern led to an
increase in research and development activities and an ever increasing number of conferences on the subject. Various professional societies added malnutrition to the agenda of the annual
meetings and even the United Nations debated the issue. The UN
General Assembly called on countries to report to the Secretary
General on what they were doing to address the protein problem
and the Secretary General was instructed to prepare a report on
global action in this area.

Unfortunately, there was relatively little to report since
the actions being taken fell far short of the rhetoric and recommendations. The increased awareness and concern had not yet
been followed by serious commitment on the part of the LDCs to
do something about malnutrition, and in the absence of such commitment, programming was limited to scattered ad hoc activities
which had usually been initiated by individuals on the basis of
opportunities rather than in response to an analysis of overall
need. Thus, many countries initiated supplementary feeding
programs for children because of the availability of free or
low cost foods. Nutrition education programs were often undertaken on the basis of logic. Attempts were made to develop new
low cost nutritious foods because this was being done elsewhere
with alleged success, and there were local technology and raw
material which could be used to create similar indigenous products.

Some of these activities did, of course, have some positive impact, but hardly anywhere did they produce a measurable
impact on the malnutrition problem.

In the early 1970s, I interviewed a number of policy makers in developing countries as to why there wasn't more being
done about the malnutrition problem. I asked them questions
such as why there was no policy covering food and nutrition,
whether there was really concern about the plight of poor
people, and why more wasn't being done in the way of programming.

The language and wording of the responses differed, but
the meaning was the same. Yes, they knew about the relationship between early malnutrition and retarded development. Yes,
of course, they cared--and they did want to do something about
it. But there was a lack of guidance being provided by the
nutrition community:

They didn't really know the magnitude of the problem or
what percentage of cases were relatively serious in terms of
mortality, morbidity, and diminished performance.

There was no consensus (and even confusion) as to what
should be done. Some advocated greater emphasis in agriculture;
some recommended fortifying the food supply; some called for intensive nutrition education.

There was little advice on which activities should be
undertaken if all could not be afforded. How could one choose
intelligently from among the alternatives?

There was little evidence that a given action would indeed
have the desired impact. Where were the models out of past experience?

There was a paucity of data on what these actions would
cost and where the money would come from. The "pilot" project
usually seemed low in cost, but the cost of a national program
might be exhorbitant. (Nutritionists were, alas, very naive
about national budgeting.)

This pointed out the need for an alternative approach to
nutrition programming. Clearly, there was a need to both
broaden and raise the level of concern about malnutrition. The
problem could not be adequately dealt with by a nutrition
branch buried in a health ministry.

At least three actions had to be taken before there could
be serious commitment and meaningful programs:

1) Nutrition programming had to be broadened to involve
agriculture, education, and industry as well as health considerations. Agricultural planning should be concerned not only
with aggregate cereal production, but also with issues such as
how a nutritionally adequate diet for low income consumers can
be ensured. Public health programs should consider, for example, the impact of environmental sanitation on enteric disorders leading to intestinal malabsorption of nutrients and the
efficacy of combining health, nutrition and family planning
services. Education programs should consider the role of nutrition education in the school curriculum and in non-formal education programs. The industrial sector should consider whether
food fortification or new foods development are cost effective
ways to help consumers fill nutrient gaps in their diets.

2) The malnutrition problem had to be placed on the agenda
of the planning body alongside problems such as housing, education, trade and transportation, requiring attention by planners,
policy makers and budgeters. Planners had to concern themselves with the costs of addressing the malnutrition problem
and the consequences of not doing so. There was a need for a
national food and nutrition policy, supported by the government at the highest level.

3) Nutrition programming had to be <u>systematized</u> and had to follow careful analysis and planning. Methods had to be developed to undertake realistic analyses of specific problems at reasonable cost. Alternative interventions needed to be evaluated and selected on the basis of suitability to local conditions and cost effectiveness.

In recent years, these actions are beginning to be taken in an increasing number of countries. Nutrition programming has entered a new era:

Conventional wisdom has been challenged, and programs previously accepted on faith are being critically evaluated. (How much do school lunch programs really cost, and what is their impact?)

Interventions undertaken for other reasons are being assessed for their possible impact on nutrition. (How does a clean water supply affect the incidence of diarrheal disease? How does a more abundant water supply affect sanitation? Disease? Malnutrition?)

Basic staple foods are being fortified and their impact on nutrient deficiency is being measured. (What happens to the incidence of Vitamin A deficiency when the entire processed sugar supply of the country is fortified, and what does this cost?)

Nutrition status surveys are being carried out to provide information to guide programming and new simple, low-cost methodologies are being employed for this purpose.

Governments are beginning to establish nutrition units in the national planning commission or as semi-autonomous agencies with responsibility and power to develop inter-sectoral nutrition plans and to coordinate their implementation.

Special tax monies are being earmarked for nutrtion programming. Support for programs is less ad hoc. In some countries nutrition is now a line item in the national budgets. Chiefs of state have promulgated policies and launched national campaigns serving notice that they consider the problem to be of high priority.

The process of systematic, inter-sectoral nutrition programming offers new hope that a significant impact can be made on the problem of malnutrition, which now affects several hundred million people around the world. However, the process is just beginning. There is a great need for trained personnel to institute effective analysis and planning, to implement programs and to evaluate them. There is a need for practical methodologies for incorporating nutrition goals into agriculture planning and programming. There is a need to devise effective strategies for reaching the rural poor.

Above all, there is a need for constant surveillance to ensure that the process of analysis and planning be kept simple and practical, that it not become an end in itself. Proposed new activities should be measured against one goal, whether they contribute to solving problems. Countries are beginning to commit greater amounts of their own personnel and money to addressing the malnutrition problem. This trend will continue and grow in direct proportion to the degree of success experienced by these new approaches.

MOISE C. MENSAH

Relationships of Food Supplies and Nutrition to Development

Development is certainly one of the most controversial issues in terms of definition. Both national and international levels have difficulty agreeing on what is the substance of it and what kind of actions can best make national and international communities benefit from that substance.

However, for the purpose of the 1976 World Food Conference which concerns itself with practical problem solving approaches to the World Food situation, development could mean the achievement of certain economic and social targets and subsequent sustained improvement of the living conditions of people in a given community be it a village or a nation. From a global point of view, one may find it convenient to endorse a definition by J. Grunwald (1971) suggesting that development is "a level of economic maturity" that would enable developing countries to enter into a "balanced competition" with developed nations, without inefficiency-bound protectionist measures. This two-level definition of development appears useful when dealing with the World Food problem which is a global problem with essentially country specific solutions.

The degree of achievement of development goals is usually assessed through indicators, the designation and number of which vary significantly from one source to another. For practical purposes, we shall consider that development implies that:

Moise C. Mensah is Vice Chairman and Executive Secretary, Consultative Group on Food Production and Investment in Developing Countries, 1818 H Street, N.W., Washington, D.C. 20433.

1. The following basic needs are adequately met: nutrition, shelter, health, education, leisure-recreation, and security.

2. After meeting those needs, surplus income is available for savings and investment to enable subsequent economic growth and further development.

3. Income is equitably distributed across socio-economic borders hopefully through appropriate employment policies and programs so that the gap between average net household income and the actual income levels at both ends of the social spectrum is minimized.

The purpose of this paper is to show how food supplies and nutrition affect the development process, that is the attainment of the above mentioned goals whether directly or indirectly.

NUTRITION AND DEVELOPMENT

Adequate nutrition is both a measure and a goal of development. Indeed it is the first priority target of any developmental efforts. Food has a dual function: it meets a basic physiological need but also has a social dimension which depends on taste, customs, wealth, etc. While recognizing the socio-cultural role which food performs, we would like at this stage to concern ourselves essentially with the nutritional aspects of food needs and their effect on development.

The first obvious question is what are those needs? For national and international planning purposes, the most important nutritional standards are those for energy and protein which are the essential factors in determining composition and cost of food supplies and can also give indications of nutritional risks among various population groups within a given community.

Energy requirements are defined as "the energy intake that is considered adequate to meet the energy needs of the average healthy person in a specified age/sex category" (Food and Agriculture Organization, 1973). This report also defined a "safe level of protein intake" that is "the amount of protein considered necessary to meet the physiological needs and maintain the health of nearly all individuals in a specified age/sex group." This safe level is, therefore, higher than the average requirement of protein.

The Expert Committee determined that for a reference man (65 kg, 20-39 years old, healthy) energy requirement ranges from 2,700 kcal to 4,000 kcal per day depending on whether he is involved in light activity or in exceptionally active work. His average need when he is moderately active would be 3,000 kcal or 46 kcal/kg of body weight.

A reference woman (55 kg, 20-39 years old, healthy) would require 2,000 kcal to 3,000 kcal per day with 2,200 kcal if moderately active, that is 40 kcal/kg of body weight.

Adjustments of energy requirements have to be made for weight and age. The requirements of infants, children and adolescents, taking into account maintenance and growth, vary from 820 kcal per day for a less than one-year old infant to 2,500 (female)-3,000 (male) at age 15. Pregnancy and lactation cost extra calories (total energy of pregnancy = 80,000 kcal and lactation = 100,000 kcal).

"The Committee considered that there was no quantifiable basis for connecting the resting and exercise energy requirements according to the climate. When physical activity is restricted by environmental factors, the category of activity should be adjusted accordingly."

As far as protein requirements are concerned, the Committee found that there was no substantial difference between the amount of nitrogen required per unit of body weight to maintain nitrogen equilibrium in men and women. It determined the average nitrogen intake to be 77 mg per kg of body weight per day "when the nitrogen is derived from milk, egg, casein or mixed diets containing animal protein . . . for subjects consuming cereals or vegetable diets 93 mg of nitrogen per kg." Using milk and egg as a basic protein source, the safe level of protein intake varies from 1.53 g per kg of body weight for the infant to 0,57/0,52 g per kg of body weight of the adult male/female. Adjusted levels for proteins of different qualities can be made based on estimates of the quality of proteins usually consumed compared to egg and milk.

Adjustments are also made for pregnant and lactating women (additional 9 g and 17 g per person per day respectively).

Having defined what nutritional requirements are let us now turn to the question of how deficient nutrition affects development.

Nutrition Affects Population Growth

Looking at the world map, one finds that there seems to be a positive correlation between malnutrition or undernourishment and the high rate of population increase. Table 1 shows the relationship between the degree of satisfaction of energy requirements and the rate of population growth.

Several explanations have been given to that phenomenon. For example, Josué de Castro suggested on the basis of studies made by physiologists that "peoples subjected to continued food deficiency, far from having their sexual appetite reduced, demonstrate an exaltation of that instinct and show a significant increase in fecundity" (Blanc, 1975). Other explanations relate poverty induced fecundity with socio-economic and cultural factors among which lack of a decent household income is a preeminent element. Inflated fecundity combined with reduced infant mortality results in increasing the size of malnourished

TABLE 1. Energy supply and population formulation

Regions	Energy Intake As Percent of Requirement		Rates of Growth of Population Percent per Year	
	1961	1969-71	1960-70	1970-85
North America	118	126	1.3	1.0
Western Europe	118	123	0.8	0.6
Oceania	121	123	1.9	1.8
Eastern Europe and				
USSR	116	127	1.0	0.9
Africa	91	94	2.5	2.9
Latin America	100	105	2.8	2.8
Near East	89	102	2.7	2.9
Far East	92	94	2.5	2.6
Asian Centrally				
Planned Economies	86	92	1.8	1.6
World	100	104	1.9	2.0

Source: Food and Agriculture Organization (1975).

populations, aggravating their already critical malnutritional
status and making it only more difficult to solve a community's
food problem.

Malnutrition Impedes Normal Development of Individuals

Studies carried out in Uganda by Dr. Dean, in Nigeria by
the Child Health Institute of Ibadan University and in
Senegal by the Center of Khombole (International Children Center) (Blanc, 1975) compared growth performances (weight, size)
of children at different ages and under various conditions
(African cities, African rural areas, European cities).

A depression in growth performance has been observed
between six months of age and four years which seems to be
attributed at least partly to malnutrition due to the succession of food deficit periods affecting both mothers and children.

Similarly and according to Berg (1973) "studies in Japan,
Taiwan and other countries witnessing nutritional improvement
in recent years all point to remarkable increase in stature."
Berg further quotes J. R. Bengoa of the World Health Organization as suggesting that "despite genetic differences and other
disease factors, . . . short stature in a population is now
regarded as an indication that malnutrition exists and plays an
important role in physical development in many developing countries."

Apart from physical development, malnutrition appears to
slow down the process of mental development. The real effect

of malnutrition here is less known than that on physical development because genetic factors, socio-economic environment and
other elements play an important role in mental development.
However, improvement of IQ has been obtained by Kugelmass in
1944 through improved nutrition of a group of malnourished
children over two years old (Kugelmass, 1944). While moderate
calorie/protein deficiency has only a minor influence on mental
development, severe and prolonged malnutrition during the first
year of life may result in permanent mental retardation (Pan
American Health Organization, 1964), and Cravioto suggests that
a child who is subjected to severe malnutrition before six
months of age will never catch up the loss in intellectual
capacity (Blanc, 1975). Also, hungry children find it difficult to perform well at school. Insofar as "brain power" is
the most precious instrument for economic development, it is
clear that losses in intellectual capacity due to malnutrition
constitute a constraint to the economic, social and cultural
development process.

Malnutrition Affects Health and Working Capacity

Malnutrition-caused diseases are well known. They may
affect adults under severe deficiency conditions but are
more common with children: (kwashiorkor, avitaminoses, etc.).
Malnutrition also prepares the ground for infections and parasitic diseases (measles, diarrheas, intestinal parasites, etc.)
which may slow down physical growth or even lead to death.

The effects of malnutrition on health may be costly to the
community.

Nearly half-a-million hospitalized patients from thirty-seven
developing countries were officially registered for malnutrition in 1968 (actual number may be higher due to classification for nutritional ailments under other diseases). At an
average cost of $7.5 a day for ninety days for each case,
costs of treating malnutrition are on the order of $340 mil-
lion a year to the thirty-seven countries. If treatment were
provided to the approximately 10 million pre-school age children who need it . . . annual costs would be on the order of
$6.8 billion (Berg, 1973).

Malnutrition also reduces working capacity. Based on Professor Lehman's studies on effects of food rationing on working
capacity, J. Blanc has established relationships between labour
productivity and the quantity of food intake (Blanc, 1975).
She suggests that for a man under light activity conditions a
shift from 2,400 kcal ration to 2,000 kcal results in a reduction from 100 percent productivity to 30 percent. Under moderate activity conditions 3,000 kcal, 2,500 kcal and 2,000 kcal
correspond to 100 percent, 58 percent and 27 percent produc-

tivity levels respectively. Under exceptionally active conditions, 4,200 kcal, 3,600 kcal and 3,000 kcal correspond to 100
percent, 76 percent and 55 percent productivity levels respectively.

Similarly, it has been shown that low productivity in
African farming is related to inadequate energy intake during
critical farming periods. For example, in West Africa nutritional surveys suggested that out of the 4,000 kcal needed for
normal rural activities (Fox, 1953) an average farmer would get
only 1,800 kcal to 2,500 kcal maximum which means only 1,000
kcal available for work since 1,500 kcal have to be spent on
basal metabolism and thermoregulation (Blanc, 1975). Malnutrition results in economic loss not only by reducing total output
because of lower productivity, but malnutrition also causes
economic loss through a reduction of working life span, and
this may be one of the basic factors underlining the gap
between developed and underdeveloped countries. As Berg (1973)
puts it,

> though life expectancy in a poor country jumps dramatically
> over the average person who survives the perils of young
> childhood, early adult mortality is still substantially
> greater than in industrialized countries. The average ten-
> year old boy in Chad, for example, can expect a life some
> fourteen years shorten than a ten-year old Indian and twenty-
> eight years shorter than the Taiwanese of the same age. The
> twenty-year old girl from Guinea looks forwards to approxi-
> mately half as many remaining years as her Swedish counter-
> part. Clearly their potential period of productive employ-
> ment is cut short and the potential return to investments
> during childhood reduced.

In trying to analyze the relationships of nutrition to
development, we have referred to various studies which propose
some answers to the question. However, there are still a number of areas where more research is needed to improve the quality of the answers. These areas have been identified by FAO
and WHO (Food and Agriculture Organization, 1973) as follows:
possibilities for catch-up growth for children and adolescents;
basal metabolic rates to reach commonly acceptable and reliable
tables; consequences of nutrition on physical inactivity bearing in mind the adverse effect on growth, psychomotor development and socio-economic consequences; effects of climate on
requirements; nutritional infection and parasitism; energy
intake and protein requirements.

FOOD SUPPLIES AND DEVELOPMENT
The assurance of food supply is a major preoccupation at
lower levels of development as shown by Table 2 which

indicates allocation of income for food purchases by people of some countries.

TABLE 2. Allocation of income for food expenditure by selected countries, mid-1960s

Country	Per capita GNP, in dollars[a]	Percent of expenditures allocated to food	Percent of increment of expenditures allocated to food	Animal protein as percent of total protein
Ghana	170	64	76	17
Ceylon	180	56	79	18
Honduras	260	47	40	27
Malaysia	330	49	37	30
Sweden	2,620	32	20	69
USA	3,980	23	20	72

Source: Berg, 1973, p. 41.
[a] Gross National Products are for 1971.

We have already discussed how food supplies and related nutritional levels affect the health and productivity of society. Food supplies also perform other economic functions: food production can be the leading economic sector, food supply can promote employment and capital formation; food production can be a major foreign exchange earner.

Takahashi (1969) submits that agriculture development was the foundation of Japan's modern economic development by providing "the largest foothold of Japan's modern manufacturing industry in the Meiji era." In fact foodgrains (mainly rice and wheat) represented between 60 to 70 percent of total agricultural production value during the period reviewed (1874-1914). Food production enabled farmers to pay land taxes representing 80 percent of total government tax income during the first half of the Meiji decade before declining progressively to 20 percent at the end. Farmers were also the largest group of domestic purchasers of locally manufactured goods until the beginning of this century, and their productive power was the main source of capital required. Moreover, agriculture productivity was good enough to enable the release of farming labour to industry without jeopardizing food production.

The leading role of food production may even be more apparent when considering the People's Republic of China whose "agriculture today feeds a quarter of the world population on 7 percent of the globe's cultivated land . . . responded to the demands of a rising population and still was able to provide a small surplus for the rich, the arts and industrialization" Perkins, 1969). Analyzing the relationships between urbaniza-

tion, famine and the market for grain, Perkins states "clearly
the Chinese grain market has influenced agricultural productivity in general and the yields of major crops in particular. . . . For a region to specialize in cash crops or handi-
craft manufacturers, it had to be reasonably certain that a
cheap source of food would always be available." This statement related to pre-revolution China seems to still hold true
as the Chinese Government continued importing 5 to 6 million
tons of grain a year even after recovery from the 1959-61 harvest failures to ensure that inadequate food supplies will not
hamper economic development efforts.

In economically successful Korea (South), it was recognized during the preparation of the Second Development Plan,
1972-76, that "the rapid growth of the Korean economy has . . .
resulted in a wide disparity between industry and agriculture,
persistent food shortages . . . and strains on the country's
foreign exchange reserves due to food import requirements.
Thus the relative stagnancy in agriculture may become a major
constraint to continue economic development" (Suh, 1971).
Hence, top priority was given to achieving self-sufficiency in
food production during the Second Economic Development Plan
period.

Experience of international food aid has shown that
increased supplies through external sources have enabled a number of countries (particularly in South Asia and West Africa)
to save foreign exchange, to build up local currency resources,
to undertake labor intensive investment programs in urban and
rural communities thereby creating employment opportunities and
promoting capital formation particularly in rural areas.

PROSPECTS FOR INCREASED FOOD SUPPLIES

The total world demand for food will grow in volume at a
2.4 percent per year rate between now and 1985, while production will grow at 2.7 percent per year (Food and Agriculture Organization, 1975). These figures, however, hide great
discrepancies between various regions. Demand growth in Africa,
the Far East/Asia, Latin America and the Near East will be
respectively 3.8 percent, 3.4 percent, 3.6 percent, and 4 per-
cent while production will increase annually by only 2.5 per-
cent, 2.4 percent, 2.9 percent and 3.1 percent respectively. On
the opposite side, demand in developed countries will grow at
1.5 percent against 2.8 percent for production. Asian centrally planned economies would have 3.1 percent increase in
demand and 2.6 percent in production.

Food deficit in cereal terms (which are the main calorie/
protein sources) would rise from 85 to 100 million tons per year
by 1985 (three times the level of 1969-71). The projections
assume "normal production conditions" which means that the situation could be slightly better or considerably worse.

In theory, 80-100 million tons of cereals could be found somewhere around the planet to fill the deficit countries' gap. It has been suggested that the "North American Bread Basket" (USA and Canada) which has become a traditional supplier of food to the rest of the world could play an active and important role in filling part of the gap while at the same time using the food power to bring about changes in food and population policies around the world.

Whatever the amount of food aid provided from external sources, it seems obvious for financial, economic and political reasons that no independent country may keep on indefinitely depending on foreign aid for a basic need such as food. Moreover, the best way of ensuring adequate food supply to the poorer sections of the poorer countries is by helping the populations concerned produce more food by and for themselves thereby finding a short-cut solution to income distribution problems. Therefore, a major task has to be undertaken by developing countries, particularly the food deficit ones, to meet as much as possible of their food gap. It is in recognition of that fact that the World Food Conference has decided to create three new bodies: the World Food Council, the International Fund for Agricultural Development and the Consultative Group on Food Production and Investment in Developing Countries (CGFPI). The latter institution concerns itself with increasing food production in developing countries through (a) improvement of local investment resource utilization efficiency; (b) increasing the flow of external aid going to food production; and (c) coordinating external resource flows in order to increase their efficiency. Among various measures, one important step developing countries would have to take is to pay special attention to the establishment of well conceived and documented food plans which would describe the present food and nutrition status, predict the future food needs (1985 or 2000) bearing in mind nutritional requirements and propose production programs to meet these needs. The food plan would also analyze in depth policy implications including measures to break existing technical, institutional, socio-economic and political bottlenecks. It is expected that such food plans will attract interest from the international donor community and result in increased aid to national food self-sufficiency efforts.

Achievement of greater self-sufficiency at a reasonable cost may not be an impossible task. Rice production could be doubled in about 15 years (1974-90) in Asian developing countries if a "master plan for irrigation improvement" with appropriate support in inputs supply and research were implemented. The program would cost 67 billion of 1975 dollars or about 4.5 billion per year and would "achieve a long-term, stable and self-sufficient supply of rice in Asia but at the same time, it is intended as an anti-recession measure by stimulating export demand in the developed countries" (Okita and Takase, 1976).

CONCLUSION

Food supply affects economic growth and development efforts both through its consequences on nutritional levels and the direct impact of the related economic activities. The world is moving towards an era of increasing food gap in developing countries. While external food aid can and should play a significant role in helping to bridge the gap, the best the international community could do is to offer increased support to national food self-sufficiency efforts which only can provide the most durable solution to the World Food Problem.

REFERENCES

Berg, A. 1973. The Nutrition Factor. The Brookings Institute, Washington, D.C.

Blanc, J. 1975. Malnutrition et sous-developpement. University of Grenoble Press, Grenoble, France.

Food and Agriculture Organization of the UN. 1973. Energy and protein requirements: Report of a joint FAO/WHO ad hoc expert committee. Rome, Italy.

Food and Agriculture Organization of the UN. 1975. Food and Nutrition 1: No. 1, Rome, Italy.

Fox. 1953. A study of expenditures of Africans engaged in rural activities. University of London, London, England.

Grunwald, J. 1971. Some reflexians on Latin American industrialization. In P. Aydalot, Essai sur la théorie du developpement. Editions Cujas, Paris, France.

Kugelmass, I. N., L. E. Paull and E. L. Samuel. 1944. Nutritional improvement of child mentality. Amer. V. Med. Sciences 208:631.

Okita, S. and K. Takase. 1976. Doubling rice production program in Asia. Overseas Economic Corporation Fund, Tokyo, Japan.

Pan American Health Organization. 1964. Research in protein/calorie malnutrition. World Health Organization, Geneva, Switzerland.

Perkins, D. H. 1969. Agricultural Development in China 1368-1968. Edinburgh University Press, Edinburgh, Scotland.

Suh, B. K. 1971. The Strategy for Agricultural Development in Korea. Samhwa Corporation Publishers, Seoul, Korea.

Takahashi, K. 1969. The Rise and Development of Japan's Modern economy. The Jiji Press Ltd., Tokyo, Japan.

JOHN P. LEWIS

National Self-Sufficiency and International Dependency

National self-sufficiency in food is an old idea--at least a very old practice--that for the past decade or so has come into vogue again. For the medium term it is a necessary and important objective for many, probably most, poor countries. Yet for the long term, country-by-country self-reliance in food production would represent a poor way to organize the world food economy. In the short run it is beyond the reach of many countries. And even for the medium term, the objective is one that invites closer approach, not perfect achievement.

Indeed the idea of food self-sufficiency has become so fashionable lately that one must take some pains not to be carried away by it. Historically the world food economy has had a pattern of local self-reliance, but the pattern was not benign. Until about 150 years ago virtually all populated territories the size of most present-day countries grew the major share of their own food. They had no alternative. But then changes in transport technology made it feasible and cheaper to move bulk food long distances. The trade in food that has developed since, has been overwhelmingly beneficial because different territories have very different comparative advantages and disadvantages in food production. Some of these are natural. Some are related to population density and the degree to which the people are engaged in nonagricultural activities.

The current food self-sufficiency syndrome is becoming so strong that one begins to find it applied to subnational regions. Yet few are arguing that it is time for my state of

John P. Lewis is Professor of Economics and International Affairs, Princeton University, Princeton, New Jersey, USA.

New Jersey to shake loose from its food dependence on the likes
of Iowa. A recent and illuminating study of Indian food distribution established that differential food availabilities per
capita, state by state, were most strongly correlated, not with
differential incomes, but with differential food <u>outputs</u> state
by state. The policy conclusion drawn by the authors was not
that the national food distribution system needs improvement;
but that each of India's food deficit states needs to become
self-supporting (Raj et al., 1975).

This last view of subnational jurisdictions is still probably a minority view. Most of us remain content with the proposition that within national jurisdictions trade between food
surplus and food deficit areas makes abundant good sense. The
self-sufficiency we advocate we limit to the national level.
Even here we are on fairly weak theoretical ground. There is
no necessary reason why the political boundaries that get drawn
around particular nation states must encompass enough area with
comparative agricultural advantage to feed the national population adequately and efficiently. Some counter cases are obvious. Take Singapore. It is scarcely more feasible--or desir-
able--for Singapore to become self-sufficient in food than it
is for New York City to do so. Historically there have been
such larger classic cases as the United Kingdom and Japan in
which a large measure of external food dependency has been an
integral ingredient of the national development process.

Moreover, if one is contemplating the long-run rationalization of the world food economy, there is no reason to expect
the case of food-surplus <u>countries</u> and food-deficit countries
to be exceptional. On the contrary, if, as much of this conference is suggesting, the overriding problem will be the adequacy of <u>world</u> food production relative to food needs, a long
run norm of nation-by-nation self-sufficiency would aggravate
that overriding problem. It would substitute some New Jersey-
like agriculture for some Iowa-like agriculture, where the
opportunity costs are lower and the yields per unit of total
inputs, correctly priced, are higher. As a result, long-term
growth of world food production would be retarded.

These rather simple but, it seems to me, inescapable propositions lead to two conclusions. First, rather than being an
ultimate solution, the goal of national food self-sufficiency
is an interim, second-best solution for an imperfect world.
Second, beyond this interim problem, which preoccupies us and
to which these remarks now turn, lies the fascinating further
question of how the world will move beyond a way-stop of
greater national food self-sufficiency into a new and superior
pattern of food specialization and trade. This latter issue
has been little analyzed. It includes questions of what the
world costs of excessive and excessively prolonged autarky
would be; of which new areas, with further agricultural development, might become net food exporters. For example, despite

its great population burden, the Indo-Gangetic plain may have
the soils, groundwater, and sunlight to become a net food
exporter. Another question is how, in the beyond-self-suffi-
ciency era, deficit countries and areas can be assured adequate
food security. Thus the longer-run problem and prospects constitute an important field for future research.

Having finished the debunking phase of my talk, I now turn
to the "second-best, interim" objective of greater national
food self-sufficiency. I fully agree that at present this is--
and should be--an important goal for most poor countries. The
rightness and salience of the objective has two general
rationales, one global, the other national.

From a global perspective, the push of poor countries
toward food self-sufficiency becomes in the medium term a rough
but reasonable surrogate for a global production and distribution optimizing strategy. In general those poor countries with
food deficits are also the ones where there are easily secured
opportunities for increasing food production, in the sense that
the marginal returns to marginal human and other investments in
agriculture are likely to be higher there than elsewhere. For
example, the same increments in fertilizer use or in water-
management investment are, when optimally deployed, likely to
yield greater output gains in South Asia than they would either
in Japan or the USA. Furthermore, the poor food-deficit countries tend to be those with the lowest per capita incomes and
the largest masses of low-end poor. Thus there is some probability, although no assurance in the absence of implementing
policies, that production gains that occur within these countries, will have a better chance of augmenting the diets of
these poorest people of the world than would equivalent production gains occurring at more remote places on the planet.

On both production and distribution counts, therefore,
developing country food strategies that aim for self-sufficiency are likely for the time being to serve global welfare.
At the same time there is no global national case, for a poor
country, such as Pakistan that achieves self-sufficiency sooner
than most, to relax its agricultural expansion efforts.

The self-interested national, as opposed to global,
rationale for the attainment of self-sufficiency is familiar,
and there is no need to rehearse it at much length. In poor
countries large parts of the population are engaged in or
dependent on agriculture. Food still claims a large fraction
of real national income. It is the most urgent, least post-
ponable requirement. To assure the availability and accessibility of food to the people is the national government's most
pressing obligation. When a country slips into food deficit,
it can be victimized by international food-price inflation if
much of the rest of the world is doing the same. The country's
fragile balance of payments position quickly can be fractured
by food imports; its development program becomes the hostage of

stop-go food financing; and if sufficient imports cannot be
obtained and/or afforded, the consequence, along with painful
hardship, mainly for the low-end poor, is likely to be internal
turmoil. It is the rare government in such a country that is
not now determined to achieve greater food self-reliance.

It is useful to divide this felt need into two components:
secular and, if the term may be used somewhat loosely, cyclical. On the secular side, the majority of poor countries lack
exceptionally buoyant, windfall export prospects, from oil or
otherwise, and very few governments are normally prepared to
program for continuing, let alone widening, food deficits. In
the near and medium terms they will lack the foreign exchange
to service such deficits commercially. And they doubt that
concessional food assistance will be available in sufficient
quantity to cover such persistent, especially widening, short-
falls in domestic production, or, if it is available, that it
will be distributed among claimants in accordance with need.
They doubt that if both of these conditions were met, that aid
would come free of unacceptable political and other strings,
especially from bilateral donors. Thus secular self-reliance
is a widely sought goal.

In many ways the problems posed by short-run, season-to-
season and year-to-year, fluctuations in developing countries'
domestic food output are just as traumatic. In the prevalent
preoccupation with the secular relations among output, population, and incomes, the problems of fluctuation tend to be
underrated. Even if a country is on a track of secular self-
reliance, a failed monsoon or widespread and devastating floods
can expose it to wrenching shortages and to the vagaries of the
volatile international foodgrains market. It may lead to soar-
ing domestic food prices that deprive the poor, to partially
irreversible cost-push inflation and to massive strains on its
political fabric. Moreover, the poorest countries tend to have
the least savings of all kinds to cope with such setbacks. And
most of these countries are grouped in climatic zones, especially those of South Asia and Central Africa, that are especially subject to wide annual variations in the weather. For
such countries a meaningful concept of self-sufficiency must
include a built-in cushion against feast and famine.

This brings us to the subject of policy--domestic policies
of the poor countries themselves for building greater self-
sufficiency in the medium term, and policies by which external
actors can reinforce these efforts. As to secular self-reliance, restraints on population growth have a clear bearing, as
will policies that moderate and structure the growth of
national food demand, for example, by retarding the shift of
diets towards such resource-extravagant foods as beef and, in
particular, by promoting a more equitable distribution of food
between rich and poor. Clearly the main requirement for secular self-reliance is more effective promotion of agricultural

production within the developing countries--mostly through own-
country efforts but with the assistance also of the international community. As much of the dialogue of this conference
reflects, this priority is now almost universally agreed upon.
Plainly, this is not the moment for trying to spell out its
implications. But it is the most pivotal of all the policy
needs.

Nearly as pivotal is the need to smooth the fluctuations
of food supplies and prices in the poor countries. Here much
of the answer is a system of stocks that can mediate between
fluctuating output and stable consumption, by storing surpluses
in particularly good years and depleting stocks in bad years.
Countries which want to be self-reliant in their cushioning of
fluctuations, cannot in times of shortage rely on imports--even
concessional imports--or to have their buffer stocks held for
them by donor countries or even by international authorities.
They will want their first-line buffers held in-country and the
precise ownership and deployment to be subject to effective
public management in behalf of food supply and price stabilization.

The success of such a policy mechanism will depend mainly
on the poor countries' own effort, consistency of purpose, and
skills. It requires the ability to procure, build and hold
stocks to public account, to run a regime of storage, transfer,
and turnover that minimizes losses, and to manage acquisitions
and releases of stocks in a way that is in fact stabilizing
rather than destabilizing. But, given the average poverty and
low saving capacity of the poor countries, donors abroad can
also help in this process. It will greatly facilitate the
speed and scale with which in-country buffers can be built and
the degree to which countries can insulate their consumers,
especially the low-end poor, from the damaging effects of output fluctuations, if much of the needed investment in public
stocks can be provided via concessional foreign transfers.

This brings me, finally, to a word about food aid in the
context of national self-sufficiency and international dependency. The conventional wisdom is right: in the past at times
food aid undermined domestic food production incentives and
therefore slowed some of the poor countries' approach toward
self-reliance. This does not have to be; now, with both host
governments and donor governments and agencies adamantly on
guard against precisely this danger, the alleged disincentive
effects are a foolish basis upon which to rule all developmental food aid out of bounds.

The use of food aid both for stock building, as just discussed, and as "food financing" for labor surplus absorbing
construction and other generally familiar investment activities
is perfectly consistent with a policy of secular self-reliance.
It should not encroach on the internal production incentives
needed for implementing that objective. Particulary in the

case of the USA during the same medium term in which the poor
countries are seeking food self-sufficiency, such food aid can
provide an important vehicle for the continuing net transfers
that, under the doctrine of the New International Economic
Order, the same poor countries are, in my judgment, rightly
demanding. If the aid can go as grants, without unreasonable
conditions, and through either multilateral or bilateral channels be more equitably distributed than has American aid in
recent years, such transfers can play a role that actually fur-
thers, not retards, the interim objective of national food
self-sufficiency. Beyond that, especially by helping to build
a system of reliable food security based on a structure of adequate, well managed, country-by-country food stocks, it can
serve to lay groundwork for the longer-run rationalization of
the world food economy to which nation-state self-sufficiency
should eventually give way.

All of which make food aid a rather nice case in point for
my starting proposition that national food self-sufficiency,
while a worthy and needed objective for the time being, should
not be enshrined as an absolute without regard to the larger
purposes it is supposed to serve.

REFERENCES

Raj, K. N., N. Krishnaji, T. N. Krishnan, I. S. Gulati,
     P. K. G. Panikar, A. V. Jose, P. R. Gopinathan Nair. 1975.
     Poverty, Unemployment and Development Policy: A Case Study
     of Selected Issues with Reference to Kerla. Department of
     Economic and Social Affairs, United Nations, New York, USA.

3

National and International Policy

MARIO VALDERRAMA
EDGARDO MOSCARDI

Current Policies Affecting Food Production: The Case of Wheat in the Andean Region

The case of wheat in the Andean Region is illustrative of the effect of government policies on food production and trade. The amount of wheat produced and consumed in the last 15 years has been crucially determined by import policies followed by Bolivia, Colombia, Ecuador and Perú.

These countries began to import increasing quantities of wheat in the mid-1950s, probably as a consequence of two facts: 1) a food gap emerging from the rapid rise in the demand for food, which is likely to occur when economic growth is linked with both a positive marginal propensity to consume and an income elasticity of relatively high demand; and 2) externally subsidized prices, reinforced in some instances by overvalued domestic currencies. These large imports of wheat were commonly made under special agreements, such as the USA P.L. 480, to alleviate the food price increase generated by demand-pull

---

Mario Valderrama is Coordinator, Rural Development, Ford Foundation, Apartado Aereo 52986, Bogotá, Colombia.

Edgardo Moscardi is Economist for Centro Internacional de Majoramiento de Maiz y Trigo (CIMMYT), Londres 40, Mexico 6, D. F., Mexico.

This paper is based on four reports drafted by the authors with CIMMYT and Ford Foundation financing. The authors want to acknowledge the valuable comments and editing assistance received from J. R. Himes and Reed Hertford of the Ford Foundation, Bogotá. This paper, however, is the authors' full responsibility. The ideas and impressions presented are not necessarily those of either the Ford Foundation or the International Maize and Wheat Improvement Center.

inflation and reduce the need to divert scarce foreign exchange resources from the importation of capital goods. But from the point of view of importing government agencies, the P.L. 480 agreement also had the advantage of generating a profit by establishing domestic prices well above import costs while still making the consumer better off.

How did massive imports of wheat affect domestic production capacity? What was the fate of national wheat producers? A means of avoiding negative effects would have been to improve domestic wheat quality and productivity. However, this did not happen and import policies over the long haul contributed to the drastic reduction observed in domestic production and the exit of many producers from the industry.

This paper will describe the main effects of import policies followed by four countries of the Andean Region and explain their rationale.

THE FACTS

Available historical data for the Andean Region indicate that, while domestic production of wheat decreased at an average rate of about 2 percent per year, total consumption increased 6.5 percent per year, well above the rates of population growth (Table 1). Deficits have been covered by imports, which have risen at an average rate of 13 percent per year. Under these circumstances, imports have come to account for 80 percent of wheat consumption.

Due to the wheat price increase in the international markets of 1972-73, the P.L. 480 agreement reached its end; as a consequence, the four countries rely only on commercial imports to the extent that at present the value of wheat imports ranks first among food items (Table 1). An economic policy oriented toward protecting the consumer, however, has made governments spend considerable sums to subsidize imports. Due to almost 20 years of externally subsidized wheat prices, this cereal has become a basic food in the popular diet with levels of consumption per person shown in Table 1. Perú, for example, spent US$5 million per month in 1975 to subsidize wheat imports, which represented 40 percent of the final price to consumers.

With the possible exception of Bolivia, the land area devoted to wheat has been falling sharply. The area currently dedicated to growing wheat in Colombia is only a fourth of that cultivated in the 1950s; land in wheat production in Ecuador today (1976) is about half of that cultivated in 1969: and in Perú the area in wheat is down by about a fifth from its level of the late 1950s. Lands previously dedicated to wheat are now mainly in pasture, especially in Colombia and Ecuador (Table 2, Figure 1).

Not only were cultivated areas greater in earlier years, but they involved farms with different structural characteris-

TABLE 1. Basic data on wheat consumption, production, and research in the Andean Region

	Bolivia	Colombia	Ecuador	Peru
Production growth rate	-2.0 (1964-74)	-2.8 (1950-74)	-0.7 (1962-72)	-2.0 (1959-75)
Consumption growth rate	4.5 (1964-74)	6.8 (1950-74)	7.0 (1962-72)	7.6 (1959-75)
Rate of growth of imports	6.5 (1964-74)	14.0 (1950-74)	5.28 (1962-72)	27.0 (1959-75)
Imports/consumption, 1975	0.85	0.75	0.80	0.90
Order of importance in terms of value of agricultural imports, 1975	1	1	1	1
Per capita cost of wheat imports per year, 1975 (US$)	8	3	5	11
Subsidy per ton imported, 1975 (US$/Ton)	60	0	55	90
Maximum cultivated area, 1950-1975 (Ha)	80,000 (1975)	195,000 (1954)	100,000 (1969)	160,000 (1967)
Per capita consumption, 1975 (Kg)	45	24	27	62
Percentage of wheat area cultivated by small farms	80	65	50	80
Yield gap, 1975-1976 (improved cultivars/native cultivars)	1.0	2.5	3.2	1.5
Percentage of cultivated area fertilized, 1975-1976	10	15	30	10
Number of improved cultivars produced by crossing, 1955-1975	0	16	8	9
Percentage of area cultivated with improved cultivars, 1975	30	40	60	20
Average national yield, 1974-1975 (Kg/Ha)	850	1,350	1,000	1,140
Nitrogen price/wheat price, 1975 (US$/Ton)	6.0	2.7	3.1	1.1?
Price/wheat price, 1975 (US$/Ton)	-	3.7	2.8	1.1?

TABLE 2. Domestic production, imports, and consumption of wheat in four Andean countries, 1950-1975, metric tons, thousands

Years	Bolivia Output	Imports	Con.[a]	Colombia Output	Imports	Con.[a]	Ecuador Output	Imports	Con.[a]	Peru Output	Imports	Con.[a]
1950		57		102	67	169		36			246	
1951		-		130	58	188		-			198	
1952		91		140	47	187		55			242	
1953		87		143	45	188		31			260	
1954		86		146	70	216		72			256	
1955		65		167	62	229		-			306	
1956		34		160	92	252		66			295	
1957		142		157	113	270		44			298	
1958		93		129	102	231	42	41	83	138	285	443
1959		114		131	130	261	39	52	91	162	336	497
1960		108		140	108	248	47	34	77	154	360	512
1961		103		135	134	269	-	50	-	154	427	579
1962	67	-		145	136	281	78	-	110	153	415	565
1963	-	-		125	93	218	78	-	106	153	362	514
1964	52	142	197	115	159	274	67	65	101	143	393	535
1965	46	168	214	110	180	290	67	55	122	147	464	610
1966	58	165	223	110	250	360	69	68	129	145	493	638
1967	60	204	264	100	171	271	86	68	128	152	493	645
1968	45	178	223	105	231	336	91	70	163	113	626	739
1969	47	123	170	72	244	316	94	67	153	127	682	809
1970	62	133	195	56	330	386	90	70	160	125	526	647
1971	-	139	153	47	385	432	69	92	161	122	696	818
1972	51	158	209	68	416	484	56	130	-	140	853	993
1973	57	119	176	73	399	472	48	131	-	142	750	892
1974	63	149	212	48	419	467	60	154	-	142	773	850
1975	-	-	-	44	320	364	-	-	-	-	-	-

Sources: FAO Yearbooks and national sources quoted in the four reports. Figures differ depending on the sources.
Note: In general, "Consumption" is the summation of output and imports.
[a] Consumption.

222

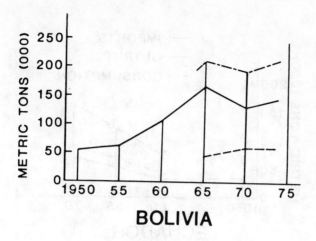

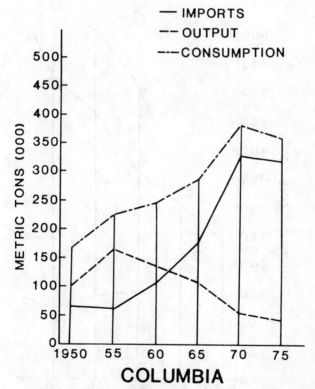

FIG. 1. Domestic production, consumption, and imports of wheat
in four Andean countries, 1950-1975. Metric tons (000).

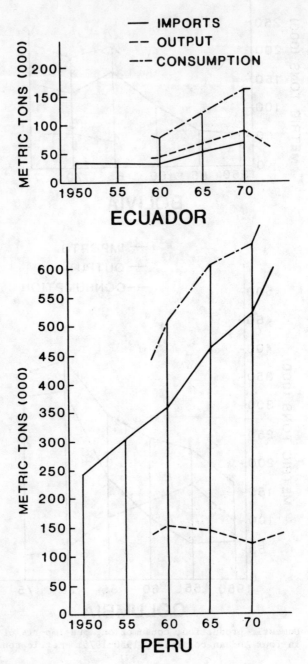

FIG. 1. (continued)

tics and greater access to available technology. At present,
close to 70 percent of the cultivated area is in small farms
with less than 10 ha.

The current genetic and technological potential would
allow for increased production. The increase in production,
nevertheless, can only come from the cooperative efforts of
research and extension services, government policy-makers, and
farmers. Currently, land area fertilized is only about 15 percent of the total area in wheat. No more than about 40 percent
of the cultivated land is sown with improved cultivars. This
area could be expanded since wheat research programs have
delivered 32 improved cultivars in the past; and it is estimated that six cultivars with good quality characteristics and
yields are ready for release to farmers. The extension and
agricultural credit infrastructures are, in general, poorly
developed, particularly for small farms that are turning out
most of the Region's wheat. Current average yields are only
slightly over 1 ton per ha.

Although the situation varies among the different countries, there are two principal factors relating to the P.L. 480
agreement that have discouraged domestic production. One was
the desire of the governments to obtain additional financing
from the agreement; second was the fact that, strictly speaking,
domestic wheat was different from imported wheat. The desire
of the governments to profit from the P.L. 480 agreement was
responsible for the lack of promotion of research on wheat,
while the inferior quality of domestically produced wheat was
responsible for the low price the millers were willing to pay
for it. Although it is true that prices fixed by the government for wheat produced locally tended to decrease in constant
value terms, they were established close to the price fixed by
the governments for imported wheat and to levels that would
allow for a rate of return comparable to those of other crops.
Imported wheat, however, had three advantages over domestic
wheat: the grain came ready for processing, it allowed for
higher flour extraction, and it had better baking quality.
These reasons, plus the fact that most mills were established
to process only imported wheat (and lacked grading and drying
equipment necessary to treat the humid, poorer quality grains
hauled directly from the field to the mills by domestic producers) made farmers incur higher transaction costs to sell their
product. In doing so they received prices well below official
levels, which explains the fact that, in practice, the profitability of wheat was lower than that of other crops. As a consequence, farmers with relatively high opportunity costs abandoned wheat production. The only farmers who continued to produce wheat were those able to obtain a net profit at low prices,
or farmers who produced regardless of whether or not profits
were made. In Colombia, for example, one region with predominantly small farms that occupied third place in production 10-

15 years ago, now ranks first, due to the decreased production
in regions where large commercial wheat farms predominated.
In Peru, 97 percent of wheat production was confined to the
highlands, and the product was not sold to the coastal mills,
but consumed within the same region.

In view of the recent increase in world prices of wheat,
governments are now interested in increasing domestic wheat
production. They have found, however, that they lack the
infrastructure to meet desired goals. Research programs do not
have enough resources to continue work on new cultivars and
cropping methods; the capacity to train production agronomists
is practically nonexistent; and seed multiplication and diffusion programs are grossly inadequate.

In summary, the wheat production capacity in the Andean
Region was reduced so drastically by import policies that relatively large investments are now needed to improve research,
extension, and production capabilities if a larger share of
total consumption is to be produced locally. Such results
could have been foreseen. What, then, was the basic rationale
for the policies that were followed? In order to learn from
past experiences and to avoid possible negative effects of
future import policies, this question is more relevant today
than ever before, since farmers in the Andean Region are in the
process of adopting non-traditional inputs whose expanded use
depends on their relative profitability.

RATIONALE OF THE POLICY
    Although a specific government policy cannot be explained
    by any single cause, it is possible to identify major
    determining factors. One factor is the policy related to
the wage level predominant in a given society. Through a relatively complicated mechanism, every society maintains a level
of wages that depends on the productivity of resources and
labor, culture, climate, customs, etc. In developing countries
low prices of food is one way to maintain wage levels within
certain limits, without drastically reducing the standard of
living. At low per capita income levels (for 1960 they were:
Colombia US$225, Ecuador US$200, Perú US$191, Bolivia US$90), a
high percentage of the household budget is used for food.
Meyer (1974, p. 6) estimated that for Bogotá 53 percent of the
total expenditure of workers in the two lowest income quartiles
was dedicated to food and beverages; the corresponding figure
for Lima was 49 percent.

    For the countries under analysis, it is well known that
the elasticity of the domestic supply for food has been and is,
to a certain extent, relatively low. Restraints on supply have
been due mainly to structural obstacles (land tenure, government policies, international structure of production, etc.) and
the consequent inadequacy of physical inputs and technology

levels needed to increase productivity. As a result, a food
gap was likely to emerge together with a general increase in
food prices generated by demand-pull inflation.

Under these circumstances, one way of ensuring low prices
for food is to concentrate food production among small farmers
who have few alternative means of employment and who produce
regardless of whether or not an adequate return is obtained for
land, capital, and other "fixed" assets. Another way of
achieving the same objective is to take advantage of opportunities to import low-cost food, as presented by the wheat surpluses in the USA.

Let us review the situation regarding wheat supplies.
North American wheat production was heavily subsidized, resulting in substantial surpluses. These surpluses were sold abroad
at international market prices (P_i), which were then artificially lower than world market prices (P_w). Therefore, purchasing countries faced two supply curves: a domestic supply
curve, S_d, and a foreign supply curve, S_i, with infinite elasticity over most of the relevant range (Figure 2). If Q_t is
the total quantity of wheat a country needs, the quantities to
be produced domestically and imported would be Q_d^* and Q_t-Q_d^*,
respectively. The immediate results of this situation were the
acquisition of a greater quantity of the product than could
have been bought at the world market price, P_w; a reduction of
levels of domestic production; and an increase in domestic consumption.

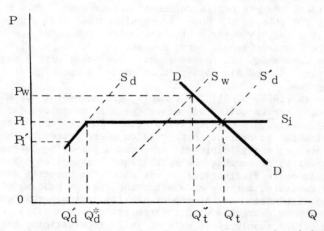

FIG. 2.   Schematic relationship between wheat produced domestically and that imported at different prices. See
text.

If governments had wished to increase national consumption
and meet that increase with domestic production, they would
have had to do so by applying additional resources and technology, so that S_d could be displaced to the right to S'_d (Figure
2). Even assuming that the new technology had allowed national
producers to turn out the required quantity at the price level
P_i, this type of decision would have been termed as inefficient
because it involved further expenses to engage additional
resources and to generate and adapt new technology at a time
when the required quantities were available in the international market at P_i. Furthermore, governments and importers
could obtain net profit from imports. It was not in the governments' interest, therefore, to develop the productive capacity to increase national production of wheat. On the contrary,
their interest was to increase total consumption and reduce
national production, so that use of imported wheat in the diet
would be greater, thus contributing to a reduction in the cost
of food and, consequently, an ability to maintain a generally
low level of wages.

EFFECTS OF THE POLICY
     This import policy produced other effects as well:
     1). Massive imports of wheat at a low price not only pro-
duced changes along the domestic supply curve of wheat faced by
consumers, but changed it into a supply curve with infinite
elasticity.
     There is evidence to support this assertion. In terms of
constant values, wheat prices tended to decrease until 1972,
while total and per capita consumption increased. This result
is only possible if the domestic supply curve is displaced to
the right, say, by using better technology. However, we know
that the domestic supply curve has not moved, but massive
imports were made. The consumer was thus faced with a supply
curve that allowed him to obtain unlimited quantities at a
given price.
     Duran (1974, p. 3), for example, estimated for Colombia
(with data series collected before the rise in prices due to
the elimination, in October 1974, of the import subsidy paid by
the Colombian government) a regression where prices to the consumer are not significant, either because prices do not vary
sufficiently, or because the established consumption habits are
such that price fluctuations do not alter the quantity demanded.
On the contrary, surveys made after the rise of prices following the elimination of the import subsidy indicate that quantities demanded decreased with the new price increases, as would
happen with a supply curve without infinite elasticity, as
shown in Table 3.
     2). The lower price also reduced domestic production of
products occupying a similar place in diets, such as corn, rice,

TABLE 3.   Quantities of wheat flour acquired before and after
           the change in price to bakeries of Bogotá, Colombia

Income strata	Quantity purchased, Kg Jan-Aug[a] 1974	March[a] 1975	Price paid US$/Kg Jan-Aug 1974	March 1975	Percent variation Q	P	Arc elasticity of demand
High	22.4	19.0	0.135	0.353	-15	162	-0.18
Medium	76.2	45.7	0.151	0.355	-40	135	-0.62
Low	42.7	33.6	0.150	0.361	-21	141	-0.29
Average	47.1	32.8	0.145	0.357	-31	146	-0.43

Source: Colombia, Ministry of Agriculture, IDEMA, 1975.
[a]The subsidy was eliminated in October 1974. US$1 = Col.$30.

potatoes, cassava, etc. In a given period of time, the total
quantity demanded of this group of products will be fixed and
the proportion consumed of each item will depend on income,
elasticity, relative price, and consumption habits. If the
price of a product such as wheat decreases, in comparison to
alternative products, consumption will increase at the expense
of other products of the group. Although the sum of the
decrease of the other products is likely to be lower than the
increase of wheat consumption, because a portion will produce a
net improvement in the diet of consumers, there is evidence
that products of direct consumption produced by small farms
have had low, and in some cases negative, rates of growth. For
Perú, the annual rates of growth of potato production from 1959
to 1969 were +5 percent, corn +7.7 percent, barley -2 percent,
and oats -9 percent; from 1963 to 1967, quinua -6 percent, and
from 1959 to 1967, cassava +6.5 percent. The production of
rice, a commercial crop, grew +14 percent from 1963 to 1969.
For the period 1950-1969, the annual rates of growth for production in Colombia were: +8 percent for rice, again a commercial crop, +3.8 percent for potatoes, -1.2 percent for beans,
and +0.5 percent for barley. A similar trend is observed for
Ecuador in barley and maize.
     3). As national producers did not have a supply curve
with infinite elasticity, the lower price P_i led them to reduce
production. Moreover, the fact that domestic wheat was of
inferior quality, because of the lack of grading and drying
equipment, made the price P'_i, with further reduction in domestic production and the exit of many farmers from the industry.
Since the farmers with more access to available technology left
production, both research and extension were discouraged and
the whole wheat production system stagnated. The domestic supply curve did not move to the right to meet a larger demand by
using new resources and better technology but remained at, or
below, the level it had in the mid 1950s.

GENERAL CONCLUSIONS

The above arguments have been intended to demonstrate that the major cause for the decrease or stagnation of wheat production in four countries of the Andean Region is not the lack of resources or technology, but rather the import policies followed by national governments. Such policies are related to the more general objective of maintaining prices and wages within certain bounds.

Due to the household budget structure that is predominant in developing countries, low food prices play an important role in its attainment. While governments usually reach that goal internally through the countries' producers, they took advantage of the international situation of low prices resulting from the world wheat surpluses.

Every action has an underlying rationale and generates its own contradictions. The new, higher world price level pointed up some of these contradictions. Since it was no longer possible to acquire wheat at the former low prices, some governments opted for maintaining low prices through subsidies to imports, thus turning this additional cost into national debt. Colombia was able to eliminate the subsidy due to its special circumstances of a rice surplus and the possibility of increasing the production of other wheat substitutes. The new, higher international prices not only prevented governments from attaining their objectives but also put heavy burdens on their national budgets through the payment of import subsidies.

The policy described has produced several side effects. On the one hand, it has not permitted the existing productive capacity to develop, as regards the use of available resources and technology. Not only are improved cultivars produced by national research programs not used extensively, but those programs lack sufficient resources to make full use of their potential. Seed multiplication facilities have low capacity, extension services are practically nonexistent, and marketing and milling systems, lacking grading and drying equipment, are geared to process imported wheat.

For those who believe that food production is limited by available resources, if these countries had followed some other policy that did not discourage the domestic production capacity, they would have needed to import less wheat, and a larger amount would have been available for use by countries truly unable to produce it.

Another contradiction is related to the generation of income within the country. The four nations under study are characterized by a large number of agricultural producers with low possibilities of productive employment on or off the farm. A policy that discourages production by preventing the use of available resources intensifies the lack of employment opportunities. In buying wheat at relatively low prices, governments limited to a certain segment of the population the possibility of earning income and, therefore, of purchasing inexpensive wheat. In this regard, the government policy produced regressive effects on income by depriving the most disadvantaged sectors of much-needed employment while favoring urban populations, importers, and mill-owners.

As may be seen from the above, the policy of importing a product that can be produced locally is far from optimum, because it does not take into account its own negative effects. A socially optimum policy should consider the effects it will cause on employment, as well as the type of producer it will affect most directly. There is likely to be greater social benefit if technology is generated and domestic resources are employed to produce a greater volume of wheat. The income thus generated, and the increased economic activity implied, might produce, through an economic multiplier, a total income higher than that obtained through low price levels of imported wheat.

An additional benefit of the alternative policy would be the reduction of dependency and the possibility of safeguarding against fluctuations of the international market. Some European countries, for example, continue to produce domestically the quantity of wheat they need internally, regardless the level of the international price, precisely to avoid the negative effects mentioned here.

In-depth studies of the social benefits of the two policies described herein should be undertaken to provide governments with terms of comparison and to suggest alternative policies that would allow for a more productive use of resources, the diffusion of available technology among farmers, and the formulation of policies for producing domestically more food at higher levels of efficiency. Governments are currently trying to reduce imports, but in the absence of such studies, they will again stimulate consumption of imported wheat if international prices decrease. Unfortunately, they will do this without taking into consideration the negative effects of such policies on their own objectives, especially now that many farmers in these countries are in the process of adopting technological changes that will shift the domestic supply curve to the right if adequate input and product policies are developed.

REFERENCES

Colombia, Ministry of Agriculture, IDEMA (Instituto de Mercadeo). 1975. Comportamiento del consumo de trigo y pastas en Bogotá, después de la eliminación del subsidio. UNEM Documento No. 3, Bogotá, Colombia.
Dion, G., N. E. Borlaug, and R. G. Anderson. 1974. Report of CIDA team investigating the present status of the wheat and barley research and production programs in Perú. CIDA, CIMMYT. Mexico, D.F., Mexico.

Durán, L. 1974. Análisis de la demanda de harina de trigo y
    semola en Colombia. M.S. thesis, Instituto Colombiano
    Agropecuario-Universidad Nacional. Bogotá, Colombia.
Krstulovic, G. 1974. Comercialización del trigo. Ministerio
    de Agricultura, Informe No. 37. Lima, Perú.
Meyer, C. A. 1974. Diferencias internacionales en los
    patrones de consumo (International comparisons of consumer
    patterns). In Ensayos, ECIEL (Programa de Estudios Con-
    juntos sobre Integración Latinoamericana), No. 1, November,
    Rio de Janeiro, Brazil.
Perú, Ministerio de Economía y Finanzas. 1975. Evaluación
    Económica 1973-1974 y Perspectivas para 1975-1976. Lima,
    Perú.
Trujillo, C. 1974. Evaluación económica de la investigación
    en trigo (Economic Evaluation of research in wheat). M.S.
    thesis, Instituto Colombiano Agropecuario-Universidad
    Nacional. Bogotá.

VLADEN A. MARTYNOV

Production of Food and Development of Agro-Industrial Integration in the USSR

The solution of the world food problem, as pointed out at the 1974 World Food Conference in Rome and during other international forums, depends primarily on a rapid growth of agricultural production. The efforts undertaken by different countries in order to stimulate agricultural development cannot be identical. But the best and most effective way of solving the food problem in economically developed countries, which possess the necessary material and financial resources for agricultural development, consists obviously in a gradual intensification and industrialisation of their agriculture. This is particularly true for the Soviet Union. Of course, any substantial growth in agricultural production demands a correlated expansion and modernization of the food marketing, distribution and trade system.

The major economic goal of the USSR is to steadily increase the standard of living of its population. Its achievement depends to a great extent on a rapid rate of increase in agricultural production. Therefore, the task of increasing agricultural production is one of the most important areas of concern of contemporary economic development for the Soviet Union.

Basically the food problem in the Soviet Union can be explained by the relative slow growth of agricultural production as compared with the rapid growth of demand for food. Agricultural output increased by 37 percent between 1961-65 and 1971-75.

Vladlen A. Martynov is Deputy Director of the Institute of World Economy and International Relations, Academy of Science, USSR.

Due to historical and economic reasons the Soviet Union
did not allocate really significant amounts of investments for
agriculture until recent years. The Soviet Union invested 320
billion roubles in agriculture between 1917 and 1975. Of this
amount 213 billion roubles was invested during the last decade
(82 billion roubles in 1965-1970 and 131 billion roubles in
1971-1975). This provided our agriculture within the last ten
years with more than 3 million tractors and 900 thousand grain
combines. Nevertheless, for the country as a whole, the amount
of fixed capital per hectare of agricultural land currently
equals only about half of what is needed. There still remain
rather wide discrepancies in the availability of fixed capital
between different state and collective farms.

The XXVth Congress of the Central Presidium of the USSR--
the supreme authority of our country--adopted a far reaching
programme of agricultural development for 1976-1980. According
to this programme investment in agriculture will amount to 172
billion roubles, equivalent to a 31 percent increase over the
preceding 5 years. This will lead to a rapid expansion of
mechanisation and the application of chemical fertilisers and
pesticides and of irrigation and drainage. It will lead to a
substantial increase in the degree of specialisation and concentration of agricultural production, including the production
of high-yielding varieties and more productive livestock
breeds. It is hoped that between 1976 and 1980 annual agricultural production will grow by at least 14 to 17 percent. The
qualitative transformation of agricultural production on a new
technological footing requires time, effort and much investment.

Experience shows that the industrialisation of agriculture
objectively calls for the accelerated development of industries
which supply agriculture with machinery and other inputs and
industries which process agricultural products. Equally important are the readjustments and reorganization of the economic
relationships between these industries and agricultural production per se. In the American literature this is known as the
agribusiness complex. In the USSR it is commonly called the
agro-industrial complex.[1]

Agribusiness emerged as a new structural phenomenon in the
early fifties. There are several descriptive models of agribusiness. In my opinion two of these are particularly important:

1) The one that concentrates on macroeconomic relations
2) The one that describes the economic organisation and
the vertical coordination of the industrial, agricultural and
marketing units at the micro level.

---

1. For purposes of convenience the term "agribusiness" will be
used in what follows.

The first mentioned model of agribusiness was suggested by the American economists J. Davis and R. Goldberg. It consisted of three segments or spheres with reference to the Soviet economy: the production of the means of production and farm services (1st sphere), the farming segment (2nd sphere), and the processing, storage, transportation and sales of agricultural products (3rd sphere). They were the first to calculate, by using input-output tables, the direct and indirect labour and material inputs necessary for the production and distribution of foods and other farm-originated final products. This model is currently often used for purposes of economic decision making and planning.

The problems of agro-industrial integration in the USSR have been a subject of long standing discussion. But it is only recently that adequate theoretical and practical efforts were brought to bear on these problems. It should be mentioned that the Soviet-American Agreement on Cooperation in Agriculture has led to the establishment of a joint working group in order to study problems of agribusiness development in the USSR and the USA.

The formation of agribusiness in countries with developed economies is a complex and manifold problem. Studies are underway to clarify the nature of agribusiness, its trends of development under different conditions, and its salient features, peculiarities and consequences. Our view is that, given the conditions of the USSR, agribusiness should primarily include such industries as are directly connected with agricultural production. That is, industries which supply typical farm inputs and production services, and related processing, storage, transportation and sales services.

The analysis of agribusiness at the macroeconomic level is of particular interest in the USSR. The centrally planned nature of the Soviet economy permits, and requires, a coordinated development of all industries comprising the country's agribusiness. The planning of agribusiness must deal with several problems. One of the most important of these problems is the optimal distribution of capital expenditures between the different spheres of production. It also calls for an integrated management system of the whole agribusiness complex. This task is quite feasible under our conditions. The USSR has already shifted towards such a management system of all the basic industries of the national economy related to the production, storage, processing and sales of agricultural products. This approach underlies the national economic plan for 1976-1980.

Agribusiness production accounted for 38 percent of the Gross National Product in the USSR as of 1974. Agribusiness gives employment to 47 percent of the labour force in the sphere of material production. Agribusiness accounted for 39 percent of the total capital expenditures in 1974. The growth

of agribusiness is demonstrated by the data in Table 1, as calculated on the basis of input-output tables.

TABLE 1.   The structure of the agribusiness complex in the USSR
           in 1966 and 1972

	Employment (millions of workers)		Fixed capital (billions of roubles)		Gross output (billions of roubles)
	1966	1972	1966	1972	1972
First sphere	3.0	4.8	14.9	20.8	43.9
industries supplying means of production to agriculture	1.6	2.3	--	14.8	27.9
Second sphere (agriculture)	31.0	29.0	67.1	112.7	108.8
Third sphere	8.5	10.1	33.7	45.3	117.3
industries processing agricultural products	4.5	5.1	--	20.6	100.7
Total	42.5	43.9	115.7	178.8	270.0

Its growth, as in other countries, is associated with a
gradual decrease in the number of workers employed in agriculture. Simultaneously the value of the gross output of the
first and third spheres increases in accordance with the
increased relative importance of these spheres in the production of final goods. In 1972 the value of final goods and services produced by the agribusiness complex equaled approximately 170 billion roubles. Fixed capital grew rapidly in all
spheres of the agribusiness complex, but particularly so in
agriculture proper. The observed structural shifts are not yet
complete. The share of agricultural labour costs in the total
of labour costs of the agribusiness sphere remains high. Much
remains to be done as to the amount and the productivity of the
equipment in all spheres of the complex.
     The first sphere of agribusiness provides the material
basis for the agricultural development of the USSR. Its rapid
growth in recent years enabled the USSR to supply the state
and collective farms with more powerful, more productive, and
increasingly specialised equipment. In 1974, for example, the
USSR produced 1429 types of agricultural equipment. This is
twice as much as was produced in 1970, and 3.5 times as much
as was produced in 1965. Mineral fertilisers are particularly
important for agricultural development. Fertiliser production
increased by 70 percent in the last five years. Total produc-

tion in 1975 equaled 90.2 million tons, or 22.0 million tons in nutrient equivalents. Nevertheless the industries that supply our national agribusiness with machinery and other inputs do not yet fully satisfy the existing demand for machinery and fertilisers. The 1976-1980 national economic plan provides for a 50 percent increase in the production of agricultural machinery and a 59 percent increase in the production of mineral fertilisers.

No less important are the industries which collect, process, transport, store and distribute agricultural products. According to the 1972 input-output table the total labour costs of the third sphere of agribusiness (excluding feed stuffs) accounted for 22.9 percent of the total of labour costs of the agribusiness complex. It absorbed more than a quarter of the total of fixed capital of the complex. About 15 percent of the total of capital expenditures in 1974 took place in the processing industries and about 6 percent in the transportation, distribution and procurement service industries.

In order to accelerate the process of agri-industrial integration it is important to strengthen the material-technical basis of this sphere. In the last five years the USSR constructed additional grain storage capacity equivalent to 20 million tons per cycle. Investments in the processing industry increased by fifty percent. Over 400 additional large scale food, meat and dairy processing facilities were built. More than 1700 were modernised and about 400 light industrial establishments were rebuilt. Slaughter capacity grew by 4.3 thousand tons per shift; milk processing by 12.3 thousand tons a shift; sugar refining by 864 thousand quintals of beet roots per day; leather foot-wear by almost 60 million pairs per year, etc. The volume of production of the food industry during these years grew by 29 percent. That of the light industries grew by 24 percent. Between 1976 and 1980 more than 31 billion roubles will be invested in these industries. This is a 25 percent increase over the 1971-1975 period.

The organisation of the distribution and procurement of agricultural products is determined primarily by the structure of crop and livestock farms. In 1974 state and collective farms accounted for 88 percent of the total of commodity production (in 1940--73 percent, in 1965--87 percent). The remaining 12 percent comes from the individually worked small-holdings by members of collective farms or other workers.[2]

State and collective farms sell about 90 percent of their output to the state purchasing organisations. There is some variation in this between commodities. Grains, cotton, sugar beet-roots and sunflower-seeds are sold exclusively to the

---

2. Their relative importance, by commodities, is as follows: potatoes (41 percent), vegetables (13 percent), wool (18 percent), meat (27 percent), eggs (11 percent).

state. But only 83 percent of potatoes, 87 percent of cattle
and poultry and 85 percent of milk are sold to the state purchasing organisation. The remaining part of production is sold
through different collective farm markets or other noncentral-
ised forms of sales at local market prices. Individually
worked smallholdings also sell their commodities through these
channels. They can also sell it to the state. In 1975 the
gross value of sales through collective farm markets equaled
6.4 billion roubles. Of this 1.4 billion roubles must be
deducted in the form of commissions going to consumer cooperatives. In recent years the share of the collective farm market
in the total sales of food commodities in the USSR has shown a
tendency to decline. In 1965 it equaled 5.3 percent, in 1970
it equaled 4.4 percent, and in 1974 it was 3.8 percent.

State purchases of agricultural products are made in two
forms. A planned (ordered) volume of production is bought at a
fixed price. Additional production is acquired at a 50 percent
premium above this price. This provides an incentive to produce more than the planned volume of production. State purchases are carried out through a specialised network of organisations and enterprises. These are coordinated by the USSR
Ministry of Procurements and its local agencies. The latter
also purchase grains. Animal produce is procured mainly by
the enterprises of the USSR Ministry of Meat and Milk Industry.
Cotton, flax and selected other crops are acquired by the USSR
Ministry of Light Industry. Apart from these Ministries, state
purchases can also be made by the USSR Ministry of Food and the
network of consumer cooperatives (Centro-sojuz of the USSR).

The industrialisation of agriculture and the formation of
agribusiness, as demonstrated by the experience of the economically developed countries, often leads to an increase in the
average cost of production. In the USSR this is furthermore
related to the rapid growth of real income of collective farm
workers and workers on the state farms. Average costs of production on our state and collective farms, increased during the
past decade (eggs are an exception because of their advanced
industrial production). The increases in costs of production
were considerable in the case of potatoes, beef, milk, cotton
and sugar beets. In order to obtain a generally higher level
of income and profitability of state and collective farms the
USSR had to increase the farm price of agricultural products
(Table 2).

The gross income of collective farms grew from 17.9 billion roubles in 1965 to 24.2 billion roubles in 1974. Higher
purchase prices alone accounted for an increase of 16.2 billion roubles in the gross income of state and collective farms
between 1971 and 1973. State farms received half of this
increase.

The increase in purchase prices did not keep up with the
growth of production costs of some agricultural products. Cur-

TABLE 2. Average state purchasing prices of basic agricultural
          commodities in 1965 and 1974

Commodity	1965 roubles per ton	1974 roubles per ton
Grains	79.2	90.2
Cotton (raw)	439.4	538.2
Sugar beets	28.5	34.2
Potatoes and vegetables	63.7	95.2
Cattle and poultry (carcass weight)	1317.2	2073.2
Milk	140.5	196.2
Eggs (in thousands)	59.4	82.1

rent farm prices guarantee the profitability of products such
as grains, cotton, sunflower seeds and eggs to state and collective farms. This profitability is less for meat and fruit,
and it is small for sugar beets, potato, vegetables and milk.
Why is this so? Basically because of their labour intensive-
ness. Agricultural wage rates increased the most. It is
therefore particularly important to change current purchase
prices so as to stimulate a more effective mechanisation, specialisation and concentration of agricultural production. Furthermore prices should be set to determine levels of net income
consistent with the planned rates of growth. Soviet economists
are now engaged in the study of price formation at all levels,
from the production of raw materials to the consumption of the
final products.

State retail prices of food products remained practically
stable in spite of the substantial increase in state purchase
prices (Table 3).

The stability of the retail prices of food products, given
a growing real per capita income and increasing purchase prices
for agricultural commodities, definitely demonstrates the
redistribution of national income in favour of the population
and of agricultural development.

In recent years increasing use has been made of different
forms of agro-industrial integration, coordination and cooperation. In May 1976 the USSR decided to accelerate the specialisation and concentration of agricultural production on the
basis of horizontal cooperation and vertical agro-industrial
integration. Experience in Russia and elsewhere demonstrates
that agro-industrial integration stands out as a most important
means of increasing agricultural productivity, specialisation
and concentration. It improves the efficiency of food marketing and food processing through the elimination of unnecessary
intermediate links in the production-consumption cycle.

TABLE 3. Indices of state retail prices of food products and
          per capita real income for the USSR in 1965, 1970 and
          1974

	1965	1970	1974
All food products	100.0	100.0	101.1
Poultry	100.0	100.0	100.0
Butter	100.0	99.9	99.9
Sugar	100.0	98.0	98.0
Potatoes	100.0	105.0	103.0
Vegetables	100.0	118.0	121.0
Bread and cereal products	100.0	99.6	99.6
Alcoholic beverages	100.0	101.0	103.0
Per capita real income	100.0	133.0	158.0

As of January 1975 the agricultural sector of the USSR had
56 agro-industrial firms and 512 agriculture related enterprises,[3] employing more than 760 thousand workers. Their fixed
capital exceeded 6 billion roubles and the annual revenue from
food processing alone equaled 2.1 billion roubles. Most were
engaged in the production and processing of vegetables, fruits,
and oil bearing or other plants. The number of agro-industrial
enterprises will continue to increase rapidly.

An agro-industrial enterprise organically integrates agricultural and industrial production. Such an enterprise has a
single integrated management system and common finances, and
functions as an independent legally recognized entity. In the
USSR the most common form of this organization is a combination
of a manufacturing establishment and state farms.

An agro-industrial firm is an organization where several
legally separate enterprises merge on the basis of rational
specialisation and cooperation, in the production, processing,
storage and distribution of agricultural products. Such firms
aim for a gradual centralization of a number of economic tasks
such as the distribution of capital expenditures and funds, the
creation of integrated transport, sales, procurement and similar services. Managerial control over these firms can be
implemented either through specially created administrative
bodies, or through the administrative staff of the principal
organization. Depending on the level of integration agro-
industrial firms can function either as large territorially
specialised amalgamations (e.g. "Ptitseprom", "Moldovoshprom",
"Dagvino" etc.) or as inter-industry amalgamations created on
the basis of a partnership-type participation of the member-

---

3. This excludes state and collective farms which possessed
subsidiary smallholdings for the processing of agricultural
products.

organisations (e.g., an amalgamated firm for the processing of
agricultural products, the production of formula feeds, etc.).

Agro-industrial firms are extremely instrumental in
achieving greater economic efficiency, specialisation and concentration of production and in the elimination of unnecessary
intermediate links in the production-consumption cycle. Let us
look, for example, at the activities of one such organisation,
an agro-industrial firm engaged in the production, processing
and distribution of vegetables and fruits. Such a firm was set
up in 1969 in the Checheno-Ingush Autonomous Republic (Northern
Caucasus) on the basis of nine state farms, three processing
plants and one trading organisation for the distribution of
vegetables and fruits in Grozny. Between 1971 and 1975 the
firm increased its marketed volume of vegetables and fruits 2.5
times. Revenue from the sales of agricultural production
increased twelvefold because of the very drastic reduction in
spoilage. The integrated management system reduced administrative costs by almost 25 percent. The shift to direct "field-
shop" or "field-plant" deliveries of agricultural products
helped to eliminate unnecessary intermediate links (14 such
organisations were engaged in procuring agricultural production
in the area before the amalgamation) and stimulated better
coordination between all system components. Management itself
became more operational and down to earth, enabling better
coordination of capital investments and the centralisation of
certain service activities such as transportation, fertilisation and maintenance.

It would be wrong to view the formation of a national
agri-business complex and the creation of different agro-
industrial firms and enterprises as merely organisational
efforts. They are part of a long-term process of economic
development, the success of which is determined by the
strengthening of the material-technical base of agriculture and
other industries. The long-term nature of agro-industrial
integration is an objectively determined feature of the whole
process of economic development.

The level of agri-business investment remains insufficient.
Many more years will be needed for the widespread establishment
of agro-industrial firms and the balanced development of all
branches of the agribusiness complex. Considerable long-term
capital investments are required to close the longstanding gap
between rural and urban infrastructure. The rural areas of the
USSR and therefore its agricultures are characterised by an
extreme territorial sparseness. This further complicates the
solution of the problem.

The productive development of our agriculture and rural
areas is but one part of the problem. The social aspect, is no
less important. Social development does not exclusively depend
on economic development. In certain aspects the causation is
the other way around, for example through changes in birth and

mortality rates, education and labour skills, lifestyles, etc.

I would like to conclude with emphasising once more that the production of food is at present one of the most important economic spheres of the economy of the USSR. Therefore considerable efforts are made by the USSR to increase agricultural production.

REFERENCES

Davis, J. H. and R. A. Goldberg. 1957. A Concept of Agribusiness. Harvard University, Boston.

Goldberg, R. A. 1968. Agribusiness Coordination: A Systems Approach to the Wheat, Soybean, and Florida Orange Economics. Harvard University, Boston.

Mighell, R. L. and L. A. Jones. 1963. Vertical Coordination in Agriculture. US Department of Agriculture, Washington.

Mighell, R. L. and W. S. Hoofnagle. 1972. Contract Production and Vertical Integration in Farming, 1960 and 1970. US Department of Agriculture, Washington.

Roy, E. P. 1963. Contract Farming. Interstate Printers and Publishers, Danville, Illinois.

Roy, E. P. 1967. Exploring Agribusiness. Interstate Printers and Publishers, Danville, Illinois.

Roy, E. P. 1972. Contract Farming and Economic Integration. Interstate Printers and Publishers, Danville, Illinois.

BARBARA A. UNDERWOOD

Food Policies in Southeast Asia Affecting the Nutrition and Health of Consumers

The implicit national and international goal of food policy is to provide all citizens with a wholesome diet in sufficient quantity and quality to be compatible with nutrition and health and at an affordable price. Few would not endorse this as an expressed goal. In reality however political and economic considerations rather than nutrition and health weigh heavy in determining national and international food policies. Politicians make food policy decisions with technical advice from economists, agriculturalists, occasionally health scientists and other professionals. Retrospective analysis of past and current food policies suggest that decisions are made based on the available technologies for influencing the food supply and the existence of organizational structures to which responsibility for implementation can be assigned. Infrequently have consumer interests as perceived by them been a part of the decision-making process.

Traditionally the assignment for implementing food policy is to departments of agriculture. The common philosophy of agriculture has been that if food is available in adequate quantity, consumer nutrition and health will be an unquestioned outcome, i.e., the "trickle-down" theory of benefit distribution. There is no question that the technology for increasing the world food supply exists as demonstrated by the application of modern agricultural techniques in developed countries. There are, however, technical constraints to the direct trans-

Barbara A. Underwood is Director, Division of Biological Health, College of Human Development, The Pennsylvania State University, University Park, Pennsylvania 16802.

fer of this technology to developing countries. There are also humane constraints related to the effect on people in the developing world now dependent upon a traditional agriculture for jobs. Additionally, health-minded nutritionists have crit- icized the "trickle-down" approach to nutrition and health which in their judgment does not assure benefit distribution to the consuming public particularly those at the highest risk of malnutrition.

Whereas food policy has been the concern of agriculture, nutrition policy, when such exists, has traditionally been assigned to departments of health. Within the government bureaucracy of developing nations, health departments lack clout compared to agriculture when resources are allocated, even though health workers have high prestige in the public's eye and tend to make program decisions more directly based on concern for consumer health. Certainly diet is determined in part by the quantity, diversity and safety of the available food supply, and consumer health is directly related to ability to choose wisely and to purchase from the supply, and to the intrafamily distribution according to nutritional needs. Obvi- ously food policy should not be determined independent of a nutrition policy if consumers' interests are to be best served. Yet, government policies aimed at food production, quality and safety, and those aimed at civic nutrition and health are assigned for implementation to segregated ministries each with professional territory and interests to protect. The segrega- tion mitigates hopes for multidisciplinary integrated programs, both in developed and in developing countries (Dwyer and Mayer, 1975). Prospects for change, however, are encouraging.

The first World Food Conference in Rome focused worldwide attention on the need to relook not at food or nutrition poli- cies in isolation but integrated. The goal is to provide an improved quality of life for all, and especially for that usu- ally neglected element of society, the poorest of the poor. This challenge has stimulated a rethinking of the criteria used in policy formulation and has tended to bring into the politi- cal arena a new coalition of technical advisors. Strict dis- ciplinary boundaries are no longer tenable if nutrition and health problems of the poorest consumers are to be effectively attacked. Professionally, sectors of agriculture, health and social welfare are in an exciting evolutionary phase. As experience accumulates, frequent evaluation of what does and does not work in reaching the poor is critical. This is the future; my charge today is to consider the present.

Current food policies affecting the nutrition and health of consumers can be grouped into those affecting the quantity, diversity and safety of the available food supply, and those affecting the purchasing power of consumers. My remarks are oriented to current policies in Southeast Asia although concep- tually much of what is reported has more universal application.

FOOD POLICIES INFLUENCING SUPPLIES TO CONSUMERS

Projection for Increased Production

In the judgment of many, prospects are favorable in Southeast Asia for a continued aggregate agricultural growth From 1954-1973 the rate of increase in agricultural products in the developing countries was 3 percent (Anonymous, 1974), an achievement accomplished through intensification and some increase in arable land. Because population over the same period increased at the rate of 2.5 percent annually, the net benefit on a per capita basis was limited to 0.4 percent. Nonetheless, these statistics suggest that more people had more to eat in 1973 than did fewer people in 1954. The true impact on the prevalence of undernutrition and related mortality is difficult to quantitate due to inadequate baseline date. The trend toward lowered mortality in preschoolers suggests an overall improvement likely to be due in part to improved nutrition.

Politicians and agriculturalists in Southeast Asia believe current food policies geared toward self-sufficiency have and will continue to be effective. Nutritionists believe supplementary policies directly supportive of consumer nutrition and health programs are critical to reducing the already widespread problems of undernutrition and specific deficiencies. Projections for Asia to 1985, based on current trends, are that need, demand and yields of food calories will be approximately in balance (Chancellor and Goss, 1976). Projections for protein are that demand and production will be in balance or exceed that of need. Some may be confused by projections of protein excess and calorie balance after years of propaganda proclaiming the great protein gap, particularly in Asia. Will the "gap" be closed or did it ever exist? Understandably the credibility of nutritionists as diagnosticians of national needs is questioned. However, the projection of a protein balance or excess is based on recalculations using the 1973 FAO/WHO reduced figures for human protein requirements (FAO/WHO Ad Hoc Expert Committee, 1973). The adequacy of these figures is questioned by some (Scrimshaw, 1976) and the lower values for requirements have not been sufficiently evaluated under existing conditions in developing countries to be confident of validity. Moreover, projections based on per capita availability fail to depict distribution distortions which can mask the true magnitude of nutritional problems of consumers on marginal incomes living under conditions of social deprivation, particularly intrafamily maldistributions. Projections also do not consider the changing food preferences of developing societies as affluence spreads.

Current Food Policies

The characteristics of current food production policies in
Southeast Asian nations are shaped in part by the countries' ability to produce sufficient rice to meet domestic
needs. Rice, the staple of the area, is produced in excess in
some countries such as Thailand and Burma, but is in deficit in
others such as Indonesia, Philippines, Singapore and Malaysia.
Production policies in rice surplus countries, while favoring
rice, tend to also provide incentives for diversification in
cropping to directly meet human food needs as well as those for
animal feed and international markets. For food surplus countries, the result of policies that support several crops has
been to improve the flow of a diversified food supply to consumers and to improve the distribution of development benefits.
Serious maldistribution continues to plague the bottom rung of
society even in food surplus areas.

Food deficit countries are less flexible in production
policies. The goal is self-sufficiency in food, the term food
being synonomous with rice in terms of allocation of production
incentives. Policies seek to create favorable production
incentives for farmers through establishing floor prices and
subsidizing needed agricultural inputs (seed, fertilizer and
pesticide packages) and by establishing ceiling prices to protect consumers. Indonesia has accomplished this with some success by maintaining a controlled buffer rice stock from which
regional market supplies could be regulated. Other cereal
crops, legumes, vegetables and fruits have only minimally
entered the support system. As a result, production of these
foods on a national scale has not significantly improved and in
the case of legumes may have deteriorated in acreage planted
(Abbot et al., 1975; Hardy et al., 1975). Legumes and pulses,
vegetable and fruit production remain essentially backyard
enterprises in food deficit Southeast Asian countries which
limits the available market supply at an affordable price.
Yet, projections to the year 2000 to hold the per capita protein supply at 1975 levels will require a 66-100 percent
increase in legumes and other vegetables, together with a 75
percent increase in cereals (Pimentel et al., 1975). Consumer
health will be further jeopardized if per capita availability
declines.

Potential for Future Food Production Policies

Since aggregate agricultural growth is projected for
Southeast Asia, there is opportunity to set new guidelines
in establishing land use policies for the future. Is it reasonable to hope that guidelines will be oriented more directly
to the nutrition and health needs of consumers? Certainly any
plans must recognize the continued pressures of population
growth and the stress these impose first and foremost on the

need for increased food energy. Further, policies must recognize the increased fuel energy costs of modern agriculture and
weigh these against the efficiency of food energy yields for
alternate crops. Energy needs in turn must be balanced against
nutrient needs. These considerations are of particular importance in Southeast Asia where the average annual population
growth rate is 2.5-2.8 percent, most countries are food deficit, most countries are fuel energy dependent, and unemployment
and undernutrition are common allies. Decision makers must ask
the questions, which crops will give the best food energy
return for the fuel energy investment, provide employment
opportunities and still be supportive of the nutrient needs of
the consumers.

The energy crisis in recent years has stimulated agriculturalists and economists to look critically at cropping efficiencies. Heichel (1976) suggested the term "cultural energy"
to summarize the aggregate of fuel energy expenditure for producing a given crop. He has plotted this against the ratio of
food energy per unit cultural energy for 24 grain, forage,
fruit and vegetable crops. Field crops such as sorghum, corn,
wheat, oats and soybean are the most efficient yielders of food
energy per cultural energy inputs. Rice, peanuts and potato
are intermediate while the vegetables and fruits aimed solely
at human consumption are extremely energy demanding in comparison to food energy yield.

Food energy deficit, though the foremost nutritional problem worldwide, most often is accompanied in segments of the
population by protein deficit. A similar evaluation of food
crops based on protein yield per unit cultural energy reveals
soybean, sorghum, oats, corn and wheat to be protein yield
efficient crops (Heichel, 1976). From a cost effective view
based on such analyses, and in a food energy and protein-scarce
world, the crops to supported for expansion should be corn,
sorghum, soybean, wheat and oats. Nutritionists have long
been advocates of increased emphasis on soybean and other
pulses in Southeast Asia as a human food indigenous to the
region and nutritionally complementary to the protein of rice.
In spite of the potential health benefits to be derived, economists and agriculturalists in food deficit countries have not
viewed legumes as economically desirable crops to promote on a
yield efficient basis. Unlike the cereal grains, no new high
yielding varieties have developed that respond to the usual
production inputs (Hardy and Havelka, 1976). In Southeast
Asia, particularly in food deficit countries, the three professional groups who are the responsible advisors to decision-
makers have talked at each other on the issue but have failed
to reach agreement. Yield responsive cereals consistently win
when decisions are finally made. New ways of analyzing the
energy and protein efficient potential of alternative crops
offer new grounds for discussions. The argument supported on

nutritional grounds should be expanded to include the economically important energy and protein efficient potentials of
legumes (Heichel, 1976; Pimental, 1975). Additionally, soybean, mung bean, ground nuts and other legumes and pulses may
also offer benefits such as: 1) the production technology is
human labor intensive and consequently income generating;
2) production inputs are less demanding, e.g., less need for
nitrogen fertilizers and for controlled water supplies;
3) products in some countries of the region stimulate cottage
industry employment in the production of fermented products and
foods, some of which are suitable for infant and child feeding;
4) the potential expanding local market and demonstrated
expanding international market could provide needed production
incentives for farmers and foreign exchange for governments.

These concepts of potential benefits need to be tested
quantitatively and qualitatively. One innovative national program testing some of these concepts is under way in the Philippines. The program includes weighing children under six years,
"Operation Timbang," and coupling this to a community government sponsored program to produce locally "Nutri Paks" containing a legume, fish powder and oil to be combined with rice and
fed children found to be in weight deficit of second or third
degree. A similar nationwide program is in the planning stages
for Indonesia. These programs should be watched closely as
potentially they could provide a model for replacing feeding
programs based on imported mixtures and foods while creating a
community level demand and market for legumes and pulses. They
also could offer a model for evaluating some of the other production benefits as outlined above.

Are changing food habits in Southeast Asia with rising
affluence reasonable to anticipate? If Japan can be used as a
predictor of projected changes, the demand for livestock meat
products could increase dramatically. The income elasticity of
demand for meat in Asia and the Far East is 1.06 compared with
.5 for most countries of the developed world (Anonymous, 1974).
At current low income levels and high meat prices, pressures
are minimal from consumers in the developing areas of Southeast
Asia on the available meat supply. The meat-ravenous developed
world, however, cannot continue to monopolize the available
resources should a substantial demand and market develop in
areas now forced to consume 50-70 percent of calories from
cereals. On the other hand, the world resources cannot support
a dietary pattern for all peoples as now characteristic of the
average American diet (Pimental et al., 1975). A shift toward
an increased consumption of grain and legume products is
inevitable for the future American diet, a shift which is
likely to have positive health benefits for Americans as well
as for the developing world who can benefit from a limited
increment in meat intake and the multiple nutritional benefits
carried. For the shift in consumption patterns in Asia to have

real nutritional benefits, a distribution system to low income
groups must be assured.

POLICIES AFFECTING THE PURCHASING POWER OF CONSUMERS

The nutrition and health of low income consumers are
directly affected by policies which influence their effective purchasing power. Market availability of food, of
course, is prerequisite to purchase but will not assure consumption if the price is beyond the reach of the consumer or if
income is insufficient to buy at any price. The vulnerable in
any society are the unemployed, underemployed and socially disrupted. Starvation on the streets of Dacca in 1975 was due to
an inability to buy rice at the market price rather than its
unavailability. Fortunately this year a bumper harvest coupled
with strict smuggling controls and massive food imports has
halved the price of rice, and starvation is no longer the major
concern in Dacca. The point is that significant fluctuations
in the prices of food, particularly the major source of calories and protein, can devastate families on subsistence
incomes. For such families, many demands to meet basic needs
compete for available income, food being only one. Policies
which offer social services to relieve any of these basic
needs, e.g., free health services, tax incentives, subsidized
housing, day care centers for children, can enhance effective
purchasing power. This, however, does not assure that available income will be wisely used for the purchase and intrafamily distribution of food.

Food Price Controls

Economists traditionally are effective in the arena of
regulatory policies for food prices. A commonly held view
is that nutrition and food habits of consumers can be manipulated through price regulation of the production, processing
and marketing channels through which food flows. The effect of
uncontrolled price on consumption patterns in the United States
was dramatically illustrated in 1974 when meat prices sky-
rocketed. Even this effect was relatively short lived for the
average American consumer who adapted and returned to his or
her seemingly insatiable desire for meat. The less affluent
have fewer options.

In the developing world fluctuating food prices for the
have-nots of society can tip the precarious balance of survival
for the high risk, the very young and old and those in the
childbearing years. For these people the alternative in
cheaper food choices inevitably is to move from a marginally
adequate cereal to a less adequate starchy root (or equivalent)
based diet. The necessity to sustain the wage earner at all
costs often forces further distortion in the intrafamily dis-

tribution of food (Gross and Underwood, 1971).

Food price control policies in Southeast Asia, like production policies, are almost exclusively restricted to rice.
Because rice is the common dietary staple, regulatory policies
provide benefit to all consumers. In the rice surplus country
of Thailand, regulation of price acts as a disincentive to
increased production though benefiting the general public, a
situation of concern to production-oriented technologists
(Anonymous, 1974). An unrestricted control policy for a common
food staple avoids the stigma of a subsidized "poor man's food"
but is an inefficient way of income transfer to the targeted
poorest of society most in need of assistance. Approaches are
needed which provide exceptional benefits to the vulnerable
without conspicuously identifying a food or a group as welfare
recipients.

Under non-military or disaster conditions few success
stories are on record for programs that effectively channel
benefits to targeted segments without associated negative
social stigma. One approach being implemented in Pakistan may
provide a model for future policy guidance. The principle
applied is to use the nationwide system of ration shops to
sell, at a subsidized price, a universally consumed staple, in
this case wheat. Shops are unrestricted in consumer access.
The wheat sold is an imported variety which, although wholesome
and nutritionally adequate, is qualitatively less acceptable to
those of increasing affluence. The more desired varieties are
available on the uncontrolled open market. Consumers have a
free choice of the quantity of staple purchased from either
market source. In effect, this approach may provide a substantial increment in purchasing power for the poorest without
identifying the commonly used staple as a welfare commodity.

Employment Policies

Insufficient earning power is a fundamental deterrent to
social development and an improved quality of life for the
majority of small farmers and landless laborers of Southeast
Asia. Unemployment and underemployment are major problems.
Most even with jobs receive insufficient pay to meet critical
basic needs. Although able to purchase sufficient food to sustain life, the diet purchasable is seldom adequate nutritionally and consequently compromises physical and social development. The high morbidity and mortality among infants and children of the poor and the shortened life expectancy of adults
attest to the fact.

Food production policies which provide employment opportunities will be necessary if the well-being of the majority of
the consuming public is to be upgraded. As in most of the
developing world, the major population in Southeast Asia is
rural and employed in subsistence agriculture. A rapidly grow-

ing number are landless laborers both rural and urban. These
groups of subsistence farmers and laborers must have an incremental increase in income generating power if their quality of
life is to be improved. Current emphasis on food self-sufficiency has generated policies favoring mechanization of agriculture and the application of modern technologies in an effort
to improve yields. It is indeed understandable that politicians and their advisors believe these policies are in the best
national development interests. Recent analysis of the consequences of such policies in several developing countries has
shown a widening disparity in income distribution, an alarming
trend with serious implications for the economically deprived
in a world universally suffering from inflation. Recognizing
these facts, both national and international groups have
renewed efforts to create programs beneficial to small farmers
while retaining the goal of improved production. Labor intensive and middle level agricultural technologies are a means of
providing employment income for more people. This approach,
however, must be weighed against the need for yield efficiencies. As yet, there have not been many success stories in
which middle level technologies have been developed, successfully employed and demonstrated to be an effective means of
income redistribution. Because of the large numbers of subsistence income people wedded to agriculture, rigorous efforts to
find programs that work are basic to improved nutrition and
health. We are, however, inexperienced in effectively designing and implementing successful nationwide programs. The poor
have been with us for a very long period in spite of a variety
of so-called "poverty programs." Newly implemented national
programs such as the one cited earlier in Pakistan involving
ration shops which indirectly redistribute income deserve close
surveillance, as do the community-oriented "Operation Timbang"
and "Nutri Paks" of the Philippines.

Hope for an improved purchasing power of the lower third
on the economic scale and as a result of policy decisions inevitably is linked to population control. An improved GNP, like
improved total food production, even when combined with policies facilitative of a more equitable income distribution is of
no avail if the mouths to be fed continue to increase at so
rapid a pace. Voluntary population control in all segments of
a society must be an integral part of all development policy.
The poor and their propensity to reproduce is a well-recognized
social problem, the solutions for which continue to elude
available technologies and programs. Effective nutrition,
health and social service programs may be a key link to voluntary compliance.

Food Safety

Consumer health is affected by the wholesomeness of the

food supply. In developed countries where most foods are
centrally processed, quality control and safety regulations,
though costly, are feasible. In the developing countries much
of the food supply does not flow through organized channels and
quality control is limited. Food safety legislation exists, or
soon will be passed, but ability to enforce legislation is negligible. Both the necessary trained manpower and the necessary
institutional structures for enforcement are lacking.

Contamination and adulteration are both major health problems in several Southern Asian countries. Vermin pose a significant hazard as do insecticide residues. Also of special
concern is contamination with aflatoxin due to poor storage
conditions. Cereals, legumes and pulses stored and processed
locally, many of which frequently are fermented, are especially
susceptible. Need for research to improve village level storage and processing procedures to minimize health hazards should
be given top priority in government programs.

Adulteration of food products en route to market through
the food system or by individual vendors is an additional major
concern in Southeast Asian countries. Practices such as the
addition of canal water to milk and the addition of calcium
salts to restore solid levels to normal before delivery to
local markets are not uncommon. Such was a personal experience
discovered only when a prescribed dietary regime based on milk
failed under hospital conditions to effectively reverse symptoms of recipient children with acute protein-energy malnutrition. In Indonesia, the practice of adulterating soybean with
coconut meal in production of tempe has caused fatal food poisoning of many consumers. In most developing countries the
infrastructure necessary to monitor and effectively control
adulteration practices is non-existent in spite of legislation
which currently may be "on the books."

The common occurrence of food poisoning from improperly
handled and stored food has contributed to adaptive food habits
with a direct consequence for nutrition and health. Special
foods fed or not fed to infants and children and to pregnant
and lactating women often lead to practices rooted in previous
negative experiences or associations. For example, in Indonesia fish is thought to cause worms in young children because
maggots often occur on improperly stored fish in the home.
Excretion of worms is common in young children so that the
association is understandable.

The future of policies and legislation to control food
safety will depend on developing the trained manpower to monitor at least that portion of the food supply that enters commercial channels. Legislation will continue to be ineffective
in controlling the safety of food outside commerical channels.
Control at this level can only be expected through research
identifying safer storage and processing procedures and education in the application of these under home conditions.

FUTURE DIRECTIONS FOR FOOD AND NUTRITION POLICIES

In Southeast Asia as elsewhere the current national and
international concern for programs to reach the poorest of
the poor and improve their quality of life present new
challenges to politicians and their advisors. Certainly one
value universally shared and encompassed in the meaning of
"quality of life" is that of well-being, e.g., health, safety
and comfort, for which an adequate, balanced and safe food supply is basic. The challenge in Southeast Asia is even greater
when confronted with the fact that funds for poverty programs
competing with other programs critical to national development
are unlikely to experience a substantial incremental growth.
Worldwide undernutrition problems are rooted in social inequi-
ties more than technical lack. Hence, to achieve the goal,
food and nutrition policies of the future will have to focus on
more effective and efficient means of addressing such inequi-
ties.

Nutritionists are naive to imagine that policies will be
influenced primarily by the health and nutritional needs of the
consuming public. Economic considerations will continue to
dominate national policy decisions, and the voice of the production-oriented economist and the technology-oriented agriculturalist will be heard above that of the consumer health-
oriented nutritionist. What is needed is for multidisciplinary
coalitions to form for the purpose of advising politicians on
alternatives to consider in reaching compromise positions from
which policies can be formulated (Dwyer and Mayer, 1975).
Analysis of alternative approaches phrased in terms meaningful
to several disciplines hold greatest potential for using
national and international resources for programs to achieve
the goals for national development while meeting consumer needs
for improved nutrition and health. The National Food and
Nutrition Consortium represents a first step in this direction
in the USA. Both national and regional variations of similar
interprofessional advisory groups are forming also in Southeast
Asia, for examples, the National Nutrition Council of the Philippines and the Interministerial Council for Nutrition of Indonesia. These coalitions must interact closely with decision
makers for ultimately it is the body politic where decisions
are made, and without their ear, the techno-bureaucratic community is ineffective.

REFERENCES

Anonymous. 1974. The World Food Situation and Prospects to
    1985. Economic Research Service. US Department of Agri-
    culture. Foreign Agricultural Economic Report No. 98.
Abbot, P. C., F. J. Levinson, E. Pollitt, J. Rohde, N. S.
    Scrimshaw, B. A. Underwood, J. D. Wrap. 1975. Nutrition

program development in Indonesia. MIT International Nutrition Planning Program. Technical Report Series No. 2.

Chancellor, W. J. and J. R. Goss. 1976. Balancing energy and food production, 1975-2000. Science 192:213.

Dwyer, J. T. and J. Mayer. 1975. Beyond economics and nutrition: The complex basis of food policy. p. 74. In P. H. Abelson (Ed.) Food: Politics, Economics, Nutrition and Research. American Association for the Advancement of Science, Washington, DC.

FAO/WHO Ad Hoc Expert Committee. 1973. Energy and Protein Requirements, FAO Technical Report Series No. 522, Food and Agriculture Organization of the United Nations, Rome.

Gross, D. R. and B. A. Underwood. 1971. Technological change and caloric costs: Sisal agriculture in northeastern Brazil. American Anthropologist 73:725.

Hardy, R. W. F. and U. D. Havelka. 1975. Nitrogen fixation research: A key to world food? p. 178. In P. H. Abelson (Ed.) Food: Politics, Economics, Nutrition and Research. American Association for the Advancement of Science, Washington, DC.

Heichel, G. H. 1976. Agricultural production and energy resources. American Scientist 64:64.

Pimental, D., W. Dritschilo, J. Krummel, J. Kutzman. 1975. Energy and land constraints in food protein production. Science 190:754.

Scrimshaw, N. S. 1976. Shattuck Lecture--Strengths and weaknesses of the committee approach. An analysis of past and present recommended dietary allowances for protein in health and disease. New England Journal of Medicine 294:136.

GONZALO ARROYO

Institutional Constraints to Policies for Achieving Increased Food Production in Selected Countries

The subject I have to talk about is not a simple one. Let me start first by clarifying some issues which will allow me to treat more specifically some examples of constraints to the implementation of food production policies in countries of Latin America, and the effects of such policies on production and food consumption.

THE CONCEPT OF AGRICULTURE

The first remark concerns the concept of agriculture. I believe that this concept, widely utilized by economists, sociologists and others, seems to lose operational utility when one wants to grasp what is happening today with food production throughout the world.

Agriculture--or, more accurately, farming itself--is only one of the four subsectors now comprising agro-industrial production: (1) production 'upstream' from the farm, industrial and other inputs; (2) farm, livestock, forestry and fisheries products, per se; (3) industrial processing and transforming of these products 'downstream' (or 'agribusiness' including food and non-food processing industries); (4) distribution of agro-industrial products to the final consumer (warehousing, wholesaling and retailing; restaurant, institutional consumption) (Malassis, 1976).

If we utilize as the only criterion value added by each subsector to the final consumption food commodity, agriculture

Gonzalo Arroyo is Associate Professor, University of Paris X, Nanterre, France.

or farming as such, the second stage of the agri-food system,
is becoming less and less important. Table 1 shows this structural change taking place in developing countries whose agriculture sectors follows, to a great extent, the pattern of
development of industrialized developed nations.

TABLE 1. Share in gross domestic product and growth rates of
agriculture and manufacturing by economic groups and
regions, 1960-1970

Economic grouping or region	Share in GDP			Average annual growth rate		
	1960	1965	1970	1960-1965	1965-1970	1960-1970
Developed market economies						
Agriculture	6.6	5.6	5.1	1.7	2.9	2.2
Manufacturing	29.8	31.6	32.7	6.4	5.3	6.2
Developing countries						
Agriculture	34.0	29.5	26.8	2.6	3.8	2.8
Manufacturing	15.5	16.8	18.1	6.6	7.3	6.8
Latin America						
Agriculture	18.5	17.4	15.2	4.0	2.8	3.3
Manufacturing	21.3	22.0	24.0	5.9	7.2	6.8
Asia, Middle East						
Agriculture	--	--	--	3.9	2.8	3.3
Manufacturing	--	--	--	9.6	11.4	10.5
Asia, East and Southeast (excluding Japan)						
Agriculture	47.4	41.4	39.8	1.6	4.8	2.6
Manufacturing	12.3	14.8	15.2	7.7	6.4	6.5
Africa (excluding South Africa)						
Agriculture	--	--	--	3.3	2.3	2.4
Manufacturing	--	--	--	10.6	4.5	4.5

Source: UNIDO, Industrial Development Survey, March 1974, p.
219.

In order to understand the diminishing importance of agriculture, it is necessary to consider the emergence in recent
decades of a world food system related to the quest of transnational agribusinesses for increased profits and international
market control of certain 'strategic' food commodities and raw
materials, and also to the increasing vertical or at least
near-integration of agricultural producers within the same system. This agri-food system signals major changes in energy,
inventory, finance, production, distribution and consumption of
food commodities.
What we want to stress here is that in both industrialized

Western countries and in underdeveloped nations, agriculture is
increasingly being submitted to agribusiness--'upstream' and
especially 'downstream'--and that traditional vertical integration is being replaced by near-integration through an indirect
control from agribusiness. Apparently autonomous farmers are
becoming in both cases, although with different effects in
terms of income and welfare, not exactly wage earners of agribusiness complexes, but what we may call 'piece-workers' for
the local processing factories and food distribution firms.
The latter exhibit an increasing capitalization process which
fosters a national and international concentration of capital
in fewer and larger transnational corporations.

This global process produces a profound modification of
the relationships between industry, distribution, and agriculture. Agriculture becomes more and more dependent even in the
case of large-scale capitalist farms on input producing and
processing agribusiness and on distribution firms, dominated by
transnational capital subject to a process of concentration in
production and marketing. The leading firms are of a diversified and conglomerate nature, frequently closely linking food
processing activities to other agricultural-related industries.

What the Federal Trade Commission concluded in 1966 about
competition among food processing firms in the USA can probably
be applied today to the world agri-food system: "competition
among conglomerates tends to have a dull edge; often it takes
on a live-and-let-live tone." Most transnationals operate in
oligopolistic markets. In underdeveloped countries they tend
to collude in partitioning the market and in conducting business in those host countries.

The case of France is quite illustrative because a considerable percentage of its active population (12.5 percent) is
composed of mostly small 'autonomous' peasants, frequently pro-
prietors of their land and of their means of production. In
1970, the fraction of the value corresponding to agricultural
products (fresh or natural) not having gone through processing
and packaging was only a third of the total value of food consumption goods, and the value added by agribusiness (national
and multinational enterprises and certain large cooperatives)
almost equaled that added by agriculture (Malassis, 1975).

In the USA this process is more advanced. Since the sixties the value added by agribusiness surpasses that of farming.
Only one fifth of the total value of food is consumed as fresh
or nonprocessed food. In 1974 the market value of agricultural
output equalled $95 billion. Farm income equalled $27 billion.
The value added by processing and distribution equalled $65
billion.

The declining share of agriculture per se in the world
agri-food system is one of the main consequences of agribusiness development. It apparently gained momentum in the early
seventies, and even more rapidly after the energy crisis and

after the spectacular increase in food prices in 1973. This
world system of production, processing, food distribution dominated by global agribusiness corporations is apparently irreversible and it is forcing itself on underdeveloped countries.
Food processing today is of great industrial significance. It
is the largest industrial sector in terms of value added in
most countries. Table 2 gives estimates of its share in total
manufacturing value added and in terms of employment.

Given the above, the concept of agriculture as an autonomous economic sector as for example in Colin Clark's three-
sector classification (primary, secondary, tertiary) is totally
inadequate in view of the actual world situation. Other areas
of analysis such as land tenure and resultant policies advocating land reform as the principal means of increasing production
are equally inadequate.

An analysis focused solely on agriculture cannot explain
the development of the agri-food system and the submission of
agricultural production to the logic of a system of transnational agribusiness. That system forces a growing specialization on peasants and farmers towards vertical or near-integration with agribusinesses dealing with the processing and
distribution of food on a world-wide basis. Because underdeveloped countries are confronted by this process of a vanishing agriculture and of a consequently vanishing free market for
agricultural commodities, any analysis of the constraints on
policy development regarding agriculture in those countries
must take account of the global transformation of the agri-food
systems and must choose, accordingly, analytical tools which
are adequate for the phenomena studied.

THE NEW INTERNATIONAL DIVISION OF LABOR

A second remark concerns the new international division of
labor. As capital investment becomes increasingly inter-
nationalized it brings with it a more rapid accumulation
of capital and considerably expanded world trade. The transnational corporations and their subsidiaries are among the most
dynamic elements furthering this process.

Their predominance implies, on the whole, a major role
for the USA in structuring a new economic order which does not
necessarily coincide with the "new international order" voted
by the United Nations Assembly controlled by Third World countries. National economies (of both industrial and Third World
countries) are integrated within a world system in different
ways and at different speeds, depending on the previous degree
of capitalization of industry and other economic sectors; the
availability, cost and training of the labor force; the abundance of natural resources and the nature and stability of
political and social institutions in each country.

For purposes of simplification, one may distinguish four

TABLE 2. Value added and employment in major agro-industries by regions and economic groups, 1960-1972

Total major agro-industries[a]	Share of ISIC category in regional total manufacturing value added (percentage)			Share of region or economic grouping in world total value added in each ISIC category (percentage)			Value (million dollars)	Share of ISIC category in regional total manufacturing employment (percentage)		Share of region or economic grouping in world total employment in each ISIC category (percentage)		Number of persons employed (000's)
	1960	1970	1972	1960	1970	1972	1972	1960	1970	1960	1970	1970
World	26	19	21	100.0	100.0	100.0	174,271	37	33	100.0	100.0	58,912
Developed market economies	22	18	19	57.4	54.4	54.0	94,060	29	25	38.6	34.5	20,324
Developing countries	48	40	39	12.6	12.4	12.9	22,416	56	51	44.6	47.7	28,112
Latin America	42	36	34	6.0	6.0	6.1	10,633	45	41	8.2	8.8	5,202
Asia	53	43	42	5.5	5.1	5.4	9,383	59	52	33.9	34.4	20,253
Centrally planned economies	28	21	20	29.9	32.8	33.1	57,613	29	26	17.0	17.6	10,381

Source: UNIDO, Industrial Development Survey. March 1974, p. 226.
[a] International Standard Industrial Classification (ISIC) groups 31, 321 and 33. This includes food, beverages, tobacco, textiles, wood products and furniture. It excludes leather, paper and rubber products.

classes of countries in the international division of labor
(Eastern Europe and socialist countries excluded):

1) Class A: Industrialized countries of North America,
Western Europe and Asia, of which the USA represents the apex.
(The parent companies and decision centers of the transnational
corporations are, without exception, to be found in these
nations.)

2) Class B: Third World nations of broad economic scope
including abundant natural resources and developing internal
markets which have already undergone a degree of industrial
development and which can offer favorable political conditions
to foreign enterprises.

3) Class C: Third World countries of lesser economic
scope, with political conditions less overtly favorable to foreign capital, but nevertheless able to attract investment in
selected sectors such as mining or the production of consumer
goods for the local, middle and upper classes.

4) Class D: Excluded countries either because they lack
natural resources and markets, or because their nationalistic
or socialistic political and social institutions do not provide
sufficient guarantees to foreign investors.

In this general framework, there is a major problem which
has had little study: the place of agriculture in the international division of labor. Earlier we mentioned the enormous
changes in the subsector grouped under the term 'agriculture',
including livestock production, forestry and fisheries. This
has been the case for both industrialized and underdeveloped
nations. The basic working hypothesis was that as capital
development increases and penetrates agriculture, especially
'traditional agriculture', the agri-food system economy ceases
to be 'agricultural' and becomes 'agro-industrial'.

We can see in Table 2 that in 1972 developed market economies contributed 54 percent of the world total value added by
agro-industries; Latin America's share was 6.1 percent and
Asia's share was 5.4 percent. The developing countries as a
whole contributed only 12.9 percent. We are unable to disag-
gregate these data but there is sufficient basis to assert in
general terms that the higher a country is situated in the new
international division of labor, the more its agri-food system
is agro-industrial. It is obvious that in the developed market economies a wide variety of sophisticated, processed,
packaged and frozen products food commodities are produced.
In the less developed, lower in the international division of
labor, relatively simple milling, refining and packing operations are undertaken. The resulting consumer foods have a
lower income elasticity of demand relative to the more sophisticated foods which are produced mostly for the high income
groups. Lall (1976) points out that food processing transna-

tionals are unevenly spread world-wide in terms of area and
activity. In terms of the procurement of raw materials such
activities are confined to areas which have a natural advantage
in producing cheap coffee, cocoa, sugar, oil seeds and selected
fruits and vegetables, or mostly in countries of Classes B, C,
and D of the international division of labor. In terms of
sales of final goods certain processed foods and beverages
(Coca-Cola, Nescafe and Unilever's margarine) are found in most
countries. The sales of a more diversified range of products
are limited to the richer countries, those with a certain
degree of development and with closer cultural and political
ties with the developed world. Such is the case of Brazil,
Argentina, and Mexico but not of Haiti, Bolivia or Paraguay.

But this general hypothesis tells us little about the
forms of integration of agriculture and 'traditional agriculture' within the world agri-food system. In order to do so we
must delineate the types of farming units and their characteristic social relationships which exist in different countries
and types of agribusiness concerns.

In Latin America, for instance, we find a variety of farming units: (1) modern capitalized farming units using advanced
technology, a hired non-resident labor force, and planned management of a technically diversified productive process;
(2) plantations with a relatively lower use of capital and
advanced technology, a significant resident labor force partly
paid through annual land allotments, and a technically diversified productive process; (3) the 'hacienda' system with relatively lower technological and capital inputs, a labor force
mostly paid through leasing arrangements and a division of work
based on product specialization; (4) family farms indirectly
integrated with agribusiness; (5) unintegrated market oriented
family farms; and (6) subsistence family unit oriented toward
self-consumption (Brant, 1976).

The first two categories admit different kinds of ownership: corporate, cooperative or private. The latter types of
farm units also admit communal land tenure. As a whole, agricultural production in Latin America is submitted to a process
of modernization particularly so in countries that fall in
classes B and C of the international division of labor.
Increasingly the more productive units belong to the first two
categories--precisely those submitted to agribusiness--and
fewer and fewer units belong to the last category which is
largely marginal in terms of cultivated area. Small land-hold-
ings are predominant among family unit farms, in spite of the
land reform programs of the sixties oriented to eradicate the
minifundia, as well as the latifundia.

If we now consider agribusinesses we shall also find it
composed of a wide array of enterprises: those owned by one
local family, 'independent' domestic corporations, corporations
controlled by domestic financial and/or industrial groups and

holdings, state-owned and state-controlled corporations, cooperative enterprises producing raw materials and finally, transnational corporations, operating through subsidiaries and joint
ventures extending their control over the previous categories
of enterprises. Transnational corporations predominant in
those line of food production which transform raw agricultural
materials and food into articles of consumption for higher
income groups. The same can be said regarding the production
of inputs such as machinery, fertilizers, hybrid seeds and
chemicals (Malassis, 1976).

AGRICULTURE AND AGRIBUSINESS: FORMS OF INTEGRATION
    A third remark concerns the different forms of integration
    or near-integration through which agriculture becomes
    'agro-industrial'. In a rather schematic way the follow-
ing can be proposed (Arroyo, 1976):

    1) Traditional direct or vertical integration of farming
activities. The traditional system was based on plantations
which in many cases were 'enclaves' within national economies
such as the tea plantations in the Far East and the banana
plantations (United Fruit Co. in Central America, etc.). The
more recent enclave plantations which use decentralized farming
operations and vertically integrated processing and distribution activities also fall within this category. Examples are
Gulf and Western's sugar plantations in the Dominican Republic, Liquigas's livestock production activities in Brazil, and
Unilever's farms in Africa and the Pacific.
    2) Direct or vertical integration of modern farms within
an agribusiness complex. This occurs in industrialized nations
where agribusiness companies manage large tracts of owned or
leased agricultural land in order to circumvent pricing problems at each stage of vertically planned operations. It occurs
in underdeveloped countries, such as Brazil, where transnational firms take advantage of the fiscal and credit incentives
offered by Governments wanting to increase production on unexploited land.
    3) Indirect vertical integration of agriculture and of
ranch land by foreign firms in countries where legal obstacles
exist in the acquisition of land. The legal device used is to
acquire or control land by means of a third person, a resident
national who acts as a strawman. Such is the case for example
with the strawberry export industry in Mexico.
    4) Near or quasi-integration of agricultural land which
is put into production by government colonization or irrigation projects. This gives rise to 'triangular agreements'
between local governments, transnational firms and peasants who
submit to the obligation of selling their production to the
foreign firm. This occurs in some Middle East and Far East
countries.

5) <u>Near</u> <u>or</u> <u>quasi</u> <u>integration</u> of agricultural production
by utilizing contract systems with independent producers.
This is the most common form in industrialized nations, where
agribusinesses process and market agricultural products such as
fruits and canned vegetables or where input supplying industries, sometimes linked with a processor, impose upon the farmers the use of certain inputs. Examples of this are the phar-
maceutical firms associated with the broiler industry and the
feed concentrate firms associated with beef and dairy farms.
The package may include credit, technical assistance, and quality control, all of which contribute to create a locally or
nationally monopsonistic market structure. In underdeveloped
countries integration is also obtained through an intermediate
governmental agency which sells to foreign firms what the small
producers and/or cooperatives and farm associations must com-
pulsorily sell to the government. This is the case with Uni-
liver's two subsidiaries United Africa and Niger France in
Africa.

AGRIBUSINESS VERTICAL INTEGRATION POLICY
        The termination of the Alliance for Progress coincided
        with the disappearance of land reform as the strategic
        core of agricultural policy. No other major policy has
emerged to take its place with respect to agricultural production in Latin America. Internationally new initiatives call
for the regulation and stabilization of the prices and availability of foods and other raw materials, as for example
through the International Commodity Reserve Fund, created as a
result of the Rome Food Conference in 1974. The current US
government policy of non-intervention in international commodity markets, except for reasons of national security, makes the
realization of above initiatives difficult.
        Many underdeveloped countries therefore detect a vacuum
concerning internationally coordinated production policies. In
its absence international production policies are shaped
through the lobbying of large corporations through the US
Department of State, and through international organizations
such as the IPC program of the FAO and the standards set for
agricultural loans at the World Bank and through the aggressive expansion of large agribusiness corporations in the Third
World countries. The strategies of transnational agribusinesses are supported by the agricultural policies as tied to foreign aid (such as the USAID programs in Central America), in
the technical assistance programs offered by developed country
governments and consulting firms, and in the content of rural
extension projects. In a similar fashion the commercial advertising and the mass media communications networks, all controlled by transnationals, continue to press for a consumption
model based on product differentiation and increased consumption of processed food and beverages.

Certain Latin American governments and landowner pressure groups are currently advocating an 'integral development' approach for agriculture. This new policy does not conflict with the transnationals' implicit policy. It also creates fewer conflicts than land reform with the dominant classes. It is not yet clear how this 'integral development' can function when, in general, agricultural prices favor industrial over rural development. If prices are increased at all, they usually favor those items which are inputs for export oriented agro-industries. The profitability of agricultural production of domestically consumed food declines relatively and the performance of agriculture when judged in terms of producing basic foodstuffs for internal consumption is disappointing, with the consequent economic and social effects on these countries.

It is important to understand what transnational agro-industrial firms have to offer in relation to increased agricultural production. In general, the positive aspects of transnationals as seen by poorer countries are that they offer capital investments, technology and know-how and access to export markets. This may help close the balance of payments gap. On the other hand, through the introduction of new methods of food manufacturing transnationals provide the consumer with improved food products. Other benefits expected are the expansion of the productive land base as for example of the Orinoco and Amazonian basins in South America and an associated increase in employment for land poor peasants.

For the advocates of free enterprise now in power in most of Latin America, agribusiness is the instrument to organize and provide technical assistance to small producers. "It can solve the major problems of marketing and financing and contract with them production, advancing them the needed funds to run their farms" (Luders, 1975).

Goldberg (1975) calls this the encouragement of 'coordination' through vertical and contractual integration. It calls for a new kind of partnership such as private-public joint ventures. Future increases in production are a function of timely provision of all inputs, including managerial ability and improved storage, transportation and distribution facilities. According to Goldberg, the coordination of the world food system by large agro-industrial firms could also solve problems such as food shortages. It could monitor expected supply-demand balances and stocks on a world-wide basis. It could buffer excessive price fluctuations through the use of futures markets. Goldberg states that farmers today are at a crossroads: either they must accept a quasi-integration with agribusiness or isolate themselves from it through OPEC-like collective bargaining arrangements. Goldberg undoubtedly prefers the first solution.

Producers in the Third World countries are faced with the same dilemma. In most of these countries small farmers are not

organized and therefore lack bargaining power. Only exceptionally can large producers act collectively in world markets, as
for example Colombia's coffee growers. Such a vacuum can only
be filled by government action. In order to understand the
options open to Third World governments within the present
international division of labor, we must analyze, even if
briefly, the costs and benefits of agro-industrial integration
of agriculture in the underdeveloped countries.

The benefits of food processing technology transferred
through transnational corporations consist in increasing the
productivity of agricultural resources and in increasing agricultural production for consumption and export purposes. As
mentioned, this can be obtained through a direct or indirect
vertical integration at the farm level, or by means of a near-
integration of agricultural production. By increasing the
demand for certain crops and by offering stable prices or long-
term contracts, the transnational processing firms can offer
the necessary incentives for the modernization of production
methods and the utilization of improved storage and transportation technologies, with the consequent favorable effects on
production and productivity.

Let us disregard for the moment any possible side-effects
of such technological innovations in order to concentrate on
the effects on production and productivity. It must be stated
from the outset that the data are insufficient to come to a
general conclusion in this respect for the underdeveloped countries or Latin America in particular. Some research is under
way, but for the moment we have only fragmentary evidence.

However, we can say that the growth of agribusiness generally induces a rise in productivity and in the production of
selected agricultural foodstuffs and raw materials in underdeveloped countries. The crucial issue is whether such
increases are consistent with national policies. It is perfectly possible to increase food production for high income
consumers, or increase the production of raw materials for
livestock production and/or increase exports at the expense of
food production for popular consumption. In the fight against
malnutrition the expansion of food processing industries dominated by transnational corporations may not be conducive for
the attainment of this goal. This is exactly what we can sur-
mise from the partial evidence available for Brazil.

BRAZIL: ADVANCED EXPONENT OF THE
TRANSNATIONALS' PRODUCTION POLICY
Brazil has been the preferred economy in Latin America for
foreign investments in the last decade. According to
Newfarmer (1975, p. 170) the subsidiaries of 26 US transnationals recorded assets of more than $490 million in the
food, paper and rubber industries in Brazil. Agricultural sup-

ply industries, machinery, fertilizers, chemicals, and biological inputs, have equally important investments there.

Brazil is a representative Class B-type country. It is
socially integrated with the new international division of
labor. It is endowed with rich natural resources. It has a
population of over 100 million. It has a strong military
regime, geared to suppress political opposition and labor force
unrest in order to foster, above all, economic growth. Its
economy has attained a certain degree of industrial development. It also presents the typical contradictions of such
countries. Rapid industrial development is accompanied by a
regressive distribution of incomes. Large sectors of the population suffer from malnutrition and are illiterate. Rural
unemployment and poverty result in uncontrolled migration to
urban areas. Political freedom is severely circumscribed, etc.

Brazil's economic performance has been frequently considered an 'economic miracle' since its Gross Domestic Product
increased between 1968 and 1974 at an annual rate of over 10
percent. (This rate of growth was lower last year.) But its
foreign debt increased from 4 to 25 billion dollars between
1968 and 1974. The minimum wage decreased in real terms by at
least 20 percent in the same period.

Brazil has abundant uncultivated land resources. The gov-
ernmant reversed its previous colonization policy of such lands
in the Amazon basin. It now promotes the acquisition of land
by business firms and the vertical integration of farm units
with these agro-industrial firms. Some say that national and
transnational corporations have acquired 20 million has. The
colonization by transnational corporations frequently leads to
the expulsion of previous settlers and Indians. Neither does
it solve the problem of unemployment in such areas, especially
in North East Brazil.

Brazil is exceptional in that land is not a constraint as
is usually so in other countries. Agricultural output therefore can increase through extending the cultivated area rather
than by intensifying production on previously cultivated land.

Table 3 shows the annual production of 4 products during
the period 1960-1970. Soya production increased seven-fold.
Cotton, rice and beans production increased slowly. Rice production grew more rapidly than population, but beans, one of
the basic ingredients of the Brazilian diet, did not keep up
with population growth.

Table 4 shows the quinquennial price indices for the
same products. Soya prices increase consistently while prices
for the other three crops consistently decrease. Table 5 gives
the exports of cotton, rice and soya through 1975. Soya
exports increased abruptly in 1972.

These facts confirm our previous statement about the
selective output increases induced by the transnationals' production policy. Soya production increases spectacularly

TABLE 3. Brazil: annual production of selected agricultural
products, 1960-1970 (thousands of metric tons)

	Cotton	Rice	Beans	Soya
1960	1,609	4,795	1,731	201
1961	1,828	5,392	1,745	271
1962	1,902	5,557	1,709	342
1963	1,957	5,740	1,942	323
1964	1,770	6,345	1,951	305
1965	1,986	7,580	2,290	532
1966	1,865	5,802	2,148	595
1967	1,692	6,792	2,548	716
1968	1,999	6,652	2,420	654
1969	2,111	6,394	2,200	1,057
1970	1,955	7,553	2,211	1,509

Source: Ministerio de Agricultura, Brasilia, Brazil.

TABLE 4. Brazil: quinquennial averages of the deflated
indices of prices received by farmers for selected
crops

Period	Products			
	Cotton	Rice	Beans	Soybeans
1959/63	100	100	100	100
1960/64	99	97	92	104
1961/65	97	93	83	105
1962/66	90	94	86	106
1963/67	86	91	75	109
1964/68	87	86	70	111
1965/69	83	85	76	111
1966/70	83	87	81	107
1967/71	81	85	80	105
1968/72	87	86	84	112

Source: Fundacao Getulio Vargas from data from the Ministerio
da Agricultura.

because it is used as an input by agribusiness and for export
purposes. Brazil has become the second largest soya exporter
in the world and soya processing mills, controlled by American
corporations, have multiplied in the seventies. On the contrary rice production increased at a yearly rate of 1.8 percent. The demand for rice increased at a much higher rate.
Rice today is being replaced by soya in Rio Grande do Sul and
by cotton, another export crop, in Goias. This is happening
because the government controlled prices of food crops have

TABLE 5. Brazil: exports of selected crops, 1960-1975 (in
          thousands of metric tons)

Years	Cotton	Rice	Soya beans
1960	95	--	--
1961	206	151	73
1962	216	44	97
1963	222	--	33
1964	217	12	--
1965	196	237	75
1966	256	289	121
1967	207	32	305
1968	274	158	66
1969	491	70	310
1970	402	91	290
1971	391	149	213
1972	--	--	1,034
1973	283	33	1,786
1974	83	57	2,724
1975	95	2	3,147

Source: Fundacáo Getulio Vargas and CACEX.

decreased relative to the prices of export crops.
     Table 6 shows the result of this policy. The quantities
of rice, corn, beans and mandioca available for internal consumption from national and foreign sources barely keeps up with
population growth.
     These data illustrate Brazil's agricultural policy as ori-
ented towards an increasing internationalization of its agriculture. Export products obtain credit, tax exemption, and
different kinds of subsidies. On the contrary, producers of
commodities for internal consumption, such as beans, obtain
support prices which are less than the market price. Beans are
produced by the small farmer. Since such holdings are uneconomical they are displaced to the interior of the country. At
the same time the use of modern inputs and mechanization of the
larger farms linked with agro-industries and foreign markets
results in a decrease in employment. Rural unemployment
increases fastest in those areas that modernize agriculture.
Additional unemployment is created by the growth of big farms,
often vertically integrated with agribusiness, in the Goias,
Matto Grosso and Amazon frontier areas.

SIDE-EFFECTS OF INTEGRATION POLICIES: ITS IMPACT ON NUTRITION
     Among the benefits expected from the introduction of a new
     technology in food manufacturing is the production of
     improved food products.

TABLE 6. Brazil: indices of the availability of selected foodstuffs for human consumption, 1960-1970

Products	1960	1961	1962	1963	1964	1965	1966	1967	1968	1969	1970
Rice	100	105	108	109	117	132	93	119	106	100	116
Corn	100	101	105	86	94	104	90	109	81	94	82
Wheat	100	87	101	87	107	79	94	93	101	104	102
Beans	100	97	92	103	100	115	104	121	110	97	96
Sweet potatoes	100	92	95	94	103	100	103	113	124	114	118
"Mandioca brava"	100	101	108	119	118	115	108	121	128	130	--
"Mandioca mansa"	100	101	108	115	134	140	136	142	144	138	--
Sugar cane	100	98	103	92	111	133	95	107	99	95	116
Red meat	100	96	93	92	93	94	93	94	100	103	101
Processed red meat	100	86	82	79	88	71	57	68	66	63	63
Milk	100	101	98	104	118	127	120	114	104	109	109
Dry milk	100	116	135	139	131	133	163	168	160	162	180
Eggs	100	102	104	107	111	113	115	115	117	120	122
Banana	100	103	112	114	120	120	119	133	135	145	149
Coffee	100	110	115	121	131	138	133	138	136	132	131

Source: Centro de Estudios Agricolas.

Food processing is not technologically complex. Basic food manufacturing techniques are well known (Horst, 1974). The food processing industry in the industrialized nations is concentrated among relatively few firms. There is nevertheless a relentless pursuit of product differentiation. Food companies spend heavily on advertising. This drives smaller firms out of the market since they are incapable of promoting their products on a national or an international scale, especially in the case of soft drinks, frozen foods and confectionery.

Such a strategy when applied in underdeveloped countries, implies induced changes in the consumption pattern of these countries. Countries with increasing per capita incomes and an increasing concentration of population in urban areas offer the necessary conditions for the introduction of a greater range of processed foods. Such "new" processed foods supposedly have a better flavor or other attributes. They are attractively packaged and heavily promoted through the media, such as television. To maintain the momentum of growth in demand the product must undergo continuously further differentiation. There are certain types of food processing, however, which require technological breakthroughs. In that case, technological transfers would be very helpful because they would improve the nutritional status of large segments of the population in Third World countries. Unfortunately, such activities are generally not profitable. They require a substantial investment in research and development. This is not in the interest of the transnational companies, as demonstrated by Inca Purina in Colombia (Ledogar, 1975).

Product differentiation and advertising, the two basic ingredients of the transnational's marketing strategy, lead to costs without corresponding benefits. Lall (1976) summarizes the distortions and socio-economic costs for the less developed countries. For example, the substitution of feed crops for pulses replaces a cheap source of protein with a more expensive one. It also reduces the total availability of protein in the country. This occurred with the displacement of 'feijao' in Brazil. Ralston Purina's promotion of poultry production in Colombia caused the displacement of beans in that country. Nestlé, the Swiss-based firm and the second largest world-wide food conglomerate, strove to replace breast feeding with bottle feeding using its infant milk formula. Such a shift, according to nutritionists, is disastrous for the health of infants. It gave impetus to the famous 'Nestlé kills babies' campaign.

In order to arrive at a general conclusion about the potential and actual contribution of the activities of international food companies in underdeveloped countries we need more evidence. However, it can be stated that the net nutritional contribution is less than claimed. It may even be negative, especially in relation to the larger and poorer strata of the population.

ECONOMIC SIDE-EFFECTS

We need to discuss two aspects. The first concerns the increasing concentration of the world food industry. This process of concentration is going to be even more rapid in the Class B and C countries. This is very detrimental for the national development those countries. They have little bargaining power and are badly prepared to deal with the tactics used by transnational capitalism.

The most widely used practices are "political" prices; arbitrary transfer prices; tied international trade between subsidiaries of the parent company; internal subsidies of branches or activities which one wants to strengthen against national or international competitors; the use of double or triple accounting systems within a single country or between host countries so as to escape taxation; the lobbying for special legislation, the corruption of civil servants and of those with political power; the licensing of technology and trademarks in countries where the transnational operates or hopes to operate in order to avoid competition; the policies of geographical relocation of industries under unfavorable political or economic conditions; the acquisition of whole industries or firms in order to obtain control over the market and then discontinuing local production; the increasing control over national financial institutions whose funds are substituted for direct external investment; alliances with local political parties so as to control labor and trade union legislation etc. All of these increase the final cost to the local consumer, reduce the nutritional status of the population and increase the surplus of real resources transferred from the underdeveloped nations to the industrialized nations (Amir, 1973).

A second aspect concerns the transformation of agriculture's productive organizational forms. It may be a mere destruction of 'traditional' agriculture resulting in the expulsion of peasants whose land is subsequently used to produce industrial or export oriented crops, as in Brazil, or through the integration of agricultural producers through different forms of vertical or near integration with agro-industries. We can hypothesize that agro-industries, because they modernize agriculture, create a labor surplus, part of which may be absorbed through industrial employment. On the other hand, they depress agricultural wages in comparison with industrial workers within those countries and with respect to the labor force in industrialized nations. The burden of reproducing the labor force is, to a certain extent, transferred to agriculture and to the less developed countries in the new world economic system.

IN CONCLUSION

The foregoing allows us to arrive at one major conclusion

regarding policies for achieving increased production in
underdeveloped countries. It is not possible for governments to design such policies without taking into account the
global agri-food system presently emerging on an international
scale. If the objective of such a policy is to increase production concurrently with the consumption and nutritional levels of the population, then the key institutional obstacle for
these governments is their lack of bargaining power within the
world agri-food system.

The dominant classes in these countries are not striving
for a new type of society. This is clearly the case for Latin
America today with the increasing role of military regimes and
the current structure of the left. As a consequence they must
depend to a great extent on world processing and input firms
for technology, capital, know-how and market knowledge and
access.

In order to achieve better results in their negotiations
with transnationals, international organizations and developed
countries, the lesser developed countries must obtain a clearer
perspective. They must strive to acquire knowledge of investment and technological agreements, of alternatives offered by
agro-industries from different countries, of national and
international food markets control of economic operations, and
on research and technical options. They must assess the contribution of multinationals in their own country and in others.
They must study the structure, strategies and mechanisms utilized by transnationals in their desire to increase their share
of the market and of profits. They must also study the viability of nationally-financed and domestically-based operations,
as well as regional or multinational projects favored by underdeveloped countries (for instance, the Andean Group and SELA).
They must devise measures in order to effectively control tendencies growing from the implantation of agro-industries
towards concentration, oligopsonistic and monopsonistic control, price fixing, etc. They must strive to impose together
with the international community, an effective Code of Conduct
upon transnationals, by which the latter can be made subject to
sovereign States, especially in those decisions which affect
the future of their economies and the wellbeing of their population.

Goldberg's dilemma can be extended to the capitalist world
at large. Not only are the farmers of the USA at a crossroads
today. It is true of the world community. Decisions today
will shape an emerging world economic system of which the agri-
food system is only a part. This global economic system has not
been yet institutionalized in political and legal terms. The
role of underdeveloped countries with their abundance of natural resources and labor force could be an important one. With
the support of their own people, they can act collectively and
increase their power in international affairs so as to obtain a

more equitable bargain. The world would be less hungry, less violent, and all would be finally better off. The political variable is unpredictable. If the present tendencies of increasing accumulation of wealth and power for the few are not reversed, all democracies could disappear. Even the world itself might end up in destruction.

REFERENCES

Amir, S. 1973. L'échange inégal, Ed .de Minuit, Paris and Palloix, Ch. 1975. L'internalisation du capital. Ed. Misféro. Paris, An American approach: Barnet, R. J. and Muller, R. E. 1974, Global Reach. Simon and Schuster. New York.

Arroyo, G. 1976. Capitalisme transnational et agriculture traditionelle; formes d'intégration. Paper presented at the University of Paris X Symposium on Transnationales et Agriculture latino-américaine. April 12-15. Nanterre, Paris.

Arroyo, G. 1972. Después del latifundio, qué? Paper presented at the X Latin American Congress of Sociology. September 10. Santiago.

Brant, V. C. 1976. Unités de production et rapports de production dans l'agriculture brénlienne. In G. Arroyo (Ed.) Les transnationales et l'agriculture in Amerique Latine. Anthropos. Paris (forthcoming).

Federal Trade Commission. 1966. The structure of food manufacturing. US Government. 147.

Goldberg, R. A. 1975. US Agribusiness breaks out of isolation. Harvard Business Review (May-June):90.

Horst, T. 1974. At Home Abroad: A Study of the Domestic and Foreign Operations of the American Food Processing Industry. Ballinger. Cambridge, Massachusetts.

Lall, S. 1976. Transfer of technology and the environment: a proposal for research into the international food processing industry in developing countries. Mimeo:4.

Ledogar, R. J. 1975. Hungry for profits. IDOC/NA. New York. 101-105.

Luders, R. 1975. Entre el colectivismo y la reforma agraria. One Pasa. (September):17.

Malassis, L. 1976. Groupes, complexes, et combinate agro-industriels: méthodes et concepts. Economies et societés 9-10:1373.

Malassis, Louis. 1975. L'agro-industrie: méthodes et concepts. Economies et societés. 13:2023.

Newfarmer, R. J. and W. Mueller. 1975. Multinational corporations in Brazil and Mexico. Subcommittee on Multinational Corporations, US Senate:170.

PAUL C. MA

Constraints in the Improvement of Consumer Food Policies

A meritorious consumer food policy should provide the consumer protection against food contamination, assure him of the high quality and of the nutritive value of the food, allow reasonable cost to be paid and provide ready accessibility at the local market whenever needed. However, such merits do not exist concomitantly. Assurance and protection involve additional cost, which ultimately has to be borne by the consumer. Regardless of the good intentions of the policies, many consumers still select food on the basis of sensory judgment and food habits or inadvertently through faddism. There are also constraints in the formulation of appropriate procedures for food safety and for high nutritive quality.

SENSORY JUDGMENT

Most consumers choose food items based on sensory qualities which include color, appearance, texture or even flavor. Color alone does represent many important quality factors such as ripeness or freshness of many fruits and vegetables and sometimes even of meats, but certainly not of the processed foods. Notwithstanding the fact that the normal canned green bean possesses a greenish yellow color because of the degradation of chlorophyll during processing, the Japanese still prefer more green color, and cupric sulfate was added to preserve the chlorophyll. In consequence of the prohibition of

---

Paul C. Ma is Director of Food Industry Research and Development Institute, P. O. Box 246, Hsinchu, 300 Taiwan, Republic of China.

cupric sulfate, it is now being replaced by Tartrazine (Yellow No. 4) and Brilliant Blue FCF (Green No. 1). Such an artificially colored product, however, is only acceptable in Japan.

A variety of natural and artificial dyes are now available on the market, and more are to come. Different countries impose different regulations governing the uses of added color in food. The regulations are rather strict in most of the developed countries but less strict worldwide. Information gathered from new research and development of additives necessitates changes of regulations and thus complicates the problem further.

The flavor of canned asparagus represents another problem. As is generally known, development of normal canned asparagus flavor requires a certain amount of tin which is usually generated from the tin-plate of the container. The presence in food products of tin, being one of the heavy metals, has been limited by national or international regulation to a range of 150 parts per million (ppm) to 250 ppm or even lower in some countries. To meet these requirements, extensive research has been carried out in Taiwan. The procedure developed and temporarily taken is to use partially lacquered cans, leaving a bare band of limited area in the center of the can allowing the liquid in the can to attack the exposed metal and thus to improve the flavor of the asparagus. A fully lacquered can would bring the metal content in control, but will incur inevitable loss of flavor.

Whether to appease sensory satisfaction in sacrifice of food safety or to uphold food safety in condemnation of flavor and color deserves in depth research in defense of consumer food policy.

FOOD HABITS

Generally speaking, no consumer food policy can change one's food habit; rather, a sound consumer food policy should be elicited in the light of food habits. Each one has his own eating pattern and prejudice which can hardly be overcome by regulation; each race, its unique habit, justifying the co-existence of Chinese, Japanese, Mexican . . . restaurants in one metropolis. After all, to many people, eating is a very personal, sensual, highly enjoyable experience--an enjoyment here and now with little worry about long-term consequence. In spite of frequent and strong warnings, few people respond by making material changes in their choice of food and drink.

No food is better than the food cooked by one's mother. Food habits are usually built up by mother, who prefers to fill the table with her favorite food and keeps the pantry full of her favorite kinds and brands of food. The family members may suffer malnutrition through eating unbalanced food cooked at home. In many developing countries, baby foods are prepared at home by mother. Because of her personal preference and lack of knowledge in nutrition and sanitation, babies eat the same food all the time and are afflicted with poor health and sickness eventually. Babies, who take the babyfood manufactured by food companies, perfectly enforced with all necessary nutrients even within one tiny bottle, will not suffer from malnutrition, although they do eat the same food for a long time through mother's preference. Children in developed countries may have nutrition problems too, because they are so used to drinking cola and eating too many snack foods, rather than eating main meals from which major nutrients are derived.

Food habits vary with geographical area which with its particular soil and climatic conditions affects agricultural production. Southern Chinese are rice eaters, while Northern Chinese eat mostly bread made from wheat, corn or sorghum. Many traditional Chinese foods are derived from soybeans. Influenced by religious belief, Chinese Buddhists in Taiwan take more vegetable than animal protein; they are definitely reluctant to eat beef. Availability of time is another important factor in the changing of food habits. In many developed countries there has been a clear trend towards meal-skipping, leading to the one-large-meal-a-day diet. There is evidence that the large quantity of food consumed in a big single meal tends to be more fattening than the same food consumed throughout the day.

In Taiwan, people's eating habits have recently undergone a striking change because of the economic improvement and social prosperity. Statistics show that during the period from 1950 to 1973 meat consumption increased 2.93 times, while the rice and cereal intake dropped significantly (Table 1). Consumer food policy should be flexible to recognize and reflect such changes, paying special attention to the prevailing average income of the people.

NUTRITION AND FOOD SAFETY

The food we eat is not only to fulfill our desire or appetite, but also, of more importance, to secure our health.

How to ensure that one's food will provide all the nutrients one needs, particularly for those of low income or those on special diets based on religious beliefs or food habits, should be our major concern.

Food safety is a topical problem of worldwide nature. Recent advances in medicine are largely responsible for curtailing the incidence of human diseases due to bacterial infection, but diseases due to organ deterioration or malnutrition, such as heart diseases, high blood pressure, kidney diseases, and many kinds of cancer, have become more prevalent. It is

TABLE 1. The changing of food consumption pattern in Taiwan
          (per capita)

Food	Food consumed (kg)/year		Calorie		Protein (gram)	
	1950	1973	1950	1973	1950	1973
Milled rice	133.6 (38.1)[c]	129.8 (28.2)	1317 (64.0)	1280 (46.5)	24.9 (54.4)	24.2 (32.8)
Other grains[a]	88.8 (25.4)	63.4 (13.8)	391 (19.0)	525 (19.1)	4.9 (10.7)	8.5 (11.5)
Beans	11.7 (3.3)	39.3 (8.6)	68 (3.3)	141 (5.1)	4.4 (9.6)	11.4 (15.5)
Fruits and vegetables	87.3 (24.9)	143.2 (31.2)	61 (3.0)	108 (3.9)	2.3 (5.0)	3.9 (5.3)
Fish & meat[b]	28.7 (8.2)	83.9 (18.2)	220 (10.7)	700 (25.4)	9.3 (20.3)	25.7 (34.0)
Total	350.1	459.6	2057	2754	45.8	73.7

Source: Data supplied by the Joint Commission on Rural Recon-
struction, Taiwan, Republic of China. [a]Includes sugar and its
products. [b]Includes milk, dairy products and animal oils and
fats. [c]Percent of total food consumed.

recognized that the latter diseases are related to some special
constituents of food and to some trace amounts of toxic substances. Due to improvement in the technique of chemical analysis, the sensitivity of the methods of chemical analysis for
these trace components has been enhanced from ppm to parts per
billion (ppb) levels. Such sensitivity does minimize the possibility of food poisoning, but it also exaggerates consumers'
awareness of unconfirmed poisonings and thus seriously hampers
the efficient utilization of some food sources.

    Nutrition and food safety are the most important features
of consumer food policy because they are not easily recognized
and measured. Food policies, although leveled to provide positive protection, often get bogged down by a number of constraints. The following are some examples of food policy constraints.

Extent of Research and Information

    Insufficient research may lead to unsound consumer food
policies or retards the development of sound policy. Although the effects on human health of cholesterol and saturated

fatty acids in food are not well understood, some premature information has already seriously affected the consumption of
highly nutritious eggs and animal fats as foods (Kaunitz, 1975).
Yang, et al. (1975) reported that the "black foot" disease, a
local disease prevalent among poor families in Taiwan, is believed to be connected with some toxic substances in drinking
water. More research, however, is needed to ascertain such a
relationship.

The shortage of protein will impose a serious problem in
the near future. Soybean is a food protein source with a large
production potential. Although a number of fabricated protein
foods made of isolated soy protein have appeared on the market,
they raise certain issues. First, these highly processed foods
are generally too expensive to be afforded by consumers with
low income. Secondly, these fabricated protein foods may have
lost, during processing, most of the other nutrients that were
originally present in soybean. Thirdly, these foods are low in
calories which the low income consumers do need. For these
reasons, the direct utilization of soybeans and other legumes
as food could be more efficient and more salutory. Not much
progress in the direct use of soybeans as food has been attained, mainly due to the lack of appropriate cooking methods,
the unpleasant flavor (mostly to the Occidentals) and the low
digestibility. Attention should also be paid to the exploitation of other protein sources such as fish protein and leaf
protein. At present a substantial amount of fish is being used
as feed rather than as food.

Food safety has been under intensive study in recent
years. On pesticide residues, the use of most of the very
effective and stable pesticides such as organo-mercuric and
organo-chlorine compounds has been prohibited in many countries, and they were replaced by some less effective but rather
easily decomposed pesticides. The higher cost of these substitutes is borne by the consumer (Li, 1976). Therefore, it remains a question whether some of the above mentioned pesticides
could be permitted and used for special circumstances and still
protect human health.

Mycotoxins have been the subject of intensive research in
many countries after aflatoxin was proved to be a carcinogen.
In the United States, other than aflatoxin, sterigmatocystin,
patulin, and penicillic acid, ochratoxin A and citrinin have
been listed as mycotoxins of major importance, although their
real toxicity is not well understood. At any rate, the production of these mycotoxins, especially in tropical areas of
high temperature and high humidity, is an important area de-
serving further investigation. The mycotoxin contamination of
some traditional Chinese fermented foods such as fermented bean
curd and "stinking" bean curd remains to be studied.

Concerning heavy metal contamination of food, studies on

mercury contamination are the most comprehensive at present.
Nevertheless, the toxicity of mercury accumulated in fish meat
has not been well established (Ganther and Sunde, 1974). Attention has also been paid to the amount of lead in foods due to
environmental pollution, but the forms in which lead exists in
foods as well as the effects of such lead on human health are
subject to further study. Cadmium, due to its ease of accumulation in human body, is another major concern. Its toxicity
is yet to be investigated. Tin is one of the less toxic elements. Because it always exists in canned foods, a proper and
safe limit has to be set through further research. Over-strict
control might severely impede the development of canned foods.

Level of Consumers' Education

The primary goal of food research should be in the consumers' interest. As the education level of people is
raised, their demands for better nutrition and better food
safety accelerate and must be answered by appropriate consumer
food policy. Nonetheless, consumers are not professionals.
They are easily fooled by commercial advertisements, and they
are over-sensitive to premature reports. Food faddism has led
the innocent people in Taiwan to believe that canned asparagus
juice can cure heart disease, decrease high blood pressure and
reduce weight. They get overwhelmingly confused on the announcement of a trace amount of mercury in vegetable oil. It
is always difficult to channel proper knowledge of nutrition
and food safety to consumers. Many people, particularly those
less educated, tend to overreact to unconfirmed information
from news media. It is therefore imperative to have food scientists transmit to the public genuine information from author-
ized research results.

The enforcement of a consumer food policy has to have the
support of the consumers, but that support can be won only if
the policy can be interpreted properly by them. Consumers'
education is vital to enlightened food policies.

Efficacy of Regulatory Service and Inspection System

Unlike the appearance, flavor and texture of food, which
are directly judged by consumers, the control of nutrition
and food safety has to be through government regulation and inspection. Based on our incomplete and meagre information about
nutrition and food safety, promulgating a law so comprehensive
as to take in every aspect of the problem seems to be an almost
impossible task for the moment. An over-strict law would
either limit the utilization of our useful food sources or
drive out certain low-cost food processes and additives. For
instance, tightening the limit of mercury content in fish would

result in the risk of losing the food fishes of relatively higher natural mercury content such as shark and swordfish. Another example is the tin content in canned foods. Trade of some
canned foods, asparagus in particular, is facing the crucial
problem of how to reduce tin content to meet international limits without sacrificing flavor. The main concern to the consumer is a compromise that will take account of his buying
power and simultaneously assure him of safety within the range
of acceptable limits. Failing to accomplish this, consumers
would have to pay an unnecessary additional cost for food or
would have to risk their own health. Strict quality control has
to depend on a reliable inspection system. Owing to the instability of some foods and to the fact that current regulations
often require limits from ppm to ppb levels, significant devia-
tion in the results could arise from slight differences in
analysis. It is therefore essential to set up a reasonable
standard of inspection, neither too strict nor too lax.

Enforcement of consumer food policy calls for efficacy of
governmental regulatory service and inspection systems. If more
than one administration is involved, they must agree on methods
used and standards adopted.

Value of Convenience Food

Modern civilization creates a busy life. Convenience foods
have become more and more popular because people lack time
to prepare their foods by the conventional way. While replacing natural foods with preserved convenience foods, shortage of
certain nutrients might also result. More research in this
field is required before its status in a consumer's food policy
can be well established.

Use of Nutrition Labeling

One recent improvement in food trade is nutrition labeling.
Nutrition labeling tells the consumers the complete content of nutrients at their first glance. However, nutrition
labeling also brings about two problems: cost and technique.
The Libby McNeill and Libby Company in the USA spent
$25,000 for data for nutrition labeling of their canned tomato
product. The technical difficulties are that different varieties, different cultural methods and harvesting at different
periods of time give different food compositions. Together with
possible degradation of nutrients during processing and storage,
these differences make a quick and correct labeling almost impossible. One possible way to solve these problems is to label
the nutritional content at a lower value, but this over-conser-
vative measure could bring about further confusion. Consumers
may worry unnecessarily about the low nutritional value and

tend to take more-than-enough nutrients by other means.

The definite place of nutrition labeling in a consumer food policy remains to be established.

FOOD COST

Every consumer wishes that the food he buys is of good quality and that the price he pays is reasonable. He sincerely hopes that such wishes could be materialized through a consumer food policy. Actually these wishes are always in conflict with each other. High quality is almost synonymous with high cost.

Food cost depends mostly on the efficiency of production of raw materials, of processing technology and of marketing. Taking canned asparagus in Taiwan as a case in point, the following are its cost components (Chang, 1975):

Raw materials	46.67%
Container (empty can)	19.09
Processing	7.94
Packaging	4.96
Marketing	6.98
Miscellaneous	14.36
	100.00%

A significant feature is the high cost of the container (19.09 percent), which is made from imported tin plant. Research is being carried out to reduce this cost of the empty tin can (Wang et al., 1976).

All efforts are being made to minimize the costs of the above components through better methods of agricultural and industrial production and also of marketing. However, to what extent such reduction will be reflected in price paid by the consumer is quite a riddle.

NATIONAL POLICY VS INTERNATIONAL ENTENTE

Each nation has its own standard in executing its consumer food policies. For example, on the use of fungicides the USA allows adding OPP (orthophenyl phenol) in lemon waxcoating, but Japan prohibited its use absolutely. The USA permits up to 700 ppm residual SO_2 in instant mashed potato, but Japan permitted only up to 30 ppm. After much negotiation, the Japanese consented to take in mashed potato powder with not more than 320 ppm SO_2 and also lemons coated with OPP-containing wax.

To facilitate and promote international trade, nations involved should negotiate among themselves to adopt uniform measures. Maybe an international conference to discuss problems relevant to consumer food policies might foster better international _entente_.

REFERENCES

Chang, H. H. 1975. The canned food industry in Taiwan. Quarterly of Bank of Taiwan 26(1):54-90 (in Chinese).
Ganther, H. E. and M. C. Sunde. 1974. Effect of tuna fish and selenium on the toxicity of methylmercury. A progress report. Journal of Food Science 39:1.
Kaunitz, H. 1975. Dietary lipids and arteriosclerosis. Journal of the American Oil Chemists' Society 52:293.
Li, G. C. 1976. Current status of pesticide residue analysis and tolerance establishment in Taiwan. To be published.
Wang, I. K., Tsai, W. C. and Wu, B. K. 1976. How to reduce the cost of empty tin can. To be published.
Yang, T. S., Hsieh, M. C., Chang, Y. C. and Hsu, C. P. 1975. Eradication of blackfoot disease in relation to drinking water and food. Food and Nutrition 1:3.

SOMNUK SRIPLUNG

EARL O. HEADY

Policies for Increasing
Food Production

Policies that promote production in all countries of the world are important for keeping food supplies in balance with food demand over the next 30-50 years. We believe that with appropriate policies and agricultural development investment that this goal can be attained in this short-run period. Our paper outlines policies that are needed to do so. However, over the longer-run, the problems of world population, hunger and supply-demand balance for food cannot be solved through in creased food production. They must be solved through fertility and population control. It is clearly evident that food pro-duction cannot keep abreast of world population growth at cur-rent rates over the next hundred years.

Hence, the world has 30-50 years of flexibility on the side of food production during which policies relating to popu-lation can be planned and implemented. The needed long-run population policies are more complex than are the short-run production policies. They must revolve especially around women. Evidence world-wide clearly indicates that when per capita in-comes rise high enough and women are given sufficient educa-tion, employment and social opportunity, they sharply curtail family size. We also must add one more complex social and eco-nomic factor. It is the development of social security systems in all countries so that parents don't have to give birth to 10

Somnuk Sriplung is Director, Division of Agricultural Economics, Ministry of Agriculture and Cooperatives, Royal Government of Thailand.

Earl O. Heady is Director, Center for Agricultural and Rural Development, Iowa State University, Ames, Iowa, USA.

children to be certain of two sons who can support them in
their old age. These two elements, social and economic attainment of women and world-wide social security programs, are the
ultimate answers to the world food problem. Greater food production is only a short-run solution.

THE SOURCES OF INCREASED FOOD PRODUCTION

Policies directed toward increasing food supplies need to
be oriented partly to the possible sources of greater food
production or availability. There are five major sources
of greater food availability for the world's people:

1) Increasing per unit yields through improved technologies such as high yielding varieties, pest control, improved
water management and laws, tenure conditions and capital supplies favoring input use, profitable price ratios, and the
availability of capital inputs such as fertilizer, pesticides,
high yield varieties, vaccines, etc. Opportunities thus for
increasing per area yields are generally highest in the developing poor countries.

2) By a more intensive use of currently cultivated land,
through multiple cropping, intercropping and related means that
more effectively use available rainfall and solar energy.
There is great opportunity here, especially with the development of water supplies and changes in water management, laws
and pricing. The possible gains from this source have been
well illustrated in Taiwan, the Indonesia intercropping system
and research at the International Rice Research Institute
(IRRI) in the Philippines. Roughly, it is the least developed
parts of the world that have climates with long or year-around
growing seasons conforming with multiple cropping possibilities. The introduction of photo-insensitivity, along with
characteristics of new high yielding varieties, permits greater
flexibility in cropping seasons.

3) By bringing uncultivated land into production. There
still are sizable areas that are not under cultivation and a
considerable area devoted to shifting cultivation. Land not
yet cultivated prevails in considerable quantities in the savan-
nahs of South America, the Amazon Basin, large parts of the
bush in Africa, outer islands of Indonesia and Malaysia. It
has been estimated that of potentially arable land, only 22 percent of that in Africa, 11 percent of that in South America and
44 percent world-wide is now under cultivation. While these
figures may somewhat overestimate possibilities, and use of
some fragile lands could cause environmental deterioration,
land is not a scarce resource in all parts of the world or
there would be less shifting cultivation in Africa and Southeast Asia. Even the USA has a large expanse of land that could

be brought into cropping under sufficient capital investment.
Capital requirements are, of course, even heavier for leveling
tropical jungles, controlling second growth and keeping the land
productive. Other problems of forest soils, woods, processing
facilities and markets also prevail in some of these locations.

4) By saving a greater proportion of crops that are produced. Estimates indicate high losses, especially in less developed countries, to rodents and birds and through spoilage in
inadequate silos and granaries.

5) By diverting a greater proportion of grains from livestock consumption to human consumption. This is, of course, a
complex and debatable alternative. In general, it implies
shifting a greater proportion of the world's grain consumption
from the rich countries where per capita consumption of meat is
high to the poorer countries where per capita direct consumption
of grain is high and grain consumed through livestock is low.
The extremes in these two sets of countries are illustrated in
Figure 1. Since this is an extremely controversial source of
increased food availability for the world, policies to implement
it are not likely to be initiated soon. It could, of course,
be implemented through two extremely different mechanisms. One
would be a set of "outright rules" that prevented grain feeding
of livestock, except in cases where the procedure allowed a
greater conversion of waste forages or other materials into
food. The second would be through economic and market institutions. If per capita incomes over the world suddenly could be
raised to the level of England, for example, consumers in Asia,
Africa, and South America would bid the price of grain to be
used as food so high that livestock feeding would take a drastic decline. World grain supplies then would be spread more
evenly among consumers world wide, greater food availability
from existing resources would prevail, and population could advance a few more steps--until it finally struck the restraints
of a world of grain consumers and vegetarians.

The figure illustrates that the highly developed countries
have a high level of grain consumption. But only a small fraction of the total is direct consumption. The major per capita
food intake is indirectly through livestock. In contrast, developing countries consume nearly all of their grain directly
as food. Their per capita grain use is small.

Policies to increase world food production partly need to
be geared to these potential sources of increased food production or availabilities. To an important extent, each of these
sources implies investments to allow realization of the production potential. But also other policies are needed which relate to the functioning of farms that serve as food producing
firms. Policies are also needed as they relate to international
trade in commodities and resources and to the agriculturally

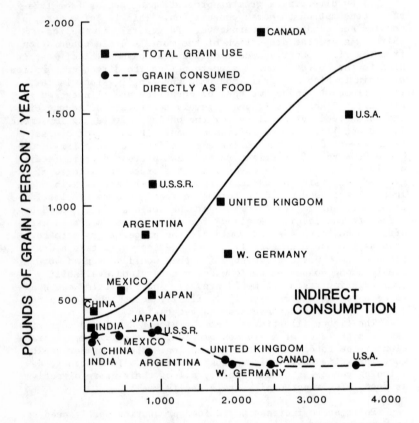

FIG. 1. Direct and indirect grain consumption by per capita income, selected countries.

related sectors that supply capital and inputs to farming and process and distribute the products of agriculture.

POLICIES RELATING TO THE ECONOMIC FUNCTIONING OF FARMS

We turn first to those policies that relate to farms as food producing firms. Over most of the world, any decision to use new and more inputs to increase production is made by the individual farmer or cultivator. If he is to produce more food economically, he must have the appropriate economic framework and incentive to do so. The framework and incentives are apparent, even if they are often lacking in many developing countries. First and foremost, the cultivator must participate in the market (administrative units termed farms in centrally planned economies excepted) if he is to be influenced by policies facilitating greater food production. The world still has millions of farms that participate in the market little or not at all because they are fully or largely subsistence units. These farms must be made large enough so that they are part of the market economy and they must be supplied with more capital so that relevant technologies do, in fact, allow more to be produced from given land and water resources. Generally, an effective capital (credit) supplying mechanism must exist or be created not only for these farms but also for others that do participate in the market but use outmoded technologies or a paucity of inputs because of limited operating funds. In too many countries, credit systems "exist on paper and in legislation" but are not effective in getting funds and inputs into the hands of farmers who most urgently need them. Somewhat typical is the credit cooperative run by the larger farmers of an area who are the major users of the public credit supplies through them, while small farmers must use the scarce traditional sources of funds. An entire treatise could be written on the nature and need of credit programs and mechanisms needed to spur production on small and unproductive farms as well as farms in general in developing countries. To attain the full potential that exists, there is still great need for publicly supported infrastructure in the form of dams, irrigation canals, roads, grain storage and other facilities that allow both the capturing of production capability and the maintenance of stable and favorable prices as output is expanded.

A further step in providing an appropriate economic framework and incentive to improve productivity is improvements needed in tenure systems. The share systems and short tenures existing in many regions of the world dampen the profitability of more productive technologies and greater input usage. Land reform in the sense of conversion of rented land to full ownership can provide a cost/returns structure that encourages improvement, but it is not necessary. Alternatives in tenure

arrangements that provide cost/return relationships paralleling
or equaling those of owned farms can be legislated (Heady,
1971). Conversion of cost/return relationships through ownership or optimal rental systems so that technological improvements are more profitable is still a needed measure for increasing world food supplies in many countries.

Price Relatives and Stability

Not only must farms participate in the market and have
capital to do so under favorable cost/return relationships
of tenure systems, but also prices of commodities must be favorable relative to prices of inputs that represent more productive technologies. Further, commodity prices must be sufficiently certain and stable that innovation is encouraged.
Price and buffer stock programs ordinarily are the policy instruments needed to attain this stability on both a seasonal
and interyear basis.

Some friction, of course, always prevails between consumers and farmers over levels of commodity prices. In some less
developed countries, politicians and administrators are prone
to heed the pressure of consumers in the large cities and favor
lower commodity prices. Frequently trade and tax policies drive
food prices down for consumers but at the expense of farmers
and farm productivity. Export taxes such as those of Ethiopia
and Thailand dampen commodity flows into the more elastic
international market and drive a greater share of the product
into the domestic market. Consumers gain but farmers are faced
with price disincentives that restrain their innovations and
investments for greater output. The large food import subsidies in countries such as Saudi Arabia likewise restrain agricultural development.

If the two goals of lower real prices for food and greater
food supplies are to be attained simultaneously, the policy instruments used must not be those that lower food costs to consumers only through lower prices to farmers. If low consumer
food prices discourage farmer innovation and restrain increases
in supplies, the long-run goal of greater production and reduced real prices for food is directly defeated. There are
numerous policy means whereby food can be priced favorably to
particular groups of consumers while farm level prices are maintained at levels favorable to improved yields. Examples are
the food stamp plan in the USA and the fair price shops in
India. In these and other cases, the public must provide a
subsidy that allows lower prices to the consumers.

Input prices also are possibilities for operation in policies aimed at keeping the price ratio favorable to innovation
and technological improvement. Even before the energy crises,
fertilizer prices were so high in countries such as Thailand

that fertilizer was used too sparingly. The inefficient input
manufacturing facilities in some countries lead to high prices
for fertilizer, pesticides and the general mix of inputs that
complement the Green Revolution. Policies to lessen input
prices and encourage greater use of known technologies can include (a) a combination of freer trade and allocation of more
foreign exchange to allow greater imports of inputs, (b) the
use of foreign capital and managerial expertise in building
more efficient input fabricating plants and in developing efficient input distribution systems, and (c) outright subsidiza-
tion of input prices. The method to be used, if needed, will
depend on the circumstances of the country. Penalties on farm
input usage, such as the fertilizer tax imposed in India a few
years back, is the antithesis of actions needed to boost world
food production.

TRADE AND SPECIALIZATION POLICIES
    We have mentioned those trade policies that use taxes or
    subsidies to dampen prices and hence food development in
    countries where they are applied. Of course, greater
freedom and an increased trade on a world-wide basis could add
to greater world food production. It could do so by allowing
realization of the greater fruits of classical comparative advantage expected under extended international trade. Important
barriers to trade do exist and cause the world's food producing
resources to be used somewhat less efficiently than they otherwise could. These barriers prevail in North America, the European Economic Community, in the barter systems of Eastern
Europe and in other countries. Even within the USSR and other
planned countries, food production is less than possible because the gains of comparative advantage among regions are
partly thwarted under the structure and organization of agriculture used.
    With a need to provide year-round employment on each farm,
Soviet farms tend to be highly diversified in all agro-climatic
regions and there is much less specialization among regions
than in North America, for example. The prevalence of small
subsistence farming over much of the world also tends to limit
gains from the interregional specialization of agriculture.
Specialization is discouraged because poor families produce a
mix of commodities needed for family consumption and because
their limited resources favor diversification as an uncertainty
strategy. If the world were to specialize interregionally in
an optimal manner for greater food production, the policies
needed are obvious even if complex. They include (a) relaxa-
tion of international trade barriers, (b) improved planning and
organizational schemes of agricultural sectors in planned economies, and (c) a vast injection of capital and managerial

services to transform small subsistence farms to commercial
units able to withstand some uncertainty as they trade through
the market with other regions.

IMPROVING TECHNOLOGY ON EXISTING CROPLAND
     A necessary policy set in all countries, if the world
     takes greater food production as a serious objective, is
     further investment in agricultural research and its effec-
tive communication to farmers. This is a necessity in both developed and developing countries. The gap between farmer technology and knowledge of scientists is now small in developed
countries. This fact prompts some agriculturists to suggest
that crop yields may now be approaching a plateau especially in
developed exporting countries. While the gap has certainly
narrowed, there are still promising possibilities such as foliar fertilization, advances in symbiotic nitrogen fixation,
controlled environmental agriculture, and others. The narrowing of the gap is not entirely negative since it arises partly
because developed farms are rapid innovators and important new
discoveries can be put into effect quickly in increasing food
output. But to the extent limits to yield increases are being
approached in some developed countries, more intensive and specialized research may be required. In North America and some
Western European countries, there may need to be much less dup-
lication in research among states and to have greater specialization on particular problems. While the societal return on
agricultural research has been shown to be high generally, the
return may decline if larger investments are required to attain
given yield increases (Schultz, 1971 and Hayani, 1975).
     The picture, of course, is greatly different in less de-
veloped countries where the gap between production possibilities and ongoing farm technology is great. The Green Revolution has not yet gone far and action programs are needed that
take it further at a greater speed. Partly this can be done by
policy elements already discussed which improve the cost/return
environment of small farms, get capital and the appropriate
bundle of inputs or practices into the hands of farmers and
cause them to be operational in the market. However, beyond
this there are still urgent needs for effective extension services that can get technical know-how to farmers in a manner
that is operational. Basically, the policy task is one of investing in more highly skilled and motivated extension personnel. Perhaps even more basic is the development of an administrative structure that functions in fact to get informational
programs organized and implemented.
     But eventually, food production policies in the less devel-
oped countries must increase research resources oriented to the
generation of new and adapted technologies to be channeled

through improved extension services. While greater investments
in regional research centers such as International Rice Research Institute, (IRRI), and Centro Internacional de Agriculture Tropical (CIAT), and Centro Internacional de Mejoramcento
de Maizy Trigo (CIMMYT) by donor countries are still needed,
these few facilities and limited research investments are still
far too few for solving the problems and advancing the technology in the many regions with an underdeveloped agriculture.
Developing countries must themselves invest more in trained
personnel and research facilities to cover diverse agroclimatic
conditions not only in adapting findings from central research
centers but also in developing independent technologies. As
with extension services, a highly important element of this
policy subset is an administrative organization that does in
fact develop research programs of great momentum. Too many research organizations in too many countries are extremely unproductive because of lacunae in administrative functions, lack of
trained personnel, inadequate salaries for scientists and political environments that are not conducive to progress and that
restrain the communication of research findings.

Not all research by donor countries and institutions is
done in the international research centers. Much more of it is
done outside of these organizations through arrangements with
universities, research institutes and government organizations
in the less developed countries. For example, a large number
of US universities have overseas research programs financed by
AID and the foundations. The same is true for educational and
research organizations in Canada and Western Europe. Generally,
however, these research programs are not highly coordinated
and one may find a half dozen institutions from one or more
countries working on the same or overlapping problems in a
given set of countries. These intercountry research resources
could be made to go much further in improving food supplies if
they were more highly coordinated on an international basis and
their duplicative efforts were reduced. The resources also
would be more productive if they concentrated less on site specific research and turned to more generalized models that allow
predictions across agroclimatic regions and national boundaries.
As an important policy step, this organizational framework needs
to be established soon.

Along with biological and physical research, which boosts
yields and serves as a land substitute, improved economic and
social research also is needed. This is especially true for
planning or sector models that can provide results indicating
the directions developmental investments should take if scarce
capital and land are to be used where their marginal economic
productivities are greatest. Examples are the Division of
Agricultural Economics-Iowa State University models of Thai
agriculture which can be used to indicate "what" and "where"

developmental investments can or should be made.

Human Capital Development

Investment in agricultural research and extension organizations that are effective in generating and adapting technical knowledge to farm conditions is part of the human capital
development which must be carried further is world food production is to be increased at rates in line with prospective population growth over the next 40 years. It must interact with
that more complex aspect of human capital development mentioned
previously, namely, education, social and economic possibilities for women, which cause extremely large families to be too
costly in terms of opportunities and careers foregone. A less
glamorous element of this human capital set is, of course, the
education and related short courses needed to place the cultivator in a position so that he can understand, manage, and implement higher yielding technologies.

Because he so often is a conservative strategist, due to
the paucity of his resources and the great hunger or other impact expected if he makes the wrong decision and is short on
food for a year, the cultivator should be surrounded with other
elements of the policy set designed to improve technology on
existing lands. As one of these elements, governments could
operate demonstration farms in such numbers that all farmers
are within walking distance of one. Government officials then
would be "put more to the test" in being certain that (a) price
ratios were profitable and conducive to innovation, (b) practices recommended were applicable, and (c) other elements of
agricultural development were feasible and operable. Another
opportunity is to subsidize inputs and technologies for operating farmers as was done effectively with fertilizers by the
Tennessee Valley Authority. Either or both systems are directed towards a large enough sample of observations so that
the uncertainty of adoption by the low income farmer will be
reduced. Typically, his thought processes and actions are in-
ductive and he "must have a large enough sample of knowledge
before him" if he is willing to act.

Of course, if the sole concern of the world was that of
more food to meet projected population growth and if equity
were given zero weight in the objective function of world leaders, an even more promising alternative exists. Farmers from
developed countries, or educated and capital supplied cultivators from other regions of a given country, could be given
franchises to initiate farming operations in those developing
nations where the gap between existing knowledge and farm practice is great. The innovative franchise could be for 10-20
years, long enough for (a) the innovative farmer to realize a
sufficient return on his investment and (b) domestic workers to

learn and be able to apply the same methods. While it is an
alternative that could be used to increase the tempo at which
world food production is augmented, its equity implications
make it a poor choice.

LAND RECLAMATION

As indicated previously, it is estimated that the world
still has a sizable amount of potentially arable land that
can be brought into production. Certainly a large increment in world food supplies would be possible if only half of
this estimated area could be brought into crops. In the majority of cases, it would involve large-scale capital investments
for clearing tropical jungles, killing second growth, developing water supplies and leveling land. This capital might be
supplied either by the domestic government or through a franchise allowing foreign investors to come in, reclaim the land,
and develop agriculture on it. The former would be preferable
where the country government can raise the capital and organize
efficient land reclamation and agricultural development projects. In case it cannot do so, the world food situation would
be bettered if the latter were allowed and encouraged. But it
would need to be surrounded by a set of necessary conditions
including (a) a franchise of a sufficient period that investing
organizations could regain their capital and a sufficient return on it, (b) the prospects of political stability which
would allow this, and (c) world grain reserves and price stability which prevent the level and uncertainty of prices from
serving as a deterrent.

It is in these respects that the world and its leaders
must begin expressing their seriousness over increased food
production relative to fertility control and population size.
If population growth is to continue at only slightly unabated
rates and if world leaders are completely serious about lift-
ing this larger population to a higher plane of nutrition, then
they must come to the hard decision of how much they are willing to invest in land reclamation for these purposes. Are they
willing to invest in land reclamation such that the supply
price of food rises by 50 to 100 percent? What other public
investments and services are they willing to forego so that
land can be reclaimed to feed a larger population at a higher
level of nutrition? Discussion of the world food and population problems is idle talk until world and country leaders begin formulating quantitative answers to these problems. To be
sure, a doubled world population can be fed an adequate diet if
we are willing to clear and drain all of the jungles, terrace
all of the mountain sides, dam up all of the streams and im-
pound all of the rainfall and use them in crop production. But
how much in terms of transportation, schools, housing and other

activities is the world or country willing to sacrifice for that
purpose? Perhaps each country should be required to answer
this question for itself.

As mentioned earlier, the rather large area of shifting
cultivation and intercropping generally does not require massive reclamation costs. It includes land not continuously in
crops as the cultivator shifts about in his "slash and burn"
technology as a source of cheap fertilizer nutrients. Hence,
continuous cropping of this land would require that this source
of fertilizer nutrients be made more costly than those purchased from commercial sources. Among numerous alternatives,
one means of accomplishing this would be to place a rent or tax
on the cultivator each time he moved to a new tract of land.
Of course, such procedures would be complicated by cultural
traditions, tribal rights and politics, and other complexities
in certain less developed regions.

GRAIN RESERVE POLICIES

It is apparent that the world does have considerable food
producing capacity which is not now being utilized. This
untapped capacity is represented especially by higher
yielding technologies not yet applied to crops, arable land not
yet or continuously in crops, and improved management of water
in conjunction with multiple cropping. More intensive use of
this untapped capacity is difficult under great instability of
commodity prices as experienced in recent years. Much arable
land not now cropped is likely to be brought into continuous
production only if prices are high enough or production costs
are sufficiently subsidized. Hence, the world's seriousness
with respect to producing more food to mesh with enlarged or
undernourished populations, will be reflected in the creation
of an effective demand for the output of land not now cropped
and grain reserve policies that will stabilize prices at sufficiently profitable levels. The mere existence of many hungry
and undernourished people in the world does not translate itself into an effective demand for commodities which could be
grown on land not now cultivated. Who is going to defray the
cost of converting this undernourishment of poor people into
effective demand? Certainly the sizable land areas in Africa,
Southeast Asia, and South America used for cropping on a shifting cultivation basis will not be brought under continuous cropping until favorable and stable prices can be attained relative
to developmental costs for these lands. Even in the USA there
are 105 million ha, nearly 60 percent of that now cropped, that
are not now planted to field crops. Certainly half or more of
this can be converted to the equivalent of Class I and II cropland under sufficiently favorable prices over time. But American farmers are unlikely to do so under extremely unstable

prices. If they did so, the market could break and bring them
losses.

There is considerable discussion, some proposed legislation, and a good many simulation or other models being developed for appropriate buffer stocks in various countries of the
world. However, these generally are directed toward the goals
and purposes of the individual country and its producers and
consumers. Goals of individual countries are not necessarily
consistent with construction of a world grain reserve program
that best conforms with greater world food production and an
optimum international and intertemporal distribution of food
among the world's consumers. In order that this may better be
accomplished, an optimal world grain reserve program must be
organized and implemented. It will require an optimal world
organization, rather than a piecemeal operation on a country-by-
country basis. Currently there is no operational structure for
its world-wide organization and operation. Whether such a
grain reserve policy with goals of price and supply stability
for the world can be attained is a challenge to world leaders.
It involves the politics of commodities and countries and may
not be an activity that can be successfully executed by the
United Nations through the FAO.

FOOD AID PROGRAMS

We have emphasized that mere existence of several million
hungry and undernourished people does not create an effective demand and favorable prices for food that could be
forthcoming from the existing supply capacity of other countries. Unless world organizations can create market or institutional means for doing so, much of the existing food supply
capacity over the world is not going to be meshed with food
needs in other parts of the world. The amounts of food aid
pledged for these purposes by various countries following the
1974 Rome Food Conference are insufficient to cause the world's
unused food resources to be fully activated in meeting present
and prospective hunger and malnutrition. If the UN could be
turned into an effective world organization bringing forth
peace among countries, and mammoth reductions in armament investments, and if these armament investments were converted to
a fund for international food aid, through the UN, then funds
would be sufficient for drawing much more of the world's potential food producing capacity into action.

But even if this were done, certain policy precautions
would need to be exercised. Under previously large international food aid programs, such as that of the USA in the 1960s
decade, an unrestricted program can have two types of detrimental effects on food production. If it is not insulated from
the market in the recipient country, it drives down prices for

domestic producers and thus dampens their incentives to improve
and produce. Second, for competing commodities, it can have
this same effect in third countries who export the same commodity through the market. There are, however, various means
whereby food aid can be sheltered from these negative economic
impacts (Srivastava, 1975).

CONCLUSIONS
        World food production can, through appropriate policies,
        be increased to upgrade diets for a larger population over
        the short-run of 30-50 years. Over the long-run, however,
the answer lies not in food production but in fertility control
and reduction in population growth rates. The ultimate answers
in fertility control are complex and revolve around education,
economic and social opportunities for women and social security
programs for the aged on a world-wide basis.
        Potential increases in world food supplies are still large
as reflected in possibilities for improving technologies on
currently cropped land, in more intensive cultivation through
improved water management and multiple cropping, in reclamation
of land not now cropped, in further public investments in research and human capital, by greater interregional specialization and trade and possibly by a redistribution of grain between
animals and people. However, realization of these possibilities requires appropriate policies in grain reserves, price
stability, tenure improvements, research investment and organization, human capital formation, market institutions that convert hunger of poor people into effective food demand, potential
franchises for improvement investments and systems of food aid
that insulate these supplies from commercial markets.

REFERENCES

Hayani, Yujiro, M. Akino, M. Shintani, and S. Yamada. 1975. A
    Century of Agricultural Growth in Japan: its Relevance to
    Asian Development. University of Tokyo Press, Tokyo,
    Japan. Ch. 6.
Heady, E. O. 1971. Farm size and optimization under tenure,
    collective and state structures. American Journal of Agri-
    cultural Economics 53:17-25.
Schultz, T. W. 1971. The allocation of resources to research.
    In Walter L. Fishel (Ed.) Resource Allocation in Agricul-
    tural Research. University of Minnesota Press, Minneapolis,
    Minnesota, USA.
Srivastava, U. K., E. O. Heady, K. D. Rogers, and L. V. Mayer.
    1975. Food aid and interantional economic growth. Iowa
    State University Press, Ames, Iowa, USA.

LUIS J. PAZ SILVA

Alternatives for Improvement in Food Marketing, Distribution and Trade Policies

Alternatives for improvement in food marketing, distribution, and trade policies are part of the central theme of the World Food Conference: "The Role of the Professional in Feeding Mankind." Within this one short sentence we have several key words which must necessarily be studied in detail and with respect to each other. In particular it seems incumbent to spell out the reasons for and who is to benefit from the proposed improvements in food marketing, distribution and trade policies. A comparison between how the world population is fed and how it should be fed will serve as a point of departure. With this in mind the paper is divided into three parts:

1) Current trends in world population and food consumption
2) The reasons for improving food marketing, distribution and trade policies
3) Policies as related to two basic development models

WORLD POPULATION AND FOOD CONSUMPTION
The world population in the year 1830 equalled approximately 1,000 million persons. One hundred years later this figure had doubled. By 1961 it had passed the 3,000 million mark. By the year 2000 the world population may reach 7,000 million. The above figures show that the time required to increase population by 1,000 million has been reduced from 100 to 10 years. There are no reasons that lead us to believe that

---

Luis J. Paz Silva is Director General, Agricultural Sector Planning Office, Ministry of Agriculture, Lima, Peru.

the current growth rate in world population will change.

How many inhabitants can the earth feed? The Committee on Resources and Man of the National Academy of Sciences of the United States calculated that, on a long term basis, the production of food can be increased ninefold over current levels of production. This increase would be possible by increasing land-based production fourfold and by increasing the production from maritime sources two and a half times. It entails farming all lands potentially capable of raising crops, and increasing the actual productivity of such lands to their maximum potential. It supposes not only a greater use of fertilizers, insecticides and fungicides but also innovations such as chemical or micro-biological synthesis of food.

The maximum sustainable level of population would be approximately 30,000 million inhabitants. Most would suffer chronically from hunger at a close to starvation level. A mass migration would have to take place toward regions which today are very scarcely populated. With the present population growth rate the above number of inhabitants would become a reality by the year 2075.

According to the International Labour Organization, the earth will be able to produce food for at most 15,000 million individuals, and then only with an immediate rationalization of the use of the earth's resources. A reduction in the number of births will only partially solve the problem. These figures refer to the level of population in relation to the possibility of producing food. However, an increase in population requires a greater use of land for residential and transportation purposes. A sizeable area of arable land must be set aside for these purposes.

The indiscriminate use of fertilizers, insecticides and other chemical products damages the earth's ecology and destroys traditionally important sources of food production. The Asiatic countries present us today with the reality of a crisis which lies ahead for the entire planet. Latin America and the Caribbean are part of this projected scenario.

Latin America had during the last 30 years one of the highest population growth rates in the world. Because of this the increase in food production per capita has been very small. In some countries it has declined. Unemployment and underemployment have increased. The demand for housing, schools, hospitals and similar items of social infrastructure has increased faster than supply. The rate of growth in population for the region as a whole was 2.8 percent annually, but countries such as Venezuela, Ecuador, Colombia, Paraguay and Peru had population growth rates of over 3.0 percent annually.

To better understand the implications of this we will make a comparison with the most populous country in the world. When China, growing at a rate of approximately 0.5 percent per annum, doubles her present population, Latin America will have reached

a population of 10,000 million inhabitants. This situation
would present itself in the year 2110. Notwithstanding this
during the World Population Conference in San Jose, Costa Rica,
some Latin American representatives insisted on the necessity
of maintaining high birth rates due to the low regional density
in population.

The increase in population is not the only problem. The
concentration of the population in urban areas also must be
analyzed and resolved. In 1900 there were only eleven cities
with more than one million inhabitants. Six of these were located in Europe. In 1985 there will be 273 cities with more
than a million inhabitants each and 147 of them will be located
in developing countries. Seventeen cities will have more than
10 million inhabitants each, and 10 of these cities will be
located in the developing countries. Calcutta will have over
40 million inhabitants.

The increase in world population and its geographical distribution are inversely related to the worldwide distribution
of income. Robert McNamara, in his address before the Board of
Governors of the World Bank, in Nairobi, observed that among
the 40 developing countries for which data are available, the
upper 20 percent of the population receives 55 percent of national income in the typical country, while the lowest 20 percent receives 5 percent. Within the developing countries, as
among the developed countries and developing countries, inequalities increase rather than decrease. These very large differences in incomes among the inhabitants of the earth, both within and between countries, give rise to absurd forms of consumption, contrary to the most elementary ethical standard.

In their book, "The Next Hundred Years," Brown and collab-
orators (1966) show that the United States, with 5.8 percent of
the world population consumes 50 percent of the earth's resources. If the entire world population would raise its living
standard to the same level as that of the United States, it
would consume annually 18,000 million metric tons of iron, 300
million metric tons of copper, 300 million metric tons of lead,
200 million metric tons of zinc, etc. These figures are much
larger than current levels of production. The annual consumption of copper, lead, zinc and tin, are greater than the currently known world reserves.

With respect to the increased demand for minerals between now and the end of this century, it is estimated that
50 percent of the increase will be due to increased per
capita consumption in the industrialized countries. Twenty
percent will be due to increased population growth in these
countries. The developing countries will account for the
remainder. Only 5 to 10 percent will be due to population
growth in these countries. In the case of food the distribution of the increase in consumption is less unequal. This is
because the poor will spend a larger proportion of income

on food rather than other goods and services.

What then should be our foremost concern? The unequal
distribution of the increase in consumption of raw materials by
the developed countries, or the rapid increase in population in
the developing countries? Between now and the end of this century the United States' population will increase by 100 million.
This increase, not considering increased per capita incomes,
will absorb a very substantial share of the total increase in
the demand for raw materials.

To provide food and services for 7,000 million people by
the year 2000 we may have to ration consumption, between countries and per person. Besides this we will need to plan population growth if mankind's bare necessities are to be satisfied
without undue depletion of the earth's resources.

In this connection one could observe that the average per
capita consumption of food grains in the United States and
Canada equals 1,900 pounds annually. Only 150 pounds are consumed directly, the remainder is consumed indirectly in the
form of livestock and poultry products. For a mainly sedentary
population such a level may be excessive, particularly so when
compared with the 400 pounds consumed by the average person in
Southern Asia. Nutritionists calculate the basic required food
intake as between 1,000 to 1,200 pounds per capita per year.
That quantity equalled the US per capita consumption in 1950.
A similar amount is currently the consumption average for many
European countries.

The increase in the standard of living in the developed
countries must inevitably reach an upper limit. It might in
fact decline after that. Given this, one wonders about the
fairness of the current distribution of world consumption.
What standard of living is a reasonable upper limit? What policies must governments take in order to avoid the rising scale
of expectations among their constituents? What is the role of
the prices of raw materials in the distribution of income among
countries?

THE REASONS FOR IMPROVING FOOD MARKETING,
DISTRIBUTION AND TRADE POLICIES

Increasing production and improvement of the marketing
system are interrelated, and both in turn reflect the
choice of a particular model of development. We will
therefore briefly touch on the different models of development
in order to gain a perspective as to the range of alternative
food marketing, distribution and trade policies.

The traditional model of development stresses economic
growth as the key aspect. Competition in economic activity
constitutes the basis of development. Economic activity is
guided by the principle of Adams Smith's invisible hand. Initiative in economic matters is the sole responsibility of

private enterprise. The touchstone of all economic activity is profit. Competition creates a Darwinian struggle of survival of the fittest. Those firms that survive, absorb an increasingly larger share of the market.

This model of development is biased in favor of Marshall's city man. Agriculture, the original source of accumulated wealth, becomes subordinate to urban development. Agriculture is made to serve the interests of the city by increasing production and releasing its labor force.

This type of hierarchical relation prevails throughout the economic system. This domination of the few is also found between developed and developing countries. Per capita income is normally taken as a proxy variable for the division between a developed and a developing economy. With the traditional model of development a country ascends the scale of per capita incomes. This in fact constitutes the fundamental objective of economic development.

There is a cultural-ideological premise in this criterion. It implies the imitation of the life style of the developed countries.

Developing countries do not possess the required technical knowledge as such, or incorporated in machines. Consequently to imitate a foreign life style both technology and capital goods have to be imported. In exchange the developing countries must export their stock of nonrenewable resources. To sustain the viability of the traditional model of development it is necessary to increase exports. This makes a developing country increasingly dependent on the developed countries.

There is an alternative to the traditional model of development. Such a model would be foremost concerned about satisfying the basic necessities of each and every individual of society. Economic activity is to be constrained by community interests. Economic activity is organized so as to reflect national objectives and controlled by the interests of the people.

Monetary gain is no longer the dominant criterion. Instead of this economic resources are allocated so as to be consistent with a detailed blueprint of objectives, detailed by regions and individual segments of society. The above approach starts with the articulation of fundamental national objectives.

It will stress nationalism in the sense of achieving cultural and economic independence. This increased self-reliance implies a drastic reduction in imports, particularly of capital goods and technological knowledge oriented services. It will stress participation in decision making at all levels, both in economic and socially oriented activities. It will stress solidarity in the sense of de-emphasizing competitive attitudes. It will eliminate all forms of domination and authoritarianism.

It will stress living conditions in the sense of first

satisfying the basic necessities and eliminating unnecessary
diversity. It will stress social security. Society will be responsible for satisfying all the basic material needs of the
members of society for as long as they live. Gainful employment is no precondition for receiving full societal support.

Labour conditions will assure equal opportunities for all;
assigned tasks will be rotated. Workers will make the basic de-
sions as to the organization of economic activity and job security. Economic activity will be made consistent with national
plans. Workers will be the collective owners of the means of
production.

Collective ownership and the establishment of non-competi-
tive relationships among enterprises implies the disappearance
of pecuniary gain as an incentive in production. It replaces
the driveshaft of the social system from that of the principle
of private property with that of the interests of the people.
Such a principle implies a subordination of the goals of economic growth and accumulation to that of production for the satisfaction of popular needs.

POLICIES AS RELATED TO TWO BASIC DEVELOPMENT MODELS

Table 1 contains a comparison of the salient features of
the traditional development model and that of production
for the satisfaction of popular needs.

In the traditional model social infrastructure will be made
to serve the interests of international trade. Roads, railways,
storage facilities and manufacturing will be predominantly established along the coast. Roads between the hinterland and
the coastal cities will be of secondary importance. Production
will be of an extractive nature. The country will export raw
materials and import capital goods. Large scale individually
owned enterprises will evolve into monopolistic market structures. The creation of additional employment opportunities depends on the commercial success of private enterprises.

There will be an increasing difference in prosperity between the rich and the poor. This influences the nature of the
supply of and the demand for goods and services. The country
will be economically vulnerable and dependent on foreign markets
Growth at times can be rapid, but disorderly, due to the uncoordinated initiatives of individual firms.

A model oriented towards the satisfaction of popular needs
will assure productive employment for all, and in accordance
with a national plan. The national plan organizes economic activity according to the priorities as determined by the people.
Social infrastructure and the location of industries will be
oriented towards the interior of the country.

All countries may be classified between these two extremes.
The traditional model exists in those former colonies which
which maintain a metropolitan oriented life style and export

TABLE 1. A comparison of the salient features of the traditional development model and that of production for the satisfaction of popular needs (An Illustration)

FEATURES	THE TRADITIONAL MODEL	PRODUCTION FOR THE SATISFAC-TION OF POPULAR NEEDS
1. Key Objective	Expansion of Individual Firms	Integral Development
2. Production Motive	Pecuniary Gain	Self-reliance
3. Desirable Goal in the Production of:		
a. Exports	Maximum	Minimum, Oriented Toward Equilibrium of Balance of Payments
b. Imports	Unconstrained	Rationed
4. Dependency	Increasing	Decreasing
5. Property	Private	Social
6. Efficiency Criteria	Maximum Monetary Profitability	Fulfillment of Goals with Maximum Economy of Scarce Resources
7. Role of Enterprises and Other Institutions	Motivated by Their Own Growth. They have the Initiative for Production	System of Institutions to Achieve National Objectives Controlled by Population at all Levels
8. Ideological Orientation	Imitation of Developed Countries	Economic, Cultural and Political Autonomy
9. Life Style	Consumerist	Humanistic

POPULAR NEEDS

PHYSICAL NEEDS -
       Food and Clothing
       Housing
       Health
       Transportation and Others

CULTURAL NEEDS -
       Education
       Recreation
       Self-realization on the Job

SOCIAL NEEDS -
       Social Security, with
       Solidarity and Integration
       Equal Distribution of Benefits
       Including Prestige
       Individual Freedom, and Others

POLITICAL NEEDS -
       Participation in the
       Decision Process

oriented production. They have been able to do so because of
low wages and fringe benefits. From the business point of view
such a development model is successful, but it is deficient
from a societal point of view. There is no job security, nor a
planned growth of employment opportunities. This tends to keep
wages below their social value.

The coastal infrastructure in such former colonies encourages the importation of foreign manufactures and consumption
habits. Indigenous production is disrupted. The easy access
to foreign goods and the imitation of foreign life styles lead
to a rapid urbanization, usually restricted to one or two large
metropolis.

Because of this industries located in such areas may become socially inefficient. For example, in Peru, the valley of
the Viru river produces both corn and poultry. But Lima is the
location of the mixed feed industry. Consequently corn has to
be transported 600 kilometers back and forth in order to provide a local supply of poultry feed. Ironically the local production of poultry production is then again exported to Lima.

A similar but more complex example is that of Uruguayan
wool. It is transported from Montevideo to New York. Here it
undergoes a first industrial processing. From New York it is
shipped to the port of Antigua in Guatemala. From here it is
sent on to a modern weaving factory in Quetzaltenango. The
fashionable Quetzaltenango wool products are sold throughout
Central America. Ironically Guatemala produces sufficient wool
to satisfy the needs of the Quetzaltenango factory. Both Uruguay and Guatemala, by adopting appropriate consumption habits
and technologies would become self-sufficient in the production
of finished wool products.

The above example shows that the economically efficient
activity of the separate elements that make up the chain of distribution between production and consumption can be socially
wasteful because of excessive transportation costs.

Former colonies that have adhered to the traditional model
of development have little or no diversification in their exports. They are very vulnerable to fluctuations in the prices
of their products in the world markets. Given the export pro-
pelled nature of such economies, the development of such countries is closely related to the prices obtained abroad.

For some countries a simple product accounts for half of
export earnings. The possibility of acquiring foreign financing (the need is greatest when export earnings are low) is very
difficult when the prices of exported raw materials decline.

Such countries cannot readily shift to the alternative
model of development outlined above because the repayment of
the accumulated foreign indebtedness imposes a continuity of
the past pattern of production. Indeed the bulk of development
programmes of such countries can receive only a second priority
because of this.

Such a vicious circle can be broken in three ways. The country may be fortunate in finding a new source of foreign exchange. The odds are not very good in this respect. A second possibility is that of countercyclical amortization of foreign indebtedness. Colombia, because of an increase in the current price of coffee, can reduce its external dependence.

A third possibility rests upon the principle of collective action among the developing countries. This was the central theme of the Fourth Conference of the United Nations on Trade and Development in Nairobi, Kenya. The developing nations have an accumulated foreign indebtedness of $130,000 million. A moratorium is to be declared for the poorer countries, and the remaining countries will be allowed to refinance their indebtedness.

Secondly, a $6,000 million common fund is to be created in order to stabilize and to regulate the prices of ten basic raw materials. Tea and coffee have been included among the latter.

Apart from price stabilizing actions the fund would also finance the construction of national storage networks, primarily for food. Individual countries would have a first line control over stocks so as to avoid the destabilizing effect of world wide calamities. Such local investments should use local resources. It should employ seasonally unemployed labor. Locally produced building materials should be utilized whenever practicable. Such self-reliance guarantees self-sufficiency of food production, not only on a national basis, but at the regional or community level.

Labor is the source of value. The full utilization of labor is the principal source for a rapid accumulation of capital at all levels throughout the economy. Imports of goods and services should be dispensed with if they displace nationally or locally employed resources. They are to be permitted only if absolutely indispensable, and if they cannot be manufactured locally. Economists should re-evaluate the principle of comparative advantage, particularly in the light of possible economies of scale and the full utilization of the man poer of a community or country.

The common fund to regulate prices for raw materials could be expanded to include the determination of a negotiated price between buyers and sellers. It would include a mechanism for periodic re-adjustments in such prices. It would also contain a built-in progressive ad valorem tax. If sellers increase the price above a given norm, they the sellers would pay a tax. The revenue so collected would augment the stabilization fund. Likewise buyers would pay a certain tax when the price of raw materials fell below the negotiated level.

In our view the developing countries must choose a development model which stresses production for the satisfaction of popular needs. The role of the professional in feeding mankind--the central theme of this World Food Conference--

will then be that of charting and aiding in the implementation
of that model.

REFERENCES

Brown, H., J. Bonner, and J. Weir. 1966. The Next Hundred
    Years. Viking, New York, USA.

MOGENS JUL

Alternatives for Improving Food Policies to Meet Consumer Needs

THE NUTRITIONAL TARGET

    To aid policy makers we have sometimes attempted to diagnose the nutritional status of a population group by conducting clinical studies. In these we have recorded weight for height, weight for age, various skin fold measurements and acute signs of nutritional deficiencies. Especially where weight for age was considered, norms usually accepted in industrialized countries have been used. Certain adjustments are necessary for racial differences but have not always been made. More importantly, one may question whether maximum growth is a necessary or even desirable goal. At any rate, the measurements have often led to the conclusion that a large section of the population was seriously malnourished. Whether justified or not this conclusion offers little guidance for a development planner. It leaves him with the impossible task of having to improve the nutrition of practically all. It is understandable that medical doctors feel obliged to plead for help for all those whose conditions could be improved. However, in low-income countries it is possible to ask for so much that little gets done.

    Even worse than inactivity, such blanket considerations may fail to point to the really seriously affected group, although a concerted effort to help that group might be within the means of planners, and advice on who most needs help is vital but missing.

    Mogens Jul is Director of The Danish Meat Products Laboratory, The Royal Veterinary and Agricultural University, Howitzvej 13, DK-2000, Copenhagen F., Denmark.

309

Recently, we have collected statistics regarding food intakes. We are aware of the inherent errors in such surveys;
e.g., the data received may be questionable, we know little
about intrafamily food distribution, food analyses are inadequate and we know little about retention of nutrients from harvest through food chain including home preparation. Accepting
these imperfections, we have compared reported intakes with
recommended daily allowances.

Here we experienced the first difficulty. The recommended
daily allowances vary widely as shown by the National Research
Council (1964, p. 68). Another complication is that over periods of recovery from disease children have requirements considerably above those of the normal healthy individual. Therefore, it has been suggested that the real target should be an
intake which would meet the high requirements of such special
groups. In our experience, comparing intake data with such
ideal intake needs suggests that intakes need to be increased
far beyond the capacity of any development effort in a low-income country.

We have collected intake data where intakes of various income groups (or expenditure groups) were known. Some of these
are illustrated in Figures 1, 2, 3, and 4 in the appendix to
this paper. Only normal recommended allowances are considered.
Yet, they suggest that in many cases the whole population is
under- or malnourished. An intervention to help everyone is
indicated, but a recommendation to that effect is hardly realistic.

As could be expected the gravest deficiencies were always
found in the very low-income groups (Figs. 1, 2, and 3). This
led us to believe that it is unwise to suggest to planners any
schemes which attempt to help the majority of a population.
The lowest income groups are often so seriously affected that
a policy to help them is urgently needed. Only such a policy
could be started, accepting the very limited resources likely
to be available.

Very few data of this nature exist. Even where they have
been collected, they are often not helpful because the income
data have not been grouped to show the situation for very low
income groups. Hence the appearance of the curves in Figure 4.

Further, we have found no case where protein intake was
less adequate than food energy intake. To us this suggests
that there is little need for special efforts to increase the
protein concentration of the food, again accepting the limited
means available. Further, where protein deficiencies exist,
they are likely to be due to maldistribution within families.
It is hardly realistic to try to compensate for the maldistribution by an overall increase in protein consumption.

In Gujarat, we found some grave deficiencies in some of
the vitamins. We have not yet ascertained whether this is

confirmed by actual deficiency diseases, but such diseases are
likely. Fortification of widely used foods is indicated if
economically possible, or vitamin supplements might be administered. A general diet modification, which would have to effect
the whole population, could not be recommended as a realistic
short or even medium term target.

The curves have led to some further conclusions. They
show that an increase in income has increased greatly nutrient
intake among the very low income groups. To us this suggests
that any step which could help these groups to increase their
income or to obtain cheaper foods of the same composition would
greatly improve their nutrient intake.

It is astounding that when we move to only slightly higher
income groups, the income elasticity of nutrient intake becomes
small. To us this means that attempting to help these groups
by increasing their income or reducing their food cost would
result in their diverting more of their income to more attractive food or to other amenities of life. Thus, programs to
help these population groups improve their nutrition by increasing income or supplies are likely to fail.

This poses a problem of an ethical nature. If groups at a
slightly higher income divert additional income to factors
other than improving their nutrient intake, is it then ethi-
cally acceptable that we make an effort directed solely toward
improving their nutrition? They themselves seem to value other
factors in life higher.

NUTRITION EDUCATION

Figures 1 to 4 suggest that for any group which is slightly above the absolute minimum of food intake, only one
course of action is feasible, namely that of improving
their understanding of the importance of improved nutrition.
This means shifting from a program of providing more income or
cheaper foods to a program of nutrition education.

Nutrition education has been a step child in nutrition
policies. We often have paid lip service to it but have
achieved little. We desparingly declare that food habits are
difficult to change, yet much evidence is on hand to show that
food habits change rapidly when the modified food pattern has
the necessary prestige value for the individual. We may then
seriously question our methods. Have we appealed to people's
sense of obligation, their better egos, etc., instead of helping to establish the prestige of more nutritious foods?

At the opening meeting of the United Nations University in
Tokyo in 1975 where world hunger problems were considered, an
interesting discussion took place. It was argued that influencing food habits was the obligation of the nutritionist
rather than that of the food technologist. I personally felt

that neither group has been very adept in efforts to change
food habits, an endeavour which might better be left with the
marketer, the public communication expert, the medicine man,
the leader of the community, the sociologist, etc.

The need for such action is clear. Ramalingaswami in
Berg, Scrimshaw and Call (1973, p. 45) quotes cases from refuge
camps where undernutrition was rampant in spite of adequate
supplies of cereals and other foods. Clearly, improving food
intake had not acquired the necessary high priority in the value scale of the individual, a situation which can only be rem-
edied by education in the widest sense.

NATIONAL FOOD AND NUTRITION POLICIES

Nutritionists tend to take for granted that every low income country should have a stated food and nutrition
policy as an integral part of each country's development
plan. To the author this seems to be asking a great deal since
none of the industrialized market economy countries have
adopted and implemented such a policy. The basic assumption
may be that one is not needed for them since sheer affluence
safeguards against food and nutrition problems. As is now realized, most countries, e.g. the USA as described by Jean Mayer
(1973), have quite serious nutritional problems. For the USA,
the National Nutrition Consortium (1974) issued some guidelines for a nutrition policy, but none has yet been adopted,
let alone implemented.

Reference is often made to the food and nutrition policy
of the United Kingdom during the Second World War. It appears,
however, that only the existence of a national emergency made
the formulation and adoption of such a policy possible. Many
attribute to that policy the fact that the United Kimgdom came
out of the war better nourished than it was at its outbreak.
No doubt the policy was well designed. Yet, it need be re-
membered that only war time conditions made possible its implementation, i.e. by the adoption of an elaborate rationing system. Besides, war time conditions created full employment and
gave everyone the means of buying the necessary foods.

Today, no industrialized market economy country can be
said to have a food policy although nutritional problems are
widespread. When one considers the need of the low income
countries for additional food supplies, it is important that
all industrialized countries adopt a food policy, which might
facilitate progress in the less developed world. So far only
Norway (1976) has adopted, but not yet implemented, such a
policy.

A great many low income countries have food and nutrition
policies, many worked out along the lines indicated by Johnston
and Greaves (1969) or by PAHO (1970). However, these policies

are general statements of intent, but actual implementation is
lacking. They often have included the establishment of a national food and nutrition council but few councils have been
effective. The main problem is that the policies normally are
overambitious, especially when one considers the meager means
in capital and trained manpower in low income countries and the
many demands with which their governments are faced. Thus,
PAHO (1970, p. 15-16) lists as desirable steps more government
action than is within the means of any low income country. The
proposals for action are often so overwhelming that frustration
rather than action results. The harsh realities were illustrated by Maaza Bekele in Berg, Scrimshaw and Call (1973, p.
22).

        In general it seems that the formulation of food and nutri-
tion policies in low income countries have been useful in creating a certain awareness of nutritional problems, but have
been overambitious and provided little guidance for action.

        It appears necessary to limit ourselves to simple pro-
posals for achieving nutritional improvements by manageable
modifications of existing or future development plans. The
author feels it useful to refer to a simple approach described
by USAID (1973a and b). By modest means and relatively little
demand on manpower the nutritional situation in a country is
analysed. Subsequently, various means of intervention are considered and their cost-benefit ratio calculated. The results
do not pretend to be the ultimate wisdom, but present the
policy maker with a choice between manageable projects, where
the cost and the benefits are known. Interestingly, in this
case, credit to small farmers was given preference over fisheries development, food fortification, developing a dairy industry, and other more traditional proposals for nutritional
improvements. This may be indicative of the problem. Plans
for nutritional improvements often concentrate on nutrition
intervention, e.g. good fortification or nutrition education.
When the whole complex of development, i.e. employment generation, infrastructure, etc., is viewed as a whole, one may get
quite a different idea as to where the greatest payoff in nutritional improvement may be found.

FEED USES OF GRAIN
        The UN World Food Conference (1974) quotes data obtained
from FAO and reproduced in Table 1. It reveals that industrialized countries use twice as much cereal for feeding domestic animals as for food. Animal products, especially
meat and milk, are such expensive commodities that it pays to
use edible grain for their production. In the words of Michel
Cepéde, former chairman of the FAO Council, the animals have
greater purchasing power than human beings.

TABLE 1. World use of cereals from U.N. World Food Conference
(1974)

	Actual consumed 1970	Projected demand 1990
	. . . million m. tons . . .	
Developed countries		
Food	160.9	164.6
Feed	371.5	565.7
Other uses	84.9	116.4
Total	617.3	846.7
Per caput (kg)	576	663
Developing market economies		
Food	303.7	547.2
Feed	35.6	101.9
Other uses	46.4	88.5
Total	385.7	737.6
Per caput (kg)	220	246
Asian centrally planned economies		
Food	164.1	225.3
Feed	15.3	61.4
Other uses	24.6	39.1
Total	204.0	325.8
Per caput (kg)	257	304
World		
Food	628.7	937.1
Feed	422.4	729.0
Other uses	155.9	244.0
Total	1207.0	1910.1
Per caput (kg)	333	357

Using Denmark as an example one may refer to Table 2. Denmark uses 89 percent of its cereal consumption for feeding domestic animals and 6 percent for human food. It is well known
that under these highly industrialized conditions conversion
factors for feed into food are poor, i.e. 5 calories in the
form of edible cereal will yield about 1 calorie in the form of
edible animal product, e.g. milk or meat. Some examples of observed conversion rates are given in Table 3. When the world
shortage of food grain is considered this appears as a luxury
production. Table 1 shows that even a modest reduction in this
practice could go a long way towards solving the present cereal
crisis in the world.

It is obviously not possible to change such practices over-
night but it seems that the problem must be faced soon. One
component of the food policy of Norway (1976) is to try to
guide agricultural subsidies in such a way as to discourage the
use of cereals for the production of animal products. This
appears to be a laudable step.

TABLE 2. Denmark's use of cereals 1971/72 in 1,000 metric tons

Feed	5,882
Food	421
Other	441
Total	6,744

TABLE 3. The energy content of edible animal products as a percentage of the feed energy required

Milk	20
Beef	8
Lamb	6
Pork	15
Eggs	15
Broilers	10

Source: Hodgson, 1971.

ANIMAL PRODUCTS IN DEVELOPING COUNTRIES

Low income countries traditionally have used whatever grains they produce directly for food. Among domestic animals, the ruminants (cattle, buffalo, sheep, goats) are raised mainly on grass land, road side grazing, forage crops, etc., all resources which can not easily be converted into human food. Thus, these animals serve to obtain food from a resource which is otherwise not available. Monogastric domestic animals (swine, poultry) are kept mainly around households, and their food is mostly meal scraps and offal, again resources not available to man. In this way, production of animal products can be supported by normal human activities without any encroachment on human food.

Many of our development efforts have, however, been directed towards helping low income countries adopt animal husbandry practices from industrialized nations, namely feeding animals fodder from irrigated land, grain, oil seeds, etc. It seems unfortunate that we, through a rather uncritical desire to teach our methods of agriculture, have contributed to converting good food grain into relatively much smaller quantities of animal products. The development seemed natural for the agriculturalist or the food technologist from the industrialized countries, since it was the accepted method. The new practices were welcomed by low income countries since the yield of animals increased so much that economies were favourable. Cheap food grain was consumed, but producing milk or meat became more remunerative. It is evident that development efforts should be reoriented towards the improvement of such production of animal products which will be sustained by the use of agricultural wastes, wasteland, etc., and one should not increase

uncritically production based on food grain or other potential
food resources.

Since most of the world's low income countries are found
in tropical climates, many possibilities exist for animal production. Thus India has favourable conditions in several areas
for growing successive crops, favouring the interspacing of
fodder crops between food crops. If leguminous crops are selected, such crops may even increase soil fertility. Other
solutions have been to develop multiple cropping, i.e. mixing a
fodder crop with a food crop, developing multipurpose crops
where seeds can be used for food and the rest of the plant for
fodder, etc.

FOOD AS A CASH CROP

When food production is considered in low income countries,
it is often felt that the food should reach those most in
need thereof. Thus, a well known nutritionist lamented
the fact that Nicaragua was exporting considerable amounts of
cattle, while at the same time protein deficiencies existed in
that country. Similarly, when a large dairy project was
planned for India by the World Food Programme, an appraisal
mission considered it an obligation of the project to supply
milk to the vulnerable groups in India's cities. Such simplistic views overlook the fact that food production can be a highly remunerative and employment intensive activity.

In the World Food Programme project mentioned above an
evaluation mission in 1975 pointed out that even at the lowest
possible prices milk is too expensive a food for low income
groups in India (WFP, 1976). Thus, buying one litre of double-
toned milk, which might represent 600 Kcal. would commit all
that a family of six has available for food expenditure per
day. It is obvious that those population groups are far better
off buying the cheapest staple, i.e. wheat and pulses where
both calories and proteins are available at about one third to
one half the price paid for them in the form of milk. When one
observes the actual behavior of low income groups, they in fact
buy very little milk. Only the most drastic price changes
could alter this fact. USAID (1973) arrives at the same conclusion that milk is not a suitable food for very low income
groups.

It is sometimes suggested that milk prices should be lowered. This might easily discourage production and result in
less milk being available. In addition a lowering of prices
would mean that the rural poor, who are every bit as badly off
nutritionally as the poor in the cities, would in fact be
forced to subsidize the latter.

Free distribution of milk is sometimes considered. Where
substantial numbers in vulnerable groups are to be reached,

enormous funds, presumably from the governments, would be required. However, adequate nutritious foods, not perishable and
easier to store and distribute, can be obtained for less than
one third of the price of the corresponding amount of milk
(WFP, 1976). Similar considerations apply to the use of meat.

It is unfortunate that irrational, emotional considerations at times have tended to divert attention from the real
potential of food production, as illustrated by World Food Programme (1976). In this evaluation study the effect of dairy development in rural areas was investigated. The study found that
mainly the landless farm labourer and the marginal farmers, i.e.
the nutritionally most deprived groups in rural areas, are active in milk production. Their nutritional status is very poor
as indicated in Figure 3. The study further determined that
these groups often obtained up to 60 to 70 percent of their income from dairying, and the efficient development of a dairy industry could increase the income of the small rural producer by
100 percent. As is illustrated by Figure 3, very low income
groups in rural areas tend to increase their food intake and intake of nutrients drastically as a consequence of an income increase, i.e. income elasticity of food intake is about 0.4.
Given the development of an efficient dairy system, this may
mean that the deprived groups in rural areas might have their
nutrient intake improved by some 40 percent, i.e. they might
move from a condition of being grossly undernourished to a situation of reasonable nutritional adequacy.

It is worth noting that many studies, i.e. Johnston and
Greaves (1969) calculate the income elasticity of food expenditure. Our findings have been that increased food expenditures
often result in the purchase of more refined foods and thus actually result in very little increase in nutrient intake. Such
a situation is illustrated by Figure 4.

Similar considerations may apply to the development of meat
industries, i.e. in Africa. It may be possible to establish a
meat industry based on the sale of meat to wealthy city dwellers
or on a remunerative export trade. These activities can result
in important employment opportunities and income increases, and
thus be very important instruments of nutritional improvement,
even though the food commodity itself is removed from the producer.

FOOD LEGISLATION
A traditional characteristic of food systems in highly industrialized countries is a very complex food legislation
and regulation system and detailed food controls. It appears that it has been accepted inter alia that such systems
will foster food development. Under the auspices of FAO and WHO
the Codex Alimentarius work was initiated. Progress has been

slow, in the views of the author unnecessarily so because of
some errors in the method of work. More importantly, however,
the purpose of the Codex Alimentarius is to provide uniform
food standards for all countries. It has been welcomed by low
income countries, since they do not have the necessary manpower
to elaborate food legislation of their own. Thus it will be
found that Johnston and Greaves (1969, p. 56) are greatly in
favour of efforts in this respect.

A word of considerable caution is called for. The Codex
Alimentarius work and much local legislative work tend to concern mainly those foods which are known from industrialized
societies, and the standards describe mainly such foods. Their
impact on the food supply systems in low income countries is
minimal because no or little enforcement system exists. Where
enforcement exists, it may often hamper rather than help development. Only where an export trade is the target may elaborate
food regulations help meet the standards of a more critical industrialized country.

A closer look at most food legislation is indicated. It
appears that many of the rules are to ensure that food traditions are not changed. Many safeguards are built into the regulations, but on close examination most of these cater to tradition rather than to food safety. Fulfilling the stipulations
of these regulations is costly. Even in industrialized countires, many requirements for food manufacture are unnecessarily
restrictive and add to cost or prevent from use foods which are
both wholesome and safe.

If the same measures are taken in low income countries,
much unnecessary cost and waste of food can result. One may
cite for instance the extraordinary caution against the use of
hydrogen peroxide in milk, although its use is safe and would
conserve as a food much milk which is now being wasted. Similarly, traditions in industrialized countries have resulted in
restrictive measures with regard to milk toning or milk filling,
although such procedures could stretch scarce dairy commodities
considerably without any ill effect for consumers or producers.
An overcautious approach to the use of new foods, pesticides,
etc., has resulted in many deaths. There is a question if it
has saved any lives.

THE DEVELOPMENT OF PROTEIN CONCENTRATES

In the last two decades, much data has indicated that protein deficiency is widespread, especially among children
in low income countries. This has led to an almost universal belief that there is a need for the manufacture of protein concentrates which could be shipped to these countries.
Such an oversimplistic assumption failed to take into account
that most countries have an adequate supply of food proteins

in their present food systems, i.e. few countries produce less than 140 percent of requirements. Thus protein distribution, not protein availability, is the real problem.

As a consequence, the world witnessed an avalanche of research efforts towards developing protein concentrates of fish, leaves, oil seeds, etc. It seemed to the author that before elaborate biochemical engineering research was started, one should have considered what such powders could be used for, if manufacturing problems were overcome. Also, even superficial calculations relating to cost of raw material and its availability, and cost of processing would have revealed that several of these powders would be prohibitively expensive. Finally, it would have been wise to consider the logistics of using such protein powders. It would then have become clear that they may be well suited for emergency feeding, but that there is practically no possibility of incorporating them into a normal diet in a low income country. Attempts to understand such basic problems would have eliminated most of the very costly experiments which have been done. As an example, one may mention the development of fish protein concentrate. Many deplored that fish of edible quality were being used for the manufacture of fish meal to be fed to domestic animals. They thought that it would be better to prepare a colourless, odourless protein concentrate, which could be fed directly to man. Two basic factors were overlooked. Fishing is highly seasonal in practically all parts of the world. Since the manufacturing process obviously would include expensive machinery, the product would have to be charged with very high overhead costs, pricing the end product out of the reach of any low income group.

Also, surplus fish used for fish meal is often landed in poor condition and not considered edible for man. With fishing methods and preservation on board to produce an edible grade fish, the cost of landing would increase by several fold and would make the process uneconomic.

Still another basic fact was overlooked. Fish meal is presently being used as an animal feed, and its whole protein value is utilized for this purpose. If the fish meal were not available, larger amounts of vegetable proteins would be required for the same feeding purposes. This means that to the same degree that fish protein could be diverted from feed use to food use, a corresponding amount of vegetable protein would be diverted from food use to feed use. On the balance, even if the project had been successful, it would have achieved nothing.

More promising was the development of leaf protein. The basic assumption was that leaf protein is converted with a rather wasteful conversion rate through the animal to milk and meat as referred to in Table 3. If the protein could be isolated and fed to man directly, the unfavourable conversion would be avoided. However, serious problems exist. The cost

of collecting leaves, suitable for the purpose, is enormous.
Growing specific leafy plants for this purpose, i.e. alfalfa,
is feasible, but it is probably equally economical to use the
same areas for growing grain or oil seeds, the protein content
of which can much more readily be used for food purposes. At
any rate, no commercial process is yet in sight, and it seems
obvious that where leaf resources exist, the domestic animal,
i.e. the cattle or the sheep, are most efficient in harvesting
the resource and converting it into high grade foods.

The most important effort has been made in the development
of oil seed concentrates, and these are useful food components
in many industrially prepared foods. The protein concentrates
from oil seeds are among the cheapest available. They have
proven to be well suited for many emergency feeding purposes,
but it has not yet been possible to fit them into products used
normally in low income countries.

THE ANALOGUES

In the industrialized countries, much effort has been made
to develop vegetable substitutes for the more expensive
animal products. Foremost, of course, was oleo margarine,
followed by a much lesser use of vegetable milk substitutes.
Recently, many oil seed concentrates or hydrolysates have been
used as meat extenders in industrialized countries, and tex-
tured products have been developed which may simply replace
meat, thereby circumventing the process of feeding animals with
a very unfavourable conversion rate. In spite of conservative
food regulations, such extenders for meat are presently widespread and may contribute towards limiting the use in industrialized countries of food grain for feed purposes.

The success of animal product substitutes has suggested
that similar products be adopted in low income countries to
save on the scarce animal resources. Such steps are useful
only if we anticipate that low income countries will accept the
same food patterns as industrialized countries, and will agree
to fulfill the increased needs for animal products through the
use of vegetable substitutes. This would not constitute an
actual improvement in the nutrition situation in low income
countries. The low income groups, presumably derive practically all their protein from vegetable sources. Little seems
to be achieved by teaching them to obtain protein from more
sophisticated and expensive, but not more nutritious, vegetable
products.

SINGLE CELL PRODUCTS

Enormous efforts have been made to develop so-called single cell proteins. Since the dry matter of these materials is made up by fat, carbohydrates and proteins, and

since the world's basic need is for more food, not just more
protein, the author has preferred the term "single cell products". There are some indications that single cell products
can be developed by fermentation of waste material, i.e. from
sugar manufacture, cellulose plants, etc. If these attempts
can be successful, sizeable recovery of otherwise wasted materials may be achieved.

The greatest effort has been in the use of mineral oil and
gas resources for single cell products. This manufacture is
energy requiring and further development is needed to decrease
energy demands. However, it must also be considered that the
world uses enormous quantities of oil and gas for energy. Mineral oil can be turned into food although with a comparatively
low yield, since much is wasted in the form of energy. Nevertheless, this seems a more appropriate use of the resources
than burning them up in passenger cars when the magnitude of the
world's food problem is considered.

Production of single cell products is already far advanced
and has resulted in quite extensive use as animal feeds. Much
attention is paid to the possibility of using these resources
as direct human food. The constraints are considerable because
of many toxicological considerations relating both to high content of nucleic acid and to residues from the substrate. In
the views of the author, use for human food is not of any immediate importance, since for a long period to come these products
can form valuable substitutes for the cereals otherwise used for
feeding animals. Thus edible cereals would be relased for human
use.

THE ROLE OF SCIENCE

In the views of the author, it seems that efforts of industrialized countries, to give aid both in the market economy
sector and in the centrally planned sector, to low income
countries face three very serious problems.

First, it seems we have considered development mainly as an
activity to be carried out by scientists. Scientists often form
the majority in the decision making bodies, and many scientists
are sent out as aid workers. In this it is generally overlooked
that scientists are trained to analyse problems, find out how
things work, etc., but are not used to finding solutions and
achieving improvements. When we consider world nutrition problems, we find that enormous studies have been made of the situation which often has been analysed with a degree of detail which
in no way is commensurate with our efforts to remedy the situation. We see a very high degree of scientific experimenting as
a component of aid work, and the author has sometimes been left
with the alarming thought that low income countries have become
the highly interesting subjects for scientific experiments, paid
for by generous aid funds.

Another problem has been found in the fact that most development aid has been based on the assumption that the development we have seen in the Western World is a desirable one. This has been the general approach of the scientist and the technician whom we have sent out to assist in development. Basically, he knows a certain trade. His asset is his knowledge of that trade, and he tries to develop the same activity in other countries as he had done at home, regardless of whether it is really needed there. We have had the problem of a technology transplant which was ultimately rejected. Instead, we should have attempted a technology transfer, but this we have not yet learned how to achieve.

Our worst failure has been our serious problems in communicating with the populations of the third World. I had a discouraging experience recently during discussion of a development project. Personnel from the project insisted that one had to choose between efficiency and integration. They maintained that when they as one expatriate group worked together in a determined team, they established a project which worked with great efficiency and obtained production results. However, they conceded and deplored that the minute the project was handed over to local personnel, it collapsed. They considered their achievement, the effective project, as a success. Since there was no trace of permanent improvement in the recipient country, that country may well be left with a feeling of frustration and resentment. The project had achieved only a considerable lack of belief in the development process in the country where help was urgently needed.

REFERENCES

Berg, A., N. S. Scrimshaw and D. L. Call. 1973. Nutrition, National Development and Planning. Massachusetts Institute of Technology Press, Cambridge, Massachusetts.

Gujarat. 1973. Incidence of Poverty in Gujarat (An Analysis Based on the Data on Consumer Expenditure). Bureau of Economics and Statistics, Government of Gujarat. Ahmedabad, India.

Guyana. Undated. The National Food and Nutrition Survey of Guyana 1971; Final draft. Undertaken by the Government of Guyana with the assistance of the Caribbean Food and Nutrition Institute and Pan American Health Organization, and the Food and Agriculture Organization of the United Nations.

Hindustan Thompson Associates Limited. 1972. A Study of Food Habits in Calcutta. Hindustan Thompson Associates Limited, Calcutta, India.

Hodgson, R. E. 1971. Place of animals in world agriculture. Journal of Dairy Science 54:442.

Johnston, B. F. and J. P. Greaves. 1969. Manual on Food and
    Nutrition Policy. Food and Nutritional Studies No. 22,
    Food and Agriculture Organization, Rome, Italy.
Mayer, J. (ed.). 1973. U.S. Nutrition Policy in the Seven-
    ties, W. H. Freeman, San Francisco, California.
The National Nutrition Consortium. 1974. Guidelines for a
    national nutrition policy. Nutrition Reviews 32:153.
National Research Council. 1964. Recommended dietary allow-
    ances; Sixth revised edition; A Report of the Food and Nu-
    trition Board. National Academy of Sciences; National Re-
    search Council. Publication 1146, Washington, D.C.
Norway Landbruksdepartementet. Undated. Om norsk ernaerings-
    og matforsynings- politikk. St. meld. No. 32 (1975-76).
Pan American Health Organization. 1970. Elements of a food
    and nutrition policy in Latin America; Report of a Techni-
    cal Group Meeting, Washington, D.C., May 19-23, 1969. Pan
    American Health Organization, Scientific Publication No.
    194. Washington, D.C.
U.N. World Food Conference. 1974. Assessment of the World
    Food Situation, Present and Future. E/Conf. 65/3.
(USAID). 1973a. Planning National Nutrition Programs: A Sug-
    gested Approach; Vol. I: Summary of the Methodology.
    Office of Nutrition, Bureau for Technical Assistance,
    Agency for International Development. Washington, D.C.
(USAID). 1973b. Planning National Nutrition Programs: A Sug-
    gested Approach; Vol. II: Case Study. Office of Nutrition,
    Bureau for Technical Assistance, Agency for International
    Development. Washington, D.C.
(WFP) World Food Programme. 1976. Second Interim Evaluation
    of WFP Assisted Project India 618, Milk Marketing and Dairy
    Development: World Food Programme. Rome, Italy.

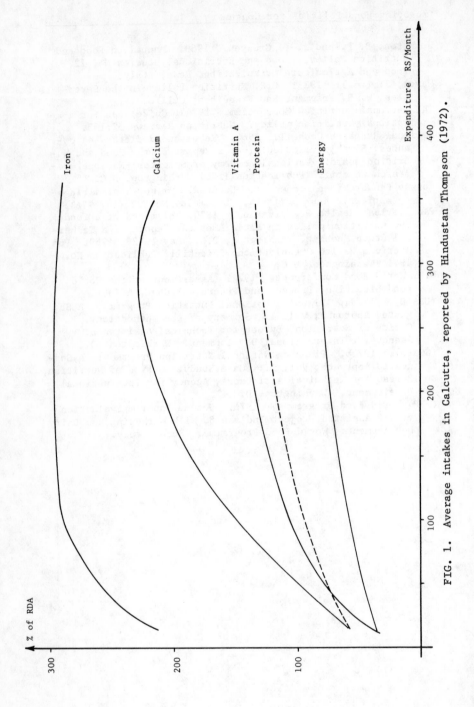

FIG. 1. Average intakes in Calcutta, reported by Hindustan Thompson (1972).

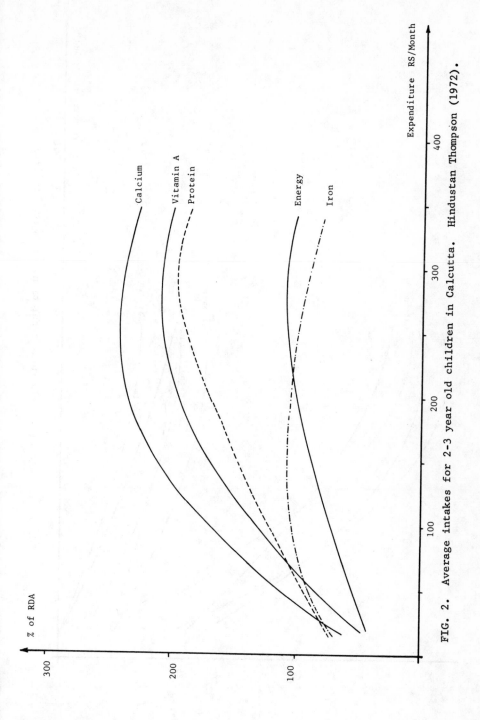

FIG. 2. Average intakes for 2-3 year old children in Calcutta. Hindustan Thompson (1972).

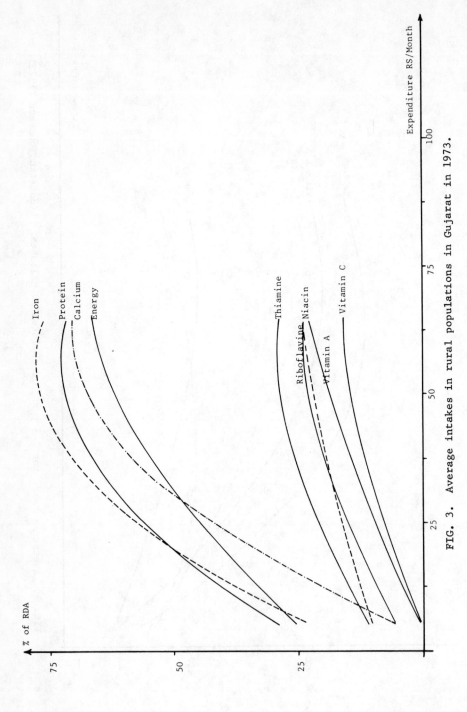

FIG. 3. Average intakes in rural populations in Gujarat in 1973.

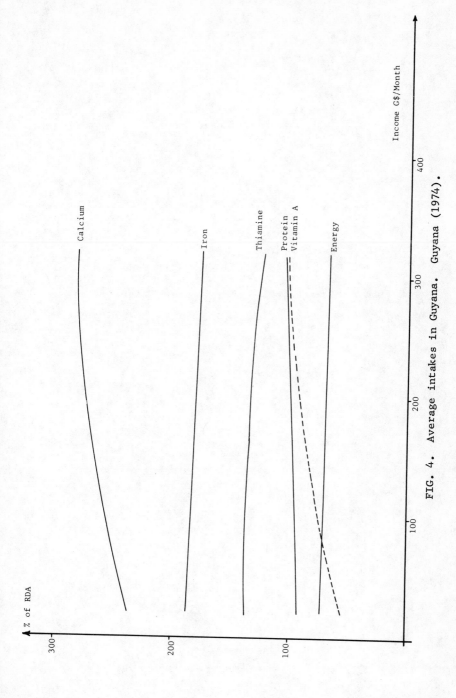

FIG. 4. Average intakes in Guyana. Guyana (1974).

4

Natural and Human Resources

M. MOHIEY NASRAT
A. AHMED GOUELI

The Productivity of the Human Work Force in Traditional Agriculture with Special Reference to Egypt

Economic development is an important issue in most countries. Accordingly, national plans are constructed to mobilize
resources for development. This requires the accumulation of
physical and human capital. Neglect of the important role of
human capital has held back economic and social progress in
many developing countries.

The effective labour force of a nation is determined by
the availability, the utilization and the productivity of
labour. Labour availability is a result of the age and sex
composition of the population. It is also determined by law,
customs, and the geographic distribution of the population.
The full utilization of this labour force is not always possible because of the several factors that cause visible or invisible unemployment. In this connection one could mention the
seasonality of production, technological change, restrictive
hiring practices, and the several macro economic variables that
determine the state of the economy. Labour productivity is
determined mainly by the workers' health and mental conditions,
their diet, their working conditions, their level of educational and vocational training, available capital resources and
last, but not least, the organization of economic activity.

The proper utilization of available human resources is of

M. Mohiey Nasrat is Head, Department of Agricultural Economics and Extension, Faculty of Agriculture, Cairo University,
Cairo, Egypt.

A. Ahmed Goueli is Head, Department of Agricultural
Economics, Faculty of Agriculture, Zagazig University, Zagazig,
Egypt.

great importance in social and economic development. There is
an urgent need for developing countries to plan the use of
their available work force for the above purposes. Because the
larger share of manpower in developing countries is as yet
employed in agriculture and related activities, rural employment problems figure large in any policy concerned with human
resources development.

In Egypt, agriculture is as yet the largest sector of the
national economy. About 70 percent of total exports are of
agricultural origin and about one-third of national income is
derived from agricultural activities. Agriculture is the major
source of employment. More than 60 percent of the population
and half of the active labour force find their livelihood in
agriculture.

THE PRODUCTION OF FOOD IN EGYPT IN RELATION TO POPULATION GROWTH

Since 1955, the population of Egypt has increased at a
rate of 2.5 percent annually. Between 1952 and 1972 the
population increased from 21 to 35 millions. Family planning programmes will not measurably decrease the rate of growth
in population, given the continuation of current social structures and customs. Egypt, therefore, faces a serious population problem, in the sense of an increasing disequilibrium
between population and resources.

This is most evident in the agricultural sector, where
agricultural land is very scarce. Accordingly, Egypt will have
to rely increasingly on foreign sources to supplement its food
production. It is estimated that by 1980 the value of wheat
imports will equal the export earnings from cotton, Egypt's
major source of foreign exchange.

Table 1 compares recent trends in population growth and
food production. Although total production of food increased,
the per caput production remained constant. There is then a
necessity for a more rapid expansion of food production in
Egypt. This can be achieved through increasing the productivity of existing resources and through an expansion of the
resource base. The improvement of the human resource base
could also contribute significantly to the achievement of this
objective.

HUMAN RESOURCES AND LABOUR FORCE

The Egyptian labour force equalled approximately 8.5 million persons in 1970/1971 relative to about 7.6 million
persons in 1966/1967 (see Table 2). Two-thirds of the
labour force is employed in the so-called commodity sectors
The remainder is employed in the group of services sectors.

TABLE 1. Population growth and the per caput production of
food, Egypt, 1960-1972 (1961-1965 = 100)

Year	Population	Food production Total	Per caput
1960	92	125	109
1961	95	85	90
1962	97	101	104
1963	100	104	104
1964	102	104	102
1965	105	106	100
1966	108	109	101
1967	111	108	97
1968	113	121	106
1969	116	123	105
1970	119	125	104
1971	122	130	105
1972	125	132	103

Source: Food and Agriculture Organization, 1974

TABLE 2. Employment by sectors, Arab Republic of Egypt, 1966-
67 through 1970-1971

Sector	1966-67	1967-68	1968-69	1969-70	1970-71
Agriculture	3,864.6	3,892.4	3,964.9	4,048.3	4,056.9
Industry	846.7	867.3	890.7	916.1	1,052.8
Electricity	18.3	18.5	20.3	22.8	30.4
Construction	307.6	259.8	338.0	387.9	365.8
Total commodity sectors	5,037.2	5,038.0	5,213.9	5,375.1	5,505.9
Transportation & communication	324.5	330.4	335.7	347.2	374.5
Finance & trade	767.7	785.8	794.3	801.7	815.6
Housing	22.6	134.3	135.8	136.3	137.0
Public utilities	31.6	32.2	32.4	33.7	35.5
Other services	1,450.2	1,506.9	1,539.1	1.580.6	1,637.5
Total service sectors	2,596.6	2,789.6	2,837.3	2,899.6	3,000.1
Total	7,633.8	7,827.6	8,051.2	8,274.7	8,506.0

Source: United Arab Republic Central Agency for Public Mobilization and Statistics. 1973.

The agricultural labour force increased from 3.9 million
persons in 1966-1967 and to 4.1 million persons in 1970-1971.
The agricultural labour force will continue to grow in the near
future because of continued population growth and the limited
rate of absorption in nonagricultural sectors. This increase
in numbers is not associated with an increase in quality. The
quality of the labour force is low and has not significantly
improved over time. This is reflected in the high illiteracy
rates among rural population. Table 3 shows for 1960 a rate of
illiteracy of 67 percent for males and 93 percent for females
in rural areas.

TABLE 3.   The educational status, by sex, of the rural area
            population (10 years or older), Egypt, 1960

Educational status	Males (1000)	Females (1000)	Total (1000)
Illiterate	3721	5276	8998
Read only	46	15	61
Read and write	1480	350	1830
Less than medium certificate	51	9	66
Medium or equal certificate	170	16	186
More than medium certificate	4	0	4
First university degree	12	0	12
Master or higher degree	2	0	2
Unknown	28	38	66
Total	6520	5705	11225

Source: Institute of National Planning.   1966.

Moreover, part of the labour force is made up of children
under fourteen years of age. Additionally social constraints
limit female participation in several agricultural activities
in parts of the country. The low quality of the labour force
and existing social constraints are reflected in the state of
technology in Egyptian agriculture. Many agricultural operations use primitive and traditional tools. This contributes to
a low productivity of the human resources in agriculture.

THE PRODUCTIVITY OF THE HUMAN WORK FORCE
        Productivity can be defined in several ways. Some are
        partial, others comprehensive. A comprehensive measure
        relates all outputs to all inputs. In agriculture, such a
measure relates the aggregate of agricultural outputs to the
aggregate of agricultural inputs. A partial productivity concept may be defined for a subsector or with respect to a single
input such as labour.

The estimation of the productivity of labour in Egyptian agriculture is not easy, because of conceptual difficulties and the lack of data. The data problems in this area are particularly acute. There is a great need for periodic surveys. But since the 1964 national cooperative survey between the Government of Egypt and the International Labour Organization no comprehensive rural area employment surveys have been undertaken. This lack of data prevents a detailed analysis of labour productivity in Egyptian agriculture. There are, however, other productivity measures of equal interest.

We use two measures of agricultural productivity. The first measure relates the gross value of agricultural production, in constant prices, to the number of persons that make up the agricultural labour force. The second measure relates the gross value of agricultural production, in constant prices, to the number of cultivated feddans (one feddan = 1.038 acres).

Table 4 contains both measures for the period 1960-1970. Throughout this period productivity per worker remained relatively stagnant, but productivity per feddan increased, with the exception of 1961, which was an abnormal year. The increase in agricultural production--with an almost constant area of cultivated land equal to 5.6 million feddans--was due to a more intensive use of land and water and other inputs such as fertilizers and improved seeds. If the effect of these inputs were eliminated, then the productivity of labour could be shown to be declining. Given the population pressure on agricultural land such a result is to be expected.

TABLE 4.   The annual gross value of agricultural output, in constant 1939 prices, per agricultural worker and per feddan, Egypt, 1960-1970

Year	Per worker per year 1939 £.E	Per fedden per year 1939 £.E
1960	41	24
1961	33	21
1962	39	25
1963	41	26
1964	43	28
1965	43	29
1966	43	30
1967	44	30
1968	42	29
1969	45	32
1970	46	33

Source: Ministry of Agriculture. Several years. Agricultural Economics Bulletin. Cairo, Egypt.

Previous studies reported similar results. Clark (1957, p. 262) stated, in relation to Egypt, "The production per acre appears to have been rising over a considerable period, at about the same rate as agricultural employment. Product per man appears, therefore, to have been approximately constant". An apparent constant low level of productivity per worker is consistent with a considerable amount of underemployment in Egyptian agriculture. Nurkse (1958, p. 35) wrote in this regard, "The highest estimates of the degree of disguised unemployment that I have seen--namely, 40 to 50 percent--are for Egypt. Naturally estimates of this sort are highly uncertain. We should not overrate the importance of this phenomenon, but it does appear to be quantitatively quite significant." The 1964 labour record survey indicates, that the degrees of underemployment in agriculture for men, women and children were respectively 12.5 percent, 25.4 percent, and 64.7 percent (Institute of National Planning, 1966, p. 196).

Egypt has gone through far reaching structural changes since 1960. Particularly in the areas of education, organization and the tendency of large numbers of workers to leave the country in order to work in other Arab countries for better pay. This last phenomenon is not restricted to skilled and educated labour, but also includes unskilled labour. Previous estimates of underemployment in Egyptian agriculture should, therefore, be used with great caution. It also makes studies about the human resource factor in Egyptian agriculture very necessary.

CONCLUSIONS

Yields per acre of crop land in Egypt are among the highest in the world. The Egyptian farmer is among the most enterprising farmers in the world. Behind him lies the accumulated experience of more than five thousand years of intensive irrigated agriculture. In spite of this productivity could be improved substantially.

As mentioned before, population in Egypt has become a very pressing problem, both in urban and rural areas. The agricultural labour force, according to published statistics, is still increasing and will continue to do so for many years to come. A reasonable balance between agricultural resources and the labour force must be achieved. This is possible through a lowering of the rate of growth in population, through a shift towards non-agricultural employment and through an expansion of the agricultural resource base, especially arable land.

In order for Egypt to achieve a greater productivity of its human resources, it should follow a multiple dimensioned policy. This would include family planning, the development of non-agricultural sectors, the expansion of cultivated area and the utilization of modern technology. Rural industries and agro-industrial complexes could be useful instruments in eliminating part of the prevailing underemployment.

In recent years skilled labour, especially in the operation and maintenance of farm machinery, has become a major constraint limiting the production of food and fiber in a modernized way. Experience then shows the need for a broad range of human resource training schemes in such areas.

The human work force in Egypt is in need of improved nutrition and health levels. Agricultural extension could play an important role in this. Agricultural extension has not played its role effectively, due to limited resources, both physical and human. The productivity of agricultural labour, however, could be greatly improved, given the progressive nature of the Egyptian farmer.

REFERENCES

Clark, C. 1967. The Conditions of Economic Progress. (3rd Ed.) Macmillan and Co., London, United Kingdom.

Nurkse, R. 1958. Problems of capital formation in underdeveloped countries. Basil Blackwell, Oxford, United Kingdom.

United Arab Republic, Central Agency for Public Mobilization and Statistics. 1973. Statistical Handbook. Cairo, Egypt.

United Arab Republic, Institute of National Planning. 1966. Research report on employment problems in rural areas. Cairo, Egypt.

United Arab Republic, Ministry of Agriculture. Several years. Agricultural Economics Bulletin. Cairo, Egypt.

United Nations, Food and Agriculture Organization. 1974. Production Year Book. Rome, Italy.

United Nations, Food and Agriculture Organization. 1975. The State of Food and Agriculture. Rome, Italy.

HENRY B. OBENG

Natural Resources Currently Available for Crop and Animal Production with Particular Reference to West Africa

Ever since the discovery of agriculture some 10,000 years ago crops and animals have been distributed geographically throughout the world mainly in accord with natural influences such as climate, land, water, plants, and human and energy resources. Such indispensable natural resources conducive to prolific and sustained crop and animal production are not always favorable in all regions of the world.

CLIMATE

Climate, including potential climatological changes, had tremendous influence on crop and animal production throughout the world. It is not only responsible for the survival of crops and animals needed for the nourishment of "Homo Sapiens" but also is one of the factors which determines the value of land, water and even energy resources for efficient production at a given location on the earth.

It has been pointed out (University of California, 1974) that the major climatic problem facing crop and animal production is the possibility that a long-term cooling trend along with a drop in precipitation is taking place plus the occurrence of large short-run variations in weather patterns. Such weather fluctuations have taken place regularly during history and, therefore, may be expected in the future. The possibility of a long-term trend is confirmed both by historical data

---

Henry B. Obeng is Director of the Soil Research Institute, Council for Scientific and Industrial Research, Kwadaso-Kumasi, Ghana, West Africa.

which indicate that a cooling trend may be expected sometime
and by man-caused effects on the atmosphere.

Man through increased industrialization is capable of modifying climate. It is a fact that CO_2 concentration in the
atmosphere is increasing day by day. This is estimated to
reach about 380 parts per million (ppm) by the year 2,000 in
contrast to 330 ppm at present (University of California, 1974).
Bryson (1974) has intimated that the increasing injection of
CO_2 and particulates into the atmosphere has led to greater
atmospheric instability and an expansion of the circumpolar
vortex as a result of high latitude cooling. The cumulative
effect at a given time can lead to reduced rainfall along the
northern edges of the monsoon regions as the monsoons are
pushed southward by the expanding circumpolar vortex. This
effect is likely to be very important if the trend is real,
since a one degree latitude southern movement is liable to
cause a 16.8 cm decline in rainfall along the southern edge of
the monsoons. The recent drought within the Sahelian region of
West Africa is reported to be a direct result of southern movement of the monsoons.

Solar radiation reaching the earth's surface can also be
lowered by atmospheric pollutants. A study (Haun, 1973) of the
wheat belt of the USA indicated that a 1 percent reduction in
solar radiation would cause a 1 percent reduction in yield. In
the case of rice, Bollman (1974) reported a 4 percent lowering
of yield as a result of a 1 percent reduction in solar radiation. Considerable yield reductions may, therefore, be brought
about by changes in solar radiation if there is continual
increase in emissions of pollutants.

The effect of man's pollution of the atmosphere through
increased industrialization may not be all that negative in
terms of crop production. It is a scientific fact that a rise
in the concentration of CO_2 increases carbon fixation (photosynthesis) in many crops. Sulphur dioxide from industrial
operations can also contribute to sulphur nutrition of surrounding crops.

LAND AND SOIL RESOURCES
Civilization depends on adequate food which in turn
depends on the availability of sufficient arable land.
Land and soil resources, however, are not limitless. At
the current rate of population growth in the world there will
be need to utilize those resources efficiently if widespread
malnutrition and starvation is to be avoided. Ways and means
will have to be found not only to slow down population growth
but to efficiently sustain production of crops and animals
through soil conservation and improved agronomic methods.

The world's land area under cultivation was estimated to
be 1461 million ha in 1970 (Table 1). This amounts to 0.4 ha

TABLE 1. Arable and potentially arable land by region and per capita, 1950, 1960, 1970, and 1985

Area	Arable land				Potentially arable	Annual growth rate by period			Hectares/ person	
	1950	1960	1970	1985		1950-60	1960-70	1970-85	1970	1985
	......million hectares......					.........percent.........			....ha......	
World	1418	1426	1461	1610	3190	.60	.25	.68	.40	.33
Europe	150	153	145	137	174	.20	(.44)a	(.44)	.31	.27
USSR	225	221	233	252	356	(.17)	.54	.54	.96	.88
Americas	313	329	355	400	1106	.51	.79	.85	.70	.56
North America	224	226	236	252	--b	.08	.44	.44	1.04	.9
Latin America	89	103	119	148	--	1.60	1.60	1.60	.42	.34
Oceania	24	28	47	95	154	1.70	6.70	6.70	3.03	3.52
Asia	463	456	467	484	628	(.20)	.24	.24	.23	.17
Africa	243	239	214	242	733	(.16)	(1.0)	.90	.62	.34

a( ) denotes negative growth rate.
bNot available.
Source: University of California (1974).

per capita with Oceania registering the highest average of 3.03
and Asia the lowest of 0.23 ha per person. The per capita need
for land is, however, greatly affected by soil productivity
which is in turn influenced to a great extent by climate,
inherent soil fertility and man's activities, especially cultivation practices and the use of pesticides, organic manures and
commercial fertilizers.

It has been suggested (University of California, 1974)
that one way of projecting the future capacity of land to satisfy the world's food needs is to consider the ratio of potentially arable land to people. "Potentially arable land" is
defined to include land presently cultivated together with all
land considered to be cultivatable and reasonably productive
for food crops adapted to a particular climate.

In Table 1, potentially arable land in the world is estimated to be about 3190 million ha of which only about 46 percent was utilized for crop and animal production. There is,
therefore, about 54 percent of potentially arable land available for development in the future. With efficient management
of such vast arable land it should be possible for food production to catch up with the yearly increase in world population.

In the projected world's potentially arable land per capita for 1985 (Table 1), the more developed nations (Europe,
USSR, North America, Australia and New Zealand) are not
expected to encounter serious difficulty in providing food
needs since they have the ability to develop and efficiently
utilize technology and capital to increase the productivity of
the available land. South America and Africa have considerable
undeveloped land and water resources but lack capital, technological know-how and sufficiently trained manpower to accomplish the task of development. They are capable with outside
technical assistance, however, of keeping pace with projected
population needs up to 1985 and beyond. Asia, on the other
hand, is not expected to be able to supply its food needs by
1985 since by that time it is estimated that she will have 58
percent of the world's people but only 20 percent of the potentially arable land.

In Table 2, a more detailed study of arable land development in four specific areas is presented (FAO, 1970). Only 45
percent of the total potential land for the combined developing
areas of Africa south of the Sahara, Asia and the Far East,
Latin America, the Near East and North West Africa was cultivated in 1962. An increase up to 53 percent has been projected for 1985. This gives an average annual growth rate of
0.7 percent. In these areas irrigated land is projected to
increase at an average annual rate of 1.7 percent from 1962 to
1985. In Asia and the Far East where the food situation is
most serious the projected growth rate of arable land is only
0.3 percent annually. However, the growth for irrigated land
is projected at 1.9 percent and the growth rate for total area
harvested is projected at 3.2 percent.

TABLE 2. Potentially arable land, arable land, irrigated land and cost of land development in four developing areas

	Africa South of Sahara	Asia and the Far East	Latin America	Near East and North West Africa	Total or average
Potentially arable land (million ha)	304.0	252.0	570.0	19.0	1,145.0
Arable land, 1962 (million ha)	152.0	211.0	130.0	19.0	512.0
Potential/arable, 1962 (percent)	50.0	84.0	23.0	100.0	45.0
Proposed arable land, 1985 (million ha)	189.0	223.0	169.0	19.0	600.0
Potential/arable, 1985 (percent)	62.0	89.0	30.0	100.0	53.0
Growth rate, 1962-85 (percent)	1.0	0.3	1.1	0.5	0.7
Irrigated area, 1962 (million ha)	1.1	44.1	10.6	16.7	72.5
Irrigated area, 1985 (million ha)	1.9	68.1	17.4	20.1	107.5
Growth rate, 1962-85 (percent)	2.4	1.9	2.2	0.8	1.7
Harvested irrigated area, 1962 (million ha)	1.1	49.5	18.2	12.8	71.6
Harvested irrigated area, 1985 (million ha)	2.1	102.7	16.2	17.8	138.8
Growth rate, harvested areas, 1962-85 (percent)	2.9	3.2	3.0	1.5	2.9
Costs, irrigation development, 1962-85	893	23,095	7,259	4,944	36,191
Drainage and flood control costs, 1962-85a	59	2,008	390	325	2,016
New land and water development costs, 1962-85	1150	27,077	12,342	7,547	48,116

(Costs ....million dollars............)

aCosts not associated with irrigation.
Source: FAO (1970).

In Table 3, world cropland area by commodity is shown together with an estimate of the 1970 production of harvested food and feedcrops for twelve commodities. As indicated in that table, nearly three-fourths of the cropland area produces cereals which account for 38.4 percent of the metric tons produced. Wheat and rice, the most widely grown cereals in the world, provided about 10 percent of this total production.

TABLE 3. World cropland area and production by commodity, 1970

Commodity	Area (million ha)	%	Production (million metric tons)	%
Total cereals	697.6	73.5	1,208.4	38.4
Wheat	210.5	22.2	317.9	10.1
Rice	134.0	14.1	307.6	9.8
Coarse grains	353.1	37.2	582.8	18.5
Maize	107.6	11.3	260.0	8.3
Millet-sorghum	71.0	7.5	64.0	2.0
Others	174.5	18.4	258.5	8.2
Root and tubers	49.5	5.2	551.1	17.5
Sugar	18.7	2.0	813.6	25.9
Pulses and nuts	60.0	6.3	42.7	1.4
Oil seeds	102.3	10.8	105.4	3.4
Vegetables	6.9	0.7	220.4	7.0
Fruits	14.1	1.5	204.3	6.5
Total	949.1	100.0	3,146.1	100.0

Source: University of California (1974).

WATER RESOURCES

A nation's rivers, streams, lakes, reservoirs, and ground-water plus the rain and snow that falls are the most important sources of water. They constitute an indispensable natural resource for quenching the thirst of man and for sustaining crops and animals, which are the basis of man's food supply. Water is, however, not evenly distributed throughout the world. Some areas of the world have it in abundance such as the humid temperate and tropical regions. In other areas, such as the deserts and arid regions, except for ground water, sources of water supply are limited and soil conditions in many cases do not make it feasible for the construction of reservoirs and dams for harvesting and storage of water. In such dry areas it becomes almost impossible to produce enough crops and animals to feed the existing population. Such areas are either completely devoid of human and animal life or where sparse population exists, famine and malnutrition is the prevailing condition.

It is obvious that the areas of the world where water conservation is of utmost importance are the savannah, the semi-
arid and arid regions. In these areas rainfall is either
poorly distributed with a very short wet season and a very long
dry season or the amount of rainfall is very small in most
years. Within these regions, irrigation is a must with sources
of water mainly originating from perennial rivers and streams
and from groundwater. Groundwater is noted to be capable of
providing the quickest and least expensive means of expanding
water supplies while other sources are under development. It
is also reported that worldwide groundwater storage in dynamic
equilibrium is very considerable, probably 3,000 times that
contained in all rivers (University of California, 1974).

It is recorded in FAO year books that irrigation land for
the world totaled 180.9 million ha in 1965 and 203.6 million ha
in 1970. Newly irrigated land within this 5-year period was
reported to average 4.5 million ha per year. If this rate of
development is projected to 1985, the area of irrigated land in
the world would increase from 203.6 million ha to 277.1 million
ha.

The estimated cost of irrigation development ranges widely
since conditions throughout the world are not the same. In
1974, it was estimated that complete irrigation development
would probably range between $1200 to $2000 per ha. At $1200,
for example, an annual development of 4.9 million ha would be
expected to require an annual investment of $5.88 billion
(University of California, 1974).

In Table 4, cultivated and irrigated land in 1970 by countries and regions is presented. It is shown that in 1970, 14
percent of cultivated land that was irrigated produced a much
greater percentage of food. Japan, China and Indonesia, all
very densely populated countries, recorded a large percentage
of irrigated land. A gross estimate of the ultimate potential
for irrigation in India, Pakistan and Bangladesh was put at
93.1 million ha compared to 36.4 million ha actually irrigated
in 1966. The irrigation potential for these parts of Asia
together with Africa and South America is estimated to be 259.1
million ha.

PLANT RESOURCES NEEDED FOR ANIMAL PRODUCTION
        The plant resources needed for efficient and sustained
        animal production consist of cereal and feed grains, hay
        and silage crops, pasture and range lands and by-products
of various processing industries. Data concerning production
of cereal and feed grains as well as pasture, range etc., by
commodity for the US are given in Tables 5 and 6, respectively.
Grains, pasture, range, hay and silage fed to livestock in 1973
in the US were grown on 63.6 million ha producing approximately
233 million metric tons of grain. Corn and wheat occupied
about two-thirds of that acreage. About 65 percent of the

TABLE 4. Cultivated and irrigated land by country or region, 1970

Country or region	Cultivated land	Irrigated land	Irri- gated	Persons per irrigated ha
	million hectares		percent	number
World	1457.00	203.61	14.0	17.8
Europe	145.00	12.29	8.5	37.6
EEC-9	52.38	5.35	10.2	46.6
Eastern Europe	46.02	2.67	5.8	38.9
USSR	232.61	11.10	4.8	21.9
North America	236.09	16.18	6.9	14.0
USA	192.32	15.38	8.2	13.3
Canada	43.77	.35	0.8	60.0
Oceania	47.00	1.60	3.4	11.9
Australia & New Zealand	45.44	1.60	3.5	9.4
Asia	463.00	145.71	31.5	14.1
Japan	5.45	2.63	48.2	39.2
China	111.20	76.00	68.3	10.0
India	164.61	27.52	16.7	19.5
Indonesia	18.00	6.80	37.8	17.1
Latin America	118.92	10.41	8.8	27.2
Mexico	23.82	4.20	17.6	12.1
Brazil	29.76	.46	1.6	202.2
Africa	214.00	6.34	3.0	54.3

Source: University of California (1974).
[a] EEC-European Economic Community.

grain produced on these lands was fed to livestock. In terms of total tonnage produced and fed to livestock, corn was by far the most important crop with 76 percent of production fed to livestock. Value of grain crops produced in 1973 was nearly $24 billion with corn providing over half and wheat about one-fourth the total. Applying the average value of 65 percent of these grains fed to livestock, the total contribution of grains to livestock feeding in 1973 was about $15.5 billion. Wedin et al. (1975) report that pasture and range, which contribute immensely to the feeding of beef cattle and sheep, and hay and silage used for feeding dairy cattle, beef cattle and lambs are grown on about 308 million ha. The major share of this acreage is permanent pasture and rangelands (Table 6).

Other plant resources in the US which are utilized in the efficient production of livestock are the commercial feeds resulting from processing of grain and oilseed crops. Soybean and cottonseed meals, for example, supply about 13.6 million

TABLE 5.   Production of US major grain crops consumed by live-
           stock, 1973

Commodity	Production ha	Production Metric tons	Value of production ($)	% as feed	Consumed by livestock metric tons
	(000)		(000,000)		(000)
Wheat	21,819	46,578	6,825	20	9,313
Rye	420	670	48	66	435
Corn	25,013	143,348	13,426	76	108,939
Oats	5,715	9,635	769	90	8,675
Barley	4,263	9,238	893	59	5,447
Sorghum	6,456	23,790	1,996	83	19,717
Total	63,686	233,259	23,957		152,526

Source: Wedin et al. (1975).

TABLE 6.   Production of forage crops consumed by livestock in
           the US

Commodity	Production ha	Production Metric tons
	(000)	(000)
Corn silage	3,549	99,654
Sorghum silage	341	8,570
Hay (all)	25,187	122,116
Cropland pasture	35,640	
Permanent pasture and range	244,620	

Source: Wedin et al. (1975).

metric tons of concentrate containing about 6.1 million metric
tons of protein (Wedin et al., 1975).

HUMAN AND ENERGY RESOURCES
      Human labor has been almost completely replaced by
   machinery in the production of food in the developed countries. This is not the case in the developing countries
where much of the food produced is still under labour intensive
cultural systems. The US is a typical example of a developed
country where human labour has been largely replaced by technologically advanced machinery in the production of food. It
is reported that from 1950 to 1970 as farm output in the US

increased by 40 percent, agricultural manpower inputs declined
by 55 percent. During the same period mechanical power and
machinery inputs expanded by 29 percent and fertilizer use
increased by 253 percent. The number of tractors increased by
36 percent with total tractor horsepower increasing by 118 percent over the same 20-year time period (University of California, 1974).

Availability of power in the developed countries far
exceeds that of developing countries. In Europe it is estimated that there are available 0.93 horsepower (hp) per ha of
arable land and in the US 1.02 hp. In the developing countries, however, the existing available power from all sources
(human, animal and mechanical) is estimated to be only 0.05 hp
per ha in Africa, 0.19 in Asia and 0.27 in Latin America.
Additional inputs of human labour and draft animal equipment in
these countries are expected to contribute more to the pool of
power. This, however, falls short of the FAO estimated 0.50 hp
which is considered to be the least needed in those countries
to achieve the full potential for high yields (University of
California, 1974). More power and better equipment are, therefore, urgently needed in the developing countries if increased
and sustained crop and livestock production are to be achieved.

A CASE STUDY OF WEST AFRICA WITH SPECIFIC EXAMPLES FROM GHANA
        West Africa lies south of the Sahara approximately between
        latitudes 5° and 20°N and consists of sixteen countries,
        namely, Senegal, Gambia, Cape Verde Islands, Guinea
Bissau, Guinea, Mali, Sierre Leone, Liberia, Ivory Coast,
Ghana, Upper Volta, Togo, Benin, Niger, Nigeria and the Came-
roon.

Climate
        Two air masses dominate West Africa. They are the north-
        erly harmattan, a desiccating, dust-laden wind which blows
in a northeasterly direction from the Sahara desert, and the
southwesterly monsoon of humid oceanic air. Both of these air
masses meet at the Inter-Tropical Convergence Zone which moves
north and south once each year. Jones and Wild (1975) report
that this zone is furthest south in January when the harmattan
blows almost to the coast reaching its northern limit ($15-25^{\circ}$N)
in August. In the north, therefore, the dominant wind for the
most of the year is the northerly harmattan and in the south,
the southwest monsoon. This results in the prevalence of a
short wet season in the north and a long wet season in the
south followed by an equally long dry season and a short dry
season, respectively.
        The mean annual distribution of rainfall is illustrated in
Figure 1. Generally, rainfall and the length of the rainy sea-

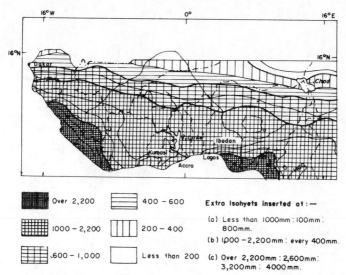

FIG. 1.   West Africa: mean annual rainfall in mm.   Scale
          1:40,000,000
          Source: Davies (1973).

son decrease from over 2200 mm in the south to less than 200 in
the extreme north, except for the relatively dry area in south-
eastern Ghana, Southern Togo and Benin where the annual rainfall near the coast is about 750 mm resulting in a savannah
vegetation.   On the whole, forest vegetation covers the areas
receiving usually more than 1000 mm mean annual rainfall.   Forest, therefore, constitutes a very small fraction of the region
with savannah and semi-arid conditions being dominant.   Water
deficiency is, therefore, the most important factor affecting
crop and animal production.   The influence of water balance on
crop distribution is as a result, very noticeable.

Within the forest zone in the south which has six to nine
months in which rainfall exceeds potential evapotranspiration,
drought stress is low and perennial crops such as oilpalm,
cocoa, coconut and rubber are predominantly grown (Figure 2).
In the Guinea savannah or the middle-belt where drought stress
is high, annual crops such as maize, yams, cassava and kenaf
are grown.   In the northern Sudanese savannah zone where precipitation fails to exceed potential evapotranspiration in even
one month of the year grasses predominate.   Some annual crops,
resistant to drought, such as sorghum, millet, groundnuts and
cotton are also grown (Figure 3).

Long dry periods characterize the Sudanese savannah zone
of West Africa especially within a narrow belt of land lying

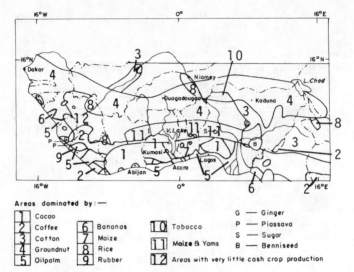

FIG. 2. West Africa: dominant cash crops. Scale
1:40,000,000.
Source: Davies (1973).

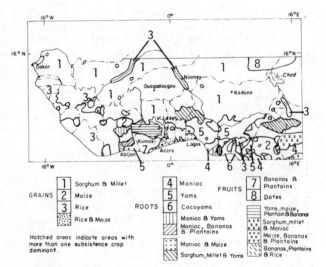

FIG. 3. West Africa: dominant subsistence crops. Scale
1:40,000,000.
Source: Davies (1973).

south of the Sahara between 12° and 17^ON latitude. This area
is known as the Sahelian zone. The severest drought occurred
from 1967 to early 1973. This resulted in severe crop failures, almost completely extinction of livestock and widespread
human starvation. The countries most seriously affected in
West Africa were Senegal, Mali, Upper Volta and Niger. Mauritania and Chad were also badly affected.

Soil Resources

     Soils are formed through the influence of climate (espe-
     cially temperature and rainfall), vegetation, parent mate-
rials (geology), relief, under drainage conditions, and time.
In West Africa, climate, geology and vegetation seem to be the
most important factors of soil formation. Due to extreme climatic conditions, most of the soils are deeply leached resulting in the complete removal of essential bases leaving only the
resistant sesquioxide minerals of aluminum, iron and manganese.
The soils are, as a result, generally infertile and concretionary with substantial areas overlying in situ developed ironpan
horizons at shallow depths. This is especially true within the
vast savannah and semi-arid regions.
     In Figure 4, an attempt has been made (Davies, 1973) to
compile a general inherent soil fertility map of west Africa
based on an interpretation of a soil map of Africa by D'Hoore
(1964). Soil fertility is here considered broadly as a term
indicative of the ability of a soil to support crops with its
inherent supply of plant nutrients.
     The grouping of the soils into high, medium, medium to
low, low and very low fertility is mainly based on the nature
and properties of the parent materials over, or in which the
soils have developed. High fertility soils which as shown in
Figure 4 are very rare and consist of vertisols and eutrophic
brown soils of tropical regions which have developed over, or
in materials of basic igneous or calcareous origin (Figure 5).
They cover approximately 10.5 million ha within both the forest
and savannah regions and are capable of sustaining high yields
of both cash and subsistence food crops. Medium fertility
soils covering some 8.5 million ha have also been developed
over or in parent materials similar to high fertility soils.
They are predominantly ferruginous tropical soils, ferrisols
and ferrallitic soils which are mostly encountered within forested areas. The medium to low fertility soils are associated
with hydromorphic and some halomorphic, ferruginous tropical
soils and ferrisols which occur under both forest and savannah
conditions (Figure 6). They are quite extensive covering
approximately 172.8 million ha within the region.
     By far, the low fertility soils are the most extensive
within West Africa. They are dominated by concretionary forest, and savannah ferrallitic and lithosolic soils, some of

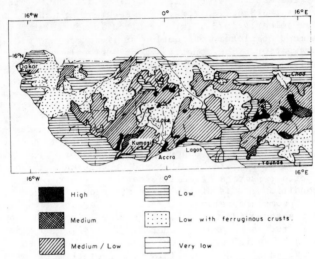

FIG. 4.   West Africa: level of inherent soil fertility.   Scale
          1:40,000,000.
          Source: Davies (1973).

which are limited in their ability to produce arable crops
because of their shallow depths to in situ developed ironpan or
impenetrable parent rock.   Together, they cover approximately
242.9 million ha.   Extensive areas of such low fertility soils
which occur within the forest zone are quite acid and concretionary covering some 129.8 million ha.   They can, however,
under good management practices be made to produce cash tree
crops like oilpalm and rubber (Figure 2).
        The less extensive group of low fertility soils cover
about 113.1 million ha within the savannah and semi-arid
regions especially the Sahelian zone which was worst hit by the
recent severe drought.   They are mainly low-level, concretionary ironpan soils highly depleted of nutrients and liable to
become waterlogged almost to the surface during the peak of the
rainy season only to dry out completely during the dry season.
They are, however, the most suitable for the extensive production of animals (Figure 7).   This is due to the predominantly
level to near-level relief and the fact that climatic conditions allow for the extensive natural growth of grasses.
Water, as intimated earlier, is a serious limiting factor to
successful rearing of animals especially during the periodic
droughts.
        The very low fertility soils are the raw mineral soils and
some immaturely developed soils of the very arid extreme northern areas of West Africa bordering the Sahara Desert.

FIG. 5. A typical vertisol (Ashaiman series) from the Accra
         Plains, Ghana.

Together, they cover some 12.1 million ha of completely barren
land almost devoid of vegetation as a result of the prevailing
extreme adverse climatic conditions.

In Ghana, an inventory of the soil resources of the nation,
which began some 30 years ago has resulted in the compilation
of an up to date soil map of the country with a comprehensive
legend in which local soil groups are correlated with similarly
developed soils in the US and French Systems as well as in the
FAO/UNESCO legend. This basic map has further been evaluated
in terms of the suitability of the soils for mechanized and
other cultivation practices and for ability to produce cash and
food crops for export, import substitution and subsistence purposes. Other suitability maps deal with erosion hazard, grazing potential, forestry, and watershed protection.

Briefly, the inventory has revealed that out of the 9.44

FIG. 6. A ferruginous tropical soil from Ghana.

million ha which constitute approximately the total land surface of Ghana, 6.72 million ha are considered to be good agricultural land for both arable and tree cash crops as well as
for food crops. However, only 2.88 million ha of this 6.72
million ha are considered suitable for mechanised cultivation
of arable crops. The remaining 3.84 million ha can only be
utilised for arable crop production under a system of hand cultivation and bullock farming with strict soil and water conservation practices enforced. Out of the total of 9.44 million ha
there are 2.24 million ha considered naturally unsuitable for
arable and tree cash crop cultivation and for pasture grazing
on a large-scale.
     These valuable soil data provide a basis for the success-
ful implementation of the Government's programme "Operation
Feed Yourself and Industries." This program is aimed at producing adequate food to feed the nation, producing raw materi-

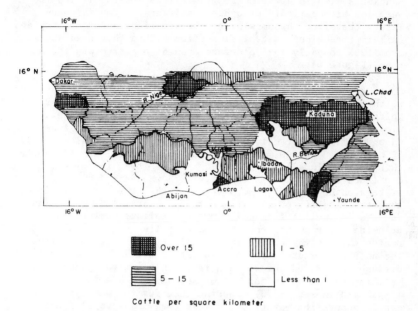

FIG. 7.   West Africa: cattle density.   Scale 1:40,000,000.
          Source: Davies (1973).

als for existing industries, and to provide export crops for
earning foreign exchange.

Water and Animal Resources

As in other regions of the world precipitation is the
source of all the water resources of West Africa. It is
responsible for groundwater and the water that accumulates in
lakes, rivers, streams and man-made dams and waterways. The
main West African rivers which are capable of supplying large
quantities of water which can be utilised through a system of
irrigation for crop and animal production are the Niger, Volta
and the Senegal. The largest and most important lake is the
man-made Volta Lake along the southern course of the Volta
River in Ghana. This lake, which is considered to be one of
the largest in the world covers an area of approximately 8,502
km^2. It is 400 km long with a storage capacity of about 120
million acre feet of water.

Rainfall in the southern forest zone of West Africa rainfall is generally adequate and well distributed for successful
crop production. This zone, however, covers just a small fraction of the region. The bulk of West Africa falls into savan-

nah and semi-arid areas where rainfall is moderately low to
very low with periodic droughts resulting in crop failures.
Water, therefore, becomes a serious limiting factor to crop and
animal production. A typical section within this area where
from 1967 to early 1973 a severe drought occurred was the Sahel
zone (Figure 8).

The Sahelian zone of Africa is a narrow belt of land lying
south of the Sahara between 12° and 17°N Latitude. The section
which falls into West Africa embraces Senegal, Mali, Upper
Volta and Niger. Other countries within it which are quite
close to West Africa are Mauritania and Chad. The area as
shown in Figure 1 receives normally an average annual rainfall
of within 600 to 200 mm but in 1968 the rainfall was well below
this average in all six countries. This low rainfall trend
continued from late 1972 to early 1973 when the drought reached
a stage unsurpassed in the history of the zone. The result was
that the majority of watering points (natural springs and hand-
dug shallow wells) from which man and animals derived their
drinking water during the dry season failed (Figures 9 and 10).
During the drought period the annual grasses which constitute
the natural pastures of the zone either wilted before flowering
or were overgrazed before maturity. This naturally caused a
striking reduction in numbers of animals in the six countries.
Temple and Thomas (1973) reported that for the whole zone total
cattle population was probably less than 50 percent of normal;
for sheep and goats, 80 percent; for camels, 95 percent; and
for horses and mules, 85 percent. Death losses were likely to
have been about 25 percent with some districts which normally
had large herds reporting death losses as high as 80 percent
(Figures 11 and 12). They also reported that some of the cattle that moved southward during the transhumance of 1971 did
not return to the zone and large numbers were evidently sold
for slaughter to neighbouring countries. The death losses and
losses in numbers due to a percentage of the herds staying outside the zone represented only a part of the disastrous effects
to the zone. Damage to crops and home gardens by excessively
large herds on the move was quite high. Existing soils were
also so degraded by sheet erosion that it will take several
years for them to regenerate.

Some death losses were normally due to diseases, but in
their weakened condition they were especially susceptible to
anthrax (Temple and Thomas, 1973). Temple and Thomas (1973)
also intimated that if a 25 percent death loss figure was
accepted as realistic and that 70 percent of the cattle population remained in the zone at the beginning of the critical
emergency period (late 1972) then there was a possibility that
over 3.5 million cattle perished. In monetary terms these cattle losses alone could reach over $400 million. The aftermath
of this calamity was that Ghana and Nigeria which served as the
main coastal markets for the zone had acute meat shortages and

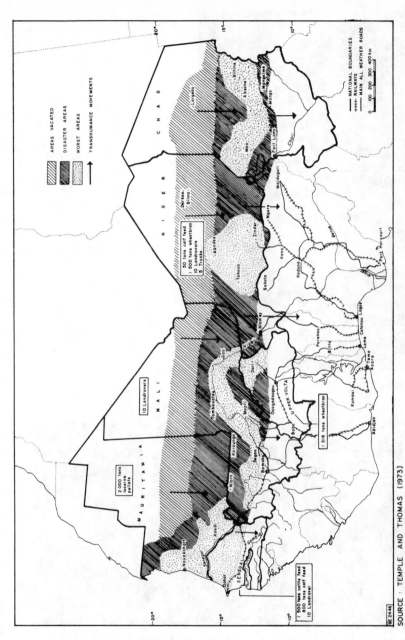

SOURCE : TEMPLE AND THOMAS (1973)

FIG. 8. Map of the Sahel Zone showing the livestock situation in July 1973 and assistance status at the beginning of September 1973

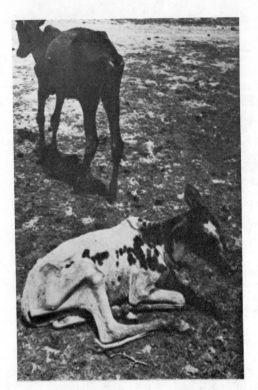

FIG. 9. These animals,
virtually skin
and bone, had
only a few
days to live
unless aid
arrived
(Temple and
Thomas, 1973).

FIG. 10. Sacks of cottonseed are dropped from a French Air
Force plane. This area would normally have some
grass cover (Temple and Thomas, 1973).

FIG. 11. Trees were denuded and grasses completely absent.
Areas like this would take several years to recover.
The very young and the older emaciated animals were
the first to suffer from starvation and lack of
water (Temple and Thomas, 1973).

FIG. 12. No species are
spared from
the scourage
of drought
(Temple and
Thomas, 1973).

had to draw on the existing meagre foreign exchange earnings to import meat from outside West Africa.

Energy Resources and Consumption

Among the sixteen countries of west Africa only five have hydro-electric dams from which most of their energy requirements are obtained. These countries with the respective dams and their maximum capacities are as follows:

Country	Hydro-electric Dam/Plant	Maximum Capacity
Cameroon	Edea	1,100,000 megawatts
Ghana	Volta	912 megawatts
Liberia	Mount Coffee Plant	399.4 megawatts
Nigeria	Kainji	900 megawatts
Sierra Leone	Guma	

There is also a planned Manantali dam for Senegal to be ready by 1980. Ivory Coast has been constructing a hydro-electric dam on the completion of which she will be able to supply all the power presently being procured from fossil fuels. Ghana under a mutual agreement supplies power to the neighbouring countries of Togo and Benin from its Volta hydro-electric dam at Akosombo. Another dam is earmarked at Kpong, only about 15 miles downstream from the Volta dam and construction is planned to start within 6 months' time.

Nigeria is the only country within West Africa which has in addition to hydro-electric power other sources of energy. Her fuel resources include sub-bituminous coal at Enugu in the East Central Site which has been mined for well over 50 years. The total reserves are reported to be minimally estimated at only 250 million tons. More impressive, however, are her petroleum reserves, estimates of which are constantly being revised with each new discovery within the offshore area. Daily production is estimated to be well over a million barrels. Nigeria oil is said to have a special value on the world market in being sulphur-free. Natural gas is also found in abundance but it is reported that at present much of it is simply put to the flame (Mabogunje, 1975).

In Figure 13, Davies (1973) provides a map illustrating, on a national basis, the total consumption of energy per head of population, converted into kilograms of coal based upon UN equivalents for other fuels. He intimates that in general the higher the standard of living within a country the higher the energy consumption. This is not always the case. For example, in countries where economies are heavily dependent on mineral development, like Liberia, considerable quantities of power may be utilised in mine working and smelting by a very small proportion of the population.

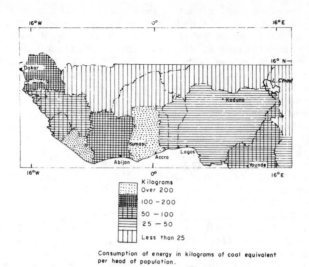

FIG. 13.   Energy consumption.   Scale 1:40,000,000.
           Source: Davies (1973).

     Compared to the developed countries the present total
amount of power available in West Africa is infinitesimal and
will not be enough to meet future energy demands for fertilizer
plants and other agro-based industries as well as for other
industrial uses. Assistance from developed countries will definitely be needed to meet energy requirements within West
Africa and other developing countries, presently and in the
future.

RESEARCH AND NATIONAL PROGRAMMES
     Prolific and sustained crop and animal production in any
     country cannot be successfully attained without the sup-
     port of well organised and equipped institutions that can
foster research and education and can deal with scientific and
socio-economic problems. In the developed countries such
institutions have been in existence for several years. The
relevant data needed to achieve high and sustained crop and
animal production are, therefore, readily available. This is
not the case with several of the developing countries where
the required human and material resources needed to successfully organise and operate such institutions are not available
due to lack of trained scientists and needed foreign currency.

Research Needs

The task for such research institutions, if in existence
or yet to be established in a developing country, will be
to mount research projects in the fields of agri-climatology
land and water resources, crop and animal production, and
socio-economic problems. In the field of agri-climatology and
water resources there will be the need to establish stations in
strategic locations to make weather observations during the
cropping seasons and to monitor the supply of both surface and
underground water. Hydrological studies to determine water
potential both in quantity and quality will also have to be
conducted. The data to be accumulated from these studies will
help in locating water supplies and in harvesting and storing
water for drinking and irrigation purposes.

In land resources studies, the first task will be to organise reconnaissance soil surveys of broad ecological zones with
a view to collecting general information on indigenous soils
and their relationships to relief, drainage, vegetation and
land-use. Detailed soil surveys of areas earmarked for immediate agricultural development will follow. The aim will be to
compile a general soil map of that particular county and other
maps detailing soils, topography, present land-use and capability of specific development areas. The accumulated data will
serve as a basis for soil fertility, soil physics, soil conservation, and erosion control studies involving, among others,
crop response to fertilization, particle size distribution,
permeability, water holding capacity, and soil and water losses. Knowledge of this kind is needed to develop effective
measures to improve the productive capacity of indigenous
soils.

In crop improvement studies, attention will need to be
focused on plant breeding so as to efficiently collect, conserve and utilise genetic resources in breeding future improved
crop varieties with higher yielding qualities and resistance to
diseases and other destructive agents.

In plant protection, research should aim at developing
better understanding of the basic nature of host-pest relationships and devising means for early detection of changes in
incidence and virulence of pests with a view to applying quick
and effective remedial measures to curtail undue crop losses as
a result of diseases, insect damage and the encroachment of
obnoxious weeds.

Animal production is the area of agriculture where very
little progress has been made in developing countries. Most of
the animals are produced under savannah and semi-arid conditions where climatic conditions are so adverse that innumerable
difficulties are often encountered in the development of efficient livestock industries. Water is often scarce, resulting
in undue wilting of the scattered annual grasses which usually
are the only sources of food available for the animals. Here,

research should be centered on the identification of potentials
for range improvement, disease control, genetic improvement and
animal nutrition.

Energy research is needed in all areas of agriculture.
The most critical needs are in the areas of engineering, pest
control, fertilization and irrigation.

Finally, socio-economic studies must be mounted with a
view to identifying all constraints due to unproductive social
habits, cumbersome land-tenure systems, low family and individual incomes, increase in nutrition-related diseases, rural population movements to urban centres and others. Ways must be
found to minimize the effects of such social and economic bottlenecks on the indigenous farmers' efforts to increase crop
and animal production.

In some developing countries the necessary research institutions to tackle the multiple problems are effectively established, often with technical and financial assistance from
international agencies and developed countries. Also, some
effective action programmes are being pursued to achieve self-
sufficiency in crop and animal production. Efforts in West
Africa, Ghana and Nigeria are typical examples. In Ghana,
where out of the nine research Institutes of the Council for
Scientific and Industrial Research, six deal with agriculture
in the special areas of animals, aquatic biology, cocoa, general crops, food and soils, sufficient data are already available to serve as an effective base for efficient agricultural
development. As a result the current Government's programmes
of "Operation Feed Yourself and Industries" are receiving the
necessary research support.

Extension and National Programmes

Useful research data alone are, however, insufficient to
achieve the desired goal of increased crop and animal production. There should be, in addition, an effective extension
service to interpret the results in such a way as to be easily
understood and applied by indigenous farmers. The lack of
trained extension workers is making the transfer of useful
research data very slow in reaching the farmers. To stimulate
as much interest in the programmes as possible the Government
of Ghana has made and is making available to indigenous farmers all the necessary farming inputs at highly subsidized
rates. Credit facilities at low interest rates, free soil surveys for small scale indigenous farmers, improved planting
materials, insecticides, fertilizers, suitable equipment for
land preparation, and crop harvesting are being provided at
practically no cost to the farmer. The programmes have had
tremendous impact on agricultural development especially within
the Forest-savannah and the Interior Savannah Zones of the
country to such an extent that Ghana is presently self-suffi-

cient in the production of maize and rice.

The picture of progress is not as bright for meat and
dairy production. The foot-slope colluvial and low-level
ironpan soils within the Interior Savannah Zone are considered
to be well suited to pasture development and large-scale livestock production. For Ghana and other developing countries
with extensive areas of such soils it is important to find ways
and means of utilizing current technological innovations with a
view to improving the indigenous forage crops and breeds of
livestock. Ways must also be found to effectively control the
tsetse fly. In this respect, it is very encouraging that under
a joint Ghana-USA project (North East Savannah Research Project) inter-disciplinary socio-economic and other studies
involving cultivation practices, water availability, burning,
overgrazing and deforestation have been mounted under the aegis
of the Council for Scientific and Industrial Research. The
purpose is to find solutions to the multiple problems militat-
ing against the efficient economic development of the vast
Interior Savannah Zone and to bring about significant increases
in crop and livestock production and thus improve the health
and economic wellbeing of the indigenous people.

REFERENCES

Bollman, F. 1974. Economic impact on rice production as a
result of climatic change. Development and Resources Corporation Monograph VI-CIAP.

Bryson, R. 1974. Climatic change and drought in the monsoon
lands. Paper presented at AAAS meeting February, 1974.
University of Wisconsin, USA.

Davies, H. R. J. 1973. Tropical Africa, An Atlas for Rural
Development. University of Wales Press, Cardiff, United
Kingdom.

D'Hoore, J. L. 1964. Soil map of Africa. CCTA Project No.
11, London, United Kingdom.

Dresch, J. 1975. Reflection on the future of the semi-arid
regions. In Richards (Ed.) African Environment. Problems
and Perspectives: 1-8. Intern. African Inst. London,
United Kingdom.

FAO/UN. 1968. State of food and agriculture. P. 118. Rome,
Italy.

FAO/UN. 1970. Provisional indicative world plan for agricultural development. Vol. 1, Rome, Italy.

Ghana Information Services Department. 1976. An official
handbook. New Times Corp., Accra, Ghana.

Haun, R. 1973. Determination of wheat growth environment
relationships. Agronomy Journal, 65:813-816. USA.

Jones, M. J. and A. Wild. 1975. Soils of the West African
savannah. Comm. Bur. of Soils CAB, Tech. Com. No. 55,
Harpenden, United Kingdom.

Mabogunje, A. L. 1975. Nigeria, physical and social geogra-
    phy--resources. In Africa, South of the Sahara, pp. 604.
    Europa Publications Ltd., London, United Kingdom.
Obeng, H. B. 1971. Soil groups of Ghana and their potential
    for agricultural development. Journal of the AAASA, Vol.
    1, No. 1: 19-27. Ethiopia.
Obeng, H. B. 1971. Soils which present problems in use and
    management in West Africa. FAO/UN World Soil Resources
    Report No. 40: 93-98. Rome, Italy.
Obeng, H. B., D. K. Acquaye and A. Bampoe-Addo. 1973. Ironpan
    geomorphic surfaces and associated soils of Ghana. Journal
    of the AAASA Vol. 1, Supplement 66-77, Addis Ababa, Ethio-
    pia.
Oyebande, L. 1975. Water resources problems in Africa. In
    Richards (Ed.). African Environment, Problems and Perspec-
    tives: Intern. African Inst., London, United Kingdom.
President's Science Advisory Commission. 1967. The world food
    problem, Vol. 2: 405-569. Washington, DC, USA.
Temple, R. S. and M. E. R. Thomas. 1973. The Sahelian drought
    --a disaster for livestock populations. World Animal
    Review 8. FAO/UN, Rome, Italy.
UNESCO. 1963. A review of the natural resources of the Afri-
    can continent. Natural Resources Research -1, UNESCO
    International Documents Service, Columbia University Press,
    New York, USA.
University of California Food Task Force. 1974. A hungry
    world: The challenge to agriculture. Division of Agricul-
    tural Sciences, University of California, USA.
USDA, Economic Research Service. 1970. Economic progress of
    agriculture in developing nations, 1950-68. Foreign Agri-
    cultural Economic Report 59. Washington, DC, USA.
USDA. 1971. Agricultural statistics, 1971. Government Print-
    ing Office, Washington, DC, USA.
Wedin, W. F., H. J. Hodgson, N. L. Jacobson. 1975. Utilizing
    plant and animal resources in producing human food. Jour-
    nal of Animal Science 41:667. USA.

ERNEST W. SPRAGUE

KEITH W. FINLAY

Current Status of Plant Resources and Utilization

It is estimated that the food deficit in the Developing Market Economies will be 100 million metric tons by 1985 if the production-growth rate is 2.0 percent per year. During the last half of the period 1967-1974, the production growth rate dropped to 1.7 percent. This means that a production-growth rate of 4.0 percent per year--or twice as large--will be necessary if the demand in 1985 is to be satisfied and the estimated 100-million-ton food deficit eliminated.

It is evident that the world may have to face a critical situation in the very near future. It will be necessary to employ imaginative and effective strategies if a production growth rate of 4.0 percent is to be achieved. This may be possible under favorable conditions, but can it be maintained?

What can we expect after 1985? There is little evidence that population growth is being reduced significantly. This can mean only one of two alternatives: 1) the need for a higher rate of production growth for several decades to come; or 2) the specter of increasing poverty, malnutrition, and social unrest.

Now that the immensity of the population explosion is becoming more apparent, there is a growing concern that our natural resources and utilization methods may be inadequate to meet the task of increasing food production at an accelerated rate; or a concern that our resource management techniques are inefficient and improper with the result that our crop germplasm

Ernest W. Sprague is Director, International Maize Program, CIMMYT, Londres 40, Mexico 6, D. F. Mexico.

Keith W. Finlay is Deputy Director General, CIMMYT, Londres 40, Mexico 6, D. F. Mexico.

has or will become vulnerable to widespread attacks by pests and diseases. With the unfavorable balance between population and food-production growth, we cannot afford any further major crop failures in large areas of the world.

GERMPLASM DEVELOPMENT

The species of plants used for human food have been evolving for a very long period of time. At first their evolution was slow and directed solely by random mutations and natural selection. After Neolithic women began to collect and domesticate some of the species, the evolution became more directed towards those plant types that best met the needs of that evolving animal, Homo sapiens.

Just as the human species is exploding in numbers, so is the development of knowledge and technology. This knowledge and technology is being applied with ever increasing sophistication to almost all areas of human endeavour.

The evolution of crop plants has been greatly accelerated and channeled into specific directions by the application of modern techniques of plant improvement, aided by a wide array of scientific disciplines such as genetics, physiology, pathology, biochemistry, etc. Perhaps one of our problems today is the use of over sophisticated techniques that do not utilize the wealth of genetic diversity that is available to us. Perhaps we do not understand what is really needed.

In modern times crop plants have been moved into a wide range of environments and geographic regions far removed from their centers of origin. This process has helped augment the genetic variability that we have today. This also indicates that the species are dynamic; they are not static; they are still evolving. Variability is still being generated, possibly at a greater rate than ever before because of the adaptive process forced on the crop species by modern plant breeders and agriculturalists.

THE CURRENT STATUS OF PLANT RESOURCES AND UTILIZATION

If the developing market economies are to achieve a 4 percent production growth rate, it will have to be based on high-potential plant resources. These resources must be managed at the research and production levels, and in a political, social, and economic environment so as to achieve maximum expression of the plant potential that is available to us today--and to strive for still greater potential for the future.

To achieve this potential will require the most imaginative use of the world's extensive store of genetic variability.

For most crop species there are reasonably comprehensive collections of the world's germplasm distributed in many different countries, but the conditions of storage, documentation, evaluation, and utilization vary widely.

During recent years there has been an acceleration in the concern for a more systematic approach to collecting and preserving plant germplasm, with special emphasis on crop species in areas threatened by modern development. The Food and Agriculture Organization of the United Nations has been taking a leading role in coordinating this international effort, and more recently the International Board for Plant Genetic Resources has been formed to focus priorities and to collect and channel funds into the priority areas.

It is important that these collections be made and maintained for the future use of mankind.

It is also important, however, that the collections be used effectively. Much is said and written about the concern for genetic vulnerability and of the need for further collections and preservation of germplasm. Often there is confusion, because the concern for genetic vulnerability results from the crop breeding techniques or resource management rather than any real danger of exhaustion of germplasm variability.

Plant breeders, in general, are not looking ahead and bringing a wide array of existing germplasm into the breeding system. Rather, they are continually reselecting in a relatively narrow gene pool, which results in even greater restriction of the genetic variability in actual use. In such location- or country-specific situations, there is a real danger of limiting genetic variability and of increasing the vulnerability of particular crop species to attack by pests, diseases, and other production hazards.

Unfortunately, many of the narrowly based breeding programs are conducted in the more developed nations where the highest yields are obtained. Because of these high yields it is often assumed that material from these programs represents the best germplasm available. There is no question that these are the highest yielding, narrow gene pools for those specific areas; however, it does not necessarily follow that it is the best germplasm for less developed countries or even for the security and future development of agriculture in the more developed world. In fact, it is perhaps urgent that the more developed nations look for more rapid ways of developing and increasing usable genetic variability to merge into their breeding programs.

In spite of the above situation, breeders are reluctant to bring new germplasm into the system. Instead, their approach to genetic vulnerability is to collect and preserve what nature and man have developed over the years with the hope that it contains the individual genes needed to solve any problem that might arise. Also, they hope that they will be able to pull out such "wonder genes" and use them for remedying the problem as simply as taking a tablet from a medicine chest. It is time for breeders to forget such wishful thinking and face the realities.

Is the breeder being realistic by developing highly specialized and narrow gene pools? Or is he taking an easy, unimaginative way out, hoping that the anticipated danger will never occur? We are all aware of examples of the wide-spread failure of crop cultivars having a narrow gene base because of the appearance of a "new" race of a pathogen; a heavy buildup of inoculum of an "old" pathogenic race; or environmental conditions that favor the spread of a pathogen or pest. Yet a look at breeding programs around the world would indicate that breeders prefer to put out fires if they start rather than developing relatively fire-proof breeding programs, cultivars, and management strategies.

To assume that a breeder can go to a germplasm bank and immediately pull out a fire extinguisher is not realistic. Although the germplasm banks undoubtedly abound with useful genes, they often occur in very low frequencies and important characters are often conditioned by a large number of additive genes. A lengthy and often complex procedure involving different environments is necessary to identify and select the required genes and incorporate them into a new cultivar in an appropriate manner to buffer the cultivar against a range of unforseen and unfavorable conditions.

The concept of germplasm preservation is based on collecting and storing samples of economically important species of historic origin. Usually such material has evolved and established itself as land races in localized areas. When any of these materials is cross-pollinated with location-specific modern cultivars, or even if two modern cultivars from different environments are crossed, it will lead to a dilution of the desirable characteristics of the modern cultivar in the environment where it is adapted.

To overcome this effect requires a great deal of time and patience. This is the main reason the average plant breeder prefers to work in a narrow, advanced gene pool with the occasional injection of a gene or two for disease resistance if the need arises.

Because of this common approach by breeders, most germplasm collections are being poorly evaluated and utilized.

The ease with which favorable genes can be identified in a collection depends on the genetic reproductive system of the species. For example, it is generally easier to identify gene effects in a self-pollinated crop than in a cross-pollinated one. Any collection of a self-pollinated crop will have relatively homozygous plants and may or may not be heterogeneous. Hopefully they will have sufficient variability to allow the scientist to more easily select types of interest to him. This is often not the case in cross-pollinated crops where each plant is genetically different. In cross-pollinated crops, many characteristics are under multigenic control, alleles are in a heterozygous condition, and the favorable recessive genes are masked.

There is no doubt that there are more favorable genes in most collections than we are able to identify, especially when the sample is grown at only one location. However, if collections could be tested in several very different environments more favorable genes could be identified. Then, by the use of appropriate pollination techniques at each site, the process of accumulating those genes could be initiated. Intercrossing the resulting progeny from each site would allow a further accumulation of favorable genes. This approach is essential in that many characters are controlled by multigenetic systems and different environments will allow more of the gene complex to express itself.

The biggest group of users of the maize germplasm bank at CIMMYT are the scientists interested in academic and fundamental studies. Other scientists want to screen the collection for disease and insect resistance or some other trait. Although the collection no doubt carries genes for resistance to diseases and insects, the chance of finding them by a simple screening of a cross-pollinated crop such as maize is unlikely. The concern to locate the genes is genuine but the approach used often offers little hope of success because the gene frequency is so low that resistance will not be expressed.

The germplasm collections of all species have much to benefit modern agriculture, but it is essential that breeders and other plant scientists realize the need to set up programs to effectively utilize the stored variability. Because of the complexity of the breeding programs and the range of environments necessary to carry out a wide range of selections for different adaptive and agronomic characteristics, the programs should be organized to provide broadly based genetic material of value to many nations. This approach contrasts with the use of a germplasm bank as the source of, single genes that supposedly will provide magic answers.

It will not be the collections per se, but the accumulations of desirable genes from the collections that will make an important contribution to world food supplies.

STRATEGY FOR EFFECTIVE USE OF GERMPLASM RESOURCES

During the process of evolution a crop genus becomes adapted to a wide range of specific environments--some lines being adapting to high cool mountains, others to lowland tropics or to the edges of deserts, etc. However, few, if any, of these individual lines will grow successfully in a wide range of different environments. Yet, through a gradual process of domestication and adaptation, a majority of crop plants are being grown today under environments and in geographic regions far removed and different from their original area of adaptation.

With the modern techniques of genetic engineering now

available to plant breeders, the vast resources of germplasm could be utilized for the development of broad based pools as a source material for the production of suitable cultivars for various agro-climatic conditions. How is this to be done? Particularly for the developing countries with limited resources and limited trained personnel? The developing countries are in urgent need of wide based, high yielding cultivars that can resist the attack of diseases and pests as well as vagaries of weather. How then can the germplasm collection be used effectively?

There are usually two reasons for the broad scale use of germplasm collections: 1) To widen genetic variability and improve the species in the environments where it has become adapted over the years; and 2) to move the species into an environment where it has previously not been able to grow and produce. Increasing evidence suggests that if there is moisture and solar energy, the breeder can adapt any species to any environment given time and access to a wide range of genetic variability. It also means that such a widely adapted cultivar will also have the capacity to make at least average production even if the environmental conditions in a growing season are somewhat unfavorable.

If germplasm from the USA Corn Belt is taken to the tropics it will be defoliated by tropical diseases. If germplasm from the tropics is taken to the Corn Belt, most of it will continue to grow vegetatively until it is killed by frost and will seldom produce any grain. This example illustrates the problem involved in the utilization of germplasm collections that have large numbers of entries collected in a multiplicity of environments. Although genotypes that are adapted to totally different environments cannot be transposed, they may have useful genes to contribute to each other. For example, although tropical maize accumulates carbohydrates as rapidly as those in the Corn Belt, they have a much lower harvest index. This suggests that there are desirable genes in Corn Belt maize that could significantly increase the grain yield of tropical maize. North American maize, on the other hand, could benefit from the inclusion of a different source of European corn borer resistance that has been identified in tropical maize.

It is of interest to take one crop--maize--and examine a method for utilizing the genes that the germplasm collection has to offer. The method is that used by CIMMYT for the production and continuous improvement of maize populations for developing countries. It can be used for the development of elite cultivars by the cooperating national programs involved in wide scale testing.

If a breeder goes to a "neutral" environment, that is, an environment that is mild enough to allow collections from any part of the world to flower and set seed, then all the types can be intercrossed. The resulting progeny may be allowed to further intercross for several generations in the neutral environment to break up linkages, or they may be selected in a series of distinctly different environments and the superior selections returned to the neutral environment for further intercrossing.

By these processes, the favored genes for each of the different environments are soon accumulated to provide a population that will grow satisfactorily in any of the environments.

A superior, widely adapted population of this type provides a vehicle for moving new genes into the breeding system more or less anywhere in the world. Possibly of more importance, if this process is executed effectively, it is possible to develop breeding material that is superior to any of the individually adapted populations that have been worked and reworked for many years in the same environments.

This does not argue that the new, widely adapted populations are able to necessarily outyield the released cultivars. It does argue that the breeder has a completely new set of genes to incorporate and up-grade his breeding populations for improvement of yield and other characteristics, which in the long run will be far superior to continuing to rework his existing breeding populations.

It is suggested that countries of the major maize-growing regions in the developed world such as North America and Europe would benefit from a similar regional cooperative program to provide superior populations adapted to their regions. These could be used by national breeders to introduce much needed desirable genetic variability. By this technique it would not be necessary for each breeder to introduce large volumes of exotic germplasm that will disrupt his program.

We believe that the current status of plant genetic resources is far more adequate for the world's food needs than is the realization of the need to develop a system to effectively use the genetic diversity that is available.

Fortunately, for the three major cereals, wheat, rice, and maize, international breeding programs are developing widely adapted, genetically broad-based populations and lines so that these resources are available to the world. Even with these crops there is a significant amount of genetic variability yet to be evaluated and made available to the world's plant breeders.

Other crop species are less advanced in this concept, but as the other international programs progress, this kind of diversity in agronomically acceptable forms will become available to increase the growth rate in production.

THE FUTURE

Although the collection, evaluation, and storage of valu-

able, threatened germplasm must proceed, more breeders
should contribute to, and benefit from, larger regional
and international breeding programs by bringing together and
concentrating desirable genes already collected as one mechanism of utilizing the existing variability.

Because of the very wide range of environmental selection
pressures that will be exerted on these genetically variable
populations, there is likely to be an increasing number of
small and continuous changes taking place. As these materials
are brought back together for recombining, the opportunities
for creating new desirable germplasm will probably outweigh the
chances of losing good germplasm.

Many attempts are presently underway to create even more
variability for use in future crop production. The first of
these--Triticale--is just starting to enter the world food system. Crosses of maize x Tripsacum, maize x sorghum, barley x
wheat, barley x rye, etc. have been produced or are being
attempted not only to intermix genetic variability within genera, but between and among genera.

The genetic resources already exist to significantly
increase the production potential of man's crop plants and to
guard against genetic vulnerability. The job of creating and
making available the necessary variability will require the
cooperation of agricultural scientists world-wide, and the rate
of progress will be limited only by our imagination and our
willingness to cooperate in this essential and exciting venture.

HERBERT KÖTTER

Constraints to Food Availability Imposed by the Human Work Force

FOOD SUPPLIES IN RELATION TO DEMAND
AND THE AGRICULTURAL LABOUR FORCE

Food Supply and Population Growth

In the 1960s food production in the developing countries
increased at a rate of 2.8 percent annually. But this
considerable achievement was largely offset by an unprecedented
rate of growth in population. The average per caput food production in these countries increased by only 0.2 percent annually between 1960 and 1970.

According to the projections prepared by the Food and Agriculture Organization for the 1974 World Food Conference, the
demand for food in the developing market economies is expected
to increase at 3.6 percent annually between 1970 and 1985.
Population growth accounts for approximately 70 percent of this
increase in the demand for food in the developing countries.

The annual rate of growth in food production was only 2.7
percent between 1961 and 1973. This barely equals the projected rate of growth in population of 2.7 percent annually for
this same period. Net cereal imports would have to increase
from 16 million tons annually during 1969-1971 to 85 million
tons annually by 1985.

The Growth of the Agricultural Labour Force

The rapid growth of population imposes two enormous

Herbert Kötter is Professor für Wirtschaftssoziologie,
University of Bonn, Federal Republic of Germany.

problems on the developing countries. On the one hand, food
production needs to be increased much faster than in the past.
On the other hand, there is the necessity to create productive
and renumerative employment for a steadily growing labour force.

In the long run self-sustained growth can be achieved only,
if nonagricultural occupations absorb an increasing share of
the human work force. But, due to a number of reasons which
cannot be discussed here, the larger part of the increase in
the labour force will have to be absorbed by agriculture until
the end of this century and even thereafter. According to a
projection of the FAO, the agricultural labour force in the
developing countries with a market economy will increase by at
least 166 million persons, or 25 percent, between 1970 and
2000. In the Far East the problem will be particularly acute,
because of an expected 40 percent increase there.

This increase of the agricultural labour force reduces,
ceteris paribus, the per caput availability of food. The relative abundance of labour with respect to other factors of production, such as land and capital, must lead to more unemployment or to a further degree of underemployment in rural areas
in general and in agriculture in particular. This sequence of
events will be inevitable, whenever agricultural labour cannot
contribute to a further increase in food production. The
growth of rural population will furthermore divert an increasing share of food production for local consumption, reducing
thereby the marketable surplus.

Absolute and Relative Overpopulation

Development policies must aim at bringing about a balance
between available resources and population. We consider
population policy a sine qua non for any long term strategy.
The population problem cannot be solved in one great leap. As
of now the increase in population has outstripped the productive
capacity of most developing countries. This gap will widen in
the next decades because of the delayed impact of population
policies such as family planning. The question is how to increase food production as quickly as possible.

The productive potential of a country is not exclusively
determined by its natural resources. The existing socioeconomic, institutional and political framework, and the whole pattern of social organization and attitudes determine to a very
high degree the will, the possibility and the capacity of the
population to make the best use of the material resources.

It may be helpful to distinguish between absolute and relative overpopulation. Absolute overpopulation exists if with a
given population, available resources and known technologies
are not sufficient, to sustain a past standard of living. Relative overpopulation exists if potentially available resources

are underutilized. Underutilization of available resources can
be due to a lack of technical know-how or due to a lack of
complementary resources such as capital. But often underutilization is due to man-made restrictions, related to deficiencies in the political and sociocultural systems. Special mention should be made of deficient land tenure structures and a
general lack of appropriate incentives to mobilize the human
work force.

MAIN OBSTACLES FOR THE ACTIVATION
OF THE AGRICULTURAL LABOUR FORCE

The Rural Poor--A Dormant Productivity Potential

The rural poor can be taken to be synonymous with the
agricultural labour force. Both can be expected to increase together. The rural poor have been untouched by the
mainstream of development. About 40 percent of the people in
developing countries live in absolute poverty. Among the 40
developing countries for which data are available, the upper 20
percent of the population receives 55 percent of national income in the typical country, while the lowest 20 percent receives 5 percent (McNamara, 1973, p. 6-7).

The deprivation of the rural poor goes beyond the maldistribution of goods and services. They cannot contribute to
socioeconomic development, because they have no access to the
resources necessary for development, in the broadest interpretation of that term. Latin American sociologists describe this
as "marginalization". It is a self-enforcing kind of cyber-
netic effect. Because the rural poor are marginal, because
they are suffering from a centuries old exploitation, malnutrition and poor health, because they are "left out" by society
and the economy, they tend to withdraw themselves. It undermines their self-reliance, and stifles incentives for increased
efforts. As a consequence they "flip out" of the social system.

It is the major thesis of this paper, that the rural poor
constitute a considerable potential for increased food production. But to do that they must be integrated into society and
into the development process. It is not our intention to be-
little the problem of a scarcity of nonhuman development resources. However, there can be little doubt that the removal
of a number of external and internal obstacles bearing upon the
underutilization of human resources, can increase the productivity of the rural poor.

Internal and External Constraints and Their Reciprocity

Motivation of the peasantry is the major factor in increasing food production. We must ask ourselves as to the

possible obstacles in this respect. There is a widely shared
view, that specific traits of peasant societies inhibit the active participation of peasants in modern development. Rogers
(1969) has listed several elements which, in his view, can be
found in all peasant societies. Most of these "characteristic
peasant traits," in my opinion, are not innate in peasant cultures, but a result of its relationship to outside society. If
such is the case, then a reorientation of this relation would
be the key in integrating peasants into society and increasing
productivity.

I will mention only a few of the factors listed by Rogers
which to me seem of paramount importance:

Perceived limited goods. The notion of perceived limited
goods implies that all desirable things in life like land,
wealth and safety, do exist only in finite quantities and cannot be increased. If the pie is limited, one can obtain a
larger share only at the expense of somebody else. This notion
is closely connected with a mutual distrust in interpersonal
relationships. If for example a peasant, having adopted innovative methods, becomes more prosperous then he must have
cheated on or exploited his neighbor.

If it can be demonstrated that all or most members of
peasant society can become more prosperous, then there exists
an important stimulus for action. Obviously the pie cannot be
enlarged without personal and group efforts. However, many are
not able to increase production without social and institutional changes in the organization of rural communities (Dams,
1975). The "Green Revolution" resulted in a situation, where
the dominant strata within the rural community obtained the
major benefits of innovations. This experience enforced the
notion of perceived limited goods and deepened mutual distrust.

Deferred gratification. The notion of deferred gratification means the postponement of immediate satisfaction in antici-
pation of future rewards. The attitude toward deferred gratification is closely connected with fatalism and low aspirations.
Participation in any long term development programme requires
deferred gratification. But if such postponement implies prolonged near starvation one should not expect too much from the
rural poor on this account.

Also their expectations for a better future have been
often disappointed. Investments did not bring about the expected results. In general, the existing structures of land-
ownership create a degree of insecurity for the peasant and
more so for the landless worker. The immediate conclusion is
that society must provide a minimum of security for those who
work the land.

Alienation. The attitude towards government at each level
alternates between dependence and hostility. "Only those in
authority can solve my problem, but they are cheating me, I am
sure." This attitude implies in substance a high degree of
alienation. A long history of exploitation has contributed to
this state of affairs. On the other hand, the existing receptivity of the peasantry with respect to the paternalistic attitudes of the rural elites, even if well intentioned, has destroyed the self-reliance of the rural poor with disastrous
consequences.

Lack of innovativeness. Rogers (1969) mentions lack of
innovativeness as a further characteristic trait of peasant
cultures. This problem is more complicated, than it appears
at first sight. Resistance against innovations can be a demonstration of rationality. Any innovation is connected with economic and social risks. Economically it may fail. Socially
it may lead to disintegration. To be sure, development implies innovations. But there seems to be a growing awareness,
that the mere transfer of technical know-how, spawned under
very different socioeconomic and cultural conditions, has inhibited a truly indigenous innovative process.

Failures have led to frustration and resistance. The
problem goes beyond the adoption of imported techniques. In my
view, we have neglected the possibility of rationalization and
further refinement and development of traditional techniques.
An unprejudiced view would teach us, that there is a lot of
wisdom in traditional techniques. Improvement of such techniques is likely to strengthen the creativity and self-reliance of rural people.

Low aspirations and achievement motivation. Low aspirations and achievement motivation seem to be inherent in peasant
societies. This is correlated with low levels of empathy, e.g.
no inclination to accept new roles within the development
process. A readiness to change attitudes, beliefs, values and
opinions is only partly a problem of intelligence. It also
reflects the experience of peasants "whose opportunities have
historically been severely limited, especially by pressures
upon their major resource, land" (Rogers, 1969, p. 34).

In concluding this section one can state, that those
sociocultural characteristics of peasant societies which impede improved productivity of human resources "are not a natural phenomenon, but the result of their marginal position within the overall society" (Kötter, 1972, p. 217). This is the
true vicious circle.

Due to marginalization peasants remain unproductive

and poor. Because they remain poor, the process of marginalization is accentuated, the more other sectors of society are
making progress. It is also an explanation, as to why development strategies, based on the assumption of the "trickle-down-
effect", more or less failed.

Any developing society, which neglects in the long run the
rural poor, deprives itself from an important development resource. It is my thesis, that the solution of the food problem
is invariably connected with the activation of this forgotten
factor.

A partly modernized agriculture may reach a high land,
capital and labour productivity. Nevertheless, the main problem remains to better utilize the abundant agricultural labour,
which by sheer growth presently reduces average per caput food
availability. Underutilized labour does not contribute substantially to production, but it proportionately increases the
demand for food. Any income distribution programme which does
not expand food production on the basis of integrating the
rural poor into the production process will largely dissipate
itself through a decline in the real purchasing power of income.

If the distribution of agricultural resources is inequi-
table, the introduction of new technologies in agriculture usually leads to an increase in production but it also "is more
likely to increase the income gap between the rich and the
poor" (Thiesenhusen). A report of the Inter-American Development Bank (1970) warns: "If income distribution does not
change, the Green Revolution . . . could cause surpluses while
many families remain undernourished". Under the existing
socioeconomic conditions of many developing countries an increase in food production is not necessarily identical with an
increased availability of food to all.

THE SOCIOPOLITICAL SYSTEM--A MAJOR STUMBLING BLOCK

Political Climate and Development Orientation
     Success in agricultural development and increased food pro-
     duction and availability depend on the mobilization of
large numbers of the rural population. A pure technological
approach to increased agricultural production will not solve
the problem. To quote Dams (1975): "The innovation process is
only achievable if a number of political, social and economic
preconditions are fulfilled". The United Nations World Food
Conference (1974) called

     on governments to bring about appropriate agrarian reforms
     and other institutional improvements in rural areas, aimed at
     organizing and activating the rural population to

participation in integrated rural development and at eliminating exploitative patterns of land tenure, credit and marketing systems, where they still prevail.

Institutional improvements in rural areas will not be sufficient. Many of the decisions affecting the rural population
are not made within the rural areas themselves. Such an approach requires, therefore, basic changes of the overall political and socioeconomic system.

Two of these seem to be of paramount importance: first, an
agricultural development strategy which gives priority to small
farmer developments; second, a definite commitment to give the
rural poor better access to productive resources, services and
social security.

Such a commitment implies considerable changes of existing
policies and power structures. It is evident then, that an inquiry into the "constraints on food availability imposed by the
human work force" ultimately comes to rest upon an analysis of
the "constraints imposed by the sociopolitical system on the
human work force".

Land Tenure--A Most Relevant Institutional Factor

It has been stated very rightly, that in many countries,
the existing land tenure sustem is the major obstacle in
achieving rural development. Existing land tenure systems oft-
en restrict a socially optimal access to land resources.
Sociopolitically unsatisfactory situations evolve when tenants
and landless workers are totally dependent on landlords. Such
a dependency is particularly obnoxious where land ownership,
political power and the judiciary are intertwined.

Specific features of land tenure arrangements may inhibit
the incentive to increase agricultural production. They may
restrict the mobility of human and non-human factors of production. They often lead to an underutilization of resources,
and under certain circumstances, to an over-exploitation or
deterioration of the original productive potential of land.

It is not possible to deal in detail with the deficiencies
of existing land tenure systems. However, one could mention
two particularly deficient forms: (1), the share-cropping system, characterized by completely dependent and exploited ten-
ants-at-will, whose social and economic position is highly in-
secure; (2), the South-American latifundio, with its landless
workers without occupational alternatives at the mercy of the
large landowner. But the situation of many small owner-operator farmers is not much better because of their dependence on
middle-men in the production and distribution of agricultural
production.

Finally, the known collective forms of agriculture are not

conducive to increased efficiency. It is not the intention of
this paper to discuss agrarian reform. But it should be made
clear, that there is no unique recipe. Agrarian reforms must
be comprehensive and adapted to specific conditions. Apart
from changes in the ownership of land, they must include other
measures, such as improved credit and marketing systems, extension services and appropriate price and tax policies.

Credit and Marketing Systems

The integration of small farmers into a market economy
requires appropriate credit and marketing systems. This
statement is certainly not new. The existing organizations
show a distinct tendency to work in favor of the "haves" and
rather than the "have-nots". Some cooperative credit schemes,
while established with the best of intentions, were soon dominated by the richer strata of the villages. The lack of credit
is one of the main reasons why the Green Revolution by-passed
the small farmer.

Education and Extension

The lack of education and training is one of the main constraints in the motivation and activation of the human
work force. However, the more fundamental problem is the
determination of the type of education and training conducive
to agricultural development. The existing programmes have an
adverse effect, because they do not relate to peasant reality.

Peasant activities are labeled as socially inferior. Due
to this, the more active and progressive youngsters who have
benefited from education, abandon such activities, only to join
the rank and file of the urban unemployed. Here again we are
confronted with a vicious circle, because the loss of those
progressive elements leads to a further deterioration of rural
areas and agriculture.

Extension services exist in most of the developing countries. For a number of reasons the usual extension worker does
not fit the requirements of small farmers' development. They
do not have a sufficient level of technical competence. More
importantly, they normally have not been trained, to identify
innovation as a technical problem within a given social context. The introduction of a new technology means more than
the use of high yielding varieties, chemicals and credit. The
new practices are quite different from traditional agriculture
and require a process of reorientation and sociocultural
change. Often the attitude of the extension worker is too
paternalistic. Hardly any provision is made for farmer consultation and active participation of farmers in the decision
making process.

It is true that the role of the extension worker is very difficult. Generally, the number of clients assigned to him, is much too large. His duties are so spread out, that he cannot fulfill a substantial role as an advisor of farmers. The prestige of being an extension worker is low. The same is true for his salary and career opportunities. As a consequence the profession is not very attractive. This leads to a negative selection process. The better qualified people look for other positions within the rural bureaucratic hierarchy.

Rural Women--The Forgotten Factor

In many developing countries more than half of agricultural labour is done by women. The fact that women constitute a large part of the agricultural work force has been neglected.

Their inferior sociocultural position is one of the reasons why their potential contribution is underutilized. They do not have access to training, nor are they a target group of the extension services. We cannot discuss this complex problem here in detail. But it best illustrates the thesis, that a better utilization of the rural labour potential goes far beyond the introduction of new technologies and technical training narrowly interpreted. It requires substantial changes in social organization, values and attitudes.

Lack of Participation

The small farmer has been more an object rather than the subject of development programmes. This lack of participation in decision-making puts limits on the activation of the agricultural labour force. Development means more than mere growth. True socioeconomic development, defined as planned dynamic sociocultural change, implies an increasing participation of all members of society; not only in the benefits, but also in the propagation and the steering of the development process.

The cry for greater social justice means more than a more equal distribution of income. It requires the participation of more and more people, at all levels, not only in the execution of activities relevant for development, but also in the decision-making process. Development planning and related measures have been superimposed from above. This has had disastrous effects on the self-reliance of rural people, a precondition for self-sustained growth.

Self-reliance has been inhibited by both the national bureaucracies through the paternalistic attitudes of bilateral and multilateral donors and agencies. This process of democratization must be a functional one. It should not remain

restricted to formally "progressive" institutions and legislation. It means the mobilization of "activity cells", the delegation of initiatives, tasks and decision-making (Behrendt,
1965, p. 524). What can be decided at the lower level, should
be handled there.

The lower level is a part of a larger system. Communication from top to the bottom, and vice versa, is needed. In
this context, the role of formal and informal groups and of
farmer organizations can hardly be overestimated. Participation through group action has political implications. Farmers'
participation at different levels means nothing less than a redistribution of political and social power.

CONCLUDING REMARKS

The intention of this paper was to touch on several of the
obstacles related to human resources that have an important bearing on the production and access to food. Hopefully, it has become clear, that several of these impediments
are deeply rooted within the sociopolitical and cultural systems of the developing societies themselves, their relations
with developed societies and within the orientation of development policies in general.

Our central thesis was the existence of an underutilized
agricultural labour potential. Its activation requires much
more than better training, technical innovations and capital
aid. Apathy, lack of a work ethic, and initiative are not innate characteristics of peasant societies. Their frequent occurrence is to the marginality of the peasant within the total
societal context. Development, therefore must be looked upon
as a system of interrelated social change. The vicious circles
of poverty and marginalization can be broken only through an increased emphasis on the principle of self-reliance.

This principle should also increasingly govern the relations between developing countries and donors. The main effort
has to be made by the developing societies themselves. Developed countries can help fill only selected gaps. Such assistance will be detrimental unless it strengthens national and
local initiatives in developing countries.

REFERENCES

Behrendt, R. F. 1965. Soziale Strategie für Entwicklungsländ-
    er. Fisher Verlag, Frankfurt, Federal Republic of Germany.
Dams, T. 1975. The integration approach of rural development
    projects: theoretical basis and practical application.
    Paper presented at the Eastern Africa Agricultural Econom-
    ics Society Conference, Kampala, Uganda. Eastern Africa
    Agricultural Economics Society.

Inter-American Development Bank. 1970. Socioeconomic progress
    in Latin America. 10th Annual Report. Inter-American De-
    velopment Bank, Washington, D.C., USA.
Kötter, H. 1972. Aspects of farmers' motivation and partici-
    pation in programme planning and implementation. In German
    Foundation of International Development. Extension and
    other services supporting the small farmer in Asia. German
    Foundation for International Development, Berlin, Federal
    Republic of Germany.
Kötter, H. 1974. Some observations on the basic principles
    and general strategy underlying integrated rural develop-
    ment. Monthly Bulletin of Agricultural Economics and Sta-
    tistics 23:No. 4, April, 1974. Food and Agricultural
    Organization, Rome, Italy.
McNamara, R. 1973. Address to the Board of Governors of the
    International Bank for Reconstruction and Development,
    Nairobi, Kenya. International Bank for Reconstruction and
    Development, Washington, D.C., USA.
Rogers, E. M. 1969. Modernization among Peasants: the Impact
    of Communication. Holt, Rinehart and Winston, Inc., New
    York, USA.
Thiesenhusen, W. 1972. Green Revolution in Latin America:
    income effects, policy decisions. Land Tenure Center Re-
    print Series No. 83. Land Tenure Center, Madison, Wiscon-
    sin, USA.
United Nations, Food and Agriculture Organization. 1974.
    World Food Conference. Publication E/Conference 65/3,
    Rome, Italy.

JAMES D. MC QUIGG

Climatic Constraints on Food Grain Production

The February 25, 1976, issue of the FAO "Food Outlook-Quarterly" includes the following statement:

The situation on the international market appears easier as exportable supplies are sufficient to meet current demand, but world cereals stock will remain low with no margin of safety. In 1976-77, world cereals supplies will again entirely depend on 1976 harvests.

This situation is caused by the fact that the potential demand for food grains remains very high and appears to be growing higher each year, while reserves have been steadily diminishing over the last decade and a half. Climate is implicated in this situation because one of the major sources of year-to-year variability of food grain (cereal) production is the year-to-year variability of large scale climatic patterns.

I believe that it is important to establish a working definition of "climate" in the context of the problem being addressed at this conference. The traditional definition of this term, which is the one I do <u>not</u> intend to use, is expressed in terms of "average weather." The definition that I <u>do</u> intend to use is expressed more in terms of the large scale, long-term variability of weather events from year-to-year or from decade-to-decade.

Climate is the sum total of the weather experienced at a

James D. McQuigg is Director of the Center for Climatic and Environmental Assessment. Federal Building, Room 116, Columbia, Missouri, 65201.

place in the course of the year and over the year. It com-
prises not only those conditions that can obviously be described as 'near average' or 'normal' but also the extreme
and all the variations (Lamb, 1972, p. 5).

In too many instances in the past, climate has either been
omitted from consideration in discussions of agricultural production or has been perceived as a constant. I have some suggestions which I hope will improve this situation.

THE IMPACT OF CLIMATIC VARIABILITY ON FOOD GRAIN PRODUCTION
Two components of year-to-year variability of grain yields
need to be considered concurrently. The first of these is
usually labeled "technology," or sometimes is referred to
as a time "trend" term. If, for example, one looks at a long
series of corn yield data from some region such as the Corn
Belt of the United States (as in Figure 1) it is apparent that
there was a comparatively flat trend in the series for the period beginning the first part of the century and ending about
World War II. Following World War II, the trend in corn yields
rose steadily until the most recent years. The flat characteristic of the yield trend line prior to World War II is the result of a comparatively static agricultural technology. The
tendency toward increasing yields since World War II is the result of better seed, better machinery, better management, and
the increased use of chemicals. These factors that are lumped
together under the term "technology" have been or will be the
subject of most of the discussions at this conference. The
second component of year-to-year variability in yields is the
result of large scale climatic variability. This shows up as
deviations above or below the underlying technology (trend)
line.
It is possible to "explain" most of the variability in a
yield data series by a regression equation somewhat similar to
the equations presented by Thompson (1969). If one has a regression model in which the components of variability attributed to technology and the component attributed to climatic
variability are expressed quantitatively, one can explain from
85 to 90 percent of the year-to-year variability of yields. A
number of other models have also been presented, such as the
one by Runge (1958, 1968).
When I was asked to prepare this paper, I was to discuss
the matter of "fitting production practices to abnormal weather
patterns." Stating the problem in this way suggests that the
weather patterns or climatic patterns associated with food
grain production are usually within some reasonable range of
"normal" and that the essential problem is to come up with management recommendations that will work during large

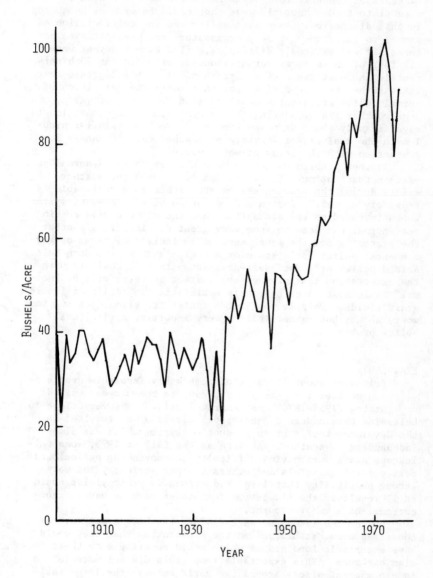

FIG. 1.   Five state average corn yield (Iowa, Illinois, Indiana, Ohio, Missouri).

meteorological anomalies. We recently took a serious look at
44 years of temperature and precipitation data for Iowa in an
attempt to find a "normal" year that could be used as an analog
in this discussion. Even when we limited the consideration of
normal to just June and July temperature and precipitation patterns, it was extremely difficult to find even one year when
all four of these terms were reasonably close to the 50th percentile in their respective distributions. This suggests that
it is rather rare to find a year that meets the definition of
normal, while it is quite usual to find that in most years,
some weather feature during the growing season occurs at levels
significantly above or below "normal." We had a similar problem in the analysis of 44 years of weather data in Kansas in
connection with the study of wheat yield.

Another problem connected with the search for a normal crop
year is that optimum yields tend to occur when the weather
events during the growing season are within some reasonable
range of "normal." Design and operation of a management system
which is based on the assumption that the climate will remain
near normal can lead to some very great difficulties, whether
the system is for the management of an individual farm, or governmental policy for a state or a region such as the Corn Belt.
A food policy or a food delivery system that is designed with
the expectation that crop season weather patterns will be "normal" is in most cases an overly optimistic projection of future
grain yields. This is not just a matter for climatologists to
worry about, but rather it is a very important agricultural
policy problem.

EXAMPLES

Following about 15 years of remarkably favorable crop season weather for corn and soybeans in the midwest United
States (1956-1970), many agriculturists came very close to
believing that modern technological advances had resulted in
the development of a grain production system which was almost
independent of weather. As late as the fall of 1973, some colleagues and I were having difficulty in convincing agricultural
policy level officials and others to take seriously the very
strong possibility that large reductions in grain yields could
still result if the midwest United States were to have a reoc-
currence of a major drought.

During the 1960s and early 1970s, the budgets of several
countries were established on the expectation that they would
have exportable food grains which would contribute to their foreign exchange. This exportable food grain did not materialize
in a number of places around the world because the large scale
weather patterns resumed their usual amount of variability,
after the decades of highly favorable low year-to-year weather

variability in the 1950s and 1960s.

The essential problem is the approach to be used to project future food grain yields. This is very important whether it is being done in the case of an individual farm, where the owner or manager is attempting to plan capital improvements or additions to the productive capacity of the farm, or whether this is being done in terms of an entire country or a group of countries, at a national or international policy level. Projections of future food grain yields need to take into account both of the major components of year-to-year variability of yields discussed above. This is the same as saying that it is necessary to project both future climate and the future technological trend in yields.

The meteorological services of a number of countries are making major efforts which will lead to the eventual capability of making deterministic climate forecasts. These are forecasts based on mathematical and/or dynamic models of the global atmophere presented for periods of one month to one year or more in advance. It appears now that it will be some time before this capability is realized. In the meantime, it is possible to prepare useful statistical estimates of the variability of future climate by using the excellent long term climatic records that exist for most parts of the world. The problem really becomes one of choosing a proper sample of past climate. In too many cases, the sample leading to such statistical estimates has been inadequate. The projection of future yields of grain has also been based on a comparatively short sample of yield records, sometimes covering only the most recent five to ten years. Where this has been the case, and where by coincidence this fairly brief period of time has also been a period of unusually favorable crop season weather, the projections of yields into the future are overly optimistic.

We recommend that anyone wanting to prepare a statistical projection of future climate should find the longest, most homogenous series of meteorological observations that it is possible to find and to proceed with the analysis using such a sample.

The problem of projecting the future trend in yields of grain is equally difficult. In several important grain producing regions of the world it is becoming increasingly clear that the trend toward higher yields which had been established for most of the period following World War II has been leveling off or even declining. The sample of data from Oklahoma shown as Figure 2 is a good example. Here the trend in wheat yields was comparatively flat until about the middle of the 1950s. There followed a rapid increase in yields due to the introduction of new wheat varieties, the establishment of governmental acreage reserves, increasing fertilizer usage, and better management. This sharp increase in yields appeared to level off after about

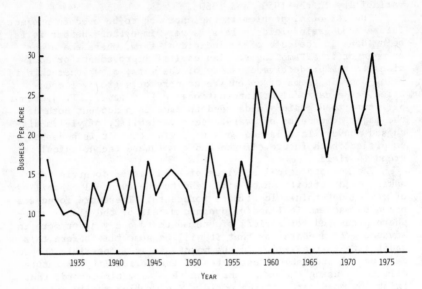

FIG. 2. Oklahoma wheat yields.

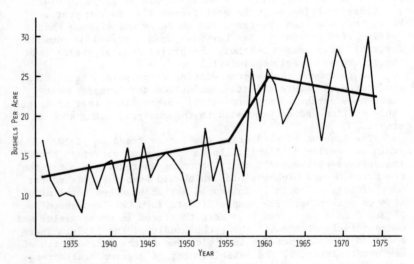

FIG. 3. Oklahoma wheat yields expressing downward technological trend line.

six or seven years. The model that we are currently using to express the technological trend line for Oklahoma is shown as Figure 3. If the trend of the past decade or two is simply projected into the future decade or so, the result may be an overly optimistic forecast of future grain yields.

In the most recent years, there have been some additional factors which need to be combined with the factors that we have considered as "technology" in the past. These additional factors mostly involve changing land use practices. In some parts of the world the practice of fallowing or the use of terraces or contour planting of crops has been abandoned. In other parts of the world, there are attempts to move food grain production to land that had formerly been considered less suitable for this purpose. Grain that in previous times would have been abandoned at harvest time has been harvested, because of the better prices for grain in recent years. In some parts of the world, such as the United States, land that had been part of the acreage reserve, funded by the government, has been released for production.

CONCLUSION

I believe it is fair to say that future food grain production, both in the developed and developing countries, may be _more_ rather than _less_ sensitive to climatic variability from year-to-year than was the case in the two decades just past. This is not to say that there will be a change in the biological and physiological response of the plants to climate, but rather this reflects a change in the response of the entire food grain producing system. This increased sensitivity will be the result of a number of factors:

1. Global grain reserves are at very low levels.
2. Further steady increases in yields resulting from improved "technology" may not fully materialize.
3. Most important, climate during the next decade or so may be subject to a greater range of year-to-year variability than has been the case in the most recent one or two decades.

The flow of meteorological information from the food-producing regions of the world (land and ocean) is rich in information about the progress of crops and fisheries during a current production season. The long time climatic records that are available from these same regions are also rich in information about year-to-year variability of crops. Both rich sources of information need to be used more effectively by producers and policy makers.

I am very pleased to have been given the opportunity to take part in this important conference. I believe that it is extremely important that the impact of climatic variability be included as one of several very important factors in future food production.

REFERENCES

Lamb, H. H. 1972. Climate Present, Past, and Future. Vol 1. Methuen and Co., Ltd., London.
Runge, E. C. A., and Odell, R. T. 1958. The relation between precipitation, temperature, and the yield of corn on the Agronomy South Farm, Urbana, Illinois. Agronomy Journal 50:448.
Runge, E. C. A. 1968. Effects of rainfall and temperature interactions during the growing season on corn yield. Agronomy Journal 60:503.
Thompson, L. M. 1969. Weather and technology in the production of corn in the US corn belt. Agronomy Journal 61: 453.

J. H. CONRAD

Constraints on Improvement of Plant and Animal Resources

To constrain is to stifle, to hold back, to restrict, or to impede. A constraint implies restriction, confinement, or limitation. In preparation for this paper, it became apparent that it was impossible to list all the constraints on improvement of plant and animal resources. Furthermore, if it were possible to list them there would not be time to discuss them. Consequently, my remarks will focus primarily on constraints in the Soil - Plant - Animal Ruminant - Livestock Production System.

RUMINANTS AS FOOD PRODUCERS

Ruminants are a special class of animals that includes cattle, sheep, goats, deer, elk, buffalo, and many wild animal species. They have, as part of their digestive system, a microbial fermentation stage in which plant materials such as grass are converted to usable nutritional forms. This unique capability enables ruminants to convert--to meat, milk, or other human food--many cellulosic plant materials and industrial by-products that would otherwise be wastes. Ruminants can even use such items as old newspapers, processed sawdust, and sugarcane bagasse. They can synthesize high-quality proteins by using the nitrogen supplied by simple, inexpensive nonprotein forms, such as urea, which humans cannot use directly. In addition, ruminants have the capability of harvesting their own food. Many millions of hectares of the

---

J. H. Conrad is Professor of Animal Nutrition and Coordinator Tropical Animal Science Programs, Department of Animal Science, University of Florida, Gainesville, Florida 32611.

earth's rangelands cannot now be harvested for food production other than by grazing with ruminants.

Currently there are two head of ruminant livestock on the world for every three people. Although 60 percent of those ruminants are in developing countries, the amount of human food they produce is about equal to that now realized from the 8 percent of the world ruminant livestock found in the USA. The potential for increasing the productivity of ruminant livestock in developing countries obviously is very great. There probably is more opportunity for improving the nutrition of the human population in these countries by increasing the productivity of their ruminant livestock than in any other way now available.

ANIMALS AS A FOOD RESERVE

Worldwide grain reserves in 1974 were estimated to represent a 27-day supply. However, many analysts have overlooked a fact of great importance--the security represented by food stored in live animals. Live animals, not including poultry, represented a 40-day food supply in 1974 compared to 27 days worth of grain reserves. This figure is based on the caloric value of meat on animals not slaughtered in that year. These are animals maintained for future consumption, breeding, traction, and milk with over 75 percent of the reserves represented by cattle (Shapiro, 1976).

RESEARCH AND CONSTRAINTS

Research is an excellent and time-tested method for identifying and solving constraints. Forages are the principal feed of ruminants throughout the world. The productivity of ruminant livestock can be increased through research to increase the productivity of forages, to develop cultivars of forage crops with greater yields and digestibility, and to develop methods of handling that will reduce the losses of forage crops during harvest and storage. More research is needed to develop biological types of ruminants that are especially suited to specific environments. Control of animal reproductive processes holds the promise of increasing the productivity per breeding animal and establishing better timing for production of young animals in relation to their food needs. Research can help identify the most limiting nutrients--minerals, protein, and energy--under a variety of grazing conditions and indicate the cost-benefit ratios from supplying levels of the various limiting nutrients during the most critical periods in the life cycle.

A report on research to meet USA and world food needs was developed by the United States Agricultural Research Policy Advisory Committee in 1975. This report identified important

problems that require research. Thirty items for research were
listed under harvested forages and seed production, 26 under
permanent rotation and irrigated pastures, 27 under range, 25
under beef cattle, 21 under lamb and mutton, 29 under dairy
cattle, and 24 under other animals. All of these address themselves to solving constraints within each category listed.
Each country in the world could develop an equally impressive
list of priority areas for research in the ruminant livestock
areas.

Numerous symposia and seminars have focused on soil fertility, tropical soils, range management, pasture and forage
management, nutritional value of forages, mineral nutrition of
grazing ruminants, supplemental feeding, breeding and crossbreeding, physiology of reproduction, improving meat quality,
identification and control of tropical diseases, and economical
and sociological factors affecting livestock production. Publications resulting from these meetings provide excellent
reviews on the information currently available and specify many
limiting constraints. Following is a very brief list of conference proceedings and reviews which emphasize constraints to
ruminant livestock production systems in the tropics: A Review
of Soils Research in Tropical Latin America, Structural Inhibitors of Quality in Tropical Grasses, Crossbreeding Beef Cattle,
Factors Affecting Calf Crop, Latin American Tables of Feed Composition, Latin American Symposium on Mineral Nutrition
Research with Grazing Ruminants, Animal Production in the Tropics, Potential to Increase Beef Production in Tropical America,
and Beef Cattle Production in Developing Countries. Specific
references to these topics are listed under references.

IDENTIFICATION OF THE CONSTRAINTS IN THE SOIL -
PLANT - ANIMAL RUMINANT-LIVESTOCK PRODUCTION SYSTEM
   It is estimated that over a billion hectares of land in
   tropical zones are suitable for grazing and that such
   areas support over 50 percent of the ruminant livestock of
the world. Production levels are low measured by any criterion
of productivity, but are especially low when compared to production levels in temperate zones. Efforts to increase offtake
through the application of technology have been relatively
ineffective. Within the ruminant livestock production system
in the tropics, there has been no development analogous to the
Green Revolution.

Major constraints can be found in the fact that the ruminant livestock production system is a very complex network of
interrelated factors ranging from soil - plant - animal relationships to people - economic - political relationships.
Oftentimes, the thrust to apply improved practices has been
directed toward single facets or uncoordinated multiple facets
that have not resulted in a beneficial response within the

overall production system. Obscure results are not surprising
when we consider that cattle are large complex mammals, that
the growing period from conception to slaughter often spans
half a decade, that the complexities of raising the animal are
compounded by the complexities of producing an adequate forage
supply under varying soil and climatic conditions, that a
highly perishable product is produced, and that extensive
financial resources are required within the production and marketing system.

An interdisciplinary approach incorporating the principles
of systems analysis is being used as a method to identify the
constraints to ruminant livestock production. The United
States Agency for International Development granted institutional development funds to four universities representing
seven disciplines to refine the methodology for identifying
constraints. The program was entitled "Expanding Competence in
the Design and Execution of Livestock Development Programs in
the Tropics Emphasizing Ruminant Livestock Production Systems."
The objective was to use a balanced, coordinated approach with
representation from several major disciplines which could supply coefficients and data for systems analysis. Areas of
expertise and the universities represented were as follows:
tropical forage production and ruminant nutrition, University
of Florida; tropical veterinary medicine and livestock production systems, Texas A and M University; sociology and information delivery systems, Tuskegee Institute; economic analysis,
Purdue University.

This consortium met at least four times annually during
the past three years. A "herd model" to simulate herd management systems was refined. A "cattle industry" model incorporating some aspects of the "herd model" was developed and
refined. Guyana, with the full cooperation of the Government
of Guyana, was selected as the tropical country in which to
utilize this method for identifying constraints to cattle production.

Using the "herd model," seven management systems were simulated within a major cattle producing area of Guyana and six
management systems in another. The "cattle industry model" was
used to simulate the aggregate behavior of producers and consumers of beef and milk as they interact in the market place
over time. Several modifications in model specifications were
made to reflect policy, program, market, and technological
changes with some examples as follows: intensive management
systems for extensive commercial subherds; subsidies on pasture
development and maintenance in the savannas; export of beef
from the savannas; long-term feeding of stocker cattle; short-
term feeding of stocker cattle; removal of transportation subsidies; and incorporation of the herd model.

This cooperative effort permitted the consortium and the
Government of Guyana to obtain a clearer perspective of the

constraints to the total cattle industry in Guyana than had
previously been done. A survey helped to provide an insight
into characteristics of producers of different classifications
which aided in structuring extension service and training.
Following a study of the cattle health problems a recommendation was made for a practical and effective veterinary diag-
nostic laboratory. A possible explanation of the production
constraints in the intermediate savanna area was found and this
was accompanied by a possible solution. A reduction in calf-
death losses was shown to be one of the most effective ways to
increase production efficiency and produce more pounds of beef.
The economic evaluation provided important insights into the
behavior of the cattle industry. A most important effect was
probably the organization of thoughts to include all the major
effects in a model in a manner in which they actually operate.

The effectiveness of the simulated herd management systems
and cattle industry analysis were severely limited by available
data and accurate coefficients. In modeling livestock production systems, forages represent the point of beginning and the
quality and quantity of available forage resources determines,
to a large extent, the output of the livestock enterprise. The
natural grasslands of the tropics and subtropics represent very
complex ecosystems with a wide range of plant species which are
selectively grazed. The selective grazing is conditioned by
stages of growth, regrowth after burning, the chemical and
physical properties of the soil, the hydrologic cycle, and the
grazing pressure imposed. For modeling purposes, estimates
were made of the monthly forage availability, monthly digestion coefficients, and the protein contents of the forage
apparently consumed. Consequently, this gave only a very rough
approximation of the quality of forage available. It was found
that more reliable coefficients are needed on forage availability, intake, and digestibility for modeling livestock production systems.

Nutritional deficiencies, protein, energy, and minerals
are often serious constraints in ruminant livestock production
systems. Mineral deficiencies have been shown to be widespread
in grazing ruminants in the tropics where adequate mineral supplementation is not furnished. One of the major advantages
from phosphorus supplementation under range conditions is the
increase in percent calf crop and the resulting increase in
the percent of calves weaned. Phosphorus supplementation as
bonemeal in a two-year study in Texas resulted in a weaned calf
crop of 81 percent as compared to 58 percent for the controls.
In a later study, the weaned calf crop was 88 percent for those
fed bonemeal compared to 64 percent for the controls (Reynolds
et al., 1953). A study conducted in Brazil resulted in a 77
percent calf crop when bonemeal was fed compared to 55 percent
for the controls. Recent trials in the Colombian llanos
demonstrated that the pregnancy rate was increased from 50 per-

cent for the controls up to 84 percent when complete minerals
were fed (Stonaker et al., 1975). Economical returns on mineral investment have been at least two to one in some studies.
In the cattle producing areas in the interior of Guyana, soil
and forage phosphorus levels are low and few cattle producers
provide mineral supplementation, especially phosphorus. However, within the time frame, it was not possible to test the
response to phosphorus supplementation in the model nor to
assess its economical returns in cattle production systems.

Using the models, it was not possible to accurately translate the effect of diseases and parasites on livestock production parameters. Diseases of livestock which affect the industry can be divided into three categories. The catastrophic
diseases are those which, when present, will cause great losses
in production and/or mortality to a high percentage of the
livestock in the area. Examples of this are foot and mouth
disease, rinderpest, and cobalt deficiency. The second type of
disease is the sporadic disease which usually affects only a
small proportion of the total herd of an area, but the local
effects can be catastrophic. Examples of this type of disease
are anthrax, blackleg, and rabies. The third group of diseases
are the chronic conditions which, under some circumstances, can
cause great economic losses by death and loss of production.
However, the effects of these diseases under the usual circumstances are difficult to ascertain because much of the loss is
not readily apparent and is expressed in slow growth rates,
lowered efficiency in feed conversion, and lowered reproductive
efficiency. Examples of this type of disease are internal parasitism, tuberculosis, and venereal trichomaniasis. The consortium was fully aware that a broad spectrum of veterinary
problems is a constraint which exists and interacts with nutritional levels and management. However, only fixed judgment
values for mortality rates and expenses for veterinary services
were considered.

It was not possible to quantify the constraints represented by people, social customs, levels of education, skills,
experience, and attitudes. However, a producer survey was conducted to gain a comprehensive understanding of the livestock
producer and current production methodology. Data were collected from cattle, swine, poultry, sheep, and goat producers.
The survey was concerned with the following topics: socio-
economic characteristics of land use, livestock breeding, herd
health data, nutritional information, marketing practices, and
involvement with and attitudes toward livestock extension programs. A review of the livestock and veterinary extension
service identified numerous constraints to the implementation
of livestock programs. These constraints are widespread in
many countries but are also difficult to quantify. Some of
these constraints were: transportation of extension workers to
the producer; availability of inputs such as feeds, minerals,

breeding stock, and vaccines; social problems relating to development of cooperatives; lack of published materials about livestock production and management; inadequate supervision and communication of personnel; and attracting and maintaining qualified personnel in the extension service.

A report by Joandet and Cartwright (1975) has outlined the concepts and limitations of modeling beef production systems. Studies to evaluate herd management practices in relevant terms of production efficiency using simulated models of beef cattle production systems have been in progress at Texas A and M University for a number of years.

The "herd model" was programmed to simulate cattle production in a major cattle producing area of Guyana and given a 12-month breeding season, unsupplemented rangeland, and no modifications of current management practices. However, a complex problem developed in trying to describe the quantity and quality of forage consumed throughout the year. Some aspects of the problem were 1) determining the proportion of the grazed area which is flooded periodically; 2) quantifying the quality of forage on both flooded and non-flooded areas throughout the year in terms of percent digestibility and crude protein; and 3) characterizing the quality of the mix of forage actually consumed by cattle from both flooded and non-flooded areas on a monthly basis.

Seven management systems were simulated within a major cattle producing area of Guyana. Results were measured in terms of slaughter weight produced per cow, slaughter weight produced per 100 kg of forage dry matter consumed, and kilograms of forage dry matter required to produce one kg of slaughter weight. A reduction in the death losses of young calves was one management practice which gave the greatest improvement in efficiency of production.

CONSTRAINTS AND THE COMMITMENT OF POLICY MAKERS

It is of little if any value to identify constraints or to conduct adaptive research if there is not a strong commitment from policy makers and politicians to increase the production of food grains and animal products.

The value of feed phosphate in ruminant livestock production has been shown to dramatically improve the percent calf crop and to provide economical returns on mineral investment of at least two to one. Feed phosphate consumption in the USA increased from 340,000 tons in 1951 to 1.3 million tons in 1970. In 1962 Brazil had some 12,000 tons of bonemeal available for livestock feeding which included 65 million head of cattle being raised on low phosphorus soils and forages. Calculations indicated this bonemeal supply represented less than a week's supply of phosphorus supplement. Phosphate deposits are found in several places in Brazil. Fifteen years later feed phosphates are not being produced from Brazilian phosphates. Plans are to construct a feed phosphate plant when the Brazilian demand reaches 30,000 tons. Meanwhile, the majority of the 85 million head of cattle are phosphorus deficient. The control of exportable Moroccan phosphate has recently been in the news. Phosphate-containing lands are changing ownership at astronomical prices. Countries which have both phosphate deposits and large ruminant livestock populations have the potential for increasing ruminant livestock production by correcting phosphorus deficiencies.

SUMMARY

Constraints on improvement of plant and animal resources are numerous and complex. Identification of and solutions to constraints on soil - plant - animal ruminant-livestock production systems offer great potential for increasing the productivity of livestock in many countries where the current productivity is relatively low.

Massive quantities of research information are currently available but adaptive or problem solving research is needed to focus on the major constraints to the development of more efficient ruminant-livestock production systems. The use of simulated models of herd systems and ruminant-livestock industries appear to be a promising technique for the identification of constraints and the selection of research priorities in ruminant-livestock production systems. More reliable coefficients in several areas are needed to make this technique function more effectively.

It is of little if any value to identify constraints or to conduct adaptive research if there is not a strong commitment from policy makers and politicians to increase the production of food grains and animal products.

REFERENCES

Centro Internacional de Agricultura Tropical. 1975. Potential to increase beef production in tropical America. Series CE-No. 10, Cali, Colombia.

Council for Agricultural Science and Technology. 1975. Ruminants as food producers--now and for the future. Special Publication No. 4, Department of Agronomy, Iowa State University, Ames, Iowa.

Cunha, T. J., A. C. Warnick, and M. Koger. 1967. Factors Affecting Calf Crop. University of Florida Press, Gainesville, Florida.

Joandet, G. E., and T. C. Cartwright. 1975. Modeling beef production systems. Journal of Animal Science 41:1238-1246.

Koger, M., T. J. Cunha, and A. C. Warnick. 1973. Crossbreed-
    ing beef cattle, Series II. University of Florida Press,
    Gainesville, Florida.
Loosli, J. K., V. A. Oyenuga, and G. M. Barbatunde (Editors).
    Animal Production in the Tropics. Heinemann Educational
    Books, Ighodaro Rd., Jericho, Ibadan, Nigeria, P.M.B. 5205.
Long, R. W.., and O. G. Bentley. 1975. Research to meet US
    and World food needs. Report of the Agricultural Research
    Policy Advisory Committee. USDA, Washington, DC.
McDowell, L. R., J. H. Conrad, J. E. Thomas, and L. E. Harris.
    1974. Latin American tables of feed composition. Atlas
    edition in English, Abridged edition in English, Spanish,
    and Portuguese, Department of Animal Science, University of
    Florida, Gainesville, Florida.
Moore, J. E., and G. O. Mott. 1973. Structural inhibitors of
    quality in tropical grasses. Anti-quality components of
    forages. Crop Science Society of America, Madison, Wiscon-
    sin.
National Academy of Sciences. 1975. World Food and Nutrition
    Study. Report of the Board on Agriculture and Renewable
    Resources. Washington, DC.
National Academy of Sciences. 1976. Nutrient requirements of
    beef cattle. Fifth Revised Edition. Washington, DC.
Reynolds, E. B., J. M. Jones, J. H. Jones, J. F. Fudge, and
    R. J. Kleberg, Jr. 1953. Methods of supplying phosphorus
    to range cattle in South Texas. Texas Agricultural Experi-
    ment Station Bulletin 773, College Station, Texas.
Sanchez, P. A. 1973. A review of soils research in tropical
    Latin America. North Carolina Agricultural Experiment Sta-
    tion. Technical Bulletin 219. Raleigh, North Carolina
    (English and Spanish).
Shapiro, K. H. 1976. The role of livestock in meeting world
    food needs and aiding overall economic development (Unpub-
    lished Report - University of Michigan, Ann Arbor).
Simposio Latino-Americano Sobre Pesquisa em Nutricão Mineral de
    Ruminantes em Pastagens. 1976. Belo Horizonte, Minas
    Gerais, Brasil.
Smith, A. J. (Editor). 1976. Proceedings of the Conference
    on Beef Cattle Production in Developing Countries. Centre
    for Tropical Veterinary Medicine, University of Edinburgh,
    Easter Bush, Roslin, Midlothian, Scotland.
Stonaker, H. H., J. Salazar, D. H. Bushman, J. Gomez, J.
    Villar, and G. Osorio. 1975. Proceedings Seminar on
    Potential to Increase Beef Production in Tropical America.
    CIAT Publication Series CE-No. 10, pps. 63-81, Cali, Colom-
    bia.

ANGELITA Y. LEDESMA

The Potentials of the Human Work Force to Produce Food

Drawn from the experiences of Third World countries, the focus of this paper is the problem of poverty and the need for human sustenance, that is, food with dignity. The paper examines the relationship between the potentials of the human work force to produce food and the structural parameters within which these potentials are fulfilled or impeded. It is significant that the literature on the positive achievements of the Green Revolution is consistently overshadowed by more pessimistic forecasts of continued hunger, malnutrition and famine in the very regions intended to be nourished and developed. Yet, if we were to assess potentials against past achievements, those of the Green Revolution are the most heralded and widely recognized. There is no doubt that the technology of the Green Revolution, itself still in a process of evolution, has achieved tremendous gains, but as the field studies carried out in different countries under UNDP/UNRISD Global-2 project indicate, the Green Revolution has failed to involve the majority of cultivators, especially the small and marginal farmers, nor has it resulted in mass welfare (Rao, 1974). Of equal concern are the divisive forces that surfaced in the social organization of communities affected by the technological transformation of their agriculture.

These problems may be partly explained by the vertical integration of rural economies into the international economy,

Angelita Y. Ledesma is Director Research and Documentation Desk, Centre for the Development of Human Resources in Rural Asia, P.O. Box 458, Greenhills, San Juan, Rizal 3113, Philippines.

resulting in their partial and lopsided development. The dual-
istic nature of the economies of the underdeveloped countries
is best reflected in agriculture, where a modernized export-
oriented sector with its great absorptive capacity exists side
by side with a traditional subsistence economy of small farmers. Under such conditions of structural inequality and uneven
strength, the best possible resources, such as those of the
Green Revolution, only enhance the inherently defective social
structures.

But problems also stem from the fact that the Green Revolution failed to generate development from within the communities. One might have expected a general upliftment of poverty
in those communities and a cumulative chain of changes that
would have restructured the allocation of resources in favor of
the disadvantaged. But this did not occur. The International
Labour Organization reports, "We have seen that the spread of
the 'Green Revolution', and more generally of the various agricultural technologies, is to accentuate the 'proletarianiza-
tion' of the rural areas of Asia. The number of the rural poor
is increasing." (ILO, 1975, p. 24).

We need to ask first a basic question: What is the objective for increasing food production? The answer to this question determines the assumptions of our food production strategies as well as their outcomes.

THE GREEN REVOLUTION EXPERIENCE OF THE HUMAN WORK FORCE
There are a number of ways to describe the rural work
force in underdeveloped countries. One could look at settlement patterns which usually follow cropping and agricultural practices. Man/land ratios indicate population densities where one may find a labor force. Or, one could try to
visualize the impact of that labor force as used in the planting of 50 million acres of land to high yielding seed varieties.
Such aggregate descriptions can be supplemented by in-depth
studies and monographs from different regions. These reveal in
detail the mosaic of activities by which rural dwellers cope
with their environment. But whether one goes to the ejidos of
Mexico or the Ujamaa villages of Tanzania, to the rubber plantations of Malaysia or to the sugar estates of the Philippines,
one always discovers a common human type trying to break away
from endemic poverty. Let us assume that the technological
breakthroughs in food production were intended to solve this
poverty. For this purpose, we will review the place of the human work force in the Green Revolution.

A comprehensive study of the social and economic implications of the Green Revolution in the wheat-growing regions of
the State of Sonora, Mexico, provides an instructive analysis
of the very complex dynamics of change (Alcantara, 1974). Invariably, its findings are reiterated in similar experiences in

other parts of the world affected by the new technology. Some of the significant findings of these studies are the following:

1) The capital-intensive nature of the new technologies associated with the Green Revolution activated transfer mechanisms which moved productive resources (land, credit, technical information, machinery) from smaller to larger farmers. In India, land tenure changes brought about eviction of tenants and displacement of sharecroppers (ILO, 1975, p. 9). In Pakistan, those who possessed extensive resources of land and water derived the greatest benefit from the new agricultural inputs (ILO, 1975, p. 9). In Mexico, the Green Revolution favored irrigated lands and thereby left 83 percent of all the farmers of Mexico who were in non-irrigated lands at a subsistence or below subsistence level as late as 1960 (Alcantara, 1974, p. 117). The concentration of resources inevitably brings with it a consolidation of strength. The consequences for the weak are self-evident.

2) The spectacular results in production yields seem to come from relatively large commercial farms, and not from subsistence or semi-subsistence farmers. This does not indicate an intensive application of labor. The lack of internal effective demand in general and in the rural areas in particular is evidence of insufficient employment. In 1971, many of the unskilled field hands attracted to Sonora could count on less than six months work per year (Alcantara, 1974, p. 267). The ILO (1975, p. 26) reports that in many Asian countries there is an increase in the number of landless farmers and a shortage of work for agricultural laborers, whether skilled or not, accompanied by a growing prosperity of the rural middle classes.

3) An increase in social tensions and class divisions appear to be inevitable under the circumstances described above. In India, in 1967-1968, only 20 percent of the total area planted to wheat consisted of the new dwarf wheats but this contributed 34 percent of the total production. There is, therefore, a strong possibility that the more progressive farmers will capture food markets, leading to a net reduction in the income of the smaller, poorer and less venturesome farmers (Wharton, 1969, p. 467). Between 1967 and 1968 there were 61 reported outbreaks of violence by landless peasants whose living conditions are as wretched today as they were when India became politically independent (ILO, 1975, p. 10). The growing prosperity of landowners and the deteriorating circumstances of small farmers have given rise to social tensions. The civil war in Pakistan was not entirely unrelated to the increasing disparity in per capita incomes between East and West Pakistan, a difference which increased from 18 percent in 1950 to 38 percent in 1970.

If social classes are defined on the basis of their control of the means of production, then the introduction of a capital-intensive technology in a situation of unequal distribution of power, predictably concentrates that control in fewer and fewer hands. As aptly put by Alcantara (1974, p. 221) "The juxtaposition of a landless and often unemployed majority, a disorganized and demoralized ejido sector, and an ever-smaller group of very powerful private farmers does not, and cannot provide the material of which social harmony is made."

Another interesting social situation described by Alcantara (1974, p. 267) is that of beneficiaries of land reform who eventually lost control over their lands during the Green Revolution. While they were not among the really poor because they received rents, the loss of their role as entrepreneurs or administrators made them compete with the mass of landless laborers for the limited field work to be done. Reduced to virtual idleness, their communities (where renting was the prevailing practice) tended to be riddled with factionalism, drunkenness, and violence. In essence, people had no community.

4) The urban-industrial bias evident from the beginning in the Green Revolution of Mexico has also been manifest in other parts of the world. This is perhaps due to the nature of the development package introduced by the Green Revolution. It may be, however, that the internal structures of recipient societies predispose them to such a bias. In Mexico, the sequence of social and political events which preceded the Green Revolution are well known. Those who supported an agriculture based on large scale private enterprise prevailed over those who espoused an agrarian socialism of a strong peasantry. After the presidency of Lazaro Cardenas who strengthened the ejido movement (the formation of communal landholdings) through the redistribution of land and income to farm laborers and smallholders, a reverse process of agricultural development took place. Agriculture was to play a new role as the "foundation of industrial greatness" (Alcantara, 1974, p. 19). Private enterprise of the growing urban middle and upper classes was to be the new base of development. The Green Revolution succeeded in financing industrialization, allowing the government to maintain urban food prices at low levels, while eventually reducing and eliminating grain imports and increasing exports of primary products (Alcantara, 1974).

This export orientation of commercial agriculture usually does not result in the development of rural areas. The expansion of plantations in the second half of the nineteenth century in South Asia provides an appropriate illustration. To this day the plantations remain modern enclaves in largely stagnant economies.

Ingrid Palmer (1972, p. 62) mentions the case of Indonesia. Here the generous credits of foreign businesses and governments financed a "rice revolution", ostensibly to save foreign exchange. This and compulsory sugar cane cultivation forced farmers to reduce soybean production, the main crop of East

Java. Had the Indonesian government been made more fully aware of the appalling protein deficiencies of the Javanese, Palmer argues, they might have bargained harder for the welfare of over 60 million people. The persistent pattern of exporting higher value products in order to import cheaper lower value food products worsens the problem of malnutrition among the rural masses (Ingrid Palmer, 1972, p. 70). Foreign exchange earnings are often a key objective in low income countries with balance-of-payments difficulties. But the nature of imports which generally go to the urban areas with their luxurious life styles, far from relieves the exhaustion of resources, both human and natural resources, in the rural areas. Even when such luxury goods are manufactured domestically, mostly by subsidiaries of foreign companies, they are no less superfluous.

The urban-industrial bias also reappears in the programs which call for large expenditures on fertilizers, machinery, pesticides, weed-killers and irrigation systems. The sources of these inputs are largely urban enterprises, domestic and foreign business firms. The chain of profit-taking by such firms diverts concern from the appalling poverty and deprivation of the countryside. Commercialization of agriculture is not tantamount to development of rural areas.

From the above, we can drawn these conclusions with respect to the human work force in areas where the Green Revolution took place. First, that the work force as a whole has not enhanced its potentials. Second, that it is in a worse state and constitutes the bulk of the rural poor who amidst harvests of plenty have themselves remained hungry. The adverse social consequences of the Green Revolution may have been unintended. But given the structural setting in which it was implemented, the results should have been foreseen.

Notwithstanding unprecedented levels of food production which testify to the potential of science and technology in solving human problems (in this instance that of physical sustenance) the Green Revolution experiences force us to consider the fact that the priority of providing for the material needs of people can, ironically, lead to their impoverishment. Economic development which aims solely at meeting the material needs of man, while suppressing the fulfillment of his other needs, must necessarily bring distortion and alienation in his life. The challenging insight is that although we refer to food, clothing, shelter as fundamental needs of man, nevertheless, there are needs beyond them, such as the need for freedom to express oneself, the need for work that permits free consciousness-formation (Galtung, 1975, p. 51). These are integral needs. They form a balance of material and non-material needs. Their fulfillment, therefore, must constitute a total man.

THE NEED FOR APPROPRIATE STRUCTURES

What kinds of structural changes, then, are needed to fulfill these integral needs of people? What kinds of human communities truly sustain and develop people's capacities to improve their lives?

When we look into the food production activities of people in underdeveloped countries, two seemingly disparate realities strike us. If they are producers of export commodities, then there is that world of villages and that of commodity markets controlled by the developed countries. If they are producers of food, then there is that region of the hinterlands and that of urban markets controlled by middlemen. Usually each sector only vaguely knows about the other, yet they are all interconnected through the mechanisms of a market system. The village producers are unable to single out the workings of the market as the cause of their small earnings and low wages. There is need, therefore, to see the international framework which links the dual economies of underdeveloped countries to those of the developed countries. These linkages could support or undermine the growth and strength of local people's communities.

Certain structural changes are now emerging at the international level. Hopefully, these trends will converge and support the changes that are evolving from the grassroots level in local communities. The 1974 Declaration on the Establishment of a New International Economic Order calls for control by the underdeveloped countries of their natural resources, and that they be enabled to process these for their own use. It asks for better terms of trade, so that they earn more from these resources. The agenda of UNCTAD IV (Nairobi, 1976) includes a proposed integrated commodities approach, in order to stabilize prices through market regulations. Such proposals are intended to narrow the gap between rich and poor nations through a redistribution of income and wealth (Gamani Corea, Development Forum, 1975).

The new relationships between developed and underdeveloped countries will generate internal changes in both and gradually forge new institutions and structures. For the underdeveloped nations, the internal changes called for are the following: (a) to meet directly the basic needs of the poorest quartile of the population; (b) to find some way of dealing with local elites (a developing country will never be able to overcome poverty if one quarter of the population appropriates three quarters of the social surplus for its own consumption); (c) to decentralize in order to promote autonomy and self-reliance at all levels, from villages to regions, to the nation itself; (d) to improve understanding about the workings of present structures and about alternative structures of the people's own creation and self-expression; (e) to counteract repression and manipulation through political mobilization.

For the developed countries, parallel internal changes are

being called for: (a) decrease their dependence on raw materials produced by underdeveloped countries (this means developing
new, less consumptive styles of living in general, and less
consumptive of nonrenewable energy resources in particular; (b)
find a way of dealing with the developed countries' instruments
of direct and structural violence in developing countries, such
as political subversion, military interventions and transnational corporations; (c) decentralize so that their people comprehend the workings of their society; (d) initiate consciousness-formation that leads towards a better understanding of the
true nature of Western liberal democracy; (e) undertake much
stronger political mobilization in the developed countries to
help change existing structure (Galtung, 1975, pp. 47-49).

Of particular relevance to our topic of discussion, the
development of the potentials of the human work force to produce food, are the new strategies which underscore the importance of self-reliance and of collective self-reliance. The
new relationships between developed and underdeveloped countries point to a shift from dependence which characterizes vertical trade and division of labor to that of self-reliance.
This means not only that underdeveloped countries rely more on
themselves, but more significantly, that the fruits of self-reliance accrue to the masses. A new type of horizontal trade
and division of labor between underdeveloped nations (that is,
among those that are at similar levels of development) would be
the basis for mutual help and cooperation. Since this is to be
founded on the cooperation of self-reliant communities, it is
called collective self-reliance.

The answer to the question we posed earlier is now quite
clear. The objective of increasing food production is above
all to meet the nutritional needs of the great masses of the
poor. Food production strategies, therefore, should not result
in the depletion of food and other resources in the very regions of their source. The work force will then be assured of
nourishment and growth. From this standpoint, self-reliance is
possible only through the direct participation of people in the
decision-making processes related to the food production system. Moreover, the strategy of self-reliance should enable
them to help define terms of trade, as well as to make decisions regarding the nature of the traded commodities and services. The people's traditional village technologies, integrated with local cultures and socioeconomic structures must be
more fully developed. Technological transfers must meet priority needs as defined by the people themselves.

With the shift from the vertical trade and division of
labor which tended to disintegrate communities, divide interests and responsibilities, to horizontal integration of self-
reliant communities, the products of economic growth would be
more evenly distributed. There will result a more balanced development of such communities. Among the characteristics of

this kind of balanced growth (Galtung, 1975, p. 48) are the expanding horizontal networks of transport and communication systems, trading patterns, exchanges of technical achievements and
knowledge which connect the villages. Another type of spatial
dispersion would be the means of producing knowledge which will
result in less reliance on urban centers of learning and in increased reliance on locally generated knowledge.

Finally, the changes generated by collective self-reliance
will lead to better horizontal cooperative bonds between developing nations. But the processes of interaction and communication must spring forth from the people themselves and from
their communities into widening circles of institutions and
structures.

FOOD PRODUCTION AS A HUMANIZING ACTIVITY

The impersonal market system in which man hitherto has
participated has indeed reduced him to that of a "factor"
of production who enters production relationships as a
"cost." The relation of cost to profits is likewise reflected
in the mutually exclusive relationships of employer and worker,
of landlord and tenant.

Let us consider man now as an <u>agent</u> of production, rather
than as a means of production; as one who expresses and recre-
ates himself in his work. Our perspective approximates the way
of Buddhism:

If the nature of work is properly appreciated and applied, it
will stand in the same relation to the higher faculties as
food is to the physical body. It nourishes and enlivens the
higher man and urges him to produce the best he is capable of.
It directs his free will along the proper course and disciplines the animal in him into progressive channels. It furnishes an excellent background for man to display his scale
of values and develop his personality. (Kumarappa, 1958)

Far reaching consequences ensue from seeing work as a means
by which he fulfills himself as a person. It implies that the
resources of man's work cannot be depleted without at the same
time depriving him of what rightfully belongs to him <u>as a per-
son</u>. In the light of this perspective, the food production
function, being one of many human activities, must be firmly
considered as a humanizing activity.

The natural structures in which food production activities
take place are the small village communities of rural people.
The village community is the living and working situation which
provides the first resources of growth. The strategy of self-
reliance proposed in the New International Economic Order is
founded on this village structure. The formation of self-reliant communities guarantees that a close relationship between

man and his resources will be maintained.

The small communities with which man can easily identify himself allow him to participate directly in decision-making processes. He is thus able to take direct responsibilities in the affairs of his community. This is the desired human resource development path followed by several underdeveloped countries. In this way, rural people in their small world of nonalienating work, of nonexploitative relationships will begin to grasp the potentialities of building life within a humanizing structure.

We conclude with the observation that in our concept of man as producer, as the agent of production, we do not lose sight of him as an integral member of a human working community. We must understand that man's potentials to produce food are inextricably linked with his experiences of social justice and expanding freedom. It is the birthright of every man to grow as a person. His activities, including his production of food, must serve to fulfill that vocation.

REFERENCES

Alcantara de, C. H. 1974. Country report: Mexico. UNDP/ UNRISD Global 2 Project on the Social and Economic Implications of Large-Scale Introduction of New Varieties of Food Grains. United Nations Publication, Geneva, Switzerland.

Corea, G. 1975. Suffering behind a Poverty Curtain . . . Development Forum. 4:1.

Galtung, J. 1975. Decision making appraisal. Symposium on a New International Economic Order Report. Ministry of Foreign Affairs, the Netherlands, De Staatsdrukkerij, The Hague.

International Labour Organization. 1975. Human resources development in rurals areas in Asia and role of rural institutions. Asian Regional Conference, Colombo, 8th Session. ILO Publication, Geneva, Switzerland.

Kumarappa, J. C. 1958. Economy of permanence. In E. F. Schumacher. Small is Beautiful. Harper & Row Publication, New York, USA.

Palmer, I. 1972. Food and the New Agricultural Technology. United Nations Research Institute for Social Development Publication, Geneva, Switzerland.

Rao, V.K.R.V. 1974. Growth with Justice in Asian Agriculture. United Nations Research Institute for Social Development Publication, Geneva, Switzerland.

Wharton, C. R., Jr. 1969. The Green Revolution: Cornucopia or Pandora's Box? Foreign Affairs, An American Quarterly Review. Council on Foreign Relations, Inc., USA.

NICOLAAS LUYKX

Alternatives for Developing and Using Natural Resources for Greater Agricultural Productivity

The intensification of food production, the reduction of losses and waste, and the ironing out of consumer imbalances in capacities to make food choices hold the key to food production resource development, conservation, and use for human sustenance.

Other sessions in this series deal with the availability of productive natural resources and the constraints on their use. In my paper, I shall concentrate on the further development of resources for greater agricultural productivity; and on the pressures of population numbers, unevenly distributed purchasing power, and policy priorities that bring us to this problem.

As we proceed, I shall emphasize the point of intensification, which is what increasing productivity per combined unit of inputs means. Soil, climate, topography, and the like have been brought into the picture because, when mixed with labor, various kinds of capital, and enterprising management skill-- and with the unforseen confluence of externalities, from the discovery of a new appropriate technology to the intervention of divine providence--they bring food commodities in from land and water and transform and transport them to the consumer.

I shall discuss, first, the backdrop of population and purchasing power relevant to the world food situation; second, some information drawn from Asia dealing with changes in the productivity of different classes of resources as agricultural development occurs; third, the dimly lit state of our knowledge

Nicolass Luykx is Director, the Food Institute, East-West Center, Honolulu, Hawaii 96822, USA.

415

regarding the present and potential supply of productive natural
resources; and, finally, I shall raise some points about investments in resource development via agricultural and food
research.

THE POPULATION AND PURCHASING POWER BACKDROP TO FOOD RESOURCES

We are familiar with the upward sweep of the exponential
curve of population growth which seems to imply either
that "the sky's the limit" or that a cataclysm is just
around the corner. More sober interpretations tell us that
evidence from demographic history in a number of countries
gives us a basis for predicting that world population is likely
to stabilize at 12-16 billion persons during the twenty-second
century (Brown, 1974, p. 191).

The numbers of people and their ability to compete, in
real terms, for food--that is, their effective purchasing power
and capacity to produce for themselves--tells us most of what
we need to know about how much food will have to be available
at various points in the future. However, we're so unsure
about how population growth and the sharing of affluence will
evolve that we must resort to broad, informed guesses. One
conservative estimate indicates that food production will just
about have to double over the next quarter century to sustain
the population in the year 2000 at present average levels of
consumption (Brown, 1974, p. 44).

An individual needs roughly 500 g of food grain per day to
meet minimum energy requirements. Most food grains such as
wheat, rice, corn, etc. have about the same caloric value per
gram. If we were to round off annual needs to an average of
200 kg per person, and amplify it by the current world population of about 4 billion persons, the aggregate minimum need for
food grain production would be 800 million tons. At the time
that preparations were being made for the 1974 Rome World Food
Conference, world cereal production was already running about
50 percent _more_ than this figure (United Nations, 1974, p. 14;
FAO, 1976, p. 10). For the world as a whole, the productive
capacity to meet minimal food needs is clearly present.

But are we talking about minimal food needs? Or are we
talking, rather, about the power people have to provide for
themselves or to obtain from others the kind, amount, and quality of food they want?

The population of this planet is unevenly distributed in
rough approximation of the distribution of productive
resources, with adjustments for income levels per person. The
four major population concentrations are North America (6 percent), Europe, including the USSR (11 percent), South Asia (21
percent), and East Asia (25 percent). Together, they comprise
almost two-thirds of the world's population.

Table 1 gives some information on population growth rates

TABLE 1. 1975 population, food supply, and income in selected major population concentrations

Region	Population mid-1975 (millions)	Proportion of world population (%)	Population growth rate (%)	Average kilocalories available per person per day	Average gross national product per person (US dollars)
North America	237	6	0.9	3,320	5,480
Europe (incl. USSR)	437	11	0.7	3,196	2,037
South Asia	838	21	2.4	2,070	120
(India)	(613)	(15)	(2.4)	(2,070)	(110)
East Asia	1,006	25	1.6	2,270	420
(P. R. China)	(823)	(21)	(1.7)	(2,170)	(160)
World total	3,967		1.9	2,470	940

Source: Population Reference Bureau, 1975 World Population Data Sheet.

and average food availability and income levels for these
regions. On all counts there are clear distinctions between
the predominantly developed regions (North America and Europe)
and the predominantly developing regions (South and East Asia).
With regard to available food stuffs and purchasing power, the
indicators show that the Asian regions listed are well below
world averages, while North American and European levels are
well above. Not only are the numbers of people unevenly distributed across the globe, but so is wealth (in inverse proportion, one might add).

Table 2, with data from the mid and latter portions of the
1960s, develops the contrasts between developing and developed
regions still further. It shows that while the poorer countries of the world contained 70 percent of the earth's population, they produced only 37 percent of the world's grain. The
richer countries, with only 30 percent of the population, produced 63 percent of the food and feed grains in that period.
Productive capacity, it can be seen, is as unevenly distributed
as income--and, indeed, production and income are two words for
the same thing.

TABLE 2.   Contrasts in grain production and population numbers,
           developed and developing countries

	World grain production[a] 1966-70 average		World population[b] 1965	
	Millions of metric tons	%	Millions of persons	%
Developed countries	619	63	999	30
Developing countries	356	37	2,281	70
Total	975	100	3,280	100

Sources: [a]West, Q. W. 1974. The World Food Situation and How
Others See It. Speech presented at Arlie House. [b]Durand,
J. D. 1967. The Modern Expansion of World Population. Pro-
ceedings of the American Philosophical Society.

One irony of the present situation is that the developed
countries are not only industrialized and affluent but they are
also the most effective producers and traders of food. North
America produced 18 percent of the world's cereals in 1974.
However, it accounted for about two-thirds of the maize and
wheat that entered into world trade in that year. Even in the
rice trade, the USA accounted for 37 percent of the world's
exports in 1974 (FAO, 1974, pp. 10, 22, 25, 27).

A further look at the relation of income and food grain
consumption indicates wide differences in the pattern of cereal

grain utilization in the world. Table 3 depicts data for the
mid-1960s for China and India, the two most populous countries
in the underdeveloped world, and contrasts these with information for the USSR and the USA in the same period. The Chinese
had 430 pounds (about 195 kg) of grain available per person
that year, on the average, while the Indians had a scant 348
pounds (about 158 kg). By contrast, the Soviets, on the average, had 1,227 pounds (about 558 kgs) of cereals available per
person, and the Americans each had an average of 1,641 pounds
(about 746 kg) available.

TABLE 3. Direct and indirect cereal consumption, selected low
and high income countries, 1964-66 averages

Country	Grain consumed directly per person (kg)	Grain consumed indirectly per person (kg)	Total grain consumed per person (kg)	Proportion consumed indirectly (%)
Low income countries				
China	142	53	195	27
India	131	27	158	17
High income countries				
USSR	156	401	557	72
USA	91	655	746	88

Source: Adapted from FAO Food Balance Sheets, 1964-66 Average, and US Department of Agriculture, as cited in L. R.
Brown, 1974. By Bread Alone. Praeger Publishers, New York.

Now, no human can consume three-quarters of a ton of rice,
noodles, bread, and other cereal products over the course of a
year. What these figures represent is the conversion of varying amounts of grain into animal products which are, in turn,
prepared as table food.

During the 1964-66 period, the Chinese consumed 25 percent
of their available cereal grains indirectly as livestock products. For the people of India, who suffered two bad crop years
in this period, the proportion was a meager 17 percent (to say
nothing of the general shortage of food at the time). For the
Soviets and Americans the situation was quite different. They
consumed 72 and 88 percent, respectively, of their available
cereal grains in the form of livestock products. As real
income increases, consumers tend to devote increasing proportions of income to foods of animal origin.

Table 4 shows how incomes have been changing, when indexed
by increases in available food per person. Taking the same
time period as used in Table 3 as a base year, changes in aver-

TABLE 4. Growth in cereal consumption, selected low and high
          income countries, 1964-66 to 1972-74

Country	Cereals available per person 1972-74 (kg)	Increase over 1964-66 (percent)
Low income countries		
China	195	2
Other developing countries	180	7
High income countries		
USSR	652	30
USA	841	16

Source: Adapted from Economic Research Service, US Department
of Agriculture Figures, as cited in L. P. Schertz. 1974.
World Food: Prices and the Poor. Foreign Affairs, Vol. 52,
No. 3.

age levels of grain availability per person are examined over
the 8-year span of 1964-66 to 1972-74. (It should be noted
that the differences between some of the figures in Table 4 and
Table 3 dealing with the same item may be attributable to differences in sources.) Over the period indicated, it can be
seen that the average increase in food grain availability per
person was only 2 percent for the Chinese and 7 percent for the
Indians. However, for the Americans, the average availability
of food grains went up 16 percent and for the Soviets it went
up 30 percent.

It is apparent from these measures that the rates of
growth in economic power for consumers in developing countries
were only a fraction of the growth rates of affluence in the
developed countries. Without the purchasing power to convert
"food need" into "effective demand", the poor will be out-bid
by the affluent for the food they need during times of critical
or chronic world-wide food shortage. The last few years have
been a critical period, although recent recovery and improvement in world food grain production have alleviated the situation. Looming large in this background, however, are the
uncertainties and unclear policy criteria with regard to the
establishment and maintenance of domestic and international
stocks of food grains as security against another world-wide
season of bad weather (Schertz, 1974, pp. 523-527). It is
awareness of the proximity of consumption levels to minimum
levels in many countries that motivates our concern with
resource productivity. In the next section we will look at
some information on changing levels of productivity as evidenced during the agricultural development of a selection of
Asian countries.

CHANGING PATTERNS OF DEVELOPMENT IN RESOURCE PRODUCTIVITY

Low productivity is the hallmark of so-called "underdeveloped" countries. The opposite situation is likewise the hallmark of the so-called "developed" countries. Table 2 highlighted this point. This is demonstrated further by the observation that rice yields in India and Nigeria are about one-third of those in Japan. Similarly, corn yields in Thailand and Brazil are about one-third of those in the USA (Brown, 1974, p. 213).

In a recently completed group study of agricultural productivity in Japan, Taiwan, Korea, and the Philippines led by Yujiro Hayami and Vernon Ruttan (Hayami et al., 1976), carefully collected and interpreted historical data demonstrate some interesting points regarding the progress of resource productivity over the course of agricultural development.

In pre-development stages, increases in total food output may take place through the addition of new resource inputs that were not previously utilized. New lands may be opened to cultivation, sparse populations may grow, and the like, leading to growth in total output without necessarily involving any recombination of resources, or changes in their quality, that increase the output-per-unit-of-input of any one of them.

"Development" begins to show only when such increases in output-per-unit-of-input take effect and are sustained (Ruttan, 1973, p. 36). The recent study of Japan, Taiwan, Korea, and the Philippines by Hayami et al. (1976) shows that it usually is a single factor of production that leads the way in bringing about improvements in total productivity during the early stages of development. In countries that were still being settled at the time that agricultural development began in earnest, such as the USA, it was labor productivity that led the way at first in promoting improvements in total output rates. In already settled countries, such as those of Northern Europe and Japan, it was improvements in land productivity that led the way. Subsequently, as development continues, other resource factors begin to show improvements in productivity. Thus, in the middle and later stages of development, the growth of total agricultural output becomes sustained by more nearly balanced increases in factor productivity rates.

The study by Hayami et al. (1976) shows that <u>intensification</u>, that is, the growth in total productivity of applied resources per combined unit of input, was a common feature associated with growth in total physical output. Thus, while new resources may have been continually initiated into the production process, many old kinds of inputs were experiencing changes in quality and were being applied in more effective amounts and combinations than previously.

It was usually when new land resources became harder to locate or develop for agriculture that population pressure on arable land became stressful. In response to these stresses, the studies show, the partial productivity of land began to

pick up, along with the acceleration in total productivity. It
was most frequently the increase in output per unit of cultivatable land that led to increasing rates of output per worker.
      The countries of Asia today are faced with limitations in
the availability of new lands that can be brought under cultivation. If they are to avoid stagnation in domestic agricultural output, new technologies--which will save land and simultaneously increase yields--will have to be adapted and introduced. Most of these, such as seeds, fertilizer, pesticides
and the like require, as a precondition, the provision of new
investments in agricultural infrastructure, including irrigation and drainage facilities, a dispersed research capacity for
the adaptation of new technologies to local circumstances, and
facilities and policies for expanded stable markets.
      The participants in the four-country Asia study (Hayami
et al., 1976) voice a warning of the massive dimensions of the
investments required, although they offer no specific figures.
These investments should be aimed, they argue, primarily at
developing irrigation facilities and research stations (especially for the development and adaptation of high-yielding
strains of crops).
      We will return to these points in the following sections.

THE CURRENT SUPPLY AND USE OF PRODUCTIVE NATURAL RESOURCES
      Agriculture is fundamentally dependent on solar energy
      and, for this reason, is distributed widely (albeit
      unevenly) over the earth's level and nearly level land
surface. Therefore, land is most often the basic resource
around which farming is organized (not to mention its significance in the organization of the cultures to which cultivators
belong).
      Table 5 indicates the proportionate distribution of the
world's leading crops on the arable surface. Cereal grains
take up three-quarters of the allocation of cultivable land to
agriculture. Within this amount, the coarse grains are roughly
balanced against wheat and rice in area terms.
      It is estimated that less than half of the 3.2 billion ha
of potentially cultivable land is currently being cropped
(Carter et al., 1974, p. 20; National Academy of Sciences,
1975, p. 65). Some 3.6 billion ha of potential grazing land
also exist. However, because no one has yet estimated the
costs involved--for land levelling, the construction of irrigation and drainage facilities, the control of diseases and
pests (such as the tsetse fly in large portions of Africa south
of the Sahara), and the maintenance of fragile ecologies by
careful management--few data are available on what is likely to
happen in the foreseeable future.
      The principal regions where sizeable land areas with
access to water could be opened are in the Amazon Basin of Bra-

TABLE 5. World cropland use and energy production by major
          crop categories, 1970

Crop category	Proportion of world cropland %	Proportion of world calorie production from crops %
All cereals	(73.5)	(74.5)
Wheat	22.2	18.8
Rice	14.1	19.6
Coarse grains	(37.2)	(36.1)
Maize	11.3	16.1
Millet-sorghum	7.5	4.0
Other coarse grains	18.4	16.0
Roots and tubers	5.2	8.8
Oil seeds	10.8	6.9
Sugar	2.0	5.0
Pulses and nuts	6.3	2.6
Vegetables and fruits	2.2	2.2
Total	100.0	100.0

Source: H. O. Carter et al., 1974. A Hungry World: The Challenge to Agriculture. University of California, Division of
Agricultural Sciences, Berkeley, California.

zil and in the Sub-Saharan region of Africa (Brown, 1974, pp.
78-79).

Irrigation facilities served some 203 million ha in 1970
out of a potential estimated land area of 344 million ha that
is amenable to irrigation (Carter et al., 1974, p. 22; National
Academy of Sciences, 1975, p. 65). These regions, however,
await decisions on whether to invest massive amounts of capital
in irrigation projects and train the manpower that could manage
the facilities in cooperation with growers. Low cost irrigation facilities in the form of locally made tubewells and pumps
have been devised in some areas subjected to the alternating
dry seasons of monsoon Asia (People's Republic of Bangladesh,
1973, pp. 142-153). Experimentation with water budget management in small-scale watersheds has produced encouraging results
for semi-arid areas (ICRISAT, 1974, pp. 64-86).

Energy for food production has traditionally come from the
sun, from organic wastes and residues, and from animal and
human power. Sunlight has driven the food production engine
throughout the evolutionary history of the earth. Mindful of
the central significance of the photosynthetic process, plant
scientists have developed crop cultivars that utilize the sun's
energy more effectively. In recent times, fossil fuels have

assumed a more important role. Tractors, pumps, fertilizer manufacturing and mixing plants, and long distance haulage all
depend on fossil fuels. The quadrupling of oil prices in 1972-
73 made the use of fossil fuel energy in some farm operations
uneconomical.

The so-called "oil crisis" hit nitrogen fertilizers in two
ways. On the one hand, oil is a feedstock in nitrogen fertilizer manufacture. On the other hand, the rise in oil prices
made the operation of fertilizer manufacturing plants more
costly. Thus, the rise in prices--if not outright physical
shortages--of nitrogen fertilizers during 1973-75 resulted in
set-backs for the "Green Revolution" in some areas. This stimulated increased research interest in making nitrogen available
to crops through natural processes, including the effective use
of organic residues and the microbial fixation of nitrogen.

Energy research includes pilot model development of simple
methane gas generators and of bio-mass conversion. Further in
the background is experimentation with means to capture solar
and wind energy. For the time being, however, agriculture will
continue to depend on fossil fuels and can only hope for marginal improvements in on-farm management efficiency to conserve
scarce and costly supplies.

Countries with domestic sources of petroleum, or with adequate foreign exchange resources, are in a less difficult situation than those without oil deposits, and without a steady
flow of exports with which to bring in foreign exchange on a
regular basis. They are caught in a tight situation that may
lead perversely to relatively costly food imports if they lose
opportunities to mechanize significant aspects of agricultural
production (FAO, 1976, p. 8).

INVESTMENT IN AGRICULTURE AND FOOD RESEARCH
        The relationship between investments in research and the
        accelerating pace of growth in resource productivity,
        while obvious to some, is generally poorly understood by
people who make policy and allocate public funds.

The public support of agricultural research and education
in the USA took on significant proportions about a century ago.
In most developing nations, with few exceptions, the development of domestic agricultural research is a post-World-War-II
phenomenon. The coordinated international effort to build
facilities, educate and train scientific manpower, and support
the exchange of information and ideas through international
networks had its beginning in the 1950s. Indeed, it was not
until 1962 that the International Rice Research Institute, the
first of the international agricultural research centers, was
founded.

There is a distinct contrast between developed and developing countries in the attention paid to research. In 1974,

three times as much money was invested in agricultural research in the developed countries as was invested in the developing countries (Boyce and Evenson, 1975, p. 3). If weighted by population figures, the contrast would be more on the order of 10:1. The same situation existed a decade earlier at the height of international assistance for research in developing countries. Even at this peak period, when foreign aid for research counting all sources reached about $100 million, this accounted for less than one quarter of what was going into the research systems of developing countries. It was equivalent, also, to just slightly more than one-twentieth of what the developed countries were putting into their own systems.

The upshot of these observations is that the developed countries are investing in, and profiting from, research. The developing countries have a weak tradition on this score. They simply don't have the resources. International assistance, although performed with good will and good effect (as far as it goes), nowhere approximates the magnitude of the investment needed if developing countries are to keep pace with the growth in absolute yields in developed countries.

Although less developed countries derive benefits from research work done elsewhere, the ultimate job of cultivar adaptation and of land and water development must be done locally. Without them, the available resources will not attain their potential productivities. There are a number of extensive and thoughtful reviews of research priorities (e.g., Brown et al., 1975; Carter et al., 1974; National Academy of Sciences, 1975), but few have addressed the problem of raising the levels of investment in developing countries to make them comparable, in time, with the per capita levels of research investment in developed countries. This would have to move step-wise through rounds of manpower and supporting-institution development, as well as the incremental development of central facilities and branch stations into dispersed networks.

Although an unpopular notion, it is probable that it would be in the best long term interest of those countries that have the resources to invest in developing regions, to do so even at the cost of reduced domestic rates of agricultural and industrial growth.

We have been accustomed to talk of "political will," but it is now time to develop the analytical instruments that can describe and evaluate the job that political will power is supposed to authorize and monitor.

REFERENCES

Barnett, H. J., and C. Morse. 1963. Scarcity and Growth: The Economics of Natural Resource Availability. The Johns Hopkins Press, Baltimore, Maryland.

Boyce, J. K., and R. E. Evenson. 1975. Agricultural Research
    and Extension Programs. The Agricultural Development Coun-
    cil. New York.
Brown, A. W. A., T. C. Byerly, M. Gibbs, and A. San Pietro,
    editors. 1975. Crop productivity--research imperatives.
    Proceedings of a conference sponsored by Michigan State
    University and the Charles F. Kettering Foundation, East
    Lansing, Michigan.
Brown, L. R. 1974. By Bread Alone. Praeger Publishers, New
    York.
Carter, H. O., et al. 1974. A Hungry World: The Challenge to
    Agriculture. University of California, Division of Agri-
    cultural Sciences, Berkeley, California.
Durand, J. D. 1967. The Modern Expansion of World Population.
    Proceedings American Philosophical Society.
FAO. February 1976. Monthly Bulletin of Agricultural Econom-
    ics and Statistics. United Nations Food and Agriculture
    Organization, Rome, Italy.
Hayami, Y., and V. W. Ruttan. 1971. Agricultural Development:
    An International Perspective. Johns Hopkins Press. Balti-
    more, Maryland.
Hayami, Y., V. W. Ruttan, and H. Southworth, Editors. 1976.
    Agricultural Growth in Japan, Taiwan, Korea, and the Phil-
    ippines. University Press of Hawaii, Honolulu, Hawaii.
International Crops Research Institute for the Semi-Arid Trop-
    ics. 1974. Annual Report 1973-74. Hyderabad, India.
Mellor, J. W. 1976. The New Economics of Growth: A Strategy
    for India and the Developing World. Cornell University
    Press, Ithaca, New York.
National Academy of Sciences. 1975. Enhancement of Food Pro-
    duction for the United States. World Food and Nutrition
    Study on Agriculture and Renewable Resources of the Commis-
    sion on Natural Resources, National Research Council, Wash-
    ington, DC.
People's Republic of Bangladesh, Planning Commission. 1973.
    The First Five Year Plan, 1973-78. Dacca, Bangladesh.
Population Reference Bureau. 1975. 1975 World Population Data
    Sheet, Washington, D.C.
Ruttan, V. W. 1973. Induced technical and institutional
    change and the future of agriculture. Proceedings of the
    Fifteenth International Conference of Agricultural Econo-
    mists. Sao Paulo, Brazil.
Schertz, L. P. 1974. World food: prices and the poor. For-
    eign Affairs. Vol. 52, No. 3.
Tsuchiya, K. 1976. Productivity and Technological Progress in
    Japanese Agriculture. University of Tokyo Press, Tokyo,
    Japan.
West, Q. W. April 1974. The World Food Situation and How
    Others See It. Economic Research Service, US Department of
    Agriculture, Washington, DC.

United Nations, Preparatory Committee of the World Food Conference. 1974. Preliminary Assessment of the World Food Situation Present and Future, New York.

SYLVAN H. WITTWER

Alternatives Available for Improving Plant and Animal Resources

The greatest challenge the world has is to provide adequate food for an expanding population. Food production must be doubled in the next 25-30 years. If people are fed it will be from improved plant and animal resources. Grain production alone must be increased at the rate of 25 million metric tons per year just to keep pace with population increases and rising demands.

Assuring our food supply involves more than production technology. It involves post-harvest handling, processing, storage, and consumer use and acceptance (Mrak, 1976; Nature, 1975). That people are malnourished is often a question of food distribution, resources, and economics. The problem is delivery. It's putting the food where the people are, and providing an income so they can buy it. Only poor people have the problem of meeting their food needs.

The immediate solution to the world food problem lies in all-out production, improved nutrition, and in education. The victory has to first be an agricultural one. It will take a Herculean effort. "We will have to find in the next 25 years, food for as many people again as we have been able to produce in the whole history of man till now" (Michigan-Kettering, 1975, p. 33). The reality of a rapidly growing world population

---

Sylvan H. Wittwer is Director, Agricultural Experiment Station; Assistant Dean, College of Agriculture and Natural Resources; and Professor of Horticulture, Michigan State University, East Lansing, Michigan, USA 48824.
Journal Article No. 7693 of the Michigan Agricultural Experiment Station.

discourages a policy of no action. There is much that can and must be done (Mayer, 1976).

BACKGROUND

There have been many recent assessments of alternatives available for improving plant and animal resources for human consumption. One is impressed by the number of studies as well as alternatives (Brown, 1975; Massachusetts Institute of Technology, 1975; Michigan-Kettering, 1975; National Academy of Sciences, 1975a, 1975b, 1975c, 1975d; Pimental, 1976; Technical Advisory Committee of the Consultative Group on International Agricultural Research, 1973, 1975; United States Department of Agriculture, 1975; University of California Food Task Force, 1974; Wittwer, 1974, 1975). Others are in progress and have been initiated by Congress through a Food Advisory Committee of the Office of Technology Assessment, by the White House through a Food and Nutrition Subcommittee, and by the National Academy of Sciences World Food and Nutrition Study.

The intent of all these efforts is to establish priorities for agricultural research which would result in an enhancement of food production, stability of supplies at high levels, and improved nutrition. All recommendations focus eventually on the cereal crops, the seed legumes, forages for livestock, the roots, tubers, sugar crops, fruits and vegetables, ruminant livestock, improved utilization of byproducts, management of resources, and reductions in resource inputs and losses. An increase of investment in research relating to the biological processes that control or limit crop and livestock productivity is a common theme. There is the consistent undertone that we know far more than is being put to use, and the ever present challenge to make operational the knowledge we now have. Thus far the bio-technical research approach has been pursued, primarily; but not without recognition of the significance of socio-economic-politico aspects of the food problem. The recommended alternatives which follow for increasing plant and animal resources for mankind are no exception. The focus is on nonpolitical technologies which lead to a stability of production at high levels, with a minimum of nonrenewable resource input, and resultant improved nutritional values.

IMPROVEMENT OF PLANT RESOURCES

Plant resources provide, directly or indirectly, up to 95 percent of the world's food supply. Increased production of crops can come from a combination of three approaches: 1), bringing more land into production; 2), enhancement of yields per hectare; and 3), increasing the number of crops produced per year.

Chief among the major food crops, in approximate order of

importance, are the cereal grains--rice, wheat, maize, sorghum, millet, barley, rye and oats; the seed legumes--field beans, chick peas, pigeon peas, soybeans, mung beans, broad beans and peanuts; the root and tuber crops--potatoes, sweet potatoes, and cassava; the sugar crops--sugarcane and sugar beets; and coconuts and bananas. A variety of fruits and vegetables are secondary staple food crops. Processed and fresh, they add personal enrichment and pleasure to eating and essential dietary nutrients. Hundreds of millions of people depend primarily on what is produced in gardens or small holdings at or very near the point of consumption. Several crops a year may be grown. Hay, pasture crops, and shrubs provide most of the feed units for herds and flocks. Wastes and byproduct utilization figure strongly in the production of swine and poultry.

Cereal grains constitute the most important food group on earth. They provide 60 percent of the calories and 50 percent of the protein consumed by the human race. Twenty percent of the protein comes from seed legumes. Research investments are needed to maximize or optimize the production of crops per unit time, with the least expenditure of land, water, fertilizer, fuel and pesticides. One looks to the biological processes that control productivity.

Greater Photosynthetic Efficiency

Emphasis on the bioconversion of solar energy comes first.

Ninety-five percent of the dry weight of plants is derived from photosynthesis (Michigan-Kettering, 1975, p. 177). It is the major outside input into our food system. It's where calories in food come from. It's a renewable process. Bioconversion of solar energy literally adds to the resources of the earth. It's non-polluting. There is no noise. The resource is essentially without limit. Current investments in photosynthesis research from all sources ($10 million in the USA) are at a surprisingly low level.

An increase in net photosynthesis and more efficient partitioning of the products of photosynthesis is a logical alternative for improving plant resources of food, feed, and fiber. Research imperatives include the identification of aspects of photosynthesis that limit the fixation of carbon dioxide. Important in such studies are improvements in plant architecture and anatomy for better light reception and carbon dioxide absorption; characterization and control of the enzymes (i.e., ribulose diphosphate carboxylase) that regulate the wasteful processes of dark respiration and light-induced (photo) respiration; identification and control of mechanisms for redistribution of photosynthates within the plant that regulate yield; and a resolution of the hormonal mechanisms that will enable the full seasonal potential productivity to be realized through control of flowering and senescence (National Academy of

Sciences, 1975c; Michigan-Kettering, 1975).

The future of the world's food supply may well reside at the door of photosynthesis and subsequent partitioning into the harvested parts. Also important are the C3 and C4 plants identified by differences in compensation points (Krezner et al., 1975). The food crops of the earth can be divided into C3 and C4 plants. Productivity under conditions of high temperatures and sunlight coupled with moisture stress is definitely favored by the C4 metabolism. The most productive plants under these climatic conditions and in terms of total digestible nutrients produced per unit land area, per unit water transpired, per unit time, are the C4 plants--maize, sugarcane, sorghum, millet. They have the highest growth rates in the world (Black, 1971). C3 crops--such as small grains, soybeans, potatoes--while inferior producers under high temperatures and sunlight and low moisture are more productive in cool-moist temperate zones.

Biological Nitrogen Fixation

Biological nitrogen fixation is the second most important biochemical process on earth. It also is non-polluting, makes no noise, is essentially without limit, and adds to the plant resources for food, feed, and fiber. The majority of world protein has its origin in this process. Biological nitrogen fixation is agriculturally important with legumes and some non-legumes, and it has potential for many crops. Industrial nitrogen fixation supplies about 40 million tons of nitrogen annually for crop production worldwide. This compares with about 90 million tons fixed biologically in agricultural soils. Of this, 35 million tons come from crop legumes, about 9 million from non-legumes, and 45 million tons from forests, permanent meadows, range, and grasslands (Michigan-Kettering, 1975). Nitrogen-fixing shrubs with a built-in supply of nitrogen are an unexploited resource for improvement of forests and rangelands (Larson, 1976). The quantity of nitrogen fixed biologically by agricultural and non-agricultural species in the USA exceeds 23 million tons annually (H. J. Evans, 1975).

The second most important research imperative for improving plant resources must reside with enhancement of biological nitrogen fixation. Again there are many options, chief among which is to establish nitrogen self-sufficiency in crops. Legumes already have the capacity to be self-sufficient or partially so through symbiotic nitrogen fixation. This may be improved and extended to cereals and grasses, and to forest, woodland, and aquatic habitats. Optimal plant-microorganismal combinations must be sought out. The photosynthetic energy flow from the plant to the nitrogen fixing organisms must be increased. Rhizobial technology, an almost forgotten science in the USA, must be re-established at the operational level of global crop production. Breeding economically important food

crops for greater nitrogen fixation has exciting possibilities
(Dart and Day, 1976). Current investments from all sources on
biological nitrogen fixation research in the USA do not exceed
$5 million. With this minimal input prompted till recently by
abundant and cheap nitrogen fertilizer, little attention has
been given to field studies (National Academy of Sciences,
1975c, 1975d). We should have a better inventory of nitrogen
fixing micro-organisms in various cropping systems and the magnitude of their respective inputs. For example, in the rice
paddies of southeast Asia biologically fixed nitrogen comes
from at least three sources--the blue-green algae, free-living
azotobacters, and other nitrogen fixing bacteria that are rhizosphere associated.

Genetic Improvement and Unconventional
Approaches to Plant Breeding

Significant advances have recently occurred in defining
techniques for isolating plant protoplasts (cells) and
and their culture. Similarly, protoplast fusion can occur
spontaneously or be chemically induced. Haploids have also
been produced from the culture of pollen grains or anthers
(Michigan-Kettering, 1975). These techniques could become a
major avenue for new species building with greater resistance
to environmental stresses, toxins, and for improvement of yields
and nutritional values of major food crops (National Academy of
Sciences, 1975d). The current minimal research investment
(less than $500,000 in the USA) suggests a great opportunity
for improving plant resources utilizing these new in vitro cultural techniques coupled with selected broad crosses and im-
munosuppressant chemicals (Internation Wheat and Maize Improvement Center, 1975; Bates et al., 1974).

Remarkable improvements in crop productivity have been
achieved through genetic improvement (Harpstead and Adams,
1976). These include hybrid corn, sorghum, and pearl millet.
The development of hybrid corn is the most spectacular of all
scientific achievements in American agriculture. The effort
still moves forward. A new record in productivity of 338 bushels from a measured, witnessed acre (212 q/ha) was achieved in
1975 (Pfeifer, 1976).

The creation and introduction of high yielding, short stat-
ured, non-lodging, photoperiodically day neutral, rice (Jennings, 1974) and wheat cultivars have contributed to a "Green
Revolution" (Dalrymple, 1975). Attention, accompanied with
great progress, is now directed in rice and wheat towards greater resistance to diseases and insects, climatic stresses, alkaline and high-salt conditions, and greater utilization of applied fertilizer. Hybrid wheat has become a reality (De Kalb
Ag-Research, Inc., 1975; Hayward, 1976). High yielding hard-
winter-type hybrids of good agronomic type and with good

milling and baking qualities are now being produced and marketed on a limited scale from the winter wheat regions of Texas,
Oklahoma, and Kansas. Triticale, the man-made crop species, is
at the brink of commercial production by farmers in the tropics
and subtropics. The best selections of both durum- and bread-
wheat-triticale types now outproduce wheat by 15-20 percent.
Triticale is also more adaptable to acid soils and tolerant of
aluminim toxicity (Wolff, 1976).

Alternatives for the future enhancement of yields of nine
major crops (maize, sugarcane, rice, wheat, soybean, pea,
potato, sugar beet, cotton) have been outlined (L. T. Evans,
1975). Experimental maximization of potato yields show production levels (100+ tons/ha) far above the maincrop yields in
Britain (S. A. Evans, 1975) and elsewhere, including the USA.
The tropical root crops (cassava, taro, yams, sweet potato,
etc.) have the greatest of all potentials for genetic improvement (Haynes, 1974). They provide the basic staple for 80 million people in tropical equatorial Africa. Only with cassava,
sweet potato, and a few species of yams is the classical plant
breeding approach of immediate application. Unconventional
techniques in plant breeding must be adopted.

Finally, great progress has been made and much is still
offered for improving the productive capacities of fruits and
vegetables (Wittwer, 1972). Hybrid coconuts with double the
yield and earlier production are a reality. Dwarf-type decidu-
ous fruit trees, spur fruiting in apples, hybrid onions, car-
rots, cabbage, spinach, melons, squash, tomatoes, peppers,
sweet corn, and cucumbers have greatly improved productive capacities, marketing qualities, consumer acceptance, and nutritional values.

Improved Utilization of Fertilizer

Only 50 percent of the nitrogen and less that 35 percent of
the phosphorus and potassium applied as fertilizer in the
USA are recovered by crops (National Academy of Sciences,
1975c). Losses of nitrogen are even greater in the tropics with
recovery averaging only 25-35 percent for rice crops.

Plant resources could be greatly improved if these enormous
losses could be even partially alleviated. One approach is the
development of improved cultivars with enhanced capacities for
ion uptake. Sulfur-coated urea for slower release of nitrogen
is another. Modulation of nitrification and denitrification is
still another. Both synthetic and natural nitrification inhibitors have been identified. One such synthetic material known
as "nitropyrine" [2-chloro-6-(trichloromethyl) pyridine], is a
highly specific bactericide that is toxic to Nitrosomonas bacteria (Laskowski et al., 1975). It reduces but does not eliminate the population of this organism. The reduction of nitrification lasts from six weeks to three months. Nitrification
inhibitors or nitrificides (both natural and synthetic) have an

important role in future plant productivity especially for the
major food crops including rice and other crops in the tropics
(Huber et al., 1976).

In sharp contrast to the nitrifying bacteria that reduce
fertilizer nitrogen utilization, other organisms--the endomy-
corrhizae--may result in large increases in the uptake of phosphate and other poorly mobile ions by agricultural crops. This
occurs from extensive fungal growth permeating the soil, absorption of ions by the fungi, and translocation of them to the
root (Michigan-Kettering, 1975, p. 251). They function as an
extension of the root. Mycorrhizae occur in most all (Cruci-
ferae and sugar beets are exceptions) agricultural crops; the
endotrophic types on food crops; and the better known ecto-
trophic types on forest trees. Those on food crops have not
been well studied. While these fungal associations improve
growth under a wide variety of conditions, remarkable increases
of yields on low fertility and marginal soils have been recorded (Morse, 1973; Sanders et al., 1975). They infect the
roots and, by still not well-defined mechanisms, help pull
phosphorus and other nutrients into the crop. Zinc uptake by
the roots of apple seedlings has been magnified 7-fold (Benson
and Covey, 1976). There are super strains of endomycorrhizae.
They should be typed and used for crop inoculation. All cereal
grains and legumes show a pronounced response.

There is a need for improved methods of fertilizer placement. Root-zone placement of nitrogen fertilizer for rice in
southeast Asia has increased the efficiency of uptake by 30-50
percent over topdressing (International Rice Research Institute, 1976). One fascinating approach has been the gradient-
mulch system for tomatoes (Geraldson, 1975). This is a high
level production-low cost concept utilizing and maintaining a
nonvariable root environment achieved by a plastic mulch, a
constant water table, and precise fertilizer placement. The
potential role of nonroot absorption in meeting the mineral nutrient requirements of food crops has been under review for 30
years (Wittwer and Bukovac, 1969). The remarkable effects of
foliar fertilization of soybeans on yield enhancement from base
yields that are already high (Garcia and Hanway, 1976) give
credence to the efficiency and effectiveness of foliar absorption. Future yield barriers may be broken by utilizing the absorptive capacities of leaves at crucial stages of reproductive
development. The rising costs and uncertainties of supplies of
nonrenewable fertilizers should be a stimulus for the further
development of this technology. Pilot programs for increasing
soybean yields by nutrient sprays in all major producing areas
of the USA are planned for the summer of 1976.

Pest Management and Crop Protection

Annual worldwide losses from pests (insects, weeds, diseases, nematodes, predators, rodents, etc.) are one-third

of the total world harvest (Michigan-Kettering, 1975). Approximately two billion kilograms of chemical pesticides are used
annually. They provide the major input (over 90 percent) for
contemporary pest control applied by growers (National Academy
of Sciences, 1975c; 1975e). Globally, however, built-in genetic resistance, antagonists, and hyperparasites provide the
foundation by which the still rather limited use of chemicals
has proven so successful. Crop protection technology in agricultural practice becomes obsolete at an alarming rate. Hence,
new strategies for pest management are in constant demand. Potentials ahead for protecting plant resources include insect
viruses and bacteria and juvenile hormones that interfere with
reproductive cycles. Egg and larvae parasites, pheromones, and
resistant cultivars are useful alternatives. The constant hope
is to stabilize yields at high levels and with reductions in
cost and in environmental and human health hazards. Allelopathy for weed control--defined as mutual harm, where chemicals
released by one plant species inhibit the growth of another--
is an emerging technology (Rice, 1974).

Alleviation of Environmental Stresses

Drought, cold, heat, salt, toxic ions, and air pollutants
limit crop productivity (Michigan-Kettering, 1975). Techniques by which crops and their environments may be manipulated
to reduce stress injury and increase productivity must be
sought. Climatic vulnerability poses one of the most serious
constraints to stabilizing yields at high levels. The most
determinant factor in food crop productivity is the weather.
Year to year variations are far more significant than any identifiable long term trends. Controlled environment agriculture
and degrees of protected cultivation hold promise for high
value crops in marginal producing areas and high concentrations
of population. A major research imperative should be to exploit the genetic potential for developing new cultivars of
crops resistant to environmental stresses.

Chemical Growth Regulants

Chemical growth regulants may duplicate genetic effects.
Interest in these compounds has now moved beyond the
parameters of horticulture and amateur gardening. The focus is
on the improvement of yields of agronomic and important food
crops. At least 30 major chemical companies are involved in
their synthesis. Seven thousand hectares of sugarcane were
treated with a variety of chemical ripeners in Hawaii in 1975.
Sugarcane ripeners are herbicides used at low doses. Vegeta-
tive growth is slowed and carbohydrates (sucrose) accumulate.
The resultant increase in productivity approximates 3 tons of
sugar per hectare per year. Similar but less promising

results have been reported for corn. The search is on for chemicals that can be used on a large scale to alleviate stress
phenomena (including those induced by air pollutants), inhibit
photorespiration, enhance nitrification, and break the soybean
yield barrier (Farm Chemicals, 1975).

Use of Land and Water Resources

Many alternatives exist for better use of land and water
for improving plant resources (National Academy of Sciences, 1975c; Michigan-Kettering, 1975; Wittwer, 1975). One can
look to technologies for maximizing yields or maximizing the
use of scarce resources. Two stand out prominently--reduced
tillage and drip irrigation.

Reduced tillage conserves soil, soil organic matter, water,
energy, and fertilizer. The concept is elimination of, or reduction in, tillage. One secret is a seed drill that disturbs
only enough soil in the stubble or sod of one crop to make an
opening for seed of the next crop. There must also be an effective weed control chemical; weeds are controlled with herbicides, not cultivation. A still newer innovation is interseeding
--sowing the seed of a second crop, such as soybeans, before the
first one, such as winter wheat, is harvested. The system can
be either labor intensive or labor saving.

Zero-tillage is the most effective management practice
ever developed for the control of wind and water erosion in the
USA Corn Belt. It has spread to more than 3 million ha in the
USA. Reduced tillage technologies now embrace 20 million ha.
More than half of America's cropland will likely be farmed
without plowing in 30 years. Much additional land can now be
used for crop production that formerly was not considered suitable. Reduced tillage is used for wheat in the Columbia Basin
of the USA, and for small grains in Britain, with an estimated
125,000 ha. It makes possible two crops of rainfed rice per
year in southeast Asia (International Rice Research Institute,
1975). It provides an improved system of land management for
highly erodible and difficult-to-manage tropical soils. Entire
issues of some journals are devoted to the topic (Imperial
Chemical Industries, Inc., 1973, 1975) and a book has been
written (Phillips and Young, 1973). The advantages of reduced
tillage that come through most clearly to the producer in temperate zones are the 1) saving of time, 2) reduction of costs,
3) greater land utilization, 4) quick turn around from one crop
to the next, and 5) taking advantage of short spells of good
planting weather.

Optimal development of plant resources comes from land
that is irrigated. Agricultural crops suffer from some degree
of water deficiency over the entire globe. Some C_4 plants may
require only half as much water per unit of dry matter produced
as do C_3 species (Berry, 1975). Billions of dollars are being

expended globally for the development of new land resources
through irrigation, but little attention is given to increasing
efficiency of water use by crops.

Drip irrigation is an improved system of water management
that irrigates the crop, not the soil. Estimates indicate a
current hectarage in excess of 50,000 for high value crops in
the USA with a worldwide total of over 100,000. There are vast
installations in Australia, Israel, Mexico, and South Africa
(Gustafson et al., 1974). Drip irrigation systems are being
added to Hawaiian sugar plantations at the rate of 5,000 ha per
year. They eventually will be installed in all plantations
(50,000 ha) currently under irrigation. This water conserving,
labor saving technology needs careful evaluation for improvement of major food crop resources.

Cropping Systems

These are viable alternatives for improving plant resources. Legumes in combination with high yield C_4 cereals demand special attention (Sprague, 1975). In the tropics
and semi-tropics, chick peas, pigeon peas, mung beans, soybeans,
and peanuts are effective components of cropping systems that
involve sorghum, sugarcane, millet, and corn. Zero or minimum
tillage is used, together with crop and weed residues maintained
as a mulch (Greenland, 1975). Higher yields of grain have been
achieved by intercropping, or interseeding, with legumes than
when grain is the sole crop. Sugarcane yields significantly
higher when it is intercropped with legumes. In addition,
there is the return from the legume (Indian Agricultural Research Institute, 1976). Legumes have a built-in nitrogen supply. The symbiotic relationship of cereal grains of high
photosynthetic efficiency with seed legumes in cropping systems
must be vigorously pursued until the desirable characteristics
of each can be combined in a single species. Rhizobial technology in southeast Asia and the Peoples Republic of China has
advanced ahead of that in the USA because of the high cost and
limited availability of nitrogen fertilizer in the agriculturally less developed countries.

Many vegetable crops can be grown in immediate succession,
and in undisturbed beds, in temperate zones with trickle irrigation (Kays et al., 1976).

There are many opportunities through newly developed technologies and cropping systems, including protected cultivation,
to increase the yields of small holdings. Vegetable and fruit
crops are seldom included in world food statistics. They are
not included in economic surveys. Production is near the site
of use. They are consumed largely by the producers. Yet they
can, and do, contribute significantly to food supplies. The
introduction of science into small farms would be to exploit
one of the greatest of opportunities for the enhancement of

global food production. Technologies can be developed for cropping systems of high yield potential but sparing of nonrenewable resources. The shifting cultivation farm averaging one
hectare in size provides food for a family. Hundreds of millions of people subsist on such food producing systems. Emphasis should be on intensive and stable production at high levels
for local consumption. It's putting food where people are
through a system that is labor intensive, but that has low resource, capital, and management inputs.

Improved storage to prevent losses of indigenous production by growers would provide production goal incentives, family food security, opportunity to manage a part of the market
system, and a means of improving and preserving seed stocks.
Improvement of subsistence agriculture--production, processing,
storage--is one great unexploited frontier. An increment of
fertilizer or pesticide in southeast Asia, for example, will
have a far greater telling effect on crop productivity than in
the USA.

Controlled Environment Agriculture

Protected cultivation of crops is the most intensive of
all agricultural food producing systems. A recent global
assessment (Dalrymple, 1973) showed a greatly expanding industry for specialty high-value crops. While the system is resource, management, and capital intensive there is the added
assurance of dependability of supply, year around production in
temperate zones, a high labor requirement, and the opportunity
for enhancement of productivity by enrichment of the enclosed
atmospheres with carbon dioxide. Controlled environment agriculture is increasingly contributing to the food supply and income of large segments of the population in agriculturally developed nations. There are 20,000 ha of plastic and glass
greenhouses in Japan. Other nations with extensive and still
growing numbers of installations are Israel, Turkey, France,
Italy, South Korea, The Netherlands, The United Kingdom, Scan-
dinavia, Bulgaria, Poland, Rumania, the USA, and the USSR.

Upgrading the Protein and Nutrient Values
of Cereal Grains, Legumes, and Root Crops

Enhancement of productivity of food crops must be linked
to improvements in nutrient content. Progress with cereal
grains has been singular (Frey, 1973; Harpstead and Adams,
1976; Johnson and Mattern, 1975; Nelson, 1973; Mertz, 1976;
Reddy and Gupta, 1974; Wolff, 1975). High-protein rice, wheat,
and barley selections have been identified. Commercial intro-
ductions with 1-4 percent more protein are in progress. High-
lysine maize for temperate zone agriculture and in the tropics
is now a reality. Commercial hybrids exist and the nutritive

values of their protein has been declared equivalent to that of
milk protein. Several selections of high-lysine sorghum close
to commercial acceptability have been created. Triticale with
its improved nutritional contributions, both in higher protein
and lysine contents than either the wheat or rye parent, is now
receiving limited commercial acceptance (Hulse and Spurgeon,
1974). Great variations exist among the nutritional components
of root crops. Sweet potato varieties in Taiwan vary in protein from 1 to 9 percent. Protein levels in the cassava of
South America range from less than one percent to more than six
(Haynes, 1974).

New Food Processing Technologies
    These provide exciting alternatives for improving plant re-
    sources. The enzymatic conversion of cellulosic wastes
and by-products to glucose is being actively pursued (Mandels
et al., 1974), with projections for an intensive pre-pilot plant
study (Westcott, 1976). Worldwide production of cellulose is
estimated at 100 billion tons per year. A significant breakthrough is the development of a high-fructose corn syrup (Nordlund, 1975). For the first time a corn-derived sweetener offers
comparable sweetness to the sucrose of sugarcane and sugar
beets. The high-fructose corn syrup has the potential of replacing by 1980 all imported raw sugar by the USA.

IMPROVEMENT OF ANIMAL RESOURCES
    Livestock numbers of the earth exceed by 2-3 times the hu-
    man population. The number of ruminants (cattle, sheep,
    goats) approximates 3.5 billion. There are about 0.6 bil-
lion swine and 5.3 billion poultry. They also constitute a
food reserve. Compared to 27 days worth of global grain reserves for 1974, there were approximately 40 days worth of animal reserves in the world--and they were far better distributed.
    Domestic animals produce meat, milk, and eggs from nutri-
ents derived from crops, forages, and by-products that have
less value elsewhere. In the USA they produce two-thirds of the
protein, one-half of the fat, one-third of the energy, four-
fifths of the calcium, and two-thirds of the phosphorus consumed by man (National Academy of Sciences, 1975c). Globally,
about 25 percent of man's protein requirements and 10 percent
of the calories are provided by livestock and poultry (National
Academy of Sciences, 1975d). Promising alternatives for improving domestic animals as food sources reside with ruminants
in making them nutritionally less competitive with man for both
protein and energy through improved forage programs. More
effective utilization of wastes and by-products appear useful
in meeting the nutritional requirements of swine and poultry,
recognizing their scavenger habits (Whyte, 1975). Increased

output from livestock has come primarily from three areas: improved nutrition (60 percent), genetic gain (30 percent), and better health (10 percent).

Ruminant Nutrition Potential

Cellulose is the world's most abundant organic compound.
Until now, its economic conversion into food has been accomplished only by ruminants (Hodgson, 1976a). Flocks (sheep, goats) and herds (beef, dairy) can grow and reproduce primarily from plant resources that cannot be consumed by man but are converted to useful products (meat, milk, hides, wool, tallow). Ruminants can also harvest their own food (Council for Agricultural Science and Technology, 1975). The rumen stomach is a fermentation vat. Virtually all feed for ruminants in developing countries is derived from natural grass and range lands and cultivated forages. Even in developed nations, 75 percent of the feed units come from forages.

Ruminant animals need not be competitive with man for either energy or protein (Hodgson, 1976b). The potential for improvement of the forest-range lands of the USA has been emphasized (McKell, 1975). It has been estimated that the carrying capacity of the approximately 300 million ha of range land in the USA could be increased by 2.4 times with intensive management, and with an improvement in environmental quality. There is an even greater potential with the nearly 1.2 billion ha of tropical and subtropical grasslands on earth where a vast array of tropical legumes are adapted. Global opportunities for improvement of crops for livestock include: improved range management, new high-yielding grasses and legumes, increasing nutritive values, improved harvesting techniques, and the merger of production and utilization systems.

An alternative to high grain rations for finishing beef cattle and maintaining all but very high producing dairy cattle is the use of nonprotein nitrogen combined with corn silage or other forages (National Academy of Sciences, 1976). The ultimate goal in ruminant animals for realization of the full potential of this resource would be control of rumen fermentation for optimizing the production of desirable end products (Blaxter, 1973).

Improved Fertility

The water buffalo is one of the world's most efficient converters of cellulose. Yet it is notoriously infertile. This is not true, however, of the swine native to the Peoples Republic of China. They apparently have a high level of fertility, early sexual maturity, and superior mothering ability; at the same time they are excellent scavengers (Whyte, 1975). Among the benefits often attributed to cross-breeding beef cattle are increased fertility and reproductive efficiency, in addition to better feed conversion and greater rates of gain.

Many alternatives exist for improving animal resources through improved fertility (National Academy of Sciences, 1975a, 1975b, 1975c; United States Department of Agriculture, 1975). A new frontier is emerging for fertility control and genetic improvement for cattle and horses. Its basis is the hormone prostaglandin $F_2\alpha$, which offers control of the reproductive cycle and greatly improves the efficiency of artificial insemination (Hafs et al., 1975). It is available now for horses and will soon be released for dairy and beef cattle. The implications of this discovery are global. It may be the long awaited technological breakthrough for improving the low fertility of the water buffalo which plays such a predominant role as a draft animal and as a source of milk and fuel for hundreds of millions of people in the tropics and semi-tropics (Technical Advisory Committee --, 1975).

Improved Animal Health

Closely allied to reproductive performance is animal health. Again, there are many challenges and options for the improvement of resources (National Academy of Sciences, 1975a, 1975c, 1975d; United States Department of Agriculture, 1975).

Prenatal immunization of the unborn dairy calf is now a reality (Wamukoya and Conner, 1971). It's an insurance against calfhood diseases.

The vaccine for control of Marek's disease of poultry was first introduced by Purchase et al., (1971). This was followed by the establishment of a new record for speed in worldwide adoption of a new technology in the agricultural sciences. It is a vaccine that will control a type of cancer in chickens. This contribution for improving an animal resource is now under study for possible adaptation to human health problems relating to the control of cancer.

CONCLUSIONS

Inflation, unemployment, and adequacy of food resources are global issues. The most viable alternatives for improvement of plant and animal resources in the USA and other agriculturally developed nations may be quite different than those for the rest of the world. In the USA we have developed food producing systems that focus on labor saving technologies requiring large capital, resource, and management inputs. Conversely, what is needed for most agriculturally developing nations, along with stable production at high levels, are food systems that are labor intensive, and that demand a minimum of resources (land, water, energy, fertilizer, chemicals), capital, management, and purchased inputs. Specific areas need identification where nonpolitical mission-oriented basic research is focused on solving production problems with economically important renewable resources. There are such technologies and I have discussed many of them briefly. We must address ourselves to these in planning future strategies for improving plant and animal resources.

REFERENCES

Bates, L. S., A. Campos, R. Rodriquez, and R. G. Anderson. 1974. Progress toward novel cereal grains. Cereal Science Today 19:283-285.

Benson, N. R., and R. P. Covey, Jr. 1976. Response of apple seedlings to zinc fertilization and mycorrhizal inoculation. HortScience 11:252-253.

Berry, J. A. 1975. Adaptation of photosynthetic processes to stress. Science 188:644.

Black, C. C. 1971. Ecological implications of dividing plants into groups with distinct photosynthetic production capabilities. Advances in Ecological Research 7:87-114.

Blaxter, K. L. 1973. The nutrition of ruminant animals in relation to intensive methods of agriculture. Proceedings of the Royal Society of London B 183:321-326.

Brown, L. R. 1975. The world food prospect. Science 190: 1053-1059.

Chancellor, W. J., and J. R. Goss. 1976. Balancing energy and food production. Science 192:213-218.

Council for Agricultural Science and Technology. 1975. Ruminants as food producers. Special Publication No. 4. Ames, Iowa.

Dalrymple, D. G. 1973. A global review of greenhouse food production. Economic Research Service, US Department of Agriculture, Foreign Agricultural Economic Report No. 89. Washington, DC.

Dalrymple, D. G. 1975. Measuring the Green Revolution: The impact of research on wheat and rice production. US Department of Agriculture, Foreign Agricultural Economic Report No. 106. Washington, DC.

Dart, P. J., and J. M. Day. 1976. Nitrogen fixation in the field other than by nodules. In N. Walker (Ed.) Soil Microbiology. Butterworth Scientific Publications, London (in press).

DeKalb Ag Research, Inc. 1975. Hybrid wheat, a special report--history, economics, opportunities. Sycamore Road, DeKalb, Illinois.

Evans, H. J., ed. 1975. Proceedings of a workshop: Enhancing biological nitrogen fixation. National Science Foundation, Division of Biological and Medical Sciences, Washington, DC.

Evans, L. T. 1975. Crop Physiology, Some Case Histories.
    Cambridge University Press, London.
Evans, S. A. 1975. Maximum potato yield in the United Kingdom.
    Outlook on Agriculture 8:184-187.
Farm Chemicals. 1975. Entering the age of plant growth regu-
    lators - special report. Farm Chemicals 138(3) (March):
    15-26.
Frey, K. J. 1973. Improvement of quantity and quality of cere-
    al grain protein. Pages 9-41 in Alternative Sources of
    Protein for Animal Production. National Academy of Sci-
    ences. Washington, DC.
Garcia, R. L., and J. J. Hanway. 1976. Foliar fertilization of
    soybeans (Glycine Max (L.) Merrill) during the seed filling
    period. Paper presented at the 28th Annual Fertilizer and
    Agricultural Chemical Dealers Conference, Des Moines, Iowa,
    January 13, 1976. Agronomy Journal (in press).
Geraldson, C. M. 1975. Evaluation of tomato production effi-
    ciency with relevance to contributing components. Florida
    State Horticultural Society Proceedings 88:152-155.
Greenland, D. J. 1975. Bringing the Green Revolution to the
    shifting cultivator. Science 190:841-844.
Gustafson, C. D., A. W. Marsh, R. L. Branson, and S. Davis.
    1974. Drip irrigation--worldwide. Pages 17-22 in Proceed-
    ings of the Second International Drip Irrigation Congress
    74. San Diego, California, July 7-14.
Hafs, H. D., J. C. Manns, and B. Drew. 1975. Onset of estrus
    and fertility of dairy heifers and suckled beef cows
    treated with prostaglandin $F_2\alpha$. Animal Production 21:13-20.
Harpstead, D. D., and M. W. Adams. 1976. Genetics of Food
    Crop Improvement, Nutrition and Agricultural Development in
    the Tropics. Pp. 443-460. Plenum Publishing Corporation,
    New York, NY.
Hayward, C. F. 1976. The status and prospects for hybrid win-
    ter wheat. Pages 84-104 in Proceedings of the Second In-
    ternational Winter Wheat Conference, Zagreb, Yugoslavia,
    June 7-19, 1975. Agricultural Experiment Station, Univer-
    sity of Nebraska, Lincoln, Nebraska.
Haynes, P. H. 1974. Tropical root crops: A modern perspec-
    tive. Span 17(3):116-120.
Hodgson, H. J. 1976a. Forage crops. Scientific American 234:
    61-75.
Hodgson, H. J. 1976b. Forages, ruminant livestock, and food.
    BioScience (in press).
Huber, D. M., H. L. Warren, and D. W. Wilson. 1976. Nitrifi-
    cation inhibitors--new tools for food production. Bio-
    Science (in press).
Hulse, J. H., and D. Spurgeon. 1974. Triticale. Scientific
    American 232:72-80.
Imperial Chemicals Industries; Plant Protection Division. 1973,
    1975. Outlook on Agriculture, Volume 7 Number 4; Volume 8
    Special Number, London.

Indian Agricultural Research Institute. 1976. Beneficial effects from the introduction of legumes in crop rotations
and intercropping systems. IARI Reporter 1(1):1-5.
International Wheat and Maize Improvement Center. 1975. Radical Research and CIMMYT's Role. CIMMYT Review, pp. 73-83.
Mexico, DF, Mexico.
International Rice Research Institute. 1975. Two crops of
rainfed rice. The IRRI Reporter 5/75 (November). Manila,
Philippines.
International Rice Research Institute. 1976. Root-zone place-
ment stretches scarce agricultural chemicals. The IRRI Reporter 2/76 (May). Manila, Philippines.
Johnson, V. A., and P. J. Mattern. 1975. Improvement of the
nutritional quality of wheat through increased protein con-
tent and improved amino acid balance. Report of Research
Findings. Agency for International Development, US Department of State, Washington, DC.
Jennings, P. R. 1974. Rice breeding and world food production.
Science 186:1085-1088.
Kays, S. J., A. W. Johnson, and C. A. Haworski. 1976. Multiple cropping with trickle irrigation. HortScience 11:
135-136.
Krenzer, E. G., Jr., D. N. Moss, and B. Crookston. 1975. Car-
bon dioxide compensation points of flowering plants. Plant
Physiology 56:194-206.
Larson, D. 1976. Nitrogen-fixing shrubs: an answer to the
world's firewood shortage? The Futurist, April 1976,
pp. 74-77.
Laskowski, D. A., F. C. O'Melia, J. D. Griffith, A. J. Regoli,
C. R. Youngson, and C. A. I. Goring. 1975. Effect of 2-
chloro-6-(trichloromethyl) pyridine and its hydrolysis
product 6-chloropicolinic acid on soil microorganisms.
Journal of Environmental Quality 4:412-417.
Mandels, M., L. Houtz, and J. Nystrom. 1974. Enzymatic hydrol-
ysis of waste cellulose. Biotechnology and Bioengineering
16:1471-1493.
Massachusetts Institute of Technology. 1975. Protein resources and technology: Status and research needs, re-
search recommendations and summary. National Science
Foundation, Washington, DC.
Mayer, J. 1975. Agricultural productivity and world nutrition. In Michigan-Kettering Crop Productivity - Research
Imperatives. Michigan Agricultural Experiment Station,
East Lansing, Michigan.
Mayer, L. V. 1976. The financial requirements of world agriculture in a food-short era. Paper presented at Food Up-
date 15, a conference sponsored by the Food and Drug Law
Institute, Camelback Inn, Scottsdale, Arizona. April
26.
McKell, C. M. 1975. Shrubs--a neglected resource of arid
lands. Science 187:803-809.

Mertz, E. T.   1976.   Breeding for improved nutritional value of
    cereals.   In M. Friedman (Ed.)   Protein Nutritional Quality
    of Foods and Feeds, Pt. 1: Assay Methods--Biological, Bio-
    chemical and Chemical.   Dekker, Marcel: New York.
Michigan-Kettering.   1975.   Crop Production--Research Impera-
    tives.   Proceedings of an International Symposium, Boyne
    Highlands, Michigan, October 20-24, 1975.   399 pp.   Michi-
    gan Agricultural Experiment Station, East Lansing, Michigan
    48824; and Charles F. Kettering Foundation, Yellow Springs,
    Ohio 45387.
Mosse, B.   1973.   Advances in the study of vesicular-arbuscular
    mycorrhizae.   Annual Review of Phytopathology 11:171-196.
Mrak, E. M.   1976.   Food science and technology--past, present,
    future.   8th Annual W. O. Atwater Memorial Lecture.   Ameri-
    can Chemical Society, New York, April 5, 1976.
National Academy of Sciences.   1975a.   Agricultural production
    efficiency.   Board on Agriculture and Renewable Resources
    of the Commission on Natural Resources, National Research
    Council, Washington, DC.
National Academy of Sciences.   1975b.   Population and food:
    Crucial issues.   Committee on World Food, Health and Popu-
    lation, National Research Council, Washington, DC.
National Academy of Sciences.   1975c.   Enhancement of food pro-
    duction for the United States.   World Food and Nutrition
    Study.   Board on Agriculture and Renewable Resources of the
    Commission on Natural Resources, National Research Council,
    Washington, DC.
National Academy of Sciences.   1975d.   Interim Report.   Report
    of the Steering Committee, National Research Council Study
    on World Food and Nutrition, Commission on International
    Relations of the National Research Council, Washington, DC.
National Academy of Sciences.   1975e.   Contemporary pest con-
    trol practices and prospects.   Report of the Executive Com-
    mittee on Pest Control: An Assessment of Present and Alter-
    native Technologies.   Environmental Studies Board of the
    Commission on Natural Resources of the National Research
    Council, Washington, DC.
National Academy of Sciences.   1976.   Urea and other non-pro-
    tein nitrogen compounds in animal nutrition.   Board on
    Agriculture and Renewable Resources of the Commission on
    Natural Resources of the National Research Council, Wash-
    ington, DC.
Nature.   1975.   21st century food needs thought - now.   (Edi-
    torial)   December 4, 1975.
Nelson, O. E., Jr.   1973.   Breeding for specific amino acids.
    Pages 303-311 in A. M. Srb (Ed.)   Genes, Enzymes, and Popu-
    lations.   Plenum Press, New York.
Nordlund, D. E.   1975.   Remarks before the New York Society of
    Security Analysts, October 15, 1975.   A. E. Staley, Mfg.,
    Co.   New York.

Pimental, D. 1976. World food crisis: energy and pests. Bulletin of the Entomological Society of America 22(1):20-26.

Pfeifer, R. P. 1976. Record yields and your operation. Crops and Soils Science Magazine 28:April/May pp. 5-7.

Phillips, S. H., and H. M. Young, Jr. 1973. No-Tillage Farming. Reiman Associates, Milwaukee, Wisconsin.

Purchase, H. G., W. Okazaki, and B. R. Burmester. 1972. Long term field trials with the herpesvirus of turkeys vaccine against Marek's disease. Avian Diseases 16:57-71.

Reddy, V., and C. P. Gupta. 1974. Treatment of Kwashiarkor with opaque-2 maize. American Journal of Clinical Nutrition 27:122-124.

Rice, E. L. 1974. Allelopathy. Academic Press, New York.

Sander, F. E., B. Mosse, and P. B. Tinker, eds. 1975. Endomycorrhizas. Proceedings of a Symposium held at the University of Leeds, England, July 22-25, 1974.

Sprague, H. B. 1975. The contributions of legumes to continuously productive agricultural systems for the tropics and semi-tropics. Technical Series Bulletin No. 12. Agency for International Development. US Department of State, Washington, DC.

Technical Advisory Committee of the Consultative Group on International Agricultural Research. 1973. Potential for International Support to Agricultural Research in Developing Countries. Rome.

Technical Advisory Committee of the Consultative Group on International Agricultural Research. 1975. Draft of a Summary Record and Chairman's Conclusions and Recommendations. Rome.

United States Department of Agriculture. 1975. Research to meet US and World Food Needs. Report of a Working Conference sponsored by the Agricultural Research Policy Advisory Committee (ARPAC). Kansas City, Missouri, July 9-11.

University of California Food Task Force. 1974. A hungry world: The challenge to agriculture. Summary Report and General Report. University of California Press. Berkeley.

Wamukoya, J. P. O., and G. H. Conner. 1976. Local immune responses in the bovine fetus vaccinated in utero with Escherichia coli antigen. American Journal of Veterinary Research 37:159-163.

Westcott, D. E. 1976. Food processing and preservation - new technology. Paper presented at a symposium on Agriculture and Food -- Progress and Prospects. Kansas City Section of the American Chemical Society, Kansas City, Missouri, February 24.

Whyte, R. O. 1975. Animal industry potential in monsoonal and equatorial Asia. Asian Productivity Organization, Tokyo, Japan.

Wittwer, S. H. 1972. Potentials for improving production ef-
    ficiency of fruits and vegetables. Proceedings of the 21st
    Annual Meeting of the Agricultural Research Institute,
    Washington, DC, October 10-11.
Wittwer, S. H. 1974. Research recommendations for increasing
    food, feed and fiber production in the USA. National
    Science Foundation, Washington, DC.
Wittwer, S. H. 1975. Food production: technology and the
    resource base. Science 188:579-584.
Wittwer, S. H., and M. J. Bukovac. 1959. The uptake of nutri-
    ents through leaf surfaces. Pages 235-261 in K. Scharres
    and H. Linser (Ed.) Handbuch der Pflanzenernährung und
    Düngung. Springer-Verlag, New York.
Wolff, A. 1975. Quality protein maize. CIMMYT Today (No. 1).
    International Maize and Wheat Improvement Center, Mexico,
    DF, Mexico.
Wolff, A. 1976. Wheat x Rye = Triticale. CIMMYT Today (No.
    5). International Maize and Wheat Improvement Center,
    Mexico, DF, Mexico.

5

Technology and Change

BEDE N. OKIGBO

Plant Technology in Today's World and Problems of Continued Widespread Adoption in Less Developed Countries

Plants as primary producers are the only organisms capable of converting solar energy through complex food chains to carbohydrates, fats, proteins and various other substances on which man and other animals depend for their survival, welfare, and existence. Without plants life on earth as we know it today would be impossible. Plants are also sources of a multiplicty of products such as oils, wood, drugs, fuel, resins, gums, paper, etc. useful to man. It is no wonder then that one of the outstanding innovations in the history of mankind was the evolution of settled agriculture, the most important element of which was the deliberate bringing into regular cultivation of plants selected from the wild to satisfy the basic human requirements for food, clothing, and shelter. The earliest estimate of the occurrence of this event in the Near and Far East is about 9,000 B.C., but there is evidence to support its having started independently at different times in different parts of the world.

According to Mrak (1966), technology is the application of scientific knowledge to practical purposes or to the solution of human needs in any particular endeavor. Technology gives man the capability of discovering, producing, processing, and utilizing materials of our environment with increasing efficiency. The range of available technology changes with time and provides man with the means of greatly modifying or controlling his environment. Mrak (1966) also maintains that the ability to generate new technology, receptivity to innovations

---

Bede N. Okigbo is Assistant Director, Farming Systems Program, International Institute of Tropical Agriculture, Ibadan, Nigeria

developed elsewhere, and dispersal of new technology varies
from place to place with the degree of development especially
with respect to education and the cultural characteristics of
people in any given environmental setting. Plant technology in
the context of this conference consists of the application of
centuries of human experience and continuously growing scientific knowledge to the art, science, and business of production
of the most important group of crop plants that are grown as
direct or indirect sources of food for man (Park and Robinson,
1975). Contributions of plants to the total calories and proteins in the human diet in various regions are shown in Table 1.

TABLE 1. Role of plant and animal products in the intake of
          calories and protein by man

Region or country	Calories		Protein	
	Plant %	Animal %	Plant %	Animal %
WORLD	90	10	69	31
Far East	94	6	86	14
- Japan	86	14	59	41
Middle East	82	12	85	15
Africa	93	7	84	16
Latin America	85	15	75	25
- Argentina	60	40	42	58
Western Europe	78	22	36	64
USSR	80	20	61	39
North America	64	36	27	73
Australia and New Zealand	58	42	32	68

This paper discusses the current state of knowledge and
practices of manipulating biological, physical, and mechanical
factors and various inputs in the production, harvesting,
processing, storage, marketing and transportation of food crops
together with the associated infrastructure for effectively
satisfying the world's current food needs with emphasis on the
problems of their continued use, development, and adoption in
the developing countries.

SCOPE OF PLANT PRODUCTION TECHNOLOGY
TODAY AND PROSPECTS FOR THE FUTURE
As already emphasized, a crop plant may be simply regarded
as a factory for the transformation of energy from the sun
in a process that utilizes carbon dioxide from the air,
hydrogen from water, and nutrients from the soil to manufacture
various useful products. The range and complexity of the activities and processes involved can best be appreciated by recognition of the ecological basis of crop production and

adoption of a systems approach to the evaluation of the processes involved. Based on ecological considerations, crop distribution and performance depend on the quality and/or quantity of 1), climatic and edaphic factors (water, rainfall, temperature, light, wind, soil conditions, and nutrients); 2), biotic factors (organisms including plants such as other crops and weeds); and 3), social environment (economic relationships in terms of supply, demand, market, etc.; historical background; political climate; and technological resources), which determine the resources allocated to a given crop, the management of its production, and its uses (FAO, 1972). These factors are in a state of dynamic change and produce different effects on the various stages of growth and parts of the plant. The systems approach considers the crop and all the factors of its production as intimately related in such a way that they interact in various ways to produce a specified end product (Clanson, 1969). Consequently crop production involves the management of all factors based on decisions of the producer with their associated risks depending on experiences and events of the past, present conditions, and objectives with possible future repercussions. A modern and efficient crop production technology should not only produce economic returns but also constitute adequate management of resources with minimal or no adverse effects on the environment. Based on these considerations, technologies for the manipulation and control of various factors of production are discussed separately below, not because they function independently but as a matter of convenience. Furthermore, since time, space, and reason necessitate that no detailed treatment can be given here, only brief discussions of the various factors are presented. In the last two decades, spectacular progress has been made in atomic science, space technology, computer technology, genetics, and understanding of life processes. Each has resulted in significant advances in agricultural technology (FAO, 1970). Some of these advances are discussed.

LAND DEVELOPMENT, SOIL MANAGEMENT, AND CONSERVATION

Since land is one of the major factors of production and the soil is the medium of anchorage of plants, and the reservoir and supplier of mineral nutrients and water (Robinson, 1975), consideration of the availability, management, and conservation of soils is a logical starting point for a discussion on plant production technology.

Land Availability and Development

The world's ability to produce enough food for the rapidly increasing population depends on the availability of land, climate, and other resources; technology for increasing yields

and efficiency of crop and livestock production; and incentives
to producers (ERS, 1974). Increased food production can be
achieved either by expanding the area of land under cultivation
or by increasing productivity per ha. The former depends on the
availability of cultivable land which is decreasing year by
year and cannot be expanded indefinitely without getting into
marginal lands. Various estimates indicate that availability
of land suitable for crop production is at least twice as much
as land currently under cultivation (FAO, 1958; Cramer, 1967;
Borgstrom, 1969; and ERS, 1974). Data on areas of land being
used for various purposes are shown in Table 2 and Figure 1.
(Figures are placed at the end of this paper.)

TABLE 2. Land used for crops and potential use, developing
          regions[a]

Region	Land suitable for crops		Land used to produce crops, 1962	
	Million ha	Percent of total land	Million ha	Percent of suitable land
Africa, South of Sahara	304	19	152	50
North West Africa	19	6	19	100
Asia & Far East	252	47	211	84
Latin America	570	29	130	23
Total or average	1,145	26	512	45

Source: Food and Agriculture Organization of the United Nations, Indicative World Plan, vol. 1, p. 49, (1967).
[a]Excludes Near East.

About 70 percent of the earth's surface is covered by oceans
and polar ice and only about 10 percent of the land surface is
currently being used for crop production (Cramer, 1967; Borgstrom, 1969). Recent studies that take into account topography,
water availability, various crops that can be grown in different cropping systems, absence of serious problems of alkalinity
and allowance for markets, transportation locations, and other
permanent facilities estimate the land surface suitable for
cultivation at about 3.2 billion ha of which 1.4 billion are
being utilized (ERS, 1974). Although about 45 percent of the
cultivable land is located in the developing countries, many
countries such as Egypt, India, and Bangladesh have such high
densities of population that they have almost reached the limit
of cultivable land available to them. Only the thinly populated areas of Africa and Latin America have the highest potential for expanding the area of land under cultivation. As a
result of difficulties and high cost in clearing large areas of
tropical forest, the presence of endemic diseases such as
sleeping sickness and river blindness, the heavy cost of

construction of irrigation and drainage structures, desalinization and land reclamation, increasing attention is being given
to techniques of increasing productivity per ha (ERS, 1974;
Schafer-Kehnert, 1973).

Land Clearance and Development

In every part of the world today, more and more land is being converted into special uses due to urbanization,
transportation, recreational and wild life reserves, and industrial, agricultural, and rural development schemes. This requires planning and projections of land use with due allowance
for population growth, economic and technological activities,
and multiple land use. Such plans should be based on accurate
surveys, identification, soil capability classification, resource inventories, and relevant maps supported by zoning and
land use legislation (Penn, 1972; Vlasin, 1974). Remote-sens-
ing techniques are of potential use in land development planning and resource use. With minimum surveys and sampling data
on land and vegetation types, mapping of soil and water sur-
faces, cropping patterns, soil and moisture characteristics, and
major soil boundaries, delineation of range lands etc. can be
carried out with minimum delay (Lindvall and Forth, 1971).
Planning for multiple land use of which agriculture is a part
should preferably be based on integrated watershed development
allowing for use of land of the greatest potential for specified activities with minimum development costs and damage to
the environment.

As population pressure builds up, more virgin forests and
jungles, marginal lands, lateritic soils, hillsides and swamps
are brought into cultivation (Tinker, 1974). In the humid
tropics where vast areas of forests are still unexploited,
clearing large areas of forest by hand labour is impossible and
expensive despite the low wages (Schafer-Kehnert, 1973). Under
these conditions heavy draft power and machines are the only
justifiable means of forest clearing. Clearing with such heavy
equipment can adversely influence soil physical and chemical
characteristics, resulting in deterioration of soil structure,
disturbance and removal of top soil, compaction and decrease in
porosity, impedance to water infiltration, poor root development, and susceptibility to erosion and flash floods (Kellog
and Orvedal, 1969; Van der Weert, 1974). Under such conditions,
special precautions should be taken to ensure minimum disturbance of the soil and all operations should be timed in accordance with the rainfall regime. Vegetable debris may be removed
by burning and windrowing, where necessary, should be limited
to short distances.

Soil Management and Conservation

The soil under natural vegetation cover attains equilibrium between destructive and favorable development

processes with adequate levels of organic matter, favourable
microbiological activity, and other processes that ensure good
physical structure and availability of plant nutrients (Bradfield, 1952; Kellog and Orvedal, 1969; Greenland, 1975).

While practices in soil management worked out in temperate
countries are not directly transferable to all parts of the
world, analytical techniques and basic soil management principles can be adapted to local conditions. These adaptations in
combination with simple tillage practices, fertilization, weed
control and other crop management practices for various soils,
climates and topographic situations will result in maintaining
adequate levels of soil organic matter, good structure, available nutrient supplies, adequate aeration and water storage
capacity, and continuous soil productivity (Kellog and Orvedal,
1969; Bradfield, 1952; Tisdal and Nelson, 1970).

Soil conservation consists of measures used to maintain
soil fertility and control of erosion by the use of such devices as terracing, contour farming, strip cropping with close
growing crops between row crops, ponds for water storage, suitable rotations with legumes and grasses, mulching with crop residues, diversion ditches for adequate drainage, prevention of
uncontrolled burning, and minimum tillage and other practices
which should go hand in hand with modern cropping systems and
soil management (Bradfield, 1952; SCS/USDA, 1968; Tisdal and
Nelson, 1920).

CROP MANAGEMENT FOR INCREASED YIELD

Bradfield (1974) indicated that crop production can be increased by increasing the area of land under cultivation,
increasing yield per hectare and by increasing the number
of crops grown per hectare per year. In each of these methods
of increasing production, the level of productivity depends on
the extent and efficiency of genetic manipulation of the crop
through breeding as demonstrated in varietal characteristics
and performance, and environmental manipulations and control of
varying degrees involving such cultural practices as tillage,
time of planting, method of planting, planting patterns and
spacings, and modifications of the wind and temperature. Other
important yield-raising practices such as plant protection,
fertilizer application, irrigation, drainage, and mechanization
are considered in greater detail below.

Tillage and Cultivation

These consist of various ways of preparing the soil for
planting with the objectives of obtaining good tilth and
fine seedbed for germination, seedling establishment and better
growing conditions, destruction of weeds and pests, and burial
of crop residues (Martin and Leonard, 1967). Tillage and

cultivations may be done by hand with hoes, or by draft animals
with plows. In modern mechanized farming, it involves plows,
harrows, discs, chisels, weeders, etc. Tillage is very expensive, especially in relation to the investments on various implements and fuel or animal power. A recent and welcome development related to this is minimum tillage, zero tillage, or
direct drilling practices which according to various authors:
1), reduces cost, time and number of planting operations; 2),
reduces soil compaction; 3), improves soil structure; 4), increases water infiltration and storage in the plough layer; 5),
reduces run-off and erosion; 6), reduces number and intensity
of annual weed growth; and 7), with mulching increases earth-
worm and microbial activity and level of soil organic matter.
Its main problems include prevalence of insect and some diseases and timing of herbicide applications. Special machines
have to be developed for minimum tillage (Kronka, 1973). While
its effects vary with the soil, crop, and climatic conditions
and continued research is still necessary, Kanuika (1976) has
guessed that by 2010 only about 5 percent of the farms in the
USA will be practising conventional tillage.

Sowing and Transplanting
        The method of planting after seedbed preparation varies
        with crop and may involve direct seed drilling, broadcast-
ing, or transplanting. Transplanting is used widely in horticulture. It enhances survival of seedlings that would otherwise be choked by weeds, reduces cost of tending the seedlings,
and may in crops like rice reduce the time the crop is in the
field thus facilitating another crop.

Spacing, Plant Population, and Number Per Stand
        There is always intra- and inter-specific competition
        among plants for nutrients, light, carbon dioxide, root
space, water, and air space in addition to cooperative interaction (Duncan, 1969). Adjustment of spacing of crops grown
in a range of environments significantly affects crop yields.
Within and between row spacings, spatial distribution and density of plants affect total yield, yield components, lodging,
response to fertilizer, and severity of disease (Holliday,
1960) (Table 3). Spacing varies with plant type, soil, and
sometimes cultural operations.

Planting Pattern
        In addition to spacing and the spatial distribution of
        crops, planting pattern also involves the number or se-
quence of cropping during the year. Planting patterns that
affect yield consist of fallowing, single or double cropping,

TABLE 3.   Influence of soybean plant population on amount of
           leaf area and time required to reach 95 percent light
           interception

	Population (plants/acre)			
	25,000	50,000	100,000	200,000
Plant spacing in inches (20 inch rows)	12	6	3	1½
Plants/foot of row	1	2	4	8
L_{95}	2.5	2.9	3.4	4.0
Days to L_{95}	62	60	55	52
Branches/plant	9.0	4.0	0.5	0.1
Yield, % of 40-inch rows[a]	108	122	115	100
% of bean weight to Total	30.7	27.3	27.2	21.0

Source: Shibles, R. M., and C. R. Weber. 1966. Interception
of solar radiation and dry matter production by various soybean
planting patterns. Crop Science 6:55-59.
[a]Percent of 100,000 plants/acre in 40-inch rows (20.8 bu).

relay cropping, intercropping, and multiple cropping. Fallowing is a cropping system in which less than one crop is grown
on a piece of land in one year to conserve water or restore
soil fertility. It allows for the extension of cultivation into marginal areas or intermittent growing of crops without fertilizer application. Monocropping is practised where the climate, the length of cropping season, and the duration of the
crop allow for only one crop a year. All the other cropping
systems permit increased production per hectare and the growing
of several crop species on a given piece of land in one year.
Continuous cropping systems usually involve growing planned sequences of crops (rotations) that help maintain soil fertility
especially where legumes are involved, reduce pests and diseases, and make for more efficient utilization of resources and
more even distribution of labour. Table 4 presents the effect
of rotations on maize yields (Schrimpe, 1965).

TABLE 4. Maize yields with various crop rotations

Method of cultivation	Average yield in bushels per acre	
	1916 to 1927	1928 to 1940
Maize in three-year crop rotation with oats and clover	60.4	66.7
Successive maize cultivation	55.1	40.7

Miscellaneous Manipulations of the Crop Environment
     Yield may be increased or production made possible by

manipulations of the time of planting to coincide with the period of optimum conditions of one or more factors (e.g. moisture or temperature) (Namken et al., 1974). Crop cultivars may be selected or treatments given to them to ensure a shorter growing season and establish more favorable light, temperature, and wind regimes (Waggoner, 1969; Mitchell, 1970). The most drastic control or modification of plants and their environment occurs in horticulture where, for example, carbon dioxide enrichment may be practised on greenhouses. Knott and Lorenz (1950) reported 1), modifications of refrigerator cars for transporting tomato seedlings from the South to the Northern United States; 2), dipping of seedlings in a synthetic latex Geon 31 to minimize transplanting shock; 3), use of growth regulators to increase fruit set and size in tomatoes; and 4), pelleting or coating of seeds for protection against seedling disease or for fertilizing. Brown (1965) discussed various yield-raising devices used in Japanese rice farms and emphasized that there is almost no end to the technologies that are generated for increased crop production. Each technology at a given time for a specified purpose may be uneconomical, but at another time or location it may become economically viable.

FERTILIZERS AND MANURES
    The fertility of the land between the Tigris and Euphrates Rivers was recorded in writing as early as 2500 BC, and by about 300 BC the value of green manure crops was recognized by the Greeks (Tisdale and Nelson, 1970). Since then the use of farm manures, green manure crops, liming, and crop rotations in the maintenance of soil fertility received much emphasis in the 19th Century and the first half of the 20th Century, but they could not support the high levels of crop and animal production now practised in many developed countries (Nelson, 1968). Since the middle of the 19th century, studies and experiments by Lawes, Gilbert, and Liebig followed by many other scientists have shown that plants require carbon, hydrogen, oxygen, nitrogen, phosphorus, potassium, sulphur, calcium, and magnesium in higher quantities than iron, manganese, boron, copper, zine, chlorine, and molybdenum that are required in very small quantities (Evans and Sorger, 1966). Nitrogen, phosphorus, and potassium are the most important of the elements that play essential roles in plant metabolism and that are constituents of proteins and/or enzymes. Carbon and oxygen are obtained from the air while hydrogen is obtained from water in the soil. All essential elements are found in the soil as components of rocks or minerals, in soil water solution, adsorbed to soil colloids, in the soil atmosphere, and in soil organisms.
    Since plants take up essential elements from the soil which are not replaced when whole crops or their parts are removed, soil fertility and productivity usually decrease with

continuous cropping. The only way of rapidly restoring soil
fertility is by the application of fertilizers or manures required by the crop. In traditional farming systems of tropical
Africa maintenance of soil fertility is accomplished through recycling of nutrients by vegetation through leaf litter which on
decomposition releases the nutrients to the soil. Regular
application of fertilizers in reasonable amounts is therefore
imperative on soils that are under continuous cultivation.

Sources and Kinds of Fertilizers

The raw materials for fertilizer synthesis consist of hydrogen (usually obtained from coal or natural gas), phosphate rock, potash, and sulphur (Nelson, 1974). These are used
in the manufacture of different types of fertilizers (Table 5).
The fertilizers are available in dry fine crystalline particles,
granules or pellets of different sizes or liquid forms. They
may be straight fertilizers containing individual nutrients or
mixtures of different ratios.

Diagnosis of Fertilizer Requirements

With experience, symptoms of nutrient deficiencies can be
observed visually, but usually chemical analysis of soil
samples and their correlation with field tests is the most reliable method.

Methods of Application

Methods of application of fertilizers include broadcasting,
drilling, banding, foliar sprays, in solution of irrigation water, or injection into the plant.

Response to Fertilizers

According to Diamond and Engelsbad (1974) best responses
to fertilizers are obtained when they are applied in the
right amounts and at times and by methods most appropriate for
the cropping system, provided that other favourable conditions
for crop growth are ensured. The response to fertilizers depends on crop species and variety, root activity, soil characteristics, depth of tillage, soil nutrient level and balance,
spacing, date of planting, time and method of application, light
intensity, etc. (Younts, 1971).

World Consumption of Fertilizers

Fertilizer consumption is very high in the developed countries and its low consumption in the developing countries
is one major constraint to increased agricultural productivity.

TABLE 5. Some commercial and experimental nitrogen fertilisers

	N	P_2O_5	K_2O	CaO	MgO	S
SOLIDS						
Highly water-soluble						
Ammonium sulphate	21	--	--	--	--	23
Ammonium nitrate	34	--	--	--	--	--
Calcium ammonium nitrate	20[a]	--	--	10	7	--
Ammonium nitrate-sulphate	30	--	--	--	--	5
Calcium nitrate	15	--	--	27	2	--
Potassium nitrate	13	--	44	--	--	--
Sodium nitrate	16	--	--	--	--	--
Urea	45	--	--	--	--	--
Urea-ammonium sulphate	40	--	--	--	--	4
Monoammonium phosphate	11	48	--	--	--	--
Diammonium phosphate	18	46	--	--	--	--
Ammonium phosphate-sulphate	16	20	--	--	--	14
Ammonium phosphate-nitrate	30	10	--	--	--	--
Nitric phosphate	20[a]	20	--	--	--	--
Ammonium polyphosphate	15	62	--	--	--	--
Ammonium polyphosphate with sulphur	12	51	--	--	--	15
Urea-ammonium polyphosphate	36[a]	18	--	--	--	--
Slowly soluble or insoluble in water						
Ureaforms	38[a]	--	--	--	--	--
Urea-Z	35[a]	--	--	--	--	--
Crotonylidene diurea	32	--	--	--	--	--
Isobutylidene diurea	32	--	--	--	--	--
Oxamide	32	--	--	--	--	--
Thiourea	37	--	--	--	--	--
Metal ammonium phosphates	8[a]	40	7	--	14	--
Sulphur-coated urea	35[a]	--	--	--	--	20
Resin-coated urea	38[a]	--	--	--	--	--
Resin-coated mixed fertiliser	14[a]	14	14	--	--	--
FLUIDS						
Anhydrous ammonia	82	--	--	--	--	--
Aqua ammonia	20[a]	--	--	--	--	--
Urea-ammonium nitrate solution	32[a]	--	--	--	--	--
Ammonium polyphosphate base solution	11	37	--	--	--	--
N-P suspension	13[a]	39	--	--	--	--
N-P-K suspension	5[a]	15	30	--	--	--

Source: Bengtson, FAO/IUFRO/F/73/25, December, 1973.
[a] Content of N or other components may vary.

The low consumption of fertilizers in developing countries is
due to lack of credit, cost/benefit ratio of fertilizer applied,
ignorance, shortage of fertilizers, etc. Fertilizer consumption per hectare in some countries of Europe and North America
is over 100-200 times the amount used in Nigeria (Brown and
Eckholm, 1974) (See Table 6.) According to Nelson (1974), 79
percent of the world's fertilizer output is consumed by the
developed countries with only 39 percent of the world population.

TABLE 6.   Fertilizer consumption per acre of arable land in 15
           most populous countries in 1972

Country	Pounds/Acre
West German	363
Japan	347
United Kingdom	239
France	231
Italy	104
United States	72
USSR	40
China	35
Brazil	32
Mexico	26
India	14
Pakistan	12
Indonesia	11
Bangladesh	7
Nigeria	1

Parker and Nelson (1969), based on studies of fertilizer
consumption and responses during 1947-63, concluded that plant
nutrients constitute a major limiting factor in agricultural
production of the developing countries and that moderate applications of 40-70 kg/ha will increase yields up to 50 percent.
The highest responses were obtained on improved crop cultivars
grown under improved management practices, adequate pest and
water management, and on good soils. They listed several developments that resulted in the production of a range of fertilizer products of higher nutrient concentration, lower price,
and much easier to transport and handle. Moreover, they emphasized 1), the need for a linkage of marketing organizations,
research workers, extension, and credit agencies; and 2) provision for retail agents to handle seed, farm equipment, and
other input sales while at the same time providing technical
services to supplement government agencies. While fertilizer
consumption has been increasing rapidly in the less developed
countries, it is very likely now that the rate of increase and
fertilizer use may be reduced by the energy crisis, increased
cost of fertilizers, and general unfavourable economic conditions.

PLANT IMPROVEMENT

Domestication
        Origin of agriculture is associated with domestication
from the wild of a few plants with desirable characteristics for use by man. According to Schwanitz (1967), De Beer
(1970), and Lawrence (1968), primitive man advanced from the
gathering stage to the artificial and deliberate selection of
certain plants after slowly accumulated observation and experience. Genetic variability was first concentrated locally from
widely dispersed plants. Later the isolation of gene concentrations imposed by tribal, ethnic, and topographic barriers
was broken by exchange and distribution of plants through trade,
various methods of transportation, and migrations of peoples
(Lawrence, 1968).
        It is interesting to note that of about 350,000 species of
plants, 1), 10-20,000 can be broadly classified as cultivated
for various purposes; 2), not more than 10,000 fit into man's
economic activities; 3), at least 3,000 species are grown for
food; 4), 100-150 species are of major commercial importance;
and 5), only 15 species contribute the bulk of man's food
(Janick et al., 1969; Burton, 1968; Fitzpatrick, 1964; Edin,
1969; Jaques, 1958; and Hill, 1952). The 14 most important
food crops consist of six grasses (rice, wheat, corn, barley,
sorghum, and sugar cane), three roots and tubers (potato, sweet
potato, and cassava), three legumes (soybeans, common bean, and
groundnut) and two fruits and nuts (coconut and bananas).
About 30 percent of man's energy comes from one grass, rice,
and 75 percent of human food comes from one or more grasses
(Burton, 1968). Many of the highly commercialized crops have
become so dependent on man that they can hardly survive in
nature. Moreover, not only has the number of cultivated plants
and other plants used by man continued to decrease, but modern
plant breeding techniques and processing for convenience foods
has further reduced the number of species in our diet and increased uniformity within each species. The uniformity has
reached such a state in some crops that concern about their
narrow genetic base and vulnerability to diseases and pests has
led to the present concern about maintaining large collections
of useful germplasm and increased plant exploration activities.
        There also is interest in diversification of plants that
are grown, studied, and processed as food as evidenced by the
recent National Academy of Sciences (1975) publication of a
list of 36 underexplored tropical plants of promising economic
value. Unfortunately, many potentially useful African species
are not covered in this publication. Concern about these neglected African food plants has recently been highlighted by
Getahum (1974) who listed 35 leafy vegetable species, 122
fruits and seeds, and 30 starchy roots and tubers eaten in
Ethiopia, and by Okigbo (1975) who listed over 90 food plants

of tropical Africa that are not receiving the attention they
deserve. Therefore, there is as much need to establish collections of germplasm of important food crops and their wild relatives as there is to increase the range of food crops under
active study and regular cultivation.

Plant Improvement
        This is the application of the principles of genetics to
     the improvement of plants involving several methods in-
cluding direct introduction, hybridization (intra- and inter-
specific), inbreeding, bulk population, back crossing, polyploidy, mutation breeding, and associated methods of selection
and evaluation. The objectives of plant breeding that have
been achieved with many species include 1), development of
plants with increased yields and production efficiency; 2), development of plants of high quality, e.g., protein content of
higher biological value as obtained in opaque 2-maize; 3),
breeding for adaptation to adverse weather conditions and environmental stresses (drought resistence, cold hardiness, etc.);
4), development of cultivars that are adapted to mechanized
handling, e.g., harvesting and planting, which require uniformity of plant type and maturity; 5), development of cultivars
that are resistant to insects, diseases, and other pests; 6),
development of cultivars that meet special needs of the consumer and processor; 7), production of cultivars that respond to
fertilizers and various inputs; 8), production of cultivars
that are early or late maturing as the case may be; and 9), development of cultivars with specific plant structure to satisfy
the needs of certain cropping systems. Major achievements in
plant breeding related to the above are summarized by
Swaminatham in Table 7.
        The scientific basis for increased yield capacity in rice
on which the Green Revolution was based was summarized by
Chandler (1973):

        1) Short, stiff-strawed cultivars resistant to lodging.
        2) Upright-leaved plants that are more efficient in light
interception and photosynthesis at high population densities.
        3) Crosses of several cultivars that manifested some hy-
brid vigour.
        4) Higher responses to fertilizer and improved management
practices.
        5) Heavy tillering that compensated for missing stands.
        6) Early maturity and insensitivity to photoperiod that
facilitated multiple cropping.
        7) Recently, the incorporation of resistance to a range of
diseases and pests and adaptation to certain soil conditions.

        These characteristics of high yielding cultivars of maize,
wheat, and rice facilitated their increasing acceptance by
farmers (Table 8). The increasing spectrum of resistance and

TABLE 7. Some significant landmarks in 20th century plant breeding

Development	Year[a]	Country of original use	Genetic principle(s) involved
1. Hybrid maize	1933	USA	Hybrid vigour
2. Hybrid sorghum	1957	USA	Hybrid vigour
3. Hybrid pearl millet	1959	USA	Hybrid vigour
4. Dwarf wheat	1961	USA	Dwarfing genes from Japanese "Norin" wheat
5. Dwarf wheat	1963	Mexico and later India, Pakistan, Middle East	"Norin" dwarfing genes and relative photo-insensitivity
6. Dwarf indica rice	1955	Taiwan	Genes for dwarfing and relative photo-insensitivity, stiff and erect leaves
7. Dwarf indica rice	1965	Philippines, India and others in Asia	Genes for dwarfing and relative photo-insensitivity, stiff and erect leaves
7. "Opaque-2" maize	1965	USA	High Lysine content
8. Hybrid barley	1969	USA	Hybrid vigour
9. "Hiproly" barley	1969	Sweden	High protein and high Lysine
10. Hybrid upland cotton	1970	India	Hybrid vigour

[a]Year of widespread use.

TABLE 8. Countries in a more favourable or less favourable situation with respect to five factors influencing dissemination of New Indica varieties in South and Southeast Asia 1968

	Water control	Avail-ability of inputs	Yield advantage over existing varieties	Disease resistance	Quality acceptability of new rice grain
MORE FAVOURABLE					
India	average	good	high	average	average
Malaysia	good	good	high	high	poor
Philippines	average	good	high	average	average
Pakistan, West	good	good	high	high	average
Viet Nam, Rep. of	average	average	high	average	average
AVERAGE					
Ceylon	good	good	low	average	average
Indonesia	average	poor	medium	average	average
LESS FAVOURABLE					
Burma	poor	poor	high	average	poor
Pakistan, East	poor	average	high	low	average
Thailand	poor	average	medium	average	poor

Source: R. W. Barker. Economic aspects of high-yielding varieties of rice. IRRI Report, FAO Study Group on Rice, CCP: RI 69/12, March 1969.

other characteristics in some International Rice Research Institute (IRRI) rice cultivars are shown in Table 9.

TABLE 9. Characteristics of IRRI improved rice varieties

| | Variety | | | | | |
	IR8	IR5	IR20	IR22	IR24	IR26
Lodging	R[a]	MR	MR	R	R	MR
Diseases						
Blast	MR	S	MR	S	S	MR
Bacterial blight	S	S	R	R	S	R
Bacterial leaf streak	S	MS	MR	MS	MR	MR
Grassy stunt	S	S	S	S	S	MR
Tungro	S	S	R	S	MR	R
Insects						
Green leafhopper	R	R	R	S	R	R
Brown planthopper	S	S	S	S	S	R
Stem borer	MS	S	MR	S	S	MR
Soil problems						
Alkali injury	S	S	S	S	MR	MR
Salt injury	MR	MR	MR	S	MR	MR
Iron toxicity	S	S	R	MR	MR	R
Reduction products	MR	MS	MR	MR	MS	MR

Source: IRRI, 1973.
[a] R, MR, MS, and S are resistant, moderately resistant, moderately susceptible, and susceptible, respectively.

Recent advances in genetic engineering of interest in plant breeding include 1), the artificial synthesis through polyploidy of triticale, a wheat x rye hybrid of higher protein content than wheat and more adapted to semi-arid areas but with less gluten; 2), parasexual hybridization that facilitates the fusion of somatic cells of otherwise incompatible species; 3), DNA transfer as accomplished by Hess in Petunia; and 4), gene transfer by a bacteriophage (Smith, 1974). These advances may in the future facilitate crosses of unrelated plant species such as maize and soybeans, thus facilitating transfer of genes for nitrogen fixation to nonlegumes.

IRRIGATION AND DRAINAGE
Irrigation and drainage constitute aspects of water management that also include conservation (Janick et al., 1969). Plants require water for growth but excess water for prolonged periods is detrimental to the growth of most crops except rice.

Irrigation
Irrigation is a major input in the Green Revolution and is

necessary because for a unit of dry matter, a plant usually consumes a certain amount of water most of which is lost through
evapotranspiration. Revelle (1970) estimated that for each ton
of maize or sugarcane, about 1000 tons of water are used by the
plant. For this reason irrigation is necessary in crop production in semi-arid and arid regions. Even in some parts of the
humid tropics supplementary irrigation may be necessary for optimum yields. Marshall (1972) gives the estimated total irrigated land area as 200 million ha about half of which is located in China and India. Most of the cultivated areas of
Egypt are irrigated. The need for irrigation is increasing all
the time and the total world irrigated area is estimated to
have doubled during the last 30 years (Marshall, 1972), mainly
as a result of the construction of more dams, wells, and reservoirs. Irrigation in dry areas or areas with a marked dry season facilitates double or multiple cropping where other factors
are not limiting. Irrigated soils in semi-arid areas are subject to salinity problems and man-made lakes are subject to
rapid siltation.

   Sources of irrigation water and methods of irrigation.
Sources of irrigation water include rivers, streams, ponds, reservoirs, wells, and multipurpose dams. Since the earliest
irrigation with the Shadulf in Egypt, various methods of irrigation have been practised. These include sprinkler, surface,
and subsurface irrigation, each of which may in turn be carried
out in different ways (Janick et al., 1969). The expense of
irrigation facilities often makes it profitable for the growing
of high yield, high value crops only.

Drainage
   This is the removal of excess water from the soil that is
   necessary in water-logged soils. Marshall (1972) indicated that the total drained land surface in the world amounts
to about 100 million ha, about 37 million of which is located
in the USA. The most intensely drained area of land is found
in the Netherlands where 1.5 million ha of the 2.5 million ha
of cultivated land is drained land (Marshall, 1972). Surface
and subsurface methods of land drainage are practised.
   While both irrigation and drainage are used in expanding
the area of land under cultivation, Brown (1965) noted that
estimates of world food production on irrigated land is less
than 10 percent, less than 5 percent of which is on land where
water is controlled on a major engineering scale. Overall
methods of water control constitute integral aspects of watershed management and soil conservation.

PLANT PROTECTION
   According to Ennis et al. (1967), several organisms com-
      pete with man for space, water, minerals, light, and above

all, food. These include various bacteria, fungi, protozoa, nematodes, mites, insects, weeds, and birds, rodents and other vertebrates. These pests cause losses in productivity and efficiency of land use, crop quality, efficiency of water management, and human efficiency. Weeds harbor pests to plants and animals. Therefore, increased crop production measures must include plant protection practices since the losses are often enormous.

Weeds

Weeds are plants that grow where they are not wanted, and especially among crop plants with which they compete for environmental factors (water, nutrients, light, space, etc.), reduce crop quality due to toxicity or other objectionable effects, reduce yields, and increase cost of production (Mitchell, 1970; Dunham, 1957). Annual losses caused by weeds in the USA during 1942-1951 were estimated at $3.8 billion (Dunham, 1957), and amounted to 3-25 percent of the annual crop production in 1950-51 (Ennis, 1967).

Methods of weed control consist of 1), mechanical, for example by hand, hoeing, plowing, mowing, etc.; 2), competition by use of smother crops; 3), cultural methods involving the use of rotations or crop sequences; 4), fire, which may be accidental or purposely set; 5), biological in which insects, bacteria, or other organisms are used to selectively keep down the weed population; and 6), chemical. Chemical weed control is the most widespread and effective method in modern agriculture and is carried out with a range of chemicals that may be inorganic salts or synthetic organic substances. The greatest advance in weed control followed the development of a range of growth regulating substances some of which are highly selective. Two main groups of synthetic organic substances, the phenoxy compounds such as 2-4 D and heterocyclic nitrogenous compounds, are used as contact, selective, non-selective, translocated, or systemic herbicides. Selectivity is based on the morphology of the plants, and the ease with which the chemicals are absorbed, translocated, or produce other physiological effects. Some herbicides are used to kill all types of weeds, and while some are more effective on grasslike plants, others are more effective on broadleaved plants. They may be applied as pre-planting, pre-emergence, or post-emergence treatments. Moreover, they may be applied in different formulations consisting of sprays (emulsions or solutions) or granular herbicides in which the active substance is used to impregnate a solid carrier. Sometimes surface-active agents are used to improve the wetting effectiveness of the herbicides. A recent development is the use of ultra-low-volume spraying techniques, which minimize the amount of water and chemical used.

Insects

Insects also cause serious losses in yield by injuring
various parts of the crop in the field or in storage. Annual losses attributed to insects in the USA in 1950-51 were
2-31 percent of total production (Ennis et al., 1967). The effectiveness of control measures is indicated by results of stem
borer control studies at IRRI in which control plots yielded
1400-2400 kg/ha, about half that of treated plots (Stakman,
1966). Damage done by insects on various plant parts by adults
and immature stages may result from chewing, rasping, sucking,
or sponging during which disease organisms may be transmitted
to the crop.

Methods of insect control include 1), legal or legislative
measures as enforced through quarantine services; 2), cultural
methods through crop rotations, time of planting, etc.; 3),
biological methods involving the use of bacteria, viruses, or
other organisms that selectively parasitise the insect; 4), genetic methods involving the use of resistant or tolerant crop
cultivars; or 5), chemical methods (inorganics, oil sprays, and
synthetic organic substances such as chlorinated hydrocarbons
like DDT, organo-phosphates such as parathion, and carbamates).
New control measures include the use of male sterility, that may
be induced by irradiation or chemicals, and attractants. The
latter are synthetic sex hormones used to attract and destroy
male insects, thus significantly reducing their populations.
The chemicals may be applied as dusts, wettable powders, fumi-
gants, or aerosols and as with herbicides, surface-active agents
may be used to improve their effectiveness.

Recent developments in insect control involve the use of
integrated control as a result of pesticide residue problems.
In this method the use of chemicals is restricted to a few strategic applications at critical periods of the development cycle
of the insect in conjunction with biological, cultural, and
other compatible control measures with minimum adverse effects
on beneficial insects and other organisms.

Other Animal Pests

As with insects, birds, rodents, and snails also cause crop
losses and chemical and other methods are used to minimize
them. For example, rodenticides or traps are used to kill rodents, while birds are more difficult to control. Certain chemicals have been tried with varying degrees of success.

Diseases

Substantial crop losses are caused by micro-organisms in
the field and in storage. Dunham (1957) estimated disease
losses in the USA during 1941-51 as annually amounting to 6.5
percent of the production or $3 billion. Organisms that cause

diseases in plants include viruses, bacteria, fungi, and nematodes. Stakman (1966) indicated that there were 200 kinds of
viruses, 200 species of bacteria, 25,000 species of parasitic
fungi, and several hundred nematodes species that attack plants.
     Control measures for disease pathogens include legal and
legislative measures, cultivation methods, genetic methods involving the use of resistant cultivars, and chemicals (fungicides, nematocides, bactericides, etc.). With the present concern about the environment, pollution and toxic residue problems, restrictions on these chemicals are similar to herbicides
and insecticides. A unique phenomenon in the use of resistant
cultivars as a method of pathogen control is the existence of
numerous physiological races requiring continuous evaluation,
screening, and production of new crop cultivars to match the
development of new races.
     In all the above control methods, the most effective are
chemical methods, but they are also detrimental to the environment and continuous effort and a lot of resources in men and
materials are devoted to the search for safer chemicals. All
the methods of control affect various operations such as seed
bed preparation, method of seeding, spacing, seed rates, fertilizer practices, cultivations, irrigation practices, harvesting, seed clearing, renovation of pastures, land clearing,
water management, etc. Thus, each input in pest control interacts with crop management practices necessitating a systems approach to the problems and recognition of the ecological implications of every action taken.

HARVESTING, STORAGE, AND PROCESSING
     Harvesting, storage, and processing consist of complex
     operations that ensure that what is produced is gathered,
     properly handled, and preserved with minimum losses in
quality and quantity. They cover vast topics which can only be
given brief treatments here. The following summary is taken
from Mitchell (1970), Hall (1970), FAO (1968), and Van Kampen
(1971).

Harvesting
     Harvesting is carried out in a range of weather, climatic
     conditions, stages of maturity, and moisture content of
various products that affect the capacities required for sequential operations of harvesting, threshing, transport, and/or
storage (Van Kampen, 1971). Van Kampen (1971) emphasized the
need of a systems approach in planning harvesting operations,
taking into account the following sequence of events: 1), harvesting; 2), transfer to containers; 3), field transport; 4),
road transport; 5), weighing; 6), unloading and conveying; 7),
cleaning; 8), storage of wet grain; 9), drying and cleaning;

10), storage of dry grain; 11), conveying; and 12), shipment.
        Harvesting of produce is based on physiological principles
affecting the prediction of the stage of maturity at which material to be handled has reached maximum dry matter accumulation
and yield to facilitate handling at minimum cost and to ensure
longevity in storage. Respiring plant tissues of different
moisture contents and texture have to be handled differently.
Thus, apart from differences in crop species, harvesting and
storage operations are different for grains, fruits, and vegetables. Harvesting may be carried out by hand or machine and
may involve separate operations of cutting, stocking, threshing,
and windrowing prior to storage. Combine harvesting involves
the use of machines that combine several operations in grain
harvesting. The moisture content at harvest determines the
method of prestorage.
        For forage crops that are grazed directly, no storage pro-
cedure is necessary. But for grain and forage to be stored, it
is necessary to select the best harvesting time for maximum retention of yield at minimum cost of prestorage operations. Usually for grains, harvesting, should be done at physiological
maturity when the grains have reached 20-25 percent moisture.
The moisture content at harvesting is affected by humidity of
the air, sunshine, and wind. When produce is harvested at high
moisture content, prestorage drying by ordinary sunshine and
air in windrows may be necessary before drying in storage. Drying with heated air may be carried out for large quantities of
produce. According to van Kampen (1971), the harvesting costs
for grain varies with operations. In a typical study he reported the following distribution of costs: drying and temporary storage, 20 percent; transport, 20 percent; combining, 43.6
percent; and field losses, 15.6 percent.

Storage
        The objectives of storage consist of avoidance of food
        losses, maintenance of food quality during the marketing
chain, preservation of food products for long periods so as to
even out supplies and minimize shortages, and hold produce so
as to secure maximum returns at times of scarcity. Storage procedures vary with the degree of perishability of the produce.
Conditions for storage of perishables are listed in Table 10.
        Losses during storage are associated with weight losses,
food loss, quality loss, monetary loss, seed loss and goodwill
loss, all of which are associated with chemical changes, development of heat, feeding by rodents, mishandling of produce, use
of poor containers, and exposure to adverse environmental conditions. Losses observed from various sources in grain storage
in India are shown in Table 11.
        Various factors that affect value and deterioration during
storage are classified by Hall (1970) as follows:

TABLE 10. Optimum storage conditions of selected fresh perishables

	Temperature °C	Relative humidity Percent	Expected storage life	Remarks
Apples (Cox's Orange Pippins)	3.5	90	3-4 months	Storage life can be extended by controlled atmosphere
Apples (Golden Delicious)	-1 to 0	90	6 months	In South Africa and the USA
Pears (Alexander Lucas)	-1 to 0	90	5-6 months	In the Federal Republic of Germany
Oranges	-1 to 1	85-90	2-3 months	Storage in darkness to prevent greening
Bananas, green	11.5 to 14.5	90-95	10-20 days	Depends on variety, Latacan types at higher temperature
Bananas, colored	13 to 16	85-90	5-10 days	To be consumed immediately after storage
Tomatoes, ripe	0	85-90	1-3 weeks	Storage in darkness to prevent greening
Potatoes, early	3 to 4	85-90	A few weeks	Storage in darkness
Potatoes, late	4.5 to 10	88-93	4-8 months	
Seed	2 to 7	85-90	5-8 months	Temperature depending on variety
Beef	-1.5 to 0	90	Up to 3 weeks	4 to 5 weeks if very strict hygienic requirements are observed
Lamb	-1 to 0	90-95	10-15 days	
Pork	-1.5 to 0	90-95	1-2 weeks	
Chicken, eviscerated	0	Over 95	7-10 days	If relative humidity is lower, water and vaporproof wrapping necessary
Fish	-1.1 to 3		4-14 days	Known as chilled storage
	-30 to -18		3-12 months	

TABLE 11. Estimates of food grain losses[a] in storage in India

Cause of loss	Wheat	Rice	Jowar	Bajra	Maize	Millets	Pulses	Ave	TOTAL
	...........................Percent.......................Million tons[b]								
Rodents	2.5	2.5	2.5	2.5	2.5	2.5	2.5	2.5	2.0
Birds	0.5	1.0	1.0	1.0	0.5	2.0	0.5	0.9	0.7
Insects[c]	3.0	2.0	2.0	1.0	3.0	0.5	5.0	2.5	2.0
Moisture	0.5	0.5	2.0	0.5	0.5	0.5	0.5	0.7	0.5

[a]Loss in food value only
[b]Based on average production in 1962-64
[c]Loss caused by insects is quantified on the basis that a kernel damaged by insects has lost half its food value.

    1) Physical: temperature, moisture.
    2) Biological: produce properties, microorganisms, insects, rodents and birds, man.
    3) Chemical: breakdown of produce, pesticides.
    4) Engineering: structures (bag storage or bulk storage), mechanical (conveying of produce and application of pesticides).
    5) Socioeconomic: finance, farming method (indigenous or nonindigenous).
    6) Politics: storage and marketing.

    Storage structures vary in scale and sophistication and may consist of straw, bamboo, wooden bins, mud and brick structures (with or without plastic lining or enveloping of grain), and concrete silos (above or below ground). Storage also may be done at the farm level for small quantities of material and in local community assembly. Distribution or transport storage involves bulk storage. Before storage threshing, cleaning, and preliminary drying are always necessary.
    Pest control measures are taken to control insects, mites, bacteria and fungi in addition to measures to control moisture. On the basis of the above operations, cost of storage is usually related to harvesting, storage structures, machinery, service installations, and operating costs in personnel, power, etc.

Processing
    Processing is one of the methods used to preserve food products and render them convenient for handling and use. Apart from home processing, which is common in traditional societies, various modern methods of commercial processing for grains, fruits, and vegetables now are used in developed countries to meet the needs of the urban population for canned and packaged convenience foods. While many conventional methods are not yet adopted in the less developed countries, new processing methods are continuously being developed in the

developed countries. Some of these and the probabilities of
their adoption are presented in Table 12

TABLE 12. Probability of widespread commercial use of selected
          new food processing methods in 1980

Food processing method	:	Probability that the process will be in widespread use in 1980
	:	--------Percent----------
Freezing by cryogenics...............:		85
Freezing by Freon or the equivalent..:		80
Boil-in-the-bag foods................:		98
Dehydrofreezing and dehydrocanning...:		90
Freeze-concentration.................:		93
Osmotic dehydration..................:		90
Continuous vacuum-drying.............:		99
Freeze-drying.......................:		99
Compaction..........................:		85
Aseptic canning.....................:		94
HTST canning........................:		95
Irradiation sterilization...........:		30
Irradiation pasteurization..........:		80
Irradiation treatment for sprout inhibition, disinfestation.........:		90
Microwaves..........................:		90
Infrared waves......................:		95
Sonic waves.........................:		90

Source: Bird, Arthur, and Goldbert, 1968.

MECHANIZATION
     Mechanization is the use of various mechanical devices of
     varying degrees of sophistication as labour-saving devices
     for the various operations and practices in crop produc-
tion ranging from land clearing and preparation to harvesting,
storage, and processing. This has been the basis of increased
productivity in modern agriculture facilitating the timely performance of operations, increases in scale of operations, and
release of manpower for other activities. Complete mechanization has taken place in agricultural production of many developed countries while in the developing countries animal and
human power are still widely used in the operation of simple
tools and mechanization is restricted to partial mechanization
of operations like threshing and transportation of produce.
The growth of mechanization in different countries as measured
by the number of tractors is shown in Table 13.
     As a result of the scale of operations and size of farms
in the developing countries, lack of credit and technicians,
and recently the energy crisis, it is now seriously felt that

TABLE 13. Number of tractors used in agriculture

	Total numbers			Increase in numbers		
	Averages			1949-1951 to 1959-1961	1959-1961 to 1966-1968	1949-1951 to 1966-1968
	1949-1951	1959-1961	1966-1968			
	Thousands			Percent per year		
Latin America	121	335	525	11	7	9
Far East	12	60	126	17	11	15
Near East	26	77	141	11	9	11
Africa	38	82	114	8	5	7
DEVELOPING COUNTRIES	197	554	906	11	7	9
DEVELOPED COUNTRIES	5816	10302	13348	6	4	5
World	6013	10856	14254	6	4	5

what is needed is appropriate technology for farmers in the developing countries involving low energy inputs, low cost biological, physical, and environmental manipulations with minium adverse effects on the environment but within the means of the farmers to operate.

ENERGY IMPLICATIONS OF IMPROVED TECHNOLOGY

As a result of inc·eased mechanization based on equipment whose main energy source is petroleum fuels, the energy input in agricultural production has continued to skyrocket and consequently, with the recent energy crisis, the cost of production has increased considerably. Heichel (1974) reviewed the comparative efficiency of energy use in crop production systems and diagrammed the energy flow in manufacturing, distribution, and growing of crops (Figure 2). Heichel (1974) also compared the cultural energy associated with various farming systems and concluded that, in primitive agriculture, the cultural energy is small while the calorie gain in production is large, and 16 calories of digestible energy are harvested for each calorie of cultural energy as for example in primitive rice production in the Philippines. In the modern agricultural system of the USA, supplementation of human labour by fossil fuels has resulted in increased calorie yield as compared with primitive agricultural systems, but the calorie gain decreased from 15 to 5 because of inefficiency in energy use. Cultural inputs of different cropping systems considered by Heichel are shown in Table 14. A similar study was carried out in the United Kingdom by Baxter (1974) in which he showed that the input/output ratio of energy in potato production is 0.87, which

TABLE 14. Relative contributions of cultural inputs to total cultural energy in several cropping systems

Cropping System	Labor	Fuel	Cultural Input (% of Total Cultural Energy)				
			Ferti- lizer	Pesti- cides	Pro- cessing	Depre- ciation	Other
Corn grain (Iowa, 1915)	20	--	--	--	--	67	13
Corn grain (Pennsylvania, 1915)	18	--	--	--	--	73	9
Corn grain (Illinois, 1969)	0.06	47	19	4	--	21	9
Corn silage (Iowa, 1915)	12	12	--	--	--	69	7
Corn silage (Iowa, 1969)	0.09	52	10	4	--	27	7
Rice (Philippines, 1970) approx.	100	--	--	--	--	--	--
Rice (Louisiana, 1970)	0.05	41	5	5	--	33	16
Sorghum (Kansas, 1970)	0.06	37	16	2	--	37	8
Soybeans (Missouri, 1970)	0.08	56	0.05	7	--	25	11
Oats (Minnesota, 1970)	0.06	51	10	0.4	--	32	7
Alfalfa Hay (Missouri, 1970)	0.12	52	4	--	--	27	17
Peanuts (No. Carolina, 1970)	0.13	41	6	12	--	23	18
Sugarbeets (California, 1970)	0.05	29	6	6	33	7	19

Source: Heichel, 1974.

represents a very low gain in productivity (see Figure 3). In
primitive cropping systems the input/output ratio is very likely not to be so close to unity since, although the output may
be lower, the input/output ratio is likely to be less than 0.5.

SUMMARY AND CONCLUSIONS
     The importance of plants as the source of food for man and
animals and the basis of life on earth and civilization is
emphasized. The current practices in use or of potential
value in the various methods of increasing and sustaining crop
plant productivity for meeting the ever increasing demand for
food by the world's rapidly increasing population have been reviewed here. It is observed that all the practices current and
potential have ecological implications related to the interaction of man and various factors in the physical, biological,
and socio-economic environments that have to be manipulated or
controlled in various degrees in order to achieve increased
productivity. Consequently a systems approach should be
adopted in the planning, research, production and consideration
of policies related to increased agricultural production.
     It is noted that food production technology of the devel-
oped countries has increasingly involved complete mechanization
based on machines powered mainly by fossil fuels and chemicals,
all of which require much more energy than the whole world can
afford or efficiently utilize as a result of the limited resources involved. Food production in the modern agriculture
of the developed countries has become specialized on just a few
commodities and so commercialized that the scale of operations
and resource endowments on which they are based are beyond the
means of millions of small, partially commercial and partially
subsistence farmers in the developing countries to adopt and
operate.
     Certain production inputs such as fertilizers are impera-
tive in increasing and sustaining yields, but ways should be
found for reducing the energy involved and quantities of fertilizers used by making maximum use of such processes as biological nitrogen fixation. Mycorrhizal phosphate nutrition and
waste recycling techniques constitute efficient utilization and
management of natural resources. Similarly, the use of pesticides may be necessary in fighting the various organisms that
rob man of his food and various products, but integrated pest
management or plant protection is the most effective and safe
method of controlling diseases and pests.
     In all crop production practices, relatively low cost,
appropriate technologies should be developed for small farmers
that minimize the use of costly inputs that are only profitable
for the scales of operation far beyond his resource endowments
or are ecologically detrimental and socially and culturally unacceptable.

Finally, it should always be borne in mind that 1), improved agricultural technology can best function as integral components of improved rural development programs, and 2), all efforts devoted to increase food production should be based on the philosophy that we are mainly buying time until various other measures such as education and general improvement of the welfare of the world's rural majority can facilitate integrated approaches to the solution of the population and food supply problem. All available resources of all governments and private bodies should be directed towards this end, at least to the extent that they are compatible policies aimed at improving the lot of the generality of mankind.

REFERENCES

Although a number of references were cited in this paper, reference list was lost in the international mails.

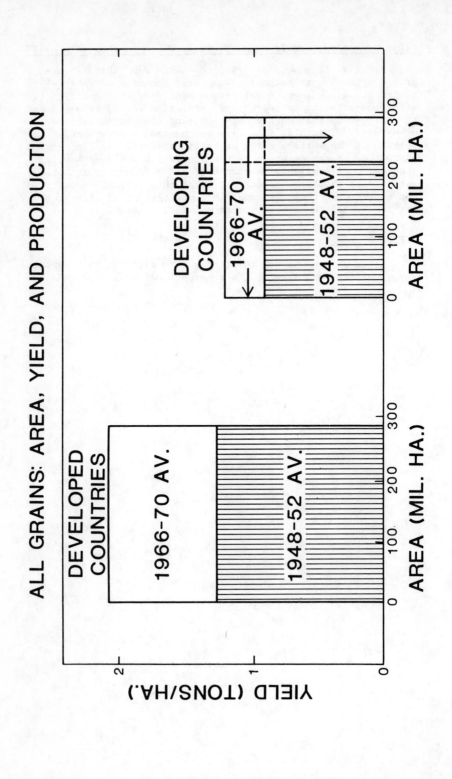

ALL GRAINS: AREA, YIELD, AND PRODUCTION

FIG. 1. In this chart the area of each rectangle, determined as the product of the amount of land in grains (in million ha or the horizontal axis) times yield per ha (in kg on the vertical scale), represents the total production of grains in million tons for an indicated group of countries at a specified time. All four rectangles may be compared in height, in width, and in area.

1. Developed countries in 1966-70 accounted for:

   a. 50 percent of area in grains
   b. 65 percent of world grain production
   c. 61 percent of the increase in grain production over the 1948-52 average
   d. None of the increase in world grain area

2. From 1948-52 to 1966-70 the LDCs:

   a. Increased grain area 35 percent, reaching nearly 300 million ha, thereby catching up with area in developed countries, which made no gain over this period.
   b. Increased grain yields 32 percent, to 1.2 tons per ha nearly equal to developed countries' 1948-52 yields which increased 63 percent by 1966-70.
   c. Increased grain production 78 percent to 356 million tons, nearly equal to the developed countries' 1948-52 production, which increased 64 percent by 1966-70.

   The increase in production in the developing countries was 156 million tons:

   45 percent from increased area
   41 percent from increased yields
   14 percent from combined effect of increased area and yields.

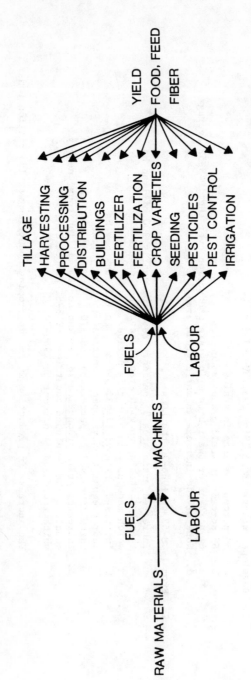

FIG. 2. Flow of energy from fuels and labour during the manufacture, distribution, and culture of food, fibre, and feed (Heichel, 1974).

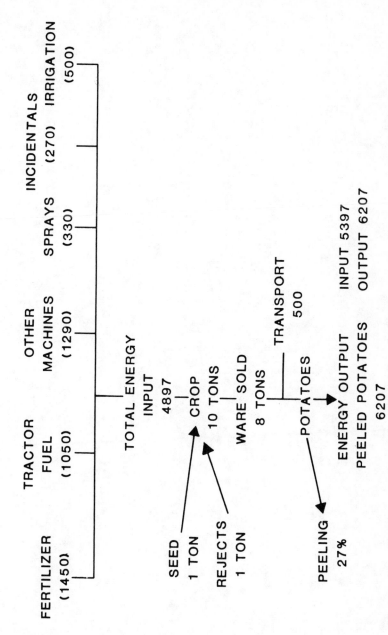

FIG. 3. Input - output energy relationships in potato production in the United Kingdom.

K. EL-SHAZLY

M. A. NAGA

Animal Technology in the World Today

In order to assess the present situation of animal production we must answer questions relative to the following:

1. The pattern of human growth in the developed and developing countries.
2. The past and present production of meat, milk, eggs and wool.
3. The per caput increase in animal production.

Figure 1 projects the increase of human population of the world from 1950 to the year 2000. It shows that while there was very little increase in population in developed countries (0.9 percent) most of the increase was due to developing countries (2.7 percent).

ANIMAL PRODUCTION

Table 1 gives the number of animals and their production in developed, developing and centrally planned economy countries. It reveals the vast difference in efficiency of production between animals in developing nations and those in developed and centrally planned economies.

Although the number of animals in developed countries is approximately one-third of those in developing countries the production is more than double in the former countries. This

---

K. El-Shazly is Deputy Minister, Ministry of Agriculture, Cairo, Egypt.

M. A. Naga is Associate Professor Animal Nutrition, University of Alexandria, Alexandria, Egypt.

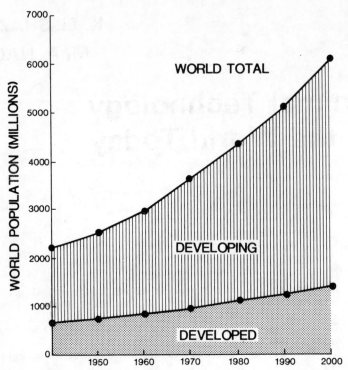

FIG. 1. World population growth.

TABLE 1. Number of animals and production[a]

	Developed countries	Developing countries	Centrally planned countries
Cattle	285,189	660,658	202,588
Buffalo	1	507	551
Sheep	351,329	432,348	258,396
Goats	15,863	307,181	70,814
Pigs	174,305	110,137	366,104
Chickens	1,618,783	1,690,655	2,335,629
Ducks	11,122	78,931	49,197
Other	15,240	74,447	35,070
Meat	53.33	20.05	36.73
Milk	207.96	78.73	130.26
Eggs	11.29	3.38	7.94
Wool	1.41	0.57	0.61

Source: Statistics Division FAO Rome (1973).
[a]Animal numbers in thousands; production in million tons.

is due to a variety of factors: disease and parasite, low
feeding standards, bad management and inferior genetic constitution. This can be clearly demonstrated (Table 2) when production (total and per caput) of meat, milk, eggs and wool is
compared for the years 1948 to 1952 and 1968 to 1972. Although
production per caput has increased to a greater rate in centrally planned countries, the actual production is much below
that in the developed countries.

There was virtually no increase in animal production per
caput in the developing countries over the last 20 years. The
production of animal protein (kg per animal unit) in 1970
shows that in Europe, North America and USSR it was 62.5, 50.0
and 44.2 kg respectively and much below the world average of
22.3 kg in the rest of the world (FAO Production Yearbook,
1972).

Using the value of minimum animal protein requirements, 29
grams per head per day, (Energy and protein requirement, Report
of a joint FAO/WHO AdHOc expert Committee 1973.), and the population in 1970 projected to 1990 we can calculate the total
human population requirements per year, assuming a carcass protein content of 17 percent (Table 3). The world meat and milk
production can in theory cover the minimum requirements up to
1990 even when other sources of animal protein e.g. fish and
eggs are discounted. In theory, it can thus be shown that the
world does not suffer as much from inadequate animal protein
production as from bad distribution depending on affluence of
the societies.

The widening gap in production between developed and
developing countries is the result of applying modern techniques in nutrition, management and breeding to animals in the
developed societies.

NUTRITION

The experiment reported by Phillips (1951) which took
place in New Zealand over 25 years ago showed that 57 percent of the improvement of animal production took place
as the result of improved nutrition while the rest of the
improvement was due to methods of breeding (culling, selection
and grading). We are not aware of similar evaluation in other
parts of the world. It would be interesting to analyze data
in different developed countries in a similar manner.

The early years of this century witnessed the important
discoveries of the vitamins, their chemical composition and
their physiological functions. Studies showed that most members of the B group acted as coenzymes for a number of important enzymes. Among the most recent discoveries is the
involvement of folic acid in the transfer of the methyl groups
from formic acid to glycine to form serine; and to the nucleo-
tide uridine to form thymidine in the synthesis of DNA; and the

TABLE 2. Increase in total and per caput animal products, 1948-52 to 1968-72

	Meat		Milk		Eggs		Greasy wool	
	1948-52	1968-72	1948-52	1968-72	1948-52	1968-72	1948-52	1968-72
Developed market								
Production Total (000 M.T.)	23,953	48,901	145,516	197,461	6,384	11,150	1,099	1,585
		204%		136%		175%		144%
Per caput (kgs)	41.7	67.4	253.5	272.0	11.1	15.4	109	202
		161%		108%		139%		116%
Developing market								
Production Total (000 M.T.)	10,618	18,050	45,635	75,366	1,212	3,026	487	571
		170%		165%		250%		117%
Per caput (kgs)	9.9	10.4	42.5	43.4	1.1	1.7	0.5	0.3
		105%		102%		154%		60%
Centrally planned								
Production Total (000 M.T.)	11,795	32,368	54,420	119,615	2,590	6,930	263	585
		274%		220%		268%		222%
Per caput (kgs)	13.9	28.0	64.0	103.4	8.0	6.0	0.3	0.5
		202%		162%		100%		167%

Source: FAO.

TABLE 3. Meat and milk supplying minimum animal protein
requirements for the world population in 1970, 1985
and 1990

	1970	1985	1990
Minimum animal protein requirements (thousand tons/day)	105	142	154
Projected world meat consumption (million tons)	107	168	197
Protein consumption from meat/day (thousand tons/day)	58	92	108
Projected world milk	389	532	597
Protein consumption from milk/day (thousand tons/day)	37	51	57
Protein consumption from meat and milk/day (thousand tons/day)	95	143	165

Source: FAO.

important role of cobalamine in methionine formation. The
requirement for vitamins has been well established and it has
been shown that requirements for growth and production are
greater than those for maintenance (Mitchell, 1962).

It has been stated for a long time that ruminants have no
need for the B group vitamins. However, vitamin B_1 deficiency
was induced within 4 days in lambs fed a high, easily ferment-
able diet (Lusby and Brent, 1972). Thiamin and the other B
group vitamins were helpful in curing the so-called molasses
toxicity in the Cuban animals (Geerken and Figueroa, 1971;
Losada et al., 1971) and in preventing the cerebrocortical
necrosis in Merino sheep fed a purified protein-free diet (Naga
et al., 1975). Crampton (1964) pointed out the importance of
expressing animal requirements in relation to their energy
intake. Perhaps in the case of ruminants and due to the intermediate role played by rumen microflora their requirements
should be related to the type of energy source. Urea fed animals synthesize less nictotinic acid in their rumen (Buziassy
and Tribe, 1960) and lose it at a higher rate than animals on
completely conventional diets (Prior et al., 1970).

The same era has witnessed the importance of macro and
micro elements for the well being of animals and their involvement in many enzymic reactions as well as their indispensabil-
ity for production and reproduction. Many of the antagonistic
and synergistic characteristics of minerals have been well
illustrated (Mitchell, 1962). Chelating compounds have been
used in the control of mineral toxicity and for the transfer
of certain elements to some specific tissues where they are
released to some natural compounds in the tissues having a
higher binding capacity than the chelating compound.

RUMEN DIGESTION AND PHYSIOLOGY
The second half of this century witnessed a concentration
of research work on rumen microbiology and physiology. It
recognized the important function of rumen microorganisms
to which animal feeds are first exposed and which undergo a
series of changes before they pass out of the rumen and down
the alimentary tract. The highlights of development in the
field of rumen digestion and physiology which resulted in major
changes in the concepts of feeding ruminants may be summarized
in the following:

Fermentation Patterns of Carbohydrates
Fermentation patterns of carbohydrates have been well
established resulting in the formation of volatile fatty
acids which are end products consisting mainly of acetic, propionic and butyric acids together with much lower concentrations of higher analogues. When cellulose and fibrous constituents form the major part of the carbohydrate feeds, acetic
acid is predominant. The proportion of acids formed are in the
range of 62 percent acetic, 22 percent propionic and 16 percent
butyric. These amounts essentially coincide with the stoichiometry for hexose fermentation suggested by Hungate (1966).
This type of ration (high roughage-low concentrate feed) stimulates the formation of acetic acid inducing higher milk production. It has been well illustrated that 40 percent of milk
fats are formed from acetic acid.
A propionic acid fermentation pattern resulting from a
high grain-low roughage diet stimulates better growth and body
fat formation and is therefore a useful technique for fattening
animals. However, the fermentation pattern and the rate at
which rumen digesta flows out were found to be closely related.
On the same diet a change from high propionic acid-low butyric
acid patterns to the opposite was noted when the ruminal rate
of outflow has spontaneously turned lower (Ishaque et al.,
1971). Contrarily, an induced higher ruminal dilution rate
(using polyethylene glycol) resulted in less propionic acid
molar proportion ratio in the rumen (Harrison et al., 1975).
It was found in our laboratory that propionic acid molar proportion increases by the increase of rumen dilution rate up to
about 5.5 percent per hour. Higher rates than that per hour
resulted in a reduction in the propionic acid molar proportion
ratio. Preston (1972) interpreted the effect of rate of outflow on the fermentation pattern as a factor for the production of propionic acid. Hence, better microbial protein synthesis results until outflow increases to the extent that it
causes a loss of carbohydrates from the rumen without complete
fermentation which does not favour microbial synthesis.
High concentrate rations rich in proteins induce higher
production of acetic acid, butric acid and higher analogues.
Branched chain volatile fatty acid (VFA), i.e. isobutyric, iso-

valeric and methylbutyric acids were found in larger concentrations when a high concentration of protein (cassein) was fed to
the animals (El-Shazly, 1952). These acids were found to be
essential requirements for cellulose degradation by cellduloly-
tic organisms. The branched chain VFA could also be formed
from carbohydrate fermentation through synthetic pathways.
However, this occurs to a much lower extent which indicates the
importance of proteins or certain amino acids for best utilization of cellulose.

VFA are absorbed through the reticulo-rumen wall and in
omasum (Gray, 1947). Very little of the VFA produced in the
rumen reach the abomasum (Badawy et al., 1958). Absorbed VFA
represent from 50 to 70 percent of the energy requirements of
the ruminants (Carroll and Hungate, 1954).

Gas Production

In the process of fermentation, carbon dioxide and methane
are also formed. The stoichiometry for hexose fermentation (Hungate, 1966) calls for the formation of a constant
quantity of methane for each molecule of hexose fermented:

$$52 \text{ Hexose} + 9 \text{ H}_2\text{O} \text{ --------- } 68 \text{ H Ac} + 18 \text{ H Prop} + 9 \text{ H But} + 21.5 \text{ CH}_4 + 64.5 \text{ CO}_2$$

Hungate (1966) also reported that most of the methane
evolving with expired gas is entirely due to rumen fermentation. A negligible fraction of rumen methane escapes to other
parts of the digestive tract. Murray et al. (1975) estimated
the methane gas collected with respiration in sheep from which
they could calculate the degree of carbohydrate fermentation in
the rumen. The loss of methane results also in a loss of
energy. Suppressing methane production, through the use of
long chain unsaturated fatty acids has therefore, caused better
utilization of energy.

Nitrogen Utilization

Results of a long and persistent research work in the
field of nitrogen utilization by ruminants have indicated
that an economic approach to ruminant feeding should be based
on maximum use of non-protein nitrogen (NPN) in the most efficient way and as little as possible of a protein which is least
degradable in the rumen and whose amino acid composition should
be complementary to the amino acids of microbial proteins. For
best utilization of NPN a readily available source of carbohydrates must be used. The use of grains as corn or barley has
been well documented. Another source of carbohydrates tested
for best utilization of urea nitrogen is molasses. The feeding
of liquid molasses and urea has been well tested (Preston and
Willis, 1970). The protein quality included in the feed is of

greatest importance (Clark et al., 1972a). Fish meal was shown
to be one of the best proteins which could be used with a
molasses--urea liquid feed. Increased maize supplementation
(up to 25 percent) was shown to improve milk yield significantly (Clark et al., 1972b).

In a recent in vitro experiment (Nour et al., 1976 unpublished) it was shown that pure starch and molasses gave best
microbial protein synthesis from urea when administered at a
maintenance level. Maize, barley and rice bran were less
effective.

Heat processing of cereals increases starch susceptibility
to α amylase and improves urea utilization when both were found
in the same medium with rumen microorganisms. When starches
are extracted, rates of ammonia utilization are increased and
reach maximum when amylolysis reaches 70 to 75 percent (Durand
et al., 1976).

Decreasing solubility of proteins in the rumen fluid and
causing them to become less degradable is another aim for best
utilization of nitrogenous compounds by the ruminant animals.
Heat, formaldehyde and tannin treatment of protein makes it
less soluble in the rumen fluid. The protein, therefore,
escapes degradation and is better utilized. Higher yields of
wool were obtained through the feeding of formalized proteins
(Chalupa and Chandler, 1972). A promising advancement in this
area is the preservation of silage with formic-formalin mixtures (Valentine and Brown, 1973). The treatment of lucerne
with 0.9 percent formaldehyde plus 0.5 percent formic acid
increased intake, digestibility and subsequent wool production
by sheep. Alfalfa-brome grass mixtures ensiled with a formaldehyde formic acid mixture gave slightly higher yields of milk
than wilted grass when fed to lactating Holstein cows (Barker
et al., 1973).

Rice gluten meal, a product of the starch industry, has a
biological value of approximately one reflecting its low solubility in the rumen liquor (Dief et al., 1968) and is a useful
tool for the physiological estimation of endogenous urinary
nitrogen in sheep. Moreover, its inclusion in the diets contributes towards the reduction of rumen ammonia concentration,
which is suitable for microbial protein synthesis in the rumen
and more economical for the nitrogen metabolism in the animal.
Setter and Roffler (1976) pointed out that any increase in
ammonia concentration over 5 mg NH_3-N per 100 ml rumen content
has little effect on the utilization of urea by rumen microorganisms.

The amino acids available for absorption from the alimentary tract are supplied by endogenous secretion, microbial protein synthesized in the rumen and feed proteins which escape
rumen degradation. The first of these should be more or less
constant under normal physiological conditions while it is pos-

sible to manipulate the other two sources. The direct measurement of essential amino acid requirements is possible through
the introduction of different levels of individual amino acids
using a duodenal canula or by introducing protected amino acids
through the rumen and estimating the free amino acid profile in
the blood and/or nitrogen retention (Chalupa, 1974). Methionine, protected from degradation in the rumen, was shown to
have a positive effect on increased wool production. Its
effect or the effect of its hydroxy analogue on milk production
were not conclusive (Chalupa and Chandler, 1972). Other amino
acids, e.g., lysine and threonine may also be effective in
increasing milk and meat production.

    An interesting method for by-passing the rumen degradation
of certain nutrients, i.e., amino acids and proteins is the
physiological conditioning of the animal by continuing bottle
feeding under specified conditions after weaning (Ørskov et al.,
1970; Brown, 1974).

    Lysine and methionine may be limiting at times (Chalupa
and Chandler, 1972; Fahmy, 1975). In our experience there are
two known cases in which the ration characteristics (other than
its protein content) contribute to the magnification of lysine
deficiency. The first case is the inclusion of cottonseed cake
in the diet. The gossypol content of cottonseed cake was
reported to be detoxified in the rumen by its incorporation
with lysine in an insoluble unabsorbable compound (Reiser and
Fu, 1962). The second case occurs on feeding regimes which
result in reduction of protozoal population density in the
rumen. Protozoa is richer than bacteria in lysine (Chalupa,
1972). By the increase of the urea concentration in the diet,
Fahmy (1975) observed a decreased blood lysine content in
sheep.

    Attention should be drawn to the need of surveying the
antitrypsin activity present in some animal feeds. It was
found that some components of the milk replacer diets which has
been long in use for this purpose contained antitrypsin activity which reached up to 23 percent (Mesbah, 1976, unpublished).
Cooking or micronization of these diets before their use
destroys the antitrypsin activity.

Energy Utilization
    Another important characteristic of the ruminant is its
    ability to digest cellulose and hemicellulose to a much
greater extent than monogastric animals. In doing so, they are
again noncompetitive with man for their energy needs.

    In a world threatened by the spread of famine, the major
source of energy in ruminant feeds should originate from roughage (feeds with a high fibre content) and from concentrate
by-products which are not consumed by man. Trends in research

and development therefore should be increasingly directed
towards the production of plants with highest photosynthetic
ability.

Unicellular algae. This group of unicellular plants (e.g.
Chlorella, Scenedismus and Spirillina) has the highest photosynthetic efficiency. Theoretically, they can produce dry matter several times more than any field crop per unit area. However, the cost of production and the digestibility of the product are limiting factors for their widespread utilization.
Suspensions of Chlorella fed to 6-month-old calves have been
shown to increase rumen digestion and improve nitrogen metabolism (Sal'Nikova and Khabibulliri, 1972). At least a part of
this effect was due to the minerals.

Hydroponic feedlot. In a system of agriculture with
cereal seeds planted in trays maintained at optimum temperature, humidity, aeration, light and periodic addition of nutrient solution, sprouts could grow 7 to 8 inches within one week.
An extrapolated production of 100 tons per acre per day of the
hydroponic feed (i.e. the green part, roots and seed husks)
could be produced and the effect of feeding this material to
dairy cattle and fattening steers has been found to be beneficial to production and digestibility (Judd and Mathews, 1974).

Forage plants. The potential for livestock development is
primarily dependent on forage production. Unfortunately not
much progress is being made in improving forage production in
most developing countries. The offtake of cattle in most parts
of Africa has been estimated to vary between 5 to 12 percent as
compared to 20 to 28 percent for Europe and North America
(Topps, 1971). According to Hutton (1974) a system for fattening beef on forages has been successfully undertaken in the
northern parts of Australia. It involves the use of legume
plants resistant to drought, which when well fertilized with
superphosphates, have made fattening on pasture a profitable
business. Rees et al. (1974) found that Pangola grass, fertilized with sulphur, led to large increases in voluntary
intake and digestibility by sheep (from 44.4 to 64.1 g/kgW
0.75/day and from 55.2 to 60.2 percent dry matter digestibility, respectively).

It is well known that roughage is very important for milk
production as it induces an acetic acid type of fermentation in
the rumen. This is beneficial for milk fat synthesis and hence
promotes milk production. A high percentage of concentrate
feeding favours higher rates of production of proionic acid in
the rumen and decreases milk fat slightly. Storry et al.
(1974) obtained responses in rumen fermentation causing higher
acetate production and increased milk fat secretion in cows

receiving a low roughage ration supplemented with 2 kg of protected tallow.

The choice of forages for animal production should be
based on their yields of total digestible nutrients (TDN) per
unit area. Napier grass, guinea grass and sugar cane have the
highest yields.

The feeding of whole sugar cane. Two alternative methods
have been used for the feeding of the whole sugar cane plant:

1. Derinded cane, using a special machine to produce a
product called "Comfith". The Comfith is ground and mixed with
cane tops to make 80 percent of a ration for fattening beef
steers or 50 percent of a ration for milking cows (Donefer,
1973).

2. Chaffed sugar cane (whole plant including tops), using
a much cheaper machine. This was reported by Preston (1974) to
give results similar to comfith-cane tops when fed to fattening
animals. A ration containing 20 kg chaffed sugar cane including tops supplemented with meat and bone meat, coconut meal, and
and urea maintained an average daily milk yield of 5 kg for 300
days showing a net income of 13.6 percent on capital. One acre
of sugar cane can support up to 5 large head of cattle. Jerez
and Preston (1972) substituted maize in dairy cattle feed at
rates of 0, 19, 37 and 57 percent of sugar cane, the rest of
the diet being rice husks and Torula yeast, and obtained a significantly greater yield of milk at the 37 percent replacement
level.

EFFICIENT UTILIZATION OF BY-PRODUCTS FROM THE AGRO-INDUSTRY

Agricultural By-products

There are millions of tons of agricultural by-products,
e.g. straws (wheat, barley, rice, etc.), corn stover, corn
cobs, cottonseed hulls, cotton stalks, etc. and industrial by-
products, bagasse, molasses from the sugar industry, fruit and
vegetable wastes from canning and dehydrating industries.
These are either wasted or inefficiently utilized every year.
The nutritive values of most of these by-products have been
studied separately or in combination with other feeds.

Methods have been developed for the treatment of poor
quality roughages in order to improve their nutritive value.
Gall (1974) reviewed these methods which include chemical,
physical and microbiological techniques. Of special interest
is the steam treatment of hard wood (Bender et al., 1970) to
improve its digestibility and feed intake by sheep. The method
was recently applied to cottonwood which was ground and steamed

at 30 pounds per square inch for 48 hours to give a product
with 34 percent higher digestibility than the 24 hour steamed
product. Treatment with steam at 100 pounds per square inch at
170°C produced the greatest digestibility (Akhtar and Walters,
1974).

Fruit By-products

An interesting fruit by-product is date pits. Work carried out at the University of Alexandria, Egypt, showed
that date pits have a TDN value of 67.3 percent and a crude
protein value of 6 percent which is however, indigestible. The
crude fat content is of the order of 8 percent and it is highly
digestible (91 percent) (El-Shazly et al., 1963). The roasting
of the seed, to make it easier to grind, resulted in a great
loss in nutritive value (38 percent TDN). Feeding ground date
seeds to replace rice bran to milking cows and buffaloes showed
insignificant differences in fat corrected milk yields (El
Shazly, unpublished results).

Other By-products

Other by-products tested for their nutritive value in
Egypt are wastes from dehydrating onions, citrus wastes
and artichoke leaves (Mohamed et al., 1971). A comprehensive
study of the food industries' wastes was made by Benbera and
Kramer (1968). They listed some of the losses related to vegetable and fruit crop processing (16 vegetables and 10 fruit
crops) identifying waste ranging from 3 to 85 percent by weight
of the original plants. Taking 20 percent as a moderate estimate of TDN, a sum of approximately 30 million tons TDN per
year could be calculated to give 10 million tons of liveweight
gain from beef.

Animal Excreta

Research in recent years has included work on the possible
use of poultry, cattle and pig manure as a source of
energy and protein. At the same time it would dispose of one
of the environmental pollutants. Three methods have been used
to deal with the processing of manure.

Drying. Drying cattle excrete can be a costly operation.
A recent report by Miller (1974) gives the results of an experiment with cattle fed on a diet containing 45 percent dried
poultry litter for 233 days and showing average daily liveweight gains of 0.6 to 0.76 kg. Muller proposes a system
whereby 45,000 broilers per year produced on deep-litter, could
feed 15 dairy cows with expected milk production of 3,500

litres, and 25 followers with 70 to 80 percent of their crude
protein and 30 to 40 percent of their TDN coming from deep litter. Smith (1974) reviewed the use of feeding dried pelleted
poultry manure. Properly dehydrated poultry excreta has 30 to
45 percent crude protein and is a source of energy. As the
only source of supplemental nitrogen it maintained milk production at 28 kg per day. Daily gains of 0.91 kg were obtained on
a beef ration supplemented with poultry excreta.

    Aerobic processing. A method of aerobic processing of
swine and cattle manure has been developed at the University of
Illinois (Day and Harmon, 1974). The method utilizes an oxi-
dation-ditch mixed liquor as a source of water to supply 30 to
46 percent crude protein for pigs. The cost of specially prepared oxidation ditches may be prohibitive for widespread use
of the technique. Savings in nutrient supply do not justify
the cost of recycling. However, if waste disposal costs are
taken into account, the economics look more favourable.

    Ensiling. Ensiling of cattle wastes by mixing with other
feeds, e.g. 57 parts cattle manure plus 43 parts ground hay,
has been studied. A ration containing 40 percent cattle wastes
and corn grain produced a higher rate of gain and feed efficiency than conventional rations. Fontenot and Webb (1974)
reviewed the value of animal wastes as feeds for ruminants and
concluded that the feeding of wastes does not adversely affect
the taste of meat or milk.

Feasibility of Utilizing Wastes
    We have only briefly mentioned some of the by-products
    that could be used as animal feeds. There are many more
important products, which differ according to the locality and
conditions. They could be utilized with advantage in animal
feeding but would require processing and industrialization for
efficient utilization.
    In some cases the treatment or processing of waste mate-
rials is costly for economic utilization. We, therefore,
believe that agro-industrial complexes utilizing available
industrial and agricultural products in an area of the country
could make processing of unconventional feeds more economically
feasible. A simple illustration of one such complex is given
in Figure 2. This is based on the treatment of poor quality
roughages but utilizes the existence of a sugar extracting factory within an agricultural area producing sugar cane, as well
as other crops (e.g. grains and cotton). In this case, straws,
stover cottonstalk and bagasse could all be treated with steam
and processed into feeds useful for milk and beef production.
Utilizing animal by-products from slaughterhouses and recy-

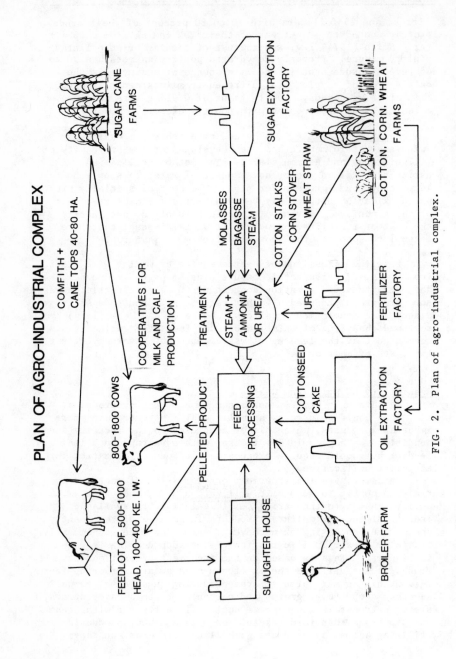

PLAN OF AGRO-INDUSTRIAL COMPLEX

FIG. 2. Plan of agro-industrial complex.

cling of animal wastes could also be included in the system.

A system for producing rumen microbial protein of high biological value which could be included in the complex has been proposed (Zaki El-Din and El Shazly, 1969). The net growth of rumen microorganisms in vitro, given ideal conditions, was shown to be five times higher than in vivo during one hour of incubation. Fermentation products, e.g. methane, could be used to heat the system and make it anaerobic, while acetic, propionic and butyric acids could be removed with good yields for the industry. Two feed products could be obtained, a single cell protein with high biological value and a high lysine content, and a fibrous meal which could be processed with other feeds for ruminants.

Anabolic Agents

Improvement in the efficiency of feed utilization through breeding and nutrition provides an important contribution to animal production in developed countries and much less so in developing countries.

The rate of protein synthesis is unquestionably the basis of production efficiency and animal health. In developing countries where there is a great potential for improvement of production efficiency through breeding and improved husbandry and nutrition, relatively quick alterations in genetical constitution could be made by importation of good genes from advanced countries through artificial insemination (Valcani, 1963) and ovum transplantation (Rowson, 1972). A selection plateau has in many cases been reached for animals in developed countries. Recent techniques have been applied to stimulate more variation in selection, e.g. the effect of stress on turkeys (Brown and Nestor, 1973).

On the other hand the use of hormone implants or oral administration has shown variable results. Effects as little as 5 percent (Blair et al., 1957) and as high as 28 percent (Hall et al., 1959) have been reported for diethyl stilbesterol (DES).

Jukes (1974) mentioned that DES usage will decrease consumers beef prices by 5 to 10 percent. A 10 percent increase in meat production (23 percent improvement in liveweight) means about 10 million tons increase. This is enough to feed about 150 to 300 million people based on levels of consumption of 190 or 95 grams per head per day respectively.

However, DES may have some adverse effects due to residues in the meat and it has been banned from many countries. It produces beneficial effects in castrated animals. Bulls may give similar growth rates as treated steers. Other anabolic agents have been examined which had no adverse effects and cause stimulation of growth in steers and bulls.

REFERENCES

Akjtar, M. A. and C. W. Walters. 1974. Feedstuffs 13:16.

Badawy, A. M., M. Campbell, D. P. Cuthberfson and W. S. Mackie. 1958. Journal of Nutrition 12:384.

Barker, R. A., D. N. Mowat, J. B. Stone, K. R. Stevenson and M. G. Freeman. 1973. Formic acid or formic acid-formalin as a silage additive. Canada Journal of Animal Science 53(3):465.

Ben-Gera, I. and A. Kramer. 1967. The utilization of food industries wastes. Advanced Food Research 17:77.

Bender, F., D. P. Heaney and A. Bowden. 1970. Potential of steamed wood as a feed for ruminants. Forest Products Journal 20(4):36.

Blair, J. W., E. S. Erwin and C. B. Roulicek. 1957. Proceeding American Society of Animal Production 8(19):14.

Brown, R. H. 1974. Calf preconditioning tests reported at Florida meeting. Feedstuffs, May 27, p. 20.

Brown, K. I. and K. E. Nestor. 1973. Some physiological responses of turkeys selected for high and low adrenal response to cold stress. Poultry Science 52:1948.

Buziassy, C. and D. E. Tribe. 1960. Australian Journal of Agriculture Research 11:989.

Carroll, E. J. and R. E. Hungate. 1954. The magnitude of the macrobial fermentation in the bovine rumen. Applied Microbiology 2:205.

Chalupa, W. 1972. Metabolic aspects of nonprotein nitrogen utilization in ruminant animals. Federation Proceedings 31:1152.

Chalupa, W. 1974. Pannel on Tracer Techniques in Studies on The Use of NPN in Ruminants, Vienna II., pp. 107.

Chalupa, W. and J. E. Chandler. 1972. Tracer Techniques on NPN for Ruminants, IEAE, Vienna, pp. 107.

Clark, J., T. R. Preston and A. Zamora. 1972a. Revista Cubana de Ciencia Agricola 6(1):19.

Clark, J., T. R. Preston and A. Zamora. 1972b. Revista Cubana de Ciencia Agricola 6(1):27.

Crampton, E. W. 1964. Nutrient-to-calorie ratios in applied nutrition. Journal of Nutrition 82:353.

Day, D. L. and B. G. Harmon. 1974. Conference of The Use of Waste Water in The Production of Food and Fiber, 6-8 March, Oklahoma City.

Dief, H. I., K. El-Shazly and A. R. Abou Akkada. 1968. The biological evaluation of urea, casein and gluten in the diets of sheep. British Journal of Nutrition 22:451.

Donefer, E. 1973. CIDA Seminar on Sugar Cane as Livestock Feed, Barbados.

Durant, M., A. Kumarresan, C. Dumay, L. Tassencourt, C. H. VanNevel, P. H. Beaumatin and L. Gueguen. 1976. Panel on Tracer Techniques on Studies the use of NPN in Ruminants, Alexandria, Egypt.

El-Shazly, K. 1952. Degradation of protein in the rumen of sheep. 1. Some volatile fatty acids, including branched-chain isomers, found in vivo. Biochemistry Journal 51:640.

El-Shazly, K., E. Ibrahim and H. A. Karam. 1963. Nutritional value of date seeds for sheep. Journal of Animal Science 22:894.

Fahmy, S. T. M. 1975. Some Metabolic Studies on Goats. Ph.D. Thesis, University of Alexandria, Egypt.

Fontenot, J. P. and K. E. Webb, Jr. 1974. The value of animal wastes on feeds for ruminants. Feedstuffs, April 8, p. 30.

Gall, F. C. 1974. Sixth Meeting of the Working Group on Dairy Industry Development, April 22-23.

Geerkeen, G. M. and V. Figueroa. 1971. Revista Cubana de Ciencia Agricola. (Eng. Ed.) 5:205.

Gray, F. V. 1947. The absorption of volatile fatty acids from the rumen. Journal of Experimental Biology 24:1.

Hall, W. H., W. S. Sherman, P. P. Appel, W. M. Reynold and H. G. Luther. 1959. The effect of low-level dielhylstilbestrol implantation, oxytetraycline and hydroxyzine on fattening lambs. Journal of Animal Science 18:710.

Harrison, D. G., E. E. Beever, D. J. Thomson and D. F. Osbourn. 1975. Manipulation of rumen fermentation in sheep by increasing the rate of flow of water from the rumen. Journal of Agricultural Science Cambridge 85:93.

Hungate, R. E. 1966. The Rumen and its Microbes. Academic Press, New York, London.

Hutton, E. M. 1974. Personal communication.

Ishaque, M. P. C. and J. A. Rook. Proceedings Nutrition Society 30:IA.

Jerez, I. and T. R. Preston. Revista Cubana de Giencia é Africola, 6(3):337.

Judd, B. Ira and J. Matthews. 1974. The hydroponic feedlot. Feedstuffs, May 6, p. 25.

Jukes, T. H. 1974. Residues in meat: Consumer regulations, producer problems. Feedstuffs, July 15, p. 26.

Losada, H., F. Dixon and T. R. Preston. 1971. Revista Cubana de Ciencia Agricola (Eng. Ed.). 5:369.

Lusby, K. S. and B. E. Brent. An experimental model for polioencephalomalacia. Journal of Animal Science 35:270.

Miller, Z. O. 1974. Pig and Poultry Research and Training Institute, Singapora, Final Report No13.SF/SIN,5, Nutrition Research 1074.

Mitchell, H. H. 1962. Comparative Nutrition of Man and Domestic Animals. Vol. 1, Academic Press, New York, London.

Mohamed, A. A., K. El-Shazly and A. R. Abou Akkada. 1971. The use of some agricultural by-products in feeding of farm animals. Alexandria Journal of Agricultural Research 19:25.

Murray, R. M., A. M. Bryant and R. A. Leng. 1975. In Tracer Techniques in Studies on the Use of NPN in Ruminants II, (Proceedings Pannel, Vienna, 1974). MEAE, p. 21.

Naga, M. A., J. Harmeyer, H. Holler and K. Schaller. 1975.
    Suspected "B" vitamin deficiency of sheep fed a protein-
    free urea containing purified diet. Journal Animal Science
    40(6):1192.
Ørskov, E. R., D. Benzie and R. N. B. Kay. 1970. The effects
    of feeding procedure on closure of the oesaphagese groove
    in young sheep. British Journal of Nutrition 24:785.
Phillips, R. W. 1951. Expansion of livestock production in
    relation to human need. Nutrition: Abstracts and Review
    21:250.
Preston, T. R. 1972. Pannel on Tracer Techniques in Studies
    on the Use of NPN in Ruminants, p. 1.
Preston, T. R. 1974. Milk and Beef Production from Sugar
    Cane in Seychelles SEY/73/002/Rep. 1.
Preston, T. R. and M. B. Willis. 1970. A new look at molasses
    for livestock feeding. Feedstuffs 42(13) March 28, 1970:
    20.
Prior, R. L., A. J. Clifford, D. E. Hague, and W. J. Visek.
    1970. Enzymes and metabolites of intermediary metabolism
    in urea-fed sheep. Journal of Nutrition 100:438.
Rees, M. C., D. I. Mirrson and F. W. Smith. 1974. The effect
    of supplementary and fertilizer sulphur on voluntary
    intake, digestibility, retention time in the rumen and site
    of digestion of pangola grass in sheep. Journal of Agri-
    cultural Science Cambridge 82:419.
Reiser, R. and H. C. Fu. 1962. The mechanism of gossypol-
    detoxification by ruminant animals. Journal of Nutrition
    76:215.
Rowson, L. E. A. 1972. International Sump. di Zootcchmic,
    Milano, April 15-17.
Sal'Nikova, M.'Y. and KH.KH. Khabilbulliri. 1972. Zhivotro
    Vodstro. 10:88.
Setter, L. D. and R. E. Roffler. 1976. Pannel in Tracer
    Techniques in Studies on the Use of NPN in Ruminants, III,
    Alexandria, Egypt.
Smith, L. W. 1974. Dehydrated poultry excreta as a crude pro-
    tein supplement for ruminants. World Animal Review 11:6.
Storry, J. E., P. E. Brumby, A. J. Hall and V. W. Johnson.
    1974. Responses in rumen fermentation and milk-fat secre-
    tion in cows receiving low-roughage diets supplemented
    with protected tallow. Journal of Research 41:165.
Topps, J. H. 1971. Ad Hoc Consultation on The Value of NPN
    for Ruminants Consuming Poor Herbages, Uganda, p. 35.
Valeani, R. 1963. World Conference on Animal Production, (2
    Publications) European Association for Animal Production,
    Rome.
Valentine, S. C. and D. C. Brown. 1973. Formaldehyde as a
    silage additive. II. The chemical composition and nutri-
    tive value of lucerne hay, lucerne silage and formaldehyde

and formic acid-treated lucerne silages. Australian Journal of Agricultural Research 24:939.

Zaki el-Din, M. and K. El-Shazly. 1969. Some factors affecting fermentation capacity and net growth of rumen microorganisms. Applied Microbiology 18:313.

ELIZABETH O'KELLY

Intermediate Technology as an Agent of Change

WHAT IS INTERMEDIATE TECHNOLOGY?

We hear a great deal about Intermediate Technology these days but there is still some confusion as to exactly what it means. Dr. E. F. Schumacher, who wrote "Small is Beautiful" may possibly have been the first person to use this term, since he introduced the concept into a report he wrote for the Indian Government as far back as 1963, and this was followed up, a year later, by a Seminar in Intermediate Technology--or Appropriate Technology as it is sometimes also called--at Hyderabad in India. Dr. Schumacher went on to found the Intermediate Technology Development Group in Britain in 1965, which is a registered charity devoted to furthering the aims of Intermediate Technology wherever this is practicable and especially in the developing countries. He is now widely recognised as one of the most distinguished exponents of the philosophy which lies behind the movement. It is not concerned solely with small technology, and I shall try briefly to show what this philosophy is and what it could do especially to help rural people.

To begin with, the term Intermediate Technology carries much wider connotations than Alternate Technology although this is often used as though it were synonomous with it. With the exception of the recent revival of interest in the use of water and wind power as alternative sources of energy to those we more often employ nowadays, Alternate Technology is usually

---

Elizabeth O'Kelly is Consultant in Intermediate Technology for Rural Development Programs in Developing Countries, 3 Cumberland Gardens, Lloyd Square, London W.C.1X 9 AF, England.

too sophisticated and too costly to be of much interest to the
countries with which Intermediate Technology is primarily concerned.   Schemes for nuclear energy, for advanced types of
solar energy and for geothermal power stations as well as for
photochemistry to replace the fossil fuels we are so rapidly
exhausting require considerable scientific knowledge and capital for development.   The aim of Intermediate Technology is
more practical.   It seeks to apply 20th century skills to discovering and developing technologies of a simple nature suited
to the actual conditions in the countries needing them with the
object of bringing about increased productivity of all kinds
whilst at the same time reducing unnecessary labour but not
employment.   Intermediate Technology aims to increase the supply of food and other necessities, to provide basic medical
care and improved school facilities and to encourage the establishment of cottage industries in the rural areas.

It should not be assumed from this, however, that the followers of Intermediate Technology are merely advocating a
return to nature and the simple life.   They are seeking to show
that Intermediate Technology, rightly applied, could act as a
bridge between the unrewarding and sometimes primitive technologies practised in many developing countries today and the more
advanced technologies of the West.   It must be emphasised, however, that in trying to narrow this gap between the two ways of
life, Intermediate Technology is not suggesting that the developing countries must be content with second best.   With the
benefit of hind sight, they now have the opportunity to avoid
many of the pitfalls into which we have been led such as our
overdependence on oil as a source of energy.   The more enlightened leaders of the developing countries have already come to
realise that the advanced technologies which we have pressed
upon them in the past are often too costly for their people.
The political climate is right for the introduction of simpler
schemes.   Large scale mechanisation in some cases has brought
as many ills as people thought it would cure.   I am told that
rusting tractors which the farmers can no longer afford to
use can now be seen in the fields of the Indian subcontinent.

The historical factors which led to the West being so
dependent upon machines of all kinds are not present in most
developing countries today.   Large scale agricultural mechanisation became necessary in Europe when, as a result of the
Industrial Revolution, large numbers of the rural population
left the land to work in the cities.   The consequence was that
those few who remained had to grow more food to feed these
towns people.   A similar situation arose in America and in
Australia and New Zealand when the great open spaces were colo-
nised by comparatively few people.   The situation in the developing countries today is quite different.   The need is to find
employment for the many who without it will go hungry.   It is
not backwardness which leads India and China to use many thou-

sands of workers on the building of a giant dam when bulldozers
could do this job far more quickly and efficiently. It is the
realisation that the money required to purchase and to operate
these machines is better spent on providing work for the people especially if there is a shortage of skilled mechanics able
to operate and maintain bulldozers.

Intermediate Technology also places great emphasis on
self-help programmes. Christian Aid, one of the largest chari-
ties in Britain concerned with overseas aid, recently exhibited
a poster which at first sight shocked by its apparent callous-
ness. It showed an obviously starving man holding a plate, and
underneath was the caption "Let the hungry feed themselves." A
second look revealed that packets of seeds and farming implements were laid upon the plate. The point was well made. We
do best to teach the people to help themselves. Ideas imposed
from above are seldom successful, and the response to village
improvement schemes is usually far better when these have orig-
inated from the villagers themselves.

In so far as it is possible, Intermediate Technology would
also advocate that the recipients of technical assistance
should make at least a token payment towards it. We are all
suspicious of something for nothing and suspect a catch in it
somewhere, as there often is. A way of achieving payment without too much hardship to the recipient is by arranging for
interest free loans with repayments spread out over as long a
period as possible. I operated such a scheme on a revolving
fund basis in West Africa where hand operated grinding mills
were obtained for more than 300 villages, and I never had a bad
debt. As the project advanced, many of the villages raised
all the money before they had even received their machines.
They were eager to have them, because they had seen from the
mills already installed the great advantages.

WHO NEEDS HELP?
If it is agreed that Intermediate Technology has something
to offer the developing countries, which countries are
they and what are their problems? The term "developing
countries" is merely a convenient way of referring collectively
to countries whose economic development is not yet equal to
that of the West. Culturally they have sometimes surpassed the
West. The term should not be equated with backwardness, nor
does it mean the same thing as another phrase often used--the
Third World. This latter phrase was coined originally to
describe those countries which were not aligned with either the
Eastern or the Western bloc and logically can include such
highly developed countries as Switzerland and Austria, both of
whom are politically neutral. Culturally, ethnically and lin-
guistically the countries of the developing world differ as
much from each other as do the countries of the West, and they

range in size from subcontinents like India with a population
of more than 531 million people to small island republics like
Haiti. Their one common factor is their need for an improved
standard of living especially for the rural people who form the
bulk of their population. Many developing countries are found
in the tropical zone, and the disastrous floods, earthquakes
and cyclones to which this region is subject are major causes
of their lack of development. Obviously they have little control over such disasters. When they are politically unstable,
as some of them undoubtedly are, the instability is often due
to the aftermath of a disaster. For example, Bangladesh broke
away from West Pakistan because of the discontent at the handling of the aid programme after the tragic cyclone in 1970
when the economy was devastated.

Attempts are often made to designate the developing countries by size, population, geographical situation, literacy
rate, and political structure, but the criterion most used is
their per capita income. In 1971, the UN produced a list of
the 25 least developed nations all of whom had a per capita
income of less than $100 a year. The figure for the United
States is $6,200 according to the World Bank. Of these coun-
tries, 16 are in Africa (Guinea, Mali, Upper Volta, Benin,
Niger, Chad, Somalia, Uganda, Rwanda, Tanzania, Burundi,
Ethiopia, Sudan, Malawi, Botswana and Lesotho); one is in the
Middle East (the Yemen Republic); five are in Asia (Afghanistan, Nepal, Sikkim, Bhutan, and Laos) and the remaining three
are islands (Western Samoa, The Maldive Islands and Haiti).
Apart from size (the Maldive Islands, for instance, would fit
into the Sudan 8,300 times and still leave room to spare),
there are certain characteristics which are common to them all
as well as to the remaining developing countries but to a lesser degree. Six families out of seven live from the land they
cultivate. They eat most of what they have grown to keep themselves alive; their land is marginal and subject to drought;
and their livestock is of poor quality. There can be little
doubt as to their need, although it can be argued that assessing their need by per capita income does not always give an
accurate picture of the situation. I have lived amongst families in both Africa and Asia who were existing quite happily on
a few pounds a year. They were able to grow all their own food
on their own land, build their houses from local materials and
exchange their surplus produce in the market for the few necessities they could not make for themselves. They had little
need for cash, although it must be admitted that this situation
will change. In fact it is changing as the West floods their
markets with consumer goods, encourages them to use proprietary
brands of baby milk instead of breast feeding their children
and opens up their countries to tourism with the wholehearted
support of their Governments.

The travellers of old were few in number, often stayed for

considerable time and sought to know the people amongst whom
they were living. The tourists of today, at the best, are
transient and at the worst demand a replica of the way of life
they have left behind them--with the possible exception of the
weather. They often fail to appreciate that the customs they
bring with them are as disturbing to the people they are visiting as the latters' often are to them. I believe that the
failure of many of our aid programmes often stems from the same
cause. We have too often sought to turn the people of the
developing countries into carbon copies of ourselves by imposing upon them the Western pattern of development. We have
failed to study their customs and cultures or to take into
account their religious and sexual taboos. In the often rigid
division of labour between the sexes, men wash the clothes in
many countries, something which we regard as women's work,
whilst the women carry the heavy loads, which we leave to men.
In many countries and especially in Asia, it is considered
improper for women to sit astride. Even in Europe until comparatively recently women rode side saddle when on horseback.
If, not knowing this, we design a pedal operated grinding mill
to relieve the women of the drudgery of grinding maize between
two stones, we will find that few of them will use it. The
followers of Intermediate Technology would therefore try to
improve existing patterns rather than superimpose new ones. It
may cost more to restore an old building than to pull it down
and build a new one, but the old building will blend far better
with the landscape.

One of the things we often fail to recognise is the extent
to which women are engaged in farming in the developing countries. The figures of 45 percent in Africa and 52 percent in
Asia have been quoted, and subsistence farming is almost
entirely in their hands, except where Islamic convention still
confines the woman to the house.

There is nothing wrong with this state of affairs. Back
in the Stone Age it was the women who dug for roots to feed
their families whilst their menfolk were away hunting. It was
the women who tanned the skins the men brought back and who
made the clay pots for cooking and for carrying water. I would
guess that it was the women who first thought of using fire to
cook food and that it was they who brought about the gradual
transition from a gathering community to an agricultural one by
cultivating the wild plants. This is the pattern still followed in the developing countries, but I recently read an
otherwise excellent book on tropical agriculture which failed
to mention the part women play. Yet their part is vital to
rural development programmes.

HOW INTERMEDIATE TECHNOLOGY CAN HELP

When considering ways in which Intermediate Technology

could assist the people of the developing countries, I
think most people would agree that help should be chiefly
in the field of rural development. Industrialisation has
ceased to be the panacea for all ills that it was once thought
to be, and Governments have come to realize that the emphasis
must be on increased agricultural production. The report of
the Select Committee on Overseas Development recently published
in Britain estimates that nearly 500 million people are now
verging on starvation because food prices have shot up and
stocks have fallen. Changes in the present agricultural pattern are urgent where there is presently low output, but I
would urge that we think carefully before we assume that large
scale mechanisation is the solution. Not only does mechanisation reduce employment, it is also impractical where farms are
less than four acres in extent and widely scattered. Such is
the case in many developing countries. A programme of land
redistribution might overcome this difficulty, but it is doubtful whether we now have the time for a very lengthy proceeding
which would be resisted fiercely by the land owners. Mechanisation is not always successful in tropical conditions as the
ground nut scheme in East Africa demonstrated. Organic matter
decomposes faster at higher temperatures than it does in temperate zones, and the soil loses many of its properties whilst
violent rainstorms wash away a large part of what remains. The
wrong use of tractors can greatly increase the soil erosion
since one of the essentials in using them is that the soil is
reasonably dry.

The most powerful argument against the indiscriminate use
of mechanisation on a large scale is that subsistence farming
is largely in the hands of the women and machines are men's
business. Mechanization means that the men will have to take
over from the women. Superficially, such a change might appear
to be beneficial to the women, in view of their very heavy
workload, but it would only be to their disadvantage because
they would lose the considerable status they enjoy as de facto
controllers of the land. If they sometimes seem reluctant to
cooperate in farming programmes, it is because they cannot
afford to experiment on their small acreage unless they can be
certain of success. The introduction of a new crop which fails
will mean that they and their families will starve. They cannot go out and buy food as we can. Nor can they afford to buy
the chemical fertilisers on which the success of the Green
Revolution is dependent, but this is not to say that they would
not use them if they could afford to do so. The women are seldom slow to adopt anything which they can see is to their
advantage, and they are much less conservative than the men.
Instead of attempting to change the whole social pattern, we
would do far better by introducing simple forms of mechanisation, which custom would allow women to use, and better hand
tools. We might also help women by making it easier for them

to gain admission to agricultural colleges and schools and by making the courses less academic and more practical. Few of the women have had the same educational opportunities as the men.

Even in those few countries where women do not play a very active part in the farming programme, food processing is almost entirely in their hands. Few of us in the West, who buy processed and packaged food realise how much time and energy goes into this heavy and monotonous task. Maize corn has to be shelled and is often then laboriously ground or pounded to make flour; millet and sorghum have to be threshed and winnowed; coconuts have to be cracked; palm nuts must be crushed to yield their oil; and padi has to be hulled, usually by pounding it in a mortar. Where the women are beginning to rebel against this type of drudgery, as they are in parts of Asia, they carry their padi to commercially operated mills and pay to have it hulled for them. Unfortunately, these power driven mills polish the rice too much, so that the vitamin content is decreased. The consequence is that malnutrition is on the increase, and the women do not realise why. There are simple hand operated machines already in use in countries like Japan which could polish rice with much less physical labour and more cheaply than the larger engine turned machines and mills. Mills worked by hand, water or wind power could still serve the developing countries admirably. These are all matters in which Intermediate Technology could both help the women and increase production. The acreage under cultivation in the Cameroons rose when the corn mills I have already mentioned took some of the back breaking labour out of grinding maize. Food storage is another problem which needs urgent attention. Fortunately, a number of organisations are attempting to do so. At present, as much as 50 percent of the hardly won harvest is lost to microorganisms, rodents and insects through poor storage techniques.

All attempts to raise agricultural production are likely to be unsuccessful, unless we can find ways and means of stopping the present drift of people to the towns. Sometimes they are in search of employment, sometimes in search of the amenities, especially the ready availability of water, which are still too often lacking in the rural areas. The water supply is something which lies well within the powers of Intermediate Technology to remedy. It costs very little to run water by gravity along an aqueduct or to dig wells. Pumps and hydraulic rams are other means of moving water and water catchment areas can increase the supply. These are projects that the villagers can often carry out for themselves, except perhaps in desert areas where more advanced technology may be necessary.

Medical facilities are all too often lacking in rural areas. Health auxiliaries could help to fill this gap, whilst programmes to teach better nutritional habits could help to prevent many tragic occurrences. For example, many thousand children go blind each year in India, Indonesia and South America because of a lack of vitamin A in their diet. Vitamin A is often present in plants growing in their backyards if their mothers only knew this.

Population control is now as vital as increased agricultural production. We need to understand that families may not want to have unnecessary mouths to feed, but they will go on having child after child until they have a sufficient number of sons to ensure a secure old age. This is especially true in those countries in the East which still practice ancestor worship, because only sons can carry out the necessary rituals. I sometimes think that our scientists would do best to concentrate on finding a means to ensure that the sex of a child can be determined at will. Then rural people would plan their families.

The development of cottage industries is a means of affording employment to rural people in their own villages. Many of them now spend the rainy season making such things as bags, mats and baskets, ropes and fishing nets out of bamboo, palm leaves, coir and rattan. Small hand operated machines could reduce the time they spend in the preparation of their materials and enable them to increase the production and income. Rural people also need help with the marketing of their products. The middleman makes most of the profit, although the Malaysian and Philippine Governments have set up organizations to sell direct which are proving most successful.

The purpose of this paper has been to explain the concept of Intermediate Technology and to show ways in which it could act as an agent of change.

I am conscious that I can be accused of having spent considerable time advocating that we should make no changes at all or that we should tread softly in attempting to do so. But what I have been trying to say is that we should try to avoid change for change's sake or because existing patterns do not conform with our own. I am not suggesting that we should put the clock back, but that we should think twice before we put it forward.

I am aware, too, that I have said very little about either the Pacific or South America because these are areas with which I am not familiar, and because in the space available it has not been possible to be too specific.

There are many people who could have put the case for Intermediate Technology more eloquently, but I have tried to put its principles into practice for more than twenty years in a number of developing countries, and I have found them to work. I hope that I have been able to convey my conviction that it is the women in the developing countries who will be the spear head of change. I may be biased, but I sincerely believe that women are the hope for the future and that anyone planning a rural development programme would be well-advised to base it on them. They will do anything to ensure that their children have a better life than they have had, and the techniques of Intermediate Technology can achieve a better life because they are geared to the needs and abilities of the rural poor.

I would like to end with an anecdote told by Idries Shah about one of the Sufi philosophers. They said to him "Your predecessor, who has just died in this village, taught us much and we are grateful to him. But he was here for thirty years and we fear that, as we have made only a little progress in that time, we may all be dead before you have completed your mission with us." Nahas, the philosopher answered. "You once hired a tiger to do your mousing. It is right to be grateful to him. But if you had had a cat, as it were, you would not have found it necessary to say what you have just said."

In planning our rural development programmes, we should try not to take a sledge hammer to crack a nut.

AMIR U. KHAN

Mechanization toward Self-Sufficiency in Food

Agriculture is the main occupation in most developing countries, yet many countries find it difficult to grow sufficient food for their populations. Potential to increase the arable land is rather limited in the developing countries. Increasing the effective cropped area by intensifying agriculture can increase food production, but this will require greater inputs of labor and power. In this context, mechanization of tropical agriculture is receiving renewed interest along a new direction.

In the late '50s, a lack of agricultural technology was felt to be a major constraint to increasing food production in the developing nations. This led to the establishment of the international research centers of which the International Rice Research Institute (IRRI) was the first. Much of the early work at these centers was directed toward generating new agricultural technology for higher yields. In 1966, IRRI released IR8, its first high-yielding, fertilizer-responsive rice variety. IR8 and subsequent varieties yielded far more than traditional varieties in Asia, particularly on experiment stations. In farmers' fields, however, yields often did not rise so sharply.

Almost a decade of experience in introducing high-yielding varieties indicates that transferring technology to the farm

---

Amir U. Khan is Head, Agricultural Engineering Department, The International Rice Research Institute, Los Baños, Laguna, Philippines. The assistance provided by Jose Samuel, Research Fellow, IRRI Agricultural Engineering Department, in preparing this paper is acknowledged.

515

level may be a more challenging problem than generating new
technology. Dr. Robert F. Chandler, in summing up his experience as the first director of IRRI, noted:

> The only real disappointment I felt was that somehow we did
> not understand sufficiently why the Asian farmer who had
> adopted the new varieties was not doing better. Somehow, I
> felt that the rice scientists who had obtained yields of 5 to
> 10 metric tons per hectare on the IRRI farm could not explain
> why so many Filipino farmers (for example) obtained on the
> average less than 1 metric ton per hectare increase in yield
> after shifting from traditional to the high yielding vari-
> eties. (Chandler, 1975)

Perhaps a better insight into the question posed by Chandler lies in one of the more searching analyses of developmental
strategies made by Owens and Shaw (1972) who identify the three
tragedies of tropical agriculture as: inadequate water control, lack of sufficient power, and lack of meaningful employment. To tap the full potential of the new seed-fertilizer
technology, availability of water and its adequate control are
the most important prerequisites. Intensification of agriculture through multiple cropping, intercropping, timely operations, and improved cultural practices requires greater inputs
of power through appropriate mechanized equipment. A decentralized rural-based industry that could support agriculture as
well as meet basic consumer needs of the rural populations
could provide meaningful employment in the countryside. In
this context, local manufacture of suitable farm equipment can
be an important rural activity that could absorb some of the
surplus farm labor in slack seasons. Thus an appropriate approach to mechanization of agriculture could not only help
raise food production but could also help develop rural industries.

MECHANIZATION AND FOOD PRODUCTION

Agricultural mechanization in the broad sense implies the
introduction of machines to utilize manual, animal, and
mechanical power for agriculture. In the developed countries, mechanization has been traditionally considered as a
means to improve labor productivity or to minimize labor inputs
in farming. Unfortunately, this sterotyped concept of mechanization has created the erroneous impression that all kinds of
mechanization are bad for the developing countries because
mechanization would lead to massive unemployment. While it
would be erroneous to say that mechanization does not displace
labor, one must realize that the displacement of labor is
highly dependent on the type and level of mechanization. The

real issue in most developing countries today is not whether to
mechanize or not to mechanize, but rather the nature of mechanization that would increase food production without creating
major socioeconomic imbalance.

Mechanization to improve the productivity of labor is
fairly well understood; however, its impact on land productivity is not as clear since mere substitution of mechanical power
for manual or animal power does not seem to increase crop
yields (Singh and Chancellor, 1974). If, however, one studies
the level of agricultural mechanization over a wide range of
countries, from the least to the most highly industrialized,
the correlation between agricultural power input and crop
yields becomes significant (Figure 1). Giles (1975) estimates
that a minimum power input of 0.5-0.8 hp/ha is essential to
produce average crop yields of about 2.5 t/ha in most developing countries. His study indicates that further increases in
food production beyond the 2.5 t/ha level will require substantially larger increases in power input per unit of increase in
yield. One way of minimizing the total power required to obtain high productivity is by providing a high level of irrigation. The exceptional cases of Taiwan and Egypt in Giles's
chart seem to support such a thesis, since these two countries
were able to reach high productivity with relatively low farm
power inputs.

In fact, we have evidence that farm mechanization of rice
production in both Western countries and in Japan began with
large-scale development of farm land and irrigation schemes
(Boesch, 1967 and Asian Development Bank, 1974). Drew and
Bondurant (1972) noted that the irrigation pump is the most important farm machine in India, where two million stationary
power units were in use in 1970. "The investment in pump power
units was twice that for farm tractors and the power used for
pumps was three times that of all tractors in India." Available data from China is even more revealing (Khan, 1976).
China's horsepower input on irrigation equipment is about 10
times the power available through farm tractors and power tillers. IRRI's 1974 Annual Report identifies lack of water control as a continuing major constraint that causes large yield
differences between experimental farms and farmers' fields when
using new varieties. It is clear that in areas where gravity
irrigation cannot be made available, lift irrigation with powered equipment will be the most important input for agricultural mechanization.

A second area in which mechanization can make a major contribution toward increased food production is more intensive
cultivation with multiple cropping and other cropping systems.
Multiple cropping is a technique of growing more than one crop
on the same land in one year. Bradfield (1971) demonstrated
as many as five crops per ha could be harvested in a year

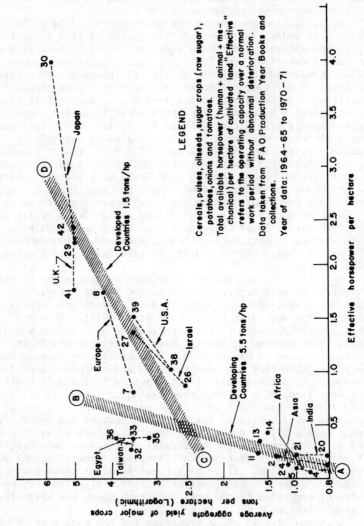

FIG. 1. Chart of agricultural mechanization (Giles, 1975).

LEGEND

Cereals, pulses, oilseeds, sugar crops (raw sugar), potatoes, onions and tomatoes.

Total available horsepower (human + animal + mechanical) per hectare of cultivated land. "Effective" refers to the operating capacity over a normal work period without abnormal deterioration.

Data taken from FAO Production Year Books and collections.

Year of data: 1964-65 to 1970-71

Developed Countries 1.5 tons/hp

Developing Countries 5.5 tons/hp

Effective horsepower per hectare

Average aggregate yield of major crops
tons per hectare (Logarithmic)

provided appropriate power equipment is available to handle timely production operations. Table 1 lists the multiple cropping indices of selected Asian countries, which indicate the great potential for increasing food production through multiple cropping.

TABLE 1. Multiple cropping indices of selected countries in Asia[a]

Countries	1960/61	1964/65	1970/71	1974/75
China	NA	NA	147.4	NA
East Pakistan (Bangladesh)	132.3	135.2	NA	140.5[b]
India	NA	115.2	117.7	123.7
Indonesia	115.9	126.2	NA	NA
Japan	139.5	132.0	126.0	NA
Philippines	136.0	NA	NA	NA
South Korea	148.3	155.7	153.4	NA
Taiwan	184.7	188.7	181.0[b]	175.0[b]
Thailand[b]	NA	126.0	129.0	NA
West Pakistan	107.5	114.7	NA	NA

$$\text{MCI} = \frac{\text{Total crop area} \times 100}{\text{Total cultivated land area}}$$

Sources: [a]Dalrumple, Dana G. 1971. Survey of multiple cropping in less developed nations. Foreign Economic Development Service, US Department of Agriculture with US Agency for International Development.

[b]The International Rice Research Institute. 1975. Proceedings of the Cropping Systems Workshop, March 18-20, Los Baños, Philippines.

As food production increases from use of the high-yielding varieties, the need to minimize post-harvest losses assumes greater significance. Appropriate farm machines, which could reduce losses in production and processing operations, can substantially increase the availability of food. Numerous studies point to excessively high post-production losses, 10 to 20 percent, in traditional harvesting, threshing, drying, processing, and storage operations. IRRI studies indicate that these

losses can be reduced by 5 to 10 percent (Samson and Duff,
1973) with appropriate farm equipment and methods.

Fertilizers and insecticides are the two leading cash inputs that have a direct bearing on food production. Ferilizer
has traditionally been applied to rice as top dressing after
transplanting, and insecticides have been sprayed. IRRI experiments indicate that applying such chemicals to the root zone
is a much more efficient way to provide nutrients and pest protection to rice plants. De Datta (1974) reported 50 percent
savings in fertilizer by using root zone application in puddled
fields. Similarly, Aquino and Pathak (1976) reported reductions in both quantity of chemicals used and frequency of application with the root zone technique. These findings have a
far-reaching potential to increase food production in the developing countries where the lack of foreign exchange and the
high cost of fertilizer and insecticide are serious constraints.
But appropriate machines are urgently needed so that small
farmers can apply chemicals into the root zone and benefit from
these developments.

TECHNOLOGICAL CONSTRAINTS

The suitability of mechanization technologies from the developed countries for the developing nations is being
seriously questioned. Two distinct agricultural mechanization technologies, the Western and the Japanese, have evolved
in the industrially advanced countries to suit agricultural,
socioeconomic, and industrial conditions. Application of such
technologies in the developing countries is not only difficult,
but creates adverse socioeconomic problems.

Recent developments in agricultural machines in the industrially advanced countries are making them increasingly unsuited to meet the mechanization needs of small farmers in the
developing countries. Tractors and other farm machines are
rapidly increasing in engine size, automation, and design sophistication. These machines are designed for mass production
and are difficult to produce in the developing countries due
to their relatively small markets. The farm equipment industry in the developing countries has not developed sufficiently to allocate resources for industrial research and development; hence, small farmers have little access to modern farm
mechanization technology that is appropriate to their requirements. The author believes that the design and development of
commercially viable machines and other utility products for
indigenous production is a major area for technical assistance.
Such assistance offers an excellent multiplier effect which can
benefit many sections of the developing countries.

Land Limitations

It has been reported (Revelle et al., 1967) that if we exclude the marginal lands which have insufficient water for one 4-month crop, then essentially no additional land is available in Asia for agricultural expansion. Therefore, ways must be found to intensify production on marginal land with better irrigation.

Small and medium-sized farm holdings of from 1 to 10 ha constitute most of the arable land in the tropics. Ironically, with all of the world's technological advances, millions of small farmers in Asia still work the land with antiquated, inefficient equipment. To the developing world, mechanization must serve the needs of small farmers through appropriate modern equipment that is locally produced. The widespread belief that the developing nations need traditional and manual implements that are slightly improved is a fallacy that has hindered the modernization of small-farm agriculture.

In the absence of appropriate modern equipment for small farms, attempts have been made to import farm equipment for joint use on small farms. In his study of the contract hire services in Malaysia and Thailand, Chancellor (1970) indicated increasing acquisition of individually owned two-wheel power tillers by farmers in Malaysia even when large-tractor contract hire services were economically available. The small farmer's desire to retain control of farm production operations and the prestige of ownership seem to favor the use of individually owned small equipment rather than the use of large contract services. The small farmer who has his own farm equipment has far more flexibility for he can use his power tiller, for example, to transport personnel and farm produce as well as for production operations.

Labor Displacement

Many have argued that it would be unwise to mechanize agriculture in the overpopulated developing economies and that development efforts should be limited to improving agriculture through better irrigation, seeds, and fertilizer. More recent studies (Johnson, 1968) indicate that even in countries of surplus labor, seasonal shortages of farm labor are a constraint, especially in the irrigated, double-cropped areas. Most farmers in dual-economy countries are being attracted to some of the conveniences that urban development offers. In some countries, such as Taiwan and Korea, the younger generation is no longer willing to accept the rigorous life of traditional farming and is rapidly moving to the cities. A continuing dependence on excessive labor inputs in agriculture will maintain low productivity of labor and will not help to raise the real

standard of living in the rural communities. The author believes that the mechanization of tropical agriculture through
relatively labor-intensive agricultural machines and mechanization techniques will help to raise food production and living
standards in Asia. Not only can properly introduced mechanization raise crop production, but it can also help create new employment in farming as well as in other rural sectors. For example, Barker (1976) studied small-scale mechanization of rice
farms in Central Luzon, Philippines, and found that labor inputs in all farming operations except land preparation have increased on the mechanized farm. The overall labor inputs on
these farms have increased from 60 to 90 mandays per ha over
a 10-year period (Fig. 2). Fortunately, the doomsday syndrome that has been predicted by many social scientists about
severe unemployment through mechanization does not seem to hold
true in areas that are being mechanized with appropriate technologies. The real issue in the developing countries is to
balance the labor displaced through appropriate mechanization
with the labor absorbed in more intensive farming operations
as well as in other sectors of the rural economies.

China has successfully applied such a strategy on a large
scale in its mechanization efforts. It is a large country,
with similar problems of other developing nations such as high
population densities, lack of capital resources, etc. Yet
China has effectively balanced the demand and supply of labor
in the rural areas among the three sectors: farming, rural
capital construction, and rural industries. Since the labor
demand in rural capital construction is easier to manipulate,
this sector has played an important role in absorbing idle farm
labor during off-seasons. The rapidly developing rural industries sector is also beginning to play an important role in
modulating fluctuations of labor demand in the rural areas.

Capital Constraints
The selling price of imported farm machines in the developing countries generally is two to four times their price
in the countries of their origin. Further, this expensive imported equipment competes with local labor, which is available
for a fraction of its cost in the industrialized countries.
Therefore, most imported machines are not economical for small-
farm operations in the developing countries. The serious shortage of foreign exchange that most developing countries are experiencing also limits the possibilities of any large-scale importation of farm machines.

The purchasing power of the small farmer in the developing
countries is rather low so the cost of mechanization must be
drastically reduced if small farms are to be mechanized. But
our intention is not to suggest subsidizing the large-scale

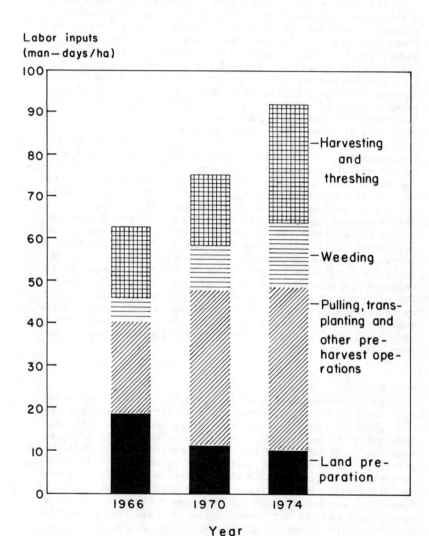

FIG. 2.   Wet season labor inputs, by type of operation and by year, for selected rice farms in the Central Luzon region and Laguna Province, Philippines (Barker, 1976).

importation of conventional equipment, but to find ways to reduce costs of locally manufactured modern equipment for small
farmers.

This can be achieved through a self-reliant approach in
which simple machines are developed for local manufacture
through an optimum use of local resources such as labor, production methods, available materials and components, etc. The
agricultural machinery development program at IRRI is based on
this specific strategy. Some of the machines developed under
this program are now being commercially produced and marketed
in many developing countries at about half the price of comparable imported machines. Many new farm machines that were
not previously available from the industrialized countries have
also been developed through the program.

We are learning that the use of locally produced small
farm equipment need not be limited to small farms, it can also
be economically used on larger farms. Large corporate farms in
the Philippines are successfully adopting the relatively new
concept of sequential farming. In this system, large farming
areas with good water control are managed in a sequential manner by conducting each operation daily on a limited acreage
with small machines throughout the year. This approach permits
year-round utilization of farm equipment with considerable reduction in capital investment. The use of locally produced
small farm equipment in such a system further reduces the investment and generates substantially more farm employment. A
135 ha farm in Laguna Province, Philippines, is successfully
operating with a total investment in equipment of only $8,500,
compared to the estimated investment for a mechanized farm of
similar size with standard 55-hp imported tractors and other
farm machines of $62,500.

IRRI MACHINERY PROGRAM

Development of power tillers, small tractors, and other
new agricultural machines is a costly process which requires a high level of engineering expertise. Most small
industries and metalworking shops in the developing nations
lack the technical capability or the capital resources for such
activity. Unfortunately, most public research institutions in
agricultural engineering in the developing countries are more
concerned with academic research than with the development of
commercial equipment. The IRRI program focuses on providing
appropriate designs for demand-oriented small rice production
and processing equipment which small firms can produce with
available resources. IRRI provides for free the complete engineering drawings and other technical assistance on farm machines to interested entrepreneurs and manufacturers in the
developing countries.

The IRRI program was focused initially on the development of small power tillers and threshers to facilitate the two most labor-consuming operations. Equipment was subsequently developed for irrigation, direct seeding, fertilizing, weed control, and processing operations such as grain cleaning and drying. This equipment is developed for farm and village-level needs. Photographs and brief descriptions of machines in the appendix illustrate the type of mechanization technology being developed under the IRRI program. Heavy emphasis is placed on successful promotion of the machinery designs. Consequently, many IRRI-developed machines are now commercially produced in Asia, Africa, and Latin America. By the end of 1975, more than 30,000 IRRI-developed machines had been commercially produced in 11 countries in Asia.

This program's impact has been particularly dramatic in the Philippines where 18 companies of an organized small-farm equipment industry produce IRRI machines. Many other manufacturers have adapted IRRI designs without direct IRRI assistance. While the direct and indirect employment generated by this program is difficult to assess, 8 cooperating manufacturers in the Philippines reported hiring 700 additional workers in 1974 in direct production. Employment that is indirectly generated in the marketing, servicing, and utilization of the machines is estimated to be many times greater than in direct production operations. The Institute is now strengthening its worldwide industrial extension activities to more effectively transfer the small-farm mechanization technology.

CONCLUSION

The IRRI machinery program clearly demonstrates that a strategy based on local production of small farm equipment can be highly successful in the mechanization of tropical agriculture. To mechanize small farms, the designs of appropriate machines must be provided to small manufacturers, entrepreneurs, and metalworking shops in the developing countries.

Indigenous production of farm machines has effectively reduced capital investments in farming and lowered mechanization costs. Fairly modern machines can be manufactured at low volume in developing nations, if they are appropriately designed to utilize local production knowhow and other resources. Considerable entrepeneurial skill is available in the developing countries that could be successfully tapped to establish local industries through technical assistance in the critical R&D areas. This selective product-oriented approach to technical assistance offers new opportunities for the development of many other sectors.

REFERENCES

Aquino, G. B. and M. D. Pathak. 1976. Absorption and translocation of Chlordimeform and Carbofuran applied in the root zone of rice plants and persistence of their residues under flooded conditions. Journal of Economic Entomology. (Submitted for publication.)

Asian Development Bank. 1974. Regional workshop on irrigation water management. ADB, P. O. Box 789, Manila, Philippines.

Barker, R. 1976. Personal communication. Agricultural Economics Dept., The International Rice Research Institute, Los Baños, Philippines.

Boesch, M. 1967. The World of Rice. E. P. Dutton & Co., New York.

Bradfield, R. 1971. Mechanized maximum cropping systems for the small farms of the rice belt of tropical Asia. Agricultural Mechanization in Asia Journal. Spring issue.

Chancellor, W. J. 1970. A survey of tractor contractor operations in Thailand and Malaysia. The Agricultural Development Council, New York.

Chandler, R. F., Jr. 1975. Case history of IRRI's research management during the period 1960 to 1972. Asian Vegetable Research and Development Center, Shanhua, Taiwan.

De Datta, S. K., et al. 1974. Increasing efficiency of ferilizer nitrogen in flooded tropical soil. Proceedings of the FAI-FAO Seminar on Optimizing Agricultural Production under Limited Availability of Fertilizer, New Delhi, India.

Drew, L. O. and B. L. Bondurant. 1972. Effects of land holding size on agricultural mechanization in India. Paper No. 72-683 American Society of Agricultural Engineers, St. Joseph, Michigan.

Giles, G. W. 1975. The reorientation of agricultural mechanization for the developing countries. Agricultural Mechanization in Asia Journal 7:2.

Johnson, S. 1968. Terminal report on the general engineering and economic research portion of Contract No. AID/csd-834. The International Rice Research Institute, Los Baños, Philippines.

Khan, A. U. 1976. Agricultural mechanization and machinery production in the People's Republic of China. Report of the Small-Scale Industries Delegation of the National Academy of Sciences, Washington, D.C.

Owens, E. and R. Shaw. 1972. Development reconsidered. Lexington Books, Massachusetts.

Revelle, R., et al. 1967. World food problem. Report of the U.S. President's Advisory Committee. U.S. Government Printing Office, Washington, D.C.

Samson, B. and B. Duff. 1973. The pattern and magnitude of
    field grain losses in paddy production. IRRI Saturday Sem-
    inar Paper, July 7, The International Rice Research Insti-
    tute, Los Baños, Philippines.
Singh, G. and W. J. Chancellor. 1974. Studies of relations be-
    tween farm mechanization and crop yields. Agricultural
    Mechanization in Asia Journal 7:1.

IRRI power tiller (5-7 hp) being used for land preparation (top photo) and transport (bottom photo).

IRRI power tiller with 10-12 hp diesel engine being used for transport.

Seeder for pregerminated paddy in puddled fields.

Prototype of IRRI power weeder (center) with commercially manufactured versions from Japan.

Manually operated lowlift diaphragm pump.

Vertical-axis windmill with tubular pump.

Contact herbicide applicator for upland operation.

Root-zone granular fertilizer applicator for lowland paddy culture.

Root-zone liquid chemical applicator for fertilizer or herbicide application in puddled fields.

Multicrop axial flow thresher mounted on self-propelled farm cart.

PTO-operated thresher for contract operation.

Two-ton capacity oscillating-screen grain cleaner.

Batch type dryer shown with kerosene burner. A rice hull fur-
nace has also been developed as an alternate heat source.

Prototype unit of an IRRI 15-20 hp riding tractor utilizing readily available automobile components with IRRI extendible lug wheels.

Moisture meter assembled for local manufacture in the developing countries.

J. R. PAGOT

Constraints in the
Introduction
of Animal Technology

A century ago in 1876, Cornevin, animal production professor of the Veterinary school of Alfort, gave the following definition of zootechny:

> It is a part of natural history dealing with domestic animals;
> its aim is to study the morphology and comparative physiology
> of breeds, varieties, individualities and at the same time
> their rational use. Its constant goal is to make the best use
> of animals. It is connected to rural economics itself a
> branch of economic policy which studies how resources are
> built up and exploited.

If the wording is a little old fashioned the concept is
still up-to-date and valid on a world wide scale.

Animal technology may differ, depending on the region but
its objective is the same: to maximise returns on capital investment and from herds, fodder and forage resources.

When a new technology is discovered somewhere in the world
there is great temptation to want its adoption on a world wide
scale. But very often transfers of technology fail utterly.
Why? The aim of this exposee is to explain the constraints to
the introduction of animal technology in tropical zones.

It should be recalled that an animal is able to manifest
its genetic potential according to climatic, sanitary, nutritional and environmental conditions. A new technique will be

---

J. R. Pagot is Director of the International Livestock
Center for Africa. P. O. Box 5689, Addis Ababa, Ethiopia.

adopted only if its use is advantageous or profitable to the breeder e.g. in reducing work or increasing production and above all if economic conditions allow him to benefit from the production increase.

The adoption of a new technique, although it may be known, requires that the constraints inherent to animals and their environment be first overcome.

IDENTIFICATION OF CONSTRAINTS

A new technique will be adopted only if it is well known; this requires a considerable spreading of expertise.

Once known, the adoption of a new technique in a new region must be considered in relation to existing animals, the nature of the physical, biological and human conditions prevailing in the region and finally the economics of production and its interaction with the other environmental conditions.

This classification is didactic because in the complex system of animal production there are permanent interactions between the different factors of production.

CONSTRAINTS OF THE PHYSICAL ENVIRONMENT

Constraints of the physical environment are particularly severe in the regions with equatorial or tropical climates.

In a tropical climate zone the local temperature is almost always over 15°C to 18°C, which is considered as the optimum level for good thermoregulation. It may reach over body temperature 41°C to 42°C; the air humidity during the dry season is below 20 percent and during the wet season is over 80 percent.

In the humid or equatorial tropics air humidity is always near or over 80 percent and the temperature almost constant between 25°C and 30°C.

The thermoregulation mechanism of animals suffers from heavy burdens and reacts well when the animals are in good condition. To reduce excess heat quantity they reduce their activity and their feed consumption, and consequently their production decreases.

It would appear that natural selection has oriented trends towards a model in which the animal shape gives weight/surface ratios favourable to a good homeostasis and that the distribution of species and breeds is not accidental.

If the climograms[1] of the areas of distribution of the zebus (Bos indicus) and taurines (Bos taurus) are compared at least for the tropical zones, it is observed that zebus are

---

1. Climogram is the polygon obtained by joining in calendar order the months of the year through the monthly average temperature and humidity. (See Figure 1.)

found in regions where the major surface area of climograms is large and are located over the 21°C line and on the lower side of the 50 percent humidity abscissa. See Figure 1.

Taurines are found in the region for which the climograms have a small surface area and are located beyond the 50 percent humidity abscissa.

In addition it appears that there exists a positive correlation between the animal's size and the surface area of the climograms. The smallest domestic animals are found throughout the humid and hot zones (cattle, sheep, goats).

The domestic animals presently existing in the tropics are well adapted to the climate of their dispersion area; the situation may be summarized as follows:

1) Zebus tolerate high temperature and low humidity but suffer from high humidity.

2) Taurines tolerate high humidity with moderate temperature but suffer from high temperature and low humidity.

Thus there are very severe constraints to the genetic improvement of tropical livestock through the importation of breeds from the temperate zones.

Many failures in genetic improvement were due to the inability of imported animals to overcome climatic constraints. Initial disorders concern the reproductive function, frigidity in males, irregular ovarian cycles in females. Later there appear cutaneous disorders, themselves under humoral control and acceleration or suppression of coat shedding (hypertrichosis).

Artificial insemination is one way to avoid importation of pure bred animals but there is a need for testing the adaptability of cross bred animals, the tendency to express physiological disorders being linked with the "percentage of improved blood".

In such operations bulls should be chosen which can tolerate high solar radiation, high temperature and humidity and can ensure good body temperature regulation.

Preference should be given to animals with dark skins to avoid sun burn in case of photo-sensitization and with short, bright hair to facilitate thermoregulation. The hair will reflect part of the heat received from the sun and air and will allow a rapid evaporation of sweat.

The animals with long and coarse hair should be culled; the Bonsma[2] test which is easy to apply is well

---

2. In the Bonsma test a pinch of hair is torn away on the side of the animal and turned round with the thumb in the palm of the hand. If the hair makes a felted ball the animal should be culled--if on the contrary the hairs spread with no tendancy to stick together the animal can be selected.

Mamou (GUINEE)

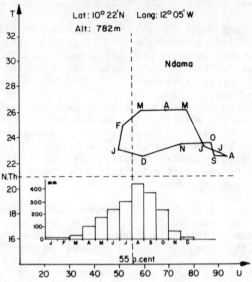

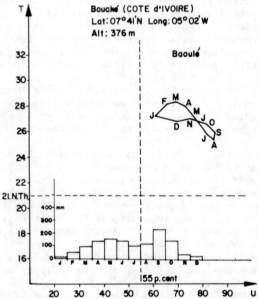

Fig. 1.   Comparison of cattle breeds of Africa, Bos taurus and
Bos indicus, and correlations with climograms and
rainfall.

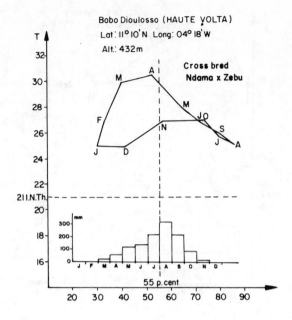

Bobo Dioulosso (HAUTE VOLTA)
Lat: 11° 10' N Long: 04° 18' W
Alt.: 432 m

Cross bred
Ndama x Zebu

55 p.cent

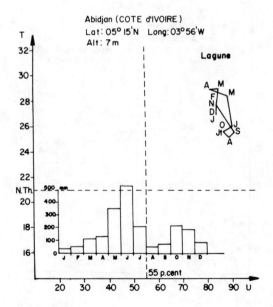

Abidjan (COTE d'IVOIRE)
Lat: 05° 15' N Long: 03° 56' W
Alt: 7 m

Lagune

55 p.cent

Fig. 1. (Continued)

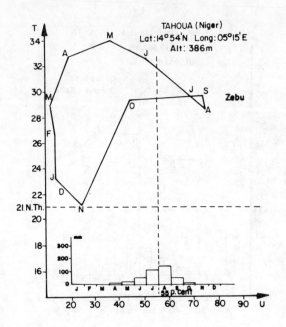

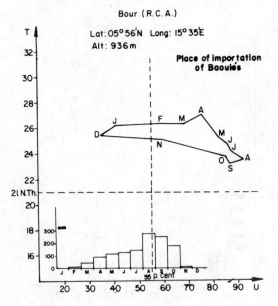

Fig. 1. (Continued)

suited to the selection of suitable animals.

BIOLOGICAL CONSTRAINTS

If an animal is able to overcome climatic constraints its production will depend on management, on the level of feeding and on health conditions. In the extensive range breeding which prevails in the dry tropical zones these factors depend on control of available and accessible water and grazing resources.

Many failures were due to the assumption that highly productive and improved animals would fare as well as local breeds when left on the range.

In the regions with a typical tropical climate there is only one rainy season thus the quantity and quality of natural accessible forage vary considerably. After rainy season abundance there is dry season scarcity. A number of factors control animal weight such as duration of grazing, quality of forage, and movement required for grazing and watering.

From the middle to the end of the rainy season water holes are numerous and grasses are abundant and of good quality. The animal can easily find the quantity of grass needed for its maintenance and growth.

In the middle of the dry season, grasses are scarce and of meagre quality, water holes are far from each other and the animal is able to find only its maintenance ration.

At the end of the dry season grasses have nearly disappeared, only a few leaves of browse are accessible and the animal, in spite of a longer daily grazing period, is unable to find sufficient for its maintenance. It also loses weight due to the amount of energy needed in its search for palatable grass and water; sometimes more than 10 km must be traveled daily.

Weight is almost at its minimum at the beginning of the rainy season when the animal will continue to lose weight because the new grasses have a very high moisture content and the ration that the animal can eat is still less than its maintenance requirement.

Research in this field has shown that loss of weight may reach 15 percent of liveweight. This is understandable when it is realized that the food value of natural grass per kilo gramme of dry matter varies from 1 to 5.

The regaining of weight during the wet season is rapid and weight will increase over the previous year's level; however, the yearly gain is small, 5 percent or less.

Concerning productivity in the Sahelian and Soudanian zones, where grazing is possible, carrying capacity is evaluated at as many hectares per animal as there are months of dry season (between 5 to 8 ha).

In all that has been said it has been assumed that intake
is balanced. However, it is often deficient. It is exceptional if the ratio of phosphorus to calcium maintains an optimum
level. Copper, zinc, molybdenum and cobalt deficiencies occur
frequently.

Tropical cattle breeders have a technique which permits
them to partially overcome the alternate abundance and scarcity: transhumance. They graze during rainy seasons on the
range far from the permanent water-holes and during the dry
seasons they graze near boreholes and well watered regions.
They migrate according to cyclical patterns which have been
well established by traditional rights. Since the herds never
stay in the same place for long, the cattle are able to find
their minimum vital requirements for growth and maintenance.[3]

The settlement of cattle populations round boreholes with
large water production produces clinical symptoms of phosphorus
deficiency and consequently botulism, since the livestock eat
the bones of dead cattle.

In the humid zones or in highlands with high agricultural
potential, fodder production, legumes in particular, is possible,
and may support intensive cattle production. However,
animal production must compete with food crops and industrial
cash crops which give a high return to the farmers.

These regions were normally the traditional market of the
dry region cattle breeders but with the general increase in
prices and demand the situation may change rapidly (compare
below).

Thus feed constraints explain the low level of precocity
of tropical livestock raised on natural rangelands. The way of
life of the cattle raisers does not permit the distribution of
supplementary feed, except salt.

If distribution of supplementary feed was possible, it
could be well worthwhile, since the genetic potential of tropical zebus and taurines is excellent; this has been shown in all
the feeding trials carried out in tropical Africa (Senegal,
Mali, Ivory Coast, Nigeria, Cameroon, Kenya, Ethiopia etc).
The livestock can with adequate feeding, gain more than 1 kg
per day, with conversion coefficients competitive with those of
improved cattle of the temperate zone.

To overcome feeding constraints caused by climatic conditions, the idea has been put forward of building up a strati-
fied system of production in which the animal would be born and
raised in the dry rangelands and finished in the humid zones

-----

3. The Tropical Cattle Unit or UBT (unit betail tropical) represents an animal of 250 kg with a daily gain of 250 gr. Its
caloric needs are evaluated in the rainy season (good grass,
small displacement) and in the dry season (meagre quality
grass, long displacements).

where fodder crops can be easily grown and where agro-industrial by-products are also available.

The classical model is the feed lot system, well known in
the US; however, it needs considerable investments, and its
technical and financial management must consist of well informed people. Several feed lots are in operation in Africa
and initial conclusions are that the use of this technique is
possible but may not be suitable for general application. In
less sophisticated models of feeding at the individual farmer's
level, small numbers of animals have been profitably handled
and were well adapted to the farmers' existing technology.

DISEASE FACTORS
       In discussing biological constraints it was assumed that
       the livestock were in good health and no factors which
       cause disease except low level of nutrition, existed.
This is not the case; the list of diseases in the tropics is a
long one. It includes all the viral and bacterial diseases of
the temperate countries in addition to diseases that have disappeared there: rinder pest, bovine pleuropneumonia, also specific tropical diseases or those diseases whose severity is
greater in the tropical than the temperate zones: trypanosomiasis, tick borne fever, blood and intestinal parasite diseases.

       Very efficient vaccines exist against the viral and micro-
bic diseases, although reactions to vaccines are very often
more severe among imported livestock than among local animals.
This is particularly the case with the living vaccines against
rinderpest and horse sickness.

       In the tick borne fevers, except East Coast fever
(theileriosis) and rickettsiosis, the local cattle, zebus in
particular, can obtain protection with little damage whereas
the reaction to immunization in imported cattle is dramatic and
death is not exceptional.

       Trypanosomiasis merits special attention. It is caused by
a multiplication in the blood of warm blooded animals of a unicellular parasite with a flagellium, which causes anaemia and
death among infected animals. Transmission is by blood sucking
insects: glossina and tabanides. They are found in humid zones
of Africa where the agricultural and fodder potentials are very
great. They have been an obstacle to the expansion of zebu
herds and also horses, in tsetse infected zones.

       To overcome this constraint a number of alternatives are
possible:

       1) The agronomic prophylaxy using clearance of vegetation
and flies habitat has been the first in use but it is expensive
unless the land is used for agricultural purposes.
       2) The protection and treatment of animals with chemical

drugs is expensive and the reaction of imported animals is
sometimes severe.

3) The clearance of vectors by insecticides has been carried out with success, but it is also very expensive and cannot
be used everywhere.

4) In other places the elimination of wild life was advocated as a good means of breaking the biological chain of
transmission of the trypanosomes.

5) The use of genetic and biological means to lessen the
population of vectors is still at the research stage, as is the
active immunization of cattle against the trypanosomes.

One other way, rather slow in its development, is the
building up of a livestock industry through the reproduction of
"trypanotolerant" strains of livestock which already exist in
the infected zones (in Guinea, Senegal, Ivory Coast, Ghana,
Nigeria). This is also possible in Zaire, Congo, and CAR,
where the national herd is the offspring of cattle imported in
the twenties from Guinea, Upper Volta, Senegal, Mali and
Dahomey.

The latest figures indicate that there exist in these regions 7.5 million cattle, 11,300 sheep and 23.6 million goats.
Although the meat and milk qualities of the various animals are
known, the mechanism of trypantolerance is still to be described; this is one of the missions of ILRAD.[4]

In conclusion it may be said that in the tropics, physical
and biological environmental conditions are very severe and
errors must be paid very promptly. For every genetic improvement there must be a corresponding improvement in management,
in particular of disease prophylaxy and of nutritional conditions.

The latter depend neither upon the animal nor upon the environment, but upon the cattle raiser, his ability, his resources and his way of life.

SOCIO-ECONOMIC CONSTRAINTS

Leaving aside the techniques of cattle raising, there is a
basic difference between pastoral and agricultural systems of production which relates to a fundamental difference in the use of livestock and land as means of production.

In respect to the pastoral system, the major features are:
a) that saving and investment are necessary in all circumstances since the herd capital is perishable and must be replaced and b) such investment is possible without recourse to

_____
4. ILRAD, the International Laboratory for Research on Animal
Diseases, located in Nairobi is responsible for research on
East Coast fever and trypanosomiasis.

any economic institutions, since one of the main products of
the herd is calves, lambs, etc.

These features can be contrasted to the conditions of production in an agricultural regime where: a) land is essentially imperishable and cannot be consumed by the management
unit except through an elaborate economic institution which
makes possible its conversion into food and b) where land cannot be increased by investment of its products (crops) except
where economic institutions exist to effect its conversion.

Looking at traditional methods of cattle raising it is
seen that the cattle breeders achieve a great deal.

In the dry rangeland zones livestock management is conducted on an extensive basis by ethnic groups with strong and
very long-standing livestock raising traditions: Peuls, Maure,
Targui, Toubous, Masais, 'etc. They utilise grass and water resources all the year round, moving their cattle along a cyclic
transhumant route.

This method of managing livestock does not lend itself to
concentrated development operations, although these people can
adopt very elaborate technology, such as vaccination against
viral and microbal diseases and chemo-prophylaxy against parasitic diseases. The results of this disease control have been
so spectacularly successful, that the overstocking of the Sahel
and the drought have been attributed to it.

In the humid zones the sociological constraints have their
origin in the fact that up to less than 40 years ago no livestock industry in real terms existed, the animals' offspring
were gathered and slaughtered at any occasion that justified a
family meeting or a village feast. In addition, as has been
mentioned above, livestock raising has always been competing
with highly productive crops.

Conditions vary, such that every case needs special consideration, but the individual reactions of tropical cattle
raisers to any innovation do not differ essentially from the
reactions of those of the other parts of the world.

Every new technique needs an investment either of work or
money. A new technique must not increase working time and it
must not disturb the normal succession of farming activities.
This is particularly important for fodder crops which must
never compete with food or cash crops.

Supplementary investment must be made by the cattle owner
either through his own means (self-financing) using the return
of his own herd, or through a related activity, or through a
banking system.

Banking systems are almost unknown. Although cooperatives
or traders are able to sell drugs and equipment to the cattle
owners for cash, only in very rare cases has a banking system
given them personal loans. Their herds are, as mentioned above,
perishable and the rangelands are either nationally or at least

collectively owned; they cannot be used for mortgages.

Investment constraints are very difficult to overcome; however, attempts have been made to organize cattle raisers, by common consent or by authoritarian methods, into cooperative structures or pastoral communes in French speaking countries, and cooperative ranches in Eastern Africa. The objective is to give power to the community to guarantee individual loans and/ or to give loans and subsidies to the community for activities of general benefit.

These models are far from being widely applied. They suppose that the socio-economic component of the systems and the motivation of the decision makers are well known. One of the tasks of the International Livestock Center for Africa (ITLA) will be to develop research in these fields.

All the constraints already studied are those which have a prior effect on production or the production itself. It is presumed that innovations will cause an increase in production, however, to be adopted they must give an increase in income.

In many regions the marketing of products is impeded by the lack of a rapid and economic means of transportation. Livestock is taken on foot, very often over a long distance, to market places and the traders, in the absence of contracts, have to submit to the will of the buyer.

The building or the improvement of roads suitable for heavy trucks and trailers has had very beneficial results in Africa, as spectacular as those in Australia.

All the facts given, presume that the society in which the cattle raisers are living and producing have technical and social structures which are able to provide them on a free or payment basis the services they require for the proper operation of their industry.

Political choices (collectivism, liberalism, socialism etc.) may impose different social structures but biological laws ignore the laws of politics.

The responsibilities of the collective whole toward the individual person cover:

1) Research for new techniques and for improvements.

2) Training of competent research workers and extension specialists.

3) Information, and permanent improvement of the expertise of all the groups and persons involved in the system of production.

OTHER CONSTRAINTS

The following statements are only an attempt to identify some of the other constraints. They must not be applied to all parts of Africa because each state has its own

problems linked with its choice of development policy and the
resources it is able to mobilize.

Scientific Research

Scientific research is a means of identifying constraints
and finding ways and means to overcome them. It is a collective responsibility.

All the governments of the tropical countries feel deeply
their need to develop their research capabilities. Many laboratories and research centers have been established; the main
constraints now are lack of funds and often lack of human resources. The training of a research worker needs about 10
years and research programmes which provide returns on a short
term basis are very often chosen in preference to the animal
production research programmes whose duration can be calculated
in decades.

The building up of universities and high level training
establishments has improved the situation during the last 10
years. However, the problems are still acute and are complicated by the fact that research workers trained abroad have to
spend some years to obtain a full understanding of tropical
problems. The magnitude of these problems is impressive and
solutions are never easily found.

The warm welcome received by ILCA's multidisciplinary and
international approach on a cooperative basis provides a justi-
fication for interafrican cooperation in the specialization of
research workers and for the operation of cooperative programmes which will make best use of the resources of all the
participants in such programmes.

The Training of Technicians

The training of technicians able to participate actively
in the development process is a governmental responsibility. The situation in this aspect is less critical than that
of research. There is room for improvement, but all governments have made laudable efforts.

Training methods are changing rapidly and attempts are being made to find ways and means of adapting to conditions prevailing in Africa.

Flexibility in training will be possible at the level of
technicians or of institutions, according to human and financial resources. An interdisciplinary approach to activities is
absolutely necessary to development.

There is a specific need for training managers able to
operate animal development projects as technicians, financial
officers and administrators.

<u>Training of Cattle Raisers</u>

Training of cattle raisers to improve their technical
knowledge will be both a collective and individual responsibility. In this field general advice should be given cau-
tiously. The number of proposed models for extension work is
the proof, if one is needed, that the ideal solution has not
yet been found and that further research is needed.

It would not be appropriate to give an appraisal of the
governmental structures of the countries which have held political and economic responsibility for less than 15 years, but it
is evident that pricing policies have an impact on marketing
and production especially if the producers don't receive an adequate return.

One may sneer at certain excesses. One may, for the sake
of one's conscience, blame the Sahelian drought on the cattle
raisers. However, those who express these views should ask
themselves the following question: "In the same conditions,
with the same resources, would I have been able to do more?".

New progress depends on bringing together successfully the
knowledge and techniques which already exist but which are normally considered on a too exclusively disciplinary basis. At
their level the cattle raisers have done their best. In the
field of research we have to find for them new systems of organization. The way will be difficult but all help is greatly
deserved.

REFERENCES

Barres, J. F. 1974. Analytical bibliography on the Sahel.
    (French/English), FFHC Action for Development, FAO and
    World Council of Churches. FAO Rome.
Boeckh, E., O. Bremaud, R. Dumas, J. E. Huhn, and R. Compere.
    1974. Etude sur la situation actuelle de l'élevage dans
    les pays du Sahel et des mesures de sauvegarde à envisager.
    Brussels: Commission des Communautés Européennes Funds Eu-
    ropeen de Developpement (FED).
Boudet, G. 1975. Rapport sur la situation pastorale dans les
    pays du Sahel. Rapport Institut d'Elevage et de Medecine
    Veterinaire des Pays Tropicaux (IEMVT).
Bunderson, V. L. 1968. Livestock Production from Rangeland
    and Ranches. Proceedings of the Seminar Animal Husbandry
    and Marketing. Nairobi.
Deramee, O. 1971. L'élevage des ruminants en Afrique au Sud
    du Sahara - bibliographie. Belgium: Centre de Documenta-
    tion Economique et Sociale Africaine.
FAO. 1966. Crop Ecological Survey in West Africa, Vol. 1.
FAO. 1972. Animal Production and Health Division. List of
    Documents relating to Livestock Production in Africa.

FAO. 1972. Marketing Service, Bibliography of Marketing and Market Studies of Livestock and Meat in Africa, April 1972.

FED. 1974. Conférence élevage Sahel: Compte rendu. Brussels: Commission des Communautes Europeennes (FED).

IEMVT. 1969. Colloque sur l'Elevage. Fort Lamy, Tchad, December 8-13, 1969. IEMVT.

IEMVT. 1973. L'embouche intensive des bovins en pays Tropicaux. Actes du Colloque Dakar, December 4-8, 1973, Maisons-Alfort IEMVT 1974.

IEMVT. 1956-1976. Etudes agrostologiques - 43 volumes par J. Andru, J. C. Bille, A. K. Botte, G. Boudet, R. Delhaye, A. K. Diallo, E. Duverger, J. F. Ellenberger, G. Fotius, A. Gaston, H. Gillet, P. Granier, M. Mosnier, B. Peyre de Fabrègnes, G. Rippstein, B. Tontain et J. Valenza.

IEMVT. 1956-1976. Travaux agrostologiques - 24 volumes par J. Andru, J. C. Bille, G. Boudet, A. Cortin, R. Demange, A. K. Diallo, J. F. Ellenberger, A. Gaston, P. Granier, H. Macher, J. Mordant, M. Mosnier, B. Peyre de Fabrègues, G. Rippstein.

IEMVT. 1956-1976. Notes de Synthèse - 4 volumes par J. André, G. Boudet, C. Devaux et B. Toutain.

IEMVT. 1956-1976. Etudes botanigues - 2 volumes J. André, A. Gaston, J. P. Lebrun et M. Mosnier.

IEMVT. 1975. Les Moyens de Lutte contre les trypanosomes et leurs vecteurs. Control Programs for trypanosomes and their vectors - Actes du colloque Paris, March 12-15, 1974 Maisons-Alfort, IEMVT.

ILCA - CIPEA. 1975. Evaluation and mapping of tropical African rangelands (Proceedings of the Seminar - Bamako - Mali March 3-8, 1975).

ILCA - CIPEA. 1975. Inventaire et cartographie des pâturages tropicaux Africains (Actes du Colloque - Bamako - Mali March 3-8, 1975).

Le Houerou, H. N. 1973. Contribution à une bibliographie écologique du region arides de l'Afrique, de l'Asie du Sud Ouest (végétation, pâturages, élevage, agriculture, nomadisme et disertisation. Actes du Colloque de Nouakchott sur la désertification 17 - 19 Décembre 1973. IFAN Dakar Editeurs.

Koechlin, J. 1961. La végétation des savanes dans le Sud de la République du Congo Brazzaville Paris ORSTON. Mémoires Inst. Etud. Centrafricaines.

Meyn, K. 1970. Beef Production in East Africa. IFO - Institut fur Wirtschaftsforschung Munchen.

Monod, T. 1975. Pastoralism in Tropical Africa. La Sociétés Pastorales en Afrique Tropicale IAI - International African Institute. Oxford University Press London Ibadan Nairobi.

Pagot, J. R. 1971. Natural Pastures, Forage Crops and Farming in the Tropical Regions of French Africa. Maisons-Alfort: IEMVT.

Pagot, J. R. 1971. Cattle Diseases in French Tropical Africa. Maisons-Alfort: IEMVT.

Pratt, D. J. 1972. Selected Bibliography on African Livestock and Rangelands, Overseas Development Administration. London.

Reinhold, B. 1971. Studien uber Fragen der Zebu-Rinderzucht in den Tropen (IFO-Institut fur Wirtschaftsforschung Munchen Afrika - Studienstelle).

Risopoulos, S. A. 1966. Management and Uses of Grasslands - Democratic Republic of the Congo. FAO.

Rockefeller Foundation. 1975. International development strategies for the Sahel New York: Rockefeller Foundation.

Stenning, D. J. 1974. Savannah nomads. A study of the pastoral Fulani of Western Bornu Province, Northern Nigeria, Oxford: University Press.

Wills, J. B. 1969. Contribution to a Bibliography of Animal Husbandry in West Africa from 1960. Ghana J. Agric. Sci. 2.

DOUGLAS ENSMINGER

Constraints to Millions of Small Farmers in Developing Countries Risking Changes in Farming Practices and Family Living Patterns

It is upon the millions of small farmers, perhaps as many as 200 million, in the Developing Countries that the world community must now depend for increases in agricultural production--enough to meet the nutritional requirements of a tenaciously increasing population.

Before proceeding with our identification and analysis of constraints, we need to have before us a working definition of a constraint. A constraint, when discussed with reference to small farm agriculture, is anything that restricts or inhibits the small farmer from either wanting to, or being prepared to, risk changing from his traditional agricultural practices to adopting and integrating new agricultural technology into his farming practices and family living pattern. Some are ready for change; others feel the risks are too great and must be motivated to change.

Thus, it is no exaggeration to say the subject you and I are now addressing is the most important topic on this World Food Conference agenda. The enlightment coming from all the other sessions will have far-reaching implications for policies and programs to remove the constraints now impeding the small farmer (Figure 1).

I have no difficulty in identifying what I believe to be

Douglas Ensminger is President, Mid-Missouri Associated Colleges and Universities; Professor, Rural Sociology, University of Missouri-Columbia; Consultant to the Ford Foundation on Rural Development; and Chairman, International Association of Agricultural Economists/FAO Committee on World Population and Food.

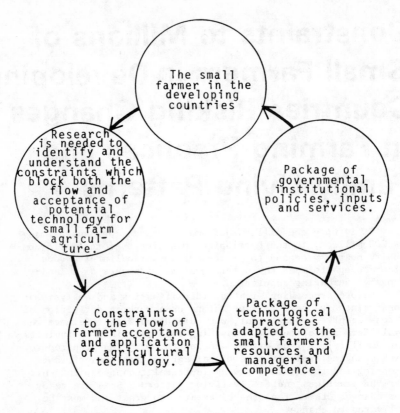

FIG. 1. The small farmer in the developing countries.

the constraints to millions of small farmers risking changes in
their farming practices and family living patterns. What I
cannot do is document adequately the underlying and interrelated cultural forces which perpetuate these constraints. I
can point out circumstantial evidence to support recommended
strategies for institutional changes which appear to offer
promise of minimizing risks to the small farmer, and I can
identify the major areas where there is need for research
related to small farm agriculture.

You will recall the story about the country agent urging
farmers to attend meetings to learn more about improved farming
practices, when one of the farmers spoke up saying, "Shucks, I
already know more now than I'm applying."

While acknowledging that we do not know as much as we

should about the interplay of these constraints to small farmers, I have a feeling we know more than the policy makers are
apparently prepared to accept.

What needs to be known about the culture of small farm
agriculture? How do we get what is presently known, and the
new knowledge that will come from research, accepted and integrated in policies and programs to modernize small farm agriculture? Modernization, as used here, refers to the process of
moving the small farmers from traditionalism toward modernization in applying agricultural science and technology. The
emphasis is on modernization--not mechanization; and there may
be a big difference. Modernization does not have to be in the
Western mold; mechanization tends to be.

HISTORY AND THE SMALL FARMER

A brief sweep of history will reveal why the small farmer
presently functions in isolation from most of the Developing Countries' agricultural policies, programs and institutions.

Throughout the Colonial era, the Colonial powers essentially disregarded food crop agriculture and supported only the
agricultural crops having high export potential. In general,
this was plantation agriculture and emphasized such crops as
coffee, tea and cocoa. Rice, in a few cases, was an export
crop. Research, institutional services and markets were developed for these cash crops. Small farmers, who were the primary
producers of the within-country food crops, were largely
ignored. Governments did little for small farmers, and the
small farmers mistrusted the governments. Governments' agricultural policies and institutional infrastructures were
focused on the export crops; the small food-crop farmers were
left to fend for themselves. Because these very policies
tended to give control of the institutions serving agriculture
to elite farmers with large holdings, the small farmers'
response was to ignore these institutions and produce only
enough to meet the family subsistence needs. They came to be
widely referred to as subsistence farmers, precisely because
they produced to subsist, not for a market.

Following the period of decolonization, there was the
emergence of the new nations, early designated as the Developing Countries. They, like the Colonial powers, also had to
have foreign exchange. Therefore, they also supported what had
come to be the traditional agricultural exports crops.

While many, if not all, of the new nations also early ver-
balized concerns about the rural poor and the need to have programs to assist the small farmers and landless laborers, few
went beyond political rhetoric. Following World War II, only
three countries went all the way in creating the conditions for
small farmers to change their values from producing to survive

to producing to improve family living. These countries were
Japan, Taiwan and South Korea. In all three cases, land reform
programs provided incentives for those who tilled the soil to
increase production for family gain. All three countries provided the conditions for making two of the basic agricultural
resources--land and water--more equitably available to all who
tilled the soil. These three countries oriented their agricultural policies to the small farmers. All gave priority to
creating national institutions and services tailored to meet
the needs of the small farmers. They: (1) directed their
agricultural research establishment to provide agricultural
technology oriented to the resources and managerial competence
of the small farmer; (2) emphasized intermediate and selective
technology which introduced mechanical power only where crucial
in the farming cycle; (3) emphasized labor intensity;
(4) introduced technology to make animal and human labor more
productive and human labor less menial and demeaning; (5) took
special pains to develop price policies and marketing institutions to provide the small farmer appropriate security against
losses in order to reduce his risks; and (6) tailored educational programs to the small farmers.

The small farmers in Japan, Taiwan and South Korea identified themselves with and interacted with the institutional
infrastructure purposely developed to serve them. The transition from traditional to modernized agriculture was facilitated. It was a move from following the traditions of the past
known security and producing to meet family subsistence needs
to an identification with and acceptance in trust of the new
institutions, policies, services and markets designed for small
farm agriculture.

Largely, the new independent nations that emerged out of
decolonization were, and remain today, dominated by an elite
power structure. Thus, they have lacked the political muscle
and will to pass and implement land reform legislation favorable to the small farmer. It is worth noting that revolutionary land reform programs were implemented in Japan and South
Korea under military rule and in Taiwan under semi-dictatorial
powers.

It is important to recognize that the political leaders in
the Developing Countries during the past 25 years were never
under severe pressure to formulate policies and develop an
institutional infrastructure to serve and modernize small farm
agriculture. The reasons are straightforward. During the fifties and up to 1972, when we emptied our storage bins of the
last of our vast and accumulated grain surpluses through the
sale of grain to Russia, the Developing Countries always knew
they could get enough food grain from the US under our Public
Law 480, "Food for Peace" program to meet their shortages, be
they chronic or of an emergency nature. Furthermore, since the
Developing Countries could pay for USA food grain in local cur-

rency and at concessional prices, they could always meet their countries' food needs. The result was greatly reduced pressure on the political leaders for reforms or policies and programs to modernize small farm agriculture.

Early in their emergence as new nations, the Developing Countries did not have to take the tough political decisions to bring the small farms into national policies and to develop programs including land reform and transformation of all institutions. The result has been that the elite farmers have become further entrenched within the institutional infrastructure. It has tended to make the big farmers richer and more politically influential and the small farmers relatively poorer and lacking in political influence.

Three events, interrelated, have contributed to the world community's now focusing attention on small farm agriculture. First was the address given in 1973 by Robert McNamara, President of the World Bank, to the Bank's Board in which he called for a new development strategy oriented to the rural poor and to small farm agriculture. Second was the World Food Conference in November 1974 which recommended that the Developing Countries give priority to assisting the small farmer increase his food production per unit of land. Third was US Foreign Aid Legislation which mandates that the Agency for International Development (AID), in giving aid to the Developing Countries, must give priority to programs to improve both the living conditions of the rural poor and small farm agriculture.

The strength of the political commitments of both the USA and Developing Countries to the small farmer is yet to be tested, but some things have changed. First, the Developing Countries are beginning to understand they can no longer look to the USA as they have the past 25 years for food aid to meet their growing food deficits. Secondly, except in Africa and Latin America, the only presently identified way for them to get the needed additional food to feed their growing populations is to now zero in on policies and programs which will influence the small farmer and help him to increase his production. This has to mean applying agricultural technology adapted to small farmers' needs and capabilities.

WHAT ARE THE CONSTRAINTS?

So, we come to the question before us. What are the constraints which keep the small farmer from risking change in farming practices and family living patterns?

It would be an easy way out to analyze the Developing Countries' agricultural development experiences in the past 25 years and highlight the failures. This would be counter-productive. What will help is to look at the record and examine the many evaluative documents and writings which bear on the experience of the Developing Countries the past two plus

decades. While I will be specific in pointing out constraints,
I must for the record, and especially for your understanding,
make clear that solid research is very limited for each and
every constraint I will identify. The inference here is clear.
The constraints we will be identifying are major inhibitors to
small farmers risking the new agricultural technology. If we
are to know enough about these constraints to be able to formulate policies and programs which will remove or minimize their
influence and create positive conditions influencing change, we
need research--and research with a sense of urgency.

Now to an analysis of what I identify as the more influential constraints.

1st Constraint: Low Level of Social and Cultural Development of Rural People

The low level of social and cultural development of the
rural people, of which the families who till the small
farms are an integral part, is the most important of all the
constraints in inhibiting modernization of small farm agriculture.

Where science and technology are highly developed, as in
the Western World, science and technology have become an integral part of the culture of the people. People in the Western
World are competent to understand the working of science. They
are innovative. They possess skills and have the needed managerial competence to organize, apply and manage technology. It
is to science and technology that people have looked for
improving the quality of their lives.

While the Developing Countries possess a small educated
elite population competent to operate in the scientific world,
the great masses of the people, especially the rural people,
live, think and derive their sense of security from the traditions of the past and are isolated from science and technology.

The constraint is the underdevelopment of the human beings
who presently have limited capacity to encompass the meaning of
science and technology and are lacking skills and managerial
competence in applying technology.

If development is to have meaning for these people, they
must themselves give leadership to change. They are the ones
who must decide they want to change; they are the ones who must
decide what changes they will make. And, they are the ones who
must make the changes. The small farmer will do all these
things only as he develops as a total human being, having a
mind to understand, to weigh evidence, to make decisions knowing there are alternatives. Finally, he must have the motivations to change--first to change self and then through self,
to make effective changes in his farming patterns.

2nd Constraint: Lack of Political
Commitment to Small Farm Agriculture

One important prerequisite for success in development in general is political commitment--political will and political muscle to effect needed changes.

Most of the Developing Countries in the past 25 years have implied in various ways, many through five year plans, that their agricultural plans and programs were for all their agriculture and all their farmers. But in effect, most programs by-passed the small farmers. The needed reforms for both land and institutions have been lacking in their national agricultural plans and development programs. Because land and institutional reforms have not been brought about in these countires, small farm agriculture remains stagnant while the elite farmers have further institutionalized their positions in the economic and political power structures.

The constraint to small farmers moving from traditional to modernizing agriculture is lack of governments' political commitment to impose and enforce both land tenure and institutional reforms.

3rd Constraint: Lack of Institutional Infrastructure
and Institutional Services for Small Farmers

In their thinking about agriculture political leaders, planners and government officials in the Developing Countries do not differentiate between the larger cash crop and small subsistence farmers. They assume whatever institutions they have to serve agriculture exist to serve all farmers. In Tanzania, an East African country where I have worked over the past three years, when political leaders and government officials talk about agriculture, they tend to think about and have in mind cash crop export agriculture.

One of the many things unique about Tanzania is President Julius K. Nyerere's understanding that the institutional infrastructure that was created in the Colonial period to serve cash crop agriculture, and which has been functioning since Tanzanian independence in 1967, cannot be changed or modified in ways to serve the needs of the country's small subsistence farmers. Through the leadership of President Nyerere, the political party TANU and the government of Tanzania are now implementing political commitments and governmental policies to transform all of Tanzania's agricultural and rural institutions so that in the future they will involve, represent and serve all of agriculture but will do this with an unqualified commitment to serve the needs of the small subsistence farmers.

If anyone doubts the need of nationwide interrelated institutional infrastructure to serve agriculture, he should study the historical development of American agriculture and then take a look at the functioning of institutions in Japan, South Korea and Taiwan. It was not until the late 1940s that the USA began its upward production trend in agriculture. It was then that our research institutions were turning out technology having high production potential. Hybrid corn was among these new technologies. By the middle forties, we had developed needed credit institutions for agriculture and a network of both public and private institutional services including extension education and the delivery of the new farm inputs. We had developed a farm-to-market transportation system and market institutions the farmers found trustworthy. Thus, by the mid-forties, the American farmers had moved away from a previous heavy reliance on following traditional farming practices to an acceptance of new agricultural technology. They placed trust in the institutions they had become a part of and found they could trust to serve their needs.

It is not an overstatement to assert that few of the small farmers in the Developing Countries will risk changing from traditional and subsistence agriculture to accepting and integrating the new technology into their farming patterns until there exist the institutions needed to serve them. The tests as to whether the institutions are capable of serving, and in fact do serve, the needs of the small farmer are two. First, can and does the small farmer relate to and interact with the institutions? Second, does the small farmer feel a sense of security and trust in the institutions and does he have direct and increasing evidence that they have his interests and needs in mind at all times?

While the institutions needed to provide services and education are essential, markets are of paramount importance to the small farmers accepting and applying the new technology. Without farm-to-market roads to assure the inputs can get to the farmers and the farm produce moved to the markets, the small farmers cannot risk change. The small hill farmer in Nepal is not interested in increasing his production beyond family needs if, in order to sell on the market, he must walk five days on trails up and down mountains.

Institutional infrastructure research and development are mandatory.

4th Constraint: Low Energy Efficiency and Output

For the millions of small farmers throughout the Developing Countries, their chief sources of power (energy) for farming are animal and human power. With few exceptions, most of the work animals are poorly fed and lack strength for heavy tillage. Largely because of malnutrition and antique hand tools, the human labor force for small farm argiculture has a high input to output ratio.

The Western approach to this low energy efficiency and

output is to prescribe replacing animal and human labor with mechanical power. From past experience we know this is not the answer. While a case can be made for selective use of mechanical power, especially in areas where multiple cropping can fit into the farming pattern, research is needed to make animal power more productive through the development of improved animal drawn implements and hand tools that make human labor more efficient.

For the Tanzanian woman who now tends the cattle and tills the crops, looks after the children and cooks the meals, the answer is not to add a tractor to increase the acreage in maize (corn). Then she would have to weed more corn with the same antique hand tools and without being freed of other responsibilities.

The emphasis in modernizing small farm agriculture should be on labor intensity. If the families of small farm agriculture are to integrate the new agricultural technology into their farming practices, it will be essential that animal and human labor be more efficient and that much of the drudgery be removed from human labor. For many countries, changes in family living and work patterns are involved. Again referring to Tanzania, if more emphasis is to be given to weeding, the men will have to accept weeding as being a part of their work and not continue to look on weeding as being women's work.

5th Constraint: Limited Agricultural Technology Adapted to the Small Farmer's Resources and Managerial Competence

With the successful transfer of the short stemmed high yielding wheat from Mexico into Northern India and Pakistan and the high expectations from the Green Revolution, agricultural research emphasis has focused on breeding high yielding varieties. These varieties will provide the high yields only when sown in association with high quantities of fertilizer and water for controlled irrigation. This new technology using high yielding varieties, fertilizer and water has limited application in better than 85 percent of small farms in the Developing Countries. These are in rain-fed areas, having limited and uncertain moisture. This is high risk agriculture and requires technology adapted to the small farmers' resources and managerial competence. This technology must have minimum dependency on oil derived agricultural inputs because most Developing Countries must import oil at high costs.

Selective and adaptive technology would minimize the use of agricultural inputs derived from oil. The reasons are twofold. First, given the world energy crisis, it would be a mistake to make agriculture in the Developing Countries too dependent on imported energy. Secondly, because of the moisture uncertainty for the small farmers in the rain-fed areas, fer-

tilizer inputs should not be the major strategy. The outcome
is too uncertain.

The need is to recognize variable climate and the farmer's
limited competence in managing sophisticated technology with
limited resources and to organize research oriented to helping
the farmer as he is, and not as he may some day become.

This means that the research must be designed to develop a
new technology to fit into both farming and family living patterns. Otherwise, it will not be adopted.

6th Constraint: Limited Understanding about Traditional Rural Cultures of Which Small Farm Agriculture is an Integral Part

Lack of understanding that small farm agriculture is an
integral part of the rural culture, both in terms of values and family patterns of living, greatly complicates program
design, program implementation and program expectations. For
the past 25 years, the emphasis on improving agricultural production in the Developing Countries, while occasionally paying
lip service to the cultural approach, has ignored the cultural
setting of small farm agriculture and persisted in taking the
Western approach that farming, wherever it took place, was an
occupation and a business.

Now in 1976, we are talking about approaching small farm
agriculture through integrated rural development. But because
so little is known about the culture of small farm argiculture
as an integral part of the rural culture, solid research findings are hard to come by as grist to be used in designing small
farm programs as an integral part of programs for integrated
rural development.

But we are not totally devoid of understanding, either
about the small farmer or the relationship of the small farmer
to his rural culture. Perhaps the most important thing we
know is that in deciding to take up new farming practices, the
small farmer's risks are both socio-cultural and economic. We
know that in many cases, even when the economic risks are minimized, the cultural rebuff to change may be greater than the
small farm family will risk.

We also know that while governments may have compelling
reasons to press small farmers to increase their production,
the small farmer as an integral part of the rural culture more
frequently than not joins in pressing the government to assist
in what, to the people, are their priorities. If development
is to take place and benefit the people, small farm agricultural development must be oriented and carried out as a part of
integrated rural development. The government must be doing the
people's business and the people must so perceive it. Unless
that happens, the people and the government do not become partners; and there is not integrated rural development.

7th Constraint: Lack of Knowledge about the Working of the Minds of the Small Farmers and the Way Their Values are Intertwined in the Rural Culture

We do not know how to design and implement educational and communication programs for small farmers. However, we do know that the Western Extension approach, which is heavily oriented to methods with strong emphasis on the "result-demonstration" is not the answer for small farm agriculture in the Developing Countries. Unless the small farmer wants to change and can be helped through the risk taking process, and then himself feel secure in the new technology and have confidence he can trust the institutions to continue to serve his interests and needs, communication messages fall on ears that do not hear.

Because of the size of the task of moving some 200 million small farmers through the process from traditional to a modernizing agriculture, research with a sense of urgency in communications and information dissemination is needed.

8th Constraint: Small Uneconomical Holdings and and Limited Off-farm Employment Opportunities

Small uneconomical holdings and landless laborers are major constraints to modernizing small farm agriculture.

A case can, and indeed must, be made for land reform programs to provide the needed incentive for those who till the soil to invest both capital and labor in improved agricultural practices. An equally strong case must be made for policies that will provide the conditions for consolidation of millions of small uneconomical holdings into units that provide the potential for small farmers to apply the new technology, and through investments in inputs, achieve economic viability.

If small farm agriculture is to emphasize labor intensity, then labor will have to be made more productive and the work less arduous. If the plight of the landless laborers, now at the bottom of the poverty heap, is to substantially improve and the small farmers are to have needed labor available at crucial points in the agricultural cycles, then national policies backed by programs must provide for off-farm employment within the rural areas. This off-farm work can be a combination of rural public works programs and small industries. Coordination of the off-farm work with the farm work will be important. Labor must be available for agriculture when needed and the off-farm work must be available in the slack farm employment periods. Difficult, through this will be, it is imperative if the small farmers are to modernize and the landless laborers are to have the right to earn enough to become free of the fear of hunger and to increase their presently low level of living.

9th Constraint: Low Level of the
Economies in the Developing Countries
The general low level of the economies in the Developing
Countries is a major impediment to modernizing small farm
agriculture; the needed massive funds to develop a national
infrastructure to serve small farm agriculture are simply not
available. Because of the low levels of the economy and the
substantial percentage of the Developing Countries' population
that lacks the income to pay for a minimum nutritional diet,
government food policies must be a compromise between low
prices for the consumers, most of whom are poor, and incentives
and minimum price guarantees for the producer. In compromises
now usually made, the incentives to the producer are generally
minimum; and the guarantees against risk and losses are simply
non-existent. This must change.
Research is urgently needed to provide policy guidance in
this crucial area.

10th Constraint: Slowness of the Evolutionary
Process of Removing Constraints
To remove and/or minimize the major constraints to small
farmers' risking change in farming methods and family patterns of living will take generations to achieve through evolutionary methods. That is not fast enough.
Since the population-food relationship is so very tenuous,
it is urgent to reduce the population pressures on resources.
The reforms needed to modernize small farm agriculture must be
made within a generation--say 25 years. This requires an
acceptance of reforms through revolutionary methods and maybe
not through revolutions.
It is just possible we could, even at this late hour, has-
ten the needed reforms without putting country after country
through revolutions to force changes. We have the experience
to draw on. We know how to concentrate brain power supported
by adequate funding and to direct it to research designed to
find solutions to problems. Maybe, just maybe, an international small farm center adequately staffed and funded could
have the needed influence to get the political leaders in the
Developing Countries to give leadership to reforms rather than
to have their countries go through a revolution. I'm enough of
an optimist to want to say, "Let's support an international
small farm institute and hope its research output and influence
will contribute to the acceptance by political leaders of the
need for far-reaching economical and institutional transforma-
tions." The political leaders do need help in identifying the
reforms needed most urgently if small farm agriculture is to be
modernized as an integral part of the process of transformation
of the traditional rural culture.

Though by nature I prefer to be optimistic, I would be intellectually dishonest if I did not share with you my deep concern that the evolutionary approach may not provide the conditions for needed land reforms and the transformation of institutions essential to modernizing small farm agriculture. Those political leaders in the Developing Countries who have functioned as the mouth piece for the small elite population have failed the small farmers and the landless laborers who make up much of the rural poor by denying them access to the nations' resources and institutions--resources and institutions which are essential if small farmers and landless laborers are to increase their production and improve their level of living.

To remove the major constraints to small farmers risking change in farming methods and family patterns of living through evolutionary methods will take generations to achieve. Because of the population pressures on the world's limited resources, we do not have time measured in generations to wait for the needed reforms.

I am not advocating that we sponsor revolutions. But I am saying we need not expect the needed reforms to be ushered in by the present elite power structures found in most Developing Countries.

As we celebrate our 200th anniversary, we should be sympathetic with the suppressed people of the world who join in revolutionary movements to free themselves from oppression by the elite and who seek equality of opportunity and sharing of their countries' resources.

DONALD L. WINKELMANN

Promoting the Adoption of New Plant Technology

The evidence is compelling. If food supplies are to stay abreast of growing populations and per capita income, farmers must increase yields. Moreover, if the lot of the world's poor is to improve, farmers in developing countries must increase yields. In short, needed increments in production and in real incomes rest on yield increases. Unless Nature turns uncharacteristically benevolent, attaining the increases will require that farmers change production technology.

Technological change in agriculture is not a new thing. New methods, new inputs, new varieties, even new crops have followed one another throughout history. What distinguishes today's scene from that of the past is today's strong sense of urgency and the emphasis on promoting change through institutional efforts.

Some of these efforts have been notable successes, others have been notable failures. Side by side are examples of new technologies which have literally swept the countryside and others which, while apparently promising much, have been rejected out of hand. Efforts to promote change could be enhanced, if factors which contribute to the rapid spread of new technologies could be identified.

The subject of this discussion is how adoption of new

Donald L. Winkelmann is Economist, International Maize and Wheat Improvement Center, Apartado Postal 6-641, Mexico 6, D.F., Mexico.

The author wishes to thank, without implicating, several CIMMYT colleagues. Opinions reflected here are not necessarily those of the International Maize and Wheat Improvement Center.

plant technology can be promoted. The focus is on developing
countries where the need for change is greatest. Most of the
observations emerge from a series of adoption studies in which
CIMMYT participated. The discussion opens with assumptions
about farmer behavior, moves to elements which might influence
farmer response to new technology, then focuses on data
selected from the adoption studies, and concludes with inference for policy makers.

THE FARMER

The farmer necessarily occupies a central role in any discussion of the adoption of new technology. He ultimately
decides on the use of a set of practices, thus is the pro-
tagonist of the drama. Agronomists, entomologists, extensionists, geneticists, and economists all play supporting roles.

By tailoring technologies so that they fit farmers' purposes, agricultural scientists make it more likely that farmers
will adopt them. Technologies which are not consonant with the
farmers' circumstances are likely to be rejected. So it is
that assumptions about farmers' purposes and circumstances are
critical. The formulation of new technologies is guided by
these assumptions.

The point of view taken in this discussion is that farmers are purposive in their behavior and are income-seeking risk
averters, that they are sensitive to the nuances of their environment, and that they are reasonably efficient in managing the
limited resources at their disposal. It is sometimes argued
that culture and tradition play a large role in shaping farmer
behavior, especially in developing countries. Our claim, which
parallels that of George Foster (1962, p. 151) is that, while
cultural elements may momentarily impede the use of a technology, the pull of economic forces will eventually dominate.
With this view of the farmer, those technologies which promise
significant increases in profits at acceptable levels of risk
will be adopted.

PROMOTING CHANGE

With profits and risk aversion as the dominant elements
shaping farmer response to technologies, there are two
avenues for influencing change. One involves changing the
environment so as to increase profits or reduce risks for given
technologies. The second involves developing whole new technologies. Virtually all nostrums for promoting change can be
grouped under one of these headings.

Environmental changes commonly recommended are those which
facilitate access to information, to inputs, and to markets.
These include extension work, credit programs, lower prices for

inputs, effective distribution of inputs, guaranteed prices, storage programs, and market roads. Most of these measures can be directly influenced by government policy.

Developing new technology usually involves research. Work on varieties emphasizes grain type, susceptibility to disease and insects, maturity dates, storability, growth patterns, and responsiveness to management. Work on agronomic practices tends to focus on fertilizers and dates of planting.

The remaining discussion is on developing new technologies. It will be argued that making technologies profitable is the dominant factor in promoting change. As a corollary, when technologies fail in diffusion it is usually because they are not sufficiently profitable or are excessively risky. This might be because of farmer access to information, inputs or markets or it could be that the proposed technology is not effective in converting inputs to product. The ensuing discussion focuses on the latter. It points to the possibility that a major difficulty is in research methodology, i.e. that insufficient attention is given to farmer circumstances in developing and testing technologies.

The argument rests on the examination of the adoption of new technology in three countries. For each, agro-climatic regions were identified and adoption rates for each region were estimated. Marked differences are evident in adoption rates between regions receiving essentially similar institutional treatments. The differences can be related to profit and risk. The inference drawn is that the recommendations did not fit farmer circumstances in some regions, hence were not adopted. To promote adoption, research methods must be changed so that farmers' circumstances play a more central role in developing and evaluating alternatives.

ADOPTION OF NEW PLANT TECHNOLOGIES

Farmers response to new technologies in Turkey, Kenya, and Mexico is the subject of this section. It will be argued that agro-climatic circumstances, with their differing implications for profits and risks, dominated the adoption of new technologies there. Farm size--with its implications for access to information and to inputs, for transaction costs, and for aversion to risk--will be shown to have been influential in the use of fertilizers in some cases.

In each of the countries a package of practices was presented to the farmers. Extension workers emphasized the complementarities among the elements of the package, and exhorted farmers to use all elements together in order to reap all potential advantages. It will be evident from the three programs reported here that farmers see these elements as separable and take them up one at a time.

Turkey

In Turkey the focus is on the country's spring wheat producing areas and on one winter wheat area. With the help
of agricultural scientists the spring wheat area was partitioned into three regions. From each of these three and from
the single winter wheat area some 200 wheat producing farmers
were selected at random and interviewed in 1973. These were
then designated as hillsides or flatlands depending on the
topography of their farms. So few flatland farmers appeared in
Thrace that the category was eliminated there. Finally each
group was arrayed by size and the array divided into two farm
size classes at the median (Demir, 1976).

Two elements dominated the new technology. The first was
high yielding varieties (HYVs) of Italian and Mexican origin
for the spring wheats and of Russian origin for the winter
wheats. The second was the application of fertilizer. Tables
1 and 2 show how farmers responded to the two elements by
region, topography, and farm size and, in the case of fertilizer, by class of wheat seeded.

TABLE 1. Adoption of HYVs among sampled farmers by size of
          farm, region, and topography (percent) in Turkey,
          1972

Region	Topography	Smaller farmers	Larger farmers	All farmers
Mediterranean	Hills	92	90	91
	Flat	95	97	96
Aegean	Hills	4	23	14
	Flat	60	77	69
South Marmara	Hills	13	32	22
	Flat	70	43	57
Thrace	Hills	62	85	70

Source: Demir (1976, p. 13).

Looking at use of HYVs of spring wheats, there are clear
differences from region to region and, with the exception of
Mediterranean Region, flatland farmers planted more HYVs than
did the hillside farmers.

What might explain these differences among profit seeking
risk averting farmers? First, the Mexican wheats lacked cold
tolerance and the Italian wheats are not as cold tolerant as
are the local varieties. Second, the Mexican wheats were susceptible to Septoria, a now-and-again fungus disease of wheat
in the Mediterranean littoral.

TABLE 2. Average fertilizer use on wheat for sampled farmers
by size, region, topography and class of seed (Kgs/ha
of nitrogen + phosphorus) in Turkey, 1972

Region	Topography	HYVs		Other	
		Smaller farmers	Larger farmers	Smaller farmers	Larger farmers
Mediterranean	Hill	133	153	-	-
	Flat	114	124	-	-
Aegean	Hill	-	64	26	30
	Flat	64	60	16	27
South Marmara	Hill	69	64	41	42
	Flat	80	65	37	48
Thrace	Hill	107	110	67	89

Source: Demir (1976, p. 16).

With this as background, consider the regions. The Mediterranean Region virtually never suffers from cold weather.
Septoria fungus there occurs less often than in the Aegean or
South Marmara Regions. Moreover, a goodly proportion of the
Aegean and South Marmara hillsides and a small proportion of
the flatlands are at altitudes where damaging cold is frequent.
Finally, these two regions as described for the study are far
more heterogeneous than was hoped, even after making the parti-
tion for topography. Each includes a mixture of disparate sub-
regions.

Juxtaposing the characteristics of the wheats with those
of the spring wheat regions, the Mediterranean Region offers no
environmental hazards to HYVs. Yields are well above those of
local varieties. Recommended varieties are used by virtually
all farmers.

Abstracting from the heterogeneity within each region, the
Aegean and South Marmara Regions presented hazards in the form
of cold weather in the higher hillsides. Moreover, for Mexican
varieties, disease in the low lying flat lands, especially in
South Marmara, is a second hazard to yields. Adoption rates
are far higher in the flatlands than in the hillsides and somewhat higher in the Aegean flatlands, where Septoria is rarely a
problem, than in South Marmara.

More recent field work in Turkey indicates that, if truly
homogeneous sub-regions were drawn within the larger Aegean and
South Marmara Regions, very high rates of adoption of HYVs
would be found in some sub-regions and very low rates of adoption in others. Two pairs of Aegean villages included in the
original survey were visited again. It was found that marked

differences in climate between paired villages accounted for
sharp differences in adoption rates.

In Thrace, 70 percent of the farmers had adopted HYVs in
1972. Why was the rate not higher, as with Mexican wheats in
Mediterranean Region? The Russian winter wheat was introduced
to Thrace in the late 1960s, some two years after the Mexican
varieties were introduced into the Mediterranean Region. It
can be argued that insufficient time had elapsed for the variety to reach all who will finally use it. For the same reason,
more large farmers had adopted than small farmers. It is common to find larger farmers among earlier adopters with differences diminishing as time passes (Gerhart, 1975; Vyas, 1975).
In the Mediterranean Region sufficient time had elapsed to
erase differences between farm size classes. In Thrace, with
some two to three years less experience with the new varieties,
a difference in adoption rates is still apparent. A survey
taken in 1975, say, would undoubtedly have shown both classes
of farmers with adoption rates on the order of 90 percent.

It can now be asked how farm size might influence income
seeking risk averters. Larger farmers have easier access to
information and inputs than have smaller farmers, face lower
per hectare transaction costs, and tend to be less averse to
risk. Each of these considerations makes larger farmers more
likely than smaller farmers to appear within the ranks of earlier adopters. In the Mediterranean Region the HYVs are sufficiently profitable and stable and have been available for sufficient time that farm size had little influence on adoption.
In Thrace, it is likely that, given two to three more years of
diffusion, the farm size differences will have narrowed to the
levels of the Mediterranean Region. For the Aegean and South
Marmara Regions, conclusions about the influence of farm size
must be tempered by the knowledge that neither region has the
desired level of homogeneity. In three zones, larger farmers
lead smaller farmers by large margins; in the fourth the order
is reversed and the margin is even larger. Whether this
reflects differences within homogeneous regions or is itself a
result of interaction between sub-regions and farm size is not
clear.

Turning to fertilizer use, there are clear differences
from region to region and between HYVs and other varieties.
The regions in which hazards are least evident, Mediterranean
and Thrace, reported the highest fertilizer use. Among farmers
using HYVs, farm size has negligible effect within regions
except for the Meditarranean Region where larger farmers use
more fertilizers. The differences are not large, certainly not
as large as the differences from region to region.

In general, the Turkish data support the view that agro-
climatic circumstances, through their impact on profits and
risk, dominate the adoption of the elements of new technology.

Kenya

For Kenya, the case is even more clear cut. A series of hybrid maizes were introduced in the 1960s in the area West of the Rift Valley. Each of these included high altitude germ plasm from the Andean Region of Latin America. A farm level study undertaken by Gerhart in 1973 examined factors influencing the adoption of hybrids and associated inputs. Three agro-climatic regions were delineated and 300 farmers were interviewed. For each region the farms were arrayed by size and divided at the median into two size classes.

Tables 3 and 4 give the percentage of farmers using hybrids and fertilizers by region and by size class. Table 3 shows sharp differences attributable to agro-climatic region but only slight differences related to size. The regional differences are easily explained. Regions 1 and 2 are areas of high elevation both above 1500 meters and with good rainfall. Region 3 is below 1500 meters and with variable rainfall. The high altitude germ plasm of the Kenya hybrids promotes good performance at high altitudes. They were developed at an experiment station in Region 2. At lower altitudes their yield advantage over local maize declines notably and finally disappears.

TABLE 3. Adoption of improved maize HYVs by region and farm size class (percent) in Kenya, 1973

	Region 1	Region 2	Region 3
Smaller half	95.7	83.7	14.9
Larger half	95.8	95.1	17.4

Source: Gerhart (1975, p. 24).

TABLE 4. Fertilizer use on maize by region and farm size (percent) in Kenya, 1973

	Region 1	Region 2	Region 3
Smaller	47.8	71.4	2.1
Larger	75.0	92.5	6.4

Source: Gerhart (1975, p. 24).

It is little wonder, then, that in Regions 1 and 2, where the hybrids yield advantage over local maizes is marked, profit seeking risk averting farmers have adopted the hybrids while in Region 3, with little if any yield advantage, they have not done so. More accurately, Region 3 farmers have not continued

to use hybrids. While only 16 percent of the sampled farmers
were using hybrids in 1973, 35 percent reported using hybrids
at some previous time (Gerhart, 1975, p. 24).

The agro-climatic differences are again evident in fertilizer use but, as contrasted with HYV use, size is also playing
a role. Fertilizer use in Region 3 is dramatically lower than
in Regions 1 and 2 and Region 1 is appreciably lower than
Region 2. Virtually all of the fertilizer was used on hybrids
(Gerhart, 1975, p. 29). It is not clear why more farmers used
fertilizer in Region 2, with lower rainfall and lesser use of
hybrids than in Region 1. Perhaps it is the influence of the
experiment station in Region 2. In each of the Regions, the
proportion of larger farmers applying fertilizer to maize is
greater than for smaller farmers.

In short, the study in Kenya West of Rift Valley reaffirms
the importance of agro-climatic region on the use of hybrids
and fertilizer. Hybrids are relatively more profitable in
Regions 1 and 2 than in Region 3, where for the lower parts of
the region there is likely to be little gain in profit at all.
Fertilizer use is influenced by agro-climatic region and by
farm size as well. The influence of farm size can be attributed to lower risk aversion and transaction costs or to better
access to inputs and information for larger farmers.

Mexico

The area studied in Mexico was that of Plan Puebla. Plan
Puebla was organized in 1967 to develop and field test a
methodology for fomenting rapid increases in the production of
a basic cereal under rainfed conditions. The organizers sought
a site with adequate infrastructure, low probability of crop
failure, small farmers, and low yields. They chose a high valley lying around the city of Puebla, two hours east of Mexico
City.

The hallmarks of the Plan were (1) research on farmers'
fields; (2) dissemination of information and inputs through
farmers groups organized for that purpose; (3) close cooperation among researchers, extensionists and evaluators; (4) col-
laboration among the Plan organization, government institutions, and farmers; and (5) emphasis on the working rules of
institutions rather than their formal rules.

While the project area is small, encompassing about
120,000 ha of cultivable land and about 80,000 ha of maize, it
is quite variable. As researchers sought to develop precise
recommendations for increasing profits, recommendations are
available for nine different soil types.

Despite the variation, the Plan area can be partitioned
into two regions. One of these, Region A, has recommendations
for eight soil types but essentially the same recommendation
applies to 45 percent of the region. The second, Region B, has

only one soil type and one recommendation.

The recommendations featured larger applications of fertilizer and greater planting densities than with the conventional technology. No change in variety was recommended as the first years of work convinced researchers that varieties were not limiting yields. The agronomic practices promised marked increases in yields. On experimental plots the increase was estimated at 1.8 tons/ha in Region A and 2.0 tons/ha in Region B (Winkelmann, 1976, p. 29).

Each year a yield survey is taken in the Plan area. Since 1971, these surveys have included yields, plant densities, and fertilizer use. In three years--1972, 1973, 1975-- farm size was also included. These surveys provided the data for analyzing several facets of the Plan.

If adoption of the recommended technology is defined strictly--as use of at least the quantity of inputs recommended--farmers have adopted on few plots. Table 5 shows the percentage of plots receiving various combinations of the recommended elements in 1975. Overall, less than 10 percent of the randomly selected plots were receiving the treatment recommended.

TABLE 5.   Percent of surveyed plots on which adoption of Plan-
            like recommendations occurred in 1975. Plan Puebla

	Region 1	Region 2
N^a	34	65
N + P^b	13	-
N P + D^c	2	11

^{a}N: At least 110 kgs/ha nitrogen in Region 1; at least 100 kgs/ha in Region 2.
^{b}N + P: N as above and at least 40 kgs/ha of phosphorus in Region 1; phosphorus not recommended in Region 2.
^{c}N + P + D: N and P as above and more than 45,000 plants ha at harvest time.
Source: Yield survey data 1975, Plan Puebla.

A variety of explanations have been offered for this apparently low level of adoption, ranging from risk (Winkelmann, 1974) to institutional shortcomings (Diaz, 1974), to the opportunity cost of labor (Villa Issa, 1976). A close look at data from the yield surveys of 1971, 1972, and 1973[1] and at experimental data suggests, however, that the chief cause

1. Yield data for 1975 were not available at the time of writing and data for 1974 were eliminated because the area suffered its earliest frost in over 50 years with substantial reductions in yields in some places.

might well be the recommendations themselves.

Several findings might explain why few farmers are planting the recommended densities. In analyses based on experimental data from the Plan, Moscardi (1976) and Hernández (1972)
suggest that yields are little influenced by planting densities
of over 40/45,000 plants. Winkelmann (1976) presents data from
the yield surveys which show yields higher with high densities
in a good year, roughly equal in an average year, and goes on
to infer that densities and yields are negatively related in a
bad year. On the average, higher densities with at least
intermediate levels of fertilizer might well pay off but in
some years they can reduce yields. Risk averters might not
accept this.

In fertilizer use, nitrogen is the most costly component
of the recommendation in Region A and its only component in
Region B. Region B has a far higher proportion of farmers
using at least recommended levels than has Region A. (Even
lowering the Region A definition to 100 kg/ha of nitrogen adds
only 2 percentage points to the proportion defined as adopting).

For both regions survey and experimental data imply that
profits increase as the farmer moves from the conventional to
the recommended strategy. But farmers need not limit their
choice to these two technologies, many other choices are open
to them. The data from 1971-73 yield surveys suggests that the
farmers of Region A would actually prefer an alternative choice
(see Table 6).

TABLE 6. Average yields on surveyed plots, 1971-73, adjusted
          for the off-farm maize cost of fertilizer[a] for three
          production technologies. Plan Puebla

	Conventional technology[b]	Intermediate technology[b]	Intensive technology[b]
Region A	1570	2668	2447
Region B	1887	2637	2892

[a]Maize cost of fertilizer at the farm gate was subtracted from
each yield.
[b]Conventional: 0-50 kgs nitrogen, 0-25 kg phosphorus, 15-
                  35,000 plants in Zones 1-4 and 15-30,000 plants
                  in Zone 5.
  Intermediate: 90-119 kgs nitrogen, 20-50 kgs of phosphorus,
                 35-60,000 plants in Zones 1-4; 80-100 kgs of
                 nitrogen, 33-66,000 plants in Zone 5.
  Intensive: 120-160 kgs of nitrogen, 40-70 kgs of phospho-
              rus, 35-60,000 plants in Zones 1-4; 101-160 kgs
              of nitrogen, 33-60,000 plants in Zone 5.
Source: Yield surveys 1971, 1972, 1973, Plan Puebla

In both regions the intensive strategy, the strategy clos-
est to the recommendations, had higher adjusted yields than had
the conventional strategy. But in the case of Region A, the
intermediate strategy gave higher average yields than the
intensive strategy. In no case would inclusion of the opportunity cost of labor have changed the order, even were family
labor valued at its estimated upper boundary. A profit seeking
farmer whose fields matched the average plots of the surveys
would choose the intermediate strategy in Region A and the
intensive strategy in Region B.

The fertilizer data were examined to see if farm size and
nitrogen use were related in 1975. In Region A the average
nitrogen use was almost exactly the same for larger and smaller
farmers, 88 kgs/ha and 86 kgs/ha. In Region B, smaller farmers
used less nitrogen on the average than did larger farmers, 108
kgs/ha to 123 kgs/ha, but the differences have little statistical significance. The same result emerges from comparing smaller and larger farmers in the proportion of each applying less
than 40 kgs/ha of nitrogen in 1975.

The yield data were then used to make frequency distributions. These are consistent with the idea that risk aversion
would not lead farmers to choose the conventional strategy. In
general the risk averter would rank the strategies in the same
way as the profit seeker (Winkelmann, 1976, p. 68).

Table 5 shows that farmers are doing roughly what would be
expected, given the earlier assumptions about behavior. More
and more farmers in Region B are moving to higher levels of
fertilizer. Meanwhile, in Region A, far fewer farmers are following the fertilizer recommendations of the Plan. Even so,
average fertilizer use has increased markedly since 1967.
While 72 percent of the farmers surveyed in 1967 used less than
40 kgs/ha of nitrogen, only 23 percent did so in 1975. In
neither case are many farmers using the planting densities
recommended.

Agro-climatic conditions again determined how a technology
fit farmer circumstances and thus had a notable effect on diffusion of new technology.

A Caveat
    For each of the countries, sharp differences in adoption
    rates are evident among agro-climatic regions. But to
what extent are these differences from region to region within
a country due to different environments?

It is probably true that institutional treatments--exten-
sion service, infrastructure, access to inputs--are somewhat
better in Turkey's Mediterranean than in Aegean Region, better
in Kenya's Region 2 than in Region 3. Still, these differences
appear to be slight as compared with the differences in adop-

tion rates. And in Plan Puebla, if such differences exist, they favor Region A where adoption rates are lowest.

In the main, the regional differences in adoption rates result from the relative suitability of the technologies. Getting the technology right is the critical step in promoting technological change.

CONCLUSIONS

There are evident patterns in adoption of improved varieties and fertilizers when farms are grouped in terms of agro-climatic region. Patterns for fertilizers also appear when farmers are grouped by size. The argument developed here is that these patterns can be explained in terms of profitability and risk without resorting to other explanations. Passing reference was made to other forms of analysis featuring many other variables. These larger models offered little insight into the process of diffusing technologies beyond that gained from the simple tables presented here.

Farmers quickly take up varieties which suit their purposes--roughly 95 percent of Turkey's Mediterranean farmers were using HYV spring wheat only five years after introduction and over 70 percent of the farmers in Thrace reported using HYVs within three years after their introduction. Larger farmers are usually among the first to adopt with smaller farmers following quickly.

Fertilizers are taken up less quickly and tend to be used in lesser amounts than recommended. Farm size generally influences fertilizer use with smaller farmers usually applying less than do larger farmers in similar agro-climatic circumstances. These actions could be a consequence of differing access to credit and inputs, differing transaction costs, or differing sensitivity to risk between larger and smaller farmers.

What does all of this imply for those concerned with promoting widespread diffusion of new technology? They can influence farmer decisions by maintaining favorable price ratios and by insuring widespread access to inputs as well as to information, in brief by influencing the environment of the farmer. There are certainly cases where such efforts would foster more rapid diffusion of technologies. But the marked influence of agro-climatic factors in adoption makes it appear that policy makers' primary concern should be to insure that research efforts lead to the evolution of technologies which truly fit the needs of those farmers for whom they have the strongest sense of concern. This is the critical requisite. To do this, research must be organized so that farmers' circumstances play a more central role in developing and evaluating alternative technologies.

REFERENCES

Demir, N. 1976. The Adoption of New Bread Wheat Technology in
    Selected Regions of Turkey--Edited and abridged by CIMMYT,
    Centro Internacional de Mejoramiento de Maíz y Trigo, Mex-
    ico City, Mexico.
Díaz, H. 1974. An institutional analysis of a rural develop-
    ment project: the case of the Puebla Project in Mexico,
    (Unpublished Ph.D. Thesis), University of Wisconsin, USA.
Foster, G. 1962. Traditional Cultures and the Impact of Tech-
    nological Change, Harper and Row, New York.
Gerhart, J. 1975. The Diffusion of Hydrid Maize in Western
    Kenya--Abridged by CIMMYT. Centro Internacional de
    Mejoramiento de Maíz y Trigo. Mexico City, Mexico.
Hernández, R. 1972. El modelo aproximativo y la matriz exper-
    imental como factores que influyen sobre el Riesgo, al
    aproximar superficies de respuesta a dos factores, (Unpub-
    lished Masters Thesis), Tesis de Maetría, Colegio de Post-
    graduados, Chapingo, México.
Moscardi, E. R. 1976. A behavioral model for decision under
    risk among small holding farmers. (Unpublished Ph.D.
    Thesis), University of California, Berkeley, California,
    USA.
Villa Issa, M. R. 1976. The effect of the labor market in the
    adoption of new production technology in a rural develop-
    ment project. The case of the Plan Puebla, Mexico, (Unpub-
    lished Ph.D. Thesis), Purdue University, West Lafayette,
    Indiana, USA.
Vyas, V. S. 1975. India's High Yielding Varieties Programme
    in Wheat 1966-67 to 1971-72. Centro Internacional de
    Mejoramiento de Maíz y Trigo, Mexico City, Mexico.
Winkelmann, D. 1975. Plan Puebla after six years, in Small
    Farmer Agricultural Study in Developing Nations. Bulletin
    No. 101, Department of Agricultural Economics, Agricultural
    Experiment Station, Purdue University, West Lafayette,
    Indiana, USA.
Winkelmann, D. 1976. The Adoption of New Maize Technology in
    Plan Puebla, Mexico. Centro Internacional de Mejoramiento
    de Maíz y Trigo, Mexico City, Mexico.

M. J. JOHN

Alternative Approaches to Adoption of Animal Technology

In India, whether land is used for agriculture, or raising livestock or fishing, it is a way of life for her people. Commercialisation of these activities and application of modern technology in production and processing have only touched the fringes. In animal agriculture the raising of crops and livestock are interlocked for mutual advantage. Diffusion of knowledge in production, processing and marketing of products is no longer the preserve of any one nation, or group of peoples. Technology knows no national barriers. It is the diffusion of the knowledge and adoption of the technology due to many constraints that remain as the hurdle to progress and human welfare around the globe.

ASSESSMENT OF PRESENT KNOWLEDGE

<u>Milk-Cattle</u>

Poor production of the Indian cow is one of both inheritance and poor management. The livestock wealth of India is immense in terms of quantity (numbers), the problem is essentially one of putting quality into cattle.

Realising the poor genetic composition of the Indian cow for milk production, and to meet the need of the army for milk, the first military dairy farm was started at Allahabad in 1899. The exotic breed Holstein-Friesian was imported. Several other

M. J. John is president of Voorhees College, Vellore, India.

Military Dairy farms were also started. On the first of April
1975 there were 24 military farms with 9835 animals. With the
culled animals from these military farms and by the use of the
superior bulls on these farms, improved and cross-bred stock
developed in the big cities of India. In the second quarter of
the century distribution of purebred bulls of Indian breeds was
a major scheme of many state governments to improve the cattle.
It made some impact on the towns and cities, but the village
cattle by and large remained unaffected by these schemes. The
average milk production of the Indian cow is 450 litres for
300 days of lactation. The vast majority of the Indian cattle
are the village herds and indiscriminate breeding is the pattern. The significant concept in livestock breeding "the cock
is half the flock" and the "bull is half the herd" is still
alien to the farmer's thinking.

    The "Key Village Scheme" and "Gaushala Development Scheme"
were introduced by the Indian Government in early Five Year
Plans to improve the stock on a broad basis. According to the
National Commission on Agriculture (1976) these schemes suffered due to several limitations, namely, a larger population
of cattle than the land could support, enormous numbers of
unproductive cattle, shortage of feed and fodder, and great
paucity of superior quality breeding bulls. Some 600 Key Village Schemes using Holstein-Friesian, Brown Swiss, and Jersey
bulls covering a population of 6 million breedable cows were
mostly failures according to the Report of the National Commission on Agriculture. Hence in the Fourth Five Year Plan,
Intensive Cattle Development Projects (ICDP) were initiated
with 5 big farms and by 1974 there were 62 ICDP projects in
operation. Cross breeding is accepted as a national policy.
The Government of India took this bold step against the background of the success of the two pilot projects: the Indo-
Swiss Project in Kerala and Brown Swiss Project in Bangalore,
and the overall impact made by Holstein-Friesian around the
Military Dairy farms and in major cities of India. These
crossbreds have shown the following advantages:

    1. A longer lactation period, about 10 months as against
6 to 8 months for the "desi."[1]
    2. A higher reproduction efficiency, conceiving within
three months after calving as against 3 to 6 months for the
"desi."[1]
    3. A lower maintenance cost, higher milk production and
greater efficiency of feed conversion and hence more economical to maintain than the "desi."

Holstein-Friesian, Brown Swiss, and Red Dane are the

----

1. "Desi" refers to local or native bird or animal.

breeds used for semen distribution. Using a Brown Swiss sire with the milk potential of 4000 kgs during the lactation period, the F1 cross gave about 2500 kgs for a lactation. For the F2 the increase averaged roughly 200 kgs for a lactation. The scheme is in the early stages and since the F2 performance was not encouraging, the effort now is to produce an F3 of 62.5 percent pure blood instead of the 75 percent in the F2. The crossbred program has come to stay as the major approach for the improvement of Indian cattle. The studies at the National Dairy Research Institute at Karnal by Singh and Rastogi (1974) have revealed that the purebred Indian Red Sindhi and Murrah buffaloe are far exceeded by the crossbred cattle in cheap milk production (Table 1).

TABLE 1. Studies of milk production in two of Indian purebred cattle, Murrah buffaloe and crossbreed Holstein cows

Breed	Age at first calving	Maintenance cost per day Rs.	Net profit in Rs taking all expenses into A/c	Cost per litre of milk paise
Red Sindhi	1241	3.61	− 3.6	55.07
Sahiwal	1287	2.81	− 80.3	54.22
Murrah Buffaloe	1390	2.81	+ 182.5	70.51
Crossbreed Cow	1011	2.37	+ 1091.3	38.27

Source: Singh Bhupal and B. K. Rastogi (1974, p. 66).

The average number of inseminations for obtaining a female calf under farm conditions with good management is only 3.6 but it takes seven or more inseminations under village conditions to obtain a female calf. Results with frozen semen are even worse.

The decentralized system of one to a few animals of the improved type in a household under the Cooperative Milk societies and Dairy corporations is the approach India is making. It is not the question of production of more milk alone but one of helping a larger number of individuals to achieve a better living standard.

Milk in India is very costly mainly because of the concentrates in the feed. Green forage of high quality and yield are needed to replace the concentrates. The Agricultural Commission places special emphasis on growing forage crops of high quality on irrigated lands. However, there are extensive areas of government and forest lands where the villagers can graze their cattle free of charges but there is no effort on the part of the farmers or of the government to improve the quality of grass on these pastured lands.

Milk-Buffaloe
    The buffaloe ranks second in world milk production and
India has 53 percent of the world's buffaloe population
(Table 2).

TABLE 2. World production of milk from each of the four major
          dairy species of domestic animals

	Thousand metric tonnes
Cows	365,230
Buffaloes	22,691
Goats	6,643
Sheep	6,368
Total	400,932

Source: Cockrill, Ross W. (1974, p. 331).

    The popularity of buffaloe as a dairy animal is due to the
high percentage of butterfat, almost double that of the cattle.
The buffaloe is an effective utilizer of low quality roughage.
It has been noted by many writers that the buffaloe seems to
possess a remarkable ability to convert coarse products into
milk, says Cockrill (1974). There are several breeds of buffaloes and some of the best ones available are in India.
Selective breeding with rigid culling within the breeds available in India is the policy adopted.
    About 40 percent of the milk produced in India in 1951,
was consumed as fluid milk while 45 percent was used in making
butter and "ghee."[2] In 1966 the fluid milk consumption rose to
44.5 percent and the utilization of milk for ghee and butter
declined to 39 percent (Table 3). The making of "ghee" and
butter is a wasteful method since adequate facilities do not

TABLE 3. Pattern of milk utilization in India

Year	Milk	Ghee	Butter	Curd	Khon[a]	Cream and ice cream	Other
1951	39.3	39.3	6.0	8.8	4.4	1.2	.4
1956	39.1	40.0	6.1	6.8	4.4	1.2	.4
1961	35.2	31.8	6.4	8.1	4.7	2.6	1.2
1966	44.5	32.7	6.3	7.8	4.9	2.6	1.2

Source: Report of the National Commission on Agriculture
(1976, p. 309).
[a]Khon is milk concentrated by boiling.

2. "Ghee" is melted butter.

exist to convert the by-products into useful human food, or
articles of industrial value. A lot of skimmed milk is produced which is not properly used.

Meat

The National Commission on Agriculture refers to the existence of some 2800 slaughter houses in the country. The
hygienic conditions in most of these slaughter houses are
appalling and animal by-products of substantial value are being
wasted. Some 720,000 tons of meat are produced annually, of
which, 54 percent is from sheep and goats, 26 percent from buffaloes and cattle, 13 percent from poultry and 7 percent from
pigs (Table 4). From the 631,000 tons in 1966 the animal meat
production rose to 721,000 tons in 1974. This is an increase
of 14 percent over the 10 year period while the population
increase over the same period was 25 percent. Hence, the per
capita availability of meat has gone down. The projected meat
production for 1985 is 1.1 to 1.4 million tons. Per capita
availability in 1971 was 1.25 kg per annum and this is expected
to rise to a point between 1.45 and 1.93 kgs by 1985.

TABLE 4. Meat production in India (in 000 tonnes)

	1965	1968	1969	1970	1971	1972	1973	1974
Beef and Buffaloe Meat	165	169	170	176	179	182	186	187
Mutton and Goat Meat	353	356	356	366	371	377	384	385
Poultry	70	69	69	83	86	90	95	95
Pig	43	51	52	52	52	52	53	54
Total	631	645	647	677	688	701	718	721

Source: Report of the National Commission on Agriculture
(1976, p. 864).

The main source of meat in India is from sheep, goats and
poultry. One may question the reliability of the figures in
the case of cattle and even in buffaloes due to the clandestine
operations in this areas as cow slaughter is banned in certain
areas for cultural and religious reasons. A look at some of
the other countries reveals how unrealistic is the approach to
this major source of animal protein. India slaughters only 2.3
percent of her cattle and buffaloe population compared to 30
percent for the United Kingdom and 40 percent for Denmark
(Tables 5 and 6).

According to the National Commission on Agriculture (1976,

TABLE 5. Percentage of animals slaughtered in India

Type of animal	Percentage of slaughtered
Cattle	0.9
Buffaloe	1.4
Sheep	32.5
Goats	36.8
Pigs	22.0
Others	6.4

Source: Report of the National Commission on Agriculture (1976, p. 867).

TABLE 6. Percentage of cattle slaughtered in some of the developed countries--1969

Country	Cattle population in thousands	No. slaughtered in thousands	Percentage
USA	112,330	40,585	36.16
UK	12,697	3,798	29.91
Denmark	2,835	1,157	40.81
Australia	20,700	7,213	34.84
New Zealand	8,839	3,051	34.52

Source: Report of the National Commission on Agriculture (1976, p. 867).

p. 890), out of the 22.8 million carcasses of "fallen"[3] animals available each year, only 53 percent are partly utilized, and the rest are wasted. If these animals were slaughtered, it would be a rich source of meat, though tough.

Sheep and Goats

Sheep and goats are the major source of meat in India and provide two-thirds of the nation's total meat production. The 40 million sheep provide annually 101 million kg of meat. Limited efforts have been made to do crossbreeding with exotic breeds to increase carcass weight and wool production. Live weight of an Indian ram ranges from 26 to 36 kgs, and that of ewes from 18 to 27 kgs. In the exotic breeds rams range from 60 to 113 kgs and ewes from 54 to 74 kgs. Regional Farms

3. "Fallen" animals are cattle not slaughtered but permitted to die a natural death as cow slaughter is banned in most states.

for crossbreeding using Merino and Romney March have been set
up for improvement of the indigeneous stock. At present the
body weight of the indigeneous stock at 6 months is only 18 kgs
while the target of the Central Sheep and Wool Research Institute is to produce a 30 to 35 kg animal at 6 months of age by
the crossbreeding program. Most of the sheep are raised in
small flocks of 10 to 50 by the small farmers and the landless
villagers, grazing them on Government lands and waste lands in
the villages.

In 1972 there were 68 million goats which were 19 percent
of the world's goat population and they provided 35 percent of
the meat and 3 percent of the milk produced in India. Some 27
million goats are slaughtered every year. Goats have an advantage over sheep. Sheep have a single lamb progeny whereas in
goats 54 percent are twins and 6 percent triplets. Also, goats
thrive on grazing. There is not much incentive to improve the
meat production of goats by crossbreeding since the exotic
breeds are all dairy animals. Selective breeding is the only
means that is being attempted. The browsing habit of goats has
a devastating effect on vegetation. In goat rearing, numbers
may vary from a single animal in a household to a flock of 100
or more. Most of the goats are raised by the weaker sections
of the society, small farmers and the landless villagers who
graze them on waste lands and forest lands.

Poultry

Among the farm animals poultry are the quickest and most
efficient converters of plant products into food of high
biological value. Although India was one of the first countries to domesticate the jungle fowl, its performance still
remains very low. The missionary organizations at Katpadi,
Martandam and Etah were the first to introduce high producing
exotic breeds at the turn of the century. During the second
World War the Military set up 10 farms with 10,000 birds for
their egg consumption needs.

In 1971, the egg production was 6040 million eggs. As a
whole 90 percent of the poultry meat is from the indigeneous
bird. Franchise hatcheries were set up in India in the 1960s
importing only the grandparent stock. This made available
genetically superior hybrid chicks. The three foreign based
hybrid stocks are that of USA, Israel and Czechoslovakia.
Efforts to evolve strains within the country under a coordinated poultry breeding project at 3 Central and 24 State farms
are under way. Progress so far is slow, reports the National
Commission on Agriculture.

In Poultry three levels of husbandry exist: (1) specialized commercial enterprises centered around urban, semi-urban
and industrial belts; (2) groups of poultry farms with medium
size flocks where a level of medium management practices exist

with some imputs and know-how of modern poultry-keeping; and
(3) back-yard poultry-keeping practiced extensively in rural
areas, with small flocks predominently of the "desi" birds.
     To the poor, the "desi" chicken that feeds on the free
range in the village is the main source of cash income and provides 90 percent of the poultry meat. In 1974 poultry meat
production was 110 million kgs from the "desi" birds and 4 million kgs from the broilers. The aim is to produce a broiler
weighing 1.5 kg at 10 weeks of age with a 2.5 feed efficiency.
     In poultry, 70 to 75 percent of the total cost of produc-
tion is the cost of feed. The technology of modern feed compu-
tation has come with the improved stock. The cost of ingredients and their availability in time are the problems. In most
rations 30 to 40 percent of the feed is food grains which compete with human food. In 1970, the cost of a metric ton of
feed was Rs 690 while in 1974 the same feed cost was Rs 1300
per metric ton. This is an increase of 88 percent at a time
when the egg price went from 25 to 32 paise--an increase of
only 28 percent. Refrigerated transport and storage for eggs
are sporadic. Two processing plants for chicken, one at
Chandigrah with a capacity of 5000 and the other at Poona with
a capacity of 8000 per day are in operation. In addition, 15
plants of 1000 bird per day capacity at wide-spread locations
supply meat to the local market. Poultry meat is very costly.
Live weight price of one kg ranges from Rs 8 to Rs 10. Dressed
chicken range from Rs 12 to Rs 15.
     In short, India has the technology for hybrid chickens,
and the balanced ration of the Western world. It is the adoption of this technology in commercial mass production that
revolutionized the poultry industry of USA making it the cheapest meat in that country. Our effort is to have the mass production benefits using the same technology but in units of 100
to a 1000 birds and have several such units in a compact area
to benefit maximum numbers of people. This method of production is showing very promising results in Kerala state and Punjab.

Pigs
     Pigs are one of the most neglected areas of meat produc-
tion. About 90 percent of the pigs raised are kept by the
socially weaker sections of the society. These animals survive
by scavenging. There is a general prejudice against eating
pork. Consumption of pork and pork products is confined to
certain tribes and castes and poor classes of people. In the
large metropolitan cities a small section of the sophisticated
people also eat pork. In the Muslim community it is a religious taboo.
     Realizing the importance of producing quality meat, and
since pigs have the shortest generation interval and high feed

conversion efficiency, the Governmemt has gone in for cross-breeding the "desi" with exotic breeds of white Yorkshire and Landrace. Some 55 breeding stations and 140 piggery development blocks are functioning. Also, 8 processing plants have been set up in the States to process the products. A factory at Borivili with a capacity for 100 pigs per day has been established. Besides the supply of fresh meat, the main products processed are bacon, ham and sausage. In 1974, some 54,000 tonnes of meat were produced from pigs; this formed 7 percent of the total meat production in the country.

Seventy-five to 80 percent of the cost of production is in feed. Feeds free of grains and cheap are needed to solve the problem of raising quality pigs. The processing plants are not used to full capacity.

Fish

India shaped like a triangle to the Southern half has a coastline of 3500 km. According to the 1961 census there were 959,337 fisher-folk in the coastal areas and 22,935 fishermen. In 1975, 1.31 million tonnes of sea fish and 0.7 million tonnes of inland fish were caught. About 25 percent of the marine catch was sundried in the traditional manner.

In 1966 India exported 19,000 tonnes of fish products worth Rs 135 millions. In 1975, 53,000 tonnes were exported with a value of Rs 1050 millions. That increase over 1966 was only 3 times in quantity exported but 8 times in value. The export was entirely from the marine catch.

The catches from reservoir fisheries is a special feature in India where dams are built to hold river water for irrigation or generation of power or both. Menon (1976) reports the existence of 265 major and medium reservoirs with a waterspread capacity of 1.2 million ha. Most of the inland catch is from these reservoirs. There is no estimate anywhere of what the catch is in small ponds, tanks, lakes, rivers and rivulets all through the country.

The problems for the inland fisheries are the scarcity of stocking material and pollution from factory effluents.

The turtle population, both sea and fresh water type, is rich and remains unexplored for food. According to Chidambaram (1976, p. 1) the world potential of fish is 118 million tonnes and 1973 catches were 65.7 million tonnes. At present three-fourths of the catch is moved throughout India in crates or baskets packed in oil. The fish are moved distances of 500 miles or more in trucks or mail train parcel vans. The Central Institute of Fish Technology has now developed a "tea packing technique" using plywood boxes with a lining by which 50 lbs. of frozen fish such as sardines are packed with an equal weight of ice and sent up to 1500 miles without repacking and icing.

Dry fish which move even into the remotest village provide

a cheap source of high quality protein for the poor and weaker
sections of the society.

Fish do not carry the stigma of beef and are acceptable to
a wider population. Application of technology in off-shore and
deep sea fishing, processing and marketing needs a lot of study
and research for adaptation to home consumption. The technology developed is mainly in the realm of the export trade to
earn foreign exchange.

SUGGESTIONS FOR INCREASED UNDERSTANDING

Protein requirement for human needs and protein availability in the dairy, meat and fish industries should be coordinated and discussed to get at a full understanding of
the situation. Meat depending upon kind and fish are consumed
by sections of the society only. Better statistics in these
areas are necessary. The use of "fallen" animals for food has
to be fully understood. Increased production and projections
have to be understood, in the light of population growth. The
part played by the vegetarians in the production and utiliza-
tions of animal proteins has to be understood. The food habits
of the people are changing fast. Most of the studies and
reports are based on the stereotypes of caste which are no
longer tenable.

WHY AVAILABLE KNOWLEDGE IS NOT BEING APPLIED

Knowledge in production, processing and marketing of products is available. The main constraint is one of finance
and foreign exchange. The feeds especially for poultry
and pigs compete with human food. When the production of food
grain is not adequate, the choice is always to use it for human
consumption and not to convert it into costly animal protein.
Land used for fodder, especially the green forage, has to compete with land for food grain production.

Cross breeding in cattle is accepted as a national policy
to increase milk production of the "desi" cattle. However, due
to the scarcity of foreign exchange importation of pedigree
bulls is a problem. Under village conditions the efficiency of
frozen semen is very low, worsened by lack of quick transport
and storage problems. Out of 75 million cows of breedable age
only 2 million are good crossbreds. The high cost of fuel oil
and electricity is a great obstacle to the expansion of refrigeration facilities which are much needed for proper processing,
storage and marketing of animal products. The socio-cultural
traditions, religious taboos and food habits of the people are
are a big block to the adoption of animal technology. In many
of the areas where technology is implemented, the human element
which plays a decisive role is not adequately taken into
account. Implementation of these programs in a Democracy is

slow, especially when the people are not fully literate.

NEEDED AREAS OF RESEARCH

A standardized process to sell meat, milk, fish and their products in the tropics without refrigeration is a great need. Studies in the use of chemical preservatives, and antibiotics need a fresh look, under Indian conditions. Popularizing the buffaloe as a meat animal in place of beef deserves special research and development. Suitable fillers to increase the volume of animal protein for use by the common man needs to be studied.

Methods for processing milk and milk products needs special consideration. Possibilities of using energy from the sun rather than other heat sources to convert milk, egg and other animal proteins into powder form to enhance keeping quality, transport and distribution need to be explored. Indigenous equipment to do the processing should also be developed.

Recycling of waste to make feeds of biological value and processes to remove toxic substances from castor cake and other materials that could be used for live stock feed, needs special study. Utilization of sewage to raise single cell proteins calls for a new look.

Research work for the production of high quality poultry within the country for egg and meat needs intensification. Dwarfism is a new concept in egg layers in India. "Mini" layers are the world's future birds; this has special significance to India where food grains are usually in short supply. Development of cheap and quality feeds without using food grains has to be studied.

BASIS FOR DECISION MAKING TO ALLEVIATE THE FOOD PROBLEM

In a country such as India where resources are limited and demands are many, the basis for decision making is essentially one of economics. Production and processing must be made attractive to the producer, and cheap to the consumer. Since funds are limited, hard decisions have to be made, to insure that minimum inputs will benefit the maximum number. The social, cultural, religious and economic background of the producer-consumer complex, with due consideration to the human elements, should be a major concern in decision making. While the intention is the application of modern technology, which by and large can be taken advantage of only with mass production, it has to be decentralized and made the smallest possible unit so that the maximum number of people can take advantage of it; this should be a guiding principle. The national policy of socialism has the guidelines, "not to let the rich become richer, nor to let the poor become poorer" and to this end, the technology has to be adapted and implemented.

REFERENCES

Cockrill, Ross W. (Ed). 1974. The Husbandry and Health of the
    Domestic Buffaloe, A Project sponsored by the Australian
    Freedom from Hunger Campaign. FAO, Rome.
Menon, K. N. and K. Chidambaram. 1976. Sea Food Export Jour-
    nal Annual. 8:1. Publication of Sea Food Exporters Asso-
    ciation of India, Cochin.
Report of the National Commission on Agriculture. 1976. Gov-
    ernment of India, Ministry of Agriculture and Irrigation,
    New Delhi, India.
Singh, Bhupal and B. K. Rastogi. 1974. Indian Journal of
    Dairy Science. 27:1.
The Wealth of India. 1970. (A dictionary of Indian Raw mate-
    rials and Industrial Products) Raw Materials Vol. VI Sup-
    plement, livestock (including poultry). Publication and
    Information Directorate, CSIR, New Delhi.

DALE E. HATHAWAY

Alternative Institutions and Other Agents of Change for Increased Food Availability

Broadly speaking, the world food problem could be looked upon, as it has been by many, as a problem of inequality between the rich and poor nations of the world, and between the wealthier and less well off within nations. While this view of the problem would suggest widespread redistribution of income between and within countries, it is not a solution likely to be quickly achieved in the world in which we live. Therefore it seems that we should concentrate on increasing the food availability in those developing countries that are faced primarily either with the option of being permanent recipients of food aid, an option which neither the recipient countries nor the donor countries view with enthusiasm; or the option of improving internal production and distribution and thus, the food availability. But the first issue is that of increasing production.

Some developing countries, because of their substantial productivity in the nonagricultural sector, have the option of using trade in order to increase food availability within their economies, and, with the proper wage policies and other internal distributional policies, their export earnings will enable them to deal adequately with the problems. Since there is a need for a division of labor among the world's population, these countries can, with adequate international trade policies, make imported food available to the less fortunate sections of their population.

Dale E. Hathaway is Director of International Food Policy Research Institute, 1776 Massachusetts Avenue, N.W. Washington, D.C. 20036.

In making this distinction, essentially I am implying that
the basic problem in most seriously affected countries is the
improvement of productivity on the millions of small traditional farms that are not now oriented toward the production of
food for markets. Thus, my major comments will focus upon the
institutional issues that appear to be crucial for increasing
the food production by the disadvantaged small farmers and rural
workers in those countries in which resources are not available
in order to provide adequate food via other options.

The key to this solution lies in increasing the productivity of the land and people engaged in agriculture in these
countries. Thus, it appears we must look at the institutional
problems that affect these productivities. This leads us directly to the use of improved technology in the production of
food by the least advanced, small farmers and rural laborers.

Since science and technology are closely linked institutionally in this problem, it seems useful to distinguish between them at this point. What we are concerned about is the
improved adaptation of technology that will enable rural people
in developing countries to produce more food, both to increase
the availability for their own family consumption and to increase the market supply of food sufficiently so that the real
price of food will be a declining proportion of the real wage
income of the urban disadvantaged population.

Science is the application of fundamental knowledge to the
principles of the growth of plants and animals. To make a distinction, technology is the application of science to meet the
particular needs and problems of improving the productivity of
plants and animals and humans in a specific institutional and
socioeconomic environment that is individual to each country,
each agroclimatic zone, and population within a country.

There are several requirements to use improved technology
as a route to increased food availability. One is the development of the basic sciences to support the technology. The
second, and most important, is the development of the appropriate technology to fit the conditions that are needed in the individual countries and technology that can and will be adopted
by the farmers themselves. The third is getting the knowledge
of the technology and its management to the farmers who must
use it. The fourth is to provide the necessary incentives for
the use of the improved technology and management by the farmers involved. Another that is often overlooked is the institutional developments that will mobilize and increase the level
of investment in food production and distribution by individual
farmers, merchants, and others involved in the farming and rural
systems.

Thus, there are a number of institutions that must be involved. First are the institutions for the training in the
basic sciences. Second are the institutions for developing and

testing the appropriate technology that can and will be used in
a specific area. Third are the institutions for training persons to take technology to the farmers and to work with the
farmers to provide them with the necessary knowledge. Fourth
are the institutions for providing information and incentives
to the farmers who in the end must make the changes that will
increase food production and make food available both for their
own families and for the societies in which they live.

INSTITUTIONS FOR TRAINING IN THE BASIC SCIENCES
        By and large, it would appear that the institutions for
        the training in the basic plant and animal sciences are in
        relatively good shape if we take a global view. We must
recognize that such institutions require a very major investment of human and physical capital, that the development of
science is capital intensive industry. It is not clear that it
would be either productive or necessary for most developing
countries to make a major investment in the further development
of the basic sciences. These investments have and are being
made in the developed economies, primarily but not necessarily
for their own purposes. The question is whether the scientific
base that exists and is available can, in fact, be used to develop the technology that will be useful in the developing
countries. With regard to this question, I could draw an anal-
ogy from my own field, economics. It is clear that there is a
need for both improved statistical theory and improved production, price and other statistics. However, it probably is not
a productive enterprise for developing countries to invest
heavily in the improvement of statistical theory as long as
their food production estimates may have an error of 20 percent
or more and where there are no adequate statistics on either
what price is being paid by farmers for crucial inputs or the
price that is being received for their output.
        One could make a similar analogy between pure economic
theory and basic economic relationships. It is clear that the
theory of the economics of agricultural development is not yet
adequate. But this problem does not merit a major research
effort in countries where we do not even know the basic relationships between a change in product price and the farmers'
response in the utilization of land, fertilizer, water and improved technology. The investment in basic science largely has
been made in the developed countries, and the major institutional efforts in this direction should be to apply this basic
science as part of the linkage to the development of relevant
technology for use in developing countries.
        Having said this I want to emphasize the continuing need
for close relations with those in the basic sciences and those
developing applied technology. Individuals primarily engaged

in the production of appropriate technology should have the
opportunity of periodically returning to some research institution working on the basic science in order to refurbish their
knowledge in the basic sciences and conversely to acquaint the
basic scientists with the problems of application at the field
level in developing countries. Thus, one of the needed institutional changes is the periodic involvement of scientists who
are developing new technology in developing countries with research programs in related basic sciences.

INSTITUTIONS FOR DEVELOPING APPROPRIATE TECHNOLOGY

Perhaps the only major institutional innovation that has
occurred in this field in the post World War II decade is
the development of the International Agricultural Research
System. Certainly this system is the intermediate link between
the basic sciences and the development and use of improved and
applied technology for the developing countries. In part, just
as the American Land Grant System was an institutional innovation more than a century ago in the United States, the development of the International Agricultural Research System, with
its crop-oriented and farming-systems oriented centers, seems
to me to be a major and significant institutional development.

After more than a decade and a half of experience with the
International Centers in their varying stages of development,
there is agreement that a crucial vital link is still weak.
This link is necessary for the system to develop the technology
needed at the local level. The weak link is the development of
effective country-level programs in applied research to produce
the technology that can and will be adopted by the farmers in
specific social, economic, cultural and agro-climatic conditions.

In developing effective applied research programs there
are three major institutional problems. First, it would seem
there has been a substantial underinvestment both by the national governments and by the external donors in the human resources necessary to build strong and effective country level
research programs for developing appropriate technology. There
are many studies that show that the returns to agricultural research are very high. My feeling, however, is that if one
could sort out the data, that the highest returns would be to
do research that produces applied technology that can and will
be adopted in specific areas. There has been a substantial
underinvestment in human and other capital necessary to produce
this kind of applied technology. Unless this can be corrected
by the appropriate national and international governmental policies, both the international investment in basic science and
in the Agricultural Centers system will be ineffective because

of the weakness of country level applied research systems.

Second, it appears there may well be a substantial mal-allocation of the scientific resources that are available within the developing countries. There are many institutional structures wherein capable scientists, in order to advance in position, salary and prestige, must leave their scientific work and become administrators. I believe this is a malallocation of resources. It is a waste of time, effort and investment in human capital to have some of a country's top scientists be forced to take difficult, burdensome, and often nonproductive administrative positions in order to obtain the recognition, salaries and the other attributes that are deserved for their contribution to their economy.

Third, there is the issue of the reward system within the scientific community of a country. I remember the words of a colleague from a developing country who was given a senior fellowship to work abroad in the US for a two-year period. His comment, which struck me as the final irony, was that "Now I will be able to work on the major problems of my country, whereas as long as I am in my country I primarily must work to establish my scientific credentials in order to insure that I will be recognized by the centralized bureaucracy and thus be eligible for promotion." Basically, the issue is: Do the individuals who control the reward system in the scientific community give these rewards for the development of technology which fits the needs of small producers?

My impression is that the developed countries have done poorly in this regard. Perhaps rich countries can afford to put a high premium on people who write exceptionally well for professional journals on esoteric subjects which are vaguely related to the problems of real farmers. I do not believe that the developing countries can afford the luxury of having a high proportion of the people capable of producing applied technology primarily writing for their peers rather than working to develop technology that will be useful to the farmers of their country. I do not question the motivation of individuals. I do question whether the institutional incentives, the professional reward system, and the bureaucratic promotional system are organized to induce the trained professionals of a country to really apply their talents to the development of improved technology for that country's small poor farmers.

Fourth, I would suspect that there is inadequate support for the working scientists who are trying to develop usable technology. By this I mean that the ratio of operating funds and funds for the hiring of field equipment, testing, personnel and so on per scientist are much higher in developed countries than is the case in the developing countries. Scientific manpower and the manpower which is capable of developing applied technology are very scarce and valuable resources indeed. The

basic principle in the allocation of scarce resources is to
supplement the scarce resources with resources that are complementary to them and cost the economy less. Yet my general observation in looking at research organizations and their budgets in many developing countries is that the scientists are
undersupported in terms of the basic help they need to do a
good scientific job and perhaps oversupported in terms of the
perquisites and other attributes that are less significant in
developing applied technology.

Finally, it seems to me that one must examine the basic
institutional structure used in the development of applied
technology. I would put the issue in the form of a question:
Is it possible to develop applied technology that meets the
needs of farmers in specific agro-climatic zones and under differing economic and social conditions via a centrally planned
and centrally directed research program? I personally doubt
it. However brilliant the scientist in the central city, he is
almost by definition not closely in touch with the real problem
and needs of the operating poor farmers in other areas. It is
the identification of the problems that face such farmers and
the application of technology to the solution of such problems
that is needed. Unless it can be proven that there are substantial efficiencies in centralizing planning and control of
such research work, it seems that the degree of centralization
involved in the development of applied technology needs to be
very carefully examined.

INSTITUTIONS FOR TRAINING AGRICULTURALISTS

It is a common statement among knowledgeable individuals
from developing countries that those institutions that
train agriculturalists are regarded as having a relatively
low status and that many of the individuals that attend these
institutions are individuals who could not gain entrance to the
higher prestige professions. This raises fundamental issues
about the values and images relating to working with the agricultural industry. In a sense, the issue emerges in the Eng-
lish word "peasant", often used as synonomous with small farmer, but which to some implies individuals who are of low status
and involved in a lesser valued occupation. Our world must
place the highest of values upon the enhancement of food production in developing countries; we must be able to change the
institutional image and the value systems relating to those who
work on the problems of agriculture and agricultural production
in such countries.

Apart from the image problem, another issue that one must
face is the question, "Is the educational system which the developing countries now have designed to fit the needs of these
countries?" By and large, the educational systems of the

developing countries are the systems that they inherited from
a colonial era. In many cases the educational institutions relating to the training of agriculturalists never worked very
well in the countries from which they were imported. It appears to me that the agricultural educational system at the
level of the university and higher level university training in
the developed countries primarily serves to train people to
leave agriculture or to avoid ever having to deal with farmers.
In my view, the educational system for developing countries
should be to train people to work in agriculture at the differing levels that are needed.

In this context one wonders why there has been little
attempt to include vocational education as a part of the standard school curriculum in developing countries. In many of the
countries of Europe vocational educational systems have had a
long history and experience of supplementing other institutions
and, in fact, have probably been one of the most productive
public investments. Vocational agricultural education has been
a corner stone of the agricultural training of many of the operating farmers and intermediate level technical people in many
of the countries that are now considered to be advanced countries. Yet in the developing countries with which I am familiar, the educational system appears to be basically organized
toward the training of public servants, not public servants to
work in rural areas, but public servants to work in central
city government bureaucracies. Thus, it seems there is a major
question of whether the institutions that are in place to train
agriculturalists to both produce the applied technology and to
produce and deliver information to farmers are really adequate
to meet the needs of the countries concerned.

I do not wish to be misunderstood on this. Most of the
systems that have been inherited by developing countries have
not been the American Land Grant System. However, most attempts
to transplant the American Land Grant System and its extension
service abroad also have failed in many countries. I believe
that the American vocational agricultural system, agricultural
college system, and agricultural extension service system is
unique to the American experience; and that attempts to transplant it as an applicable institution for the development and
the training of agriculturalists in the developing countries is
not necessarily a useful enterprise.

PROVIDING INCENTIVES FOR FARMERS
     Basically, this issue is one of extreme importance and one
     which is poorly understood. Institutional mechanisms
     must, in fact, take into account certain factors. First,
knowledge relating to new technology must be available at low
cost to the individual. There is a very high personal cost to

the individual in acquiring the information on the use and
probable outcomes of changes in technology and management practices. Such information must become more widely available, in
a form and manner which will reduce the cost to the individual
who must invest in acquiring the information in order to change
his farming practices.

Second, people in most parts of the world must have an incentive to change from things which they are accustomed to doing and about which they have knowledge. People are more likely to act effectively if it can be demonstrated to them that
change will improve their own well-being and self-interest.
In this regard, we must look at the development of better institutional structures which provide incentives in terms of
improved markets for the products that are produced and an increased availability of goods which farmers need in order to
increase production and improve their standard of living on
terms which are favorable relative to the increased effort and
risk they take.

This is the final crucial link in the chain from science
to increased production. Even if all of the other links are
strong and effective, the better technology will only increase
output if farmers use it on their farms. Institutional incentives need to be developed to encourage adoption.

There is among economists a general tendency to say that
price incentives are the major incentives to which people react. This, I think, is a dubious proposition. I would argue
that price incentives are a necessary but not sufficient condition to encourage people to adopt improved technology that will
increase food availability for themselves and the people in
the country around them. However, many people are incapable
of responding to price signals because of technological constraints, constraints upon credit, input availability and the
other constraints that have been discussed elsewhere in this
meeting. We may tend to overvalue prices as an inducement to
change and undervalue the price system as an information system that could be used to inform people how they might act to
improve their own well-being.

INCREASING INVESTMENT IN AGRICULTURAL PRODUCTION

The sources of growth in output can generally be attributed to either increased investment in agriculture or
technology which changes the productivity of the land,
labor, and investment. I have concentrated primarily upon the
technology, but the importance of investment should not be
overlooked.

It is unrealistic to assume that the necessary investment
in the infrastructure and other productive elements necessary
to support the adoption of improved technology and to achieve

its maximum potential will come from either external lenders or
national governments. It also is unrealistic to assume that
poor farmers on the margin of subsistence will be able to rapidly increase their rate of monetary savings and investment.
Therefore, new institutions and new policies must be developed
to use the major available resource--underutilized local labor
--in this investment. This is not a new idea, nor do I have
any new suggestions to make, but most nations have been less
than successful in its execution. Yet it equals in importance
the institutional problem of producing and encouraging the increased adoption of improved technology, because the two generally are complementary.

SUMMARY AND CONCLUSIONS
      Basically, little of this is new. My main conclusion is
      that the major and crucial linkage to the improvement of
      food availability in those developing countries where food
availability must primarily come via the improvement of production among small and least advantaged of the farmers depends
on the ability of institutions to develop and increase the rate
of adoption of improved technology on millions of small farms.
The basic scientific structure in the world appears adequate if
not always effective. The intermediate structure is largely in
place in the form of the International Agricultural Centers to
convert the science to a general level of applied technology
for the principal food crops and geographical areas. What
appears to be weakest is the country level development of usable technology and the incentives for adoption on a widespread
basis by many farmers. My essential point is that to deal with
this weak linkage we should concentrate more on certain key institutions. Those institutions are the applied research institutions in the developing countries; the development, utilization, and reward system for the manpower engaged in applied research; and the development of the agricultural education institutions that are used primarily to train individuals to develop applied research and to carry that applied research to
the farmers who eventually must be the adopters. In summary,
I think there is no overall generalization about the necessary
institutional changes. What I have attempted to do is to highlight the parts of the institutional structure that need serious and continuing examination, greater investment, and much
more serious attention if, in fact, those developing countries,
whose major route to increasing food availability lies in increasing production in small farms, are to succeed in their
objective.

Workshop Reports

Impacts of the World Food Situation

IMPACTS OF FOOD SITUATION ON PEOPLE

This report summarizes both verbal and written contributions of panelists and participants during workshop sessions. The most direct consequences of the world food situation are their effects on people. Adverse food situations may be caused directly by inadequate supplies of food or indirectly by social customs and human preferences.

ASSESSMENT

Malnutrition of the infant is related to the nutritional level of the mother, to supplemental food provided and to weaning practices. Infants who are malnourished during the early critical months of growth and development have higher susceptibility to disease and parasitism and higher mortality rates than normally nourished babies.

Malnourished surviving children do not reach their full potential of physical growth or mental development. The retardation of physical growth, especially of the lower limbs becomes permanent at maturity. Although there is still controversy on the permanency of mental retardation, malnutrition contributes to low learning ability and poor performance in school.

Malnourished adults have reduced physical capacity and work output and are more affected by infectious and parasitic diseases. They become caught in a vicious cycle of low productivity both causing and resulting from malnutrition. The social effects of this cycle depress the entire community as they affect housing, land use, community functions and human attitudes. These socio-economic restraints limit development more than do technological inadequacies and they are passed from generation to generation.

CONSTRAINTS

Although the constraints to food development are severe in all developing countries, yesterday's constraints must be priorities for today's research and action. Poverty and low food intake are primary factors in the cycle of malnutrition, deprivation and isolation, each as causes and indicators of the others.

Rural people must frequently sell much needed food at low prices at harvest time to pay debts and then buy it back later at higher prices on credit. Often, the need for a quantity of food compels them to sell high protein meat, milk, eggs or fish to buy larger amounts of carbohydrate foods. The exportation of food from a country may not reflect the actual food situation within it.

Governmental policies to assist agricultural development, and in many instances the food production impetus of the Green Revolution, have assisted the wealthy with their greater resources and flexibility at the expense of the poor. Similarly, capital intensive technology has enabled the wealthy to expand their productive enterprizes replacing the only resource of the poor, their labor. In turn, employment generating schemes often do not generate actual income but rather substitute subsistence purchasing power for subsistence food production capability.

Income distribution is tied to land ownership and not to land tillage, making agricultural employment highly seasonal and unstable. The need for food drives rural people to farm unsuited land, deforest mountain slopes and overgraze grasslands while their lack of investment capital and/or skills prevents any soil resource conservation. Agricultural productivity of marginal lands is low and is depressed further by raising plants of low yield and animals of low growth potential, because of plant and animal diseases, weeds, insect pests, rats and the vagaries of weather.

The lack of storage facilities for food grains spells losses either from rat, insect, mold and bacterial destruction, or the choice of selling at low price at harvest and buying back later at high cost. The lack of processing facilities for perishable products simply means that they are wasted during times of surplus. Inadequate distribution facilities frequently mean that there is need in one part of a country while there is surplus in another.

Professionals in food production development working in the midst of these constraints may be further hampered by inadequate training and/or experience to cope with the complexity of the problems. They may be further hampered by lack of coordination with professionals working in related areas of development as in population control, public health or community development.

Whatever gains may be made through creative enterprise and
diligent labor are all too often consumed by population growth.
A combination of low productive capacity per adult caused by
malnutrition and a high infant and child mortality rate work
against any programs of population limitation because children
are needed to ensure continuity of the labor force to support
the family.

International policies and programs frequently act as further constraints on the already burdened developing countries.
These countries are receiving inadequate prices for their principally agricultural raw materials in world trade and are paying too much for imports. Food aid programs designed to assist
developing countries to develop their own productive capabilities have in some areas depressed development and fostered
dependence on the donor countries or on their own national governments.

ALTERNATIVES

The alternatives considered were principally addressed to
professionals in food production development. Professionals were defined broadly to include persons recognized
by their communities as having greater expertise in their areas
of operation than the people with whom they work. Although
they commonly have some training related to their responsibilities, professionals are not limited to the highest academically
trained or politically authoritative persons in these communities. The role of professionals is to contribute to overcoming
some of the constraints and reducing the negative impacts of
the food situation.

Promotion and Support of Sustained Agricultural Development

Maximum productivity of the land and maximum production of
food are the basic but not the only goals of professionals. Gains in food production through technological advances
must be balanced against losses of social values, consumption
of costly imported fossil fuels and environmental degradation.
Agricultural technology must be so introduced and applied that
it favors small farmers and enhances their productivity. Professionals must assess as far as possible the benefits and
costs of alternative solutions. In their rural efforts, they
must help to develop farming into an attractive occupation and
make rural life appealing without placing undue emphasis on
exportable crops. In achieving this, governmental input into
policies and interventions which favor and, as necessary, subsidize small farmers and the rural poor will probably be necessary.

Relationships of Professionals to Their Communities

Professionals in food development must be sensitive to the social values and physical needs of the people and avoid making authoritative or burdensome demands upon them. People of rural communities in developing countries look to professionals from outside their communities as experts who tell them what to do rather than to whom they express their needs. It is very important that professionals obtain the involvement of their communities in decision making. Within the limited ranks of available professionals, it is more important that field staffs be strong than that headquarters staffs be large. Experienced professionals should be rotated through field assignments instead of filling these positions entirely with new recruits. Field assignments must be of sufficient length that professionals can develop coherent viable programs which will continue after they are replaced by new workers. Continual emphasis must be placed on village level agricultural development as the basis of food production, and rewards for village level workers must be commensurate with their contributions.

Cultural Aspects of Rural Development

Professionals working in rural communities must become practical rural sociologists as well as practical technologists. They must emphasize development of indigenous and locally available foods, and secondarily motivate people within the context of their cultures to produce and utilize introduced foods. They must also recognize the extent to which economy of labor, efficiency and maximum productivity are compatable with local structures and work within this framework.

The Training of Community Leadership

Professionals must seek out functional leaders in their communities and work through them in reaching the people. They must be both motivators and educators, working through the homes to reach adults and through the schools to reach children. The greatest long range effectiveness is gained in training local leaders in their communities.

The Development and Application of Appropriate Technology

In most developing countries, labor intensive rather than capital intensive or imported energy intensive technology must be emphasized. In much of the world, simpler and more applicable technology must still be developed and adapted in ways that the farmers will understand and utilize to improve the quality of rural life.

Protection of Food through Production, Storage and Distribution

Both research and development in protection of the food
supply must be given major emphasis in the developing
countries. Imported technologies are seldom adaptable or economically feasible. Basic efforts in crop production must
include development and adoption of genetically resistant varieties, pest and disease control, and protection of stored
grains from adverse weather, rats and contamination. Processing of perishable products through local industries is needed
to prevent alternate periods of waste and scarcity. Animals of
genetically improved growth potential must be protected against
diseases and parasites through the use of sanitation, vaccines
and drugs. Food distribution improvement is largely dependent
on the development of infrastructures.

The Role of Women

Professionals must include both men and women in all food
development programs and in educational opportunities.
Special attention should be given by professionals in developed
countries that in much of the world the applicable terminology
is "the farmer, she" and not "the farmer, he."

Protection of People from Environmental Pollutants

Professionals must balance long range ecological views
with short range pressures in advocating the use of agricultural chemicals including fertilizers and the disposal of
plant residues and animal wastes. These products must be utilized as resources to increase production and not permitted to
contaminate water or food supplies with chemical residues or
disease agents. Especially in the developing countries, many
of the major infectious and parasitic diseases of people have
animal reservoirs.

Population Limitation and Food Development

A primary strategy in developing food sufficiency and
enhancing economic and social development must be effective population limitation. Governmental policies must foster
population control and methods of contraception must be within
the reach of all people. There is evidence that the reduction
of high infant mortality through improved nutrition and better
health is a key motivating factor toward smaller families.
Active family planning programs must enable and accelerate this
natural process.

Interrelationships of Professionals
in Different Areas of Responsibility

Professionals working in the same communities in areas of food production, nutrition, public health and population control must be alert to each others' goals, constraints and methods so that they coordinate their efforts and cooperate at all levels. There is real need for professionals to join together as cadres of workers, as free as possible from political restraints.

International Aid in Development of Food Production

International food aid and concessional sales must be used as emergency measures and provided in ways that will promote local food production. Market policies in international trade must be fostered which promote its flow to areas of greatest need at times of need. International assistance to indigenous development is the most important of all aid programs.

Other Involvements in Food Development

Governments in developing countries must frequently intervene directly to reach rural and poor people who may not otherwise benefit from food development programs. Countries with food surpluses are called upon to use these resources to benefit needy nations and in no ways to capitalize on their distress. Private agencies in food development are urged to accelerate their efforts and to integrate them into overall community programs. Large national and multinational industries are recognized for their contributions to development and cautioned to avoid exploitive or disruptive social practices.

Summary of the Professionals' Role

The tasks of professionals in food production development are multifaceted and interwoven with the needs, values and aspirations of needy people. They must function at community levels in planning, promoting and implementing food production programs within their own expertise. Finally they must participate in assessing the impact of their efforts in a sensitive and objective manner.

PANELISTS

Chairperson   Ivan D. Beghin   Guatemala City,
                                             Guatemala
Rapporteur   George W. Beran   Ames, Iowa

Subplenary Speaker	Fernando Monckeberg B.	Santiago, Chile
Subplenary Speaker	Jean A. S. Ritchie	Addis Ababa, Ethiopia
Panelist	Faith Abeyawardene	Peradeniya, Sri Lanka
Panelist	Donald J. Bogue	Chicago, Illinois
Panelist	Khorsand Bondari	Athens, Georgia
Panelist	Harold F. Breimeyer	Columbia, Missouri
Panelist	Maxine M. Burch	Omaha, Nebraska
Panelist	Nena R. Bustrillos	Laguna, Philippines
Panelist	Amirul Islam	Dacca, Bangladesh
Panelist	Urailuckshna Mahaguna	Bangkok, Thailand
Panelist	Mudambi V. Rajagopal	Nsukka, Nigeria
Panelist	James H. Steele	Houston, Texas
Panelist	Nedeljko Suljmanac	Belgrade, Yugoslavia

PARTICIPANTS

Leland G. Allbaugh
Jessica Alles
Janice Beran
Dwight S. Busacca
Karen A. Carpenter
William K. DuVal
Amat El-Rahim El Gorafy
Robert V. Enochian
Beverly B. Everett
M. A. B. Fakorede
John Falloon
Henry J. Frundt
Mary Hastings-Roberts
Seve Tile Imo
Patricia Anne Jester
C. J. Johanns
John J. Jonas
Wadie W. Kamel

Scott Knudson
James L. Koster
Perez Labour
Julie Ann Lickteig
Terence Henry Martin
Alex Eugene Maruu-Soka
Diane McComber
Luis Antonio Mejia
Richard M. Kwandawire
Elizabeth Mulley
Adinah Robertson
Barbara Schick
A. L. Shewfelt
Wesley G. Smith
Ronald E. Stenning
Dan Keith Vander Linden
J. E. Wiebe

IMPACTS OF FOOD SITUATION ON ENVIRONMENT

The environment has come under stress as the increase in human population has accelerated. Some elements of soil, water, air, vegetation and animal life (including microbes) have already suffered irreparable damage. Demand for food production causes a great threat to the environment and care must be exercised to maintain a high food production potential. Professionals should point out alternative technologies which provide adequate food and yet are environmentally safe and conducive to conservation of resources.

MANAGING THE PLANT-ANIMAL SYSTEMS AND COMPONENTS

Success of food production technologies in temperate zones has led some to conclude that we have perfected technologies applicable worldwide. This is not true. Insufficient information exists on soil, crop, animal and vegetation management in large parts of the world, and we also have insufficient knowledge about the interaction between technology levels and the environment. More information is needed, for example, on the behavior of tropical soils under agriculture, the niche of animals in the agroecosystem and their protection, the animal-vegetation interactions, the adaptation of labor intensive technology, and the safe application of modern technology.

Few improvements in crop and animal production can be made by single individuals or even by single scientific disciplines. Scientists should work together to develop and promote "packages of practices". Cooperation is required to develop natural or induced resistance to pests in crops and animals and to exploit all other biological controls associated with natural enemies of pests including sequences of crops. Every effort should be made to integrate programs of controls used against

crop and animal pests, to develop resistant or tolerant crop
varieties and breeds of animals, and to extend them into marginal areas. Maximum advantage should be taken of all self-
protective devices available in nature. We should recall previous systems of crop and animal husbandry which might be
effective for food production especially in countries where
labor is abundant and capital is not.

PLANT NUTRIENTS AND WATER

Plant nutrient supply in most soils in the world is so low
it limits production. Use of organic and inorganic fertilizers must be promoted. Such practices, however, need
not degrade the environment. Uncertainties concerning future
availability and prices of farm inputs, particularly those
which involve substantial fossil fuel costs, make it necessary
to explore new technologies such as systems of reduced tillage
which conserve soil and water, and to continue a search for
crop plants which are more economical of water use.

Imaginative ways of recovering plant nutrients and other
products from agricultural, industrial, and human wastes must
be tried. These should be explored while observing sound public health practice and should aim to restore and protect the
productivity of streams, lakes, estuaries, and oceans, especially the spawning areas, by international agreement where
needed. Some civilizations have used wastes effectively and
still do. No potential technology should be overlooked in supplying potable water for household and animal use and satisfactory water for agriculture and other industries.

There is a serious lack of knowledge about sources of
underground water and their recharge rates. This leads to
inadvertent extraction of water which is replenished slowly or
not at all. Use of such water resources must be coordinated
with recharge practices to preserve the aquifers as resources.
The world should expend at least as much effort in locating,
classifying and monitoring the water resources as it spends on
the identification and classification of soil resources, inadequate as this is.

Spread of irrigation in many parts of the world has been
accompanied by the increase of water borne diseases, schistosomiasis being especially important. Increased attention
should be given to development of technologies to contain and
eventually to reduce the incidence of this and other water
borne diseases.

Water conservation has aspects of amount and quality. The
quantity of water is related to the management of watersheds
and streams and distribution systems. Water quality in some
streams is poor because waste water from industry and human
habitation is not circulated back to the land for re-use of
plant nutrients and purification by filtration through soil.

Salinity resulting from irrigation is a serious quality problem. Continued attention must be directed toward control of
salinity in irrigated regions by conventional and innovative
means.

Other constraints on water conservation include information about the normal supplies from all sources, knowledge of
the most efficient plant and animal users of water, and efficient water use practices. Information also is needed on the
minimum quantity which can be used effectively, the timing of
use, effectiveness of soil or organic mulches in preventing
evaporation, usefulness of supplemental irrigation and identification of plants with favorable transpiration ratios.

The crucial link in effective and efficient water use is
an extension network which deals specifically with improved
water use alone or in conjunction with instruction on other
superior practices. Research is needed on methods of bringing
resource information to the general public as well as to the
small farmer.

PREVENTING SOIL DESTRUCTION
The most widely expressed concern of food production on
environment is the erosion of soil and permanent loss of
flora and fauna. Pollution by pesticides also may be a
consequence of highly productive agriculture. Both may cause
damage to the soil resource itself and cause additional damage
off-site to the atmosphere, water supplies, fish, etc. Eventually they may cause serious social problems.

A principal constraint to adequate soil conservation is
that conservation incentives are over-ridden by high prices.
The economic imperative to produce food in some countries is so
great, as are the need for fuel and feed for livestock, that
practices which are destructive to the environment are
employed. Lack of information about cultivation of semi-arid
as well as tropical forest land has led to the growth of deserts.

Some constraints are social in nature. One example is the
subdivisions of land for inheritance leading to tracts too
small and disoriented for adequate erosion control. Another
limitation occurs when small farmers are forced to till marginal land extremely subject to erosion because the best land
is held by a minority and is not developed to its full potential. Better extension education could alleviate problems of
erosion where control methods are known at the experiment stations.

An economic constraint to erosion control is the need for
land to remain out of production temporarily while appropriate
structures and practices are installed. Another is land transferred from agriculture to other uses and its perpetual loss
for food production.

There are many circumstances when short-term production
gains are made at the expense of the environment or of future
productivity. Usually farmers do not consider these "external
or deferred" costs of short-term gains nor can they be expected
to. It must be a public responsibility to design policies and
institutions to assure that these external costs are not
neglected in decisions about the use of agricultural resources.
Full use of the scientific community (local and/or international) must be made <u>before</u> new resource areas are opened for
use so that current knowledge may help avoid resource catastro-
phes. Support for new research on resources must continue.

RATIONAL EMPLOYMENT OF PESTICIDES

One of the major constraints in preventing pesticide pollution is ignorance. We do not know where they go, how
long they last, how they degrade, whether or not resistance in the target pest develops and what their future effects
might be even on subsequent crops.

Food production in some countries is of such critical need
that fertilizers and other chemicals are used without a full
appreciation of the potential hazards. Enough studies should
be conducted world-wide to alert people of the consequences of
careless use. Lack of international recognition and control of
"dangerous" pesticides is also a constraint. Recognizing the
potential danger of pesticides which have been banned in the
public interest in some countries, it is suggested that the
buyers of pesticides be supplied with all of the information
used as a basis for the ban. Requirements on testing and
developing new pesticides with the accompanying economic costs
slow the discovery and release of new products. Positive
actions by governments are in order to help develop new compounds.

Acknowledging that pesticides may have effects on non-
target organisms, it is suggested that studies continue on all
likely secondary effects. An international network to supply
information on the proper use of all pesticides is suggested so
new observations anywhere might be made available immediately
to everyone. Local extension systems should be developed to
deliver this information to actual users, many of whom may be
unable to read the printed instructions.

One must remember that farming was practiced before most
pesticides became available. Management systems should incorporate pest control independent of chemicals wherever possible
and perhaps consider maximum use of cultural practices and
labor for the control of pests. Pesticides do alter the agroecosystem so any practices lessening the dependence upon a pesticide will tend to extend its useful life.

SOME HUMAN DIMENSIONS
High levels of food production also have desirable side
effects and these should be studied more closely. Bringing poorly drained land under cultivation may reduce the
incidence of various diseases by eliminating either the pathogens or the vectors. More food of higher quality also reduces
disease through better nutrition. It is important to know
which foods have high vitamin, mineral and amino acid contents.
Increases of these food sources should have the greatest impact
upon human health. New and unconventional food sources may
enhance the environment by reducing need to produce common
sources.
The capacity of the earth to produce food has both economic and physical limits. These limits are lower if a pleas-
ing environment is to be maintained. Because increased production of food tends to be at the expense of the environment, an
early stabilization of population is crucial to providing a
moderately good quality of life for all. Stabilization cannot
come too soon.

PANELISTS

Chairperson	Leon Hesser	Washington, DC
Rapporteur	John Pesek	Ames, Iowa
Subplenary Speaker	Pierre Crosson	Washington, DC
Subplenary Speaker	James D. McQuigg	Columbia, Missouri
Panelist	Olugbemiro Akerejola	Zaria, Nigeria
Panelist	Stanley M. Barnett	Kingston, Rhode Island
Panelist	Javier Bernal	Bogota, Colombia
Panelist	Chester E. Evans	Fort Collins, Colorado
Panelist	Jerome Goldstein	Emmaus, Pennsylvania
Panelist	R. Jacobsohn	Bet-Dagen, Israel
Panelist	John Marangu	Kankakee, Illinois
Panelist	Pierce Ryan	Dublin, Ireland
Panelist	Donald N. Sibley	Quezaltenango, Guatemala
Panelist	E. C. Stakman	St. Paul, Minnesota
Panelist	E. P. Theron	Natal, South Africa
Panelist	Derek E. Tribe	Victoria, Australia

PARTICIPANTS

Thomas F. Azi	Helen E. Clark
Craig W. Bair	Raymond P. Coppinger
William B. Bryan	Abraham H. Epstein
Donald P. Carter	Roger G. Feldman

Leopold Gahamanyi
Pauk Gazi
William Goemaat
Wilfred J. Grieser
Stanley Howard Hargrove
Paul Jacobson
Amri Jahi
James L. Jarvis
Epeli Kanaimawi
Don Kirkham
Kyung Won Lee
Joseph K, Lendiy
Eugene R. Maahs
Dean McKee
Darrel S. Metcalfe

Don Miles
Kenneth A. Nielsen
Phyllis J. Olson
Jean Ongla
Hisatomo Oohara
Diane G. Pazos
Norman Rask
Carmen J. Romero
Jamilton P. Santos
Walter H. Schuller
John M. Sekerak
Gustave C. Strain
Dave Williams
Robert L. Zimdahl

IMPACTS OF FOOD SITUATION ON
NATIONAL AND WORLD DEVELOPMENT

Development was defined as widespread improvement and
modernization. Development is a combination of at least the
following: more food, more jobs, more opportunity, more industrialization, better nutrition, greater labor productivity,
better health, increases in gross national product, more per
capita real income and more participation by the lowest 40 percent in the society, economy and development.

An issue arose immediately over the relationship between
the food situation and development. For some, adequate food
for the underfed was synonymous with development. For others,
acute food shortages and a requirement to feed the hungry with
high priced food disrupted development, that is, investment
and modernization programs. Emergency food imports at high
prices and public distribution of food in famine areas can be
so costly as to divert virtually all foreign exchange and
national resources from industrialization and modernization.

THE SITUATION
    The food situation was interpreted in various terms by
    different workshop members as follows:

1) The sudden appearance of food shortage and food price
increases around the world since 1972.

2) The long-run prospects for instability, i.e., both
shortages and surpluses in the world food market. During the
next two decades free world market prices received by major
grain exporters will probably be in some years above and in
other years below the level which would encourage agricultural
investment and output expansion.

3) The wide differentials between the generally heavy

618

consumption of meat and prepared food with high fossil fuel
energy input in the developed countries and the persistent and
occasionally damagingly low per capita consumption of unbalanced diets by millions in the less developed countries (LDCs).

4) The disappearance of grain stocks and the lack of
security of consumption and the great uncertainty and probable
instability of retail and farm level food prices in a world
without food reserves.

5) Local hunger, isolated starvation, persistent malnutrition, stunted human development, high death rates, misery,
langor and blindness among millions of people, especially rural
people living on subsistence and unemployed people in urban
areas.

THE ISSUES

If the hungry are not fed, some panelists predicted drastic consequences in the short-run; others in the long-run.

If the poor are not fed, development may never take place
even in the long-run because the population will be rendered
incapable by malnutrition. If the hungry are not fed they may
attack and destroy the civilizations of the rich countries in
the near future. If the poor masses in the LDCs are not fed,
they may rebel and overthrow the government systems which are
unresponsive to their needs.

Some expressed very real fears that if all the hungry of
the world are fed, dependent populations will expand rapidly
and persistently require large transfers which would preempt
resources vitally needed to make long-run improvements, such as
job creation, industrialization, reform and modernization. The
dilemma is that no investments can be made toward self-reliance
and development in some countries if all the dependent are fed
adequately and no progress can be made if the poor are not fed
because revolution and debilitation of the population would
result. It was sincerely hoped by all that the dilemma could
be avoided and that feeding the hungry in the short-run could
be made compatible and complementary with development in the
long-run.

THE CONSTRAINTS

An issue emerged around the constraint imposed by low producer food prices. Many felt higher food prices worsened
the food situation for the hungry. Others felt that
higher prices to producers are required to increase food production. Government subsidies for agricultural inputs and food
consumption were offered as a costly but effective means of
keeping consumer prices low and yet creating incentives for
production of larger amounts of food.

Market shortages of food can be alleviated by higher

prices. Consumption is reduced, conservation is encouraged and diets shift to more plentiful and less desirable foods as high prices attach to those foods in short supply. Higher food prices worsen the diets of the poor and make the budgets of food relief agencies less able to cover the need. Higher food prices tend to raise wages and prices of all outputs in the long-run including exports, thus reducing ability to import food. On the other hand, increasing food supply depends on using more inputs in agriculture and on adopting improved techniques, which is encouraged by increased producer prices. Higher producer prices are needed in many cases to justify more fertilizer, more pest control and more care which lead to more production of food in the future.

Reduced population growth and even reduced total future populations in some areas would make prospective future food supplies more nearly adequate. A more adequate food supply would increase the chances of providing the population with higher levels of living, including more nonfood goods and services per capita. Current efforts by LDC political leaders and professionals to reduce high birth rates, especially among the poor and disadvantaged, need to be assisted, supported and encouraged by all professionals.

The population problem is so large and difficult that mere admonition, dictatorial orders or unreasonable requirements by developed countries (DC) governments or central LDC governments will not suffice and may prove counterproductive. Contraceptive means should be made available free to all people. Family planning programs, i.e., birth spacing counseling and birth limitation decision assistance, are more accepted and effective if operated by members of target groups themselves through local governments or social groups. Higher social status for women, more equal education, more equal opportunity for men and women and greater old age security provided by the larger social group rather than the family would reduce the desire of a number of couples to have more than two children.

Professionals of all kinds should and can contribute greatly to population control by designing direct programs or supporting programs which either make possible or make acceptable lower birth rates.

THE POSSIBILITIES

Appropriate technology offers large and varied potential to increase the adequacy of food consumption in LDCs.

Effective supply can be increased not only by making appropriate changes in production techniques and making strategic investments in agriculture but also by reducing loss and destruction of food during storage, transport, processing or retailing and preparation. Food production in LDCs is generally far below biological potential but also a large fraction of what is produced (sometimes half) is lost before it can be eaten.

Changes must be made in habits, traditions and attitudes of professionals, technicians and scientists as well as leaders, merchants, housewives and farmers. The changes should move current agricultural techniques, merchandising and storage practices and food preparation methods toward those which result in less loss and malnutrition and increase the effective supply of food and hence reduce its real price. Identification, creation, improvement and introduction of techniques which are appropriate must be a local LDC responsibility and should have top priority for government expenditure and for the attention of professionals.

Suitable technology uses available resources more effectively; that is, appropriate technology economizes on whatever resources are scarce locally, such as land or water, by designing effective ways to increase output by increasing the use of less scarce resources such as labor, sunshine, cement, fertilizer or machines. Technology is important or strategic because it raises the output potential by removing constraints and opening up greater potential. The use of technologies is appropriate because it makes relatively small and acceptable changes in the food production, marketing and consumption system. The level of employment of people or the level of any one capital input is changed at a rate which institutions, markets and attitudes can adapt.

Professionals must assist in not only the provision of appropriate technology but with the acceptance of the adjustment it requires in market prices, employment levels, profit rates and institutions. All classes of professionals have an important role in discovering, installing and adapting the system to more efficient and appropriate technology which will permit more adequate nutrition and also greater supplies of nonfood goods and services.

Improvements in the efficiency of the food system contribute significantly to general economic development. When food available for consumption increases more than the inputs of labor, land and materials then the resource efficiency of the food system improves. Adoption of appropriate and productive technologies can reduce the resource cost per unit of food consumed. Then less of the countries' total resources are required to produce food and more resources are available to be employed in nonfood activities. A higher level of total goods and services in the economy are possible since in most LDCs the efficiency of production, storage, processing and utilization of food can be sharply improved.

Professionals of all types can and should encourage and contribute to increased resource productivity and reduced waste in the food system. To obtain general economic development from improvements in the food system also requires market com-

petition so resources are paid only normal wages and gains in
efficiency are distributed among producers, merchants and consumers. If monopoly power exists and gains are captured excessively by landlords or merchants, then only part of the economic development potential of food system improvements will be
obtained. Only if the upper 10 percent of the LDC population
receives limited increases in income can the poorest 40 percent
improve its diet as a result of increases in food production
and storage efficiency.

Increased effective demand among the poor resulting from
broad based rural economic development reduces malnutrition and
increases food supply in many nations. The cause of much malnutrition is not lack of food but lack of jobs and income to
buy food. The food supply would be larger in several countries
(e.g., Uruguay, Paraguay and Brazil) if there were more effective demand so a larger quantity of food could be sold. To the
extent that rural economic development including high labor
participation creates jobs for the unemployed and additional
income for the underemployed, the hungriest people would
increase their incomes and purchase of food products, thereby
reducing their own malnutrition and increasing the total demand
for food. If a larger volume of food is sold, this will
encourage production. With effective retail demand for food
increased, there should be opportunity and incentive for food
producers if marketing margins stay constant. Especially the
production of vegetables and fruits is often limited to that
quantity that can be sold. If effective demand increases, some
food production can usually increase.

All professionals have an important role in improving the
food situation by assisting in expanding employment, increasing
real income, improving nutrition from improved income, increasing market demand for food and translating increased effective
retail food demand to increased farm level demand. More jobs
in rural areas increase the income and security of small farmers thereby often increasing their ability and willingness to
adopt new techniques which result in increased total output.
Industrialization often improves food system inputs and reduces
their cost, thereby increasing food production and reducing
waste.

RECOMMENDATIONS TO PROFESSIONALS

Local shortages of food, even for one or two years, can
have a long-term impact on national and world development
by two distinctly different routes:

1) Poor harvests and temporary loss of an area's ability
to import enough food can, via malnutrition, seriously damage
the physical and mental ability of the human population. This
can lead to exploitative, destructive use of land and the envi-

ronment which will permanently reduce the area's capacity to produce. Well designed relief of that situation can maintain the potential for national and world development. Professionals in LDCs and DCs should creatively design world trade, food aid and food reserves so as to insure that policy makers world-wide have available and understand reasonable and effective means to relieve local temporary food shortages and maintain national and world development potential. Food aid programs should and can be designed and administered by professionals to create capital and generate investment and to maintain or improve incentives for local food producers to expand production. Professionals should and can relieve food shortages without perpetuating or increasing the local food deficit or creating windfall profits to local or international merchants or speculators.

2) The shock of a food crisis which threatens development, shoots up prices and increases civil unrest will usually attract the attention of political leaders to the food system and increase their sense of priority concerning its resolution. Professionals should be prepared to take advantage of this priority and attention and to present well-designed programs to adjust producer incentives, develop appropriate technology and modify constraining basic structures such as land tenure and market monopolies.

The 1976 World Food Conference at Ames, Iowa, should support the principles established at the Rome Food Conference of November, 1974, and the 7th Special Session of the United Nations General Assembly in September, 1975. This Conference urges fellow professionals to work out the details of food reserves, meat consumption limitation, self-reliance by the LDCs, interdependence among all nations, massive implementation of available appropriate technology, internal reforms to improve equity and to develop unconventional food sources such as indigenous plants and animals. Professionals can provide specific and locally appropriate means to increase food supply, control food demand growth and improve the distribution of available food. Whether we like it or not, the privileged classes of LDCs, including professionals and leaders, have the major responsibility to reduce hunger and obtain progress among the lowest 40 percent of their populations.

PANELISTS

Chairperson	Quentin M. West	Washington, DC
Rapporteur	Arnold A. Paulsen	Ames, Iowa
Subplenary Speaker	Martin J. Forman	Washington, DC
Subplenary Speaker	Earl O. Heady	Ames, Iowa
Subplenary Speaker	John P. Lewis	Princeton, New Jersey

Panelist	Bruno Benvenuti	Wageningen, Netherlands
Panelist	I. K. Djokoto	Kumasi, Ghana
Panelist	Gary E. Hansen	Honolulu, Hawaii
Panelist	Daryl J. Hobbs	Columbia, Missouri
Panelist	Tadeusz Jakubczyk	Warsaw, Poland
Panelist	Berl A. Koch	Manhattan, Kansas
Panelist	Donald G. McClelland	Washington, DC
Panelist	H. O. Mongi	Mbeya, Tanzania
Panelist	Robert W. Rinden	Oskaloosa, Iowa
Panelist	John Scott	New York, New York
Panelist	Carlos L. Solera	Dunn Loring, Virginia
Panelist	Tan Bock Thiam	Kuala Lumpur, Malaysia

PARTICIPANTS

Mela Gad Aluke	Howard C. Madsen
Mina M. Baker	Dean B. Mahin
Sushma Barewal	Gordon McCleary
Wilma D. Brewer	Corinne W. Mitchell
William J. Brune	Nancy J. Moon
David S. Burgess	Alexander Sciberras
Donald M. Deichman	J. T. Scott
Heliodoro Diaz-Cisneros	Melvina E. Sokan
Cesar Duran	Melvin Sprecher
Steven Falken	Rosa Stone
William R. Fene	Yutse Thomas
Charles French	Jean B. Thompson
Rodger D. Garner	Jerome V. Vanice
Walter W. Goeppinger	Henry Vigues
Joseph Havelka	Roberto Villeda
Zoe E. Kay	M. Luca Yankovich
H. O. Kunkel	Duane E. Young
John C. Lorentzen	Bernard E. Youngquist

National and International Policy

FOOD PRODUCTION POLICIES

We recognize the purposes of food production policies to
be: (1) to provide adequate nutrition for the population of a
country; (2) to generate increased employment and income;
(3) to provide, where possible, surplus food products for
export to obtain foreign exchange; (4) to develop food processing and distribution industries using local materials, as well
as industries utilizing byproducts, in order to improve employment opportunities and the quality of life of the people in the
country; and (5) to improve self-reliance in food and agricultural raw materials in order to ensure the availability of
materials for food processing within the producing countries.

We realize that however significant our policy alternatives may be, our efforts will be largely wasted if they are
not heard, understood and acted upon by the policy-makers in
the various nations. Thus, we recognize each participant has
the responsibility, upon the return to his/her post, to work
hard to transmit the findings of this Conference to the policy-
makers. We also urge the organizers of this Conference to
transmit the proceedings directly to the political and educational leaders in the various countries, as well as to international organizations, for their study and, where appropriate,
action.

We also recognize, as agricultural professionals, our
legitimate concerns are with increasing food production. However, we must underline a conviction that even the most optimistic outcomes of our efforts will not be adequate if population growth is not brought under control.

Food production policies can, and usually will, have differential impacts (1) on various sectors (e.g., consumer versus
producer) of a society, (2) on short- and long-run consequences
and (3) on existing political subdivisions. These differential

625

impacts will almost always--if not always--mean that conflicts
are an inherent part of any food production policy. In most
cases, the best that can be hoped for is a workable compromise.

TAXONOMY OF CONSTRAINTS

Why is it that these goals and objectives have exceeded
our abilities and capabilities to transform them into
realities? That is, what constraints prevent our attempts
and desires for improving food production and nutrition, especially in the developing countries? We recognize that some of
the constraints are of application to all, or nearly all,
developing countries. (To some extent, of course, each constraint is nation-oriented.) Also, we realize that each constraint is nearly always one of an interacting web of constraints.

We have outlined a taxonomy of constraints, primarily to
point out the diversity and complexity of the various constraints. We realize that our list is incomplete and lacking
in specificity. However, this taxonomy must include these
types of constraints: economic (land, labor and capital);
socio-cultural (including structures); educational-research
(humanistic, biological and social); technological-entrepre-
neurial; and political-administrative-legal. In the next section we will recommend some general policy guidelines and
strategies for overcoming, or at least alleviating, these constraints.

SOME GENERAL POLICY GUIDELINES

We recognize, but do not elaborate on, the reality that
food production policies are only a segment (although a
major segment) of resource, input, conservation and processing policies which constitute the agriculture-food policy
chain. In turn, this policy network must be interwoven
(whether through a market, indicatively planned, or centrally
planned political economy) with other major national and international policies.

Moreover, we realize that this overall (macro) perspective
must also be turned upside down, so to speak, so that policy
needs and expectations can be perceived from the micro (individual, corporation, community or cooperative) perspective,
too.

We do not elaborate on the concept of strategies, but it
should be noted that to specify "What should be done?" leads
directly and importantly to the question of "how should we proceed both to enact and to implement these policies?" As general propositions, we desire to stress:

1) The importance or recognizing and making operational
the interdisciplinary aspects of strategy.

2) The need to distinguish (especially for political leaders) the essential differences between long-run and short-run strategies.

3) The necessity of fitting the strategy to the specific constraint.

4) The necessary interaction among researcher, producer, and consumer.

5) The essence of effective policy is determined by the quality of its implementation.

SOME SPECIFIC ALTERNATIVE POLICIES (not in order of priority):

Institutional Structures

1) Creation of a continuing interdisciplinary task force of producers, consumers and other professionals engaged in the production, processing and distribution of food to monitor the nation's food situation and make policy recommendations.

2) Establishment of interministerial machinery to identify problems and to take action to overcome constraints.

Research, Development and Extension

1) Where suitable resources exist, there should be more emphasis on integrated animal-crop production (including research) which will utilize land not suited for crop production and by-product feed and food resources, as well as contribute to a more stable and efficient farming system.

2) More emphasis on research and specific production policies geared to the more rapid acceleration of agricultural production under natural rain conditions (as compared to controlled-water conditions) in the tropics and sub-tropics.

3) Continued research on development of "package demonstrations" adapted to a local situation, including research on how these practices will be accepted and should be applied.

4) Continued search for new varieties, processes and machines that are useful, as viewed by the food producer.

5) Research on methods to reduce waste and enhance nutritional quality in production and distribution processes.

6) Research on increasing food from fish and other aquatic sources.

7) Develop an adequate institutional infrastructure for a balanced program of research, development and transfer of appropriate technologies for improving food supplies and nutrition.

8) In order to overcome constraints of personnel, equipment, foreign exchange and information, close cooperation should be established between research and development institu-

tions in different countries. This will help in the training
of personnel, availability of equipment, and interchange of
know-how in the areas of pre- and post-harvest technologies to
accelerate development.

Incentives for Food Production

1) Provide stable prices at a level that will encourage
food production; and organize equitable marketing services.
2) Establish legal and administrative procedures which
will make possible limited liability loans (i.e., to cooperatives) at realistic rates, loan evaluation, service and collection procedures; make available inputs to promote the efficient
use of technological improvements.
3) Improve government regulations, eliminating those
which inhibit production more than they yield equity, health or
safety benefits.
4) Adopt policies to increase the security and prestige
of farming as an occupation. Such policies should include
crop-failure insurance and other financial incentives to recognize the most productive farmers.

Regionalize and Decentralize the Development Process

Regionalize and decentralize the development process,
including, where appropriate, the "intensive development
zone" approach. This involves the development of a basic,
rural infrastructure (including feeder-roads, water electricity, education, housing and health services).

Implement Alternative Organizations

Implement alternative organizations and structures of production in the various social, economic and resource situations in a country. Examples are peasant collectives, contracts with multinational firms, formation of regional corporations controlled by local producers, national purchasing and
processing organizations and land reform to provide large numbers of adequately-sized units (including the necessary infrastructure).

Coordinate Policies

Coordination of food development policies between common
interests and problems. More specifically, the impact of
foreign trade and foreign aid policies of food-surplus countries should be closely related to the interests and needs of
the less-developed countries (LDCs), both in the short- and
long-run.

Provide "Impact Analysis"
    Provide an "impact analysis" of proposed economic and
    technological policies. These should be broad in nature
but should include short- and long-range consequences, as well
as biological, economic and sociological consequences.

PANELISTS

Chairperson	R. J. Hildreth	Chicago, Illinois
Rapporteur	Ross B. Talbot	Ames, Iowa
Subplenary Speaker	Gonzalo Arroyo	Nanterre, France
Subplenary Speaker	Vladlen A. Martynov	Moscow, Russia
Subplenary Speaker	Henry B. Obeng	Kumasi, Ghana
Subplenary Speaker	Somnuk Sriplung	Bangkok, Thailand
Panelist	R. S. Gowe	Ottawa, Canada
Panelist	Quentin A. L. Jenkins	Baton Rouge, Louisiana
Panelist	Gurdev S. Khush	Manila, Philippines
Panelist	Roy D. Laird	Lawrence, Kansas
Panelist	H. A. B. Parpia	Rome, Italy
Panelist	J. B. Penn	Washington, DC
Panelist	Howard W. Ream	Madison, Wisconsin
Panelist	Jose Salaverry-Llosa	Lima, Peru
Panelist	Abdelmajid Slama	Tunis, Tunisia
Panelist	E. J. Wellhausen	Mexico City, Mexico

PARTICIPANTS

Muhamad Al-Amri
Mohammed Ashraf
Adierson E. Azevedo
Charles L. Cramer
Frank Crane
Egbert deVries
Doeke C. Faber
D. Dale Gillette
Antonio E. Goncalves
Harold D. Guither
Clare I. Harris
W. Lee Honeyman
P. K. Hoogendyk
Randall J. Jones
Bun Eng Lao
Mark Love
Chung Chi Lu
Carl C. Malone
Marshall A. Martin

Francisco Mayorga
Richard J. McConnen
W. H. M. Morris
Alice V. Murray
Kenneth Nicol
Allan P. Rahn
C. Joan Reynolds
David E. Sahn
Victor E. Smith
Darl E. Snyder
O. Stavrakis
John C. S. Tang
Alberto Valdes
Aubrey D. Venter
Sharon B. Webster
Zenon M. Wozniak
William H. Yaw
Delmar Ray Yoder

DISTRIBUTION AND
MARKETING POLICIES

INTRODUCTION AND PROBLEM DEFINITION
     The basic role of food marketing and distribution is to
move the desired amounts and types of food from producers
     to consumers. Marketing and distribution begin when a
farmer starts developing his future production plans and ends
when the consumer receives the food product.
     It is recognized that marketing presumes that there are
markets. It is also recognized that marketing is closely
related to income distribution. Improved marketing, in the
form of marketing efficiency, should not be viewed as an end in
itself. It must form part of a total system to deliver a
larger, more nutritious volume of food to needy people. It
must also provide a higher income to producers. Many different
functions are performed in distributing the production inputs
to the farmer and marketing the food products to the consumer.
These marketing functions include assembly, storage, transportation, grading and standards, processing and packaging, credit
and finance, dissemination of price information, wholesaling
and retailing, promotion and advertising and transfer of ownership.
     These functions are necessary in the marketing and distri-
bution of farm products and in the creation of a variety of
consumer utilities. In principle, the functions are necessary
to distribute food from the peasant farmer to nearby village
consumers as well as in the distribution of food in the sophisticated systems of world trade. In many cases, the traditional
marketing system of market-oriented industrial societies which
spawned these functions do not fulfill the objective of efficiently moving food to consumers in many developing countries.
     The importance of each of the marketing functions depends
on particular situations and upon the level of development as

630

well as upon the farm commodities in question. Advertising,
for example, may be relatively unimportant in many developing
countries and particularly in those countries with chronic food
shortages. Yet, the basic physical marketing functions such as
assembly, transportation and storage are important in all countries. Ghana and Iowa both must have transportation to move
food from producers to consumers; however, the transportation
problems in Ghana and Iowa are different. Ghana has insufficient roads to move the food off the farms to nearby villages.
The fundamental transportation problem in Iowa is to coordinate
the movement of a large production mass off the farms and out
of processing plants into a widely dispersed national and
international market. It must also be done in a manner such
that shippers do not attempt to move all the produce during a
short period of time, thereby temporarily overloading the
transportation system.

Many problems exist in current food marketing and distribution systems in developing countries. One central problem in
poor countries is the lack of capital. Another is the lack of
serious attention paid to the marketing system by government
leaders and in development plans. Systematic attention is
needed if the marketing system is to serve as a means of
encouraging increased food production in these countries--a
goal that lies at the heart of world food strategy. Among the
general problems identified in this workshop, for numerous
countries of the world, were:

Lack of coordination in production, marketing and consumption.

Lack of price information for producers and consumers.

High cost, inefficient marketing systems burdened by an
excessive number of retailers and poorly located processing
plants.

Lack of infrastructure including roads, ports, transportation and storage.

Inadequate or lacking grades and standards.

Unnecessarily costly packaging and containers for food.

Lack of credit for producers.

Lack of effective competition in food distribution.

Inadequate food reserves.

Excessive waste in food distribution.

Destabilizing and counter productive government policies.

Unproductive attempts to redistribute income through the
marketing and distribution system.

Low level of training of people employed in marketing.

Lack of consumer organizations in developing countries.

It was generally agreed that these marketing and distribution problems exist in varying degrees in all countries. The
identification of constraints impeding solutions to these prob-

was, however, limited to those in developing countries.

CONSTRAINTS
    One of the major constraints to solving food marketing and
    distribution problems in developing countries is the fail-
    ure or inability to view production, marketing and distri-
bution and consumption as a total system. Attempts to improve
food marketing and distribution are typically made on a piecemeal basis. If several problems exist simultaneously, attempts
to solve one problem might only aggravate the seriousness of
others. Frequently, there is a failure or inability to recognize that a national marketing system improvement strategy
should be consistent with an overall development strategy.
    Social pressures force politicians to think in terms of
quick, short-run government actions. These actions may be
destablizing and may result in effects opposed to those initially desired. In the past in Brazil, for example, when surplus supplies of rice have occurred, the government restricted
the amount of credit available to rice producers. This
restraint on credit forced farmers to reduce the production of
rice the following year, thereby creating a shortage of rice
and higher rice prices. In responding to the demands of consumers to reduce rice prices, the supply of credit is again
expanded renewing the cycle of surpluses and shortages.
    Another constraint is a lack of market incentive, which
may result from a combination of circumstances including the
inability of local marketing systems to express the desires of
consumers and the needs of producers.
    Regional blocks such as the European Common Market also
create constraints to improving the marketing and distribution
of food. Levies imposed on imported foods to protect domestic
producers tend to reduce prices paid to more efficient producers of similar products. The lower prices received by the more
efficient producers lower both income and output in developing
countries.
    The inability or failure to provide the proper infrastruc-
ture including roads, transportation and storage, combined with
a lack of credit institutions often forces farmers to market
all their products at one time at depressed prices; or it may
prevent them from marketing their products altogether. Post-
World War II experience is replete with attempts to utilize the
marketing infrastructure of industrialized countries in the
agricultural production systems in developing countries and
massive failures have resulted. One such failure has been the
lack of a minimum food reserve, in developing countries, to
meet emergency and disaster demands.
    A lack of consumer knowledge of relative food costs and
nutritional values inhibits consumers from maximizing the value
received from their income spent on food.

The lack of producer organization and organized markets may contribute to the lack of price information to both producers and consumers. Producer cooperatives have been successful in many cases but they are not a universal panacea to overcoming constraints to improved marketing organization and efficiency.

ALTERNATIVE SOLUTIONS

Poor people may not have access to the existing food supply because of high marketing costs or because available food supplies are bid away by other domestic or foreign consumers. Government has a role to provide these people with food. Alternative methods are currently being tested by several governments to reduce marketing costs and thereby increase the prices paid to farmers and decrease the prices paid by consumers. Some of these alternatives also attempt to systematically coordinate production, marketing and consumption by providing price supports, finance and risk reduction.

The Government of Mexico is experimenting with the "markets on wheels" concept. The government agency, CONASUPO, provides price supports and builds storage facilities in the production areas for basic food commodities such as corn and beans. This enables the farmer to receive higher prices. This agency also provides "markets on wheels" by providing trucks to take perishable products to town and sell the products directly to consumers at prices below those in supermarkets.

A similar experiment is being conducted in Brazil. This experiment, which involves less direct government intervention, also attempts to increase the income of small farmers and to facilitate the movement of food from the farm to the consumer by providing two basic marketing functions, namely, information and finance. A public corporation called COBAL buys and sells basic food products. The Extension Service provides information. COBAL, for example, will inform the Extension Service that COBAL desires to purchase 20,000 tons of corn in a certain area. The Extension Service will locate farmers who are willing to provide the corn. COBAL provides a cash advance for the corn. If the producer can sell his corn at a higher price in the market at delivery time, he sells the product and reimburses COBAL. If the market is less than the guaranteed price, the farmer delivers the corn to COBAL to satisfy the advance payment.

Taiwan has a national policy for rice production and marketing that attempts to improve the welfare of both small rice growers and consumers. More than 90 percent of the farmers in Taiwan grow rice. Almost all Chinese people eat rice daily. The government developed a program to collect approximately one-third of the off-farm rice stock. The remaining two-thirds of the rice stock is left in the hands of private dealers. The government fixes a minimum price for rice at approximately the cost of production plus a 20 percent profit. The stocks are used to stabilize prices for the benefit of consumers. Farmers get about 80 percent of the consumers' dollars paid for rice. The profit margin for middlemen is narrow but, because the volume of business is large, the private rice marketing industry remains profitable.

Another attempt to reduce consumer prices in several countries involves no government intervention. Instead, this method is based upon consumer cooperatives.

Subsidized food prices have been used in Ghana and Egypt to reduce food prices. The subsidy approach has generally been unsuccessful in these two countries because smuggling of substantial quantities of the low-priced foods into surrounding countries, where food is priced at the higher market price, has reduced food supplies.

These institutional developments are examples of efforts to reduce two basic marketing costs: the physical cost of marketing and any monopoly extraction that may exist. Alternative solutions to food problems of many nations could include marketing boards as well as commodity agreements. Regional groups of countries might attempt to develop intergovernmental coordinating efforts for marketing or for bargaining on food supplies to meet critical local needs.

The work group concluded that efforts to solve the income distribution problem through the marketing system are, in themselves, unlikely to be successful. Solutions to the low income problem are more likely to be successful through a national income policy.

Many attempts have been made to improve the infrastructure of developing countries. Improvements in infrastructure, such as access roads, markets and processing facilities, where carefully planned, have opened up markets and thereby stimulated production. A key to the success of the Kaira milk scheme in Gujerat State, India, was the construction of a milk plant that permitted dairy farmers, formerly selling only to villages, to enter the Bombay market. A large increase in milk production followed. Success with the Kaira scheme led the government of India to undertake the "Operation Flood" program throughout India. The plant was only one element in a comprehensive program. More poorly conceived efforts elsewhere have resulted in building unneeded facilities.

NEEDED RESEARCH

Many efforts have been made to adopt marketing technologies and functions which have evolved in industrial nations. Research is needed to determine the transferability of these technologies. These technologies may well serve the marketing and distribution needs of higher income classes in developing countries. They may fail, however, in adequately servicing the needs of low income people. Research is needed to explore additional changes in existing marketing technologies to better serve the needs of low income people. These alternative methods may include lower cost processes, packages relevant for developing countries and other distribution technologies. Studies are also needed to determine the economic feasibility of proposed investments in marketing and distribution facilities and in proposed infrastructure investments.

Providing an adequate food supply to developing nations is a problem not only for the developing nations but for the entire international community. Supplemental efforts to solve this problem should, therefore, be explored by the international community. Alternative methods of providing food reserves along with alternative methods of financing these reserves should be explored. In addition, the impact of these reserves on production and prices paid to farmers should be investigated.

Domestic food reserves, if any, in developing countries could be augmented by a grain reserve to meet disasters and emergencies. Chronic food shortages post a different question, as do bigger stocks and so-called commercial reserves. Research on alternative methods of accumulating and dispersing such reserves is badly needed. Some investigations of this question have been completed but more are needed. Perhaps needed even more is the political will to implement existing knowledge to increase and stabilize food supplies in the world. This stability inevitably will assist in supplying food to hungry people. An integral part of a world food distribution system is an early warning system of pending disasters in needy nations.

Finally, though this statement has emphasized local marketing questions, it is important to stress the need for international trade in solving many of the world's food problems. Without international attention--more specifically, without international trade--the world is not likely to attain many of its desired objectives in relation to reliable and nutritious food supplies.

PANELISTS

Chairperson	Jimmye S. Hillman	Tucson, Arizona
Rapporteur	C. Phillip Baumel	Ames, Iowa
Subplenary Speaker	Khaled El-Shazly	Cairo, Egypt
Subplenary Speaker	Mogens Jul	Copenhagen, Denmark
Subplenary Speaker	Luis J. Paz Silva	Lima, Peru
Panelist	Antonio Bacigalupo	Bogota, Colombia
Panelist	Byron L. Bondurant	Columbus, Ohio

Panelist	Keith O. Campbell	Sydney, Australia
Panelist	J. Maud Kordylas	Accra, Ghana
Panelist	Robert C. T. Lee	Taipei, Republic of China
Panelist	Jose Pastore	Sao Paulo, Brazil
Panelist	Shlomo Reutlinger	Washington, DC
Panelist	Dusan J. Tomic	Beograd, Yugoslavia
Panelist	Antonio Turrent-Fernandez	Chapingo, Mexico
Panelist	Gerald C. Wheelock	Normal, Alabama
Panelist	Harold L. Wilcke	St. Louis, Missouri

PARTICIPANTS

Dyaa Abdou
Lucile F. Adamson
Dale G. Anderson
Don Ault
Dale Bawden
William G. Boggess
Steve Carpenter
Lynn K. Engstrand
Lindley Finch
John Henry Foster
Gene A. Futrell
William R. Gasser
Merlyn H. Grott
Nile Harper
Sarkar Hiren
Mohamed Mahrous Ismail
Cathy Lynn Jabara
George Jacoby
Jean Marie Johnson

Young W. Kihl
J. L. F. Kriek
Coy G. McNabb
William H. Meyers
Safiah B. Mohamed
George Nassif
Wallace E. Ogg
John J. Piderit
Richard W. Rundell
Charles Sand
O. J. Scoville
Harvey R. Sherman
Bhag Singh Sidhu
Ralph H. Smuckler
Kathy Stephenson
Budiningsih Sunyoto
Sopin Tongpan
J. William Uhrig
Charles L. Wright

CONSUMER POLICIES

The scope of the topic was identified as those policies which affect consumers' well-being and protection. It was agreed that the discussion for the three sessions would relate to the following:

Food quality, standards and monitoring with respect to nutritional value, e.g., quality control, enrichment, labeling; sensory factors, e.g., appearance, taste, texture; and accessibility and safety, e.g., home-grown and conventional foods, non-processed and processed locally marketed products, contamination and spoilage.

Consumer capability, relating to potentials for: consumer nutritional understanding, e.g., cultural food patterns, beliefs and preferences, nutritional education; purchasing power, e.g., income increasing enterprises; assimilation, e.g., biological utilization restricted by infections or parasitic diseases caused by environmental conditions such as water supply.

ASSESSMENT

The first session's discussion of assessment tended to center on developing countries. Three major points were brought out as limiting the adequacy of policies for securing consumers' nutritional well-being and safety:

1. Policies generally do not result from broad analyses of cost and benefits and thus may unintentionally have detrimental effects. For example, agriculture and food policies generally emphasize increasing yields with less consideration given to total impact on the quality of the diet. Failure to consider the impact on the consumer may also result in imple-

mentation of aid programs which result in a decrease in the
quality of the consumer's diet.

2. Policies do not always take into sufficient consideration the multiple goals of individual countries, the locally
available foods and food habits and the analysis of local and
regional use of simple technologies.

3. Differences in the needs and interests of households,
communities and markets in food surplus and food deficit countries are often inadequately considered in policy formulation.

CONSTRAINTS, POTENTIALS AND POLICY ALTERNATIVES

The following proposals represent different avenues
through which potentials for feeding the world's population may be realized more adequately by incorporation of
nutritional considerations at all levels and stages of policy
formulation.

For the most part, the alternative policies presented are
to be interpreted as additions to ones already existing in
order that the needs of consumers are better and more fully
represented. Policies that, for example, allocate a greater
portion of limited resources to consumer areas rather than to
export income producing areas may foster individual and family
capacities to respond in ways that in the long-run compensate
for short-run production losses.

A Basic Constraint

Inadequate representation of consumer, and especially food
and nutrition concerns, has limited recognition of consumer aspects as a major component of food policy at local/
regional/national levels. Consumers' food and nutrition concerns should be represented as part of multiprofessional advisory inputs into policy determination at all levels. A coordinated planning and action process which weighs concerns related
to consumer education and consumer organizations, production
and distribution systems and purchasing power is needed. Each
professional involved in food policy development must assume
responsibility for contributing to the careful consideration of
consumer needs in policy development at all levels.

The Food Quality Constraint

Emphasis on cash crops for export in agricultural production policies has led, in many countries, to the neglect of the
production of a variety of highly nutritious foods resulting in
a less diverse food supply. Often this has affected the nutritional adequacy of diets as well as introducing less acceptable
food products.

In the consumer interest, increased emphasis should be
given to nutritional requirements of the total population
in agricultural production planning. This requires the further
study of consumption patterns, needs and the nutritional
requirements of families, households and communities.

Low priority has been given to such crops as vegetables
and fruits meant solely for human consumption. While these
products may be relatively high in cost per calorie and protein
energy yield, they provide nutrients vital to consumer health
and nutrition.

Policies are needed to promote local production of vegetable and fruit crops through community and/or household gardens.
This is likely to be a concern of ministries in addition to
agriculture, such as people's welfare and education, and to
involve assistance and integration of educational programs at
local levels by appropriately trained personnel in agriculture,
education and health.

Lack of emphasis on post-harvest procedures, compared with
production, has resulted in inadequate recognition of the high
proportion of food lost in the post-harvest stage, from farm to
consumer.

Increased attention should be given to:

1. Simple methods of food preservation, packaging, storage and processing, taking into account local possibilities and
environmental conditions.

2. Community and household methods of food storage and
food preservation.

3. Local food preservation industries including those
based on appropriate technologies and on local cooperatives.

4. Training of personnel in respect to 1, 2 and 3.

5. Research in relation to 1, 2 and 3, including safety
of chemical methods.

6. Time and methods of harvest.

7. Organization of local/regional distribution systems,
such as cooperatives.

Emphasis on the relatively expensive production of animal
compared with vegetable protein has meant that consumers with
greater purchasing power compete more successfully for animal
protein and the grain resources they represent. Therefore, the
relation to utilization of the total food resource represented
by animal proteins has not been adequately considered in food
production policies.

More attention should be given to the complementary uses
of animals (including fish) and crops (including edible roots)
in food systems:

1.   Search for trade-off possibilities which yield the
smallest increases in grain prices to low income consumers.

2.   Make provisions for emergency grain stocks.

3.   Increase the protein content of local/regional food
systems.

4.   Explore substitutes for feed grains. Increase use of
forages and crop residues, agro-industry by-products, wood-
industry by-products, animals wastes and other products not
directly usable by humans, for animal production.

5.   Explore the potential of inland fisheries as a source
of protein.

6.   Continue efforts to rationalize the harvesting of fish
and other marine species in international waters.

7.   Explore protein sources through animal research
(including small animals and the more exotic or unconventional
sources).

The adverse impacts of the introduction and long-term
importation of mass produced and/or low cost food aid products
on nutritious food availability and safety often leads to:
thwarting of incentive for local food production; developing
consumption habits for foods that cannot economically be produced locally; and increasing the incidence of certain health
problems.

Policies relating to food production and/or food aid
should place increasing emphasis on efforts to:

1.   Identify and restrict the production and promotion of
food products whose effect substantially reduces the safety and
nutritive quality of food, or its adequacy for specific groups.

2.   Plan ahead to minimize the adverse impacts of the
integration of local and global food systems. For example, use
long-term trade agreements or aid agreements and programs which
promise to end the need for aid.

3.   Use food transfers as part of a package containing
food, technology and capital.

4.   Include development of protective measures for small
scale food and income producing enterprises of households in
national planning.

Research and technological lags due to concentration on
export crops and a limited number of food cereals have thwarted
development on other consumer-related issues and limited the
opportunity to provide adequate bases for recommendations and
actions.

Increased research and development emphases are needed
with regard to: production of pulses and high quality plant
protein sources, improved quality (protein, vitamins) of basic
dietary staples, combinations of available commodities into
more nutritious groupings, socio-cultural significance of foods

and food combinations, and food and nutrition related communication processes.

Limited attention to soil conservation practices that may decrease food quality and agricultural productivity in the long-run is another constraint.

Increased attention should be given to ecological effects with respect to soil conservation and practices, avoiding the loss of topsoil and vital nutrients and recognizing the role of cover crops and the related significance of animal protein.

The Consumer Capability Constraint

Lack of adequate purchasing power of urban or rural families often makes it impossible for consumers to obtain an adequate diet even when food is available.

Policies that lead to the generation of income or to needed redistribution of income should be adopted where appropriate and may include these considerations and programs:

1.   Home industries or other income generating program to promote self-reliance and maintenance of exchange processes.
2.   Creation of farmers' and consumers' cooperatives to increase income and to lower farm supply and food prices.
3.   Intervention programs such as subsidies, price controls, minimum daily allotments and food stamps.
4.   Develop credit programs for women and high risk families to promote development of small enterprises (such as a few chickens or a milking goat or two) to produce both for the market and for household consumption.

Limited education, training and communication technologies have thwarted optimal utilization of food, resulting in:

1.   Shortage of trained personnel, including nutritionists, to facilitate the efficient utilization of food after production.
2.   Neglect of social and cultural problems such as special needs of vulnerable groups.
3.   Limited knowledge and ability of consumers to achieve potential utilization of available nutritional and other resources.

Greater efforts should be made to provide education and training at both the professional and subprofessional levels in food sciences and technology, human nutrition and dietetics and home economics, emphasizing socio-cultural aspects. Aid agencies should give greater assistance to institutions concerned with aid to the establishment of new departments and teacher centers. Trained personnel concerned with nutrition and post-harvest problems should be included in extension and community health programs.

Frequent omission of post-harvest policies in external aid programs, whether by advisers from abroad or those from within, by-passes consideration of nutritional, socio-cultural and other aspects of consumer needs.
Advisers and aid-giving bodies should give full attention to educational needs previously listed.

Limited attention to quality and safety of mass produced processed foods may affect nutritional status and health of consumers, particularly in urban areas.
As food industries develop:

1. Research is needed to identify appropriate product criteria.
2. Effective inspection procedures and information labeling need to be developed and their use enforced.
3. Educational programs in product selection should be developed.
4. Consumer response should be encouraged.

Unsafe water supplies and other environmental conditions contributing to infections or parasitic diseases reduce utilization of available food.
Programs to help people provide (or adapt to) healthful living environments should be given priority including improvement of water supplies and education for healthful and safe home practices.

PANELISTS

Chairperson	Eleanora A. Cebotarev	Guelph, Canada
Rapporteur	Ruth Deacon	Ames, Iowa
Subplenary Speaker	M. J. John	Vellore, India
Subplenary Speaker	Paul C. Ma	Taiwan, Republic of China
Subplenary Speaker	Barbara A. Underwood	University Park, Pennsylvania
Panelist	Farah Hassan Adam	Shambat, Sudan
Panelist	Veronica Arthur	Ames, Iowa
Panelist	Francis Aylward	Reading, England
Panelist	Luke Jinchang Im	Seoul, Korea
Panelist	P. Mahadevan	Rome, Italy
Panelist	Joseph Nemeth	Budapest, Hungary
Panelist	Kenneth O. Rachie	Cali, Colombia
Panelist	C. D. Van Houweling	Rockville, Maryland
Panelist	Jan Zalewski	Warsaw, Poland

PARTICIPANTS

Maria Teresa Aguirre
L. David Brown
H. Dean Bunch
Loretta Clifton
Julio A. Echevarria
Josefa Eusebio
Richard E. Felch
Charles P. Gratto
Don F. Hadwiger
Paul G. Hill
Radziah H. J. Ishak
Robert E. Johanson
Faisal Kasryno
Ann F. Lincoln
Jane A. Love
Chi-Lin Luh
Charles P. Lutz
Karen Sue Morgan

Bonita D. Neff
Susan Newcomer
Merlin L. Pfannkuch
Russell Pounds
Abbas Sadrai
Kenneth G. Seipel
Della Sprecher
Richard C. Staples
Virginia P. Steelman
Nancy Steorts
Mark M. Sterner
Lester J. Teply
A. Ellen Terpstra
Donald E. Thompson
Ann V. Wade
H. D. Woite
Li-An Yang

Natural and Human Resources

PHYSICAL RESOURCES FOR FOOD PRODUCTION

To achieve the objective of this Conference of involving scientists and educators in world food problems, this workshop identified the major physical resources which act as constraints to the production of food. The challenge is formidable and requires a coalition of professionals if solutions to food production problems are to be achieved.

LAND

To make rational decisions and to achieve optimal management, priority should be given to the development of a global land resources inventory. Making best use of this resource should be based on land use assessment, land use planning, the application of soil conservation practices, and fertilizer needs with the greatest potentials for an increased cultivated land base in Africa, Asia and South America.

Soil Surveys

Modern soil surveys would result in a more precise measurement of the amount of potentially arable land, and specific information on the types and extent of soils would assist in evaluating present food production capabilities in relation to possible cropping patterns. Application of survey information to on-site conditions which optimize plant growth and development under natural ecological conditions is necessary for increasing the world's food production capacity. While considerable information on certain soil associations in various parts of the world has been assembled from previous soil survey activities, there is a question about its application and use for orderly land use planning.

Land Use Assessment

By assessing present land use, the production levels for a
variety of cropping alternatives can be estimated. Furthermore, estimates of the possible yield improvements that
might come from the application of research results can be
made. Such an assessment could give the human and capital
requirements for development of different kinds of land. The
particular land use constraints to higher yields could be identified in terms of particular production inputs such as drainage and land modification.

Land Use Planning

A vigorous assessment of present use of land would serve
as a basis for developing future land use alternatives.
The most effective investment opportunities for increasing food
production from a country's land base could result from planning, but there is always the possibility that plans may conflict with the ideas of those who own the land or who are
attempting to put the plans into effect. Land use planning
should result in the best use of land consistent with needs for
agriculture, housing, industry, recreation, etc.

Soil Conservation

There is a need to develop a coordinated worldwide soil
conservation program which would reduce wind erosion,
reduce water erosion, minimize salinization, reduce water logging, limit urban sprawl and reduce pollution. Conservation
measures should include but not be limited to tillage systems,
efficient use of agricultural and urban wastes, proper placement of terraces, application of effective drainage and cropping practices (including the role of forests and soil building
crops) and integration of animal agriculture with various cropping systems. New low cost conservation methods need to be
developed, and an economic analysis conducted on costs and benefits before implementing a soil conservation program.

Fertilization

There is the potential for greatly increasing the productive capacity of land through fertilization and the application of advanced management techniques although there are
some attendant problems. With limited phosphorus reserves,
research is needed to learn suitable methods for the conservation of this nutrient. A goal for plant breeders is to develop
food crops which will result in significant yield increases
with small increments of added fertilizers. Multi-cropping,
using different varieties of plants to take advantage of fertilizers leaching into various strata of the rhizosphere, holds

potential for minimizing pollution by fertilizers and increasing food production. There is a need for a better understanding of the relationship between nitrogen fixing plants and the soil microflora as related to the growth of cultivated crops. Synergistic effects from mutually compatible crops, the phenomenon of nitrogen fixation by certain tropical grasses and legume interplanting hold promise for increased crop production in the future. The possible accumulation of toxic factors in soil due to excessive use of fertilizers or pesticides needs to be recognized as a constraint to future food production.

WATER

As with land, water resource inventories need to be made in order to provide a basis on which to make rational decisions and to optimize management strategies. Underground water surveys should estimate total resources and potentials for recharging. Surface water inventories should include potential for storage during periods of flood.

Irrigation

Water conservation can be achieved by improved technology of water application. The trickle method is a good example of such technologies which should be improved and adopted where applicable. There is a great need to avoid water losses by evaporation during storage and during transport through canals. Prior to irrigation of some soils, it may be necessary to leach salts by applying water. This leaching process needs to be understood as a reclamation technique rather than wastage of water. Excessive irrigation and improper drainage can lead to water logging or salinity problems, resulting in decreased productivity. Proper management of water application and proper land preparation for irrigation are important factors in realizing increased yields of food crops. Economics of irrigation facility installation are a major deterrent to increased use of irrigation in cropping systems.

Dry Land Agriculture

There is a critical need to conserve water in dry land farming as well as in irrigated production systems. The best methods of conserving soil moisture by tillage methods (relationship of fallowing and no-till systems to soil moisture retention) need to be identified and applied. Plant breeders will be able to contribute to physical resource conservation by breeding or selecting drought resistant food plant cultivars. Development of low cost soil and water conservation practices is important to increasing production under dry land conditions.

AQUATIC SOURCES OF FOOD
     To insure continued supplies of edible fish and other
     aquatic foods, an international institute of fisheries
     should be established. Such an institute would monitor
pollution levels in all water systems (rivers, lakes, seas and
oceans) and would take steps to insure continued food productivity in these water systems. Another need is to identify and
to protect endangered aquatic species, so that valuable food
sources are not eliminated either by overfishing or by pollution. The cultivation of aquatic species for food is a reality, and there is a need for more information on aquaculture
practices, to make them a more significant part of the food
production system.

WEATHER
     The most influential physical factor in agriculture,
     because it is least subject to control, is weather. Cur-
     rently there is considerable interest in the fluctuations
of weather patterns and changes in climate. To evaluate the
impact of such fluctuations and changes more information is
needed. This need should be met through the establishment of
an agricultural metereological network that is worldwide in
scope. The worldwide network would be linked directly to
regional weather analysis centers, and such centers would provide weather information of direct use in increasing food production.

ENERGY
     Alternate sources of energy for use in agriculture are
     needed to replace fossil fuels. Fossil fuels, particu-
     larly petroleum, have freed men and animals from much bur-
densome labor in agriculture, but there is a critical need for
careful consideration of suitable alternative sources of
energy. Until alternative sources are available, it would
appear incumbent to conserve fossil fuels. Plants are prime
users of solar energy, but usage can be improved by proper management techniques such as seeding rates and multiple cropping.
Also, there is a potential for breeding plants that have
increased efficiency for use of solar energy resulting from
modifying the leaf arrangement, changing the number of leaves
and/or by increasing the photosynthetic efficiency.
     The identification of methods and the development technol-
ogy for producing food crops with minimal energy expenditure
are other alternatives for minimizing fossil fuel use. Minimum
tillage and trickle irrigation are two techniques that conserve
physical resources as well as energy.

Nitrogen Sources

Ammonia is one of the preferred nitrogen sources that is used in high energy agriculture as practiced in the United States and some other western countries. The production of ammonia by reduction of gaseous nitrogen is an energy consuming process when done artificially. There is, however, a great potential for increased use of biologically fixed nitrogen. Better understanding and use of nitrogen fixation by micro-organisms are essential steps in decreasing the fossil fuel dependence of agriculture.

Recycling of Agricultural Wastes

Recycling is an important conservation technique that can utilize human, animal and plant nutrients; enhance soil tilth; abate pollution and yield heat energy by direct burning or through methane fermentation.

MANAGEMENT

Perhaps the weakest link in the process of discovering new knowledge and applying that knowledge to agricultural food production is the transfer of that knowledge to farmers who can effectively use it to manage their resources. In the area of physical resources for use in agriculture, nothing appears more important than the management techniques practiced by individual farmers. Identification and discovery of useful and economic management systems that apply to long term physical resource needs are vital, but the application of these management techniques by individual farmers is also most important.

SOCIO-ECONOMIC IMPACTS ON PHYSICAL RESOURCES

The interdisciplinary make up of this Conference and Workshop made it abundantly clear that the subject of physical resource availability could not be adequately treated by considering only the scientific and technological needs for these resources. Physical resources for food production often depend upon socio-economic conditions such as the high cost of land reclamation. The use of prime land for agriculture may not be feasible because of the lack of transportation and communication infrastructures.

Farm Size

The size of farm units may not be optimal for efficient food production or for soil conservation, but in attempting to remedy the situation through changes in farm land organization or in land tenure systems there are usually fewer

alternative solutions than might be expected. The existing
socio-economic conditions will limit any simplistic solutions
and may override change of any kind.

Planning

Many land use alternatives can only be properly evaluated
on a socio-economic basis. The use of physical resources
in general can be evaluated best by careful and explicit delineation of economies involved in production. One of the constraints in planning is the identification of data needed to
properly evaluate alternatives. Good economic models for planning and evaluating alternatives are needed. Such models would
identify gaps in knowledge and specify data that will form the
basis for program decision making in the future.

Cooperation for the Long Term

For introduction of any new technology involving improved
efficiency of resource use, there is a need for close
cooperation between professional biologists, physical scientists or engineers and social scientists. The implementation
of sound management practices of land, water and energy
resources often involves changes in the traditional cultural
patterns and may cause shifts in national priorities. In the
press of short-run problems, governments often fail to perceive
and to act upon long-run goals, such as an enduring agricultural production base. It is encumbent upon governments to
identify and devise strategies for preserving agricultural productivity if they are to meet the world's future needs for
food.

PANELISTS

Chairperson	Roger L. Mitchell	Manhattan, Kansas
Rapporteur	John P. Mahlstede	Ames, Iowa
Subplenary Speaker	Nicolaas Luykx	Honolulu, Hawaii
Subplenary Speaker	R. J. Olembo	Nairobi, Kenya
Panelist	Jose E. G. Araujo	San Jose, Costa Rica
Panelist	M. M. Elgabaly	Cairo, Egypt
Panelist	Arne Eskilt	Arendal, Norway
Panelist	Ljubomir R. Lazarevic	Nemanjina, Yugoslavia
Panelist	Orlando Olcese	Guatemala City, Guatemala
Panelist	Felicitas Piedad-Pascual	Iloilo City, Philippines
Panelist	E. W. Russell	Reading, England

| Panelist | Philip H. Spies | Stellenbosch, South Africa |
| Panelist | D. Sundaresan | Karnal, India |

PARTICIPANTS

Jerry Adem Afuh
Antonio M. Arantes-Licio
Roger J. Blobaum
Kimberly Bobo
Cornelius Bodine, Jr.
N'Guetta Bosso
Adhemar Brandini
Waltraud A. R. Brinkmann
Alvaro Bueno
Alvaro Cordero
Aurora G. Corpuz
George R. Dawson
S. A. Ewing
L. S. Fife
Pilar A. Garcia
Theodore A. Granovsky
William H. Greiner
Philip Hand
Vernon K. Jones
Karl Kaukis

S. MacCallum King
Daniel Kitivo
Willard Latham
E. D. Ludlow
Reginald Lemange Marandu
Joseph C. Meisner
A. Lee Meyer
Yordan V. Mladenov
Lawrence Mzee
Joseph Naghski
Lowell G. Nelson
H. Wayne Pritchard
John Putman
Charles L. Rhykerd
Edward C. A. Runge
H. M. Stahr
George W. Thomson
Enrique Torres
Howard H. Wilkowske
Madison J. Wright

MAINTAINING AND IMPROVING
PLANT AND ANIMAL RESOURCES

People of the world depend on plants and animals for food.
In developing countries, these are produced primarily by peasant cultivators or herdsmen controlling only a few hectares of
land. Potentially arable land is limited in amount. Most
arable land not now under cultivation is remote from centers of
population with food deficits. Food for an expanding population, therefore, must come largely from increasing the production of lands now cultivated. Nonarable lands, however, will
continue to be important sources of food, both in quantity and
quality, as products of grazing ruminant animals. For at least
the remainder of this century, people will depend upon the same
plant and animal species now grown for food. Thus, maintaining
and improving these plant and animal resources are essential to
feeding the human population of the world.

MANAGEMENT

Yields of crops can be greatly increased by management to
remove such constraints as inadequate fertility, pest damage and drought stress. Feed availability is the principal factor limiting production of livestock. The productivity
of existing breeds of animals can be increased by continued
emphasis on forage production, on factors improving nutrition
and on parasite and disease control. Gains from improved management can be enhanced by the breeding of plants and animals
that have an increased potential to respond. Improving plants
and animals for food processing and for meeting the nutritional
requirements of people, especially for protein, is also an
important breeding goal.

GENETICS

Improving the genetic potential of plants and animals grown for food is urgent if hunger is to be minimized.

Genetic variability is the ultimate and effectively irreplaceable source of improvement and adaptation of plants and animals. Food demands of increasing world populations and present trends of adopting new technologies threaten extinction of many breeds, primitive cultivars and even wild species seriously reducing genetic resources available to breeders. The loss of genetic resources may include genes needed to counter new diseases or other pests that unpredictably limit potential for both short- and long-range improvement.

Current Efforts

The World Food Conference of 1976 recognizes and commends the governments, international agencies (particularly, the Consultative Group on International Agricultural Research assisted by the Technical Advisory Committee, FAO, the International Board for Plant Genetic Resources, and UNESCO Man and Biosphere Program and working groups of animal scientists assembled by FAO) and others who have recognized that genetically variable populations of wild and primitive cultivated plants and indigenous animal breeds and species now face extinction. Their efforts have made significant contributions toward the collection, maintenance and utilization of plant and animal germ plasm selected because of potential importance to human welfare.

Need for Germ Plasm Collections

Several reports made at this Conference dramatically show the great contributions that improved varieties of rice, wheat, maize, pearl millet, sorghum, peanuts and other crops have made to food supplies in the world. These new varieties were produced by use of germ plasm from existing collections. Expected population growth makes major increases in food supplies imperative. Unfavorable weather and unpredictable disease and insect outbreaks could greatly reduce food production and bring hunger to millions. Major investments to support comprehensive, national and global efforts to collect and preserve threatened genetic resources are an immediate need. Cost of such a comprehensive program will be small in terms of human benefits.

Still greater investments are needed in evaluating the genetic resources, systematically documenting their traits and using them in breeding programs. Well supported national and international centers are required to give both the depth and scope required to make rapid improvements by combining desired

traits. Heterozygous and heterogeneous populations from such
centers can be grown and selected in the environments and production conditions of various countries.

Need for Implementation

Commercial industry, many different public institutions
and effective extension organizations must be encouraged
and assisted to implement the increase of seed or improved crop
varieties and breeding stock of animals developed by breeders.
These agencies have essential roles in supplying cultivators
and herdsmen and helping them, in turn, improve their production systems so they achieve rewards of greater and more stable
income for the increased food produced.

Need for Research

Achieving cultivar improvement that benefits the small
cultivator of developing countries requires teams of plant
scientists to conduct the adaptive research and evaluations
needed to identify selections that fit the production situations. Then trained extension workers are necessary to guide
their effective adoption and use on farms. All other investments will produce little food unless this investment in
trained leadership is made to serve the needs of each country.
Improvement of plant and animal resources is a building
operation. Each improved strain or cultivar is the base for
further improvement by breeding procedures that add genes to
increase potential or reduce weaknesses of any trait. Research
on physiology, genetic control of metabolic systems, genetic
and environmental interactions, the nature of disease and
insect resistance, stress tolerance and other biological factors is essential to understanding the potential of genetic
resources and developing effective selection procedures to permit breeding progress. New scientific advances from research
in such areas as somatic hybridization and genetic engineering
using techniques to manipulate genetic material may help meet
specific improvement goals. Rapid progress in biological
research requires major investments internationally and within
nations to train capable scientists and to support them in the
continuing programs essential for sustained productivity.
Strong international cooperation among scientists and programs
is vital to success.

PLANT PROGRAMS

Prompt and widespread attention should be given to plant
programs to insure:

1. That the collection of genetically variable wild pro-

genitor species of actual or potential crop plants and primitive cultivars be accelerated and that adequate support be given for their preservation and effective utilization in breeding programs.

2. That those countries in which wild relatives and primitive cultivated forms of important food and feed crops occur establish ecosystem preserves of sufficient size to protect populations and allow their continuing co-evolution. Ecosystem preserves are the only feasible means of preserving the germ plasm and natural conditions for studying the biology of interactions of insect predators and pathogens, of plant pathogen antagonists and hyperparasites and of indigenous mycorrhizal fungi and microorganisms with nitrogen fixing capabilities.

3. That special emphasis be given to the collection of genetic material which might result in improvement of nutritional quality, yield of nutrients, disease resistance, insect resistance and tolerance to climatic and other environmental stresses; also of special interest are those crops which complement each other as sources of nutrients, which might have uniquely beneficial properties as food and feed sources and which require a minimum input of external resources.

4. That more species be included in the germ plasm collections than are currently being collected, especially forage grasses and legumes, pulses, oilseeds, tropical fruits and vegetables and other specialized crops which are important foods in developing countries; that attention be directed toward appropriate microbial collections which might be useful in the production and utilization of foods and feed crops.

5. That the program be worldwide with each nation being encouraged to participate; that an inventory, catalog and retrieval system be established so the material will be available to qualified scientists of all nations, and that adequate replication in different locations be maintained to prevent catastrophic losses.

6. That teams of plant scientists, food technologists and other related scientists cooperate in the evaluation of new genetic combinations to increase their effectiveness in improving food and feed production both in quantity and quality.

7. That support be given for the development of a scientific discipline to provide a subject matter base for research and training in the systematic collection, evaluation, preservation and utilization of germ plasm with early emphasis on new methods for preserving germ plasm.

ANIMAL PROGRAMS

Prompt and widespread attention should be given to animal programs to insure:

1. That efforts for conservation of desirable animal

germ plasm be expanded with emphasis on those breeds or lines which possess exceptional attributes such as disease resistance, adaptation to extreme environmental conditions, superior growth rate or food producing qualities which appear to be in danger of loss.

2. That adequate support be given to promptly increase efforts for listing and describing genetic variants and breeds within species so this basic information will be available for establishing programs of animal gene conservation and other research purposes.

3. That zoological gardens or natural preserves be established or maintained to protect those species which are nearly extinct; that heterogeneous outbred populations (gene pools) be established to include and retain genes which may be lost.

4. That support be given to research and development of methods for the long-term storage of semen and fertilized ova as methods to preserve genes.

5. That support be given for the development of scientific programs to provide basic information for research and training in the collection and preservation of animal germ plasm.

6. That breeding programs be implemented following the establishment of adequate nutrition, health and husbandry standards; that the establishment of additional animal research centers be encouraged to study the role of animals in food production compatible with efficient crop production, to develop improved strains and to provide basic information for germ plasm evaluation programs.

PANELISTS

Chairperson	D. G. Hanway	Lincoln, Nebraska
Rapporteur	Allen H. Trenkle	Ames, Iowa
Plenary Speaker	Glenn W. Burton	Tifton, Georgia
Subplenary Speaker	J. H. Conrad	Gainesville, Florida
Subplenary Speaker	Don Winkelmann	Mexico City, Mexico
Subplenary Speaker	S. H. Wittwer	East Lansing, Michigan
Panelist	A. Gordon Ball	Guelph, Canada
Panelist	Ricardo Bressani	Guatemala City, Guatemala
Panelist	George A. Clayton	Edinburgh, Scotland
Panelist	J. C. Craddock, Jr.	Beltsville, Maryland
Panelist	Alfonso G. Flores-Mere	Lima, Peru
Panelist	Kanji Gotoh	Sapporo, Japan
Panelist	U. J. Grant	Ithaca, New York
Panelist	Bruce M. Koppel	Honolulu, Hawaii

Panelist	Malcolm H. MacDonald	San Jose, Costa Rica
Panelist	Robert O. Whyte	Kelantan, Malaysia
Panelist	Yukio Yamada	Chiba, Japan

PARTICIPANTS

Rezai Abdolmujid
Rufus O. Adegboye
Horace H. Autenrieth
Wilbur P. Ball
William L. Baran
Stephen Edgar Beebe
J. Artie Browning
E. A. Butler
Naomi N. Capinpin
Don Duvick
Paul J. Fitzgerald
Henry A. Fitzhugh
Thomas W. Freeze
S. R. Freiberg
Maebelle Godown
John Greig
Dale D. Harpstead
John N. Hathcock

Keith W. Johnson
Fuh-Kiang Koh
Lyle Lapham
Cesar E. Lopez
Allen Nipper
Arne Nordskog
Loren E. Noren
John M. Poehlman
Mark B. Rhea
Raul L. D. Ribeiro
Michael F. Richter
David J. Sammons
Emanuel A. Serrao
Willis H. Skrdla
Aroonpironjn Sutas
Freda S. Tepfer
L. D. Williams

HUMAN RESOURCES

This workshop addressed the issue of human resources as related to world food problems. Panelists emphasized that these resources included men, women and children, and also recognized that improving human resources was not synonymous with greater numbers. Indeed, for most countries, rapidly expanding populations were regarded as liabilities rather than assets.

After a brief discussion of population and labor force projections, the panelists focused on improvements that might be implemented in the short- and medium-run to improve the human resource base. Discussion concentrated on developing countries and centered on relevant educational, nutritional-health and family planning strategies that could bring about significant improvements in food production. The group further recognized that enhancing the quality of human beings was both an end and a means of development.

During the discussions, several concepts surfaced repeatedly. The problem of motivation--of policy makers, agricultural bureaucracies, teachers and farmers--appeared to be a central feature related to the potential progress that could be achieved in improving agriculture. Similarly, a sensitivity toward, and knowledge of, local agricultural systems appeared as a prerequisite for solving significant issues at either the national or farm level. The needs for broader participation, for greater self-reliance, for additional decentralization of decision making, and for a more acute awareness of the interconnected social and political system in which farmers operate, were also stressed. Finally, the perceived low status of those connected with agriculture was cited as an important impediment to the full realization of the human potential that exists in many countries.

The workshop focused specifically on six human resource
problem areas which panelists thought had important consequences for the solution of world food problems: urban bias;
lack of incentives; compartmentalization of program planning
and delivery systems; quality of life in rural areas; the
shortage of relevant educational materials; and population, or
numbers of people.

URBAN BIAS

Policy makers in many developing countries lack an understanding of the importance of agriculture to the nation's
economy. Few have lived in rural areas and so are unfa-
miliar with the problems of the small farmer and the rural family and community.

The school curriculum is designed for urban children and
has little relevance for those living in the countryside.
Often the curriculum is patterned after that of the previous
colonial power, with undue emphasis on preparation for the university. Sometimes a European or American model has replaced a
more adequate native system. The necessity of developing all
levels of education simultaneously often prevents the allocation of sufficient funds to eradicate illiteracy in rural areas
or to develop the kinds of education programs that would aid
the rural poor in improving their lot.

Several countries are requiring experience in rural living
of their politicians; some require service to rural areas as a
part of training for health service professions or for all high
school graduates. It was recognized that wide application of
this principle to include all those making policies affecting
rural people or preparing to serve them in agriculture, health,
education or welfare would help overcome a pervasive urban
bias.

The decentralization of education and health institutions
with greater local control was recommended as one way of insuring more appropriate programs. Reforms in the educational system that would be helpful in removing urban bias are:

1. Reorganize the curriculum for all schools (urban and
rural) to include an understanding of the contribution of agriculture to the nation's economy.
2. Develop educational materials appropriate for rural
areas of the specific country. Students can learn to read,
write and do calculations if the program relates to their daily
pursuits.
3. Incorporate vocational education in agriculture, local
crafts and other supporting services in the primary schools.

Extension workers need a broad enough education to identify problems in agriculture, to understand the interrelated-

ness of production and local cultural patterns and to feel comfortable in fostering farmer participation in decision making.
They must be alert to guard against changing the food available
to families in undesirable ways through the introduction of
cash crops.

INCENTIVES

Present public policies tend to favor the larger farmers.
The small farmer needs assurance (and evidence) that
improved practices will bring financial rewards.

In many countries land reforms are a prerequisite to
improved incentives. In addition to credit at reasonable cost,
water and roads are necessary to aid in production and in marketing.

The salary structure for agricultural researchers, teachers and extension workers is too low to attract or retain professionals to work in rural areas. In some countries this
results in a low prestige position for the agricultural profession and failure to attract competent personnel. Agricultural
scientists are too few in number in most developing countries.

COMPARTMENTALIZATION

The bureaucracy at federal, district and local levels
tends to attack problems in isolation rather than recognizing an interrelatedness among them. Several ministries
may be involved, each with representatives dealing with the
farmer, few of whom are prepared for a realistic approach.
Hence, program coordination is needed at both national and district levels.

A distribution of research, training and supervisory services among several nonrelated agencies and ministries serves
the local agriculture worker poorly and fails to capitalize on
his or her full potential.

QUALITY OF LIFE

Although the aspirations of people vary from country to
country, the panelists agreed that certain basic ingredients should be available to all: adequate food, clothing
and shelter; health services; education for literacy, vocation
and understanding and enjoyment of life; and ammenities such as
water, roads, electricity and recreation.

Undesirable conditions of living in rural areas encourage
the migration to the cities and fail to attract the health,
education and agricultural personnel needed. It is a paradox
that increased education for agricultural production may simply
provide a "ticket to town" for many best able to serve rural
regions.

Care should be taken to include the rural poor in any local program to prevent deepening the chasm between them and the rural rich. The cycle of poverty and marginal production must be broken to foster and utilize the human resources, that now are a drain on the economy, as well as for humanitarian reasons.

The allocation of funds for the building of roads, for transportation, for a communications network, for water systems and for electricity is necessary to provide decent living conditions. The use of para-professionals for health service delivery would assist many rural populations (i.e., the "barefoot doctor" concept).

Educational programs are needed for literacy, for vocational training, for village support services as well as for agriculture and for nutrition and family health. More and better trained extension workers are needed in agriculture and for rural family living.

The quality of rural life is enhanced when the rural people themselves--both women and men--have an opportunity to participate fully with professionals in program development.

Some countries may be able to provide regional centers, with transportation networks to the surrounding villages and countryside, for more specialized health, education and recreational facilities.

SHORTAGE OF RELEVANT EDUCATIONAL MATERIALS

A shortage of educational materials relevant to the local community occurs in most rural regions of the world. This results in part from the inadequate funding of research and the lack of attention to the need for books and curricula based on rural life.

The panelists suggested a number of measures basic to materials development that might help to increase the availability of materials:

1. Research on foods available in local areas for better utilization of resources for health of people.

2. Specific information by country on what foods each can and does produce, food needs and numbers to be fed as basic to the development of materials.

3. Periodic evaluation of educational programs on the local level and of those training the educators.

4. In some areas of the world two or more countries with similar resources might share responsibilities for research and for preparing educational materials.

5. In most countries there is a core of information already available that might be assembled for immediate use.

POPULATION

In many countries of the world there are excessively large populations, growing at rapid rates with consequent impacts on food supplies, income, employment and quality of life. At the same time there are inadequate numbers of trained personnel in certain key scientific areas related to agriculture and inadequate number of persons competent to design and implement world development programs. As food production increases, population increases, tending to offset the advantage of improved agricultural practices.

Poverty is the parent of the problem as well as the result. It was noted that economic development results in improved living conditions which, in turn, result in fewer children per family.

In some areas of the world, migration out of rural areas is a solution; in many, this only adds to unemployment and miserable living conditions in the urban areas.

Educating families to the effect that having fewer children will ensure a higher level of living for those who are born may be an effective approach to changing the pattern but is too slow to help in the near future. Some countries are providing monetary incentives to encourage few children; India is trying legislation along a variety of frontiers to achieve the same end.

It was recognized that it is important to improve nutrition and health first, so parents can be assured that children who are born will survive. The lessening of the drudgery for women and the provision of education and outside employment of women tends to reduce the birth rate.

PANELISTS

Chairperson	Walter P. Falcon	Stanford, California
Rapporteur	Helen LeB. Hilton	Ames, Iowa
Subplenary Speaker	Herbert R. Kotter	Bonn, Republic of Germany
Subplenary Speaker	Angelita Y. Ledesma	San Juan, Philippines
Subplenary Speaker	Moise C. Mensah	Washington, DC
Subplenary Speaker	M. Mohiey Nasrat	Giza, Egypt
Panelist	John O. Callaghan	Dublin, Ireland
Panelist	Harold O. Carter	Davis, California
Panelist	Freda U. Chale	Dar es Salaam, Tanzania
Panelist	Santiago Fonseca Martinez	Montevideo, Uruguay
Panelist	Mary Gaobepe	Lusaka, Zambia
Panelist	Donald G. Green	Honolulu, Hawaii

Panelist	Sumati Rajagopal Mudambi	Nsukka, Nigeria
Panelist	Ned S. Raun	Washington, DC
Panelist	Aree Valyasevi	Bangkok, Thailand
Panelist	Guillermo Varela	Bogota, Colombia
Panelist	Marjorie Grant Whiting	Washington, DC
Panelist	Eugene A. Wilkening	Madison, Wisconsin

PARTICIPANTS

Luis Aguilar
Kolawole Alli
Robert E. Anderson
Sinforoso A. Atienza
Jesse Ausubel
Eleanor Brohl
       Bunce
Carlos Cenzano
Charles A. Cesaretti
Raymond Clark
Gunars Dambe
Olga Echeverry
Paul Fuglestad
Wayne A. Fuller
Steve Griffin
H. Douglass Gross
Flemming Heegaard
Stanley E. Held
Guido Heredia
Tahira K. Hira
Bruce Thomas Holland

Bambang Ismawan
Grant L. Kuhn
Mary E. Lapham
Warren E. Larson
Doris J. Longacre
Avelino Luna
Daronk Margerita
Marjorie M. McKinley
Martha Meyer
Eleanor M. Miller
Murray B. Nelson
Eleanor O'Cansey
Stella A. Ombwara
Edward Pidgeon
Jon O. Ragnarsson
Jose Ramirez
Peter M. Ranum
Bruno W. Schlachtenhaufen
Evelyn B. Spindler
Dorothyann W. Strange
Leila M. Young
Anthony F. Zimmerman

Technology and Change

INSTITUTIONAL RESOURCES

PROBLEM CONTEXT

    Institutions, broadly defined, refer to the patterns of
relations among people, including relations among organizations of people. The concept of institution includes
customary ways of doing things, as well as reference to specific organizations. By definition, institutions are products
of relatively stable and routine patterns of interpersonal and
interorganizational behavior. Institutions are thus limited in
their flexibility and capacity to innovate. This characteristic of institutions is both a strength and a constraint.

    "Institutional resources" encompasses the "people prob-
lems" associated with the task of overcoming the gap in food
demand and supply. It is people who eat, people who reproduce
people, people who produce food, people who become organized
into formal and informal groups, people who discover new knowledge, and people who accept or reject the knowledge available
to close the food-population gap. In sum, institutions and
institutional practices inadequate to the task can be enormous
barriers to closing the food-population gap. Effective institutions are a major requirement for making progress in closing
the gap. This proposition is supported by the repeated finding
that presently available food production technology is not
being fully utilized.

    The Workshop discussed models for providing <u>technical
assistance</u> on the one hand and the concept of <u>institutional
building</u> on the other. The failure to explicitly recognize the
differences between these two concepts is a problem in itself
and suggests a need for scientists to focus more attention on
the science, or art, of national and international institutional change and development. In brief, the technical assistance orientation is one of adapting to existing institutions

665

in order to get technology adopted, and is short range in planning and action horizons (even though this approach may contribute very significantly to long-term changes in food production as well as institutions). Institution building is essentially long-range in nature and has the objective of deliberately introducing organizational change in order to develop indigenous ways of doing things that will become institutionalized. The time frame for substantive institution building is measured in decades.

From a societal perspective, government is the key institutional system. Government affects the capacity of the institutional systems involved in the total food production and utilization system to do what is necessary and what people know how to do technologically in order to close the food-population gap. The government institutional system embraces the political leadership as well as professional public officialdom and its attendant bureaucracy.

Food production and utilization scientists are not able to demand or require changes in the governmental system as a precondition to further efforts to close the gap in food demand and supply. Efforts should be focused on the institutional systems directly related to the food problem, fully recognizing the impact of the governmental system and the need to develop and exploit opportunities for changing that system as appropriate within each country. Effective food policy is a need in every country and governments are urged to address the relevant questions. Food policy includes food production and utilization, which implies a concern with institutional systems beyond those involved with the development and adoption of production technology. Institutions for population control, health services, nutrition, and other services are recognized as being integral parts of the food problem. This report, however, because of the experiences of the Workshop Panel, focused primarily on institutions related to food production and--to a lesser extent--food utilization, which implies the involvement of scientists from home economics and the health professions as well as agriculture.

RECOMMENDATIONS

The remainder of this report is devoted to a discussion of alternatives related to the following institutional systems:

1. The entire institutional system for identifying the needs as well as implementing the development and delivery of food production and food utilization information to all the users in the food system.

2. The institutional infrastructure involved in providing adequate and timely inputs--such as credit, seed, fertilizer, and breeding stock--to the farmer.

3. The institutional systems involved in organizing, managing, and allocating land and water resources.

4. The system of economic and noneconomic incentives required to motivate the farmer to produce more food, and processors and consumers to reduce food loss.

5. The institutional structures and practices necessary to improve the storage, processing, utilization, transportation, and marketing of increased food resources.

The following alternatives are offered in a context which recognizes a broad continuum of agricultural regions in the world, some of which are primarily concerned with subsistence food production, some with the objectives and potential for creating a national cash-farm agriculture, and some with the potential to enter into the world food market. The alternatives may have different implications or require different programs for different countries, depending upon their food production objectives and potentials.

Alternatives for Improving the Food Production and Utilization Information System

A major effort should be made to improve the institutional system for developing and delivering appropriate information in order to increase food production and utilization. A key point in improving this institutional system is the establishment of linkages between the information developer (usually the researcher), the information deliverer (often extension), and the information users (farmers, households, and the agricultural infrastructure).

An interrelated system of organizations and committed personnel is required to develop and deliver useable information and technology. At least five functions must be fulfilled: 1) research and development of new technology; 2) adequate local testing of technological developments; 3) dissemination of information to users; 4) adoption of new practices; and 5) a continuous system of feedback and interaction among all the actors in this system, with an emphasis on the involvement of the farmer.

There are many institutional arrangements for creating this interrelated system of agricultural information development and delivery, none of which is universally the "best" arrangement. In short, the institutional structure must be "built" to fit the country, though the requirement of effective linkages is universal.

The emerging system of international research centers provides one nucleus on which to build national, and perhaps international, models of information development and delivery. One way of visualizing such a system is indicated in Figure 1.

"A" is a national university or research institute. "B"

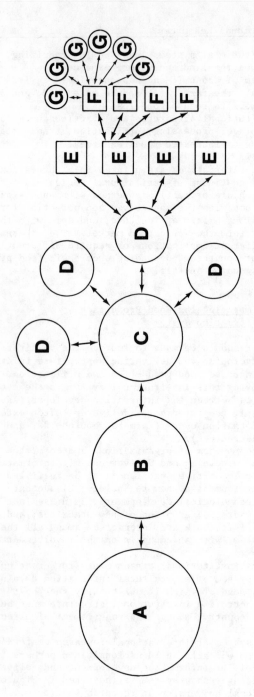

FIG. 1. Model of agricultural information development and delivery.

is the experiment station focusing work on problems farmers
have with each major crop. "C" is a substantion for each different agro-climate (environment). "D" is the first stage of
on-farm testing by research staff assisted by extension personnel and cooperating farmers. "E" is a series of trials to ver-
ify data from research at "D". "F" becomes the experimental
package in larger farm plots to check the reliability of the
package and also to generate added seed stock (in the case of
plants). "G" are demonstrations conducted by extension personnel.

Staff from "B" must be involved in all functions through
"F", and they must follow what is happening in step "G". In
this way they are aware of production problems and the priority
problems that should be researched. They also identify problems that should be researched at "A".

Special small production teams form part of the staffing
pattern at "B" and all "C" locations, supported by the research
staff at "B". Extension staff members are requested to locate
cooperating farmers for all of the "D", "E", and "F" locations
and to participate in the research at these steps. This array
of locations provides a reasonable sample of such variables as
environment and cropping systems and provides confidence in
developing recommendations and encouraging extension to pursue
function "G".

In all functions "D" through "G", farmers should be
brought into the program physically and emotionally. With such
involvement the farmer is more likely to understand different
practices and to value them accordingly. Moreover, it puts the
farmer, the extension personnel, and the researcher in a joint
decision-making process. Similar versions of this model can be
developed where the ultimate target users are households (home-
makers) or managers and owners of the infrastructure.

Training of Personnel Involved in the Development and Delivery
of Information Related to Food Production and Utilization

A general institutional constraint within the agricultural
information development and delivery system is the present
training being received by students in developing countries and
by students attending universities in the developed countries.
The major concern can be summarized as follows:

Substantial numbers of students are receiving advanced
agricultural training without having had enough (or any) experience in farming, thus creating research and extension personnel who cannot put "science into practice" or establish credi-
ble relationships with farmers. A similar situation prevails
in home economics and with other community service professionals involved in the total food-population gap.

Efforts should be made by the developing countries, as
well as the relatively developed countries, to modify training

so as to increase the _experiential_ component. Further, the
experiential component must focus on the range of technology
appropriate for the country. Developed countries can contribute to the resolution of this institutional constraint by
recognizing the needs of international students and by being
flexible in their institutional requirements and arrangements.
Developed countries are beginning to experience the problem of
having students in agricultural curricula who do not have
direct agricultural experience. Thus, modifying curricula to
accommodate the needs of students from developing countries
may, to some extent, be in the developed countries' own best
interest.

Professionals currently involved in research and extension
roles also need opportunities for additional training that will
focus on knowledge needed to more effectively interact with and
involve farmers and others who are part of the agricultural
infrastructure.

Institutions offering training in technical agriculture
and related subjects (such as home economics) should include in
the curricula courses which give an understanding of overall
development and the role of agriculture within the total economy. Such understanding would be useful as agricultural and
related scientists interact with government policy makers.

Institutional Structure for Agricultural Inputs

There is no one institutional arrangement that will assure
adequate, economical, and timely provision of the inputs
required for a more productive agriculture. Where possible
within the governmental system of a country, it may be useful
to consider some mix of public and private systems. There is
great need to increase the input of the farmer into the development and decision-making of the institutional structures
which organize and deliver agricultural inputs.

Institutional Systems for Land and Water
Organization, Management, and Allocation

The objective in land and water organization, management,
and allocation should be to encourage the wise use of all
land and water, with special concern for agricultural land and
water. While land reform and land tenure are major issues in
many countries, the relationship between the system of land
tenure and total food production is somewhat tenuous. The best
land-tenure system for producing adequate food may be dependent
upon factors unique to a given country's socio-economic-politi-
cal and cultural systems, _plus_ the physical characteristics of
the land resource.

There is a need to build into the institutional systems
concerned with the nation's land and water resources the per-

spective of long-range and overall natural resource planning.
Such planning, based on resource capabilities, competitive
needs for the resources, protection and quality of the
resources, and the government's social policies, would set a
framework for choosing the most effective relationships between
people and the resources of land and water. This would require
linkages among several institutions, including those concerned
with urban and industrial development.

Institutional System of Incentives
    More attention needs to be given to both economic and non-
    economic incentives for all people involved in food pro-
duction and utilization--the farmer, research and extension
personnel, persons providing inputs, and consumers. Examples
of constraints and abstract solutions are readily identifiable,
but concrete alternatives are the prerogative of the individual
countries.
    From an institutional viewpoint, the objective is to build
into the development of programs for food production and utilization an overt effort to match established goals and objectives with meaningful rewards. This suggests the need to
include in the "food-system" team social scientists who can
bring to bear on the situation the body of knowledge that
exists with respect to incentives and human motivation. The
persons expected to "respond" to incentives should have input
into the process of developing them.

The Political-Governmental System
    Considering suggestions for alternative governmental sys-
    tems was deemed inappropriate for the World Food Confer-
ence. What the Conference considered, and what is needed
institutionally, is renewed efforts in the forging of relationships between the governmental system and the food production,
food utilization, and social scientists. Governments are much
more receptive to information about food production because of
the change in the world food situation in the last 2 to 4 years
years.
    Scientists, therefore, should renew efforts to develop the
information base for assessing the total food production system in countries and participate in the development of an
information gathering and planning system which will assist in
the establishment of food production and utilization policies.
A key problem to be overcome is the absence of, or lag in
acquiring, timely and useful information in food policy planning on a national and international basis. Priority should be
given to an institutional system that would assure such knowledge on a worldwide basis.

SUMMARY
     The message to scientists is clear: The food-population
     gap cannot be closed unless the institutional changes
     necessary within and among countries are made. Some of
the changes needed are clear, though the means for achieving
them are not. Part of the effort in institutional change must
be short run in nature--a "make-do" approach. A second part of
the effort is to develop within each country a vision of the
institutional framework needed and to work toward that framework in the long-run. To do this, professionals with understanding of institutions must become involved with the scientists more directly concerned with the development and
dissemination of technology.

PANELISTS

Chairperson	K. R. Tefertiller	Gainesville, Florida
Rapporteur	Ronald C. Powers	Ames, Iowa
Subplenary Speaker	Dale E. Hathaway	Washington, DC
Subplenary Speaker	Elizabeth O'Kelly	London, England
Subplenary Speaker	Ernest W. Sprague	Mexico City, Mexico
Panelist	Shawki M. Barghouti	Amman, Jordan
Panelist	Francis C. Byrnes	New York, New York
Panelist	John M. Cormack	Winnipeg, Canada
Panelist	J. S. Kanwar	Hyderabad, India
Panelist	W. Keith Kennedy	Ithaca, New York
Panelist	M. T. Kira	Giza, Egypt
Panelist	Herbert F. Lionberger	Columbia, Missouri
Panelist	P. T. Obwaka	Njoro, Kenya
Panelist	Lander Pacora Coupen	Lima, Peru
Panelist	Magatte Sow	Dakar, Senegal
Panelist	H. H. Stonaker	Fort Collins, Colorado

PARTICIPANTS

Fitri Aini	T. W. Edminster
Gerald C. Anderson	William C. Ehlke
Gary A. Apel	Richard A. Farley
Hanumappa Ramappa Arakeri	John W. Gibler
Orville W. Arends	Paul T. Gibson
John Blackmore	Marcel R. Harper
Harold E. Butz	Zane R. Helsel
John W. Casey	John N. Hilgerson
Neville P. Clarke	K. Robert Kern
Kenneth R. Colton	Joseph A. Keys
E. Paul Creech	Alphonse J. Kunkel
Davis W. Dickerson	Margaret E. McWilliams

Egil Oyjord
Adalberto Palma-Gomez
James W. Robertson
Anthony S. Rojko
W. Neill Schaller
Samuel F. Scheidy

Frederick G. Smith
Charles S. Taylor
George R. Town
Sarah A. Zimmerman
Lawrence W. Zuidema

SELECTION AND USE
OF TECHNOLOGIES

THE WORKSHOP ASSIGNMENT

Major emphasis was to be placed on assessing the effectiveness of the development and/or selection, communication (dissemination, diffusion), use, and results of technology. In the main, technology was to be taken as given. An exception to this rule was those cases where the technology selected was believed inappropriate for specified goals. In general, the workshop was not responsible for "cataloging" all the technology available in the many areas related to food and to population control.

The assessment was to be broad, including the areas of population control and food production, processing, distribution, and use. The service infrastructures, including education, service, and technology delivery and marketing systems, were also to be assessed.

CHANGING GOALS

While the major emphasis of The World Food Conference was on food, this workshop considered technology and its application and results in a broader sense. Historically, the discussion of technology for food has been limited to food production. Now meeting world food needs is being discussed in direct relation to other goals, especially population control. In addition, the discussion of food production and population control is being linked directly to other goals such as quality of life, with particular emphasis on providing employment opportunities and parity of economic and social services, cultural programs, and employment in rural areas.

More specific food production goals are being related by some to:

1. Improved _per capita_ food consumption and nutritional levels.
2. Increased agricultural income and more equitable distribution of income among farmers.
3. Additional employment opportunities in farming and elsewhere in the rural sector.
4. Increased participation, power, and influence of rural residents, including farmers, in political decision-making processes, especially those that involve economic growth and the distribution of rewards.

The increasing emphasis on small-scale and marginal farmers is one illustration of changing goals.

Though there was only limited discussion and no attempt to integrate or rank goals, the Workshop recognized that: (1) broader range of food-related goals is being proposed by some currently; (2) some of these goals may conflict with each other; and (3) national, and in some cases international, priorities must be set involving food-related goals as well as their relationship to other societal developmental goals.

FOOD, A PRIORITY PROBLEM

At a very general level, the alternatives to effective development, selection, diffusion, and use of appropriate technology for food production and population control are:

1. Continued stagnation and persistance of a low level of agricultural production and income.
2. Continued population growth that will outdistance agricultural production and result in mass starvation in many places in the world.
3. More and more people who will experience food shortages and face starvation, resulting in increasing political unrest, further political instability, and perhaps revolution.

The most general recommendation of the Workshop, therefore, was that countries seeking to increase food production and lower population growth rates should be assisted, on a high priority basis, in formulating essential policies and in the development of national programs and infrastructures to assure the application of appropriate technology to increase available food and to lower the population growth rate.

The offering and acceptance of aid should not be tied to the purchase of specific materials or machines nor to the use of specific experts. The food and population control research, technology, and program needs of the host country should determine how available resources are used. Presently available resources should be augmented by additional funding, including consideration of alternatives such as the use of funds for purposes other than debt-servicing payments.

The Workshop agreed that a crisis situation exists and international organizations and nation-states, in general, have not committed themselves by placing a high priority on, and developing policies and programs which support, the development and dissemination of technology to meet food needs and to control population.

The Workshop recommended that increased priority be given to the concurrent development and implementation of technology in at least four areas: (1) production of food; (2) processing, distribution, and consumption of food, with emphasis on nutrition; (3) population control; and (4) adequate and effective infrastructure and delivery and support institutions to facilitate 1, 2, and 3.

RESEARCH AND ADAPTATION SYSTEMS

There is a great need for continuing to build research networks among countries, within regions, and worldwide so that food- and population-related research will be more efficient, available, and of greater use.

There is a wealth of research and technology already existing in many areas related to food and to population problems. Increased emphasis should be placed on procedures and systems that will make these data retrievable, adaptable, and useable under varying conditions to meet divergent needs. Emphasis must be on appropriate technology.

The need for retrievable and useable information systems exists for program and diffusion technology as well as for the more commonly discussed "hard" technology. For example, many experimental programs related to food and population control are being carried out around the world. There is a need to collect and collate the results (including success and failure elements) of these programs to answer "why!" questions and to formulate action generalizations. Further, there is need to establish an effective means of communicating the results of these programs to policy makers, program directors, and workers in all countries. The potential for establishing international and/or regional centers for these purposes should be explored.

Continued emphasis and support should be given to the international and regional research centers. They should increase programs involving field trials, training, and outreach functions. The potential for creating "outlying" research "sub-stations" in selected countries in the regions served should be investigated.

RESEARCH FOCUS

Technology is crucial to increasing food production. The expertise and other resources to produce and extend this technology are limited. Based on these concerns several recommendations were made:

1. Increased attention must be given to a more rationalized process of determining research priorities and allocating and planning the use of limited personnel, financial, and other resources. These resources must be used to develop technology that will increase food production (including that of small farmers) and help control population. Too often priorities on research and technology are left to the whims of the scientist or research leader who often appears to have little knowledge or concern for the needs of the peasants. Priorities are often given to the production of journal articles to impress scientific peers and administrators. The reward systems must be restructured to provide incentives to make the technology produced more relevant to the needs of developing countries. Increased emphasis should be placed on, and incentives provided for, the adaptation of existing technology.

2. Increased awareness, concern, and attention must be given to the needs of the users of technology. In each developing country or agricultural region a structure needs to be developed that interfaces with the agricultural infrastructure and local production units to identify the real technology needs at each level. Consideration should be given to: the availability and feasibility of developing needed complementary technology, intermediate technology, and supporting services; motivations and incentives for users; and probable impact on family living and social organizational patterns. From this interface the required technology should be determined and sought.

The following were among the more specific suggestions for making research and technology more relevant to user needs: 1) involve ultimate users in determining technology needs; 2) require researchers to live and work with ultimate users for substantial periods of time; 3) facilitate or create more effective "linker" roles between researchers and ultimate users; 4) place increased emphasis on adapting research technology; 5) analyze "technology" currently being used by indigenous groups; 6) make sure technology recommended is area specific and adapted to the farmer's resource and management competence; and 7) make technology supportive of labor intensive agriculture, especially for small farm application.

RESEARCH AREAS
    A great deal of basic research and technology is available. High priority should be given to their adaptation and use. There is a tendency among developing countries to unnecessarily duplicate research done in developed and other

developing countries. Professionals trained in developed countries tend to continue their "thesis" research when they return
home despite other high priority agricultural research needs.
Both of these tendencies should be recognized and corrected.

Additional high priority research is needed. Though a
complete inventory of research needs was not delineated the
following high priority research areas were discussed:

1. Most research and technology appears to be devoted to
agricultural production. There is need for much additional
research and technology applied to nutrition and food processing, marketing, distribution, storage (including household),
and preparation.

2. Additional research should be undertaken related to
needs of the small scale farmer.

3. Research efforts should be increased to analyze the
effectiveness of existing institutional and specific infrastructures that deal with food and population issues and programs at all levels within developing countries, and also on a
worldwide basis.

4. Additional research should be conducted on change
agencies, change agents, and program methods and effectiveness.
The following are among the most important research areas:
1) relative effectiveness of alternative organizational structures; 2) alternative planning processes; 3) the impact on program effectiveness of involving user groups in problem definition, planning, and implementation; 4) communication within
change organizations; 5) effective linkage systems between
"research" and "extension"; 6) the impact of various combinations of "extension" methods; 7) interaction and effectiveness
of change agent and farmer behavior; 8) where relevant, the
existing and potential role of the private, commercial sector
in diffusing technology; and 9) the decision making processes
of farmers.

5. Given the energy crisis and the world's limited oil
reserves, research should be initiated that would minimize
dependency on oil derivative inputs, especially for fuel use in
agriculture. Emphasis, for example, should be placed on breeding nitrogen-fixing plants and increasing the effectiveness of
existing ones, developing further and more efficient uses of
solar energy, perfecting reduced tillage techniques, and
improving multi-cropping systems.

6. Research should be undertaken to determine how to
select and orient technical advisors and other experts to maximize their usefulness.

THE POSITIVE, "PACKAGE" APPROACH
          Historically (including this Conference), emphasis has
          often been placed on limiting factors or constraints to

solving food and population problems. In future decisions
regarding the selection and diffusion of technology, emphasis
should be given to specifying conditions that will have to prevail for the specified technologies to be accepted and integrated into farming and family and community patterns of living. Conditions such as the following may be relevant:
government policy, administration policy and structure; availability of inputs and infrastructures for delivery; transportation; education and management services; credit; markets; price
incentives; and risk reduction and guarantee programs. Based
on this type of analysis, decisions must be made regarding the
creation of conditions that will facilitate the adoption of the
technology.

A HOPE

It is hoped that in the future those who engage in
research and in the development of technology in the areas
of food and population will develop the capability and the
deserved credibility and that they will establish the relationships that may allow them to have greater influence on national
policies and programs to the end that more effective and efficient progress can be made toward solving the food and population problems of the world.

PANELISTS

Chairperson	C. A. Williams	Normal, Alabama
Rapporteur	George M. Beal	Ames, Iowa
Subplenary Speaker	Willard W. Cochrane	St. Paul, Minnesota
Subplenary Speaker	Douglas Ensminger	Columbia, Missouri
Subplenary Speaker	Amir U. Khan	Manila, Philippines
Panelist	Azril Bacal	Lima, Peru
Panelist	Joseph A. Beegle	East Lansing, Michigan
Panelist	Melvin G. Blase	Columbia, Missouri
Panelist	Jenaro Collazo-Collazo	Rio Piedras, Puerto Rico
Panelist	Mercedes B. Concepcion	Manila, Philippines
Panelist	Robert M. Dimit	Brookings, South Dakota
Panelist	Rom Moav	Jerusalem, Israel
Panelist	Edgardo C. Quisumbing	Quezon, Philippines
Panelist	A. W. van den Ban	Wageningen, Netherlands
Panelist	Harri E. Westermarck	Helsinki, Finland
Panelist	D. Keith Whigham	Urbana, Illinois
Panelist	F. G. Winarno	Bogor, Indonesia

PARTICIPANTS

James A. Anderson	James W. McKinsey
Charles N. Bebee	William C. Morris
Bartely P. Cardon	A. Tunde Obilana
Armand DeLaurell	Orville I. Overboe
Mary Ann Farthing	Carolyn Sue Palmore
Dean F. Gamble	Doris E. Phillips
Syamal K. Ghosh	Wattana Pratoomsindh
John B. Herrick	Michael W. Sands
Francis E. Horan	Beyene Seifu
John W. Ingels	Telilia Tesfaye
Keith Kirkpatrick	William N. Thompson
Gerald E. Klonglan	Donald E. Tynan
John Mandom Kum	R. Venkatachalam
Rene Q. Lacsina	Richard Weisskoff
Jonathan J. Lu	Frederick Earl Wepprecht
Charles A. Martinson	Michael B. Whiteford
Herbert F. Massey	Mervin J. Yetley

TECHNOLOGY FOR FOOD PRODUCTION AND PRESERVATION

To increase the production of food to feed a growing population it will be necessary to increase the area of land utilized in the production of crops or meat and to increase the productivity of land presently under cultivation. Much of this increase in production must take place in the developing countries. New technologies, or the transfer of existing technology, will be needed to bring food production in developing countries to a level that will provide food security. A great resource of technology presently exists that is not being utilized in many countries. Ways must be found to destroy the barriers that prevent the adoption of this technology.

Much of the existing technology is in the developed countries and may not be applicable to the conditions that occur in developing countries. This is especially true of many technologies that are developed in temperate zones and then transferred to tropical areas. Much research is needed to develop new technology. The greatest constraints are the frequent failure to consider the social and economic impact of a technology, and the low economic and educational level of many of the recipients. These constraints result in a failure to understand the technology and to comprehend the potential benefits from its adoption.

Although evidence of the need for change exists and the results of the failure to change should be apparent, not all governments have established positive policies to increase the production of food. The lack of such policies, including domestic and international monetary policies, prevents the development of food processing and marketing systems, adequate research and extension facilities, and other institutional structures to encourage the expansion of the country's ability to produce food.

There are many different constraints to the adoption and development of technology. Some apply generally, while others apply more specifically to certain countries or situations. Constraints that will impede the development or adoption of technologies, in general, include:

1. The lack of adequate land resources, both in quality and quantity.
2. Inadequate water for irrigation of crops as well as for other uses by people and animals.
3. Lack of storage facilities to preserve harvested crops and processed foods. (Losses in food are evident at the farms and in every step of the food production and marketing system.)
4. Diseases and pests that are a constant threat to the expansion of crop and animal production. This is especially true of the tropics where the control measures utilized in temperate zones do not suffice.
5. The high cost of energy. In many countries this constraint is formidable because so much of the energy must be imported.
6. Inadequate or improperly directed government policies which prevent the acquisition of needed inputs to expand the production of food.
7. Inadequate food processing and marketing structures at the local, national, and international level.
8. Inadequate research facilities and personnel, and extension personnel.
9. Insufficient planning for the introduction and development of new technology with respect to the people who will be the recipients. People must want to change for a program to be successful. This is especially true when a technology is transferred from one culture to another.

How to solve problems and overcome constraints is difficult to determine. A summary of alternative suggestions for solving problems and overcoming constraints follows:

1. In general, much technology is available that could solve many of the existing problems. The real challenge is to find ways to transfer or adopt technology already developed. The search for new technology, however, should be continued for the solution of future problems and for technology that is appropriate to the problems of developing countries.
2. Develop more efficient systems of water use. Trickle irrigation systems provide an example. Crops that are more efficient utilizers of water should be introduced.
3. Storage systems should be developed that would include superior methods of preserving perishable foods and feeds. With aggressive efforts on the part of extension and local food-industry personnel, much could be done, with little cost,

to improve "on the farm" storage of crops. People could more
fully utilize accepted food-preservation techniques to conserve
food and provide a reserve for food-short periods. Care must
be taken so that new technology does not create new health
problems where improper preservation may result in toxic conditions.

   4. Ways must be found to counteract the continual threat
of diseases and pests to animal and crop production. The
greatest potential is in the development of plants and animals
that have resistance to specific diseases and pests, but the
use of chemicals or other practices must be explored to assist
in maximizing production.

   5. The development of new energy sources is needed if
developing countries are going to meet their needs. Research
is needed to develop alternate energy sources so that dependency upon fossil fuels will be minimized. Solar energy, hydro
energy, methane produced from animal and crop wastes, wind, and
other sources of energy should be explored. More efficient use
of waste materials, such as recycling animal wastes, or the use
of crop wastes for feeding ruminant animals, are examples of
more efficient animal systems.

   6. Government policies must be adopted that provide
incentives to the farmer to increase the production of food for
farm and nonfarm citizens, and to research and extension workers to motivate them to develop a more efficient food production system. Little progress can be made unless there is economic benefit to the farmer when production is increased.

   Agribusiness industries that contribute to increased production of the farmer should be encouraged. For example,
advanced technology cannot be fully utilized by the small
farmer. In the Philippines, poultry production is an integrated system involving the farmer and agribusiness. Business
organizations and cooperatives provide the chicks and feed to
farmers, farmers feed the poultry, and industry and cooperatives market the finished product. Thus, the advanced technology needed to hatch and inoculate the chicks and market the
poultry is provided by the businesses and the technology of
feeding and husbandry is provided by the farmers. Similar systems have been developed for agriculture and cattle raising.
This combination has increased income to all and raised the
nutritional level of the country.

   7. In countries where nutrition is a problem, there are
many domestic species of plants and animals that have not been
fully developed. Much of the emphasis has been applied to cash
crops which may provide, primarily, foreign exchange, not additional food for the people. There should be increased research
to increase yields and quality of locally grown crops such as
cassava and millet. Many domestic animals such as goats are
common in most countries as scavengers but have not been
improved through organized breeding programs. Much research

and extension information is needed in this field.

8. Local food industries should be encouraged to supplement the production of farmers. Fermentation, single-cell protein, processing of fish products, and other industries not relying upon land can add to the total food production of a country.

9. Alternatives must be developed so government policymakers have a choice in developing a food policy. Both small and large farmers are involved in the food production system. The social and economic impact must be a part of the study of alternatives for a food production policy. Technology for the large farmer may not be applicable to the small farmer, but both are essential to expanded production. The risks for all must be considered. A positive attitude and the will to increase production must be developed.

In summary, the overriding constraint is the problem of transferring technology from one country to another and from one culture to another. To overcome this obstacle, careful planning and understanding of each other's cultures are necessary. The people who will receive the new technology must be included in the planning for it. The aim should be to provide access to technology for all people.

PANELISTS

Chairperson	Richard H. Forsythe	Camden, New Jersey
Rapporteur	Clarence W. Bockhop	Ames, Iowa
Subplenary Speaker	B. N. Okigbo	Ibadan, Nigeria
Subplenary Speaker	J. R. Pagot	Addis Ababa, Ethiopia
Subplenary Speaker	Mario Valderrama	Bogota, Colombia
Panelist	Jose A. Eusebio	Laguna, Philippines
Panelist	James N. Kerri	San Diego, California
Panelist	T. W. Kwon	Seoul, Korea
Panelist	Richard Phillips	Manhattan, Kansas
Panelist	W. R. Pritchard	Davis, California
Panelist	A. M. Satari	Bogor, Indonesia
Panelist	Gurdip Singh	Haryana, India
Panelist	Rex L. Smith	Gainesville, Florida
Panelist	F. C. Stickler	Moline, Illinois
Panelist	W. Sybesma	Zeist, Netherlands
Panelist	Charles A. Taff	College Park, Maryland

PARTICIPANTS

Ray H. Anderson	Diane D. Birt
Primo V. Arambulo III	Barbara J. Bobeng
Roy G. Arnold	James W. Bolcsak

Wesley F. Buchele
Mofazzal H. Chowdhury
Gilbert F. Copper
Zafrallah T. Cossack
W. W. Cravens
Melvin G. Dorr
Richard A. Falb
James J. Foley
Jere E. Freeman
Henry A. Fribourg
Vinod K. Gael
George R. Gist
Christy M. Hanegraaf
Paul R. Henderlong
Joyce L. Hochmuth-Nowell
Warren C. Hyer, Jr.
Allen D. Jedlicka

Kamal B. Kardosh
Tebaho Kitleli
Mary Ann Lewis
Donald L. McCune
Joseph P. Murphy
Mary A. Musil
Howard H. Olson
Javier Perez-Villasenor
Donald M. Roberts
Ray Shorter
Gajendra Singh
John L. Strauss
Larry F. Strikeleather
William H. Tallent
Nan Unklesbay
Robert K. Waugh